T0245637

EVERYMAN'S LIBRARY

EVERYMAN,

I WILL GO WITH THEE,

AND BE THY GUIDE,

IN THY MOST NEED

TO GO BY THY SIDE

THE DIARY OF SAMUEL PEPYS

EDITED AND INTRODUCED
BY KATE LOVEMAN

SELECTED FROM
THE COMPLETE DIARY
(XI VOLUMES)
EDITED BY ROBERT LATHAM
AND WILLIAM MATTHEWS

EVERYMAN'S LIBRARY
Alfred A. Knopf New York London Toronto

379

THIS IS A BORZOI BOOK
PUBLISHED BY ALFRED A. KNOPF

This edition, selected by Kate Loveman from the Latham-Matthews text, first included in Everyman's Library 2018

The Latham-Matthews edition in XI volumes first published in Great Britain by Bell and Hyman, London, and in the United States by the University of California Press, Berkeley, 1970–83.

Selections from the diary of Samuel Pepys previously published in Everyman's Library in 1906 (2 vols) and 1955 (1 vol).

 Published in the United States by Alfred A. Knopf, a division of Penguin Random House LLC, New York, and in Canada by Penguin Random House Canada Limited, Toronto. Distributed by Penguin Random House LLC, New York. Published in the United Kingdom by Everyman's Library, 50 Albemarle Street, London W1S 4DB and distributed by Penguin Random House UK, 20 Vauxhall Bridge Road, London SW1V 2SA.

www.randomhouse/everymans
www.everymanslibrary.co.uk

ISBN 978-1-101-90792-4 (US)
978-1-84159-379-1 (UK)

A CIP catalogue reference for this book is available from the British Library

Book design by Barbara de Wilde and Carol Devine Carson

Typography by Peter B. Willberg

Typeset in the UK by Input Data Services Ltd,
Isle Abbotts, Somerset

Printed and bound in Germany by GGP Media GmbH, Pössneck

CONTENTS

INTRODUCTION

When Samuel Pepys began his diary in 1660, he was a minor government clerk, struggling to pay his rent and watching anxiously as the last of England's republican regimes collapsed. When he ended his diary nine years later, he was a wealthy and powerful naval administrator whose expertise was valued by Charles II. The intervening years had seen a succession of national celebrations and disasters: the restoration of the monarchy, the Great Plague, the Great Fire of London, and a punishing naval war with the Dutch. Pepys vividly records his experience of living through these events, along with eyewitness accounts that he obtained from his wide network of contacts. His desire to improve himself – intellectually, socially, financially, and perhaps even morally – drove his diary-keeping and resulted in an intimate account of a life lived in dangerous times. Meanwhile, his fascination with the city around him produced a record of daily life in seventeenth-century London that is unrivalled in its breadth and detail. Much of the power and the pleasure of reading Pepys's diary come from the ways in which national dramas are interwoven with his personal and domestic concerns. For example, in 1667 Pepys was dealing with a threatened Dutch invasion, hurriedly sending additional ships to help the defence. At the same time he also sent his wife and father to hide his money in the country. After the danger passed, there were farcical scenes as the family attempted to locate and dig up the badly buried gold – trying to do so at night, without alerting the neighbours to what was going on. Stealthy excavation was made even more difficult as Pepys's father, who was supposed to be able to identify where the gold was buried, was hard of hearing. 'I was out of my wits almost', commented Pepys.[1] What makes Pepys's journal unusual among seventeenth-century diaries is his decision not to foreground the end result of this night (most of the gold was retrieved), but to focus on the arguments, exertion, problem-solving and cooperation that led to that result. In writing he captures his experiences and discoveries, so that we discover with him.

1. 10 Oct. 1667.

BEFORE THE DIARY

Samuel Pepys was born in London in 1633, during the reign of Charles I. His father John worked as a tailor, while his mother Margaret had been a washmaid before her marriage. Pepys was the oldest of their eleven children to live to adulthood. His surviving siblings – Tom, Paulina, and John – appear in his diary, usually because Samuel had determined that one or other was in need of a job, a spouse, or a reprimand. The family lived in Salisbury Court, off Fleet Street. The streets surrounding Salisbury Court were part of 'the City', the area of the metropolis within and around the medieval city walls that was run by the elected representatives of the Corporation of London. To the west of the City lay the up-market leisure and residential district around Covent Garden. Continuing west brought you to the heart of Westminster, to the Houses of Parliament and the King's residence at Whitehall Palace. Pepys was nine when civil war broke out between Charles I and Parliament. On 30 January 1649, when the King was executed by the remnants of the parliament, Pepys enjoyed a day off from his studies at St Paul's School to witness the event. 'I was a great roundhead when I was a boy', he later recalled in his diary – though it was not something he wanted others to recall.[1] Pepys worked hard at St Paul's. He obtained a scholarship to the University of Cambridge, beginning his studies at Magdalene College in 1651. His time there helped him to acquire the knowledge and manners expected of a gentleman, but that was not all puritan Cambridge had to offer. In 1653, the college authorities punished him after he was discovered 'in drink'. He also visited a local bawd, Elizabeth Aynsworth, learning 'a very lewd song' from her and, presumably, other things.[2]

After leaving Cambridge in 1654, Pepys went to work in Westminster for Sir Edward Mountagu. Although many of Pepys's immediate family were artisans and tradesmen, on his father's side he was connected to Huntingdonshire gentry: Mountagu was the son of Pepys's great aunt, and willing to assist his younger cousin. He was a figure of note in Oliver Cromwell's regime, sitting on Cromwell's Council of State. In 1656 Mountagu became a general-at-sea, taking joint command of the parliamentarian naval forces.

1. 1 Nov. 1660.
2. *Fifth Report of the Royal Commission on Historical Manuscripts, Part 1* (London: Eyre and Spottiswoode, 1876), p. 482. Diary entry, 7 Oct. 1667.

Pepys acted as Mountagu's secretary and helped to manage his affairs while he was away from London. He also took on a second job as a clerk at the Exchequer in Westminster, dispensing and receiving government money. Pepys's prospects, however, were seriously threatened by an illness that had worsened since university: bladder stones. By March 1658, the pain was unbearable. To save his life, he risked an agonizing operation with a high mortality rate. The operation was successful, but he remained wary of a recurrence of the stone, carefully monitoring his lower body for pain. His diary would become a resource in tracking his health and testing potential remedies.

By the time Pepys endured his operation, he was no longer a bachelor. In December 1655 he had married Elizabeth St Michel, the fifteen-year-old daughter of a French Protestant immigrant. Elizabeth is not named in the diary – Pepys refers to her as 'my wife'. While this implies (accurately) that he was not inclined to imagine her identity outside of his influence, it was also a sign of his affection: this was a love match, albeit a tempestuous one. Elizabeth had no money, no influential family connections, and she lacked the education to keep up with her new husband's broad range of intellectual pursuits. But she was, like him, capable, intelligent, and keen to better herself. Just occasionally Pepys became aware that he had underestimated her: 'she is very cunning, and when she least shows it, hath her wit at work', he concluded after she matched him point for point in a quarrel over the household accounts and the lowness of each other's family origins.[1] Elizabeth certainly knew how to use the little power she had to win arguments with her husband. The greatest of these began in October 1668 when she discovered his affair with her paid companion, Deb Willet. Elizabeth had far more to lose than Samuel: if their marriage broke down, she was the one who would be left with little to support herself. In her rage and grief, she employed just about all the tactics at her disposal to make her husband feel her pain and to ensure his fidelity. She demanded that he take oaths to prevent future lapses – a strategy Pepys himself used to constrain his desire for 'pleasure'. Knowing his concern for his reputation, she threatened to shame him by declaring the affair, or else to damage his status by publicly converting to Catholicism. She even suggested that they remove themselves from the temptations of the city by going to live in the country (not a proposal she would

1. 28 Feb. 1665.

much have enjoyed, as she loved London just as much as he did). Elizabeth evidently had a shrewd sense of her husband's character. Although their simmering disputes frequently erupt in the pages of the diary, they would prove an effective partnership, together successfully navigating the challenges presented by their rapidly changing society.

RESTORATION

At the point Pepys started his diary there was no government in control of the country. Strife between elements in the army and the parliament meant 1659 had seen four regimes within the year, as well as a failed royalist rising and riots in the capital. The year 1660 began under the republican 'Rump' parliament, which was widely seen as unrepresentative of the electorate. Popular agitation succeeded in persuading the most powerful army leader, George Monck, that the Rump's government was untenable. Monck compelled the Rump to readmit to parliament MPs whom the army had long prevented from sitting, and to proceed to free elections for a new parliament. The new Convention parliament quickly resolved to invite Charles Stuart, exiled in the Netherlands, to take the throne. Charles II's arrival was widely celebrated, since many people who were otherwise wary of the restoration of the monarchy welcomed the stability it promised.

One of the most pressing matters was a religious settlement. During the 1640s and 1650s, the Church of England had been remodelled: bishops were abolished, the Book of Common Prayer was forbidden, and attendance at church was no longer compulsory. Presbyterians in the church and in parliament still wanted to see a national church, but one governed by meetings of elected officers, rather than by bishops appointed by a monarch. However their efforts foundered. Self-governing 'Independent' congregations formed, opposed to the idea of a state church. Sects with much more controversial views also proliferated: Quakers, for example, valued an individual's direct relationship with the Holy Spirit over the guidance of the Bible and, shockingly, allowed women to preach. Before Charles's return in 1660, he promised to allow 'Liberty to Tender Consciences', with the details to be determined by parliament.[1] This calculatedly ambiguous phrase was

1. *King Charles II his Declaration to All his Loving Subjects . . . Dated from his Court at Breda in Holland, the 4/14 of April 1660* (Edinburgh, 1660).

taken to mean that the religious freedoms secured in the civil wars would continue, at least for the vast majority of Protestants. However the Cavalier parliament elected in early 1661 strictly curtailed those freedoms: it reinstated the Church of England as it had existed prior to 1642, forced out committed Presbyterians, and implemented laws to penalize and jail those who worshipped outside the state church. The harshness of this settlement remained a source of strife and prompted anti-government plots.

Meanwhile, the nation faced external challenges, not least from the Dutch. In 1665 long-running disputes with the Dutch Republic over trade and colonial expansion led to the official declaration of the Second Anglo-Dutch War. Parliament was initially generous in voting to finance the war effort, but grew increasingly suspicious of Charles's plans and became reluctant to grant further supply. The extravagance and lax morals of Charles's court, especially the King's ostentatious spending on his mistresses, did not endear him to parliament or the public. The economic damage wrought by the plague and Great Fire further weakened the country. At the end of the 1660s hostility to Charles's rule appeared to be growing rather than diminishing.

In the midst of uncertainty, disasters, and economic crisis, Samuel Pepys was doing exceptionally well for himself. In June 1660, Mountagu (who had facilitated Charles's return) got Pepys appointed as Clerk of the Acts to the Navy Board. The Navy Board oversaw shipbuilding, supplies for the fleet, and the payment of seamen. As Clerk of the Acts Pepys served as the Board's secretary, handling correspondence and keeping records. The job came with a fine house at the Navy Office in Seething Lane in the east of the City, where Pepys would live among his colleagues. Pepys was diligent and ambitious. He set out to learn about every aspect of the navy related to his post in order to perform to the best of his ability and expand his role – for he was increasingly convinced most of his colleagues were incompetent. He began to encroach on the duties of other naval officials by, for example, drawing up large contracts with merchants. His own efficiency and the esteem of Mountagu (now Lord Sandwich) gained him other supplementary and lucrative positions in the administration. Besides the salary that came with his post, he also profited from the gifts and payments offered by merchants who were keen for him to smooth their business with the navy. In the seventeenth century, an official who had exerted himself to provide an efficient service might legitimately take a gift in return – but what distinguished a generous gratuity from a bribe was unclear. In his diary, Pepys recorded the 'gifts' he received, along with his justifications for accepting them and the obligations they placed him under. From a man unable to pay his rent in the early months of 1660, he had amassed thousands of pounds by 1668, which he judged would be enough to live well on if he lost his post.

METHOD AND MOTIVES

Pepys's diary was his private record of his affairs and observations, kept in conjunction with other personal documents such as his financial accounts, and more public records such as his office memoranda and letterbooks. In the nine years that he kept his diary, Pepys revealed its existence to only two people: a lieutenant he served with on board ship in 1660 and his close colleague Sir William Coventry – and he immediately had second thoughts about telling Coventry.[1] Pepys did not want to have his diary used against him, nor be required to produce information from it against his will. He wrote it in shorthand, which he used chiefly for the privacy it afforded. However, this shorthand was far from a secret code. It was a popular system devised by Thomas Shelton, whose most successful manual, *Tachygraphy* (1635), was published many times during the century. Had Pepys wanted the greater security of a code, he would have used one, for he devised ciphers as part of his work for Mountagu. He did, however, make further efforts to disguise one element of his diary: his sexual encounters. Initially he simply wrote about these in shorthand; in early 1664 he started to use French when describing them; this then became a mix of French, English, and Spanish with occasional use of other languages. In 1667 he began to include random letters in some of the passages with erotic content, making them more difficult to read. Pepys's uses of polyglot and obfuscating letters are inconsistent – not all erotic passages are rendered in this way, nor are all the passages in this language explicitly sexual. The polyglot appears (at least until he begins deliberately garbling passages) to be more about enjoying the frisson of the illicit, exotic, and secret than masking shameful content. In fact, the information that seventeenth-century correspondents most often rendered in cipher was frequently not disguised at all in the diary, for Pepys commonly wrote names, places, headings, and dates in longhand. The diary would therefore not have stood up to a determined attempt to read

1. 11 April 1660; 9 March 1669.

it by his close contemporaries in the government, especially as knowledge of shorthand was regarded as a valuable skill in a secretary or clerk. What shorthand did offer was a good measure of security against the diary being read by the people most likely to come across it in his papers – his household servants, his relatives, and, most importantly, his wife.

Pepys's shorthand entries were the culmination of a process of recording and reflection. William Matthews, who worked extensively on Pepys's manuscripts, has untangled the process. Each day Pepys kept notes of his expenses. To these he might add comments on his movements and encounters, which served as rough drafts for diary entries. He could also draw on other records, including 'to do' lists and correspondence. Writing up entries into his journal book sometimes happened at intervals of several days or of over a week. In an extreme case, Pepys's famous account of the Great Fire was not completed until four months after the event, for his diary had been among his possessions sent to safety and it took time to clear the backlog of entries.[1] There were a couple of occasions when Pepys bound his notes into his diary in lieu of writing up full entries. In this edition, an example can be seen in the entries for 9–17 June 1668, which cover Pepys's trip to the West Country. The influence of Pepys's notes on his writing can be detected most strongly in his early diary entries, with their accounts of trips to alehouses, money spent, friends seen, and food consumed: here the 'spine' of Pepys's notes on expenses is less fleshed out than in later years. He became a more fluent writer, elaborating his notes, as he grew more practised in diary-keeping. Significantly, as Matthews uncovered, Pepys's diary entries are not spontaneous, careless effusions – writing was, minimally, a two-stage process, and he had opportunities to craft what he wrote.

It is not hard to understand why Pepys chose to begin a diary on 1 January 1660. This was the start of a new year, a new decade, and it was clear to Pepys and those around him that they were living in momentous times. Pepys had been writing to his patron Mountagu, reporting on matters such as the apprentices' riots and the latest rumours about the army leaders. His new journal served as another repository for such observations, one in which he could elaborate with more freedom on what he had seen and which allowed him to foreground his own interests, rather than those of

1. *The Diary of Samuel Pepys: A New and Complete Transcription*, ed. Robert Latham and William Matthews, I, c–ciii.

his patron. Seventeenth-century diarists often wrote out of a desire to better understand God's guiding hand in the world around them and, if possible, to understand the state of their souls. However, there is little sign of powerful godly motivations driving Pepys's diary-keeping. God is thanked and praised in matters such as the state of Pepys's health or finances. Bad behaviour and immoral thoughts prompt a 'God forgive me', yet Pepys's religious state and God's hand in affairs are not dwelt upon. From the start, the diary was a worldlier document.

Pepys frequently used the diary to vent his spleen, articulate his anxieties, and affirm his next move. Mark Dawson has persuasively argued that the diary was a means of 'social accounting', allowing Pepys to monitor his social progress and the effects of his decision-making on his status.[1] In 1663, for example, Pepys was torn about whether he should dare to adopt the courtly fashion of wearing a wig. He outlined the financial, practical, and status considerations in his diary and – having taken the plunge – recorded the results of various 'test-runs' in his new wig. The first audience, Pepys's maids, were encouraging ('they conclude it to become me'). As his confidence grew, he worked his way up to appearing before the Duke of York. The Duke's wry comment that 'Mr. Pepys was so altered with his new perriwigg that he did not know him' quelled Pepys's doubts but also highlighted the overtness of his social transformation.[2] When Pepys lacked the power or resources to resolve an issue himself, his gathering of information in his diary and other records afforded him a sense of control – he had done all that was possible and carefully considered his actions. Occasionally, Pepys was explicit that he was writing with a mind to future defence of his conduct. On 19 October 1666, in the middle of the Second Anglo-Dutch War, Pepys and the other Navy Board members warned the Duke of York (the Lord High Admiral) that they were completely out of money and could no longer obtain essential supplies. After describing the interview, Pepys wrote, 'This I set down for my future justification, if need be.' He wanted to be able to refer back to his record if – as indeed proved to be the case – the Board's conduct during the war was criticized. Pepys's imagined future reader here was himself. Tellingly, he rarely introduces individuals in any detail or explains institutions or procedures with which he is familiar. Although it is apparent that in later life he did consider the possibility that others

1. Mark S. Dawson, 'Histories and Texts: Refiguring the Diary of Samuel Pepys', *Historical Journal*, 43 (2000), 407–31 (pp. 422–5).
2. See 9 May, 31 Oct., 3 Nov., 9 Nov. 1663.

might read his diary, the signs that he was mindful of a wider readership as he wrote are few.

While much of the content of Pepys's diary reflects his strategic mindset, it is also clear that he thought of it not only as a record of great events, as a means to further his ambitions, and as a stock of ammunition for self-defence – it was also a store of pleasures. Relishing delights – trips to the theatre, rides in a fine coach, music, dancing, and the pursuit of women – became one of the diary's defining characteristics. When Pepys ended his diary, it was chiefly because he feared going blind and believed that keeping a diary worsened his eye trouble. Revealingly, he could also see little need for a private account, 'now my amours to Deb are past, and my eyes hindering me in almost all other pleasures'.[1] Pepys's love of 'great pleasure' is part of his diary's appeal but it can also be one of his most repellent traits, since his sexual pleasures were often predatory. Although he had some eager partners, Pepys frequently targeted girls and women who could not easily refuse his advances. Other records of the time suggest that Pepys's tendency to target female servants was not unusual. Nonetheless much of his behaviour would have been regarded as repugnant, even as criminal, by his contemporaries, had it become known. After sneaking into the home of Mrs Bagwell, the wife of a ship's carpenter, Pepys struggled with her and 'enfin je avais ma volonté d'elle' ('finally I had my will of her'). Pepys's sole recorded thought about this afterwards was to comment on the 'mighty pain' in his finger, injured during the struggle.[2]

Despite Pepys's ongoing scrutiny of his actions, there are many moral and emotional blind spots in his account. His decision to prevent his brother Tom's engagement in 1662, for example, appears to have seriously annoyed several members of his family, yet Pepys had trouble recognizing or understanding this. He professed to be baffled by one relative's hostility and was enraged when he later discovered that his brothers had been plotting to circumvent his decision.[3] In another case, Elizabeth's tactics in the aftermath of Pepys's affair with Deb Willet included revealing that she had rejected advances by Pepys's patron Lord Sandwich *and* Sandwich's son.[4] Yet Pepys – who was given to jealousy – apparently had no suspicions of these men and made surprisingly little comment

1. 31 May 1669.
2. 20 and 21 Feb. 1665.
3. 1 July 1663 and 20 March 1664
4. 10 Nov. 1668.

on Elizabeth's revelations. His focus on his own concerns naturally dominates his diary, but his account is rich enough to give us tantalizing glimpses of what he misses, and of others' lives potentially as enthralling as his.

LATER LIFE AND PUBLICATION

Pepys concluded his diary – very much against his will – on 31 May 1669. To end this record was 'almost as much as to see myself go into my grave'. There was a greater bereavement to come for soon after, in November 1669, Elizabeth died of a fever contracted on the way home from a continental holiday. Yet the bleak future Pepys foresaw for himself in the last pages of his diary did not come to pass: he was mistaken in believing that he was growing blind, that his pleasures would be sorely limited, and that his contact with Deb Willet was over. He remained able to read and write (albeit sometimes with difficulty) until his death. His surviving papers show he continued to enjoy pleasures such as the theatre, music, and 'amours'. Deb did not disappear from his life. She married a clergyman, for whom Pepys obtained a post as a naval chaplain. There is no diary to tell us what was afoot, but this was a suspicious pattern: on each of the two ships that Deb's husband served on in the early 1670s was another husband who had risen through his wife's relationship with Pepys.[1] Pepys never remarried, but in 1670 he began a partnership with Mary Skinner, a merchant's daughter from his parish. This lasted the rest of his life. Meanwhile, his rise in government continued. His efficiency and successful politicking saw him become the admiralty's principal administrator in 1673. In the 1680s Pepys served as Secretary for the Affairs of the Admiralty under both Charles II and James II (the erstwhile Duke of York). This position was roughly equivalent to a secretary of state. During his career he oversaw large shipbuilding programmes and introduced long-lasting reforms to professionalize the navy. When the Revolution of 1668–9 forced James into exile, Pepys – long known as James's man – was forced to resign. This was a bitter blow, but it did mean that he had more time for one of his favourite pursuits, the development of his fine library. In particular, he was keen to amass material that could be used for an extensive history of the navy; this was a work he had begun to consider

1. Loveman, 'Samuel Pepys and Deb Willet after the Diary', *Historical Journal*, 49 (2006), 893–901.

during the diary period and never quite got around to writing.

Pepys died in 1703 from the kidney and bladder problems that had troubled him throughout his life. By this time, he had come to see his library as a gift to posterity and he set out conditions in his will for the collection's 'unalterable preservation and perpetuall security'.[1] He instructed his heir, his sister's son John Jackson, that his library should go by preference to his old college Magdalene in Cambridge, where it was to be under the control of the master. Among some 3,000 volumes were Pepys's diary and three versions of the shorthand manual detailing the system used to write it. Pepys gave great thought to the preservation of his library and no doubt also to the fate of the diary that was so dear to him. Like his library collection, the diary was both a reflection of himself and a valuable historical resource. Experience had taught him that private papers could be used to damage an individual's reputation after death, as well as in life. By leaving his diary to his former college, Pepys was trying to secure not just its safety, but also its sympathetic reception. The instructions in his will specified that only the master of the college could remove books, and then only as far as his lodge. Therefore volumes normally had to remain in the room that contained Pepys's donated library, meaning the diary would be encountered amidst the evidence of his generosity and scholarship. The home Pepys intended for his diary also meant any readers would most likely have certain qualities in common with Pepys: they would be male Cambridge scholars – and diligent ones at that, since they would have to commit to deciphering the shorthand. Furthermore, the college authorities would have an interest in ensuring that, if parts of the diary were published, this would not be in a way than unduly maligned its writer's reputation. This was largely how events played out, after the diary remained unnoticed for decades. It took over 120 years from Pepys's death for the diary to be printed, appearing in a censored form suited to nineteenth-century priorities and sensibilities, with all sexually explicit material excised. Even today, most editions of the diary available in print or electronically are based on flawed nineteenth-century texts. It was not until the late twentieth century that the diary became available in full. Between 1970 and 1983, Robert Latham, William Matthews, and their team of experts published the complete diary, together with scholarly notes and extensive editorial material.

1. The National Archives, London, PROB 1/9, Will of Samuel Pepys, Codicil, 13 May 1703.

THIS EDITION

This selection is based on the text of Latham and Matthews's magisterial edition, with revised and new notes intended to suit a wide readership. In selecting from the wealth of diary entries, I have sought to show the variety of Pepys's experiences, while choosing entries which fit together to follow the developing plots in his domestic, professional, and political affairs. Unlike other selections, this book prioritizes offering full days' entries, rather than supplying truncated entries for each day. Without access to full entries it is difficult to appreciate the diary as literature and as history. If Pepys's accounts of his days are routinely curtailed or his prose condensed, this risks giving a distorted sense of his writing style and of the information he provides. Any internal cuts to entries in this selection are therefore kept to a minimum and discreetly signalled.[1] The main text is the version produced from Pepys's shorthand by William Matthews. Matthews transcribed the shorthand based primarily on modern-day spellings. However, Pepys's spellings are retained when he writes in longhand. Seventeenth-century spellings are also used in cases where the shorthand indicates both a seventeenth-century pronunciation and a spelling that Pepys uses elsewhere in longhand (e.g. 'fallow' for 'follow'). Matthews necessarily intervened a good deal when it came to adding punctuation since in shorthand Pepys's punctuation is largely confined to parentheses and to a symbol indicating a pause or break. The paragraphing is Pepys's own.[2] I have not sought to revise Matthews's excellent work. However, when a phrase in the printed edition raised a query, this was checked against the manuscript; it has led in particular to corrections to Pepys's entries for 9–17 June 1668.

Changes to the editorial material of the complete edition have been more extensive. The footnotes in this book draw on material from across Latham and Matthews's apparatus, including their glossary and the 'Companion' volume that contains biographical and historical information. I have checked this material, silently correcting any mistakes, rewording it for a general readership, and updating it where new evidence is available from research done in

1. The method here therefore differs from an earlier selection of the Latham and Matthews text (first published in 1985 and subsequently issued by Penguin), which silently cuts phrases, sentences, and paragraphs.
2. Transcription methods are detailed in *The Diary of Samuel Pepys: A New and Complete Transcription*, ed. Latham and Matthews, I, lv–lxii.

the past forty years. Unfortunately, space constraints mean it has not been possible routinely to supply sources in the notes, but a select bibliography of some principal sources follows this introduction. Where the diary has text in languages other than English, I have translated this. While Pepys's early editors chose to omit sexual passages, Latham and Matthews exercised another form of discretion in not translating his erotic polyglot. Here for the first time translations of Pepys's polyglot are provided for readers. I have given these translations in seventeenth-century sexual idioms, using language found in Pepys's own English and in what he would call the 'mighty lewd' books of his time.[1]

Research for this edition has turned up new discoveries, identifying people and places and resolving cryptic allusions. Examples include the identity of Pepys's first portrait painter; the fate of the would-be bride in Tom Pepys's thwarted engagement; and the text of the amusing tongue-twister that helped seal Pepys's life-long friendship with John Evelyn during the plague.[2] The evening Pepys spent laughing with friends over this tongue-twisting poem was, he wrote, 'one of the times of my life wherein I was the fullest of true sense of joy'.[3] Discoveries and moments of this kind are, in one sense, small. Yet Pepys's brilliance as a historical witness and an evocative writer comes in large part from his appreciation of the seemingly trivial, fleeting, or frivolous. He was willing to remark on the unremarkable; to record what others did not see or would not risk recording; and to hazard his reputation by leaving his diary to posterity – to us.

Kate Loveman

1. See 9 Feb. 1668 for one such book.
2. See notes for 27 Nov. 1661, 23 Aug. and 22 Oct. 1662, and 10 Sept. 1665.
3. 10 Sept. 1665.

SELECT BIBLIOGRAPHY

Pepys, Samuel, *The Diary of Samuel Pepys: A New and Complete Transcription*, ed. Robert Latham and William Matthews, 11 vols (London: HarperCollins; Berkeley and Los Angeles: University of California Press, 2000; 1st pub. London: Bell, 1970–83).

Calendar of State Papers Domestic Series Charles II, 1660–69, ed. Mary Anne Everett Green (London: HMSO, 1860–94), via British History Online, Version 5.0 <http://www.british-history.ac.uk>

Davies, J. D., 'Montagu, Edward, first earl of Sandwich (1625–1672)', *Oxford Dictionary of National Biography*, Oxford University Press, 2004; online edn, Jan. 2008 <http://www.oxforddnb.com/view/article/19010>

Davies, J. D., *Pepys's Navy: Ships, Men and Warfare 1649–1689* (Barnsley: Seaforth, 2008).

Fox, Frank L., *The Four Days' Battle of 1666: The Greatest Sea Fight of the Age of Sail* (Barnsley: Seaforth, 2009; 1st pub. as *A Distant Storm*, Rotherfield: Press of Sail Publications, 1996).

The History of Parliament <http://www.historyofparliamentonline.org>

Journals of the House of Commons and *Journals of the House of Lords*, via British History Online, Version 5.0 <http://www.british-history.ac.uk>

Knighton, C. S., *Pepys and the Navy* (Thrupp: Sutton, 2003).

Latham, Robert, general ed., *Catalogue of the Pepys Library at Magdalene College, Cambridge*, 7 vols (Woodbridge and Cambridge: Brewer, 1978–94).

Loveman, Kate, *Samuel Pepys and his Books: Reading, Newsgathering, and Sociability, 1660–1703* (Oxford: Oxford University Press, 2015).

OED Online, Oxford University Press, June 2017 <www.oed.com>

Ollard, Richard, *Cromwell's Earl: A Life of Edward Mountagu, 1st Earl of Sandwich* (London: HarperCollins, 1994).

Ollard, Richard, *Pepys: A Biography* (London: Sinclair-Stevenson, 1974, repr. 1991).

Tomalin, Claire, *Samuel Pepys: The Unequalled Self* (London: Viking, 2002).

CHRONOLOGY[1]

1633	23 February: Born in Salisbury Court, Fleet Street
	3 March: Baptized in St Bride's, Fleet Street
c. 1644	At the grammar school, Huntingdon
c. 1646–50	At St Paul's School, London
1649	Saw Charles I beheaded
1650	Awarded leaving exhibition
1651–4	At Magdalene College, Cambridge
1651, 1653	Awarded scholarships
1654	Takes his B.A.
?1654	Appointed secretary or domestic steward to Edward Mountagu in Whitehall Palace
1655	1 December: Married to Elizabeth St Michel in St Margaret's, Westminster
?1656	Appointed clerk to George Downing, Teller of the Receipt in the Exchequer
1658	26 March: Operated on for the stone
	c. August: Moves to Axe Yard
1659	May: Carries letters to Mountagu in the Baltic
1660	1 January: Begins diary
	April–May: Accompanies Mountagu's fleet to Holland to bring over Charles II
	28 June: Resigns clerkship in Exchequer
	29 June: Appointed Clerk of the Acts to the Navy Board
	23 July: Sworn in as Mountagu's deputy as clerk in Privy Seal Office
1661	*23 April: Coronation of Charles II*
	5 July: Uncle Robert Pepys dies
1662	15 February: Admitted as Younger Brother of Trinity House
	17 August: Resigns deputy-clerkship in Privy Seal
	20 November: Appointed to Tangier Committee
1664	15 March: His brother Tom dies
	8 April: Appointed to Corporation for the Royal Fishery
1665	15 February: Elected Fellow of the Royal Society
	22 February: Second Dutch War begins
	20 March: Appointed Treasurer of Tangier Committee

1. From *The Diary of Samuel Pepys*, ed. Latham and Matthews, X, 623–6 (with amendments).

Spring: Great Plague begins in London
3 June: Battle of Lowestoft
5 July: Moves family to Woolwich
21 August: The Navy Office moves to Greenwich
October: Takes lodgings at Greenwich
4 December: Appointed Surveyor-General of the Victualling

1666 January: Navy Office and Pepys household move back to London
March: Sandwich arrives in Spain as Ambassador
1–4 June: Four Days Fight
25 July: St James's Day Fight
2–5 September: The Great Fire of London

1667 25 March: His mother dies at Brampton
10–13 June: Dutch raid on Thames and Medway
13 June: Sends his gold to Brampton
21 July: End of Second Dutch War
28 July: Resigns Surveyorship of Victualling
7–12 October: Visits Brampton to recover his gold
22 October: Defends Navy Board before parliamentary Committee on Miscarriages

1668 27 February: His sister Paulina marries John Jackson
5 March: Defends Navy Board before House of Commons
5–17 June: His holiday tour to West Country
September: Sandwich returns
25 October: Elizabeth discovers him *in flagrante* with Deb

1669 31 May: Discontinues his diary
June–October: Travels to France and Low Countries
10 November: Elizabeth dies; he erects a monument to her in St Olave, Hart Street

1670 30 March: His brother John appointed Clerk to Trinity House

1672 24 January: Admitted as Elder Brother of Trinity House
17 March: Third Dutch War begins
28 May: Death of Sandwich in Battle of Sole Bay

1673 29 January: Navy Office destroyed by fire; he moves to Winchester Street
15 June: Duke of York resigns as Lord High Admiral under terms of Test Act (March) excluding Roman Catholics; office put in commission
18 June: Appointed Secretary to Admiralty Commission; is succeeded at Navy Board by his brother John and Thomas Hayter as joint Clerks
4 November: Elected M.P. for Castle Rising, Norfolk

1674 January: Moves to Derby House, new headquarters of Admiralty
9 February: End of Third Dutch War

1676 1 February: Appointed Governor of Christ's Hospital
22 May: Elected Master of Trinity House
1677 15 March: His brother John buried
8 August: Elected Master of Clothworkers' Company
1679 5 February: Elected M.P. for Harwich
21 May: Resigns as Secretary to Admiralty and Treasurer for Tangier
22 May–9 July: In Tower on suspicion of treasonable correspondence with France
July: Moves to W. Hewer's house in York Buildings, now no. 12 Buckingham Street
1680 30 June: Proceedings against him abandoned
c. September: His brother-in-law John Jackson dies
3, 5 October: Takes down at King's dictation story of his escape after Battle of Worcester
4 October: His father buried at Brampton
1682 May: Accompanies Duke of York to Edinburgh
1683 30 July: Sets out for Tangier as secretary to expedition under Lord Dartmouth to evacuate colony
1683–4 December–February: Visits Spain
1684 30 March: Returns to England
10 June: Appointed King's Secretary for the affairs of the Admiralty
1 December: Elected President of Royal Society
1685 *6 February: Death of Charles II; accession of Duke of York as James II*
19 May: Takes seat as M.P. for Harwich, having been elected for both Harwich and Sandwich
20 July: Nominated Master of Trinity House by King under new charter
1686 March: Special Commission 'for the Recovery of the Navy' begins to sit
30 November: Resigns Presidency of Royal Society
1688 Spring: Moves to house now no. 14 Buckingham Street
29 June: Called as witness in Trial of Seven Bishops
October: Special Commission dissolved
5 November: William of Orange lands
23 December: James II takes flight to France
1689 16 January: Defeated in parliamentary election at Harwich
13 February: William and Mary become joint sovereigns
20 February: Resigns his Secretaryship
May–July: Detained on suspicion of Jacobitism
26 August: Resigns Mastership of Trinity House
1690 25–30 June: Imprisoned on suspicion of Jacobitism
Publishes his *Memoires relating to the state of the Royal Navy* [*1679–88*]

1699	27 April: Made freeman of city of London for services to Christ's Hospital
1701	c. June: Retires to Hewer's house at Clapham
1703	26 May: Dies at Clapham
	4 June: Buried at St Olave, Hart Street
1722	4 October: His nephew and heir, John Jackson, buried
1724	July: His library moved from Clapham to Magdalene College, Cambridge
1766	His account of the King's escape after the Battle of Worcester first published by Sir David Dalrymple
1825	His diary first published by Lord Braybrooke from the transcription by John Smith
1841	His Tangier Journal first published by John Smith
1884	His monument erected in St Olave's
1903	The Samuel Pepys Club founded in his honour
1970–83	His diary published in full for the first time by Robert Latham and William Matthews

NOTES ON THE TEXT

SYMBOLS:

[ ] Square brackets enclose Latham and Matthews's editorial emendations when Pepys has accidentally or consciously omitted a letter or word. In this selection, they also signal editorial summary of Pepys's movements.

⟨⟨ ⟩⟩ Double angle-brackets enclose text inserted by Pepys into the margin as an addition.

⟨ ⟩ Single angle-brackets signal other additions, where Pepys interlined text or crowded words into the spaces between entries.

◆ A diamond in this selection signals text has been omitted. These cuts are usually complete sentences or paragraphs. In cases where the text resumes mid-sentence, the initial letter has been silently capitalized.

CURRENCY: In the seventeenth century one pound (1*l*) was worth twenty shillings (20*s.*) and a shilling contained twelve pence (12*d*).

DATES: The Julian ('Old Style') calendar was used in seventeenth-century England. This ran ten days behind the Gregorian ('New Style') calendar that was widely used on the continent but not adopted in England until 1752. The diary text and the footnotes employ the Julian calendar.

In England, the year officially began on 25 March, although New Year celebrations were widely held during the first week of January. Pepys's headings sometimes refer to dates in January, February, and March according to the legal year. For example, the month we would call 'January 1662', Pepys might write either as 'January 1661' or 'January 1661/2'.

WHO'S WHO: In addition to the identifications of individuals given in the footnotes, at the end of this volume there is a list of people who recur often or under various names.

ACKNOWLEDGEMENTS

Particular thanks for help with the editorial work for this selection are due to Steve Loveman, David Clark, Sarah Knight, Gareth Wood and, at the Pepys Library, Jane Hughes and Catherine Sutherland. The University of Leicester also supported the project through granting me academic study leave for a semester.

Kate Loveman

AS THE DIARY BEGINS ...

In January 1660 Samuel Pepys is living in Westminster, close to his work at the Exchequer. London is at the centre of renewed and alarming power struggles over the control of England, Scotland, Wales, and Ireland. Government over the previous year has been tumultuous, even in the context of two decades of wars and revolts. The year 1659 began under the reign of the Protector Richard Cromwell, who had assumed power after the death of his father Oliver. Richard's rule soon collapsed and in the spring of 1659, with the support of much of the army, the Rump Parliament was recalled to govern.

'The Rump' was the parliament that had presided over the execution of Charles I. It was made up of the MPs who had remained after parliament was purged by the army in 1648 to remove men seen as insufficiently hostile to the royalists. However, these remaining MPs had themselves subsequently been expelled by Oliver Cromwell in 1653.

The restored Rump's hold on power was weak. In October 1659, John Lambert and other disaffected officers – seeking arrears in pay and a return to 'godly' government – surrounded the Houses of Parliament with troops, once again expelling the Rump and returning the country to direct army rule.

Other officers in the army and navy soon rallied to the Rump's cause. The formidable General George Monck, commander of English forces in Scotland, declared for the Rump. Vice-Admiral John Lawson announced his support on 13 December and, to enforce the point, prepared his fleet to blockade London. The Common Council of London – the City of London's elected governing body – called for a free parliament without army interference or restrictions on MPs. In late December, the Rump was allowed to meet again.

So 1660 begins in great uncertainty. If government by the Rump is seen by many as preferable to rule by army appointees, the Rump's claims to be a legitimate, representative parliament are now widely rejected. Meanwhile, Monck has started the march south to England with his troops. Although he has declared for the Rump, his intentions concerning the government are far from clear. Moderate MPs 'secluded' in the army purge of 1648 are seeking readmission to parliament. London's Common Council continues to defy the Rump and demand a representative parliament through the return of the secluded MPs or a new election. A free parliament might lead to a return to monarchy and to Stuart rule, but there are other possibilities. With troops quartered around the city and an army advancing from the north, events on London's streets will be critical to the outcome of the crisis.

THE DIARY
OF SAMUEL PEPYS

$16\frac{59.}{60.}$

Blessed be God, at the end of the last year I was in very good health, without any sense of my old pain[1] but upon taking of cold.

I lived in Axe-yard, having my wife[2] and servant Jane,[3] and no more in family then us three.

My wife, after the absence of her terms for seven weeks, gave me hopes of her being with child, but on the last day of the year she hath them again. The condition of the State was thus. *Viz.* the Rump, after being disturbed by my Lord Lambert,[4] was lately returned to sit again. The officers of the army all forced to yield. Lawson lie[s] still in the River and Monke is with his army in Scotland. Only my Lord Lambert is not yet come in to the Parliament; nor is it expected that he will, without being forced to it.

The new Common Council of the City doth speak very high; and hath sent to Monke their sword-bearer, to acquaint him with their desires for a free and full Parliament, which is at present the desires and the hopes and expectation of all – 22 of the old secluded members[5] having been at the House[6] door the last week to demand entrance; but it was denied them, and it is believed that they nor the people will not be satisfied till the House be filled.

My own private condition very handsome; and esteemed rich, but endeed very poor, besides my goods of my house and my office, which at present is somewhat uncertain. Mr Downing master of my office.[7]

1. Pepys had been operated on for a bladder stone on 26 March 1658.
2. Elizabeth, née St Michel, aged 19.
3. Jane Birch, from Dymock in Gloucestershire, aged 18.
4. John Lambert was a general and a Councillor of State, but not a peer. "Lord" was used as title of respect to men in powerful office.
5. MPs forced out in the army purge of 1648, prior to the execution of Charles I.
6. The House of Commons.
7. George Downing, one of the four Tellers of the Exchequer.

JANUARY 1. 16 $\frac{59.}{60.}$ Lords=day.

This morning (we lying lately in the garret) I rose, put on my suit with great skirts,[1] having not lately worn any other clothes but them.

Went to Mr. Gunnings church at Exeter-house, where he made a very good sermon upon these words: That in the fullness of time God sent his Son, made of a woman, &c., shewing that by "made under the law," is meant his circumcision, which is solemnised this day.[2]

Dined at home in the garret, where my wife dressed the remains of a turkey, and in the doing of it she burned her hand.

I stayed at home all the afternoon, looking over my accounts.

Then went with my wife to my father's; and in going, observed the great posts which the City hath set up at the Conduit in Fleet-street.[3]

Supped at my father's, where in came Mrs. The. Turner[4] and Madam Morris and supped with us. After that, my wife and I went home with them, and so to our own home.

2. In the morning, before I went forth, old East brought me a dozen of bottles of sack and I gave him a shilling for his pains.[5]

Then I went to Mr. Sheply, who was drawing of sack in the

1. His "skirts" were probably lower parts of a coat, though it is possible Pepys was at the cutting-edge of fashion in wearing loose "petticoat breeches" that resembled skirts.
2. Peter Gunning conducted services at Exeter House Chapel in the Strand using the Church of England's Book of Common Prayer, which was now illegal. The sermon text (loosely recalled by Pepys) is Galatians 4.4.
3. John Pepys, Samuel's father, was a tailor with a house and shop at Salisbury Court, off Fleet Street. Posts and chains were set up across the main thoroughfares as part of the City's defences.
4. Theophila ("The") was the 8-year-old daughter of John and Jane Turner who lived in Salisbury Court. The Turners were relatives of Pepys on his father's side. "Mrs", meaning "mistress", was a polite title for both unmarried and married women.
5. East was a servant of Pepys's master, Edward Mountagu, whose London lodgings were in Whitehall Palace. The wine was a New Year's gift.

wine-cellar to send to other places as a gift from my Lord,[1] and told me that my Lord hath given him order to give me the dozen of bottles.

Thence I went to the Temple[2] to speak with Mr. Calthropp about the 60*l*: due to my Lord; but missed of him, he being abroad.[3] Then I went to Mr. Crew's and borrowed 10*l*: of Mr. Andrewes for my own use;[4] and so went to my office, where there was nothing to do. Then I walked a great while in Westminster-hall,[5] where I heard that Lambert was coming up to London. That my Lord Fairfax was in the head of the Irish brigades but it was not certain what he would declare for.[6] The House was today upon finishing the act for the Council of State, which they did, and for the indemnity to the soldiers, and were to set again thereupon in the afternoon.[7] Great talk that many places have declared for a free Parliament; and it is believed that they will be forced to fill up the House with the old members. From the Hall I called at home, and so went to Mr. Crew's (my wife, she was to go to her father's), thinking to have dined; but I came too late. So Mr. Moore[8] and I and another Gentleman went out and drank a cup of ale together in the new market, and there I eat some bread and cheese for my dinner. After that, Mr. Moore and I went as far as Fleet-street together and parted, he going into the City, I to find Mr. Calthrop, but failed again of finding him: so returned to Mr. Crews again,

1. Edward Mountagu, Pepys's first cousin once removed, whom he had served as secretary since c.1654. He was "my Lord" by virtue of his appointments under Cromwell, and having been a naval commander. Out of favour with the government, he was now at Hinchingbrooke, his home near Huntingdon. Edward Shipley was his steward.
2. The area around Temple church in the west of London, a centre for the legal trade.
3. Lestrange Calthorpe, a lawyer, was acting for his brother Sir James Calthorpe, who owed Mountagu money.
4. John Crew, Mountagu's father-in-law, lived in Lincoln's Inn Fields. Pepys pays many visits to him in the diary. John Andrews was his steward.
5. Westminster Hall (often just "the Hall") was part of the Palace of Westminster and adjoined the entrance to the House of Commons. It was a good place to get the latest news, being also the site of law courts and bookstalls.
6. Thomas Fairfax (Commander-in-Chief of the parliamentary army 1645–50) had, in collusion with Monck, raised a rebellion in Yorkshire against Lambert. The Irish Brigade was made up of troops previously stationed in Ireland, who now backed Fairfax in large numbers.
7. The Commons selected men for a new Council of State, the executive body responsible for enacting parliament's policies. MPs also voted on terms to indemnify those members of the army who had "interrupted" the Rump Parliament in October 1659.
8. Henry Moore, a lawyer, was a member of John Crew's household with whom Pepys dealt frequently.

and from thence went along with Mrs. Jemimah[1] home and there she taught me how to play at Cribbige. Then I went home, and finding my wife gone to see Mrs. Hunt,[2] I went to Will's[3] and there sat with Mr. Ashwell talking and singing till 9 a-clock, and so home. There, having not eat anything but bread and cheese, my wife cut me a slice of brawn which I received from my Lady,[4] which proves as good as ever I had any. So to bed, and my [wife] had a very bad night of it through wind and cold.

4. Early came Mr. Vanly to me for his half-year's rent, which I had not in the house, but took his man to my office and there paid him.[5] Then I went down into the Hall and to Will's, where Hawly brought a piece of his Cheshire cheese, and we were merry with it. Then into the Hall again, where I met with the Clerk and quarter-master of my Lord's troop,[6] and took them to the Swan and gave them their morning's draught, they being just come to town. Mr. Jenkings[7] showed me two bills of exchange for money to receive upon my Lord's and my pay. It snowed hard all this morning and was very cold, and my nose was much swelled with cold. Strange, the difference of men's talk: some say that Lambert must of necessity yield up; others, that he is very strong, and that the Fifth-monarchy men[8] will stick to him if he declares for a free Parliament. Chillington was sent yesterday to him with the vote of pardon and indemnity from the Parliament.

From the Hall I came home, where I found letters from Hinchingbrooke[9] and news of Mr. Sheply's going thither the next week. I dined at home, and from thence went to Wills to Shaw, who promised me to go along with me to Atkinson about some money; but I found him at cards with Spicer and D. Vines, and could not get him along with me. I was vexed at this and went and walked in the Hall, where I heard that the Parliament spent this day in fast

1. Jemima Mountagu, nearly 14, was the eldest child of Pepys's patron. She was staying with a medical practitioner while being treated for a malformed neck.
2. Elizabeth Hunt and her husband John were Pepys's neighbours in Axe Yard.
3. An alehouse near Westminster Hall.
4. Jemima Mountagu, wife of "my Lord".
5. Pepys leased his house from Valentine Wanley. In this case he paid his rent by illicitly borrowing from his office at the Exchequer.
6. Mountagu had been appointed to command a regiment of horse in 1658, but was dismissed from his post on the fall of Richard Cromwell. Pepys still referred to the regiment as "My Lord's".
7. Quartermaster's clerk.
8. The Fifth Monarchist sect anticipated the imminent arrival of King Jesus; its members were prepared to take up arms to prepare the way for His coming.
9. Edward Mountagu's house near Huntingdon.

and prayer; and in the afternoon came letter[s] from the North, that brought certain news that my Lord Lambert his forces were all forsaking him and that he was left with only 50 horse and that he did now declare for the Parliament himself. And that my Lord Fairfax did also rest satisfied and had laid down his arms, and that what he had done was only to secure the country again my Lord Lambert his raising of money, and free Quarter.[1]

I went to Will's again, where I found them still at cards and Spicer had won 14*s* of Shaw and Vines.

Then I spent a little time with G. Vines and Maylard at Vines's at our vials.[2]

So home, and from thence to Mr. Hunt's and sat with them and Mr. Hawly at cards till 10 at night, and were much made of by them.

Home and so to bed; but much troubled with my nose, which was much swelled.

9. For these two or three days, I have been much troubled with thoughts how to get money to pay them that I have borrowed money of, by reason of my money being in my Uncles hands.

I rose early this morning, and looked over and corrected my brother John's speech which he is to make the next Apposition;[3] and after that I went towards my office and in my way met with W. Simons, Muddiman, and Jack Price[4] and went with them to Harpers,[5] and in many sorts of talk I stayed till 2 of the clock in the afternoon. I found Muddiman a good scholar – an arch rogue – and one that, though he writes new[s]-books for the Parliament, yet he did declare that he did it only to get money; and did talk very basely of many of them. Among other things, W. Simons told me how his uncle Scobell[6] was on Saturday last called to the bar for entering in the journal of the House, for the year 1653, these words – "This day his Excellence the Lord Generall Cromwell dissolved this House." Which words the Parliament voted a forgery, and demanded of him how they came to be entered: he answered that

1. Conditions of "free quarter" would have allowed Lambert's troops to take what they needed (or wanted) from the local populace.
2. Viol: a stringed fretted instrument, held between the knees like a modern cello and played with a bow.
3. John Pepys, aged 18, was at St Paul's School. On Apposition Day, senior pupils gave orations to compete for exhibitions to Oxford or Cambridge universities. John's speech was in Greek.
4. Symons and Price were underclerks to the Council of State. Henry Muddiman was a journalist.
5. A tavern in Westminster, very close to Pepys's home.
6. Henry Scobell, Clerk of the Parliaments.

they were his own handwriting and that he did it by virtue of his office and the practice of his predecessors; and that the intent of the practice was to let posterity know how such and such a Parliament was dissolved, whether by the command of the King or by their own neglect, as the last House of Lords was;[1] and that to this end he had said and writ that it was dissolved by his Excellence the Lord Generall. And that for the word "dissolved," he never at that time did hear of any other term; and desired pardon if he would not dare to make a word himself, which it was six years after before they came themselfs to call it an Interrupcion.[2] But they were so little satisfied with this answer, that they did choose a committee to report to the House whether this crime of Mr. Scobells did come within the Act of Indemnity[3] or no.

Thence I went with Muddiman to the Coffee-house, and gave 18*d* to be entered of the Club.[4] Thence into the Hall, where I heard for certain that Monke was coming to London, and that Bradshaw's lodgings[5] were preparing for him.

Thence to Mrs. Jem and found her in bed, and some was afraid that it would prove the small-pox. Thence back to Westminster-hall, where I heard how Sir H. Vane was this day voted out of the House and to sit no more there; and that he would retire himself to his house at Raby, as also all the rest of the nine officers that had their commissions formerly taken away from them were commanded to their farthest houses from London during the pleasure of the Parliament.[6] Here I met with Quarter Maister of my Lord's troop and his clerk Mr. Jenings, and took them home and gave a bottle of wine and the remainder of my collar of brawn, and so good-night. After that, came in Mr. Hawly, who told me that I was missed this day at my office and that tomorrow I must pay all the money that I have, at which I was put to a great loss how I should

1. The House of Lords had dwindled to about six members by the time of Charles I's execution; it had been abolished in March 1649.
2. When Lambert prevented members from meeting on 13 Oct. 1659 he was reported in the House of Commons Journal to have "interrupted" the session.
3. A law passed in 1659, preventing prosecution of anyone who had tried since 1653 to alter the government from "a Commonwealth or Free State".
4. The Rota club met at Miles's coffeehouse (the Turk's head) in New Palace Yard, Westminster, to debate republican models for government.
5. In fact it was the Prince's Lodgings at Whitehall that were prepared for Monck.
6. In October 1659 the withdrawal of the nine officers' commissions had led them to suspend the Rump. Sir Henry Vane (a leading republican who was not in fact one of the officers) was now targeted because of his association with the army during that time.

get money to make up my cash, and so went to bed in great trouble.[1]

10. Went out early, and in my way met with Greatorex, and at an alehouse he showed me the first sphere of wire that ever he made, and indeed it was very pleasant.[2] Whence to Mr. Crews and borrowed 10*l*; and so to my office and was able to pay my money. Thence into the Hall; and meeting the Quarter Maister, Jenings and Captain Rider, we four went to a cook's to dinner. Thence Jenings and I into London, it being through heat of the sun a great thaw and dirty, to show our bills of return; and coming back, drank a pint of wine at the Star in Cheapside. So to Westminster, overtaking Captain Okeshott in his silk cloak, whose sword got hold of many people in walking.

Thence to the Coffee-house, where were a great confluence of gentlemen; *viz.* Mr. Harrington, Poultny cheareman, Gold, Dr. Petty &[c]., where admirable discourse till 9 at night.[3] Thence with Doling to Mother Lam's,[4] who told me how this day Scott was made Intelligencer, and that the rest of the members that were objected against last night, their businesses were to be heard this day sennit.[5] Thence I went home and wrote a letter, and went to Harpers and stayed there till Tom carried it to the post-boy at White-hall. So home to bed.

13. Coming in the morning to my office, I met with Mr. Fage and took him to the Swan.[6] He told me how high Haslerigg and Morly the last night began at my Lord Mayor's to exclaim against the City of London, saying that they have forfeited their charter.[7] And how the Chamberlain of the City did take them down, letting them

1. John Hawley was Pepys's fellow clerk at the Exchequer. Pepys had taken Exchequer money to pay his rent on 4 January.
2. Probably an armillary sphere showing the movements of celestial objects. Ralph Greatorex was an inventor and mathematical-instrument maker.
3. The contributors included James Harrington, founder of the club, and William Petty, a physician and political economist who later became a friend of Pepys.
4. Thomas Doling was Messenger to the Council of State and an old friend. Mother Lamb's was an alehouse.
5. Thomas Scott, a republican, had been given control of the intelligence service. The "rest of the members" were Henry Vane's associates who had collaborated with the army. Their fate was to be debated in a sennight (a week).
6. Valentine Fage, Pepys's apothecary, sat on the Common Council of London so was well informed on the latest developments.
7. The City's charter was allegedly forfeit because its Common Council had been campaigning for a free parliament. Sir Arthur Hesilrige (principal leader of the Rump) and Col. Herbert Morley were members of the parliamentary committee appointed to deal with the City.

know how much they were formerly beholding to the City, &c; he also told me that Monke's letter that came to them[1] by the sword-bearer was a cunning piece, and that which they did not much trust to;[2] but they were resolved to make no more applications to the Parliament, nor to pay any money, unless the secluded members be brought in or a free Parliament chosen.

Thence to my office, where nothing to do. So to Will's with Mr. Pinkny, who invited me to their feast at his Hall the next Monday.[3] Thence I went home and took my wife and dined at Mr. Wade's. And after that we went and visited Catau.[4] From thence home again, and my wife was very unwilling to let me go forth; but with some discontent, would go out if I did; and I going forth towards White-hall, I saw she fallowed me, and so I stayed and took her round through White-hall, and so carried her home angry. Thence I went to Mrs. Jem. And found her up and merry, and that it did not prove the small-pox but only the swine-pox; so I played a game or two at cards with her and so to Mr. Vines, where he and I and Mr. Hudson played half-a-dozen things, there being there Dick's wife and her sister. After that I went home and found my wife gone abroad to Mr. Hunt's, and came in a little after me. So to bed.

16. In the morning I went up to Mr. Crews, and at his bedside he gave me direction to go tomorrow with Mr. Edwd. to Twickenham,[5] and likewise did talk to me concerning things of state and expressed his mind how just it was that the secluded members should come to sit again. I went from thence, and in my way went into an alehouse and drank my morning draught with Matt Andrews and two or three more of his friends, coachmen. And of one of them I did hire a coach to carry us tomorrow to Twickenham.

From thence to my office, where nothing to do; but Mr. Downing, he came and found me all alone; and did mention to me his going back into Holland,[6] and did ask me whether I would go or no; but gave me little encouragement but bid me consider of it and asked me whether I did not think that Mr. Hawly could perform the work of the office alone or no. I confess I was at a great

1. The Common Council.
2. It was not clear from the letter whether Monck was for the Rump or a free parliament.
3. George Pinckney was a parish clerk; his Hall was that of the Company of Parish Clerks.
4. Catau ("Kate") Sterpin, a maidservant in the New Palace Yard.
5. Edward Mountagu, jun., aged 12, was to go to school there.
6. Downing was the diplomatic resident there, as well as being Pepys's employer at the Exchequer.

loss all the day after to bethink myself how to carry this business.

At noon Harry Ethell came to me and went along with Mr. Maylard by coach as far as Salsbury Court; and there we set him down and we went to the Clerkes,[1] where we came a little too late; but in a closet[2] we had a very good dinner by Mr. Pinkny's courtesy. And after dinner we had pretty good singing and one Hazard sung alone after the old fashion; which was very much cried up, but I did not like it.

Thence we went to the Greene Dragon on Lambeth hill, both the Mr. Pinknys, Smith, Harrison, Morrice that sang the bass, Sheply and I, and there we sang of all sorts of things and I ventured with good success upon things at first sight and after that played on my flagelette;[3] and stayed there till 9 a-clock, very merry and drawn on with one song after another till it came to be so late.

After that, Sheply, Harrison and myself, we went towards Westminster on foot, and at the Golden Lion, near Charing-cross, we went in and drank a pint of wine, and so parted; and thence home, where I found my wife and maid a-washing.

I sat up till the bell-man came by with his bell, just under my window as I was writing of this very line, and cried, "Past one of the clock, and a cold, frosty, windy morning." I then went to bed and left my wife and the maid a-washing still.

17. Early, I went to Mr. Crew's; and having given Mr. Edwd: money to give the servants, I took him into the coach that waited for us and carried him to my house, where the coach waited for me while I and the child went to Westminster-hall and bought him some pictures. In the Hall, I met Mr. Woodfine and took him to Will's and drank with him. Thence the child and I to the coach, where my wife was ready, and so we went towards Twickenham. In our way, at Kinsington, we understood how that my Lord Chesterfield had killed another gentleman about half an hour before and was fled.[4] We went forward and came about one of the clock to Mr. Fuller's,[5] but he was out of town; so we had a dinner there and I gave the child 40*s* to give to the two Ushers.

After that we parted and went homewards, it being market-day at Brainford. I set my wife down and went with the coach to Mr.

1. The Parish Clerks' Hall.
2. A private room or study.
3. Flageolet: a wind-instrument (resembling a recorder) with four holes at the front and two at the back.
4. This was a duel over the price of a mare.
5. William Fuller, schoolmaster at Twickenham.

Crews, thinking to have spoke with Mr. Moore and Mrs. Jane, he having told me the reason of his melancholy was some unkindness from her after so great expressions of love, and how he had spoke to her friends[1] and had their consents. And that he would desire me to take an occasion of speaking with her, but by no means not to heighten her discontent or distaste whatever it be, but to make it up if I can.

But he being out of doors, I went away and went to see Mrs. Jem, who was now very well again. And after a game or two at cards, I left her. So I went to the Coffee club[2] and heard very good discourse; it was in answer to Mr. Harrington's answer, who said that the state of the Roman government was not a settled government, and so it was no wonder that the balance of propriety[3] was in one hand and the command in another, it being therefore always in a posture of war; but it was carried by Ballat that it was a steady government; though, it is true by the voices, it had been carried before that it was an unsteady government. So tomorrow it is to be proved by the opponents that the balance lie in one hand and the government in another.

Thence I went to Westminster and met Shaw and Washington, who told me how this day Sydenham was voted out of the House for setting any more this Parliament, and that Salloway was voted out likewise and sent to the Tower during the pleasure of the House.[4]

Home, and wrote by the post[5] and carried [it] to White-hall; and coming back, turned in at Harper's, where Jack Price was, and I drank with him and he told me, among other things, how much the Protector[6] is altered; though he would seem to bear out his trouble very well, yet he is scarce able to talk sense with a man. And how he will say that "Who should a man trust, if he may not trust to a brother and an Uncle;"[7] and how much those men have to answer before God Almighty for their playing each the knaves with him as they did. He told me also that there was 100000*l* offered, and

1. Relations.
2. The Rota, at Miles's Coffeehouse.
3. Property.
4. Col. William Sydenham and Maj. Richard Salwey had collaborated with the army in October–December 1659.
5. An inland postal service, overseen by the government, left London three nights a week. This was Tuesday, one of the postnights.
6. Richard Cromwell, out of power since May 1659. Price was an underclerk of the council.
7. The brother (-in-law) was Charles Fleetwood and the uncle John Desborough; both were leaders of the movement that had led to Richard Cromwell's fall.

would have been taken, for his restitution, had not the Parliament come in as they did again. And that he doth believe that the Protector will live to give a testimony of his valour and revenge yet before he dies, and that the Protector will say so himself sometimes.

Thence I went home, it being late and my wife in bed.

24. In the morning to my office; where after I had drank my morning draught at Will's with Ethell and Mr. Stevens, I went and told part of the excise money till 12 a-clock. And then called on my wife and took her to Mr. Pierce's,[1] she in the way being exceedingly troubled with a pair of new pattens,[2] and I vexed to go so slow, it being late. There when we came, we found Mrs. Carrick very fine, and one Mr. Lucy, who called one another husband and wife; and after dinner, a great deal of mad stir; there was pulling off Mrs. Bride's and Mr. Bridegroom's ribbons, with a great deal of fooling among them that I and my wife did not like;[3] Mr. Lucy and several other gentlemen coming in after dinner, swearing and singing as if they were mad; only, he singing very handsomely. There came in afterwards Mr. Southorne, clerk to Mr. Blackburne,[4] and with him Lieutenant Lambert, Lieutenant of my Lord's ship; and brought with them the declaration that came out today from the Parliament, wherein they declare for law and gospel, and for tithes; but I do not find people apt to believe them.

After this, taking leave, I went to my father's; and my wife staying there, he and I went to speak with Mr. Crumlum[5] (in the meantime, while it was 5 a-clock, he being in the school, we went to my cousin Tom Pepy's shop, the turner in Paul's churchyard, and drank with him a pot of ale); he gave my father directions what to do about getting my brother an exhibition, and spoke very well of my brother.

Thence back with my father home, where he and I spoke privately in the little room to my sister Pall[6] about her stealing of things, as my wife's scissors and my maid's book, at which my father was much troubled.

Hence home with my wife and so to White-hall, where I met

1. James Pearse, navy surgeon. He and his wife Elizabeth were good friends of Pepys.
2. Wooden-soled overshoes, needed to walk in dirty city streets.
3. This was a mock-wedding, replicating the custom of pulling off ribbons from the bridegroom that accompanied putting the couple to bed.
4. Robert Blackborne, Secretary to the Navy Commissioners, c.1653–60.
5. Samuel Cromleholme, High Master of St Paul's School.
6. Paulina, aged 19.

with Mr. Hunt and Luellin[1] and drank with them at Marshes, and afterwards went up and writ to my Lord by the post.

This day the Parliament gave order that the late Committee of Safety[2] should come before them this day sennit, and all their papers and their model of Government that they had made to be brought in with them. So home and talked with my wife about our dinner on Thursday.

30. This morning, before I was up, I fell a-singing of my song *Great, good, and just*, &c.[3] and put myself thereby in mind that this was the fatal day, now ten year since, his Majesty died.[4]

Scull the waterman came and brought me a note from the Hope,[5] from Mr. Hawly with direction about his money, he tarrying there till his master[6] be gone.

To my office, where I received money of the excise of Mr. Ruddyer; and after we had done, went to Will's and stayed there till 3 a-clock; and then, I taking my 12*l*-10*s*. 00*d* due to me for my last Quarter salary, I went with them by water to London, to the house where Signor Torriano used to be, and stayed there a while with Mr. Ashwell, Spicer and Ruddier. Then I went and paid 12*l*. 17*s*. 06*d* due from me to Captain Dick Mathews according to his direction the last week in a letter. After that I came back by water, playing on my Flagelette; and not finding my wife come home yet from her father's, I went and sat a while and played at cards with Mrs. Jem, whose maid had newly got an ague and was ill thereupon.

So homewards again; have great need to do my business; and so pretending to meet Mr. Shott the wood-monger of White-hall, I went and eased myself at the Harp and Ball. And thence home, where I sat reading till bed-time, and so to bed.

There seems now to be a general cease of talk, it being taken for granted that Monke doth resolve to stand to the Parliament and nothing else. I spent a little time this night in knocking up nails for my hats and cloaks in my chamber.

1. Peter Llewellyn, a friend recently dismissed as underclerk to the Council of State but soon to be reappointed.
2. The Committee of Safety (composed mostly of military officers) ruled during the "interruption" of the Rump, October–December 1659.
3. A setting of the Marquis of Montrose's poem "Upon the Death of King Charles the First". It begins "Great! Good! and Just! could I but Rate / My Griefs, and Thy too Rigid Fate").
4. It was eleven years since Charles I's execution.
5. The Hope Reach, part of the River Thames east of Tilbury.
6. Downing, who was returning as ambassador to the Dutch Republic.

FEBRUARY.

2. I drank at Harpers with Doling; and so to my office, where I found all the officers of the regiments in town waiting to receive money that their soldiers might go out of town; and what was in the exchequer they had. At noon, after dining at home, I called at Harpers for Doling, and he and I met with Luellin and drank with him at the Chequer at Charing-cross; and thence he and I went to the Temple to Mr. Calthrops chamber, and from thence had his man by water to London-bridge to Mr. Calthrops, a grocer, and received 60*l.* for my Lord.[1] In our way we talked with our waterman, White, who told us how the watermen have lately been abused by some that have desire to get in to be watermen to the State, and have lately presented an address of 9 or 10000 hands to stand by this Parliament; when it was only told them it was a petition against Hackny coaches. And that today they have put out another to undeceive the world and to clear themselfs; and that among the rest, Cropp, my waterman and one of great practice, was one that did cheat them thus.[2] After I had received the money, we went to the Bridge Taverne and drunk a Quart of wine and so back by water, landing Mr Calthrop's man at the Temple; and we went homewards, but over against Somerset-house, hearing the noise of guns, we landed and found the Strand full of soldiers. So I took my money and went to Mrs Johnson, my Lord's sempstress; and giving her my money to lay up, Doling and I went upstairs to a window, and looked out and saw the Foot face the Horse and beat them back, and stood bawling and calling in the street for a free Parliament and money. By and by a drum was heard to beat a march, coming towards them; and they all got ready again and faced them, and they proved to be of the same mind with them; and so they made a great deal of joy to see one another. After all this, I took my money and went home on foot and lay up my money; and changing

1. Lestrange Calthorpe, the lawyer, and Edward Calthorpe of the Grocer's Company were paying off a debt due from their kinsman.
2. The bogus petition was presented to the House of Commons on 31 January. It pledged support to the Rump and declared against the King and a House of Lords. The day after, the Council of State prepared its list of official watermen, positions that gave freedom from forced service in the navy. The watermen of the Thames competed for business with the hackney carriage drivers. The reply to the address, presented on 2 February, declared for a free parliament.

my stockings and shoes, I this day having left off my great skirt-suit and put on my white suit with silver lace coat; and went over to Harpers, where I met with W. Simons, Doling, Luellin and three merchants; one of which had occasion to use a porter, and so they sent for one and James, the soldier, came; who told us how they had been all day and night upon their guard at St. James's and that through the whole town they did resolve to stand to what they had began, and that tomorrow he did belive they would go into the City and be received there.

After all this, we went to a sport called Selling of a Horse for a Dish of Eggs and Herrings;[1] and sat talking there till almost 12 a-clock and then parted: they were to go as far as Allgate. Home and to bed.

3. Drank my morning draught at Harpers and was told there that the soldiers were all quiet, upon promise of pay. Thence into St. James's Park, and walked there to my place for my Flagelette and there played a little, it being a most pleasant morning and sunshine. Back to White-hall, where in the guard-chamber I saw about 30 or 40 prentices of the City who were taken at 12 a-clock last night and brought prisoner hither.[2] Thence to my office, where I paid a little more money to some of the soldiers under Lieutenant-Collonell Miller (who held out the Tower against the Parliament after it was taken away from Fich by the Committee of Safety, and yet is continued in his office);[3] about noon Mrs. Turner came to speak with me and Joyce,[4] and I took them and showed them the manner of the House's sitting, the doorkeeper very civilly opening the door for us. Thence with my Cosen Roger Pepys;[5] it being term time, we took him out of the Hall to Priors, the Renish wine-house, and there had a pint or two of wine and a dish of Anchoves, and bespake three or four dozen of bottles of wine for him against his Wedding. After this done, he went away and left me order to call and pay for all that Mrs. Turner would have. So we called for nothing more there, but went and bespoke a shoulder of mutton at Wilkinsons,[6] to be dressed as well as it could be done, and sent a bottle

1. Possibly a game of chance.
2. They had risen in support of the soldiers' mutiny on 2 February.
3. On 12 Dec. 1659, Lt-Col. John Miller, faithful to the Committee of Safety, had resisted an attempt by Col. Finch, his superior officer, to hand over the Tower of London to parliamentary agents.
4. Jane Turner and Joyce Norton were relatives.
5. Roger Pepys of Impington, a barrister at the Middle Temple and eldest son of Pepys's great-uncle. He was about to marry for the third time.
6. A cookshop kept by William Wilkinson in Westminster.

of wine home to my house. In the meantime, she and I and Joyce went walking all over White-hall, whither Generall Monke was newly come and we saw all his forces march by in very good plight and stout officers. Thence to my house, where we dined; but with a great deal of patience, for the mutton came in raw and so we were fain to stay the stewing of it. In the meantime, we sat studying of a posy[1] for a ring for her, which she is to have at Rog Pepys his wedding. After dinner I left them and went to hear news; but only found that the Parliament-house was most of them with him[2] at White-hall, and that in his passage through the town he had many cry to him for a free Parliament; but little other welcome. I saw in the Palace-yard how unwilling some of the old soldiers were yet to go out of town without their money; and swore, if they had it not in three days as they were promised, they would do them more mischief in the country then if they had stayed here; and that is very likely, the country being all discontented. The town and guard are already full of Monkes soldiers. I returned, and it growing dark, I and they went to take a turn in the park, where Theoph (who was sent for to us to dinner) outrun my wife and another poor woman, that laid a pot of ale with me that she would outrun her. After that, I set them as far as Charing-cross and there left them and my wife; and I went to see Mrs. Ann, who begun very high about a flock-bed I sent her,[3] but I took her down. Here I played at cards till 9 a-clock. So home and to bed.

7. In the morning, I went early to give Mr. Hawly notice of my being forced to go into London; but he having also business, we left our office business to Mr. Spicer and he and I walked as far as the Temple, where I halted a little and then went to Pauls schoole; but it being too soon, I went and drank my morning draught with my Cosen Tom. Pepys the turner, and saw his house and shop. Thence to school, where he that made the speech for the seventh-form, in praise of the Founder, did show a book that Mr. Crumlum had lately got, which is believed to be of the Founder's own writing.[4] After all the speeches, in which my Brother John came off as well as any of the rest, I went straight home and dined; then to the

1. A motto or verse inscribed on a ring.
2. Monck.
3. Ann, Jemima Mountagu's maid, was angry about a mattress stuffed with flocks (coarse wool) that Pepys had sent to her.
4. At St Paul's School, speeches were made on Apposition Day by students competing for exhibitions to go to university. The founder of the school was John Colet (d. 1519).

Hall, where in the Palace I saw Monk's soldiers abuse Billing[1] and all the Quakers that were at a meeting-place there; and indeed, the soldiers did use them very roughly and were to blame. So after drinking with Mr. Spicer, who had received 600*l* for me this morning, I went to Captain Stone and with him by coach to the Temple-garden (all the way talking of the disease of the stone); where we met Mr. Squib, but could do nothing till tomorrow morning. Thence back on foot home, where I found a letter from my Lord in Character,[2] which I construed; and after my wife had shown me some ribbon and shoes that she had taken out of a box of Mr. Mountagus, which formerly Mr. Kipps had left her when his master was at sea, I went to Mr. Crew and advised with him about it, it being concerning my Lord's coming up to town, which he desires upon my advice the last week in my letter. Thence, calling upon Mrs. Ann, I went home and wrote in Character to my Lord an answer to his letter. This day Mr. Crew told me that my Lord St. John's[3] is for a free Parliament, and that he is very great with Monke – who hath now the absolute command and power to do anything that he hath a mind to do.

Mr. Moore told me of a picture hung up at the Exchange,[4] of a great pair of buttocks shitting of a turd into Lawsons mouth, and over it was writ "The thanks of the House."[5]

Boys do now cry "Kiss my Parliament" instead of "Kiss my arse," so great and general a contempt is the Rump come to among all men, good and bad.

11. This morning I lay long abed; and then to my office, where I read all the morning my Spanish book of Rome.[6] At noon I walked in the Hall, where I heard the news of a letter from Monke, who was now gone into the City again and did resolve to stand for the sudden filling up of the House; and it was very strange how the countenance of men in the Hall was all changed with joy in half an hour's time. So I went up to the Lobby, where I saw the Speaker reading of the letter;[7] and after it was read, Sir A. Haslerig[8] came

1. Edward Billing, a prominent Quaker.
2. Cipher.
3. Oliver St John, a leading Presbyterian MP and member of the Council of State.
4. The Royal Exchange, the City's chief forum for trading.
5. John Lawson (commanding the fleet) was a republican and friend of the Rump.
6. A guide for pilgrims, *Las cosas maravillosas dela sancta ciudad de Roma* (1651).
7. Monck and his officers had decided on resistance to the Rump. They sent the parliament a letter requiring it to fill up vacant seats in the House by 17 February and reminding it of its declared intention to dissolve.
8. Arthur Hesilrige, a leader of the Rump.

out very angry; and Billing standing at the door, took him by the arm and cried, "Thou man, will thy beast carry thee no longer? thou must fall." The House presently after rose, and appointed to meet again at 3 a-clock. I went then down into the Hall, where I met with Mr. Chetwind,[1] who had not dined no more then myself; and so we went towards London, in our way calling at two or three shops, and could have no dinner; at last, within Temple-bar, we found a pullet ready-roasted, and there we dined. After that, he went to his office in Chancery-lane, calling at the Rolles,[2] where I saw the lawyers pleading; then to his office, where I sat in his study singing while he was with his man (Mr. Powells son) looking after his business. Thence we took coach for the City to Guild-hall, where the hall was full of people expecting Monke and Lord Mayor to come thither, and all very joyful. Here we stayed a great while; and at last, meeting with a friend of his, we went to the Three Tun tavern and drank half a pint of wine; and not liking the wine, we went to an alehouse, where we met with company of this third man's acquaintance and there we drank a little: hence I went alone to Guild-hall to see whether Monke was come yet or no, and met him coming out of the chamber where he had been with the Mayor and Aldermen; but such a shout I never heard in all my life, crying out "God bless your Excellence." Here I met with Mr. Lock,[3] and took him to an alehouse and left him there to fetch Chetwind; when we were come together, Lock told us the substance of the letter that went from Monke to the Parliament. Wherein, after complaints that he and his officers were put upon such offices against the City as they could not do with any content or honour. That there are many members now in the House that were of the late tyrannical Committee of Safety. That Lambert and Vane are now in town, contrary to the vote of Parliament. That there was many in the House that do press for new oaths to be put upon men; whereas we have more cause to be sorry for the many others that we have already taken and broken. That the late petition of the Fanatique people presented by Barebone, for the imposing of an oath upon all sort of people, was received by the House with thanks.[4] That therefore he doth desire that all writts for filling up of the House be issued by Friday next, and that in the meantime

1. James Chetwind, Chancery clerk.
2. The Court of the Master of the Rolls.
3. Matthew Lock, Monck's secretary.
4. Praisegod Barebone presented a petition to parliament on 9 February demanding the imposition of an oath abjuring the monarchy.

he would retire into the City, only leave them guards for the security of the House and Council. The occasion of this was the order that he had last night to go into the City and disarm them and take away their charter;[1] whereby he and his officers see that the House had a mind to put them on things that should make them odious; and so it would be in their power to do what they would with them. He told us that they had sent Scott and Robinson to him this afternoon, but he would not hear them.[2] And that the Mayor and Aldermen had offered him their own houses for himself and his officers, and that his soldiers would lack for nothing. And endeed I saw many people give the soldiers drink and money, and all along in the streets cried, "God bless them" and extraordinary good words. Hence, we three went to a merchant's house hard by, where Lock writ a note and left; where I saw Sir Nich. Crisp and so we went to the Star taverne (Monke being then at Bensons),[3] where we drank and I wrote a letter to my Lord from thence. In Cheapside there was a great many bonefires, and Bow bells and all the bells in all the churches as we went home were a-ringing. Hence we went homewards, it being about 10 a-clock. But the common joy that was everywhere to be seen! The number of bonefires, there being fourteen between St. Dunstan's and Temple-bar. And at Strand bridge I could at one view tell 31 fires. In King-streete, seven or eight; and all along burning and roasting and drinking for rumps – there being rumps tied upon sticks and carried up and down. The buchers at the maypole in the Strand rang a peal with their knifes when they were going to sacrifice their rump. On Ludgate-hill there was one turning of the spit, that had a rump tied upon it, and another basting of it. Indeed, it was past imagination, both the greatness and the suddenness of it. At one end of the street, you would think there was a whole lane of fire, and so hot that we were fain to keep still on the further side merely for heat. We came to the chequer at Charing-cross, where Chetwind wrote a letter and I gave him an account of what I had writ for him to write. Thence home and sent my letter to the post-house in London, and my wife and I (after Mr. Hunt was gone whom I found waiting for me at my house) went out again to show her the

1. Without a charter, the City of London and its Common Council had no legal authority. There appears to be no direct evidence of an attempt against the charter itself, but the Rump had repeatedly moved against the City.
2. MPs Thomas Scott and Luke Robinson had been sent with a conciliatory message.
3. Thomas Benson kept a tavern in Cheapside.

fires; and after walking as far as the Exchange, we returned and to bed.

21. In the morning, going out, I saw many soldiers going toward Westminster; and was tol[d] that they were going to admit the secluded members again. So I to Westminster-hall, and in Chancery-row I saw about 20 of them, who had been at White-hall with generall Monke, who came thither this morning and made a speech to them and recommended to them a commonwealth, and against Ch. Stuart.[1] They came to the House and went in one after another, and at last the Speaker came. But it is very strange that this could be carried so private, that the other members of the House heard nothing of all this till they found them in the House, insomuch that the soldiers that stood there to let in the secluded members, they took for such as they had ordered to stand there to hinder their coming in. Mr. Prin[2] came with an old basket-hilt sword on, and had a great many great shouts upon his going into the hall. They sat till noon, and at their coming out Mr. Crew saw me and bid me come to his house; which I did, and he would have me dine with him, which I did, and he very joyful; told me that the House had made Generall Monke generall of all the forces in England, Scotland, and Ireland. And that upon Monkes desire, for the service that Lawson had lately done in pulling down the Committee of Safety, he had the command of the Sea for the time being. He advised me to send for my Lord forthwith, and told me that there is no Question but, if he will, he may now be imployed again; and that the House doth entend to do nothing more then to issue writs and to settle a foundation for a free parliament. After dinner I back to Westminster-hall with him in his coach. Here I met with Mr. Lock and Pursell, Maisters of Musique;[3] and with them to the Coffee-house into a room next the Water by ourselfs; where we spent an hour or two till Captain Taylor came to us, who told us that the House had voted the gates of the City to be made up again and the members of the City that are in prison to be let at liberty; and that Sir G. Booth's case be brought into the House tomorrow.[4]

1. Monck read a statement defining the terms on which secluded members were to be restored to their places.
2. William Prynne, a Presbyterian MP who had been imprisoned for his opposition to the Commonwealth in the early 1650s.
3. Matthew Locke the composer (to be distinguished from Monck's secretary of the same name), and either Thomas or the elder Henry Purcell, uncle and father respectively to the famous Henry Purcell.
4. Sir George Booth had led the Presbyterian-Royalist rising of August 1659 and was now a prisoner in the Tower.

Here we had variety of brave Italian and Spanish songs and a Canon[1] for 8 *Voc*:, which Mr. Lock had newly made on these words: *Domine salvum fac Regem*,[2] an admirable thing.

Here also, Captain Taylor began a discourse of something that he hath lately writ about Gavelkinde in answer to one that hath writ a piece upon the same subject.[3] And indeed, discovered a great deal of study in antiquity in his discourse. Here, out of the window it was a most pleasant sight to see the City from [one] end to the other with a glory[4] about it, so high was the light of the Bonefires and so thick round the City, and the bells rang everywhere. Hence home and wrote to my Lord; afterward came down and found Mr. Hunt (troubled at this change) and Mr. Spong, who stayed late with me, singing of a song or two, and so parted. My wife not very well, went to bed before.

This morning I met in the hall with Mr. Fuller of Christ's.[5] And told him of my design to go to Cambrige, and whether.[6] He told me very freely the temper of Mr. Widdrington; how he did oppose all the fellows in the college, and that there was a great distance between him and the rest; at which I was very sorry, for that he told me he feared it would be little to my Brothers advantage to be his pupil.

MARCH.

2. This morning I went early to my Lord at Mr. Crew's, where I spoke to him.[7] Here were a great many too, come to see him, as Secretary Thurlow who is now by this Parliament chosen again as Secretary of State.[8] There was also generall Monkes trumpeters to give my Lord a sound of their trumpets this morning. Thence I went to my office and wrote a letter to Mr. Downing about the business of his house. Then going home, I met with Mr Eglin, Chetwind and Thomas, who took me to the Leg in King's-street,

1. A kind of round.
2. "Lord save the King".
3. "Gavelkind" was the custom of dividing an estate equally among all male heirs. Silas Taylor's *The History of Gavel-kind* was published in 1663.
4. Circle of light.
5. Thomas Fuller, fellow of Christ's College, Cambridge. Pepys was consulting him about a tutor for his brother John.
6. Whither, i.e. to which college.
7. Mountagu had arrived in London at the end of February, and been appointed a General of the Fleet with Monck.
8. John Thurloe had been a Secretary of State under the Protectorate.

where we had two brave dishes of meat, one of fish, a carp and some other fishes, as well done as ever I eat any. After that to the Swan tavern, where we drank a Quart or two of wine, and so parted. So I to Mrs. Jem. and took Mr. Moore with me (who I met in the street) and there I met W. How and Sheply. After that to Westminster-hall, where I saw Sir G. Booth at liberty. This day I hear the City Militia is put into a good posture, and it is thought that Monke will not be able to do any great matter against them now, if he had a mind.

I understand that my Lord Lambert did yesterday send a letter to the Council, and that tonight he is to come and appear to the Council in person. Sir Arth. Haslerigg doth not yet appear in the House. Great is the talk of a single person, and that it would now be Charles, George, or Richard again.[1] For the last of which, my Lord St. Johns is said to speak high. Great also is the dispute now in the House in whose name the writs shall run for the next Parliament – and it is said that Mr. Prin in open House said, "In King Charles's."

From Westminster-hall, home. Spent the evening in my study, and so after some talk with my wife, then to bed.

6. Shrove=tuesday.

I called Mr. Sheply and we both went up to my Lord's lodgings at Mr. Crew's, where he bade us to go home again and get a fire against an hour after – which we did at White-hall, whither he came; and after talking with him and I about his going to sea, he called me by myself to go along with him into the garden, where he asked me how things were with me and what he hath endeavoured to do with my uncle to get him to do something for me;[2] but that he would say nothing to. He likewise bade me look out now, at this turn, some good place; and he would use all his own and all the interest of his friends that he hath in England to do me good. And asked me whether I could without too much inconvenience go to sea as his Secretary, and bade me think of it. He also begin to talk of things of state, and told me that he should now want one in that capacity at sea that he might trust in. And therefore he would have me to go.

He told me also that he did believe the King would come in, and

1. Charles II, George Monck, or Richard Cromwell.
2. The uncle was Robert Pepys of Brampton, in whose will Pepys hoped to feature significantly.

did discourse with me about it and about the affection of the people and City – at which I was full glad.◆

This day I hear that the Lords do entend to sit, and great store of them are now in town and I see in the Hall today.

Overton at Hull doth stand out, but can it is thought do nothing; and Lawson it is said is gone with some ships thither, but all that is nothing.[1]

My Lord told me that there was great endeavours to bring in the Protector again; but he told me too, that he did believe it would not last long if he were brought in; no, nor the King neither (though he seems to think that he will come in), unless he carry himself very soberly and well. Everybody now drink the King's health without any fear, whereas before it was very private that a man dare do it. Monke this day is feasted at Mercers-hall, and is invited one after another to all the twelve halls in London.[2]

Many think that he is honest yet, and some or more think him to be a fool that would raise himself, but think that he will undo himself by endeavouring it.

My mind, I must needs remember, hath been very much eased and joyed in my Lord's great expression of kindness this day; and in discourse thereupon, my wife and I lay awake an hour or two in our bed.

10. In the morning went to my father, whom I took in his cutting-house; and there I told him my resolution to go to sea with my Lord and consulted with him how to dispose of my wife; and at last resolved of letting her be at Mr. Bowyers.[3] Thence to the Treasurer of the Navy, where I received 500*l* for my Lord; and having left 200 of it with Mr. Rawlinson at his house for Sheply, I went with the rest to the Sun taverne on Fish-street hill, where Mr. Hill, Stevens and Mr. Hater of the Navy Office had invited me; where we had good discourse and a fine breakfast of Mr. Hater.[4] Then by coach home, where I took occasion to tell my wife of my going to sea, who was much troubled thereat and was with some dispute at last willing to continue at Mr. Bowyers in my absence. After that to see Mrs. Jemi: and paid her maid 7*l*:; and then to Mr. Blackburne, who

1. Maj.-Gen. Robert Overton, Governor of Hull, was trying to organize a republican rising. Lawson, also a republican, had just been displaced from command of the fleet. Both yielded to the new regime within a week.
2. The halls of the twelve great livery companies.
3. Robert Bowyer ("my father Bowyer"), Usher of the Receipt of the Exchequer and a trusted friend of Pepys. His house was at Huntsmoor in Buckinghamshire.
4. Thomas Hayter, a clerk in the Navy Office, was soon to work for Pepys there.

told me what Mr. Creed did say upon the news of my coming into his place,[1] and that he did propose to my Lord that there should be two Secretarys: which made me go to Sir H. Wright's where my Lord dined and spoke with him about it; but he seemed not to agree to the motion. Hither W. Howe[2] comes to me and so to Westminster; in the way he told me what I was [to] provide and so forth against my going. He went with me to my office, whither also Mr. Mage comes half-foxed[3] and played the fool upon the viallin, that made me weary. Then to White-hall and so home and set many of my things in an order against my going. My wife was up making of caps for me, and the wench[4] making an end of a pair of stockings that she was knitting of. So to bed.

17. This morning bade Adieu in bed to the company of my wife. We rose and I gave my wife some money to serve her for a time, and what papers of consequence I had. Then I left her to get her ready and went to my Lord's with my boy Eliezer[5] to my Lord's lodging at Mr. Crews. Here I had much business with my Lord; and papers, great store, given me by my Lord to dispose of as the rest. After that, with Mr. Moore home to my house and took my wife by coach to the Chequer in Holborne; where after we had drunk &c., she took coach and so farewell. I stayed behind with Tom Alcock and Mr. Anderson my old chamber fellow at Cambrige his brother,[6] and drank with them there, who were come to me thither about one that would have a place at sea. Thence with Mr. Hawly to dinner at Mr. Crews. After dinner, to my own house, where all things were put up into the dining-room and locked up, and my wife took the key along with her. This day, in the presence of Mr. Moore (who made it) and Mr. Hawly, I did (before I went out with my wife) seal my will to her, whereby I did give her all that I have in the world but my books, which I gave to my Brother John, excepting only French books, which my wife is to have.[7]◆

22. Up very early and set things in order at my house, and so took leave of Mrs. Crispe and her daughter (who was in bed) and of Mrs. Hunt. Then to my Lord's lodging at the gate and did so there, where Mr. Hawly came to me and I gave him the key of my house

1. Pepys was taking John Creed's place as Mountagu's secretary at sea.
2. William Howe, a clerk in Mountagu's service.
3. Half-drunk.
4. The maid, Jane Birch.
5. Pepys's footboy, Eliezer Jenkins.
6. I.e. the brother of Charles Anderson, Pepys's roommate at Cambridge.
7. Elizabeth's father was French and she was fluent in the language.

to keep; and he went with me to Mr. Crews and there I took my last leave of him. But the weather continuing very bad, my Lord would not go today. My Lord spent this morning private in sealing of his last will and testament with Mr. Wm. Mountagu. After that I went forth about my own business to buy a pair of riding gray serge Stockings – a sword and belt and shoes. And after that took Wotton and Brigden to the Popes-head tavern in Chancery-lane, where Gilb. Holland and Shelston was; and we dined and drank a great deal of wine, and they paid all.[1]

Strange how these people do now promise me anything; one a Rapier, the other a vessel of wine or a gown, and offered me his silver hatband to [do] him a courtesy. I pray God keep me from being proud or too much lifted up hereby.

After that to Westminster and took leave of K. Sterpin, who was very sorry to part with me; and after that, of Mr. George Mountagu, and received my warrant of Mr. Blackburne to be Secretary to the two Generalls of the Fleete. Then to take my leave of the clerks of the Councell; and thence Doling and Luellin would have me go with them to Mount's chamber, where we sat and talked and drank and then I went away. So to my Lord (in my way meeting Chetwind and Swan and bid them farewell), where I lay all night with Mr. Andrews.[2]

This day Mr. Sheply went away on board and I sent my boy with him; this day also Mrs. Jemim: went to Marrowbone,[3] so that I could not see her.

Mr. Moore being out of town tonight, I could not take leave of him nor speak to him about business, which troubled me much.

I left my small keys therefore with Mr. Andrews for him.

23. Up early. Carried my Lord's Will in a black box to Mr. Wm. Mountagu for him to keep for him. Then to the Barbers and put on my Cravatt there. So to my Lord again, who was almost ready to be gone and had stayed for me.

Hither came Gill. Holland, and brought me a Stick=rapier – and Shelston a sugar-loaf; and had brought his wife, which he said was a very pretty woman, to the Ship tavern hard by for me to see, but I could not go. Young Reeve also brought me a little Perspective glasse[4] which I bought for my Lord; it cost me 8*s*. So after that my

1. These were all local tradesmen.
2. John Andrews, steward to Lord Crew.
3. Marylebone.
4. Probably a telescope.

Lord in Sir H. Wrights coach with Captain Isham, and Mr. Tho. and John Crew with him. And I and W. Howe in a Hackny to the Towre, where the barges stayed for us.

My Lord and the Captain in one, and W. How and I and Mr. Ibbott and Mr. Burr in the other, to the Long Reach, where the *Swiftsure* lay at Anchor (in our way we saw the great breach which the late high water had made, to the loss of many 1000*l* to the people about Limehouse). As soon as my Lord on board, the guns went off bravely from the Ships; and a little while after comes the Vice-admirall Lawson and seemed very respectful to my Lord, and so did the rest of the Comanders of the frigates that were thereabouts.

I to the Cabbin allotted for me, which was the best that any had that belonged to my Lord. I got out some things out of my chests for writing, and to work presently, Mr. Burr and I both. I supped at the Deck table with Mr. Sheply. We were late, writing of orders for the getting of ships ready, &c.; and also making of others to all the Seaports between Hastings and Yarmouth to stop all dangerous persons that are going or coming between Flanders and there.

After that to bed in my cabin, which was but short; however, I made shift with it and slept very well; and the weather being good, I was not sick at all; yet I know not when I shall be.

26. This day it is two years since it pleased God that I was cut of the stone at Mrs. Turner's in Salisbury-court. And did resolve while I live to keep it a festival, as I did the last year at my house, and for ever to have Mrs. Turner and her company with me. But now it pleases God that I am where I am and so am prevented to do it openly; only, within my soul I can and do rejoice and bless God, being at this time, blessed be His holy name, in as good health as ever I was in my life.

This morning I rise early and went about making of an establishment of the whole fleet and a list of all the ships, with the number of men [and] guns: about an hour after that, we had a meeting of the principal commanders and seamen to proportion out the number of these things. After that to dinner, there being very many commanders on board. All the afternoon very many orders were made, till I was very weary.

At night Mr. Sheply and W. Howe came and brought some bottles of wine and something to eat at my Cabbin, where we were very merry, remembering the day of being cut of the stone. The

Captain Cuttance[1] came afterwards and sat drinking a bottle of wine till 11 a-clock at night, which is a kindness he doth not usually do to the greatest officer in the ship. After that to bed.

APRILL.

2. Up very early, and to get all my things and my boy's packed up. Great concourse of commanders here this morning to take leave of my Lord upon his going into the *Naseby*,[2] so that the table was full; so there dined below many commanders and Mr. Creed, who was much troubled to hear that he could not go along with my Lord, for he had already got all his things thither, thinking to stay there; but W. Howe was very high against it, and he indeed did put him out, though everybody was glad of it. After dinner I went in one of the boats with my boy before my Lord, and made shift before night to get my cabin in pretty good order. It is but little; but very convenient, having one window to the sea and another to the Deck and a good bed. This morning comes Mr. Edw. Pickering, like a coxcomb as he always was.[3] He tells me that the King will come in, but that Monke did resolve to have the doing of it himself, or else to hinder it.

6. This morning came my brother-in-law Balty to see me and to desire to be here with me as Reformado, which did much trouble me.[4] But after dinner (my Lord using him very civilly at table), I spoke to my Lord and he promised me a letter to Captain Stokes for him, that he should be there. All the day with him, walking and talking; we under sail as far as the Spitts. In the afternoon, W. How and I to our Viallins, the first time since we came on board. This afternoon I made even with my Lord to this day, and did give him all the money remaining in my hand.

In the evening, it being fine moonshine, I stayed late, walking upon the Quarter-deck talking with Mr. Cuttance, learning of some sea terms; and so down to supper and to bed – having an hour before put Balty into Bur's cabin, he being out of the ship.

1. Roger Cuttance, commander of the *Naseby* and an ally of Mountagu.
2. Mountagu was transferring from the *Swiftsure* to the *Naseby*, his flagship. The fleet remained in the Thames and in the Downs (off the Kent coast) until 11 May.
3. Pickering was a relative of Mountagu's by marriage.
4. Balthasar St Michel, aged about 20. A reformado served without a formal commission but with an officer's rank.

11. A gentleman came this morning from my Lord of Manchester to my Lord for a pass for Mr. Boyle,[1] which was made him. I eat a good breakfast by my Lord's order with him in the great cabin below. The wind all this day was very high – so that a gentleman that was at dinner with my Lord that came along with Sir John Bloys (who seemed a fine man) was forced to rise from table. This afternoon came a great paquet of letters from London directed to me; among the rest, two from my dear wife, the first that I have since my coming away from London. All the news from London is that things go ever further toward a King. That the Skinners Company the other day at their entertaining of Generall Monke had took down the Parliament arms in their Hall and set up the Kings.

In the evening my Lord and I had a great deal of discourse about the several Captaines of the fleet and his interest among them, and had his mind clear to bring in the King. He confessed to me that he was not sure of his own Captain[2] to be true to him, and that he did not like Captain Stokes. At night W. Howe and I at our viallins in my cabin, where Mr. Ibbott and the Lieutenant were late. I stayed the Lieutenant late, showing him my manner of keeping a Journall.[3] After that, to bed.

It comes now in my mind to observe that I am sensible that I have been a little too free to make mirth with the Minister of our ship, he being a very sober and an upright man.

21. This day dined Sir John Boys and some other gentlemen, formerly great Cavaliers; and among the rest, one Mr. Norwood, for whom my Lord gave a convoy to carry him to the Brill;[4] but he is certainly going to the King – for my Lord commanded me that I should not enter his name in my book. My Lord doth show them and that sort of people great civility. All of their discourse and others' are of the King's coming, and we begin to speak of it very freely. And heard how in many churches in London and upon many signs there and upon merchants' ships in the river they have set up the King's arms.

In the afternoon the Captain would by all means have me up to

1. Probably Charles Boyle, 2nd son of the Earl of Cork.
2. Roger Cuttance.
3. The Lieutenant was David Lambert, whom Pepys knew from a previous voyage to the Baltic in 1659. This is one of only two times that Pepys records telling someone about his diary-keeping.
4. Boys and Henry Norwood were going to Brielle in Holland. Both now carried letters from Mountagu to the King.

his cabin; and there treated me huge nobly, giving me a barrel of pickled oysters, and opened another for me, and a bottle of wine, which was a very great favour.

At night singing with W. Howe, and under the barber's hands in the coach.[1] This night there came one with a letter from Mr. Edwd. Mountagu[2] to my Lord, with command to deliver it to his own hand. I do believe that he doth carry some close business on for the King.

This day I had a large letter from Mr. Moore, giving me an account of the present dispute at London that is like to be at the beginning of the Parliament, about the House of Lords, who do resolve to sit with the Commons, as not thinking themselfs dissolved yet – which whether it be granted or no, or whether they will sit or no, it will bring a great many inconveniencys. His letter I keep, it being a very well-writ one.

29. *Sunday.* This day I put on first my fine cloth suit, made of a cloak that had like to have been beshit behind a year ago the very day that I put it on.

After sermon in the morning, Mr. Cooke came from London with a packet, bringing news how all the young lords that were not in arms against the Parliament do now sit. That a letter is come from the King to the House; which is locked up by the Council till next Tuesday, that it may be read in the open House when they meet again, they having adjourned till then to keep a fast tomorrow – and so the contents is not yet known.

13000*l* of the 20000*l* given to Generall Monke is paid out of the Exchequer – he giving 12*l* among the teller-clerks of the Exchequer.

My Lord called me into the great Cabbin below, where I opened my letters and he told me that the Presbyterians are quite mastered by the Cavaliers, and that he fears Mr. Crew did go a little too far the other day in keeping out the young Lords from sitting.[3] That he doth expect that the King should be brought over suddenly, with[out] staying to make any terms at all, saying that the Presbyters did intend to have brought him in with such conditions as if

1. A large room normally used by the captain.
2. A relative of Pepys's patron, son of the 2nd Baron Mountagu of Boughton.
3. Elections had just been held for a new parliament (the Convention Parliament). Cavaliers controlled the powerful committee that scrutinized the returns and determined who was qualified to sit in the Commons. Meanwhile, a number of lords who had succeeded to their titles after the House of Lords ceased to sit in 1649 wanted to be admitted to that House. Mountagu's father-in-law Crew joined with other Presbyterian MPs in opposing this.

he had been in chains. But he shook his shoulders when he told me how Monke had betrayed them, for it was he that did put them upon standing to keep out the Lords and the other members that came not within the Qualifications – which he[1] did not like; but however, he[2] hath done his business, though it be with some kind of baseness.

After dinner I walked a great while upon the deck with the Chyrurgeon[3] and Purser and other officers of the ship; and they all pray for the King's coming, which I pray God send.

MAY.

2. In the morning at a breakfast of Radyshes at the Pursers cabin. After that to writing – till dinner – at which time comes Dunne from London with letters that tell us the wellcome Newes of the Parliaments votes yesterday, which will be remembered for the happiest May-day that hath been many a year to England.

The King's letter was read in the House, wherein he submits himself and all things to them – as to an act of Oblivion to all, unless they shall please to except any; – as to the confirming of the Sales of the King's and Church lands, if they see good.[4]

The House, upon reading the letter, order 50000*l* to be forthwith provided to send to His Maiesty for his present[5] supply. And a committee chosen to return an answer of thank[s] to His Majesty for his gracious Letter. And that the letter be kept among the Records of the Parliament. And in all this, not so much as one Noe. So that Luke Robinson[6] himself stood up and made a recantation for what he hath done and promises to be a loyall subject to his Prince for the time to come.

The City of London have put out a Declaracion, wherein they do disclaim their owning any other governments but that of a King, Lords, and Commons. Thanks was given by the House to Sir Joh.

1. Mountagu.
2. Monck.
3. The surgeon, James Pearse.
4. This was Charles's Declaration of Breda. He offered an act of oblivion to pardon offences committed against his father and himself during the civil wars and interregnum. In matters of religion there would be "Liberty to Tender Consciences" with a parliamentary act to follow. Parliament would also decide upon the ownership of confiscated royalist and church lands.
5. Immediate.
6. A republican MP.

Greenevill, one of the bedchamber to the King, who brought the letter; which they continued bare[1] all the time it was reading.

Upon notice made from the Lords to the Commons of their desire that the Commons would join with them in their vote for King, Lords, and Commons, the Commons did concur and voted that all books whatever that are out against the government of King, Lords, and Commons should be brought into the House and burned.

Great joy all yesterday at London; and at night more bonefires then ever and ringing of bells and drinking of the King's health upon their knees in the streets, which methinks is a little too much. But everybody seems to be very joyful in the business – insomuch that our sea-commanders now begin to say so too, which a week ago they would not do. And our seamen, as many as have money or credit for drink, did do nothing else this evening.

This day came Mr. North (Sir Dudly North's son)[2] on board to spend a little time here, which my Lord was a little troubled at; but he seems to be a fine gentleman and at night did play his part exceeding well at first sight.

After Musique I went up to the Captain's cabin with him and Lieutenant Ferrers, who came hither today from London to bring this news to my Lord; and after a bottle of wine, we all to bed.

3. This morning my Lord showed me the King's declaration and his letter to the two Generalls to be communicated to the fleet. The contents of the letter are his offer of grace to all that will come in within 40 days, only excepting them that the Parliament shall hereafter except. That the sales of lands during these troubles, and all other things, shall be left to the Parliament, by which he will stand. The letter dated at Breda, April $\frac{4}{14}$ 1660, in the 12th year of his Raigne.[3] Upon the receipt of it this morning by an express, Mr. Phillips, one of the messengers of the Council from Generall Monke, my Lord summoned a council of war, and in the meantime did dictate to me how he would have the vote ordered which he would have pass this council. Which done, the commanders all came on board, and the council set in the coach (the first council of war that hath been in my time), where I read the letter and

1. Bareheaded – with hats removed as a sign of respect.
2. Charles North, eldest son of Sir Dudley.
3. Charles dated his reign from the death of his father.

declaration; and while they were discoursing upon it, I seemed[1] to draw up a vote; which being offered, they passed.[2] Not one man seemed to say no to it, though I am confident many in their hearts were against it.

After this was done, I went up to the Quarter-deck with my Lord and the commanders, and there read both the papers and the vote; which done, and demanding their opinion, the seamen did all of them cry out "God bless King Charles" with the greatest joy imaginable.

That being done, Sir R. Stayner, who had invited us yesterday, took all the commanders and myself on board him to dinner; where dinner not being ready, I went with Captain Hayward to the *Plimouth* and *Essex*, and did what I had to do there and returned, where very merry at dinner. After dinner, to the rest of the ships (I stayed at the *Assistance* to hear the harper a good while) quite through the fleet. Which was a very brave sight, to visit all the ships and to be received with the respect and Honour that I was on board them all. And much more to see the great joy that I brought to all men; not one through the whole fleet showing the least dislike of the business. In the evening, as I was going on board the Vice-Admirall, the Generall begun to fire his guns, which he did all that he had in the ship; and so did all the rest of the commanders, which was very gallant, and to hear the bullets go hissing over our heads as we were in the boat. This done and finished my Proclamation, I returned to the *Nazeby*, where my Lord was much pleased to hear how all the fleet took it; and in a transport of joy showed me a private letter of the King's to him and another from the Duke of Yorke[3] in such familiar style as to their common friend, with all kindness imaginable. And I found by the letters, and so my Lord told me too, that there hath been many letters sped between them for a great while, and I perceive unknown to Monke. And among the rest that have carried these letters, Sir John Bois is one, and the Mr. Norwood which had a ship to carry him over the other day, which my Lord would not have me put down his name in the book. The King speaks of his being courted to come to The Hague, but doth desire my Lord's advice whether to come to take ship. And

1. Pretended.
2. The vote thanked "his Majesty" for his declaration on behalf of the officers of the fleet and pledged their loyalty to him; it also resolved that the King's letter, declaration, and the vote itself would be read to the fleet.
3. James, Duke of York, the King's brother and heir. He would become Pepys's patron.

the Duke offers to learn the seaman's trade of him, in such familiar words as if Jack Cole[1] and I had writ them. This was very strange to me, that my Lord should carry all things so wisely and prudently as he doth, and I was over-joyful to see him in so good condition; and he did not a little please himself to tell me how he had provided for himself so great a hold in the King.

4. After this to supper, and then to writing of letters till 12 at night and so up again at 3 in the morning. My Lord seemed to put great confidence in me and would take my advice in many things. I perceive his being willing to do all the Honour in the world to Monke and to let him have all the Honour of doing the business, though he will many times express his thoughts of him to be but a thick-skulled fellow; so that I do believe there is some agreement more then ordinary between the King and my Lord to let Monke carry on the business, for it is he that must do the business, or at least that can hinder the business if he be not flattered and observed. This my Lord will hint himself sometimes.

My Lord, I perceive by the King's letter, hath writ to him about his father[2] Crew, and the King did speak well of him; but my Lord tells me that he is afeared that he hath too much concerned himself with the Presbyterian[s] against the House of Lords – which will do him a great discourtesy.

I wrote this morning many letters, and to all the copies of the vote of the council of Warr I put my name; that if it should come in print, my name may be at it.

I sent a copy of the vote to Doling,[3] inclosed in this letter:

"Sir,

He that can fancy a fleet (like ours) in her pride, with pendants loose, guns roaring, caps flying, and the loud *Vive le Roy's* echoed from one ship's company to another, he and he only can apprehend the joy this enclosed vote was received with, or the blessing he thought himself possessed of that bore it, and is

Your humble servant."

About 9 a-clock I got all my letters done, and sent them by the messenger that came yesterday.

This morning came Captain Isham on board with a gentleman going to the King, by whom very cunningly my Lord tells me he

1. Pepys's school friend.
2. Father-in-law.
3. Messenger to the Council of State.

intends to send an account of this day's and yesterday's actions here, notwithstanding that he hath writ to the Parliament to have leave of them to send the King the answer of the Fleete.

Since my writing of the last Paragraph, my Lord called me to him to read his letter to the King, to see whether I could find any slips in it or no.[1]◆

The rest of the afternoon at nine-pins. In the evening came a packet from London; among the rest, a letter from my wife which tells me that she hath not been well, which did exceedingly trouble me; but my Lord sending Mr. Cooke this night, I wrote to her and sent a piece of gold inclosed to her, and writ also to Mrs. Bowyer and enclosed a half-piece to her for a token.

After supper at the table in the coach, my Lord talking concerning the uncertainty of the places of the Exchequer to them that have them now, he did at last think of an office which doth belong to him in case the King doth restore every man to his places that ever have been patent,[2] which is to be one of the clerks of the Signett, which will be a fine imployment for one of his sons.

After all this discourse, we broke up and to bed.

In the afternoon came a Minister on board, one Mr. Sharpe, who is going to the King; who tells me that Commissioners are chosen, both of Lords and Commons, to go to the King; and that Dr. Clarges is going to him from the Army and that he will be here tomorrow.

My letters at night tell me that the House did deliver their letter to Sir John Greenville in answer to the King's standing, and that they gave him 500*l* for his pains, to buy him a Jewell. And that besides the 50000*l* ordered to be borrowed of the City for the present use of the King, the twelve companies of the City do give every one of them to his Majesty, as a present, 1000*l*.

8. All the morning busy. After dinner there came several persons of Honour, as my Lord St. Johns and others, for convoy to Flushing, and great giving of them salutes. My Lord and we at nine-pins: I lost nine shillings. While we were in play, Mr. Cooke comes on board with letters from London, bringing me news of my wife: that he went to Huntsmore to see her, and brought her and my father

1. Pepys at this point reproduces Mountagu's letter to the King as best he can remember it. In his letter Mountagu congratulates the King and approves of the plan for him to take ship at Scheveningen, near The Hague.
2. I.e. Mountagu had identified a position that would be his to give if the King restored the rights of anyone who controlled or held a position conferred by letters patent.

Bowyer to London where he left her at my father's very well; and speaks very well of her love to me. My letters today tell me how it was entended that the King should be proclaimed today in London with a great deal of pomp. I have also news who they are that are chosen of the Lords and Commons to attend the King.

And also the whole story of what we did the other day in the fleet at reading the King's declaration; and my name at the bottom of it.[1] After supper, some music and to bed – I resolving to rise betimes tomorrow to write letters to London.

10.◆ At night, while my Lord was at supper, in comes my Lord Lauderdale and Sir J. Greenville, who supped here and so went away. After they were gone, my Lord called me into his cabin and told me how he was commanded to set sail presently for the King,[2] and was very glad thereof; and so put me to writing of letters and other work that night till it was very late, he going to bed. I got him afterwards to sign things in bed. After I had done some more work, I to bed also.

14. In the morning, when I waked and rose, I saw myself out of the Scuttle[3] close by the shore, which afterwards I was told to be the Duch shore. The Hague was clearly to be seen by us.

My Lord went up in his night gowne into the Cuddy[4] to see how to dispose thereof for himself and us that belong to him, to give order for our removall today.

Some masty[5] Duchmen came on board to proffer their boats to carry things from us on shore &c., to get money by us.

Before noon, some gentlemen came on board from the shore to kiss my Lords hands. And by and by Mr. North and Dr. Clerke[6] went to kiss the Queen of Bohemia's[7] hands from my Lord, with a dozen of attendants from on board to wait on them; among which I sent my boy – who, like myself, is with child[8] to see any strange thing.

1. The newsbook *The Faithfull Post* of 8 May, printed the fleet's declaration, subscribed '*Samuel Pepys*, Secretary'.
2. By a resolution of both Houses of Parliament, he was to await orders from the King. However, Grenville urged the importance of going to Scheveningen immediately to collect the royal party.
3. An opening in a ship's deck or side.
4. A room in which officers took their meals.
5. Burly.
6. Dr Timothy Clarke, a physician who would become Pepys's good friend.
7. Elizabeth, daughter of James I and widow of Frederick, Elector Palatine, titular King of Bohemia.
8. Eager.

After noon they came back again, having kissed the Queen of Bohemia's hand, and was sent again by my Lord to do the same to the Prince of Orange.[1] So I got the Captain to ask leave for me to go, which my Lord did give; and I, taking my boy and Judge Advocate[2] with me, went in company with them. The weather bad; we were soundly washed when we came near the shore, it being very hard to land there.

The shore is, as all the country between that and The Hague, all sand. The rest of the company got a coach by themselfs. Mr. Creed and I went in the fore-part of a coach, wherein there was two very pretty ladies, very fashionable and with black paches,[3] who very merrily sang all the way and that very well. And were very free to kiss the two blades that were with them.

I took out my Flagelette and piped, but in piping I dropped my rapier=stick; but when I came to The Hague, I sent my boy back again for it and he found it, for which I did give him 6*d.* but some horse had gone over it and broke the scabbard. The Hague is a most neat place in all respects. The houses so neat in all places and things as is possible.

Here we walked up and down a great while, the town being now very full of Englishmen, for that the Londoners[4] were come on shore today.

But going to see the Prince, he was gone forth with his Governor; and so we walked up and down the town and Court to see the place; and by the help of a stranger, an Englishman, we saw a great many places and were made to understand many things, as the intention of the Maypoles which we saw there standing at every great man's door, of different greatness according to the Quality of the person. About 10 at night the Prince comes home, and we found an easy admission. His attendance very inconsiderable as for a prince. But yet handsome, and his tutor a fine man and himself a very pretty boy. It was bright Mooneshine tonight. This done, we went to a place we had taken up to sup in – where a sallet[5] and two or three bones of mutton were provided for a matter of ten of us, which was very strange. After supper the Judge and I to another house to bed, leaving them there; and he and I lying together in

1. The future William III of England, now 9 years old. He was son of Mary, elder daughter of Charles I.
2. John Fowler, Judge-Advocate of the fleet.
3. Shapes of material worn on the face.
4. Representatives of the City.
5. Salad.

one of their press-beds, there being two more in the same room, but all very neat and handsome; and my boy sleeping upon a bench by me, we lay till past 3 a-clock; and then rise and up and
⟨⟨15⟩⟩ down the town to see it by daylight. Where we saw the soldiers of the Prince's guard, all very fine, and the Burgers of the town with their arms and musquets as bright as silver; I meeting this morning a Schoole-Master that spoke good English and French, he went along with us and showed us the whole town. And indeed, I cannot speak enough of the gallantry of the town. Everybody of fashion speak French or Latin, or both. The women, many of them very pretty and in good habitt, fashionable, and black spots.

He went with me to buy a couple of basketts, one of them for Mrs. Pierce, the other for my wife.

After he was gone (we having first drank with him at our lodging), the Judge and I to the *grand Salle*,[1] where we were showed the place where the States-generall[2] sit in council. The hall is a great place, where the flags that they take from their enemies are all hung up. And things to be sold, as in Westminster-hall, and not much unlike it but that not so big – but much neater.

After this to a bookseller's and bought, for the love of the binding, three books – the French Psalms in four parts – Bacon's *organon*, and Farnaby's *Rhetoric*.[3]

After that, the Judge, I, and my boy by coach to Scheveling again – where we went into a house of entertainment and drank there, the wind being very high; and we saw two boats overset there and the gallants forced to be pulled on shore by the heels – while their trunks, portmanteaus, hats, and feathers were swimming in the sea. Among others, I saw the Ministers that came along with the Commissioners[4] sadly dipped – Mr. Case among the rest. So they came in where we was; and I being in haste, left my Copenhagen knife there and so lost it.

Having stayed here a great while, a Gentleman that was going to kiss my Lord's hand from the Queen of Bohemia and I hired a Duch boat for four Rix Dollers[5] to carry us on board. We were fain

1. The Great Hall ("Zaal").
2. The central assembly of the provinces that made up the Dutch Republic.
3. An edition of Francis Bacon's *Novum organum* (on natural philosophy) and Thomas Farnaby's handbook of rhetoric for schoolboys, *Index Rhetoricus* (Amsterdam, 1648).
4. The commissioners sent by Parliament and the City of London.
5. Dutch or North German silver coin.

to wait a great while before we could get off from the shore. The sea being very rough.

The Duchman would fain have us all paid that came into our boat, besides us two and our company, there being many of our ship's company got in who were on shore. But some of them had no money to give them, having spent all on shore.

Coming on board, we found all the Commissioners of the House of Lords at dinner with my Lord; who after dinner went away for shore.

Mr. Morland, now Sir Samuel, was here on board, but I do not find that my Lord or anybody did give him any respect, he being looked upon by him and all men as a knave. Among others, he betrayed Sir Rich: Willis that married Dr. Foxes daughter, that he had paid him 1000*l* at one time, by the Protector and Secretary Thurloes order, for intelligence that he sent concerning the King.[1]

In the afternoon my Lord called me on purpose to show me his fine clothes which are now come hither; and indeed, are very rich – as gold and silver can make them. Only his sword he and I do not like.

In the afternoon my Lord and I walked together in the Coach two houres, talking together upon all sorts of discourse – as Religion, wherein he is I perceive wholly Scepticall, as well as I, saying that indeed the Protestants as to the Church of Rome are wholly fanatiques. He likes uniformity and form of prayer.[2]

About State business, among other things he told me that his conversion to the King's cause (for so I was saying that I wondered from what time the King could look upon him to be become his friend), from his being in the Sound, when he found what usage he was likely to have from a Comonwealth.[3]

My Lord, the Captain, and I supped in my Lord's chamber –

1. Samuel Morland had been Pepys's tutor at Cambridge before working for the Protectorate under Secretary of State Thurloe, while passing information to the royalists. He had just been knighted by the King for his services. Willys was a royalist conspirator who had worked as a double agent for Thurloe. Morland told Charles that Willys had schemed to have Charles assassinated.

2. Mountagu appears to have meant that, while mainstream Protestants disparaged members of separatist groups and sects as "fanatiques", all Protestants were "fanatiques" in relation to the Roman Catholic Church. He therefore seemed fundamentally sceptical about claims to religious authority (which Pepys says is his own position), while also seeing reasons for uniformity in worship and set forms of prayer.

3. In spring 1659 Mountagu had been sent with a fleet to the Baltic to facilitate negotiations between Sweden and Denmark. The Rump parliament, mistrusting him, then dispatched Commissioners to take over the negotiations and govern the fleet's actions.

where I perceive that he did begin to show me much more respect then ever he did yet.

After supper my Lord sent for me, entending to have me play at cards with him; but I not knowing Cribbige, we fell into discourse of many things, till it was so rough sea and the ship seeled so much that I was not able to stand; and so he bid me go to bed.

17.◆ Before dinner, Mr. Edward[1] and I, W. Howe – Pim and my boy, to Skeveling, where we took coach, and so to The Hague, where walking, intending to find one that might show us the King incognito, I met with Captain Whittington (that had formerly brought a letter to my Lord from the Mayor of London) and he did promise me to do it; but first we went and dined – at a French house, but paid 16*s* for our part of the club. At dinner, in came Dr. Cade, a merry mad parson of the King's. And they two after dinner got the child[2] and me (the others not being able to crowd in) to see the King, who kissed the child very affectionately. There we kissed his and the Duke of Yorkes and the Princesse Royalls[3] hands. The King seems to be a very sober man; and a very splendid Court he hath in the number of persons of Quality that are about him; English, very rich in habit. From the King to the Lord Chancellor,[4] who did lie bed-rid of the goute: he spoke very merrily to the child and me. After that, going to see the Queen of Bohemia, I met with Dr. Fuller,[5] who I sent to a tavern with Mr. Edwd. Pickering, while I and the rest went to see the Queen – who used us very respectfully. Her hand we all kissed. She seems a very debonaire, but plain lady.◆

22.◆ News brought that the two Dukes are coming on board, which, by and by they did in a Duch boat, the Duke of Yorke in yellow trimming, the Duke of Glocester[6] in gray and red.

My Lord went in a boat to meet them, the Captain, myself and others standing at the entering Port.

So soon as they were entered we shot the guns off round the fleet. After that, they went to view the ship all over and were most exceedingly pleased with it.

They seem to be both very fine Gentlemen.

After that done, upon the Quarter Deck table under the awning,

1. Edward Mountagu, son of Pepys's patron.
2. Edward Mountagu, jun.
3. Mary, Princess Dowager of Orange, sister to Charles II.
4. Sir Edward Hyde.
5. Thomas Fuller, historian and clergyman.
6. Gloucester was the King's youngest brother.

the Duke of Yorke and my Lord, Mr Coventree and I spent an houre at allotting to every ship their service in their return to England;[1] which having done, they went to dinner, where the table was very full – the two Dukes at the upper end, my Lord Opdam next on one side, and my Lord on the other.

Two guns[2] given to every man while he was drinking the King's health, and so likewise to the Dukes healths.

I took down Monsieur D'esquier to the great Cabbin below and dined with him in state alone, with only one or two friends of his.

All the dinner the Harper belonging to Captain Sparling played to the Dukes.

After dinner, the Dukes and my Lord to see the Vice and Rere-Admirall; and I in a boat after them.

After that done, they made to the shore in the Duch boat that brought them, and I got into the boat with them. But the shore was so full of people to expect their coming as that it was as black (which otherwise is white sand) as everyone would stand by another.

When we came near the shore, my Lord left them and came into his own boat, and Generall Penn[3] and I with him – my Lord being very well pleased with this day's work.

By the time we came on board again, news is sent us that the King is on shore; so my Lord fired all his guns round twice, and all the fleet after him; which in the end fell into disorder, which seemed very handsome.

The gun over against my Cabbin I fired myself to the King, which was the first time that he hath been saluted by his own ships since this change. But holding my head too much over the gun, I have almost spoiled my right eye.

Nothing in the world but going of guns almost all this day. In the evening we begun to remove Cabbins; I to the Carpenters Cabbin and Dr. Clerke with me – who came on board this afternoon, having been twice duckt in the sea today coming from shore, and Mr. North and John Pickering the like. Many of the King's servants came on board tonight; and so many Duch of all sorts came to see the ship till it was quite dark that we could not pass one by another, which was a great trouble to us all.

This afternoon Mr. Downing (who was knighted yesterday by

1. The Duke of York had been appointed Lord High Admiral. William Coventry, the Duke of York's secretary, was soon to be one of Pepys's closest associates in the work of the navy.
2. Gunshots fired as a salute.
3. William Penn, soon to be a navy colleague and neighbour of Pepys.

the King) was here on board and had a ship for his passage into England with his lady and servants. By the same token, he called me to him when I was going to write the order to tell me that I must write him *Sir G. Downing*.

My Lord lay in the Roundhouse[1] tonight.

This evening I was late, writing a French letter myself by my Lord's order to *Monsieur Kragh, Embassador de Denmarke a la Haye*,[2] which my Lord signed in bed. After that, I to bed and the Doctor, and slept well.

23. The Doctor and I waked very merry, only my eye was very red and ill in the morning from yesterday's hurt.

In the morning came infinite of people on board from the King, to go along with him.

My Lord, Mr. Crew, and others go on shore to meet the King as he comes off from shore.

Where (Sir R. Stayner bringing His Majesty into the boat) I hear that His Majesty did with a great deal of affection kiss my Lord upon his first meeting.

The King, with the two Dukes, the Queen of Bohemia, Princesse Royalle, and Prince of Orange, came on board; where I in their coming in kissed the Kings, Queen and Princesses hands, having done the other before. Infinite shooting off of the guns, and that in a disorder on purpose, which was better then if it had been otherwise.

All day nothing but Lords and persons of Honour on board, that we were exceeding full.

Dined in a great deal of state, the Royall company by themselfs in the coach, which was a blessed sight to see.

I dined with Dr. Clerke, Dr. Quarterman, and Mr. Darcy in my Cabbin.

This morning Mr Lucy came on board, to whom and his company of the King's guard in another ship my Lord did give three dozen of bottles of wine. He made friends between Mr. Pierce and I.[3]

After dinner, the King and Duke upon the [4] altered the name of some of the Shipps, *viz.* the *Nazeby* into *Charles* – The *Richard*, *James*; the *Speaker*, *Mary* – The *Dunbar* (which was not in

1. The uppermost cabin at the stern of the ship.
2. At The Hague.
3. Pepys had fallen out with the surgeon James Pearse after Pearse had taken young Edward Mountagu on an unsanctioned overnight trip.
4. ?supply "quarter-deck table".

company with us) the *Henery – Winsby*, *Happy returne – Wakefield*, *Richmond – Lamport*, the *Henretta – Cheriton*, the *Speedwell – Bradford*, the *Successe*.

That done, the Queen, Princess Royall, and Prince of Orange took leave of the King, and the Duke of Yorke went on board the *London*, and the Duke of Glocester the *Swiftsure* – which done, we weighed Ancre, and with a fresh gale and most happy weather we set sail for England – all the afternoon the King walking here and there, up and down (quite contrary to what I thought him to have been), very active and stirring.

Upon the Quarter-deck he fell in discourse of his escape from Worcester.[1] Where it made me ready to weep to hear the stories that he told of his difficulties that he had passed through. As his travelling four days and three nights on foot, every step up to the knees in dirt, with nothing but a green coat and a pair of country breeches on and a pair of country shoes, that made him so sore all over his feet that he could scarce stir.

Yet he was forced to run away from a miller and other company that took them for rogues.

His sitting at table at one place, where the master of the house, that had not seen him in eight years, did know him but kept it private; when at the same table there was one that had been of his own Regiment at Worcester, could not know him but made him drink the Kings health and said that the King was at least four fingers higher then he.

Another place, he was by some servants of the house made to drink, that they might know him not to be a Roundhead, which they swore he was.

In another place, at his Inn, the master of the house, as the King was standing with his hands upon the back of a chair by the fireside, he kneeled down and kissed his hand privately, saying that he would not ask him who he was, but bid God bless him whither that he was going. Then the difficulty of getting a boat to get into France, where he was fain to plot with the master thereof to keep his design from the four men and a boy (which was all his ship's company), and so got to Feckam in France.

At Roane he looked so poorly that the people went into the rooms before he went away, to see whether he had not stole something or other. In the evening I went up to my Lord to write letters for England – which we sent away, with word of our coming, by

1. In September 1651, after his defeat there.

Mr. Edw. Pickering. The King supped alone in the coach. After that I got a dish, and we four supped in my cabin as at noon.

About bed-time my Lord Bartlet[1] (who I had offered my service to before) sent for me to get him a bed, who with much ado I did get to bed to my Lord Middlesex in the great Cabbin below; but I was cruelly troubled before I could dispose of him and quit myself of him.

So to my Cabbin again, where the company still was and were telling more of the King's difficultys. As, how he was fain to eat a piece of bread and cheese out of a poor boy's pocket.

How at a Catholique house, he was fain to lie in the priests hole a good while in the house for his privacy.

After that our company broke up, and the Doctor and I to bed. We have all the Lords Commissioners on board us, and many others. Under sail all night and most glorious weather.

25. By the morning we were come close to the land and everybody made ready to get on shore.

The King and the two Dukes did eat their breakfast before they went, and there being set some Shipps diet before them, only to show them the manner of the Shipps diet, they eat of nothing else but pease and pork and boiled beef.

I had Mr. Darcy at my cabin and Dr. Clerke, who eat with me and told me how the King had given 50*l* to Mr. Sheply for my Lord's servants, and 500*l* among the officers and common men of the ship. I spoke with the Duke of York about business, who called me Pepys by name, and upon my desire did promise me his future favour.

Great expectation of the King's making some Knights, but there was none. About noon (though the Brigantine that Beale made was there ready to carry him), yet he would go in my Lord's barge with the two Dukes; our captain steered, and my Lord went along bare with him. I went, and Mr. Mansell and one of the King's footmen, with a dog that the King loved (which shit in the boat, which made us laugh and me think that a King and all that belong to him are but just as others are) went in a boat by ourselfs; and so got on shore when the King did, who was received by Generall Monke with all imaginable love and respect at his entrance upon the land at Dover. Infinite the Croud of people and the gallantry of the Horsmen, Citizens, and Noblemen of all sorts.

1. Berkeley, one of the peers sent by the House of Lords to present an address to the King.

The Mayor of the town came and gave him his white staffe, the badge of his place, which the King did give him again. The Mayor also presented him from the town a very rich Bible, which he took and said it was the thing that he loved above all things in the world.

A Canopy was provided for him to stand under, which he did; and talked awhile with General Monke and others; and so into a stately coach there set for him; and so away straight through the towne toward Canterbury without making any stay at Dover.

The Shouting and joy expressed by all is past imagination. I seeing that my Lord did not stir out of his barge, I got into a boat and so into his barge, whither Mr. John Crew stepped and spoke a word or two to my Lord; and so returned. We back to the ship; and going, did see a man almost drowned, that fell out of his boat into the sea but with much ado was got out.

My Lord almost transported with joy that he hath done all this without any the least blur and obstruccion in the world that would give an offence to any, and with the great Honour that he thought it would be to him.

Being overtook by the Brigantine, my Lord and we went out of our barge into it; and so went on board with Sir W. Battin[1] and the Vice- and Rear-Admiralls.

At night my Lord supped, and Mr. Tho. Crew, with Captain Stoakes. I supped with the Captain, who told me what the King had given us. My Lord returned late and at his coming did give me order to cause the marke to be gilded, and a Crowne and *C. R.* to be made at the head of the Coach table,[2] where the King today with his owne hand did mark his Highth – which accordingly I caused the painter to do; and is now done, as is to be seen.

JUNE.

7. I to bed, and about one in the morning W. Howe called me up to give him a letter to carry to my Lord that came to me today, which I did. And so to sleep again. About 3 in the morning the people begun to wash the deck and the water came pouring into my mouth, which wakened me; and I was fain to rise and get on my gown, and sleep leaning upon my table.

This morning Mr. Mountagu went away again.

1. Sir William Batten, soon to be a colleague and neighbour of Pepys at the Navy Office.
2. The table in the captain's state room.

After dinner came Mr. John Wright and Mr. Moore, with the sight of whom my heart was very glad. They brought an order for my Lord's coming up to London – which my Lord resolved to do tomorrow.

All the afternoon getting my things in order to set forth tomorrow. At night walked up and down with Mr. Moore, who did give me an account of all things at London. Among others, how the Presbyters would be angry if they darst, but they will not be able to do anything.

Most of the commanders on board and supped with my Lord.

Late at night came Mr. Edw. Pickering from London, but I could not see him this night.

I went with Mr. Moore to the Maister's Cabbin, and saw him there in order to going to bed.

After that to my own Cabbin to put things in order and so to bed.

8.◆ To Gravesend.[1] A good handsome wench I kissed, the first that I have seen a great while.

Supped with my Lord. Drank late below with Penrose, the Captain: to bed late, having first laid out all my things against tomorrow to [put] myself in a walking garbe. Weary and hot, to bed to Mr. Moore.

9. Up betimes. 25*s* the reckoning for very beer. Paid the house and by boats to London, six boats. Mr. Moore, W. Howe and I, and then the child in the room of W. Howe.

Landed at the Temple. To Mr. Crews. To my father's and put myself into a handsome posture to wait upon my Lord. Dined there.

To Mr. Crews again. In the way met Dr Clerke and Mr. Pierce.

To White-hall with my Lord and Mr. Edw. Mountagu. Found the King in the parke.[2] There walked. Gallantry great.

To Will How till 10 at night. Back and to my fathers.

10. *Whitsunday.* Up and to my Lord's. To Mr. Merstons,[3] where Monsieur Impertinent. At my father's found my wife. After dinner, my wife and I to walk in Lincolnes-Inn walks. After prayers she home and I to my Lord. Stayed there: and so to my father's, where I met Mr. Fairebrother. To bed with my wife.

1. By horse.
2. St James's Park, near Whitehall Palace.
3. Robert Mossom, whose services based on the Book of Common Prayer Pepys attended, along with his friend "Monsieur Impertinent" (Mr Butler).

18. To my Lord, where much business and some hopes of getting some money thereby. With him to the parliament-house, where he did entend to have gone to have made his appearance today, but he met Mr. Crew upon the stairs and would not go in.

He went to Mrs. Browns and stayed till word was brought him what was done in the House.[1] This day they made an end of the twenty men to be excepted from pardon to their estates.[2]

By barge to Stepny with my Lord, where at Trinity-house[3] we had great entertainment.

With my Lord there went Sir W. Pen, Sir H. Wright, Hetly, Pierce, Creed, Hill, I and other servants.

Back again to the Admiralty and so to my Lord's lodgings, where he told me that he did look after the place of the Clerk of the Acts for me.[4] So to Mr. Crews and my father's and to bed. My wife went this day to Huntsmoore for her things,[5] and I was very lonely all night.

This evening my wife's brother Balty came to me to let me know his bad condition and to get a place for him, but I perceive he stands upon[6] a place for a gentleman that may not stain his family; when God help him, he wants bread.

29. This day or two my maid Jane hath been lame, that we cannot tell what to do for want of her. Up and to White-hall, where I got my warrant from the Duke to be Clerk of the Acts. Also, I got my Lord's warrant from the Secretary for his Honour of Earle of Portsmouth and Vicount Mountagu of Hinchingbrooke.[7]

So to my Lord to give him an account of what I had done. Then to Sir Geffery Palmer to give them to him to have bills drawn upon

1. Mountagu was due to receive the thanks of the House, but his visit was presumably postponed by a message from the King asking the Commons to speed the passage of the Act of Indemnity and Oblivion.
2. The Act of Indemnity was a general pardon covering crimes committed during the civil wars and interregnum, with certain exceptions. Some men, directly involved in the execution of Charles I, were exempted entirely from pardon. The Commons was now identifying others who would be exempted from punishment by the death penalty, but not by confiscation of their estates.
3. Trinity House was the public body in charge of safe navigation. This being Trinity Monday, the corporation met to elect officers for the year.
4. This was the position that Pepys held until 1673 and in which he made his reputation as an administrator. The Clerk of the Acts was secretary to the Navy Board, which conducted the civil administration of the navy.
5. Home of the Bowyers, with whom she had been staying while Pepys was at sea.
6. Holds out for.
7. The Secretary of State issued a warrant as part of the process of approving letters patent to grant a title or office. Earl of Portsmouth was Mountagu's initial choice of title; he later changed his mind and decided on Earl of Sandwich.

them[1] – who told me that my Lord must have some good Latinist to make the preamble to his patent, which must express his late service in the best terms that he can; and he told me in what high flaunting terms Sir J. Greenville hath caused his to be done in, which he doth not like; but that Sir Rd. Fanshaw hath done Generall Monkes very well.[2]

Back to Westminster; and meeting Mr. Townsend in the palace – he and I and another or two went and dined at the Leg there. Then to White-hall, where I was told by Mr. Huchinson at the Admiralty that Mr. Barlow my Predecessor, Clerk of the Acts, is yet alive and coming up to town to look after his place[3] – which made my heart sad a little. At night told my Lord thereof and he bade me to get possession of my patent; and he would do all that could be done to keep him out. This night my Lord and I looked over the list of the Captains, and marked some that my Lord hath a mind to have put out. Home and to bed. Our wench very lame, abed these two days.

JULY.

2. Infinite of business, that my heart and head and all was full.

Met with Purser Washington, with whom and a lady, a friend of his, I dined at the Bell Taverne in King's-street; but the rogue had no more manners then to invite me thither and to let me pay my club.[4] All the afternoon with my Lord, going up and down the town. At 7 at night he went home, and there the Principall officers of the Navy; among the rest, myself was reckoned one.[5] We had order to meet tomorrow to draw up such an order of the Council as would put us into action before our patents were passed – at which my heart was glad.[6]

1. Palmer was the Attorney-General who oversaw the next stage of producing bills (warrants) to confirm letters patent.
2. Grenville was to be made Earl of Bath and Monck made Duke of Albemarle.
3. Thomas Barlow had been appointed in 1639 and had a legal claim on the post.
4. Share of the bill.
5. The four Principal Officers of the Navy Board were the Treasurer (Sir George Carteret), the Comptroller (Sir Robert Slingsby), the Surveyor (Sir William Batten), and the Clerk of the Acts (Pepys). In 1660 there were also three Commissioners (Sir William Penn, Lord Berkeley of Stratton, and Peter Pett).
6. The members of the Navy Board could not act officially until letters patent were passed affirming their positions. An order of the Privy Council could empower them to act in the meantime.

At night supped with my Lord, he and I together in the great dining-room alone by ourselfs, the first time that ever I did it in London. Home to bed. My maid pretty well again.

4. Up very early in the morning; and landing my wife at White-Friars stairs,[1] I went to the bridge[2] and so to the Treasurer's of the Navy, with whom I spoke about the business of my office; who put me into very good hopes of my business. At his house comes Comissioner Pett; and I and he went to view the houses in Seething-lane belonging to the Navy, where I find the worst very good; and had great fears in my mind that they will shuffle me out of them, which troubles me.[3]◆

10. This day I put on first my new silk suit, the first that ever I wore in my life. This morning came Nan Pepys's husband Mr. Hall to see me, being lately come to town – I had never saw him before. I took him to the Swan tavern with Mr. Eglin and there drank our morning draught. Home, and called my wife and took her to Dr. Clodius's to a great wedding of Nan Hartlib to mynheer Roder, which was kept at Goring-house with very great state, cost, and noble company.[4] But among all the beauties there, my wife was thought the greatest. After dinner I left the company and carried my wife to Mrs. Turner's. I went to the Atturny-generalls and had my bill,[5] which cost me seven pieces. Called my wife and set her home. And finding my Lord in White-hall garden, I got him to go to the Secretarys;[6] who did, and desired the despatch of his and my bills to be signed by the King.

His bill is to be Earle of Sandwich, Viscount Hinchingbrooke, and Baron of St. Neots.

Home, with my mind pretty quiet, and to bed – not returning, as I said I would, to see the bride put to bed.

17. This morning (as endeed all the mornings nowadays) much business at my Lord's.

There came to my house before I went out, Mr. Barlow, an old

1. Landing stage.
2. London Bridge, the only bridge across the Thames in the London area.
3. The Principal Officers were allotted houses attached to the Navy Office, between Crutched Friars and Seething Lane. Pepys fears the others may find a pretext to prevent him moving in.
4. Nan Hartlib was daughter to the writer Samuel Hartlib senior, Pepys's neighbour in Axe Yard. Her new husband was a wealthy Dutch merchant.
5. Warrant.
6. The Secretary of State's office.

consumptive man and fair-conditioned[1] – with whom I did discourse a great while; and after much talk, I did grant him what he asked – *viz.*, 50*l* per annum if my salary be not encreased and 100*l* per annum in case it be to 350*l*.; at which he was very well pleased to be paid as I received my money, and not otherwise.[2]

Going to my Lord's I find that my Lord had got a great cold and kept his bed. And so I brought him to my Lord's bedside, and my Lord and he and I did agree together to this purpose what I should allow him.

That done and the day proving fair, I went home and got all my goods packed up and sent away. And my wife and I and Mrs. Hunt went by coach, overtaking the carts a-drinking in the Strand – being come to my house and set in the goods; and at night sent my wife and Mrs. Hunt to buy something for supper; they bought a Quarter of lamb; and so we eat it but it was not half roasted.

Will, Mr. Blackburnes nephew, is so obedient that I am greatly glad of him.[3] At night, he and I and Mrs. Hunt home by water to Westminster.

I to my Lord; and after having done some business with him in his chamber in the Nursery, which hath been now his chamber since he came from sea, I went on foot with a link-boy[4] to my house – where I find my wife in bed and Jane washing the house, and Will.[5] The boy sleeping and a great deal of sport I had before I could wake him. I to bed, the first night that I ever lay here with my wife.

23. This morning, Mr. Barlow comes to me and he and I went forth to a Scrivener in FanChurch-street, whom we find sick of the gout in bed, and signed and sealed our agreement before him.

He urged to have these words (*in Consideration whereof*) to be interlined, which I granted, though against my will.

Met this morning at the office; and afterward Mr. Barlow by appointment comes and dined with me. And both of us very pleasant and pleased. After dinner to my Lord, who took me to Secretary Nicholas; and there, before him and Secretary Morris, my Lord

1. Barlow appeared to be suffering from a wasting disease and to be well off – factors relevant to the bargain Pepys was about to strike.
2. Pepys's patent revoked Barlow's claim on the post of Clerk of the Acts; however, by paying Barlow he made sure his appointment would not be challenged.
3. William Hewer (aged 17) was the nephew of Robert Blackborne, a former naval official, who had introduced him to Pepys. Hewer was to become Pepys's colleague in the navy, life-long friend, and surrogate son.
4. Torchbearer.
5. Pepys's current footboy, not Will Hewer.

and I, upon our knees, together took our oaths of Allegiance and Supremacy and the oath of the Privy Seale – of which I was much glad, though I am not likely to get anything by it at present; but I do desire, for fear of a turn-out of our office.[1] That done and my Lord gone from me, I went with Mr. Cooling and his Brother and Sam Hartlibb,[2] little Jenings and some others to the King's-head tavern at Charing-cross; where after drinking, I took boat and so home. Where we supped merrily among ourselfs (our little boy proving a droll); and so after prayers, to bed.◆

AUGUST.

2. To Westminster by water with Sir W. Batten and Sir W. Penn (our servants in another boat) to the Admiralty; and from thence I went to my Lord's to fetch him thither. Where we stayed all the morning about ordering of money for the victuallers and advising how to get a sum of money to carry on the business of the Navy. From thence, dined with Mr. Blackburne at his house with his friends (his wife being in the country and just upon her return to London), where we were very well treated and merry.

From thence, W. Ewre[3] and I to the office of Privy Seale, where I stayed all the afternoon and received about 40*l* for yesterday and today, at which my heart rejoiced for God's blessing to me, to give me this advantage by chance – there being of this 40*l* about 10*l* due to me for this day's work. So great is the present profit of this office above what it was in the King's time; there being the last month about 300 bills, whereas in the last King's time it was much to have 40.[4] With my money, home by coach.

It being the first time that I could get home before our gates were shut since I came to the Navy Office.

When I came home, I find my wife not very well of her old pain in the lip of her *chose*,[5] which she had when we were first married.

1. Sandwich became a Clerk of the Privy Seal and Pepys became his deputy, taking their oaths before the two Secretaries of State. Based in Whitehall Palace, the Office of the Lord Privy Seal prepared documents needed for issuing letters patent (which affirmed royal grants of appointments and privileges). Fees were paid to the clerks and their deputies for this service.
2. Son of the writer Samuel Hartlib.
3. Hewer.
4. The number of new appointments at the start of Charles's reign meant the fees Pepys received at the Privy Seal were unexpectedly high.
5. "her thing". Elizabeth suffered recurring pain from a cyst in her labia.

I went and cast up the expense that I laid out upon my former house (because there are so many that are desirous of it and I am in my mind loath to let it go out of my hands, for fear of a turn). I find my layings-out to come to about 20*l*, which with my fine[1] will come to about 22*l* to him that shall hire my house of me.

To bed.

10. I had a great deal of pain all night and a great looseness upon me, so that I could not sleep. In the morning I rose with much pain and to the office I went and dined at home; and after dinner, with great pain in my back, I went by water to White-hall to the Privy Seale; and that done, with Mr. Moore and Creed to Hideparke by coach and saw a fine foot-race, three times round the park, between an Irishman and Crow that was once my Lord Claypooles footman (by the way, I cannot forget that my Lord Claypoole[2] did the other day make enquiry of Mrs. Hunt concerning my house in Axeyard and did set her on work to get it of me for him, which methinks is a very great change): Crow beat the other above two miles.

Returned from Hide-parke; I went to my Lord's and took Will (who waited for me there) by coach and went home taking my lute home with me [which] hath been all this while since I came from sea at my Lord's for him to play on. To bed, in some pain still.

For this month or two, it is not imaginable how busy my head hath been, so that I have neglected to write letters to my Uncle Robt. in answer to many of his, and to other friends; nor endeed have I done anything as to my own family; and especially this month, my waiting at the Privy Seale makes me much more unable to think of anything, because of my constant attendance there after I have done at the Navy Office. But blessed be God for my good chance of the Privy Seale; where I get every day, I believe, about 3*l* per diem.[3] This place I got by chance and my Lord did give it me by chance, neither he nor I thinking it to be of the worth that he and I find it to be.

Never since I was a man in the world was I ever so great a stranger to public affairs as now I am, having not read a newsbook or anything like it, or enquired after any news, or what the Parliament doth or in any wise how things go. Many people look after my house in axe-yard to hire it of me, so that I am troubled with them; and I have a mind to get the money to buy goods for my

1. Payment for a lease.
2. John Claypole was a son-in-law of Oliver Cromwell.
3. Per day.

house at the Navy Office, and yet I am loath to put it off, because that Mr. Man bids me 1000*l* for my office, which is so great a sum that I am loath to settle myself at my new house, lest I should take Mr. Man's offer in case I find my Lord willing to it.

16. This morning my Lord (all things being ready) carried me by coach to Mr. Crews, in the way talking how good he did hope my place would be to me and, in general, speaking that it was not the salary of any place that did make a man rich, but the opportunities of getting money while he is in the place: where he took leave and went into the coach, and so for Hinchingbrooke: my Lady Jem and Mr. Thomas Crew in the coach with him.

Thence to Whitehall about noon, where I met with Mr. Madge, who took me along with him and Captain Cooke (the famous singer) and other Maisters of Musique to dinner at an ordinary[1] above Charing-cross, where we dined, all paying their club. Thence to the Privy Seal, where there hath been but little work these two days. In the evening, home.

18. This morning I took my wife toward Westminster by water and landed her at White-friars, with 50*s*. to buy her a petticoat. And I to the Privy Seale. By and by comes my wife to tell me that my father hath persuaded her to buy a most fine cloth of 26*s* per yard and a rich lace, that the petticoat will come to 5*l*, at which I was somewhat troubled; but she doing it very innocently, I could not be angry.

I did give her more money and sent her away; and I and Creede and Captain Hayward (who is now unkindly put out of the *Plymouth* to make way for Captain Allen to go to Constantinople, and put into his ship the *Dover*, which I know will trouble my Lord) went and dined at the Leg in King's-street, where Captain Ferrers, my Lord's Cornett,[2] comes to us – who after dinner took me and Creed to the Cockepitt play, the first that I have had time to see since my coming from sea, *The Loyall Subject*, where one Kinaston, a boy, acted the Dukes sister but made the loveliest lady that ever I saw in my life – only, her voice not very good.[3] After the play done, we three went to drink, and by Captain Ferre[r]s means, Mr.

1. An establishment serving fixed-price meals.
2. Captain Robert Ferrers, a member of Sandwich's household, had once been a cornet in his regiment.
3. *The Loyal Subject* was a tragicomedy by John Fletcher, written in 1618 and now performed at the Cockpit Theatre, Drury Lane. Edward Kynaston, playing Olympia, was 17.

Kinaston and another that acted Archas the Generall[1] came to us and drank with us. Thence home by coach; and after being trimmed, leaving my wife to look after her little bich, which was just now a-whelping, I to bed.

28. At home looking over my papers and books and house as to the fitting of it to my mind till 2 in the afternoon. Some time I spent this morning beginning to teach my wife some skill in Musique, and find her apt beyond imagination.

To the Privy Seale where great stir of work today. Collonell Scroope is this day excepted out of the Act of Indemnity, which hath been now long in coming out, but it is expected tomorrow.[2] I carried home 80*l* from Privy Seale by coach; and at night spent a little more time with my wife about her Musique with great content.

This day I heard my poor mother hath these two days been very ill, and I fear she will not last long.[3]

To bed – a little troubled that I fear my boy Will[4] is a thief and hath stole some money of mine – perticularly a letter that Mr. Jenkins did leave the last week with me with half a crown in to send to his son.

29. Office day. Before I went to the office, my wife and I examined my boy Will about his stealing of things, as we doubted[5] yesterday; but he denied all with the greatest subtility and confidence in the world. To the office; and after office, then to the church, where we took another view of the place where we had resolved to build a gallery; and have set men about doing it.[6] Home to dinner; and there I find that my wife hath discovered my boy's theft and a great deal more then we imagined. At which I was vexed and entend to put him away.

To my office at Privy Seale in the afternoon; and from thence at night to the Bull-head with Mount, Luellin and others; and thence to my father's; and he being at my uncle Fenner's, I went thither to him, and there sent for my boy's father and talked with him about

1. Probably Thomas Betterton, who would become the most celebrated actor of the period.
2. Adrian Scroope was one of the regicides. Debates about the application of the Act to particular cases had delayed its publication.
3. Margaret Pepys lived until 1667.
4. Pepys's current footboy (surname unknown), rather than Will Hewer.
5. Suspected.
6. A new gallery in St Olave's church containing pews for the navy officers and their families.

his son and had his promise that if I will send home his boy, he will take him notwithstanding his indentures.

Home at night; and find that my wife hath found out more, of the boy's stealing 6*s*. out of W. Ewres closet and hid it in the house of office[1] – at which my heart was troubled. To bed and caused the boy's clothes to be brought up to my chamber. But after we were all a-bed, the wench (which lies in our chamber) called us to listen of a sudden; which put my wife into such a fright that she shook, every joynt of her, and a long time that I could not get her out of it. That noise was the boy, we did believe, was got in a desperate mood out of his bed to do himself or Wm. some mischief. But the wench went down and got a candle lighted; and finding the boy in bed and locking the doors fast, with a candle burning all night, we slept well, but with a great deal of fear.

31. Early to wait upon my Lord at White-hall; and with him to the Duke's[2] chamber. So to my office in Seething-lane. Dined at home; and after dinner to my Lord again; who told me that he is ordered to go suddenly to sea and did give me some orders to be drawing upon against his going.[3] This afternoon I agreed to let my house[4] quite out of my hands to Mr. Dalton (of the wine-cellar to the King, with whom I have drunk in the old wine-cellar two or three times) for 41*l*. At night, made up even at Privy Seale for this month against tomorrow to give up possession; but we know not to whom – though we most favour Mr. Bickerstaffe, with whom and Mr. Mathewes we drank late after office was done at the Sun, discoursing what to do about it tomorrow against Baron;[5] and so home and to bed. Blessed be God all things continue well with and for me; I pray God fit me for a change of my fortune.

1. The privy.
2. The Duke of York (the Lord High Admiral). Pepys now worked under him in the navy.
3. Sandwich was to bring the King's sister, Mary, from the Dutch Republic.
4. In Axe Yard.
5. Charles Bickerstaffe and Hartgill Baron both laid claim to a clerkship in the Privy Seal Office – Baron was confirmed the next day. Pepys continued in his post.

SEPTEMBER.

1. *Saturday.*◆

Mr. Moore and I and several others being invited today by Mr. Goodman, a friend of his, we dined at the Bull-head upon the best venison pasty that ever I eat of in my life; and with one dish more, it was the best dinner I ever was at. Here rise in discourse at table a dispute between Mr. Moore and Dr. Clerke, the former affirming that it was essentiall to a Tragedy to have the argument[1] of it true, which the Doctor denyed and left to me to be judge – and the cause to be determind next Tuesday morning at the same place upon the eating of the remains of the pasty, and the loser to spend 10*s.*

All this afternoon sending express to the fleet to order things against my Lord's coming – and taking direction of my Lord about some rich furniture to take along with him for the Princesse.

And talking of this, I hear by Mr. Townsend that there is the greatest preparacion against the Prince de Ligne's coming over from the King of Spaine that ever was in England for any Imbassador.[2]

Late home; and what with business and my boy's roguery, my mind being unquiet, I went to bed.

4. I did many things this morning at home before I went out – as looking over the Joyners, who are flooring my dining-roome – and doing business with Sir Wms. both[3] at the office. And so to White-hall and so to the bull head where we had the remaynes of our pasty, where I did give my verdict against Mr. Moore upon last Saturdays wager. Where Dr. Fuller[4] coming in doth confirme me in my verdict.

From thence to my Lord's and dispatcht Mr. Cooke away with the things to my Lord. From thence to Axeyard to my house; where standing at the door, Mrs. Diana[5] comes by, whom I took into my

1. Subject matter.
2. He came as Spanish ambassador-extraordinary to congratulate Charles on his restoration.
3. Sir William Batten and Sir William Penn.
4. Thomas Fuller the historian; he and Pepys decided that tragedies need not be historically true.
5. Probably Diana Crisp, who had been a neighbour in Axe Yard.

house upstairs and there did dally with her a great while, and find that in Latin "*nulla puella negat.*"[1]

So home by water; and there sat up late, putting my papers in order and my money also, and teaching my wife her Musique lesson, in which I take great pleasure.

So to bed.

21. *office day.* There all the morning and afternoon till 4 a-clock. Then to White-hall, thinking to have put up my books at my Lord's, but am disappointed for want of a chest which I have at Mr. Bowyers.[2] Back by water about 8 a-clock; and upon the water saw [the] corps of the Duke of Gloucester brought down Somersett-house stairs to go by water to Westminster to be buried tonight.[3] I landed at the old Swan and went to the Hoope taverne and (by a former agreement) sent for Mr. Chaplin, who with Nich Osborne and one Daniel came to us and there we drank off two or three quarts of wine, which was very good (the drawing of our wine causing a great quarrell in the house between the two drawers which should draw us the best, which caused a great deal of noise and falling out till the maister parted them and came up to us and did give us a large account of the liberty that he gives his servants all alike, to draw what wine they will to please his customers); and eat above 200 wallnutts. About 10 a-clock we broake upp. And so home; in my way I called in with them at Mr. Chaplins, where Nich. Osborne did give me a barrell of Samphire[4] and showed me the Keyes of Mardyke fort, which he that was commander of the fort sent him as a token when the fort was demolished;[5] which I was mightily pleased to see and will get them of him if I can.

Home, where I find my boy (my mayd's brother) come out of the country today; but was gone to bed and so I could not see him tonight.[6]

I to bed.

22. This morning I called up the boy to me and find him a pretty well-looked boy, and one that I think will please me.

1. "No girl says 'no'": a line from Martial, *Epigrams*, Book 4, 71.
2. Pepys was moving the books he had kept at Axe Yard via Sandwich's Whitehall lodgings to Seething Lane.
3. The King's youngest brother had died of smallpox on 13 September.
4. A seaside plant, commonly used as a pickle.
5. Mardyke fort in Flanders, held by Commonwealth troops, was demolished in 1659.
6. Wayneman Birch, aged 11, from Dymock, Gloucestershire.

I went this morning to Westminster by land along with Luellin, who came to my house this morning to get me to go with him to Captain Allen to speak with him for his brother to go with him to Constantinople; but could not find him. We walked on to Fleetstreete, where at Mr. Standings in Salsbury-court we drank our morning draught and had a pickled herring. Among other discourse here, he told me how the pretty woman that I always loved at the beginning of Cheapeside that sells children's coates was served by the Lady Bennett (a famous Strumpet), who by counterfeiting to fall into a swoune upon the sight of her in her shop, became acquainted with her and at last got her ends of her to lie with a gallant that had hired her to Procure this poor soul for him. To Westminster to my Lord's; and there in the house of office vomited up all my breakfast, my stomach being ill all this day by reason of the last night's debauch. Here I sent to Mr. Bowyers for my chest and put up my books and sent them home. And stayed here all day in my Lord's chamber and upon the leads[1] gazing upon Diana, who looked out at a window upon me. At last I went out to Mr. Harpers, and she standing over the way at the gate, I went over to her and appointed to meet tomorrow in the afternoon at my Lord's.[2] Here I bought a hanging jack.[3] From thence by coach home (by the way at the New Exchange I bought a pair of Short black stockings to wear over a pair of silk ones for mourning; and here I met with The. Turner and Joyce buying of things to go into mourning too for the Duke, which is now the mode of all the ladies in towne), where I writ some letters by the post to Hinchingbrooke to let them know that this day Mr. Edwd Pickering is come from my Lord and says that he left him well in Holland and that he will be here within three or four days.

To bed, not well of my last night's drinking yet. I had the boy up tonight for his sister to teach him to put me to bed, and I heard him read, which he doth pretty well.

25. To the office, where Sir W. Batten, Collonell Slingsby, and I sat a while; and Sir R. Ford[4] coming to us about some business, we talked together of the interest of this kingdom to have a peace with Spain and a war with France and Holland – where Sir R. Ford talked like a man of great reason and experience. And afterwards

1. Roof coverings that could serve as a walkway.
2. Diana failed to come as arranged.
3. A turnspit for roasting meat.
4. A merchant, of Seething Lane.

did send for a Cupp of Tee (a China drink) of which I never had drank before) and went away.[1]◆

28. *office day.* This morning Sir W. Batten, Collonell Slingsby, went with Collonell Birch and Sir Wm Doyly to Chattam to pay off a ship[2] there. So only Sir W. Pen and I left here in town.

All afternoon at home among my workmen; work till 10 or 11 at night; and did give them drink and were very merry with them – it being my luck to meet with a sort of Drolling workmen upon all occasions. To bed.

29. All day at home to make an end of our dirty work of the playsterers; and indeed, my Kitchin is now so handsome that I did not repent of all the trouble that I have been put to to have it done.

This day or yesterday I hear Prince Robt. is come to Court; but welcome to nobody.[3]

OCTOBER.

3. With Sir W. Batten and Pen by water to White-hall, where a meeting of the Dukes of Yorke and Albemarle, my Lord Sandwich and all the Principal Officers, about the Winter gard;[4] but we determined of nothing.

From thence to my Lord's, who sent a great iron chest to White-hall; and I saw it carried into the King's closet, where I saw most incomparable pictures. Among the rest, a book open upon a deske which I durst have sworn was a reall book, &c.

Back again to my Lord and dined all alone with him, who doth treat me with a great deal of respect. And after dinner did discourse an houre with me and advise about getting of some way to get himself some money to make up for all his great expenses – saying that he believed he might have anything that he would ask of the King.

This day Mr. Sheply and all my Lord's good[s] came from sea – some of them laid at the Wardrobe[5] and some brought to my Lord's house.

1. Tea was a new and expensive import; the first printed adverts for it appeared in 1658. The brackets are Pepys's own.
2. To pay the wages due to the crew at the end of a commission.
3. Prince Rupert, first cousin of Charles II. During the civil wars and afterwards he had quarrelled with many of the royalists.
4. The reduced number of ships patrolling the seas during winter months.
5. The office of the King's Great Wardrobe, of which Sandwich was Master.

From thence to our office, where we met and did business: and so home and spent the evening looking upon the painters that are at work in my house.

This day I heard the Duke speak of a great design that he and my Lord of Pembrooke have, and a great many others, of sending a venture to some parts of affrica to dig for gold=ore there. They entend to admit as many as will venture their money, and so make themselfs a company. 250*l* is the lowest share for every man.[1] But I do not find that my Lord doth much like it.

At night Dr Fairebrother (for so he is lately made of the Civil law)[2] brought home my wife by Coach, it being rainy weather, she having been abroad today to buy more furniture for her house.

7. *Lordsday.* To White-hall on foot, calling at my father's to change my long black Cloake for a short one (long cloaks being now quite out); but he being gone to church, I could not get one, and therefore I proceeded on and came to my Lord before he went to Chappell; and so went with him, where I heard Dr. Spurstow preach before the King a poor dry sermon; but a very good Anthemne of Captain Cookes afterwards.

Going out of the Chappell, I met with Jack Cole my old friend (whom I had not seen a great while before), and have promised to renew acquaintance in London together. To my Lord's and dined with him; he all dinner time talking French to me and telling me the story how the Duke of Yorke hath got my Lord Chancellors daughter with child, and that she doth lay it to him, and that for certain he did promise her marriage and had signed it with his blood, but that he by stealth had got the paper out of her Cabinett. And that the King would have him to marry her, but that he will not.[3] So that the thing is very bad for the Duke and them all; but my Lord doth make light of it, as a thing that he believes is not a new thing to the Duke to do abroad. Discoursing concerning what if the Duke should marry her, my Lord told me that among his father's many old sayings that he had writ in a book of his, this is one: that he that doth get a wench with child and marries her

1. The Company of the Royal Adventurers into Africa received its charter on 18 Dec. 1660. Initially set up to mine gold in West Africa, it soon began to trade in slaves. It was predecessor to the slaving corporation the Royal Africa Company.
2. William Fairbrother, a friend, had recently received his doctorate in law.
3. The Duke and Anne Hyde had contracted a marriage in 1659 and had a religious ceremony on 3 Sept. 1660. Their son was born on 22 October. Sandwich's version of events is exaggerated, but the Duke had denied he was contracted to Anne. The marriage was not made public until December.

afterward it is as if a man should shit in his hat and then clap it upon his head.

I perceive my Lord is grown a man very indifferent in all matters of Religion, and so makes nothing of these things.

After dinner to the Abby,[1] where I heard them read the church-service, but very Ridiculously, that endeed I do not in my mind like it at all. A poor cold sermon of Dr. Lambs, one of the Prebends, in his habitt, came afterwards; and so all ended. And by my troth a pitiful sorry devocion it is that these men pay.

So walked home by land. And before supper I read part of the Maryan persecution in Mr. Fuller.[2] So to supper, prayer, and to bed.

11. In the morning to my Lord's, where I met with Mr. Creed, and with him and Mr. Blackburne to the Rhenish wine-house – where we sat drinking of healths a great while, a thing which Mr. Blackburne formerly would not upon any terms have done.[3] After we had done there, Mr. Creed and I to the Leg in King-street to dinner, where he and I and my Will had a good udder to dinner; and from thence to walk in St. James's Park – where we observed the several engines at work to draw up water, with which sight I was very much pleased.

Above all the rest, I liked best that which Mr. Greatorex brought, which is one round thing going within all with a pair of stairs round; which being laid at an angle of 45 doth carry up the water with a great deal of ease.[4] Here in the park we met with Mr. Salsbury, who took Mr. Creed and me to the Cockpitt to see *The Moore of Venice*, which was well done. Burt acted the Moore;[5] by the same token, a very pretty lady that sot by me cried to see Desdimona smothered.

From thence with Mr. Creed to Hercles pillers, where he and I drank; and so parted and I went home.

13. To my Lord's in the morning, where I met with Captain Cuttance. But my Lord not being up, I went out to Charing-cross to see Major-Generall Harrison hanged, drawn, and quartered – which was done there – he looking as cheerfully as any man could

1. Westminster Abbey.
2. Thomas Fuller's *The Church-History of Britain* described the persecution of Protestants under Mary I. Pepys owned the 1656 edition and knew the author.
3. Puritans objected to the drinking of healths as a pagan custom.
4. Ralph Greatorex's design was probably a version of the Archimedean screw – a rotating spiral screw inside a tube.
5. Shakespeare's *Othello* was performed at the Cockpit Theatre in Drury Lane with Nicholas Burt in the title role.

do in that condition.[1] He was presently cut down and his head and his heart shown to the people, at which there was great shouts of joy. It is said that he said that he was sure to come shortly at the right hand of Christ to judge them that now have judged him. And that his wife doth expect his coming again.

Thus it was my chance to see the King beheaded at White-hall and to see the first blood shed in revenge for the blood of the King at Charing-cross. From thence to my Lord's and took Captain Cuttance and Mr. Sheply to the Sun taverne and did give them some oysters. After that I went by water home, where I was angry with my wife for her things lying about, and in my passion kicked the little fine Baskett which I bought her in Holland and broke it, which troubled me after I had done it.

Within all the afternoon, setting up shelfes in my study. At night to bed.

20. This morning one came to me to advise with me where to make me a window into my cellar in lieu of one that Sir W. Batten had stopped up; and going down into my cellar to look, I put my foot into a great heap of turds, by which I find that Mr. Turners house of office is full and comes into my cellar, which doth trouble me; but I will have it helped.

To my Lord's by land, calling at several places about business. Where I dined with my Lord and Lady; where he was very merry and did talk very high how he would have a French Cooke and a Master of his Horse, and his lady and child to wear black paches;[2] which methought was strange, but he is become a perfect Courtier; and among other things, my Lady saying that she would have a good Merchant for her daughter Jem, he answered that he would rather see her with a pedlar's pack at her back, so she married a Gentleman rather then that she should marry a Citizen.

This afternoon, going through London and calling at Crowes the upholster in Saint Bartholmew – I saw the limbs of some of our new Traytors set upon Aldersgate, which was a sad sight to see; and a bloody week this and the last have been, there being ten hanged, drawn, and Quarterd. Home; and after writing a letter to my Uncle by the post, I went to bed.

1. He was executed as a regicide.
2. Fashionable shapes of material worn on the face.

NOVEMBER.

1. This morning Sir W. Pen and I were mounted earely. And have very merry discourse all the way, he being very good company.

We came to Sir Wm. Battens,[1] where he lives like a prince, and we were made very welcome. Among other things, he showed us my Lady's closet, where there was great store of rarities. As also a chaire which he calls King Harrys chair, where he that sits down is catched with two irons that come round about him, which makes good sport.[2] Here dined with us two or three more country gentlemen; among the rest, Mr. Christmas my old Schoolfellow, with whom I had much talk. He did remember that I was a great roundhead when I was a boy, and I was much afeared that he would have remembered the words that I said the day that the King was beheaded (that were I to preach upon him, my text should be: "The memory of the wicked shall rot");[3] but I found afterward that he did go away from schoole before that time.

He did make us good sport in imitating Mr. Case, Ash, and Nye, the ministers[4] – which he did very well. But a deadly drinker he is, and grown exceeding fat. From his house to an alehouse near the church, where we sat and drank and were merry; and so we mounted for London again – Sir W. Batten with us. We called at Bowe and drank there, and took leave of Mr. Johnson of Blackwall, who dined with us and rode with us thus far.

So home by moone-light, it being about 9 a-clock before we got home.

7. *office day.* This day my father came to dine at my house; but being sent for in the morning, I could not stay but went by water to my Lord; where I dined with him, and he in a very merry humour (present Mr. Borfett and Childe).

At dinner he, in discourse of the great opinion of the virtue, gratitude (which he did account the greatest thing in the world to him and hath therefore in his mind been often troubled in the late times how to answer his gratitude to the King, who raised his

1. Batten's country house at Church Hill, Walthamstow, Essex.
2. A variety of joke chair.
3. A loose recollection of Proverbs 10.7.
4. Two leading Presbyterians and a leading Independent preacher respectively. Pepys had seen Thomas Case in the Dutch Republic.

father) did say that that was it that did bring [him] to his obedience to the King. And did also bless himself with his good fortune, in comparison to what it was when I was with him in the Sound[1] – when he darst not owne his correspondence with the King. Which is a thing that I never did hear of to this day before; and I do from this raise an opinion of him to be one of the most secret men in the world – which I was not so convinced of before.

After dinner he bade all go out of the room, and did tell me how the King hath promised him 4000*l* per annum for ever and hath already given him a bill under his hand (which he showed me) for 4000*l* that Mr. Fox is to pay him.[2] My Lord did advise with me how to get this received and to put out 3000*l* into safe hands at use,[3] and the other he will make use of for his present occasion. This he did advise with me about with much Secresy.

After all this he called for the Fiddles and books, and we two and W. Howe and Mr. Childe did sing and play some psalmes of Will. Lawes[4] and some songs. And so I went away.◆

20. About 2 a-clock my wife wakes me and comes to bed; and so both to sleep and the wench to wash.[5]

I rise and with Will to my Lord's by land, it being a very hard frost and the first we have had this year. There I stayed with my Lord and Mr. Sheply, looking over my Lord's accounts and to set matters straight between him and Sheply.[6] And he did commit the viewing of those accounts to me – which was a great joy to me to see that my Lord doth look upon me as one to put trust in.

Then to the Organ, where Mr. Childe and one Mr. Mackworth (who plays finely upon the viallin) were playing, and so we played till dinner.[7] And then dined – where my Lord in a very good humour and kind to me.

After dinner to the Temple, where I met Mr. Moore and discoursed with him about the business of putting out my Lord's 3000*l*; and that done, Mr. Sheply and I to the new Play-house near

1. When Pepys and Mountagu were in the Baltic in 1659.
2. This was a grant to support Sandwich's title. Stephen Fox administered the finances of the royal household.
3. At interest.
4. Henry and William Lawes, *Choice Psalmes put into Musick, for Three Voices* (1648).
5. It was washday, requiring day-and-night effort.
6. Shipley was steward at Hinchingbrooke.
7. Sandwich had recently had an organ set up in his Whitehall lodgings.

Lincolnes Inn fields (which was formerly Gibbons's tennis-court), where the play of *Beggers' bush* was newly begun.[1] And so we went in and saw it. It was well acted (and here I saw the first time one Moone,[2] who is said to be the best actor in the world, lately come over with the King); and endeed it is the finest play-house, I believe, that ever was in England.

From thence, after a pot of ale with Mr. Sheply at a house hard by, I went by link home, calling a little by the way at my father's and my uncle Fenner's, where all pretty well. And so home, where I found the house in a washing pickle; and my wife in a very joyful condition when I told her that she is to see the Queene[3] next Thursday.

Which puts me in mind to say that this morning I found my Lord in bed late, he having been with the King, Queene, and Princesse at the Cockpitt[4] all night, where Generall Monke treated them; and after supper, a play – where the King did put a great affront upon Singleton's Musique,[5] he bidding them stop and bade the French Musique play – which my Lord says doth much out-do all ours.

But while my Lord was rising, I went to Mr. Foxes and there did leave the Gilt Tankard for Mrs. Fox;[6] and then to the Counting-house to him, who hath invited me and my wife to dine with him on Thursday next, and so to see the Queene and Princesses.

22. This morning came the Carpenters to make me a door at the other side of my house, going into the Entry – which I was much pleased with.

At noon my wife and I walked to the old Exchange;[7] and there she bought her a white whiske[8] and put it on, and I a pair of gloves; and so we took coach for White-hall to Mr. Foxes – where we found her[9] within, and an alderman of London paying a 1000*l* or 1400*l* in

1. *The Beggar's Bush*, a comedy by Fletcher and Massinger. The theatre was the Theatre Royal, Vere St, at which Thomas Killigrew's players (the King's Company) acted from 8 Nov. 1660 to the beginning of May 1663. During this period Pepys generally refers to it as "the Theatre".
2. Michael Mohun.
3. The Queen Mother, Henrietta Maria, had returned to England in October.
4. The private royal theatre in Whitehall Palace.
5. A group of court musicians led by John Singleton.
6. A gift from Sandwich to Stephen Fox for facilitating his payment of £4,000 from the King.
7. The Royal Exchange, site of upmarket shops.
8. A neckerchief.
9. Mrs Elizabeth Fox.

gold upon the table for the King, which was the most gold that ever I saw together in my life.

Mr. Fox came in presently and did receive us with a great deal of respect. And then did take my wife and I to the Queenes presence-Chamber. Where he got my wife placed behind the Queenes chaire and I got into the Crowd; and by and by the Queen and the two princesses came to dinner. The Queen, a very little plain old woman and nothing more in her presence in any respect nor garbe then any ordinary woman. The Princesse of Orange I have often seen before. The Princess Henriettee[1] is very pretty, but much below my expectation – and her dressing of herself with her haire frized short up to her eares[2] did make her seem so much the less to me.

But my wife, standing near her with two or three black paches on and well dressed, did seem to me much handsomer then she.

Dinner being done, we went to Mr. Foxes again, where many gentlemen dined with us, and most princely dinner – all provided for me and my friends; but I bringing none but myself and wife, he did call the company to help to ⟨eate⟩ up so much good victualls. At the end of the dinner, my Lord Sandwich's health in the gilt tankard that he did give Mrs. Fox the other day.

After dinner I have notice given me by Will, my man, that my Lord did enquire for me; so I went to find him, and met him and the Duke of Yorke in a Coach going towards Charing-Crosse. I endeavoured to fallow them, but I could not; so I returned to Mr. Fox and after much kindness and good discourse, we parted from thence.

I took Coach for my wife and I homewards; and I light at the Maypoole in the Strand and sent my wife home.

I to the new playhouse and saw part of *The Traytor* (a very good Tragedy); where Moone did act the Traytor very well.[3]

So to my Lord's and sat there with my Lady a great while talking. Among other things, she took occasion to enquire (by Madam Dury's late discourse with her) how I did treate my wife's father and mother. In which I did give her a good account. And she seemed to be very well opinioned of my wife.

1. Henriette, younger sister of Charles II and Mary, Princess of Orange.
2. Corkscrew curls were in fashion.
3. *The Traitor* by James Shirley. Mohun played the plotter Lorenzo.

From thence to White hall at about 9 at night. And there, with Loud the page that went with me, we could not get out of Henry the 8ths gallery into the further part of the boarded gallery where my Lord was walking with my Lord Ormond. And we had a key of Sir S. Morland, but all would not do; till at last, by knocking, Mr. Harrison the Dore=keeper did open us the door.

And after some talk with my Lord about getting a Katch[1] to carry my Lord St. Albans goods to France – I parted and went home on foot, it being very late and dirty. And so weary to bed.

DECEMBER.

4. To White-hall to Sir G. Carteret's Chamber, where all the officers met;[2] and so we went up to the Duke of Yorke and he took us into his Closet and we did open to him our project of stopping the growing charge of the fleet, by paying them in hand one moyety and the other four months hence. This he doth like; and we returned by his order to Sir G. Carteret's chamber, and there we did draw up this design in order to be presented to the parliament. From thence I to my Lord's and dined with him and told him what we have done today.

Sir Tho. Crew dined with my Lord today and we were very merry with Mrs. Bockett, who dined there still, as she hath always done lately. After dinner Sir Tho. and my Lady went to the play-house to see *The Silent Woman*.[3] I home by water; and with Mr. Hater in my chamber all alone, he and I did put this morning's design into words. Which being done, I did carry it to Sir W. Batten's where I found some gentlemen with him (Sir W. Pen among the rest, pretty merry with drink) playing at Cards; and there I stayed looking upon them till one a-clock in the morning; and so Sir W. Pen and I went away, and I to bed.

This day the parliament voted that the bodies of Oliver, Ireton, Bradshaw, and ,[4] should be taken up out of their graves in the abby and drawn to the gallows and there hanged and buried under it. Which (methinks) doth trouble me, that a man of so great

1. Ketch (a ship).
2. Sir George Carteret, Treasurer of the Navy, had lodgings at Whitehall. This was a gathering of the officials of the Navy Board.
3. Ben Jonson's *Epicœne*, at the Theatre Royal, Vere St.
4. Supply "Pride". Oliver Cromwell, Henry Ireton, John Bradshaw, and Thomas Pride were regicides who had died before the Restoration.

courage as he was should have that dishonour, though otherwise he might deserve it enough.

5. This morning the Proposall which I writ the last night I showed to the Officers this morning, and was well liked of. And I wrote it fair for Sir G. Carteret to show to the King; and so it is to go to the Parliament.

I dined at home; and after dinner went to the new Theatre and there I saw *The Merry Wifes of Windsor* acted.[1] The humours[2] of the Country gentleman and the French Doctor very well done; but the rest but very poorly, and Sir J. Falstaffe as bad as any.

From thence to Mr. Will Mountagu's chamber to have sealed some writings tonight between Sir R. Parkhurst and myself, about my Lord's 2000*l*;[3] but he not coming, I went to my father's. And there found my mother still ill of the stone and hath just newly voided one, which she hath let drop into the Chimny; and could not find it to show it me. From thence home and to bed.

15. All day at home looking upon my workmen. Only, at noon Mr. Moore came and brought me some things to sign for the Privy Seale and dined with me; we have three eales, that my wife and I bought this morning of a man that cried them about, for our dinner. And that was all I did today.

16. In the morning to church; and then dined at home. In the afternoon I to White-hall, where I was surprized with the news of a plott against the King's person and my Lord Monkes – and that since last night there is about 40 taken upon suspicion;[4] and among others, it was my lot to meet with Simon Beale the Trumpet, who took me and Tom. Doling into the guard in Scotland-yard and showed us Major-Generall Overton.[5] Where I heard him deny that he is guilty of any such things, but that whereas it is said that he is found to have brought many armes to towne, he says it was only to sell them, as he will prove by oath.

From thence with Tom. Doling and Boston and D. Vines (who we met by the way) to Prices and there we drank; and in discourse I learned a pretty trick to try whether a woman be a maid or no, by

1. Shakespeare's comedy.
2. Amusing or whimsical characters.
3. Sandwich was loaning to Parkhurst money that he had received from the King.
4. Hatched by discontented sectaries and soldiers, the plot's aims were said to include the burning of Whitehall Palace and the killing of the King and Albemarle (Monck).
5. Robert Overton, a republican arrested for alleged involvement in the plot.

a string going round her head to meet at the end of her nose; which if she be not, will come a great way beyond.

Thence to my Lady and stayed with her an hour or two talking of the Duke of York and his Lady, the Chancellor's daughter, between whom she tells me that all is agreed and he will marry her. But I know not how true yet.

It rained hard, and my Lady would have had me have the coach, but I would not; but to my father's, where I met my wife and there supped; and after supper by linke[1] home and to bed.

25. *Christmas day.*

In the morning very much pleased to see my house once more clear of workmen and to be clean; and endeed it is so far better then it was, that I do not repent of my trouble that I have been at.

In the morning to church; where Mr. Mills[2] made a very good sermon. After that home to dinner, where my wife and I and my brother Tom (who this morning came to see my wife's new mantle put on, which doth please me very well)[3] – to a good shoulder of Mutton and a Chicken. After dinner to church again, my wife and I, where we have a dull sermon of a stranger which made me sleep; and so home; and I, before and after supper, to my Lute and Fullers *History*,[4] at which I stayed all alone in my Chamber till 12 at night; and so to bed.

31. At the office all the morning. And after that home; and not staying to dine, I went out and in Paul's churchyard I bought the play of *Henery the fourth*.[5] And so went to the new Theatre (only calling at Mr. Crews and eat a bit with the people there at dinner) and there saw it acted; but my expectation being too great, it did not please me as otherwise I believe it would; and my having a book I believe did spoil it a little.

That being done, I went to my Lord's, where I found him private at cards with my Lord Lauderdale and some persons of Honour; so Mr. Sheply and I over to Harpers and there drank a pot or two, and so parted – my boy taking a catt home with him from my Lord's, which Sarah[6] hath given him for my wife, we being much troubled with mice.

1. Torch.
2. Daniel Milles, Rector of St Olave, Hart Street.
3. Tom Pepys, aged 26, was a tailor like his father.
4. Thomas Fuller's *Church-History of Britain*.
5. Probably Part 1 of Shakespeare's history play.
6. Housekeeper at Sandwich's Whitehall lodgings.

At Whitehall enquiring for a coach, there was a Frenchman with one eye that was going my way; so he and I hired the coach between us and he set me down in Fanchurch-street. Strange how this fellow, without asking, did tell me all what he was, and how he hath run away from his father and come into England to serve the King, and now going back again &c.

Home and to bed.

1661

$16\frac{60.}{61.}$

At the end of the last and the beginning of this year I do live in one of the houses belonging to the Navy office as one of the principall officers – and have done now about half a year. After much trouble with workmen, I am now almost settled – my family being, myself, my wife, Jane, Will Ewre, and Wayneman, my girl's brother.

Myself in a constant good health – and in a most handsome and thriving condition. Blessed be Almighty God for it. I am now taking of my sister Paulina to come and live with me. As to things of state – the King settled and loved of all. The Duke of Yorke lately matched to my Lord Chancellor's daughter which doth not please many. The Queene[1] upon her return to France – with the Princesse Henrietta. The Princesse of Orange lately dead, and we into new mourning for her.[2]

We have been lately frighted with a great plot, and many taken upon it and the fright of it not quite over. The parliament, which hath done all this great good to the King, beginning to grow factious, the King did dissolve it December 29. last – and another likely to be chosen speedily.[3]

I take myself now to be worth 300*l* clear in money. And all my goods and all manner of debts paid, which are none at all.

JANUARY. $16\frac{60.}{61.}$

3. Early in the morning to the Exchequer, where I told over what money I have of my Lord's and my own there, which I find to be 970*l*: thence to Will's, where Spicer and I eat our dinner of a roasted leg of porke which Will did give us. And after that, I to the Theatre, where was acted *Beggars bush*[4] – it being very well done; and here

1. Henrietta Maria, the Queen Mother.
2. The King's eldest sister had died of smallpox on 24 Dec. 1660.
3. The parliament's offence was not its factiousness but its illegal origin as a convention summoned before the return of the King.
4. Fletcher and Massinger's comedy, acted at the Theatre Royal, Vere St.

the first time that ever I saw Women come upon the stage.[1] From thence to my father's, where I find my mother gone by Bird the carrier to Brampton, upon my uncles great desire, my aunt being now in despair of life.[2] So home.

7. This morning news was brought to me to my bedside that there hath been a great stirr in the City this night by the Fanatiques, who have been up and killed six or seven men, but all are fled.[3] My Lord Mayor and the whole City have been in armes, above 40000.[4] To the office; and after that to dinner, where my brother Tom came and dined with me; and after dinner (leaveing 12*d* with my servants to buy a cake with at night, this day being kept as Twelfeday), Tom and I and my wife to the Theatre and there saw *The Silent Woman*, the first time that ever I did see it and it is an excellent play. Among other things here, Kinaston the boy hath the good turn to appear in three shapes: 1, as a poor woman in ordinary clothes to please Morose; then in fine clothes as a gallant, and in them was clearly the prettiest woman in the whole house – and lastly, as a man; and then likewise did appear the handsomest man in the house.[5] From thence by link to my Cosen Stradwickes, where my father and we and Dr. Pepys[6] – Scott and his wife, and one Mr. Ward and his. And after a good supper we have an excellent cake, where the mark for the Queene was cut;[7] and so there was two queens, my wife and Mrs. Ward; and the King being lost, they chose the Doctor to be King, so we made him send for some wine; and then home: and in our way were in many places strictly examined, more then in the worst of times, there being great fears of these fanatiques rising again. For the present I do not hear that any of them are taken.

1. The Restoration led to women appearing regularly on the English public stage for the first time. The first record of a performance by a female member of one of the Restoration companies was on 8 Dec. 1660 when an unknown woman played Desdemona in Thomas Killigrew's production of *Othello* at the Theatre Royal.
2. Anne Pepys, wife of Pepys's uncle Robert, lived at Brampton, Huntingdonshire.
3. This was a rising of the Fifth Monarchists, led by Thomas Venner. They sought to end the monarchy and, ultimately, to establish Christ's kingdom on earth. Around fifty of them terrified London for the next three days.
4. A slip for 4,000.
5. A production of Jonson's comedy *Epicœne* at the Theatre Royal. Edward Kynaston played the title role, a boy who masquerades as a woman and tricks old Morose into marriage before his identity is revealed at the end of the play.
6. Dr Thomas Pepys, the diarist's cousin.
7. This was a Twelfth Night party. The cake served usually contained a bean and pea, the finders of which were made King and Queen.

Home, it being a clear Mooneshine and after 12 a-clock at night. Being come home, we find that my people have been very merry, and my wife tells me afterward that she hath heard that they had got young Davis and some other neighbours with them to be merry; but no harme.

9. waked in the morning about 6 a-clock by people running up and down in Mr. Davis's house, talking that the Fanatiques were up in armes in the City,[1] and so I rise and went forth, where in the street I find everybody in arms at the doors; so I returned (though with no good courage at all, but that I might not seem to be afeared) and got my sword and pistol, which however I have no powder to charge, and went to the door, where I found Sir R. Ford; and with him I walked up and down as far as the Exchange, and there I left him. In our way, the streets full of trainebands,[2] and great stories what mischief these rogues have done; and I think near a dozen have been killed this morning on both sides. Seeing the city in this condition, the shops shut and all things in trouble, I went home and sat, it being office day, till noon. So home and dined at home, my father with me. And after dinner he would needs have me go to my uncle Wights[3] (where I have been so long absent that I am ashamed to go): I found him at home and his wife; I can see they have taken my absence ill, but all things are past and we good friends; and here I sat with my aunt till it was late, my uncle going forth about business – my aunt being very fearful to be alone. So home to my lute till late, and then to bed – there being strict guards all night in the City, though most of the enemy they say are killed or taken.

10. This morning my wife and Pall went forth early. I stayed within and there comes Mr. Hawly to me and brings me my money for the Quarter of a year's salary of my place under Downing that I was at Sea.[4] So I did give him half, whereof he did in his noblenesse give the odd 5*s*. to my Jane. So we both went forth (calling first to see how Sir W. Pen doth, who I find very ill); and at the hoope by the bridge we drank two pints of Woremoode and sack[5] – talking of

1. Venner's band, who had been hiding in nearby woods, returned to the City early in the morning.
2. The City militia.
3. William Wight, half-brother of Pepys's father, a fishmonger living in the east of the City.
4. Wages due from Pepys's clerkship at the Exchequer during his voyage to fetch the King.
5. Wormwood and white wine.

his wooing afresh of Mrs. Lane and of his going to serve the Bishop of London.

Thence by water to White-hall and found my wife at Mrs. Hunts; and leaving her to dine there, I went and dined with my Lady, and stayed to talk a while with her.

After dinner Will comes to tell me that he hath presented my piece of plate to Mr. Coventry, who takes it very kindly and sends me a very kind letter, and the plate back again – of which my heart is very glad.[1] So to Mrs. Hunts, where I find a Frenchman, a lodger of hers, at dinner; and just as I came in was kissing my wife, which I did not like, though there could not be any hurt in it.

Thence by Coach to my uncle Wights with my wife; but they being both out of doors, we went home. Where after I had put some papers in order and entered some letters in my book which I have a mind to keep, I went with my wife to see Sir W. Pen, who we find ill still – but he doth make very much of it. Here we sat a great while; at last comes in Mr. Davis[2] and his lady (who takes it very ill that my wife never did go to see her) and so we fell to talk: among other things, Mr. Davis told us the perticular examinations of these Fanatiques that are taken. And in short it is this –

Of all these Fanatiques that have done all this, *viz.*, routed all the train-bands that they met with – put the King's lifeguard to the run – killed about 20 men – broke through the City gates twice – and all this in the daytime, when all the City was in armes – are not in all above 31. Whereas we did believe them (because they were seen up and down in every place almost in the City, and have been about Highgate two or three dayes, and in several other places) to be at least 500. A thing that never was heard of, that so few men should dare and do so much mischief. Their word was "King Jesus, and the heads[3] upon the gates!" Few of them would receive any Quarter but such as were taken by force and kept alive, expecting Jesus to come and reign here in the world presently, and will not believe yet but their work will be carried on, though they do die.

The King this day came to towne.

1. Pepys had sent William Coventry a silver dish and cup on Coventry's appointment as Secretary to the Lord High Admiral, the Duke of York. Gifts of plate were customarily made on receiving appointments or titles.
2. John Davis, a clerk in the Navy Office.
3. The regicides' heads.

30th. *Fast day.*

The first time that this day hath been yet observed.[1] And Mr. Mills made a most excellent sermon – upon "Lord, forgive us our former iniquitys."[2] Speaking excellently of the justice of God in punishing man for the sins of his ancesters.

Home, and John Goods comes; and after dinner I did pay him 30*l* for my Lady. And after that, Sir Wm. Pen and I into Moorefields and have a rare walk, it being a most pleasant day. And besides much discourse, did please ourselfs to see young Davis and Whitton, two of our clerks, going by us in the field – who we observe to take much pleasure together; and I did most often see them at plays together.

Back to the old James in Bishops-gate-street, where Sir Wm. Batten and Sir Wm. Rider met him about business of the Trinity-house: so I went away home, and there understand that my mother is come home well from Brampton. And have a letter from my brother John – a very ingenious one; and he therein begs to have leave to come to town at the Coronacion.

Then to my Lady Batten's, where my wife and she are lately come back again from being abroad and seeing of Cromwell, Ireton, and Bradshaw hanged and buried at Tiburne.[3] Then I home.

FEBRUARY.

14. *Valentine's day.* Up earely and to Sir W. Battens. But would not go in till I had asked whether they that opened the doore was a man or a woman.[4] And Mingo,[5] who was there, answered "a Woman;" which, with his tone, made me laugh.

So up I went and took Mrs. Martha[6] for my Valentine (which I do only for complacency), and Sir W. Batten, he go in the same manner to my wife. And so we were very merry.

About 10 a-clock we with a great deal of company went down by our barge to Deptford; and there only went to see how forward

1. A fast-day commemorating the execution of Charles I, instituted in December 1660.
2. A loose recollection of Psalms 79.8.
3. Their corpses were disinterred, hung up, and then buried under the gallows.
4. On Valentine's Day, one custom required that a man took the first woman he saw as his valentine. A present was then due to her. Each year tactical manoeuvring by both sexes took place to ensure the best choice of partner (and present).
5. Batten's black servant.
6. Batten's daughter.

Mr. Pett's yacht is.[1] And so all into the barge again, and so to Woolwich on board the *Rosebush*, Captain Brown's ship, that is brother-in-law to Sir W. Batten – where we had a very fine dinner dressed on shoare. And great mirth and all things successefull – the first time I ever carried my wife a-shipboard – as also my boy Waineman, who hath all this day been called "young Pepys", as Sir W. Pen's boy "young Pen".

So home by barge again; good weather, but pretty cold.

I to my study and begun to make up my accounts for my Lord, which I entend to end tomorrow.

To bed.

The talk of the towne now is, who the King is like to have for his Queene – and whether Lent shall be kept with the strictnesse of the King's proclamacion;[2] which it is thought cannot be, because of the poor, who cannot buy fish – and also the great preparacion for the King's crowning is now much thought upon and talked of.

23. This my *Birth day, 28 yeeres.*

This morning Sir W. Batten, Pen, and I did some business; and then I by water to White-hall – having met Mr. Hartlibb[3] by the way at Alderman Backwells: so he did give me a glass of Rhenish wine at the Steeleyard. And so to White-hall by water. He continues of the same bold impertinent Humour that he was alway of and will ever be. He told me how my Lord Chancellor hath lately got the Duke of Yorke and Duchesse, and her woman, my Lord Ossery, and a Doctor, to make oath before most of the Judges of the kingdom concerning all the circumstances of their marriage.[4] And in fine, it is confessed that they were not fully married till about a month or two before she was brought to bed; but that they were contracted long before, and time enough for the child to be legitimate; but I do not hear that it was put to the Judges to determine whether it was so or no.

To my Lord and there spoke to him about his opinion of the Light, the Sea-marke that Captain Murford is about and doth offer

1. Peter Pett, shipwright and Navy Commissioner at Chatham, was building this yacht.
2. The proclamation prohibited the consumption and sale of meat during Lent.
3. Samuel Hartlib, jun., underclerk to the Privy Council.
4. At a special meeting of the Privy Council on 18 February, the Duke had brought evidence to prove that he had been contracted in marriage to Anne Hyde on 24 Nov. 1659 and then lived in clandestine marriage with her until a Church of England ceremony on 3 Sept. 1660.

me an eighth part to concern myself with it.[1] And my Lord doth give me some incouragement in it – and I shall go on. I dined here with Mr. Sheply and Howe. After dinner to White-hall chappell with Mr. Childe; and there did hear Captain Cooke and his boy make a tryall of an Anthemne against tomorrow, which was rare Musique.

Then by water to White-fryers to the play-house, and there saw *The Changeling*,[2] the first time it hath been acted these 20 yeeres – and it takes exceedingly. Besides, I see the gallants do begin to be tyred with the Vanity and pride of the Theatre=actors, who are endeed grown very proud and rich.

Then by linke home – and there to my book awhile and to bed.

I met today with Mr. Townsend, who tells me that the old man is yet alive in whose place in the Wardrobe he hopes to get my father – which I do resolve to put for.[3]

I also met with the Comptroller, who told me how it was easy for us all, the principall officers, and proper for us, to labour to get into the next parliament – and would have me to aske the Dukes letter.[4] But I shall not endeavour it – because it will spend much money, though I am sure I could well obtaine it. This is now 28 years that I am born. And blessed be God, and a state of full content and great hopes to be a happy man in all respects, both to myself and friends.

MARCH.

1. All the morning at the office. Dined at home, only upon fish, and Mr. Sheply and Tom. Hater with me. After dinner Mr. Sheply and I in private talking about my Lord's ententions to go speedily into the country; but to what end we know not. We fear he is to go to sea with this fleet now preparing. But we wish that he could get his 4000*l* per annum[5] settled before that he doth go.

Then he and I walked into London. He to the Wardrobe and

1. Probably the erection of a lighthouse in the Humber. By investing in lighthouses, owners could profit from charges made to shipping.
2. A tragedy by Thomas Middleton and William Rowley, performed by William Davenant's actors (the Duke's Company) at Salisbury Court, Whitefriars.
3. Pepys was trying to get his father the position of yeoman tailor of the King's Wardrobe.
4. I.e. the Lord Admiral's recommendation to the electors of an Admiralty borough.
5. Granted by the King, *see* 7 Nov. 1660.

I to White-fryers and saw *The Bondman* acted – an excellent play and well done – but above all that ever I saw, Baterton doth the Bondman the best.[1]

Then to my father's and find my mother ill. After staying a while with them, then I went home – and sat up late, spending my thoughts how to get money to bear me out in my great expense at the Coronacion, against which all provide – and Scaffolds[2] setting up in every street.

I have many designs in my head to get some, but know not which will take.

To bed.

25. *Lady=day.* This morning came workmen to begin the making of me a new pair of stairs up out of my parlour, which, with other work that I have to do, I doubt[3] will keep me this two months; and so long I shall be all in dirt – but the work doth please me very well. To the office then. And there all the morning. Dined at home; and after dinner came Mr. Salsbury to see me and showed me a face or two of his paynting; and endeed, I perceive that he will be a great master.

I took him to White-hall with me by water; but he would not by any means be wooed to go through bridge[4] and so we were fain to go round to the old swan.

To my Lord's and there I showed him the King's picture,[5] which he entends to copy out in little. After that, I and Captain Ferrers to Salsbury-court by water and saw part of *The Queenes maske.*[6] Then I to Mrs. Turners and there stayed talking late – The. Turner being in a great chafe about being disappointed of a room to stand in at the coronation.

Then to my father's and there stayed talking with my mother and him late about my dinner tomorrow.

So homewards and took up a boy that had a lanthorn, that was picking up of rags, and got him to light me home. And had great discourse with him how he could get sometimes three or four bushels of rags in a day, and gat 3*d* a bushel for them. And many

1. *The Bondman* by Philip Massinger was one of Pepys's favourite plays. Thomas Betterton became Samuel and Elizabeth's favourite actor.
2. Stands for spectators.
3. Fear.
4. The channels between the arches of London Bridge were narrow and dangerous.
5. A portrait of Charles, painted 1659–60, and attributed to Pieter Thys; now in the UK's Government Art Collection.
6. *Loves Maistresse: or, The Queens Masque*, by Thomas Heywood, at the Duke's Company's theatre.

other discourses, what and how many ways there are for poor children to get their livings honestly.

So home and to bed – at 12 a-clock at night, being pleased well with the work that my workmen have begun today.

26. Up early to do business in my study.

This is my great day, that three year ago I was cut of the stone – and blessed be God, I do yet find myself very free from pain again. All this morning I stayed at home looking after my workmen, to my great content, about my stairs. And at noon by coach to my father's, where Mrs. Turner, The, Joyce, Mr. Morrice, Mr. Armiger, Mr. Pierce the surgeon and his wife – my father and mother and myself and my wife.

Very merry at dinner. Among other things, because Mrs. Turner and her company eate no flesh at all this Lent and I had a great deal of good flesh, which made their mouths water.

After dinner, Mrs. Pierce and her husband and I and my wife to Salisbury-Court;[1] where coming late, he and she light of[2] Collonell Boone, that made room for them; and I and my wife sat in the pit and there met with Mr. Lewes and Tom. Whitton – and saw *The Bondman* done to admiration. So home by coach – and after a view of what the workmen have done today, I went to bed.

31. *Sunday.*

At church, where a stranger preached like a fool.

From thence home and dined with my wife; [she] staying at home, she being unwilling to dress herself, the house being all dirty.

To church again. And after sermon I walked to my father's and to Mrs. Turner's – where I could not woo The to give me a lesson[3] upon the Harpsicon[4] and was angry at it.

So home; and finding Will abroad at Sir W. Battens, talking with the people there (Sir W and my Lady being in the country) – I took occasion to be angry with him; and so to prayer and to bed.

1. The Duke's Company's playhouse.
2. Came across.
3. A piece of music.
4. Harpsichord: a keyboard instrument (resembling a grand piano) where striking the keys plucks the strings.

APRILL.

8. Up early, my Lady Batten knocking at her door that comes into one of my chambers – I did give directions to my people and workmen; and so about 8 a-clock we took barge at the Tower – Sir Wm. Batten and his Lady, Mrs. Turner, Mr. Fowler[1] and I. A very pleasant passage. And so to Gravesend, where we dined; and from thence a coach took them and I and Fowler, with some others come from Rochester to meet us, on horseback – at Rochester, where light at Mr. Alcocks and there drank and had good sport with his bringing out so many sorts of cheese. Then to the hill=house at Chatham,[2] where I never was before. And I find a pretty pleasant house – and am pleased with the armes that hang up there. Here we supped very merry, and late to bed; Sir Wm. telling me that old Edgeborow, his predecessor, did die and walk in my chamber – did make me somewhat afeared, but not so much as for mirth sake
⟨⟨9⟩⟩ I did seem.[3] So to bed in the Treasurer's chamber and lay and sleep well – till 3 in the morning, and then waking; and by the light of the moon I saw my pillow (which overnight I flung from me) stand upright, but not bethinking myself what it might be, I was a little afeared. But sleep overcame all, and so lay till high morning – at which time I had a caudle[4] brought me and a good fire made. And in generall, it was a great pleasure all the time I stayed here, to see how I am respected and honoured by all people; and I find that I begin to know now how to receive so much reverence, which at the beginning I could not tell how to do.

Sir Wm. and I by coach to the Dock and there viewd all the store-houses and the old goods that are this day to be sold, which was great pleasure to me; and so back again by coach home – where we had a good dinner. And among other strangers that came, there was Mr. Hempson[5] and his wife, a pretty woman and speaks Latin. Mr. Allen and two daughters of his, both very tall and the youngest very handsome, so much as that I could not forbear to love her

1. John Fowler, Judge-Advocate of the fleet.
2. An Elizabethan house near the dockyard, used for the accommodation of official visitors.
3. Kenrick Edisbury, Surveyor of the Navy, 1632–8, had lived at Hill House.
4. A warm drink with wine or ale, eggs, and spices.
5. William Hempson, Clerk of the Survey at Chatham.

exceedingly – having, among other things, the best hand that ever I saw.[1]

After dinner we went to fit books and things (Tom Hater being this morning come to us) for the Sale by an inch of candle.[2] And very good sport we and the ladies that stood by had to see the people bid. Among other things sold, there was all the State's armes;[3] which Sir W. Batten bought, entending to set up some of the images in his gardens and the rest to burn on the Coronacion night. The sale being done, the ladies and I and Captain Pett and Mr. Castle took barge; and down we went to see the *Sovereigne*;[4] which we did, taking great pleasure therein – singing all the way; and among other pleasures, I put my Lady, Mrs. Turner, Mrs. Hempson, and the two Mrs. Allen's into the lantern[5] and I went in to them and kissed them, demanding it as a fee due to a Principall officer. With all which we were exceeding merry, and drank some bottles of wine and neat's tongue,[6] &c. Then back again home and so supped; and after much mirth, to bed.

21. In the morning we were troubled to hear it rain as it did, because of the great show tomorrow.[7] After I was ready, I walked to my father's. And there find the late mayde to be gone and another come by my mother's choice, which my father doth not like; and so, great difference there will be between my father and mother about it. Here dined Dr. Tho. Pepys and Dr. Fayrebrother. And all our talk about tomorrow's Shewe – and our trouble that it is like to be a wet day.

After dinner comes in my Cozen Snow and his wife, and I think [to] stay there till the Shewe be over. Then I went home; and all the way is so thronged with people to see the Triumphall Arches[8] that I could hardly pass for them.

So home, people being at church; and I got home unseen.◆

My mind a little troubled about my workmen, which being

1. Capt. John Allen, Clerk of the Ropeyard at Chatham; his younger daughter was Rebecca.
2. An auction-sale by candle of government property. The successful bidder was the one who made the highest offer before the candle went out.
3. Carvings of the coats of arms of the Commonwealth.
4. The *Royal Sovereign*, the largest warship in the fleet.
5. There were huge lanterns at the stern of the ship.
6. Ox or cow's tongue.
7. The royal entry held the day before the coronation.
8. Four temporary triumphal arches were constructed, each with elaborate allegorical decorations.

foraigners[1] are like to be troubled by a couple of lazy rogues that worked with me the other day that are Citizens: and so my work will be hindered, but I must prevent it if I can.

22. *King's going from the Tower to White-hall*

Up earely and made myself as fine as I could, and put on my velvet coat, the first day that I put it on though made half a year ago: and being ready, Sir W. Batten, my Lady, and his two daughters and his son and wife, and Sir W. Penn and his son and I went to Mr. Young's the Flagg-maker in Cornhill; and there we had a good room to ourselfs, with wine and good cake, and saw the Shew very well – in which it is impossible to relate the glory of that this day – expressed in the clothes of them that rid – and their horses and horse-cloths. Among others, my Lord Sandwich.

Imbroidery and diamonds were ordinary among them.

The Knights of the Bath was a brave sight of itself. And their Esquires, among which Mr. Armiger[2] was an Esquire to one of the Knights. remarquable was the two men that represent the two Dukes of Normandy and Aquitane.[3]

The Bishops came next after the Barons, which is the higher place;[4] which makes me think that the next parliament they will be called to the House of Lords. My Lord Monke rode bare[5] after the King, and led in his hand a spare horse, as being Maister of the Horse.

The King, in a most rich imbrodered suit and cloak, looked most nobly. Wadlow, the vintner at the Devil in Fleetstreet, did lead a fine company of Souldiers, all young comely men, in white doublets. There fallowed the Vice-Chamberlin, Sir G. Carteret, a company of men all like turkes; but I know not yet what they are for.[6]

The Streets all gravelled; and the houses, hung with Carpets before them, made brave show, and the ladies out of the windows. One of which, over against us, I took much notice of and spoke of her, which made good sport among us.

So glorious was the show with gold and silver, that we were not able to look at it – our eyes at last being so much overcome with it.

1. Men not enrolled as freemen of the City. Freemen could properly object to their employment as skilled workers within the City.
2. Probably William Armiger, a distant relative of Pepys.
3. Wearing what John Evelyn called "fantastique habits", they personified the royal claims to these duchies.
4. The bishops did not take part. Pepys may have been reconstructing events using a list from one of a couple of pamphlets that make the same mistake.
5. Bare-headed.
6. They appear to have been a company of the royal foot guard.

Both the King and the Duke of Yorke took notice of us as he saw us at the window.

The show being ended, Mr Young did give us dinner – at which we very merry, and pleased above imagination at what we have seen. ⟨Sir W. Batten going home, he and I called and drank some Mum[1] and laid our wager about my Lady Faulconbrige's name, which he says not to be Mary; and so I won above 20*s*.⟩

So home – where Will and the boy stayed and saw the show upon tower hill – and Jane at T. Pepys the Turner and my wife at Charles Glascockes in Fleetstreete. In the evening, by water to White-hall to my Lord's. And there I spoke with my Lord. He talked with me about his suit, which was made in France and cost him 200*l*, and very rich it is with imbroidery.

23. I lay with Mr. Sheply, and about 4 in the morning I rose.

Coronacion day.

And got to the abby, where I fallowed Sir J. Denham the surveyour[2] with some company that he was leading in. And with much ado, by the favour of Mr. Cooper his man, did get up into a great scaffold across the north end of the abby – where with a great deal of patience I sat from past 4 till 11 before the King came in. And a pleasure it was to see the Abbey raised in the middle, all covered with red and a throne (that is a chaire) and footstoole on the top of it. And all the officers of all kinds, so much as the very fidlers, in red vests.

At last comes in the Deane and prebends of Westminster with the Bishops (many of them in cloth-of-gold Copes); and after them the nobility all in their parliament-robes, which was a most magnificent sight. Then the Duke and the King with a scepter (carried by my Lord of Sandwich) and Sword and mond[3] before him, and the crowne too.

The King in his robes, bare-headed, which was very fine. And after all had placed themselfs – there was a sermon and the service. And then in the Quire[4] at the high altar he passed all the ceremonies of the Coronacion – which, to my very great grief, I and most in the Abbey could not see. The crowne being put upon his head, a great shout begun. And he came forth to the Throne and there passed more ceremonies: as, taking the oath and having things read

1. Spiced ale.
2. Sir John Denham, poet and Surveyor-General of the King's Works.
3. Orb (royal jewel in the form of a globe).
4. Choir.

to him by the Bishopp, and his lords (who put on their capps as soon as the King put on his Crowne) and Bishopps came and kneeled before him.

And three times the King-at-armes went to the three open places on the scaffold and proclaimed that if any one could show any reason why Ch. Steward should not be King of England, that now he should come and speak.

And a Generall pardon also was read by the Lord Chancellor; and meddalls flung up and down by my Lord Cornwallis – of silver; but I could not come by any.

But so great a noise, that I could make but little of the Musique; and endeed, it was lost to everybody. But I had so great a list to pisse, that I went out a little while before the King had done all his ceremonies and went round the abby to Westminster-hall, all the way within rayles, and 10000 people, with the ground coverd with blue cloth – and Scaffolds all the way. Into the hall I got – where it was very fine with hangings and scaffolds, one upon another, full of brave[1] ladies. And my wife in one little one on the right hand.

Here I stayed walking up and down; and at last, upon one of the side-stalls, I stood and saw the King come in with all the persons (but the Souldiers) that were yesterday in the cavalcade; and a most pleasant sight it was to see them in their several robes. And the King came in with his Crowne on and his sceptre in his hand – under a Canopy borne up by six silver staves, carried by Barons of the Cinqueports – and little bells at every end.

And after a long time he got up to the farther end, and all set themselfs down at their several tables – and that was also a rare sight. And the King's first Course carried up by the Knights of the bath. And many fine ceremonies there was of the Heralds leading up people before him and bowing; and my Lord of Albimarles going to the Kitchin and eat a bit of the first dish that was to go to the King's table.[2]

But above all was these three Lords, Northumberland and Suffolke and the Duke of Ormond, coming before the Courses on horseback and staying so all dinner-time; and at last, to bring up (Dymock) the King's Champion, all in armor on horseback, with his Speare and targett carried before him. And a herald proclaim that if any dare deny Ch. Steward to be lawful King of England, here was a Champion that would fight with him; and with those

1. Handsome.
2. The food was tasted to ensure it was not poisoned.

words the Champion flings down his gantlet; and all this he doth three times in his going up toward the King's table. At last, when he is come, the King Drinkes to him and then sends him the Cup, which is of gold; and he drinks it off and then rides back again with the cup in his hand.

I went from table to table to see the Bishops and all others at their dinner, and was infinite pleased with it. And at the Lords' table I met with Wll. Howe and he spoke to my Lord for me and he did give him four rabbits and a pullet; and so I got it, and Mr. Creed and I got Mr. Michell to give us some bread and so we at a Stall eat it, as everybody else did what they could get.

I took a great deal of pleasure to go up and down and look upon the ladies – and to hear the Musique of all sorts; but above all, the 24 viollins.

About 6 at night they had dined; and I went up to my wife and there met with a pretty lady (Mrs. Frankelyn, a Doctor's wife, a friend of Mr. Bowyers) and kissed them both – and by and by took them down to Mr. Bowyers.[1] And strange it is, to think that these two days have held up fair till now that all is done and the King gone out of the hall; and then it fell a-raining and thundering and lightening as I have not seen it do some years – which people did take great notice of God's blessing of the work of these two days – which is a foolery, to take too much notice of such things.

I observed little disorder in all this; but only the King's Footmen had got hold of the Canopy and would keep it from the barons of the Cinqueports; which they endeavoured to force from them again but could not do it till my Lord Duke of Albemarle caused it to be put into Sir R. Pye's hand till tomorrow to be decided.[2]

At Mr. Bowyers, a great deal of company; some I knew, others I did not. Here we stayed upon the leads[3] and below till it was late, expecting to see the Fireworkes; but they were not performd tonight. Only, the City had a light like a glory round about it, with bonefyres.

At last I went to Kingstreete; and there sent Crockford to my father's and my house to tell them I could not come home tonight, because of the dirt and a coach could not be had.

And so after drinking a pot of ale alone at Mrs. Harpers, I returned to Mr. Bowyers; and after a little stay more, I took my

1. Robert Bowyer, Pepys's good friend, had a house in Westminster.
2. The barons had the honour of carrying the canopy for the King, which the footmen tried to snatch, leading to a scuffle. The footmen were punished.
3. Roof walkways.

wife and Mrs. Frankelyn (who I proferred the civility of lying with my wife at Mrs. Hunts tonight) to Axe yard. In which, at the further end, there was three great bonefyres and a great many great gallants, men and women; and they laid hold of us and would have us drink the King's health upon our knee, kneeling upon a fagott; which we all did, they drinking to us one after another – which we thought a strange Frolique. But these gallants continued thus a great while, and I wondered to see how the ladies did tiple.

At last I sent my wife and her bedfellow to bed, and Mr. Hunt and I went in with Mr. Thornbury (who did give the company all their wines, he being yeoman of the wine-cellar to the King) to his house; and there, with his wife and two of his sisters and some gallant sparks that were there, we drank the King's health and nothing else, till one of the genlemen fell down stark drunk and there lay speweing. And I went to my Lord's pretty well. But no sooner abed with Mr. Sheply but my head begun to turne and I to vomitt, and if ever I was foxed[1] it was now – which I cannot say yet, because I fell asleep and sleep till morning – only, when I waked I found myself wet with my spewing. Thus did the day end, with joy everywhere; and blessed be God, I have not heard of any mischance to anybody through it all, but only to Serjeant Glynne, whose Horse fell upon him yesterday and is like to kill him; which people do please themselfs with, to see how just God is to punish that rogue at such a time as this – he being now one of the King's Serjeants and rode in the Cavalcade with Maynard, to whom people wished the same fortune.[2]

There was also this night, in Kingstreet, [a woman] had her eye put out by a boy's flinging of a firebrand into the coach.

Now after all this, I can say that besides the pleasure of the sight of these glorious things, I may now shut my eyes against any other objects, or for the future trouble myself to see things of state and shewe, as being sure never to see the like again in this world.

24. Waked in the morning with my head in a sad taking through the last night's drink, which I am very sorry for. So rise and went out with Mr. Creed to drink our morning draught, which he did give me in Chocolate to settle my stomach.[3] And after that to my wife, who lay with Mrs. Frankelyn at the next door to Mrs. Hunts.

1. Drunk, befuddled.
2. Sir John Glynne and Sir John Maynard were eminent lawyers who had served in high office under Oliver Cromwell.
3. Chocolate, a new and exotic drink in Britain, was held to aid digestion. This is Pepys's first recorded taste of it.

And they were ready, and so I took them up in a coach and carried the lady to Pauls[1] and there set her down; and so my wife and I home – and I to the office.

That being done, my wife and I went to dinner to Sir W. Batten; and all our talk about the happy conclusion of these last solemnitys.

After dinner home and advised with my wife about ordering things in my house; and then she went away to my father's to lie, and I stayed with my workmen, who do please me very well with their work.

At night set myself to write down these three days' diary; and while I am about it, I hear the noise of the chambers and other things of the Fireworkes, which are now playing upon the Thames before the King. And I wish myself with them, being sorry not to see them.

So to bed.

MAY.

19. *Lords day.* I walked in the morning toward Westminster; and seeing many people at Yorke-house, I went down and find them at Masse, it being the Spanish Embassadors; and so I got into one of the gallerys and there heard two masses[2] – done, I think, in not so much state as I have seen them heretofore. After that into the garden and walked a turn or two; but find it not so fine a place as I alway took it for by the outside. Thence to my Lord's and there spoke with him about business; and then he went to White-hall to dinner – and Captain Ferrers and Mr. Howe and myself to Mr. Wilkinsons at the Crowne. And though he had no meat of his owne, yet we happened to find our Cooke Mr. Robinson[3] there, who had a dinner for himself and some friends; and so he did give us a very fine dinner.

Then to my Lord's, where we went and sat talking and laughing in the drawing-room a great while. All our talk about their going to sea this voyage,[4] which Captain Ferrers is in some doubt whether he shall go or no. But swears that he would go if he were sure never

1. St Paul's Cathedral.
2. The Catholic envoys' chapels (with those of the Queen Mother and later Queen Catherine) were the only places where Catholic services could legally be held. The presence of unprivileged persons (such as Pepys) was forbidden.
3. "Our Cooke" in that Pepys bought cooked meats from his shop.
4. A fleet was preparing to leave for the Mediterranean.

to come back again. And I giving him some hopes, he grew so mad with joy that he fell a-dancing and leaping like a madman.

Now it fell out so that the balcone windows were open; and he went to the rayle and made an offer to leap over and asked what if he should leap over there. I told him I would give him 40*l* if he did not go to sea. With that, though I shut the door and W. Howe hindered him all we could, yet he opened them again and with a vault leaps down into the garden – the greatest and most desperate frolic that ever I saw in my life. I run to see what was become of him, and we find him crawled upon his knees – but could not rise. So we went down into the garden and dragged him to the bench, where he looked like a dead man – but could not stir. And though he had broke nothing, yet his pain in his back was such as he could not endure. With this, my Lord (who was in the little new room) came to us in an amaze and bid us carry him up; which by our strength we did and so laid him in Easts bed by the doore[1] – where he lay in great pain. We sent for Doctor and Chyrurgeon, but none to be found; till by and by, by chance comes in Dr Clerke – who is afeared of him.[2] So we sent to get a lodgeing for him; and I went up to my Lord, where Captain Cooke, Mr. Gibbons, and others of the King's Musique were come to present my Lord with some songs and Symphonys,[3] which were performed very finely; which being done, I took leave and supped at my father's – where was my Cozen Beck, come lately out of the country.

I am troubled to see my father so much decay of a suddaine as he doth, both in his seeing and hearing – and as much, to hear of him how my Brother Tom doth grow disrespectfull to him and my mother.

I took leave and went home. Where to prayers (which I have not had in my house a good while), and so to bed.

23. This day I went to my Lord, and about many other things at White-hall – and there made even my accounts with Mr. Sheply at my Lord's. And then with him and Mr. Moore and John Bowles to the Renish wine-house, and there came Jonas ⟨Moore⟩ the Mathematician to us. And there he did by discourse make us fully believe that England and France were once the same continent, by very good arguments. And spoke very many things, not so much to prove the Scripture false, as that the time therein is not well

1. East was Sandwich's porter.
2. I.e. afraid for him – but Ferrers recovered over the next week.
3. Instrumental introductions to vocal compositions.

computed nor understood.[1] From thence home by water and there shifted myself into my black silke sute (the first day I have put it on this year); and so to my Lord Mayors by coach, where a great deal of Honourable company – and great entertainment.[2]

At table I had very good discourse with Mr. Ashmole, wherein he did assure me that froggs and many other insects do often fall from the Sky ready-formed.[3]

Dr. Bates's singularity, in not rising up nor drink the King's nor other healths at the table, was very much observed.[4]

From thence we all took coach and to our office. And there sat till it was late.

29. *Kings birth day.*

Rose earely; and having made myself fine and put six spoons and a porringer of Silver in my pocket to give away today, Sir W. Pen and I took Coach and (the weather and ways being foule) went to Waltamstowe.[5] And being come thither, heard Mr. Ratcliffe (my former schoolefellow at Pauls, who is yet a mere boy) preach upon "Nay, lett him take all, since my Lord the King is returned," &c:[6] he reads all, and his sermon very simple – but I looked for no better. Back to dinner to Sir Wms; and then after a walk in the fine gardens, we went to Mrs. Brown's, where Sir W. Pen and I were godfathers and Mrs. Jordan and Shipman godmothers to her boy. And there, before and after the Christening, we were with the women above in her chamber; but whether we carried ourselfs well or ill, I know not – but I was directed by young Mrs. Batten. One passage,[7] of a lady that eate wafers with her dog, did a little displease me. I did give the midwife 10*s* and the nurse 5*s* and the maid of the house 2: but for as much as I expected to give the name to the Childe, but did not, it being called John, I forbore then to give my plate – till another time, after a little more advice.[8]

1. Commentators sought to determine the age of the earth and the chronology of human history from biblical sources, yet these contained inconsistencies. Moore thought the study of the earth could be applied to help resolve these issues.
2. This was an Ascension Day dinner.
3. Elias Ashmole was a member of the Royal Society, which had discussed the "generation of insects" the day before.
4. William Bates objected, like many puritans, to the drinking of toasts.
5. Pepys and Penn were going to the christening of Sir William Batten's nephew. Wealthy godparents traditionally gave silver plate to the child.
6. A loose recollection of 2 Samuel 19.30. The preacher was about 27 – a year younger than Pepys.
7. Occurrence.
8. It was common for a godfather to name a male child, often giving it his own name. In this case the baby had been named after his father.

All being done, we went to Mrs. Shipmans, who is a great butterwoman; and I did see there the most of milke and cream, and the cleanest, that ever I saw in my life. After we had filled our bellies with cream, we took our leaves and away. In our way we had great sport to try who should drive fastest, Sir W. Batten's coach or Sir W. Pen's charriot, they having four and we two horses, and we beat them. But it cost me the spoiling of my clothes and velvet coate with dirt.

Being come home, I to bed; and gave my breeches to be dried by the fire against tomorrow.

JUNE.

10. earely to my Lord – who privately told me how the King hath made him embassador in the bringing over the Queen. That he is to go to Algier &c. to settle that business and to put the fleet in order there; and so to come back to Lisbone with three ships, and there to meet the fleet that is to fallow him.[1]

He sent for me to tell me that he doth intrust me with the seeing of all things done in his absence as to this great preparation, as I shall receive orders from my Lord Chancellor and Mr. Edw. Mountagu. At all which, my heart is above measure glad – for my Lord's honour, and some profit to myself I hope.

By and by out with Mr. Sheply, Walden, parliament-man for Huntingdon, Rolt, Mackworth, and Alderman Backwell to a house hard by to drink Lambeth ale. So I back to the Wardrobe and there find my Lord going to Trinity-house,[2] this being the solemn day of choosing Master; and my Lord is chosen – so he dines there today.

I stayed and dined with my Lady; but after we were sat, comes in some persons of condition; and so the children and I rise and dined by ourselfs, all the children and I, and were very merry – and they mighty fond of me. Then I to the office, and there sat a while. So home; and at night to bed – where we lay in Sir R. Slingsby's lodgings – in the dining-room there, in our green bed – my house being now in its last work of painting and whiting.

1. Charles's match with Catherine of Braganza had been publicly announced on 8 May. Sandwich was to go with a fleet to Portugal to conclude the marriage treaty. He had instructions to stop at Algiers and make a treaty for free passage of ships.
2. The public body in charge of safe navigation.

13. I went up and down to Alderman Backwells, but his servants not being up, I went home and put on my gray cloth suit and faced white coate, made of one of my wife's pettycoates – the first time that I have had it on. And so, in a riding garbe, back again and spoke with Mr. Shaw at the Aldermans; who offers me 300*l*, if my Lord pleases, to buy this cloth with – which pleased me well.[1] So to the Wardrobe and got my Lord to order Mr. Creed to imprest[2] so much upon me, to be paid by Alderman Backwell.

So with my Lord to White-hall by water. And he having taken leave of the King, comes to us at his lodgeings and from thence goes to the garden Staires and there takes barge. And at the stairs was met by Sir R. Slingsby,[3] who there took his leave of my Lord; and I heard my Lord thank him for his kindness to me, which Sir Robert answered much to my advantage.

I went down with my Lord in the barge to Deptford; and there went on board the Duch yacht and stayed there a good while, W. Howe not being come with my Lord's things, which made my Lord angry. By and by he comes and so we set sayle; and anon went to dinner. My Lord and we very merry. And after dinner I went down below and there sang and took leave of W. Howe, Captain Rolt, and the rest of my friends; then went up and took leave of my Lord, who gave me his hand and parted with great respect.

So went, and Captain Ferrers with me, into our wherry. And my Lord did give five guns, all they had charged, which was the greatest respect my Lord could do me and of which I was not a little proud. So with a sad and merry heart I left them, sailing pleasantly from Erith, hoping to be in the Downes tomorrow earely.

We toward London in our boat. Pulled off our Stockings and bathed our legs a great while in the River – which I had not done some years before.

By and by we came to Greenwich; and thinking to have gone on the King's Yacht, the King was in her, so we passed by; and at Woolwich went on shore in the company of Captain Poole of Jamaica[4] and young Mr. Kenersly and many others. And so to the Taverne, where we drank a great deal, both wine and beere. So we parted thence and went home with Mr. Falconer, who did give us

1. Pepys was buying cloth for Sandwich to take to Algiers to give as presents. Alderman Edward Backwell was a powerful goldsmith-banker and a financial agent for the crown.
2. Money paid in advance by the government to a public servant.
3. Comptroller of the Navy.
4. Jonas Poole had been on the 1654 voyage on which the English captured Jamaica. "Young Poole" who entertained Pepys later in the day was his son.

cherrys and good wine. So to boat and young Poole took us on board the *Charity* and gave us wine there, with which I had full enough; and so to our wherry again. And there fell asleep till I came almost to the tower; and there the Captain and I parted. And I home – and with wine enough in my head went to bed.

30. *Lords day.*

To church; where we observe the trade of briefes[1] is come now up to so constant a course every Sunday, that we resolve to give no more to them. A good sermon; and then home to dinner, my wife and I all alone.

After dinner, Sir Wms. both and I by water to White-hall; where having walked up and down, at last we met with the Duke of Yorke according to an order sent us yesterday from him, to give him an account where the fault lay in the not sending out of the ships. Which we find to be only the wind hath been against them, and so they could not get out of the River. Hence I to Grayes Inn walk all alone; and with great pleasure seeing the fine ladies walk there – myself humming to myself (which nowadays is my constant practice since I begun to learn to sing) the *trillo*;[2] and find by use that it doth come upon me. Home, very weary, and to bed – finding my wife not sick but yet out of order, that I fear she will come to be sick. This day the Portuguese Embassador came to White-hall to take leave of the King, he being now going to end all with the Queene and to send her over.

The weather now very fair and pleasant, but very hot. My father gone to Brampton to see my Uncle Robt., not knowing whether to find him dead or alive. Myself, lately under a great expense of money upon myself in clothes and other things; but I hope to make it up this summer, by my having to do in getting things ready to send with the next fleet for the Queene.

Myself in good health; but mighty apt to take cold, so that this hot weather I am fain to wear a cloth before my belly.[3]

1. Briefs were charitable collections authorized by the Lord Chancellor.
2. The accelerated repetition of the same note.
3. End of the first manuscript volume.

JULY. 1661.

2. To Westminster-hall and there walked up and down, it being term-time.[1] Spoke with several; among others, my Cosen Rogr. Pepys, who was going up to the parliament-house and enquired whether I had heard from my father since he went to Brampton – which I had done yesterday, who writes that my uncle is by fits stupid and like a man that is drunk, and sometimes speechless.

Home; and after my singing master had done and took Coach and went to Sir Wm. Davenant's opera – this being the fourth day that it hath begun, and the first that I have seen it.[2] Today was acted the second part of *The Siege of Rhodes.*[3] We stayed a very great while for the King, and the Queene of Bohemia. And by the breaking of a board over our heads, we had a great deal of dust fell into the ladies' necks and the men's haire, which made good sport. The King being come, the Scene opened; which endeed is very fine and magnificent, and well acted, all but the Eunuches, who was so much out that he was hissed off the stage.[4]

Home and wrote letters to my Lord to Sea; and so to bed.

6. Waked this morning with news, brought me by a messenger on purpose, that my Uncle Robert is dead – and died yesterday. So I rose, sorry in some respect; glad in my expectations in another respect. So I made myself ready. Went and told my Uncle Wight – my Lady – and some others thereof. And bought me a pair of boots in St. Martins and got myself ready; and then to the post-house and set out about 11 or 12 a-clock, taking the messenger with me that came to me; and so we rode and got well by 9 a-clock to Brampton, where I find my father well. My Uncles corps in a coffin, standing upon joynt-stooles in the chimny in the hall; but it begun to smell, and so I caused it to be set forth in the yard all night and

1. Term time for the law courts, when Westminster Hall was busy.
2. By the "opera" Pepys means the new theatre in Portugal Row, Lincoln's Inn Fields, to which Davenant had transferred the Duke's Company. The stage had a proscenium arch and movable scenery.
3. The first part of Davenant's operatic drama *The Siege of Rhodes* had been acted in 1656. He then revised it and published it with the second part in 1663. It became one of Samuel and Elizabeth's favourites.
4. The eunuch was played by John Downes, who became a theatre historian. In *Roscius Anglicanus* (1708) he attributed his forgetting his lines to the "August *presence*" of Charles II.

wached by two men. My aunt I find in bedd in a most nasty ugly pickle, made me sick to see it. My father and I lay together tonight, I greedy to see the Will but did not aske to see it till tomorrow.

7. *Lords day.* In the morning my father and I walked in the garden and read the Will; where though he gives me nothing at present till my father's death, or at least very little, yet I am glad to see that he hath done so well for us all – and well to the rest of his kindred.[1] After that done, we went about getting things, as ribbands and gloves, ready for the burial. Which in the afternoon was done; where it being Sonday, all people far and near came in and in the greatest disorder that ever I saw; we made shift to serve them what we had of wine and other things; and then to carry him to the church, where Mr. Taylor buried him and Mr. Turner preached a funerall Sermon – where he spoke not perticularly of him anything, but that he was one so well-known for his honesty, that it spoke for itself above all that he could say for it. And so made a very good sermon.

Home with some of the company who supped there; and things being quiet, at night to bed.

⟨⟨8⟩⟩ I fell to work, and my father, to look over his papers and
⟨⟨9⟩⟩ clothes. And continued all this week upon that business –
⟨⟨10⟩⟩ much troubled with my aunts base ugly humours. We had
⟨⟨11⟩⟩ news of Tom Trices putting in a caveat against us in behalfe
⟨⟨12⟩⟩ of his mother, to whom my Uncle hath not given anything,
⟨⟨13⟩⟩ and for good reason therein expressed; which troubled us
also.[2] But above all, our trouble is to find that his estate appears nothing as we expected and all the world believes. Nor his papers so well sorted as I would have had them, but all in confusion, that break my brains to understand them. We missed also the Surrenders of his Coppyhold land, without which the land could not come to us but to the heire-at-law.[3] So that what with this and

1. Robert Pepys left his house at Brampton and most of the estate to Pepys's father, with it to pass to Pepys after his father's death. Pepys was also left an annuity, initially of £30. He and his father were appointed executors.
2. Robert Pepys felt cheated by his wife over the financial arrangements that had accompanied their marriage, and so he left her and his step-sons nothing. The step-sons (Jasper and Thomas Trice, both lawyers) therefore put in a caveat against the will, suspending its execution. This affair caused Pepys much worry and litigation.
3. Most of Robert Pepys's land was held in copyhold, i.e. on terms based on the customs of the manor. The surrenders (documents by which the copyhold land was transmitted) were missing, which meant that the land would pass to the heir-at-law, Thomas Pepys (Robert's eldest brother). This was a second source of strife for Pepys arising from the will.

the badness of the drink and the ill opinion I have of the meat, and the biting of the gnatts by night – and my disappointment in getting home this week – and the trouble of sorting all the papers, I am almost out of my wits with trouble. Only, I appear the more contented, because I would not have my father troubled.

The latter end of the weeke, Mr. Philips comes home from London; and so we advised with him and had the best counsel he could give us. But for all that, we were not quiet in our minds.

22. Up by 3 and going by 4 on my way to London. But the day proves very cold; so that having put on noe stockings but thread ones under my boots, I was fain at Bigglesworth to buy a pair of coarse woollen ones and put them on. So by degrees, till I came to Hatfield before 12 a-clock – where I had a very good dinner with my hostesse at my Lord of Salsburys Inn; and after dinner, though weary, I walked all alone to the Vine-yard, which is now a very beautiful place again; and coming back, I met with Mr. Looker my Lord's gardener (a friend of Mr. Eglins), who showed me the house,[1] the chappell with rare pictures, and above all the gardens, such as I never saw in all my life; nor so good flowers nor so great goosburys, as big as nutmegs.

Back to the Inne and drank with him; and so to horse again, and with much ado got to London and set him up in Smithfield; so called at my uncle Fenners, my mother's, my Lady's; and so home, in all which I find all things as well as I could expect. So, weary and to bed.

23. Put on my mourning. Made visits to Sir W. Pen and Batten. Then to Westminster and at the hall stayed talking with Mrs. Michell[2] a good while; and in the afternoon, finding myself unfit for business, I went to the Theatre and saw *Breneralt*;[3] I never saw before. It seemed a good play, but ill acted; only, I sat before Mrs. Palmer, the King's mistress, and filled my eyes with her, which much pleased me.[4] Then to my father's, where by my desire I met my Uncle Thomas and discourse of my Uncles Will to him, and did satisfye as well as I could. So to my Uncle Wights, but find him out of doors; but my aunt I saw and stayed a while; and so home –

1. Hatfield House, a Jacobean mansion.
2. Ann Mitchell, a bookseller in Westminster Hall and long-time friend of Pepys.
3. *Brennoralt*, a tragicomedy by Sir John Suckling; first performed c.1640 and now acted at the Theatre Royal.
4. Barbara Palmer had been the King's mistress for over a year, and been married to her husband Roger, a lawyer, for slightly longer. Her political influence was to prove formidable.

and to bed. Troubled to hear how proud and Idle Pall is grown, that I am resolved not to keep her.

24. This morning in bed my wife tells me of our being robbed of our silver tankard; which vexed me all day for the negligence of my people to leave the door open.

My wife and I by water to White-hall, where I left her to her business; and I to my Cosen Tho. Pepys[1] and discoursed with him at large about our business of my uncles Will. He can give us no light at all into his estate. But upon the whole, tells me that he doth believe that he hath left but little money, though something more then we have found, which is about 500*l*.

Here came Sir G. Lane by chance, seeing a bill upon the doore to hire the house, with whom my Cosen and I walked all up and down; and endeed it is a very pretty place. And he doth entend to leave the agreement for the house, which is 400*l* fine and 46*l* rent a year to me between them.[2] Then to the Wardrobe; but came too late and so dined with the servants. And then to my Lady, who doth show my wife and me the greatest favour in the world – in which I take great content.

Home by water, and to the office all the afternoon; which is a great pleasure to me again – to talk with persons of Quality and to be in command; and I gave it out among them that the estate left me is 200*l* a year in land, besides money – because I would put an esteem upon myself.

At night home and to bed, after I had set down my Journall ever since my going from London this journy, to this houre.

This afternoon I hear that my man Will hath lost his cloak with my tankard, at which I am very glad.

AUGUST.

24. At the office in the morning and did business. By and by we are called to Sir W. Battens to see the strange creature that Captain Holmes hath brought with him from Guiny; it is a great baboone, but so much like a man in most things, that (though they say there is a Species of them) yet I cannot believe but that it is a monster

1. Thomas Pepys ("the Executor"), living in St Martin-in-the-Fields.
2. That is, Pepys was to draw up the terms of the lease between Lane (a clerk to the Privy Council) and Thomas Pepys. A "fine" was a payment for a lease.

got of a man and she-baboone.[1] I do believe it already understands much english; and I am of the mind it might be tought to speak or make signs.

Hence the Comptroller and I to Sir Rd. Fords and viewed the house again; and are come to a complete end with him, to give him 200 per annum for it.[2]

Home; and there met Captain Isham enquiring for me to take his leave of me, he being upon his voyage to Portugall, and for my letters to my Lord – which are not ready. But I took him to the Miter and gave him a glass of sack, and so Adieu. And then I straight to the Opera and there saw *Hamlet Prince of Denmarke*, done with Scenes very well. But above all, Batterton did the Prince's part beyond imagination.[3]

Thence homeward, and met with Mr. Spong and took him to the Sampson in Pauls churchyard and there stayed till late; and it rained hard, so we were fain to get home wet. And so to bed.

25. *Lords=day.* At church in the morning; and dined at home alone with my wife very comfortably; and so again to church with her, and had a very good and pungent sermon of Mr. Mills concerning the necessity of Restitucion.

Home, and I find my Lady Batten and her daughter to look something askew upon my wife, because my wife doth not buckle to them and is not sollicitous for their acquaintance, which I am not troubled at at all.

By and by comes in my father (he intends to go into [the] country tomorrow); and he and I, among other discourse, at last called Pall up to us and there in great anger told her before my father that I would keep her no longer; and my father, he said he would have nothing to do with her. At last, after we had brought down her high spirit, I got my father to yield that she should go into the country with my mother and him and stay there a while, to see how she will demean herself. That being done, my father and I to my Uncle Wights and there supped, and he took his leave of them. And so I walked with [him] as far as Pauls and there parted, and I home – my mind at some rest upon this making an end with Pall, who doth trouble me exceedingly.

1. Robert Holmes had recently returned from West Africa. The creature may have been a chimpanzee or a gorilla.
2. This was a plan to buy Sir Richard Ford's house in Seething Lane to add to the Navy Office.
3. Betterton was performing in an adaptation of Shakespeare's play by Sir William Davenant, staged at the Lincoln's Inn Fields Theatre.

26. This morning before I went out I made even with my mayd Jane, who hath this day been my maid three yeares and is this day to go into the country to her mother.[1] The poor girl cried, and I could hardly forbear weeping to think of her going; for though she be grown lazy and spoiled by Palls coming, yet I shall never have one to please us better in all things, and so harmlesse, while I live. So I paid her her wages and gave her *2s-6d* over, and bade her Adieu – with my mind full of trouble for her going.

Thence to my father; where he and I and Tho. together, setting things even and casting up my father's account; and upon the whole, I find that all he hath in money of his owne due to him in the world is but 45*l*.; and he owes about the same Summ. So that I cannot but think in what a condition had he left my mother if he should have died before my Uncle Robt. ⟨Hence to Tom. Trice for the probate of the Will and had it done to our minds; which did give my father and me good content.⟩

From hence to my Lady's at the Wardrobe and dined; and thence to the Theatre and saw *The Antipodes*,[2] wherein there is much mirth but no great matter else.

Thence with Mr. Bostock, whom I met there (a clerk formerly of Mr. Phelps's) to the Divell tavern and there drank; and so away, I to my uncle Fenners, where my father was with him at an alehouse. And so we three went by ourselfs and sat talking a great while about a brokers daughter that he doth propose for a wife for Tom, with a great portion; but I fear it will not take, but he will do what he can. So we broke up; and going through the street, we met with a mother and some friends of my father's man Ned's, who are angry at my father's putting him away – which troubled me and my father, but all will be well as to that.

We have news this morning of my Uncle Tho. and his son Tho being gone into the country without giving notice thereof to anybody; which puts us to a stand, but I fear them not.[3]

At night at home I find a letter from my Lord Sandwich, who is now very well again of his feaver but not yet gone from Alicante, where he lay sick and was twice let blood; his letter dated the 22. July. last – which puts me out of doubt of his being ill. In my coming home, I called in at the Three Crane tavern at the

1. Jane Birch was returning to her home in Dymock, Gloucestershire. She came back to work for the Pepyses in March 1662.
2. A comedy by Richard Brome, at the Theatre Royal.
3. Thomas Pepys and his son Thomas "the turner" were in dispute with Pepys over Robert Pepys's bequest of the Brampton estate.

Stockes by appointment, and there met and took leave of Mr. Fanshaw, who goes tomorrow, and Captain Isham, toward their voyage to Portugall. Here we drank a great deal of wine, I too much and Mr. Fanshaw till he could hardly go. So we took leave one of another.

27. This morning to the Wardrobe and there took leave of my Lord Hinchingbrooke and his brother and saw them go out by Coach toward Rye in their way to France; whom God blesse.[1] Then I was called up to my Lady's bedside, where we talked an houre about Mr. Edwd. Mountagus disposing of the 5000*l* for my Lord's preparation for Portugall, and our fears that he will not do it to my Lord's honour, and less to his profit;[2] which I am to enquire a little after.

Thence to the office and there sat till noon. And then my wife and I by Coach to my Cosen Tho. Pepys the Executor to dinner; where some ladies and my father and mother – where very merry; but methinks he makes but poor dinners for such guests, though there was a poor venison=pasty.

Thence my wife and I to the Theatre and there saw *The Joviall Crew*,[3] where the King, Duke and Duchesse, and Madam Palmer were; and my wife, to her great content, had her full sight of them all, all the while. The play full of mirth. Thence to my father's and there stayed to talk a while; and so by foot home by mooneshine.

In my way and at home, my wife making a sad story to me of her brother Balty's condition, and would have me to do something for him; which I shall endeavour to do, but am afeared to meddle therein for fear I shall not be able to wipe my hands of him again when I once concern myself for him. I went to bed, my wife all the while telling me his case with teares, which troubled me.

31. At home and the office all the morning; and at noon comes Luellin to me and he and I to the taverne, and after that to Bartlemew faire;[4] and there, upon his motion, to a pitiful alehouse, where we had a dirty slut or two come up that were whores; but my very heart went against them, so that I took no pleasure but a great deal

1. Sandwich's son Edward Mountagu (now Viscount Hinchingbrooke) and his brother Sidney were going to school in Paris.
2. Edward Mountagu, son of Baron Mountagu of Boughton, was managing Sandwich's affairs while he was abroad.
3. A comedy by Richard Brome, at the Theatre Royal.
4. The huge fair annually held in West Smithfield around the feast of St Bartholomew (24 August).

of trouble at being there and getting from thence, for fear of being seen. From thence he and I walked toward Ludgate and parted. I back again to the fair all alone and there met with my ladies Jemimah and Paulina, with Mr. Pickering and Madamoiselle,[1] at seeing the Monkys dance, which was much to see what they could be brought to do; but it troubled me to sit among such nasty company. After that, with them into Christs: Hospitall,[2] and there Mr. Pickering bought them some fairings and I did give every of them a bauble, which was the little globes of glass with things hanging in them, which pleased the ladies very well.

After that, home with them in their Coach; and there was called up to my Lady, and she would have me stay to talk with her, which I did, I think a full houre. And the poor lady did with so much innocency tell me how Mrs. Crispe had told her that she did entend, by means of a lady that lies at her house, to get the King to be godfather to the young lady that she is in childbed now of.[3] But to see in what a manner my Lady told it me, protesting that she sweat in the very telling of it, was the greatest pleasure to me in the world, to see the simplicity and harmelessnesse of a lady.

Then down to supper with the ladies, and so home; Mr. Moore (as he and I cannot easily part) leading me as far as Fanchurch-street to the Miter, where we drank a glass of wine; and so parted and I home – and to bed.

Thus ends the month. My mayde Jane newly gone, and Pall left now to do all the work till another mayde comes; which shall not be till she goes away into the country with my mother. Myself and wife in good health. My Lord Sandwich in the Straits and newly recovered of a great sickness at Alicante. My father gone to settle at Brampton. And myself under much business and trouble for to settle things in the estate to our content. But which is worst, I find myself lately too much given to seeing of plays and expense and pleasure, which makes me forget my business, which I must labour to amend.

No money comes in, so that I have been forced to borrow a great deal of money for my own expenses and to furnish my father, to leave things in order. I have some trouble about my Brother Tom,

1. Sandwich's daughters, their relative Edward Pickering, and their governess Mlle Le Blanc.
2. Christ's Hospital was a school for poor children, within the area covered by the fair.
3. Lady Sandwich had given birth to a daughter, Catherine, on 20 August.

who is now left to keep my father's trade, in which I have great fears that he will miscarry – for want of brains and care.

at Court things are in very ill condition, there being so much æmulacion, poverty, and the vices of swearing, drinking, and whoring, that I know not what will be the end of it but confusion. And the Clergy so high,[1] that all people that I meet with, all do protest against their practice. In short, I see no content or satisfaccion anywhere in any one sort of people.

The Benevolence proves so little, and an occasion of so much discontent everywhere, that it had better it had never been set up.[2] I think to subscribe 20*l*. We are at our office quiet; only, for lack of money, all things go to wrack. Our very bills[3] offered to be sold upon the Exchange at 10 per cent losse. We are upon getting Sir R. Fords house added to our office. But I see so many difficultys will fallow, in pleasing of one another in the dividing of it and in becoming bound personally to pay the rent of 200*l* per annum – that I do believe it will yet scarce come to pass.

The season very sickly everywhere of strange and fatall feavers.

SEPTEMBER.

7. At the office all the morning. At noon Mr. Moore dined with me; and then in comes Wll. Joyce to answer a letter of mine I writ this morning to him about a mayde of his that my wife had hired; and she sent us word that she was hired to stay longer with her master. Which mistake he came to clear himself of, and I took it very kindly. So I having appointed the young ladies at the Wardrobe[4] to go with them to a play today, I left him and my brother Tom, who came along with him to dine; and my wife and I to them and took them to the Theatre, where we seated ourselfs close by the King and Duke of Yorke and Madam Palmer (which was great content; and endeed, I can never enough admire her beauty); and here was *Barthlemew fayre*, with the Puppet Shewe, acted today, which had not been these forty years (it being so satyricall against puritanisme, they durst not till now; which is strange they should already dare to do it, and the King to countenance it); but I do

1. Arrogant, high-handed.
2. In July, Parliament had ordered collections towards "a Free and voluntary Present" for the King.
3. Bills of exchange.
4. Sandwich's daughters.

never a whit like it the better for the puppets, but rather the worse.[1]

Thence home with the ladies, it being, by reason of our staying a great while for the King's coming and the length of the play, near 9 a-clock before it was done; and so in their Coach home and, still in discontent with my wife,[2] to bed; and rose so this morning also.

8. *Lords day.*

To church, it being a very wet night last night and today. Dined at home. And so to church again with my wife in the afternoon. And coming home again, find our new mayde Doll asleep that she could not hear to let us in, so that we were fain to send the boy in at a window to open the door to us.

So up to my chamber all alone. And troubled in mind to think how much of late I have addicted myself to expense and pleasure, that now I can hardly reclaime myself to look after my great business of settling Gravely business,[3] till it is now almost too late. I pray God give me grace to begin now to look after my business; but it always was, and I fear will ever be, my foible, that after I am once got behindhand with business, I am hard to set to it again to recover it.

In the evening I begun to look over my accounts; and upon the whole, I do find myself, by what I can yet see, worth near 600*l.*; for which God be blessed – which put me into great comfort. So to supper and bed.

30. This morning up by mooneshine; at 5 a-clock to White-hall to meet Mr. Moore at the Privy Seale; but he not being come as appointed, I went into King-Streete to the Red Lyon to drink my morning draught and there I heard of a fray between the two Embassadors of Spaine and France; and that this day being the day of the entrance of an Embassador from Sweden, they were entended to fight for the precedence.[4] Our King, I heard, hath ordered that no Englishman should meddle in the business, but let

1. Ben Jonson's *Bartholomew Fair* had been performed earlier in 1661 without the episode featuring the puppet show in Act 5. In it, the puritan Zeal-of-the-Land Busy disputes with a puppet over whether it (the puppet) is a profane idol. He loses.
2. He was angry because Elizabeth had been out the previous day and not told him where or why.
3. Business relating to his Uncle Robert's will.
4. The French and Spanish ambassadors each wanted to follow first after the King's coach in the procession. That position was given to the monarchy held to be the most senior by foundation, so to lose it was to cede a major claim to status.

them do what they would; and to that end, all the Souldiers in the town were in arms all the day long, and some of the train-bands in the City and a great bustle through the City all the day. Then I to the Privy Seale; and there, Mr. Moore and a gentleman being come with him, we took coach (which was the business I came for) to Chelsy to my Lord Privy Seale and there got him to seal that business.[1] Here I saw by day-light two very fine pictures in the gallery, that a little while ago I saw by night. And did also go all over the house, and find it to be the prettiest contrived house that ever I saw in my life. So to coach back again. And at White-hall light and saw the soldiers and people running up and down the streets. So I went to the Spanish Embassadors and the French,[2] and there saw great preparations on both sides; but the French made the most noise and vaunted most, the other made no stir almost at all; so that I was afeared the other would have had too great a conquest over them.

Then to the Wardrobe and dined there; and then abroad, and in Cheapeside hear that the Spaniard hath got the best of it and killed three of the French coach-horses and several men and is gone through the City next to our King's coach. At which it is strange to see how all the City did rejoice. And endeed, we do naturally all love the Spanish and hate the French.

But I, as I am in all things curious, presently got to the waterside and there took oares to Westminster-palace, thinking to have seen them come in thither with all the coaches; but they being come and returned, I run after them with my boy after me, through all the dirt and the streets full of people; till at last at the mewes[3] I saw the Spanish coach go, with 50 drawne swords at least to guard it and our soldiers shouting for joy. And so I fallowed the coach, and then met it at Yorke-house, where the Embassador lies; and there it went in with great state. So then I went to the French house, where I observe still that there is no men in the world of a more insolent spirit where they do well or before they begin a matter, and more abject if they do miscarry, then these people are. For they all look like dead men and not a word among them, but shake their heads.

The truth is, the Spaniards were observed not only to fight most desperately, but also they did outwitt them; first in lining their owne harnesse with chains of iron, that they could not be cut –

1. Pepys served as Sandwich's deputy in his clerkship at the Privy Seale, with Henry Moore as Pepys's assistant.
2. York House and Exeter House, on the south and north sides of the Strand respectively.
3. The Royal Mews, Charing Cross.

then in setting their coach in the most advantageous place, and to appoint men to guard every one of their horses, and others for to guard the coach, and others the coachmen. And above all, in setting upon the French horses and killing them, for by that means the French were not able to stir.

There were several men slain of the French, and one or two of the Spaniards, and one Englishman by a bullett – which is very observable, the French were at least four to one in number. And had near 100 case of pistolls among them, and the Spaniards had not one gun among them; which is for their honour for ever, and the others disgrace.

So having been very much dawbed with dirt, I got a coach and home – where I vexed my wife in telling of her this story and pleading for the Spaniard against the French.[1]

So ends this month. Myself and family in good condition of health. But my head full of my Lord's and my own and the office business – where we are now very busy about the business of sending forces to Tanger.[2] And the fleet to my Lord of Sandwich, who is now at Lisbone to bring over the Queene – who doth now keep a Court as Queen of England.

The business of Argier hath of late troubled me, because my Lord hath not done what he went for, though he did as much as any man in the world could have done.[3]

The want of money puts all things, and above all things the Navy, out of order; and yet I do not see that the King takes care to bring in any money, but thinks of new designs to lay out money.

OCTOBER.

10. At the office all the morning. Dined at home; and after dinner, Sir W. Pen and my wife and I to the theatre (she first going into Covent-garden to speak a word with a woman to enquire of her mother, and I in the meantime with Sir W. Penn's coach, staying at W. Joyces), where the King came today; and there was *The*

1. Elizabeth was French on her father's side.
2. Tangier had just been gained by Britain as part of the marriage treaty with Portugal. It was seen as of great importance in defending trade in the Straits of Gibraltar from North African pirates.
3. Sandwich had bombarded the town of Algiers in an effort to secure a treaty to protect British shipping. However, the assault was hampered by bad weather and no treaty had yet been achieved.

Traytor[1] most admirably acted – and a most excellent play it is. So home and entended to be merry, it being my sixth wedding night;[2] but by a late bruise in one of my testicles I am in so much pain that I eat my supper and in pain to bed; yet my wife and I pretty merry.

26. This morning Sir W. Pen and I should have gone out of town with my Lady Batten to have met Sir Wm. coming back from Portsmouth at Kingston; but could not, by reason that my Lord of Peterborough (who is to go Governor of Tanger) came this morning with Sir G. Carteret to advise with us about completing of the affairs and preparacions for that place. So at the office all the morning. And in the afternoon Sir Wm. Pen, my wife and I to the Theatre and there saw *The Country Captaine*,[3] the first time that it hath been acted this 25 years – a play of my Lord Newcastles, but so silly a play as in all my life I never saw, and the first that ever I was weary of in my life. So home again; and in the evening news was brought that Sir R. Slingsby our Comptroller (who hath this day been sick a week) is dead; which put me into so great a trouble of mind, that all the night I could not sleep, he being a man that loved me and had many Qualitys that made me to love him above all the officers and Comissioners in the Navy. Coming home, we called at Dan. Rawlinson's and there drank good sack; and so home.

30. All the morning at the office. At noon played on my Theorbo[4] and much pleased therewith – as it is now altered with a new neck. In the afternoon Captain Lambert called me out by appointment and we walked together to Deptford; and there in his ship the *Norwich* I got him to show me every hole and corner of the ship, much to my informacion and the purpose of my going. So home again; and at Sir W. Battens heard how he had been already at Sir R. Slingsby's (as we were all invited and I entended this night to go); and there he finds all things out of order and no Such thing done tonight; but pretending that the Corps stinks, they will bury it tonight privately, and so will unbespeake[5] all their Guests and there shall be no funerall – which I am sorry for, that there

1. A tragedy by James Shirley, at the Theatre Royal.
2. Samuel and Elizabeth had married in a civil ceremony, as required by the Commonwealth government, on 1 Dec. 1655. However, they habitually celebrated their wedding night on 10 October – this probably marked a religious service that had pre-dated the December ceremony.
3. A comedy by the Marquess of Newcastle and James Shirley, performed at the Theatre Royal.
4. A type of lute with an extended neck to carry bass strings.
5. Uninvite.

should be nothing done for the honor of Sir Robt.; but I fear he hath left his family in great distraction. Here I stayed till late at Cards with my Lady and Mrs. Martha, and so home. I sent for a bottle or two of wine thither.

At my coming home, I am sorry to find my wife displeased with her maid Doll:, whose fault is that she cannot keep her peace, but will alway be talking in an angry manner, though it be without any reason and to no purpose. Which I am sorry for – and do see the inconvenience that doth attend the increase of a man's fortune, by being forced to keep more servants, which brings trouble.

Sir Henery Vane, Lambert, and others are lately sent suddenly away from the tower, prisoners to Scilly; but I do not think there is any plot as is said; but only a pretence, as there was once pretended often against the Cavaleers.[1]

NOVEMBER.

2. At the office all the morning; where Sir John Minnes[2] our new Comptroller was fetched by Sir Wm. Pen and myself from Sir W. Battens and led to his place in the office – the first time that he hath come hither. And he seems a good fair-condition[ed] man and one that I am glad hath the office.

After the office done, I to the Wardrobe and there dined; and in the afternoon had an hour or two's talk with my Lady with great pleasure; and so with the two young ladies by Coach to my house and gave them some entertainment; and so late at night sent them home with Captain Ferrers by Coach.

This night my boy Wainman, as I was in my chamber, [I] overheard him let off some Gunpouder; and hearing my wife chide him below for it, and a noise made, I call him up and find that it was powder that he had put in his pocket, and a mach carelessely with it, thinking that it was out; and so the match did give fire to the powder and had burned his side, and his hand that he put into his pocket to put out the fire.[3] But upon examination, and finding him in a lie about the time and place that he bought it, I did extremely

1. The republican prisoners were dispersed to the Channel Islands and Scilly Isles following reports of an alleged Presbyterian rising in Worcestershire.
2. Sir John Mennes, Slingsby's replacement, held the office of Comptroller of the Navy until 1671.
3. The powder was probably for fireworks to celebrate on 5 November, the anniversary of the failed Gunpowder Plot.

beat him. And though it did trouble me to do it, yet I thought it necessary to do it. So to write by the post, and to bed.

3. *Lords day.* This day I stirred not out, but took physique[1] and it did work very well; and all the day, as I was at leisure, I did read in Fuller's *Holy Warr*[2] (which I have of late bought) and did try to make a Song in the prayse of a Liberall genius[3] (as I take my own to be) to all studies and pleasures; but it not proving to my mind, I did reject it and so proceeded not in it. At night my wife and I had a good supper by ourselfs, of a pullet=hashed; which pleased me much to see my condition come to allow ourselfs a dish like that. And so at night to bed.

20. To Westminster-hall by water in the morning, where I saw the King going in his barge to the parliament-house, this being the first day of their meeting again. And the Bishops I hear do take their places in the Lords' house this day.[4] I walked long in the Hall, but hear nothing of newes but what Ned. Pickering tells me, which I am troubled at, that Sir J. Mennes should send word to the King that if he did not remove all my Lord Sandwichs Captaines out of this fleet, he believed the King would not be master of the fleet at its coming home again – and so doth endeavour to bring disgrace upon my Lord. But I hope all that will not do, for the King loves him.

Hence by water to the Wardrobe and dined with my Lady, my Lady Wright being there too (whom I find to be a witty but very conceited woman and proud);[5] and after dinner Mr. Moore and I to the Temple, and there he read my bill and likes it well enough.[6] And so we came back again, he with me as far as the lower end of Cheapside; and there I gave him a pint of Sack and parted. And I home, and went seriously to look over my papers touching T. Trice, and think I have found some that will go near to do me more good in this difference of ours then all I have before. So to bed, with my mind cheery upon it; and lay long reading Hobbs his *liberty and necessity*,[7] and a little but a very shrewd piece. And so to sleep.

1. Medicine, especially a laxative.
2. Thomas Fuller's *The Historie of the Holy Warre*, about the Crusades. Pepys owned the 1651 edition.
3. Natural ability or inclination.
4. The act of 1642 that excluded the bishops had been repealed in July.
5. Anne Wright, Lady Sandwich's sister.
6. Henry Moore was helping Pepys in his legal disputes over Robert Pepys's will. This was a Chancery bill against Thomas Trice, Robert's step-son.
7. Thomas Hobbes's *Of Libertie and Necessitie* (first published 1654), a treatise on free will and predestination.

27. This morning our maid Dorothy and my wife parted – which though she be a wench for her tongue not to be borne with, yet was loath to part with her. But I took my leave kindly of her; and went out to Savill's the painter and there sat the first time for my face with him.[1] Thence to dinner with my Lady. And so after an hour or two's talk in Divinity with my Lady – Captain Ferrers and Mr. Moore and I to the Theatre and there saw *Hamlett*, very well done.[2] And so I home and find that my wife hath been with my aunt Wight and Ferrers to wait on my Lady today, this afternoon, and there danced and were very merry; and my Lady very fond, as she is alway of my wife. So to bed.

29. I lay long in bed, till Sir Wms. both sent me word that we were to wait upon the Duke of Yorke today and that they would have me to meet them at Westminster-hall at noon; so I rose and went thither and there I understand that they are gone to Mr. Coventry's lodgings in the old palace-yard to dinner (the first time I knew that he hath any); and there I met them two and Sir G. Carteret, and had a very fine dinner and good welcome and discourse; and so by water after dinner to White-hall to the Duke, who met us in his Closett; and there he did discourse to us the business of Holmes,[3] and did desire of us to know what hath been the common practice about the making of forrayne ships to strike sail to us: which they all did do as much as they could, but I could say nothing to it, which I was sorry for; so endeed, I was forced to study a lie: and so after we were gone from the Duke, I told Mr. Coventry that I had heard Mr. Selden often say that he could prove that in Henry the 7ths time he did give commission to his Captains to make the King of Denmark's ships to strike to him in the Baltique.[4]

From thence Sir W. Pen and I to the Theatre but it was so full that we could hardly get any room; so he went up to one of the boxes and I to the 18*d* places and there saw *Love at first sight*, a play

1. Daniel Savile of Bell Alley, Cheapside. Pepys had chosen a senior member of the Painter-Stainers' Company to execute his first portrait: Savile sat on Company's Court of Assistants in this year and became the Master in 1669. He painted both Pepys and his wife, but the pictures have not survived.
2. This was probably Davenant's adaptation at Lincoln's Inn Fields Theatre, as his company had exclusive rights to perform *Hamlet*.
3. Captain Robert Holmes was in trouble over his failure to force a ship carrying the Swedish ambassador to strike (lower) sail to his warship when it was in the mouth of the Thames. By not striking sail, the ambassador contested British claims to territorial waters.
4. John Selden, the great legal authority, was the author of *Mare clausum* (first published 1635). This made ambitious claims for Britain's sovereignty over the seas. He had died in 1654.

of Mr. Killigrews, and the first time that it hath been acted since before the troubles;[1] and great expectation there was, but I find the play to be a poor thing; and so I perceive everybody else to do. So home, calling at Pauls churchyard for a *Mare Clausum*, having it in my mind to write a little matter, what I can gather about the business of Striking sayle and present it to the Duke, which I now think will be a good way to make myself known.[2] So home and to bed.

DECEMBER.

3. To the paynters and sat and had more of my picture done; but it doth not please me, for I fear it will not be like me. At noon from thence to the Wardrobe; where dinner not being ready, Mr. Moore and I to the Temple about my little business at Mr. Turner's[3] and so back again; and dinner being half-done, I went in to my Lady, where my Lady Wright was at dinner with her. And all our talk about the great happiness that my Lady Wright says there is in being in the fashion and in variety of fashions, in scorn of others that are not so, as citizens wifes and country-gentlewomen – which though it did displease me enough, yet I said nothing to it. Thence by water to the office through bridge, being carried by him in oares that the other day rowed in a scull faster then my oares to the Tower, and I did give him 6*d*.:[4] at the office all the afternoon, and at night home to read in *Mare Clausum* till bedtime; and so to bed. But had a very bad night by dreams of my wife's riding with me, and her horse throwing her and breaking her leg. And then I dreamt that I had one of my testicles swelled, and in such pain that I waked with it; and had a great deal of pain there a very great while, till I fell asleep again; and such apprehensions I had of it that when I rose and trussed up myself, thinking that it had been no dream – till in the daytime I found myself very well at ease and remembered that I did dream so; and did dream that Mr. Creed was with me and that I did complain to him of it, and he said he had the same

1. The boxes held the most expensive seats in the Theatre Royal, while the 18*d* seats were some of the least expensive. Thomas Killigrew's comedy *The Princess, or Love at First Sight* was first acted c.1637.
2. Pepys probably bought the 1652 English translation of Selden's Latin work. His planned essay is untraced; it may never have been written.
3. The legal dispute with Trice.
4. I.e. Pepys had previously seen one of the two men who was currently rowing him "in oares" (a boat rowed by two men) make a trip faster in a scull (rowed by one man) than Pepys's two-man boat had then managed.

pain in his left which I had in my right stone – which pleased me much to remember.

7. This morning came Captain Ferrers and the German, Emanuel Luffe (who goes as one of my Lord's footmen, though he deserves much a better preferment) to take their leave of me. And here I got the German to play upon my Theorbo, which he did both below and in my wife's chamber, who was in bed. He plays rarely. And I find by him that my lute is a most excellent lute. I did give them a mince-pie and Coller of brawn and some wine for their breakfast, and were very merry; and sent for Mr. Adams our neighbour to drink Mr. Sheply's health. At last we all parted. But within a Quarter of an houre after they were gone and my wife and I were talking about buying of a fine Scallop[1] which is brought her this morning by a woman to be sold, which is to cost her 45*s*, in comes the German back again, all of a goare blood; which I wondered at and tells me that he is afeared that the Captain is killed by the watermen at Tower stayres. So I presently went thither and find that upon some rude pressing of the watermen to ply the Captain, he struck one of them with his Cane; which they would not take, but struck him again and then the German drow his sword and run at one of them. But they were both soundly beaten. The Captain is however got to the Hoy[2] that carries him and the pages to the Downes, and I went into the alehouse at the Stairs and got them to deliver the Captains feathers, which one from the Captain was come to demand; and went home again and there find my wife dressing of the German's head and so did give him a Cravett for his neck and a Crowne in his purse, and sent him away again. Then came Mr. Moore and he and I to Westminster, and so to Worster-house to see Mr. Mountagu[3] before he goes away (this night); but could not see him, nor do I think he hath a mind to see us, for fear of our demanding of money of him for anything. So back to White-hall and eat a bit of meat at Wilkinsons; and then to the Privy Seale and sealed there, the first time this month. And among other things that passed, there was a patent for Roger Palmer (Madam Palmer's husband) to be Earle of Castlemaine and Baron of Limbricke in Ireland. But the honour is tied up to the males got on the body of this wife, the Lady Barbary – the reason whereof everybody knows.[4] That done,

1. Scalloped lace collar.
2. Small passenger and cargo ship.
3. Edward Mountagu, currently managing Sandwich's affairs.
4. I.e. the title was intended to pass via the King's sons.

by water to the office, where I find Sir W. Pen hath been alone all this night and was just rose; and so I to him, and with him I find Captain Holmes, who hath wrote his case and gives me a Copy, as he hath many among his friends, and presented the same to the King and Councell – which I shall make use of in my attempt of writing something concerning the business of Striking Sayle which I am now about. But he doth cry out against Sir John Mennes as the veriest knave and rogue and Coward in the world. Which I was glad to hear, because he hath given out bad words concerning my Lord, though I am sorry it is so. Here Captain Cox then came in, and he and I stayed a good while and so good-night. Home, and wrote by the post to my father; and so to bed.

14. All the morning at home, lying abed with my wife till 11 a-clock – such a habitt we have got this winter, of lying long abed. Dined at home. And in the afternoon to the office. There sat late; and so home and to bed.

25. *Christmas day.* In the morning to church; where at the door of our pew I was fain to stay, because that the Sexton had not opened the door. A good sermon of Mr. Mills. Dined at home all alone. And taking occasion, from some fault in the meat, to complain of my maid's Sluttery,[1] my wife and I fell out, and I up to my Chamber in a discontent. After dinner my wife comes up to me and all friends again; and she and I to walk upon the Leads; and there Sir W. Pen called us and we went to his house and supped with him. But before supper, Captain Cock came to us half-drunck and begun to talk; but Sir W. Pen, knowing his humour and that there was no end of his talking, drinks four great glasses of wine to him one after another, healths to the King &c., and by that means made him drunk, and so he went away; and so we sat down to supper and were merry; and so after supper home and to bed.

31. My wife and I this morning to the paynters;[2] and there she sat the last time and I stood by and did tell him some little things to do, that now her picture I think will please me very well. And after her, her little black dogg sat in her lap and was drawn, which made us very merry. So home to dinner, and so to the office and there late, finishing our estimate of the debts of the Navy to this day; and it comes to near 374000*l.*

So home; and after supper and my barber had trimmed me, I sat

1. Untidiness, dirtiness.
2. Daniel Savile.

down to end my Journall for this year; and my condition at this time, by God's blessing, is thus:

My health (only upon ketching cold, which brings great pain in my back and making of water, as it use to be when I had the stone) very good, and so my wife's in all respects.

My servants, W. Hewer, Sarah, Nell, and Waynman. My house at the Navy Office. I suppose myself to be worth about 500*l* clear in the world, and my goods of my house my owne, and what is coming to me from Brampton when my father dies – which God defere. But by my uncles death, the whole care and trouble of all and settling of all lies upon me; which is very great because of lawsuits, especially that with T. Trice about the inter[e]st of 200*l* – which will I hope be ended soon.

My chiefest thoughts is now to get a good wife for Tom – there being one offered by the Joyces,[1] a cousin of theirs, worth 200*l* in ready money. I am also upon writing a little treatise to present to the Duke, about our privilege in the seas as to other nations striking their flags to us. But my greatest trouble is that I have for this last half-year been a very great spendthrift in all manner of respects, that I am afeared to cast up my accounts, though I hope I am worth what I say above.[2] But I will cast them up very shortly.

I have newly taken a solemn oath about abstaining from plays and wine, which I am resolved to keep according to the letter of the oath, which I keepe by me. The fleete hath been ready to sail for Portugall, but hath lack[ed] wind this fortnight.[3] And by that means my Lord is forced to keep at sea all this winter till he brings home the Queen – which is the expectacion of all now – and the greatest matter of public talk.

1. William and Anthony Joyce, tallow chandlers and brothers who were both married to cousins of Pepys.
2. On 24 May 1661, Pepys had calculated he was worth £500 in money, plus other goods.
3. A fleet, carrying troops to garrison Tangier, was due to rendezvous with Sandwich's fleet.

1662

JANUARY. $\frac{1661}{62.}$

6. *Twelfe day.* This morning I sent my lute to the painter's; and there I stayed with him all the morning, to see him paint the neck of my lute in my picture – which I was not much pleased with after it was done. Thence to dinner to Sir Wm. Pens (it being a solemn feast-day with him, his wedding day; and we have, besides a good chine[1] of beef and other good cheer, eighteen mince-pies in a dish, the number of the years that he hath been married); where Sir W. Batten and his Lady and daughter was, and Collonell Treswell and Major Holmes,[2] who I perceive would fain get to be free and friends with my wife; but I shall prevent it, and she herself hath also a defyance[3] against him. After dinner they set in to drinking, so that I could stay no longer but went away home; and Captain Cock, who was quite drunk, comes after me and there sat awhile, and so away. And anon I went again after the company was gone, and sat and played at Cards with Sir W. Penn and his children; and so after supper, home. And there I hear that my man Gul:[4] was gone to bed; and upon enquiry I hear that he did vomit before he went to bed, and complained his head aked. And thereupon, though he was asleep, I sent for him out of his bed; and he rose and came up to me, and I appeared very angry and did tax him with being drunk; and he told [me] that he had been with Mr. Southerne and Homewood at the Dolphin and drank a Quart of sack, but that his head did ake before he went out. But I do believe that he hath drunk too much; and so I did threaten him to bid his Uncle dispose of him some other way. And sent him down to bed and do resolve to continue to be angry with him. So I to bed to my wife and told her what hath passed.

14. All the morning at home – Mr. Berchenshaw, by appointment yesterday, coming to me, and begun composition of Musique.[5] And

1. Rib.
2. Robert Holmes. He had been dismissed as captain of the *Royal Charles* in November due to the controversy over striking sail, but was a major through his military service.
3. Strong dislike, a "declaration of hostilities".
4. Gulielmus (William) Hewer.
5. John Birchensha, a violist and musical theorist, had devised mathematical rules for composing.

he being gone, I to settle my papers and things in my chamber; and so after dinner, in the afternoon to the office and thence to my chamber about several businesses of the office and my own; and then to supper and to bed. This day my brave vellum covers to keep pictures in came in, which pleases me very much.

15. This morning Mr. Berchenshaw came again; and after he had examined me and taught me something in my work, he and I went to breakfast in my chamber, upon a Coller of brawne. And after we had eaten, he asked me whether we have not committed a fault in eating today, telling me that it is a fast-day, ordered by the parliament to pray for more seasonable weather – it having hitherto been some summer weather, that it is, both as to warmth and every other thing, just as if it were the middle of May or June, which doth threaten a plague (as all men think) to fallow; for so it was almost the last winter, and the whole year after hath been a very sickly time, to this day. I did not stir out of my house all day, but con'd my Musique; and at night, after supper to bed.

23. All the morning with Mr. Berchenshaw and after him Mr. Moore, in discourse of business; and at noon by Coach by invitacion to my Uncle Fenners, where I find his new wife, a pitiful, old, ugly, illbread woman in a hatt, a midwife.[1] Here were many of his and as many of her relations, sorry mean people. And after choosing our gloves,[2] we all went over to the Three Crane taverne, and (though the best room of the house) in such a narrow dogghole we were crammed (and I believe we were near 40) that it made me loathe my company and victuals; and a sorry poor dinner it was too.

After dinner I took aside the two Joyces and took occasion to thank them for their kind thoughts for a wife for Tom; but that considering the possibility there is of my having no child, and what then I shall be able to leave him, I do think he may expect in that respect a wife with more money, and so desired them to think no more of it. Now the jest was, Anthony mistakes and thinks that I did all this while encourage him (from my thoughts of favour to Tom) to pursue the mach, till Will Joyce told him that he was mistaken. But how he takes it, I know not; but I endeavoured to tell it him in the most respectful way that I could.

This done, with my wife by Coach to my aunt Wights, where I left her and I to the office; and that being done, to her again and

1. Thomas Fenner's first wife, Pepys's mother's sister, had died in August 1661. He had married Hester Ayres on 11 Jan. and this was their wedding dinner.
2. Wedding favours for the guests.

sat playing at cards after supper, till 12 at night; and so by moonshine home and to bed.

26. *Lords=day.* To church in the morning and then home to dinner alone with my wife; and so both to church in the afternoon and home again; and so to read and talk with my wife, and to supper and bed.

It having been a very fine clear frosty day – God send us more of them, for the warm weather all this winter makes us fear a sick summer.

But thanks be to God, since my leaving drinking of wine, I do find myself much better and to mind my business better and to spend less money, and less time lost in idle company.

FEBRUARY.

3. After musique practice I went to the office, and there with the two Sir Wms. all the morning about business. At noon I dined with Sir W. Batten with many friends more, it being his Wedding=day. And among other Froliques, it being their third year, they had three pyes, whereof the middlemost was made of an ovall form in an Ovall hole within the other two, which made much mirth and was called the middle peace; and above all the rest, we had great striving to steal a spoonefull out of it; and I remember Mrs. Mills the minister's wife did steal one for me and did give it me; and to end all, Mrs. Shippman did fill the pie full of White wine (it holding at least a pint and a half) and did drink it off for a health to Sir Wm. and my Lady, it being the greatest draught that ever I did see a woman drink in my life.

Before we had dined came Sir G. Carteret, and we went all three to the office and did business there till night. And then to Sir Wm. Batten again, and I went along with my Lady and the rest of the gentlewomen to Major Holmes's, and there we had a fine supper; among others, excellent lobsters, which I never eat at this time of the year before. The Major hath good lodgings at the Trinity-house. Here we stayed late, and at last home. And being in my chamber, we do hear great noise of mirth at Sir Wm. Battens, tearing the ribbands from my Lady and him.[1] So I to bed.

1. Pulling ribbons from the married couple was one of the ways weddings were celebrated.

10. Musique practice a good while. Then to Pauls churchyard, and there I met with Dr: Fullers *Englands worthys* – the first time that I ever saw it; and so I sat down reading in it, till it was 2 a-clock before I thought of the time's going. And so I rose and went home to dinner, being much troubled that (though he had some discourse with me about my family and armes) he says nothing at all, nor mentions us either in Cambrige or Norfolke.[1] But I believe endeed, our family were never considerable.

At home all the afternoon; and at night to bed.

14. *Valentine's day.* I did this day purposely shun to be seen at Sir W. Battens – because I would not have his daughter to be my Valentine, as she was the last year, there being no great friendship between us now as formerly. This morning in comes W. Bowyer, who was my wife's Valentine, she having (at which I made good sport to myself) held her hands all the morning, that she might not see the paynters that were at work in gilding my chimny-piece and pictures in my dining-room.[2]◆

24. Long with Mr. Berchenshaw in the morning at my Musique practice, finishing my song of *Gaze not on swans* in two parts, which pleases me well.[3] And I did give him 5*l* for this month or five weeks that he hath taught me, which is a great deal of money and troubled me to part with it. Thence to the painter's and sat again for my picture in little. And thence over the water to Southwarke to Mr. Berchenshaws house and there sat with him all the afternoon, he showing me his great Card of the body of Musique,[4] which he cries up for a rare thing; and I do believe it cost much pains, but is not so usefull as he would have it. Then we sat down and set *Nulla nulla sit formido*,[5] and he hath set it very finely. So home and to supper; and then called Will up and chid him before my wife for refusing to go to church with the maids yesterday, and telling his mistress that he would not be made a slave of – which vexes me. So to bed.

1. Thomas Fuller's *The History of the Worthies of England* (1662) sought to record the "Persons of Quality" and "Memorable Persons" of each county. Pepys probably read it in Joshua Kirton's bookshop.
2. Custom required she took the first man she saw as her valentine.
3. This was the poem "Beauties Excellency", which had been mostly set by Birchensha. The words, ascribed to Henry Noel, featured in Henry Lawes's *Ayres and Dialogues . . . The First Booke* (1653), which Pepys owned.
4. Birchensha's rules for composition, or part of them.
5. A song about the perils of love; the first line translates as "Let there be no, no fear at all, although Cupid is blind". Pepys retained a manuscript of the song in his library, but it is probably a different setting.

27. This morning came Mr. Berchensha to me; and in our discourse, I finding that he cries up his rules for most perfect (though I do grant them to be very good, and the best I believe that ever yet were made) and that I could not persuade him to grant wherein they were somewhat lame, we fell to angry words, so that in a pet he flung out of my chamber and I never stopped him, being entended to have put him off today whether this had happened or no, because I think I have all the rules that he hath to give, and so there remains nothing but practice now to do me good – and it is not for me to continue with him at 5*l.* per mensem.[1]

So I settled to put his rules all in fair order in a book, which was my work all the morning till dinner. After dinner to the office till late at night; and so home to write by the post, and so to bed.

MARCH.

1. This morning I paid Sir Wm. Batten 40*l*, which I have owed him this half year, having borrowed it of him.

Then to the office all the morning. So dined at home. And after dinner comes my uncle Thomas, with whom I have some high words of difference; but ended quietly, though I fear I shall do no good by fair means upon him.[2]

Then my wife and I by coach, first to see my little picture that is a-drawing,[3] and thence to the Opera and there saw *Romeo and Julett*, the first time it was ever acted.[4] But it is the play of itself the worst that ever I heard in my life, and the worst acted that ever I saw these people do; and I am resolved to go no more to see the first time of acting, for they were all of them out[5] more or less. Thence home, and after supper and wrote by the post – I settled to what I have long entended, to cast up my accounts with myself; and after much pains to do it and great fear, I do find that I am 500*l* in money beforehand in the world, which I was afeared I was not. But I find that I have spent above 250*l* this last half year, which troubles me much. But by God's blessing, I am now resolved to take up, having furnished myself with all things for a great while, and

1. Per month.
2. This was the dispute over Robert Pepys's will.
3. A new miniature drawn by Daniel Savile.
4. Shakespeare's play was acted for the first time since the Restoration by the Duke's Company at the Lincoln's Inn Fields Theatre.
5. Unable to remember their lines.

tomorrow to think upon some rules and obligations upon myself to walk by.

So with my mind eased of a great deal of trouble, though with no great content to find myself above 100*l* worse now then I was half a year ago, I went to bed.

3d. All the morning at home about business with my brother Tom and then with Mr. Moore; and then I set to make some strict rules for my future practice in my expenses, which I did bind myself in the presence of God by oath to observe, upon penaltys therein set down. And I do not doubt but hereafter to give a good account of my time and to grow rich – for I do find a great deal more of content in those few days that I do spend well about my business then in all the pleasures of a whole week, besides the trouble which I remember I always have after them for the expense of my money.

Dined at home and then up to my chamber again about business; and so to the office – about despatching of the East India ships, where we stayed till 8 at night; and then after I had been at Sir Wm. Pens awhile, discoursing with him and Mr. Kenard the Joyner about the new building in his house, I went home, where I find a vessel of oysters sent me from Chatham. And I fell to eat some and then to supper; and so after the barber had done, to bed.

I am told that this day the Parliament hath voted 2*s* per annum for every chimney in England, as a constant Revenue for ever to the Crowne.[1]

12. At the office from morning till night, putting of papers in order, that so I may have my office in an orderly condition. I took much pains in sorting and folding of papers. Dined at home, and there came Mrs. Goldsborough about her old business, but I did give her a short answer and sent her away.[2]

This morning we have news from Mr. Coventry that Sir G. Downing (like a perfidious rogue, though the action is good and of service to the King, yet he cannot with any good conscience do it) hath taken Okey, Corbet, and Barkestead at Delfe in Holland and sent them home in the *Blackmore*.[3]

Sir Wm. Pen, talking to me this afternoon of what a strange thing it is for Downing to do this – he told me of a speech he made

1. The Chimney-Money (Hearth Tax) Bill.
2. This concerned a debt owed to Robert Pepys of Brampton.
3. John Okey, Miles Corbet, and John Barkstead were regicides who fled abroad. They had been arrested by special command of Downing, envoy extraordinary at The Hague and himself an ex-rebel who had previously served Okey.

to the Lords States of Holland,[1] telling them to their faces that he observed that he was not received with the respect and observance now, that he was when he came from that Traitor and Rebell, Cromwell – by whom I am sure he hath got all he hath in the world – and they know it too.

26. Up earely – this being, by God's great blessing, the fourth solemne day of my cutting for the stone this day four year. And am by God's mercy in very good health, and like to do well, the Lord's name be praised for it. To the office and Sir G. Carterets all the morning, about business. At noon came my good guest[s] Madam Turner, The, and Cosen Norton, and a gentleman, one Mr. Lewin of the King's life-guard; by the same token he told us of one of his fellows, killed this morning in the dewell. I had a pretty dinner for them – *viz*: a brace of stewed Carps, six roasted chicken, and a Jowle of salmon hot, for the first course – a Tanzy[2] and two neats' tongues and cheese the second. And were very merry all the afternoon, talking and singing and piping on the Flagelette. In the evening they went with great pleasure away; and I with great content, and my wife, walked half an houre in the garden; and so home to supper and to bed.

We had a man-cook to dress dinner today, and sent for Jane to help us.[3] And my wife and she agreed at 3*l* a year (she would not serve under) till both could be better provided; and so she stays with us – and I hope we shall do well if poor Sarah[4] were but rid of her ague.

30. *Easterday*. Having my old black suit new-furbished, I was pretty neat in clothes today – and my boy, his old suit new-trimmed, very handsome. To church in the morning. And so home, leaving the two Sir Wms. to take the Sacrament – which I blame myself that I have hitherto neglected all my life, but once or twice at Cambrige. Dined with my wife, a good shoulder of veal, well dressed by Jane and handsomely served to table – which pleased us much and made us hope that she will serve our turns well enough.

My wife and I to church in the afternoon and seated ourselfs, she below me; and by that means the precedence of the pew which my Lady Batten and her daughter takes, is confounded. And after sermon she and I did stay behind them in the pew and went out by

1. The governing body of the province of Holland.
2. Egg pudding flavoured with tansy herb.
3. Jane Birch, who had left Pepys's service on 26 Aug. 1661.
4. The current maid.

ourselfs a good while after them – which we judge a very fine project hereafter, to avoyd contention.[1]

So my wife and I to walk an hour or two on the leads; which begins to be very pleasant, the garden being in good condition.

So to supper, which is also well served in. We had a lobster to supper, with a crabb Pegg Pen[2] sent my wife this afternoon; the reason of which we cannot think, but something there is of plot or design in it – for we have a little while carried ourselfs pretty strange to them.

After supper, to bed.

APRILL.

2. Mr. Moore came to me and he and I walked to the Spittle, an hour or two before my Lord Mayor and the Blewe coate boys came, which at last they did, and a fine sight of charity it is endeed.[3] We got places and stayed to hear a sermon; but it being a presbyterian one, it was so long, that after above an hour of it we went away; and I home and dined, and then my wife and I by water to the Opera and there saw *The Bondman* most excellently acted; and though we had seen it so often, yet I never liked it better then today, Ianthe acting Clerora's part very well now Roxalana is gone.[4] We are resolved to see no more plays till Whitsontide, we having been three days together. I met Mr. Sanchy, Smithes, Gale and Edlin at the play; but having no great mind to spend money, I left them there. And so home and to supper; and then dispatch some business, and to bed.

19. This morning before we sat, I went to Allgate; and at the Corner shop, a drapers, I stood and did see Barkestead, Okey, and Corbet drawne toward the gallows at Tiburne; and there they were hanged and Quarterd. They all looked very cheerfully. But I hear they all die defending what they did to the King to be just – which is very

1. Seating order in church signalled gradations of social status and was a common source of strife in parishes.
2. Sir William Penn's daughter Margaret.
3. This was one of the Spital (Hospital) sermons given at Easter in Spitalfields. It was attended by the boys of Christ's Hospital, a charitable school for poor children of Londoners. They wore blue uniforms.
4. Massinger's play at the Lincoln's Inn Fields Theatre. "Ianthe" was Mary Saunderson, a leading actress in the Duke's Company, here nicknamed after the part she played in *The Siege of Rhodes*. "Roxalana" was Hester Davenport, so-called after her part in the same play.

strange. So to the office. And then home to dinner. And Captain David Lambert came to take his leave of me, he being to go back to Tanger, there to lie.

Then abroad about businesse and in the evening did get a bever,[1] an old one but a very good one, of Sir W. Batten; for which I must give him something, but I am very well pleased with it. So after writing by the post, to bed.

21. This morning I attempted to persuade my wife in bed to go to Brampton this week; but she would not, which troubles me. And seeing that I could keep it no longer from her, I told her that I was resolved to go to Portsmouth tomorrow.[2] Sir W. Batten goes to Chatham today and will be back again to come for Portsmouth after us on Thursday next.

I went to Westminster and several places about business. Then at noon dined with my Lord Crew; and after dinner went up to Sir Tho. Crew's chamber, who is still ill. He tells me how my Lady Duchess of Richmond[3] and Castlemayne had a falling out the other day; and she call[ed] the latter Jane Shoare, and did hope to see her come to the same end that she did.[4]

Coming down again to my Lord, he told me that news was come that the Queene is landed; at which I took leave, and by coach hurried to White-hall, the bells ringing in several places; but I find there no such matter, nor anything like it. So I went by appointment to Anthony Joyces, where I sat with his wife and Mall Joyce an hour or two; and so, her husband not being at home, away I went and in Cheepeside spied him and took him into the coach home; and there I find my Ladys Jemimah and Anne and Madamoiselle[5] come to see my wife. Whom I left, and to talk with Joyce about a project I have of his and my joyneing to get some money for my brother Tom and his kinswoman, to help forward with her portion if they should marry: I mean, in buying of tallow of him at a low rate for the King, and Tom should have the profit.[6] But he tells me the profit will not be considerable, at which I was

1. A beaver fur hat.
2. The trip was ostensibly for navy business, but timed to coincide with the celebrations surrounding Queen Catherine's arrival from Portugal. In the event, her arrival was delayed.
3. Dowager Duchess, and Lady Castlemaine's relation.
4. Jane Shore, mistress of Edward IV, was reputed to have fallen to begging and died in a ditch.
5. Sandwich's daughters and their governess.
6. Joyce was a tallow chandler. The plan was for Pepys to purchase tallow for the navy from him and the profit to go to Tom Pepys's marriage settlement.

troubled. But I have agreed with him to serve some in in my absence.

He went away, and then came Mr. Moore and sat late with me, talking about businesses; and so went away and I to bed.

22. After taking leave of my wife, which we could hardly do kindly, because of her mind to go along with me – Sir W. Penn and I took coach and so over the bridge to Lambeth – W. Bodham and Tom Hewet going as clerks to Sir W. Penn, and my Will for me. Here we got a dish of buttered eggs, and there stayed till Sir G. Carteret came to us from White-hall, who brought Dr Clerke with him, at which I was very glad.[1] And so we set out. And I was very much pleased with his company, and were very merry all the way. He, among [other] good Storys, telling us a story of the monkey that got hold of the young lady's cunt as she went to stool to shit, and run from under her coats and got upon the table, which was ready laid for supper after dancing was done. Another about a Hectors crying "God damn you, rascall!" We came to Gilford and there passed our time in the garden cutting of Sparagus for supper, the best that ever I eat in my life but in that house last year. Supped well, and the Doctor and I to bed together – calling Cosens, from his name and my office.

25. All the morning at Portsmouth at the pay; and then to dinner and again to the pay; and at night got the Doctor to go lie with me, and much pleased with his company; but I was much troubled in my eyes, by reason of the healths I have this day been forced to drink.

28. The Doctor and I begun Philosophy discourse, exceeding pleasant. He offers to bring me into the college of the Virtuosoes and my Lord Brunkard's acquaintance.[2] And to show me some anatomy, which makes me very glad. And I shall endeavour it when I come to London. Sir W. Penn much troubled, upon letters come last night; and this morning showed me one of Dr Owen to his son, whereby it appears his son is much perverted in his opinion by him; which I now perceive is one thing that hath put Sir Wm so

1. Pepys knew Timothy Clarke from the voyage to Holland in 1660. He was now a physician to the royal household.
2. Founded in 1660, this "college of the Virtuosoes" became known as the Royal Society, its first royal charter being granted in July 1662. Clarke was one of the first fellows and Viscount Brouncker would become its first President in 1663.

long off of the hookes.[1] By coach to the Pay-house, and so to work again. And then to dinner. And to it again, and so in the evening to the yard and supper and bed.

MAY.

1. Sir G. Carteret, Sir W. Pen, and myself, with our clerks, set out this morning from Portsmouth very early and got by noon to Petersfield, several of the officers of the yard accompanying us so far. Here we dined and were merry.

At dinner comes my Lord Carlingford from London, going to Portsmouth; tells us that the Duchess of Yorke is brought to bed of a girle,[2] at which I find nobody pleased. And that Prince Robert, the Duke of Buckingham and [3] are sworne of the Privy Councell.

He himself made a dish with egges of the butter of the Sparagus; which is very fine meat, which I will practise hereafter.

To horse again after dinner, and got to Gilford – where after supper I to bed, having this day been offended by Sir Wm Pens foolish talk, and I offending him with my answers; among others, he in discourse complaining of want of Confidence,[4] did ask me to lend him a grain or two, which I told him I thought he was better stored with then myself, before Sir George. So that I see I must keep a greater distance then I have done. And I hope I may do it, because of the interest which I am making with Sir George.

To bed all alone, and my Will in the truckle-bed.

2. earely to coach again and to Kingston, where we baited a little; and presently to coach again and got earely to London; and I find all well at home, and Mr. Hunt and his wife had dined with my wife today – and been very kind to my wife in my absence. After I had washed myself, it having been the hottest day that hath been this year, I took them all by coach to Mrs. Hunts; and I to Dr Clerkes lady and give her her letter and token. She is a very fine woman, and what with her person and the number of fine ladies

1. William Penn, jun., (the future Quaker leader) had been sent down from Christ Church, Oxford, for nonconformity in October 1661. Dr John Owens, the Independent divine, had been among his mentors.
2. Princess Mary, later Queen.
3. Prince Rupert, the Duke of Buckingham, and the Earl of Middleton.
4. "Confidence" meant "self-assurance", but also "over-boldness" or "presumption".

that were with her, I was much out of countenance and could hardly carry myself like a man among them. But however, I stayed till my courage was up again; and talked to them and viewed her house, which is most pleasant; and so drank and good-bye. And so to my Lord's lodgings, where by chance I spied my Lady's coach, and find her and my Lady Wright there; and so I spoke to them. And they being gone, went to Mr. Hunts for my wife, and so home. And to bed.

15. To Westminster; and at the Privy Seale I saw Mr. Coventrys seal for his being Comissioner with us – at which I know not yet whether to be glad or otherwise.[1] So, doing several things by the way, I walked home; and after dinner to the office all the afternoon. At night all the bells in the towne rung, and bonefires made for the joy of the Queens arrivall; who came and landed at Portsmouth last night. But I do not see much thorough joy, but only an indifferent one, in the hearts of people, who are much discontented at the pride and luxury of the Court, and running in debt. So to bed.

20. Sir W. Penn and I did a little business at the office, and so home again. Then comes Deane Fuller[2] after we had dined, but I got something for him; and very merry we were for an houre or two, and I am most pleased with his company and goodness. At last parted, and my wife and I by coach to the Opera and there saw the second part of *Seige of Rhodes*, but it is not so well done as when Roxalana was there – who, it is said, is now owned by my Lord of Oxford.[3] Thence to tower wharfe and there took boat; and we all walked to halfe-way-house and there eat and drunk – and were pleasant; and so finally home again in the evening, and so good-night – this being a very pleasant life that we now lead, and have long done; the Lord be blessed and make us thankful. But though I am much against too much spending, yet I do think it best to enjoy some degree of pleasure, now that we have health, money and opportunities, rather then to leave pleasures to old age or poverty, when we cannot have them so properly.

21. My wife and I by water to Westminster; and after she had seen her father (of whom lately I have heard nothing at all what he does,

1. William Coventry, Secretary to the Lord High Admiral (the Duke of York), had been made a Commissioner on the Navy Board. He was to become Pepys's staunchest ally.
2. William Fuller, dean of St Patrick's, Dublin.
3. Davenant's play, performed at Lincoln's Inn Fields. Hester Davenport (who had previously played Roxalana) had left to be mistress to the Earl of Oxford.

or her mother), she came to me to my Lord's Lodgeings, where she and I stayed, walking into White-hall garden; and in the privy Garden saw the finest smocks and linen petticoats of my Lady Castlemaynes, laced with rich lace at the bottomes, that ever I saw; and did me good to look upon them. So to Wilkinsons, she and I and Sarah,[1] to dinner, where I had a good Quarter of Lamb and a salat. Here Sarah told me how the King dined at my Lady Castlemayne – and supped – every day and night the last week. And that the night that the bonefires were made for joy of the Queenes arrivall, the King was there; but there was no fire at her door, though at all the rest of the doors almost in the street; which was much observed. And that the King and she did send for a pair of scales and weighed one another; and she, being with child, was said to be heavyest. But she is now a most disconsolate creature, and comes not out of doors – since the King's going.

But we went to the Theatre to *The French Dancing Maister*, and there with much pleasure we saw and gazed upon her. But it troubles us to see her look dejectedly, and slighted by people already. The play pleased us very well; but Lacy's part, the Dancing Maister, the best in the world.[2]

Thence to my brother Tom's in expectation to have met my father there tonight, come out of the country. But he is not yet come, but here we find my Uncle Fenner and his old wife, whom I have not seen since the wedding dinner, nor care to see her.[3] They being gone, my wife and I went and saw Mrs. Turner, whom we find not well. And her two boys, Charles and Will, come out of the country, grown very plain boys after three years being under their father's care in Yorkeshire. Thence to Toms again and there supped well, my she-Cosen Scott being there; and my father being not come, we walked home. And to bed.

31.◆ This month ends with very fair weather for a great while together. My health pretty well, but only wind doth now and then torment me about the fundament extremely. The Queene is brought a few days since to Hampton Court; and all people say of her to be a very fine and handsome lady and very discreet, and that the King is pleased enough with her: which I fear will put Madam Castlemaines nose out of Joynt. The Court is wholly now at

1. Sandwich's housekeeper.
2. This performance at the Theatre Royal may have been a version of *The Varietie* by the Marquess of Newcastle or James Shirley's *The Ball, or French Dancing Master*. It starred John Lacy, an expert dancer and comedian.
3. For the wedding dinner, *see* 23 Jan. 1662.

Hampton. A peace with Argiers is lately made; which is also good news.[1] My father is lately come to towne to see us, and though it hath cost and will cost more money, yet I am pleased with the alteracions on my house at Brampton. My Lord Sandwich is lately come with the Queene from Sea, very well and good repute. Upon an audit of my estate I find myself worth about 530*l de Claro.*[2] [The] Act for Uniformity is lately printed, which it is thought will make mad work among the presbyterian ministers.[3] Spirits of all sides are very much discontented; some thinking themselfs used, contrary to promise, too hardly; and the other, that they are not rewarded so much as they expected by the King. God keep us all. I have by a late oath obliged myself from wine and playes, of which I find good effect.

JUNE.

3. Up by 4 a-clock. And to my business in my chamber – to even accounts with my Lord and myself; and very fain I would become master of 1000*l*., but I have not above 530*l* towards it yet.

At the office all the morning, and Mr. Coventry brought his patent and took his place with us this morning. Upon our making a Contract, I went, as I use to do, to draw the heads thereof; but Sir W Pen most basely told me that the Controller is [to] do it, and so begun to imploy Mr. Turner about it, at which I was much vexed and begun to dispute; and what with the letter of the Dukes orders, and Mr. Barlows letter, and the practice of our predecessors, which Sir G. Carteret knew best when he was Comptroller, it was ruled for me.[4] What Sir J. Minnes will do when he comes I know not, but Sir W. Penn did it like a base raskall, and so I shall remember him while I live.

After office done, I went down to the Tower wharfe, where Mr.

1. The treaty with Algiers had been secured by John Lawson in Sandwich's absence.
2. Clear.
3. *An Act for the Uniformity of Publique Prayers* required all clergy to use the forms of prayer and service as laid out in the revised Book of Common Prayer. Clergymen refusing to do so after 24 Aug. 1662 were to be ejected from their livings. Presbyterian clergy and their followers were thereby forced out of the state church.
4. The Comptroller had long ceased to draft contracts. The Clerk of the Acts, in taking over this and other work, had assumed the major share of business in the office. Pepys marshalled evidence from the Duke of York and Thomas Barlow (his predecessor as Clerk of the Acts) to defend his territory. Turner was clerk to the current Comptroller, Mennes.

Creed and Sheply was ready with three chests of Crusados, being about 6000*l*, ready to bring on shore to my house; which they did, and put it in my further cellar – and Mr. Sheply took the key.[1] I to my father and Dr Williams and Tom Trice, by appointment in the old Bayly, to Short's the ale house, but could come to no terms with T. Trice.[2] Thence to the Wardrobe, where I find my Lady come from Hampton Court, where the Queene hath used her very civilly; and my Lady tells me is a most pretty woman – at which I am glad.

Yesterday (Sir R. Ford told me) the Aldermen of the City did attend her in their habitts, and did present her with a gold Cupp, and 1000*l* in gold therein. But he told me that they are so poor in their Chamber, that they were fain to call two or three Aldermen to raise fines to make up this sum – among which was Sir W. Warren.[3]

Home and to the office; where, about 8 at night, comes Sir G. Carteret and Sir W. Batten. And so we did some business. And then home and to bed, my mind troubled about Sir W. Penn – his playing the rogue with me today. As also about the charge of money that is in my house, which I had forgot. But I made the maids to rise and light a candle and set it in the dining room to scare away thiefs.[4] And so to sleep.

14. Up by 4 a-clock in the morning and upon business at my office. Then we sat down to business; and about 11 a-clock, having a room got ready for us, we all went out to the Tower hill; and there, over against the Scaffold made on purpose this day, saw Sir Henry Vane brought.[5] A very great press of people. He made a long speech, many times interrupted by the Sheriffe and others there; and they would have taken his paper out of his hand, but he would not let it go. But they caused all the books of those that writ after him to be given the Sheriffe; and the Trumpets were brought under the scaffold, that he might not be heard.

Then he prayed, and so fitted himself and received the blow. But the Scaffold was so crowded that we could not see it done. But Boreman, who had been upon the Scaffold, came to us and told us

1. These coins were part of Catherine of Braganza's dowry and in the charge of Sandwich's servants.
2. The dispute over Robert Pepys's will.
3. Men chosen to serve on London's Court of Aldermen who wanted to avoid the duty would pay a fine. Calling up reluctant representatives was an established fund-raising tactic.
4. The money remained safe and was moved a couple of days later.
5. Henry Vane the younger was a leading republican, imprisoned since 1660. He had been convicted of treason against Charles II for his actions under the Commonwealth.

that first he begun to speak of the irregular proceeding against him; that he was, against Magna Charta, denied to have his excepcions against the Endictment allowed. And that there he was stopped by the Sheriffe. Then he drow out his paper of Notes and begun to tell them; first, his life, that he was born a Gentleman, that he was bred up and had the Qualitys of a Gentleman, and to make him in the opinion of the world more a Gentleman, he had been, till he was seventeen year old, a Goodfellow.[1] But then it pleased God to lay a foundacion of Grace in his heart, by which he was persuaded against his worldly interest to leave all preferment and go abroad, where he might serve God with more freedom. Then he was called home and made a member of the Long parliament; where he never did, to this day, anything against his conscience, but all for the glory of God. Here he would have given them an account of the proceedings of the Long parliament, but they so often interrupted him, that at last he was forced to give over; and so fell into prayer for England in Generall, then for the churches in England, and then for the City of London. And so fitted himself for the block and received the blow. He had a blister or Issue upon his neck, which he desired them not to hurt. He changed not his colour or speech to the last, but died justifying himself and the cause he had stood for; and spoke very confidently of his being presently at the right hand of Christ. And in all things appeared the most resolved man that ever died in that manner, and showed more of heate then cowardize, but yet with all humility and gravity. One asked him why he did not pray for the King: he answered, "Nay," says he, "you shall see I can pray for the King: I pray, God bless him."

The King had given his body to his friends; and therefore he told them that he hoped they would be civil to his body when dead; and desired they would let him die like a gentleman and a christian, and not crowded and pressed as he was.

So to the office a little, and so to Trinity-house all of us to dinner. And then to the office again, all the afternoon till night; and so home and to bed. This day I hear my Lord Peterborough[2] [is come] unexpected from Tanger, to give the King an account of the place, which we fear is in none of the best condition. We have also certain news today that the Spaniard is before Lisbone with thirteen sayle; six Duch, and the rest his own ships – which will, I fear, be ill for Portugall.

1. A boon companion (implying hard drinking).
2. Governor of Tangier.

I writ a letter of all this day's proceedings to my Lord at Hinchingbrooke, who I hear is very well pleased with the work there.

15. *Lords day.* To church in the morning and home to dinner – where came my Brother Tom and Mr. Fisher, my Cosen Nan Pepys's second husband, who I perceive is a very good-humord man, an old Cavalier. I made as much of him as I could, and were merry. And am glad she hath light of so good a man. They gone, I to church again; but my wife not being dressed as I would have her, I was angry and she, when she was out of doors in her way to church, returned home again vexed. But I to church: Mr. Mills, an ordinary sermon. So home and find my wife and Sarah[1] gone to a neighbour church – at which I was not much displeased. By and by she comes again and, after a word or two, good friends. And then her brother came to see her; and he being gone, she told me that she believed he was married and hath a wife worth 500*l* to him, and did enquire how he might dispose that money to the best advantage; but I forbore to advise her till she could certainly tell me how things are with him, being loath to meddle too soon with him.[2] So to walk upon the leads and to supper and bed.

22. *Lords day.* This day I first put on my slasht doublet,[3] which I like very well. Mr. Sheply came to me in the morning, telling me that he and my Lord came to town from Hinchingbrooke last night. He and I spent an hour in looking over his accounts, and then walked to the Wardrobe, all the way discoursing of my Lord's business. He tells me, to my great wonder, that Mr. Barnwell[4] is dead, 500 in debt to my Lord.

By and by my Lord came from church and I dined, with some others, with him; he very merry, and after dinner took me aside and talked of state and other matters. By and by to my brother Toms and took [him] out with me homewards (calling at the wardrobe to talk a little with Mr. Moore); and so to my house, where I paid him all I owed him and did make the 20*l* I lately lent him up [to] 40*l*, for which he shall give bond to Mr. Sheply, for it is his money.

So my wife and I to walk in the garden, where all our talk was against Sir W. Penn; against whom I have lately had cause to be much prejudiced against. By and by he and his daughter came out

1. The maid.
2. Balthasar St Michel was in fact not yet married. He wed Ester (or Hester) Watts on 4 Dec. 1662 at St Benet, Paul's Wharf. Pepys did not attend.
3. A close-fitting jacket slashed to reveal the lining.
4. Sandwich's steward at Hinchingbrooke.

to walk, so we took no notice of them a great while; at last, in going home spoke a word or two, and so good-night and to bed. This day I am told of a Portugall lady at Hampton Court, that hath dropped a child already, since the Queenes coming. But the King would not have them searched whose it is; and so it is not commonly known yet. Coming home tonight, I met with Will Swan,[1] who doth talk as high for the fanatiques as ever he did in his life; and doth pity my Lord Sandwich and me that we should be given up to the wickedness of the world, and that a fall is coming upon us all. For he finds that he and his company are the true spirit of the nation, and the greater part of the nation, too – who will have liberty of conscience in spite of this act of uniformity, or they will die; and if they may not preach abroad, they will preach in their own houses. He told me that certainly Sir H. Vane must be gone to Heaven, for he died as much a martyr and saint as ever any man died. And that the King hath lost more by that man's death then he will get again a good while. At all which, I know not what to think; but I confess I do think that the Bishops will never be able to carry it so high as they do.

30.◆ *Observations*

This I take to be as bad a Juncture as ever I observed. The King and his new Queene minding their pleasures at Hampton Court. All people discontented; some that the king doth not gratify them enough; and the others, Fanatiques of all sorts, that the King doth take away their liberty of conscience; and the heighth of the Bishops, who I fear will ruin all again. They do much cry up the manner of Sir H. Vanes death, and he deserves it. They clamour against the Chimny-money and say they will not pay it without force. And in the meantime, like to have wars abroad – and Portugall to assist, when we have not money to pay for any ordinary layings-out at home.

Myself all in dirt about building of my house and Sir W. Batten's a storey higher. Into a good way; fallen on minding my business and saving money, which God encrease; and I do take great delight in it and see the benefit of it. In a longing mind of going to see Brampton, but cannot get three days time, do what I can.

In very good health, my wife and myself.

1. Pepys had friendly dealings with him while working at the Exchequer in 1660.

JULY.

4. Up by 5 a-clock; and after my Journal put in order, to my office about my business, which I am resolved to fallow, for every day [I] see what ground I get by it. By and by comes Mr. Cooper, Mate of the *Royall Charles*, of whom I entend to learn Mathematiques; and so begin with him today, he being a very able man and no great matter, I suppose, will content him. After an hour's being with him at Arithmetique, my first attempt being to learn the Multiplicacion table, then we parted till tomorrow: and so to my business at my office again – till noon; about which time Sir W. Warren[1] did come to me about business and did begin to instruct me in the nature of Firre, timber and deals,[2] telling me the nature of every sort; and from that, we fall to discourse of Sir W. Batten's corruption and the people that he imploys, and from one discourse to another of that kind; I was much pleased with his company and so stayed talking with him all alone at my office till 4 in the afternoon, without eating or drinking all day; and then parted and I home to eat a bit, and so back again to my office. And toward the evening came Mr. Sheply, who is to go ⟨out⟩ of town tomorrow; and so he and I with much ado settled his accounts with my Lord; which though they be true and honest, yet so obscure that it vexes me to see in what manner they are kept. He being gone, and leave taken of him as of a man likely not to come to London again a great while, I eat a bit of bread and butter, and so to bed. This day I sent my brother Tom, at his request, my father's old Basse viall[3] which he and I have kept so long; but I fear Tom will do little good at it.

6. *Lords day.* Lay long in bed today with my wife, merry and pleasant. And then rose and settled my accounts with my wife for housekeeping, and do see that my kitchen, besides wine, fire, candle, soap, and many other things, comes to about 30*s* a week or a little over.

To church, where Mr. Mills made a lazy sermon; so home to dinner, where my brother Tom dined with me. And so my wife and

1. William Warren was a timber merchant. Pepys came to work closely with him in navy business, to their mutual advantage.
2. Sawn timber used for decks etc.
3. Bass-viol: a stringed instrument resembling a cello.

I to church again in the afternoon. And that done, I walked to the Wardrobe and spent my time with Mr. Creede and Mr. Moore, talking about business; so up to supper with my Lady – who tells me with much trouble that my Lady Castlemayne is still as great with the King and that the King comes often to her as ever he did. At which, God forgive me, I am well pleased.

It begun to rain, and so I borrowed a hat and cloak of Mr. Moore and walked home, where I found Captain Ferrer with my wife; and after spending a matter of an hour with him, he went home and we all to bed.

⟨Jack Cole, my old friend, found me out at the Wardrobe; and among other things, he told me that certainly most of the chief Ministers of London would fling their livings;[1] and that soon or late the issue thereof would be sad to the King and Court.⟩

9. Up by 4 a-clock and at my multiplication table hard, which is all the trouble I meet withal in my arithmetique. So made me ready and to my office – where all the morning busy. And Sir W. Penn came to my office to take his leave of me;[2] and desiring a turn in the garden, did commit the care of his building to me and offered all his services to me in all matters of mine. I did (God forgive mee) promise him all my service and love, though the rogue knows he deserves none from me, nor I entend to show him any; but as he dissembles with me, so must I with him. Dined at home, and so to the office again, my wife with me; and while I was for an hour making a hole behind my seat in my closet, to look into the office, she was talking to me about her going to Brampton – which I would willingly have her do but for the cost of it; and to stay here will be very inconvenient because of the dirt that I must have when my house is pulled down.[3]

Then to my business till night; then Mr. Cooper and I to our business, and then came Mr. Mills the Minister to see me – which he hath but rarely done to me, though every day almost to others of us; but he is a cunning fellow and knows where the good victualls is and the good drink, at Sir W. Batten. However, I used him civilly, though I love him as I do the rest of his coat.[4] So to supper and to bed.

19. Up early and to some business; and my wife coming to me,

1. Due to the Act of Uniformity.
2. He was going to Ireland.
3. The roof was to be taken off to add a storey.
4. Profession.

I stayed long with her, discoursing about her going into the country; and as she is not very forward, so am I at a great loss whether to have her go or no, because of the charge; and yet in some considerations, I could be glad she was there, because of the dirtiness of my house and the trouble of having of a family there. So to my office, and there all the morning; and then to dinner, and my brother Tom dined with me, only to see me. In the afternoon I went upon the River to look after some tarr I am sending down[1] and some Coles, and so home again. It raining hard upon the water, I put ashore and sheltered myself while the King came by in his barge, going down toward the Downes to meet the Queene,[2] the Duke being gone yesterday. But methought it lessened my esteem of a king, that he should not be able to command the rain.

Home, and Cooper coming (after I had despatch[ed] several letters), to my Mathematiques. And so at night to bed, to a chamber in Sir W. Pens – my own house being so foule that I cannot lie there any longer. And then the chamber lies so as that I come into it over my leads without going about. But yet I am not fully content with it, for there will be much trouble to have servants running over the leads to and fro.

20. *Lordsday.* My wife and I lay talking long in bed; and at last she is come to be willing to stay two months in the country, for it is her unwillingness to stay till the house is quite done that makes me at a loss how to have her go or stay.

But that which troubles me most is that it hath rained all this morning, so furiously that I fear my house is all over wet; and with that expectation I rose and went into my house, and I find that it is as wet as the open street, and that there is not one dry footing above nor below in my house. So I fitted myself for dirt and removed all my books to the office, and all day putting up and removing things, it raining all day long as hard within doors as without. At last to dinner; we had a calf's head and bacon at my chamber at Sir W Pens, and there I and my wife concluded to have her go, and her two maids and the boy; and so there shall be none but Will and I left at home, and so the house will be free, for it is impossible to have anybody come into my house while it is in this condition; and with this resolution, all the afternoon we were putting up things in the further cellar against next week, for them to be gone. And my wife and I went into the office and there measured

1. For the navy.
2. The Queen Mother, visiting from France.

a silk flag that I have found there, and hope to get it to myself, for it hath not been demanded since I came to the office. But my wife is not hasty to have it, but rather to stay a while longer and see the event, whether it will be missed or no.

At night to my office and there put down this day's passage in my Journall and read my oaths, as I am obliged every Lord's day; and so to Sir W. Pens to my chamber again, being all in dirt and foule, and in fear of having ketched cold today with dabbling in the water.

That which hath most vexed me today was that by carrying the key to Sir W. Pens last night, it could not, in the midst of all my hurry to carry away my books and things, it could not be found; and at last they found it in the fire that we made last night. So to bed.

28. Up early; and by 6 a-clock, after my wife was ready, I walked with her to the George at Holborne conduict, where the Coach stood to carry her and her maid to Bugden;[1] but that not being ready, my brother Tom stayed with them to see them gone; and so I took a troubled, though willing, godbwy,[2] because of the bad condition of my house to have a family in it. So I took leave of her and walked to the waterside, and there took boat for the Towre, hearing that the Queene-Mother is come this morning already as high as Woolwich and that my Lord Sandwich was with her; at which my heart was glad (and I sent the waterman, though yet not very certain of it, to my wife to carry news thereof to my Lady):[3] so to my office all the morning, abstracting the Dukes instruccions in the Margin thereof.[4]

So home all alone to dinner, and then to the office again, and in the evening Cooper comes; and he being gone, to my chamber a little troubled and melancholy; to my lute late, and so to bed – Will lying there at my feet, and the wench in my house in Will's bed.

1. Buckden, Huntingdonshire, where Robert Pepys had owned land. Elizabeth then went on to Brampton.
2. God be with ye, goodbye.
3. Sandwich had gone to escort the Queen Mother from France. His ship had been rumoured lost in a storm before word had reached London that he was safe.
4. Issued by the Duke of York in January 1662, the "Instructions" described the duties of the Navy Board. Pepys now summarized the contents in the margin.

AUGUST.

1. Up, my head akeing, and to my office; where Cooper read me another lecture upon my modell,[1] very pleasant.

So to my business all the morning, which encreases by people's coming now to me to the office. At noon to the Exchange;[2] where meeting Mr. Creede and Moore, we three to a house hard by (which I was not pleased with) to dinner; and after dinner and some discourse ordinary, by coach home, it raining hard. And so at the office all the afternoon, till evening to my chamber; where, God forgive me, I was sorry to hear that Sir W Pens maid Betty was gone away yesterday, for I was in hopes to have had a bout with her before she had gone, she being very pretty. I have also a mind to my own wench, but I dare not, for fear she should prove honest and refuse and then tell my wife.

◆ And so to bed – being in pain in my cods with the little riding in a coach today from the exchange – which doth trouble me.

15. Up very early, and up about seeing how my work proceeds, and am pretty well pleased therewith; especially, my wife's closet will be very pretty. So to my office and there very busy all the morning, and many people coming to me. At noon to the Change and there hear of some Quakers that are seized on, that would have blown up the prison in Southwarke where they are put.[3] So to the Swan in old Fish streete, where Mr. Brigden and his father-in-law Blackbury, of whom we have bought timber in the office but hath not dealt well with us, did make me a fine dinner, only to myself. And after dinner comes in a Jugler, which showed us very pretty tricks. I seemed very pleasant, but am no friend to the man's dealings with us in the office. After an hour or two's sitting after dinner, talking about office business, I went to Pauls churchyard to my booksellers,[4] where I have not spent any time a great while. And there I hear the next Sunday will be the last of a great many Presbyterian

1. A model of a ship. Richard Cooper was teaching Pepys about a ship's workings.
2. The Royal Exchange (often simply "the Change") at Cornhill. The midday trading hour, officially ending at noon, was the best time to meet merchants and learn news.
3. About eighty Quakers had been arrested for attending an illegal religious meeting.
4. Joshua Kirton's bookshop.

ministers in towne, who I hear will give up all. I pray God the issue may be good, for the discontent is great. Home to my office till 9 at night, doing business; and so to bed – my mind well pleased with a letter that I find at home from Mr. Coventry, expressing his satisfaction in a letter I writ last night and sent him this morning, to be corrected by him in order to its sending down to all the yards as a Charge to them.

17. *Lords=day.* Up very earely, this being the last Sunday that the Presbyterians are to preach, unless they read the new Comon Prayer and renounce the Covenant,[1] and so I had a mind to hear Dr Bates's farewell sermon,[2] and walked thither – calling first at my brother, where I find that he is come home after being a week abroad with Dr Pepys, nobody knows where; nor I, but by chance, that he was gone, which troubles me. So I called only at the door, but did not ask for him; but went to Madam Turners to know whether she went to church and to tell her that I would dine with her. And so walked to St. Dunstans, where, it being not 7 a-clock yet, the doors were not open; and so I went and walked an hour in the Temple garden, reading my vows; which it is a great content to me to see how I am a changed man, in all respects for the better, since I took them – which the God of Heaven continue to me and make me thankful for.

At 8 a-clock I went and crowded in at a back door among others, and the church being half-full almost before any doors were open publicly; which is the first time that I have done so these many years, since I used to go with my father and mother. And so got into the Gallry besides the pulpit and heard very well. His text was, "Now the god of peace" – the last *Hebrews* and the 20 verse[3] – he making a very good sermon and very little reflections in it to anything of the times. Besides the sermon, I was very well pleased with the sight of a fine lady that I have often seen walk in Grayes-Inn walks. And it was my chance to meet her just at the door going out, and very pretty and sprightly she is; and I believe the same that my wife and I some years since did meet at Temple barr gate and have

1. In addition to imposing the Book of Common Prayer, the Act of Uniformity required clergymen to declare against the Solemn League and Covenant, the alliance agreed by the English and Scottish parliaments in 1643. The treaty included clauses tending to a Presbyterian religious settlement, such as the rejection of bishops. As all men over 18 had been required to swear to uphold the Covenant, the new Act required many clergy to go back on their oaths.
2. Dr William Bates, Rector of St Dunstan-in-the-West and a great Presbyterian preacher.
3. Hebrews 13.20–21.

sometimes spoke of. So to Madam Turner's and dined with her. She had heard parson Herring[1] take his leave; though he, by reading so much of the Common Prayer as he did, hath cast himself out of the good opinion of both sides.

After dinner to St. Dunstan's again, and the church quite crouded before I came, which was just at one a-clock; but I got into the gallery again, but stood in a crowd and did exceedingly sweat all the while. He pursued his text again very well, and only at the conclusion told us after this manner – "I do believe that many of you do expect that I should say something to you in reference to the time, this being the last time that possibly I may appear here. You know it is not my manner to speak anything in the pulpit that is extraneous to my text and business. Yet this I shall say, that it is not my opinion, faction, or humour that keeps me from complying with what is required of us, but something which after much prayer, discourse and study yet remains unsatisfied and commands me herein. Wherefore, if it is my unhappinesse not to receive such an illuminacion as should direct me to do otherwise, I know no reason why men should not pardon me in this world, and am confident that God will pardon me for it in the next." And so he concluded.

Parson Herring read a psalme and Chapters before sermon; and one was the Chapter in the *Acts* where the story of Ananias and Saphira is.[2] And after he had done, says he, "This is just the case of England at present; God, he bids us to preach, and men bid us not to preach; and if we do, we are to be imprisoned and further punished: all that I can say to it is that I beg your prayers and the prayers of all good Christians for us." This was all the exposition he made of the chapter, in these very words and no more.

I was much pleased with Dr Bates's manner of bringing in the Lord's Prayer after his owne, thus – "In whose comprehensive words we sum up all our imperfect desires; saying – Our Father" &c. Church being done and it raining, I took a hackney-coach and so home, being all in a sweat and fearful of getting cold.

To my study at my office, and thither came Mr. Moore to me and walked till it was quite dark. Then I writ a letter to my Lord Privy Seale as from my Lord, for Mr. [Moore] to be Sworne directly as Deputy to my Lord, he denying to swear him as Deputy together with me. So that I am now clear of it, and the profit is now come

1. John Herring, Vicar of St Bride, Fleet Street.
2. Acts 5. Ananias and Sapphira present money as an offering to God, but keep back part for themselves. The Apostle Peter charges them with betraying God and the pair are miraculously struck dead.

to be so little that I am not displeased at my getting off so well.[1]

He being gone, I to my study and read; and so to eat a bit of bread and cheese and so to bed.

I hear most of the Presbyters took their leaves today. And the City is much dissatisfied with it. I pray God keep peace among us and make the Bishops careful of bringing in good men in their room, or else all will fly a-pieces; for bad ones will not down[2] with the City.

18. Up very earely, and up upon my house to see how work goes on, which doth please me very well. So about 7 a-clock took horse and rode to Bowe, and there stayed at the Kings-head and eat a breakfast of eggs till Mr. Deane of Woolwich[3] came to me; and he and I rid into Waltham Forrest and there we saw many trees of the King's a-hewing and he showed me the whole mystery of off=square,[4] wherein the King is abused in the timber that he buys, which I shall with much pleasure be able to correct. After we had been a good while in the wood, we rode to Ilford; and there, while dinner was getting ready, he and I practised measuring of the tables and other things till I did understand measure of timber and board very well. So to dinner; and by and by, being sent for, comes Mr. Cooper,[5] our officer in the Forrest, and did give me an account of things there and how the country is backward to come in with their carts. By and by comes one Mr. Marshall, of whom the King hath many carriages for his timber, and they stayed and drank with me. And while I am here, Sir Wm. Batten passed by in his coach homeward from Colchester, where he hath been seeing his son-in-law Lemon, that lies a-dying; but I would take no notice of him, but let him go. By and by I got a-horseback again and rode to Barking, and there saw the place where they ship this timber for Woolwich; and so Deane and I home again. And parted at Bow, and I home just before a great showre of rain as God would have it.

I find Deane a pretty able man, and able to do the King service;

1. Pepys thus surrendered his role as Sandwich's deputy at the Privy Seal Office to Moore.
2. Agree.
3. Anthony Deane, Assistant-Shipwright at Woolwich, became a close friend over Pepys's naval career.
4. Apparently still mysterious to Pepys as he had trouble remembering the method's name: he corrected his original longhand "over-square" to "off-square", a term not traced elsewhere. Exactly which abuse he meant is uncertain, but it was one of several customary ways of measuring timber that favoured the seller over the buyer.
5. William Cooper, timber purveyor.

but I think more out of envy to the rest of the officers of the yard (of whom he complains much) then true love, more then others, to the service. He would fain seem a modest man, and yet will commend his own work and skill and vie with other persons, especially the Petts.[1] But I let him alone, to hear all he will say.

Whiled away the evening at my office, trying to repeat my rules of measuring learnt this day; and so to bed – with my mind very well pleased with this day's work.

20. Up earely and to my office. And thence to my Lord Sandwich, who I find in bed and he sent for me in; and among other talk, doth tell me that he hath put me into commission with a great many great persons in the business of Tanger, which is a very great Honour to me and may be of good concernment to me.[2] By and by comes in Mr. Coventry to us, who my Lord tells that he is also put into the commission, and that I am there; of which he said he was glad and did tell my Lord that I was endeed the life of this office, and much more to my commendation, beyond measure. And that whereas before he did bear me respect for his sake, he doth do it now much more for my own – which is a great blessing to me – Sir G. Carteret having told me what he did yesterday concerning his speaking to my Lord Chancellor about me.[3] So that on all hands, by God's blessing, I find myself a very rising man. By and by comes my Lord Peterborow[4] in, with whom we talked a good while, and he is going tomorrow towards Tanger again. I perceive there is yet little hopes of peace with Guyland,[5] which is of great concernment to Tanger. And many other things I heard which yet I understand not, and so cannot remember.

My Lord and Lord Peterborough going out to the Sollicitor-Generall about the drawing up this commission, I went to Westminster-hall with Mr. Moore; and there meeting Mr. Townsend, he would needs take me to Fleetestreete to ⟨one⟩ Mr. Barwell, Squire Sadler to the King, and there we and several other Wardrobe-men dined. We had a venison pasty, and other good plain and handsome dishes. The mistress of the house a pretty well-carriaged

1. A family of shipwrights holding positions in the navy dockyards.
2. The Privy Council's Committee for Tangier was charged with oversight of Britain's new colony. Pepys's fellow committee members included lords, and his membership brought him not just esteem but profit.
3. Carteret had praised Pepys to Lord Chancellor Clarendon in the expectation that Sandwich would learn of this.
4. Governor of Tangier.
5. Al-Khiḍr Ghaylān, or "Guyland" to the English, a Moroccan warlord who controlled the region around Tangier.

woman, and a fine hand she hath. And her maid a pretty brown lass. But I do find my nature ready to run back to my old course of drinking wine and staying from my business; and yet, I thank God, I was not fully contented with it, but did stay at little ease. And after dinner hasted home by water and so to my office till late at night. In the evening Mr. Hayward came to me to advise with him about the business of the Chest, which I have now a mind to put in practice, though I know it will vex Sir Wm. Batten – which is one of the ends, God forgive me, that I have in it.[1]

So home and eat a bit, and to bed.

23. Up earely and about my works in my house to see what is done and design more. Then to my office; and by and by we sat till noon at the office. After sitting, Mr. Coventry and I did walk together a great while in the garden, where he did tell me his mind about Sir G. Carteret's[2] having so much the command of the money, which must be removed. And endeed, it is the bane of all our business. He observed to me also how Sir W. Batten begins to struggle and to look after his business; which he doth indeed a little, but it will come to nothing. I also put him upon getting an order from the Duke for our inquiries into the Chest, which he will see done. So we parted; and Mr. Creede by appointment being come, he and I went out together, and at an ordinary in Lumbardstreete dined together; and so walked down to the Styll yard and so all along Thames streete, but could not get a boat: I offered 8*s* for a boat to attend me this afternoon and they would not, it being the day of the Queenes coming to town from Hampton Court.[3] So we fairly walked it to White-hall; and through my Lord's lodgings we got into White-hall garden, and so to the bowling-greene and up to the top of the new banquetting-house[4] there over the Thames, which was a most pleasant place as any I could have got. And all the show consisted chiefly in the number of boats and barges – and two Pageants, one of a King and another of a Queene, with her maydes of honour sitting at her feet very prettily. And they tell me the Queene is Sir Rich. Fords daughter. Anon came the King and Queene in a barge under a Canopy, with 10000 barges and boats

1. The Chatham Chest was a fund for the relief of disabled seamen and Pepys wanted to address its mismanagement. Edward Hayward had formerly been Treasurer of the Chest, while Batten was the current chair of the Governors who ran the fund.
2. Treasurer of the Navy.
3. Queen Catherine's first arrival in London.
4. Summer-house.

I think, for we could see no water for them – nor discern the King nor Queen. And so they landed at White-hall bridge, and the great guns on the other side went off.

But that which pleased me best was that my Lady Castlemayne stood over against us upon a piece of White-hall – where I glutted myself with looking on her. But methought it was strange to see her Lord and her upon the same place, walking up and down without taking notice one of another; only, at first entry, he put off his hat and she made him a very civil salute – but afterwards took no notice one of another. But both of them now and then would take their child, which the nurse held in her armes, and dandle it. One thing more; there happend a scaffold below to fall, and we feared some hurt but there was none; but she, of all the great ladies only, run down among the common rabble to see what hurt was done, and did take care of a child that received some little hurt; which methought was so noble.

Anon there came one there, booted and spurred, that she talked long with. And by and by, she being in her haire, she put on his hat, which was but an ordinary one, to keep the wind off. But methought it became her mightily, as everything else do.

The show being over, I went away, not weary with looking on her; and to my Lord's lodgings, where my brother Tom and Dr Tom Pepys were to speak with me. So I walked with them in the garden and was very angry with them both, for their going out of town without my knowledge. But they told me the business, which was to see a gentlewoman for a wife for Tom of Mr. Cooke's providing, worth 500*l*, of good education; her name Hobell and lives near Banbury;[1] demands 40*l* per annum joynter.[2] Tom likes her; and they say had a very good reception, and that Cooke hath been very serviceable therein and that she is committed to old Mr. Young of the Wardrobes' tuition.[3]

After I had told them my mind about their folly in going so unadvisedly, I then begun to enquire after the business; and so did give no answer as to my opinion till I have looked further into it by Mr. Young.

By and by, as we were walking in my Lord's walk, comes my

1. Elizabeth Hobell, 18-year-old daughter of John Hobell, a gentleman of Banbury (d. 1655). (She had a younger sister Martha, a possible but less likely candidate.) Both sisters were due to inherit a third of their father's estate on marriage.
2. £40 per year jointure (the estate reserved to support the wife in her widowhood).
3. She was under the care of John Young, Yeoman Tailor of the King's Wardrobe, a relative. Mr Cooke, the go-between, was a servant of Sandwich's.

Lord; and so we broke our discourse and went in with him. And after I had put them away, I went in to my Lord and he and I had half an hour's private discourse about the discontents of the times, which we concluded would not come to anything of difference, though the presbyters would be glad enough of it; but we do not think Religion will so soon cause another warr.◆

Here we broke off, and I bid him good-night. And so with much ado (the streets being at 9 a-clock at night crammed with people going home to the City, for all the borders of the River have been full of people as the King hath come, to a miracle) got to the palace-yard and there took boat and so to the Old Swan; and so walked home and to bed, very weary.

SEPTEMBER.

1. Up betimes at my lodging, and to my office and among my workmen. And then with Sir W. Batten and Sir W Pen by coach to St. James's, this being the first day of our meeting there weekly by the Duke's order; but when we came, we find him going out by coach with his Duchesse, and he told us he was to go abroad with the Queene today (to Durdans it seems, to dine with my Lord Barkely, where I have been very merry when I was a little boy).[1] So we went and stayed a little at Mr. Coventry's chamber and I to my Lord Sandwichs, who is gone to wait upon the King and Queene today. And so Mr. Paget being there, Will Howe and I and he played over some things of Lockes[2] that we used to play at sea, that pleased us three well – it being the first musique I have heard a great while – so much hath my business of late taken me off from all my former delights.

By and by, by water home and there dined alone; and after dinner, with my brother Tom's two men I removed all my goods out of Sir W. Pen's house into one room, that I have with much ado got ready at my house. And so I am glad to be quit of any further obligation to him. So to my office; but missing my key, which I had in my hand just now, makes me very angry and out of order, it being

1. Durdans, a country house near Epsom, Surrey, was owned by Lord Berkeley of Berkeley. Pepys would have known it when staying as a boy with his cousins at Ashtead.
2. Probably Matthew Locke's *Little Consort of Three Parts* (1656) that Pepys had enjoyed with Howe in 1660.

a thing that I hate in others and more in myself, to be carelesse of keys, I thinking another not fit to be trusted that leaves a key behind their heels. One thing more vexes me – my wife writes me from the country that her boy plays the rogue there and she is weary of him; and complains also of her maid Sarah, of which I am also very sorry.

Being thus out of temper, I could do little at my office; but went home and eat a bit, and so to my lodgings to bed.

3. Up betimes; but now the days begin to shorten and so whereas I used to rise by 4 a-clock, it is not broad daylight now till after 5 a-clock, so that it is 5 before I do rise. To my office; and about 8 a-clock I went over to Redriffe and walked to Deptford, where I find Mr. Coventry and Sir W Pen beginning the pay – it being my desire to be there ⟨to⟩day, because it is the first pay that Mr. Coventry hath been at and I would be thought to be as much with Mr. Coventry as I can. Here we stayed till noon, and by that time paid off the *Breda*; and then to dinner at the Taverne, where I have obtained that our commons[1] is not so large as they used to be, which I am glad to see. After dinner, by water to the office; and there we met and sold the *Weymouth*, *Successe*, and *Fellowship* Hulke. Where pleasant to see how backward men are at first to bid; and yet when the candle is going out, how they bawl and dispute afterward who bid the most first.[2]

And here I observed one man cunninger then the rest, that was sure to bid the last man and to carry it; and enquiring the reason, he told me that just as the flame goes out the smoke descends, which is a thing I never observed before, and by that he doth know the instant when to bid last – which is very pretty. In our discourse in the boat, Mr. Coventry told us how the Fanatiques and the Presbyters that did entend to rise about this times did choose this day as the most auspicious to them in their endeavours against monarchy – it being fatal twice to the King, and the day of Olivers death.[3] But blessed be God, all is likely to be quiet I hope.

After the sale I walked to my brother's, in my way meeting with Dr Fairbrother, of whom I enquired what news in church matters. He tells me, what I heard confirmed since, that it was fully resolved by the King and Council that an indulgence should be granted the

1. Food provided for the group.
2. The highest bid made before the candle extinguished was the winning bid.
3. The royalist army had been defeated twice on 3 September – at Dunbar in 1650 and at Worcester in 1651 – and Cromwell had died on 3 Sept. 1658.

presbyters; but upon the Bishop of Londons speech (who is now one of the most powerful men in England with the King), their minds was wholly turned.[1] And it is said that my Lord Albemarle did oppose him most; but that I do believe is only in appearance. He told me also, that most of the presbyters now begin to wish they had complied, now they see that no Indulgence will be granted them, which they hoped for. And that the Bishop of London hath taken good care that places are supplied with very good and able men, which is the only thing that will keep all quiet.◆

9. At my office betimes; and by and [by] we sat, and at noon Mr. Coventry, Sir J. Mennes, Mr. Pett and myself by water to Deptford, where we met Sir G. Carteret, Sir W. Batten and Sir W. Penn at the pay of a ship; and we dined together on a haunch of good venison boiled, and after dinner returned again to the office and there met several tradesmen by our appointment, to know of them their lowest rates that they will take for their several provisions that they sell to us. For I do resolve to know that, and to buy no dearer; that so, when we know the lowest rate, it shall be the Treasurer's fault and not ours that we pay dearer.

This afternoon, Sir John Minnes, Mr. Coventry, and I went into Sir John's lodgings, where he showed us how I have blinded all his lights and stopped up his garden-door; and other things he takes notice of that he resolves to abridge me of, which doth vex [me] so much, that for all this evening and all night in my bed, so great a fool I am and little master of my passion, that I could not sleep for the thoughts of my losing the privilege of the leads and other things which in themselfs are small and not worth half the trouble. The more fool am I, and must labour against it for shame – especially I that use to preach up Epictetus's rule of *τὰ ἐφ ἡμιν καὶ τὰ οὐκ ἐφ ἡμῖν*.[2]

Late at my office, troubled in mind; and then to bed, but could hardly sleep all night.

27. Up betimes and among my workmen, and with great pleasure see the posts in my entry taken down, beyond expectation; so that now, the boy's room being laid into the entry doth make my coming

1. The proposed indulgence (a royal declaration) would reportedly have allowed Presbyterian ministers to remain in their posts if the Book of Common Prayer was read in their churches. It was defeated at a Privy Council meeting on 28 August, principally by Gilbert Sheldon, Bishop of London.
2. "Of things, some are in our power, others are not", from Epictetus, *Enchiridion*, 1.1. Pepys sometimes gets the diacritics wrong when writing Greek.

in very handsome, which was the only fault remaining almost in my house.

We sat all the morning. And in the afternoon I got many jobbs done to my mind, and my wife's chamber put into a good readiness against her coming – which she did at night, for Will did, by my leave to go, meet her upon the road and at night did bring me word she was come to my brother's by my order. So I made myself ready and put things at home in order, and so went thither to her. Being come, I find her and her maid and dog very well – and herself grown a little fatter then she was. I was very well pleased to see her; and after supper, to bed and had her company with great content – and much mutual love. Only, I do perceive that there hath been fallings-out between my mother and she, and a little between my father and she; but I hope all is well again. And I perceive she likes Brampton house and seat better then ever I did myself. And tells me how my Lord hath drawn a plot of some alterations to be made there, and hath brought it up, which I saw and like well. I perceive my Lord and Lady have been very kind to her. And Captain Ferrers, so kind that I perceive [I] have some jealousy of him; but I know what is the Captain's manner of carriage, and therefore it is nothing to me. ⟨She tells me of a Court[1] like to be in a little time, which troubles me, for I would not willingly go out of towne.⟩

29. *Michaelmas day.* This day my oaths for drinking of wine and going to plays are out, and so I do resolve to take a liberty today and then to fall to them again. Up and by coach to White-hall, in my way taking up Mr. Moore and walked with him, talking a good while about business in St. James's parke. And there left him and to Mr. Coventry's, and so with him and Sir W. Penn up to the Duke; where the King came also and stayed till the Duke was ready. It being Collar day[2] – we had no time to talk with him about any business. They went out together and so we parted; and in the parke Mr. Cooke by appointment met me, to whom I did give my thoughts concerning Tom's match and their journy tomorrow. And did carry him by water to Toms, and there taking up my wife, maid, dog and him, did carry them home – where my wife is much pleased with my house, and so am I fully. I sent for some dinner and there dined (Mrs. Margt Pen being by, to whom I had spoke to go along with us to a play this afternoon) and then to the King's Theatre,

1. A manorial court at Brampton.
2. A day on which knights of chivalric orders wore their insignia at court.

where we saw *Midsummers nights dreame*,[1] which I have never seen before, nor shall ever again, for it is the most insipid ridiculous play that ever I saw in my life. I saw, I confess, some good dancing and some handsome women, which was all my pleasure.

Thence set my wife down at Madam Turners and so by coach home; and having delivered Pegg Pen to her father safe, went home, where I find Mr. Deane of Woolwich hath sent me the modell[2] he had promised me. But it so far exceeds my expectation that I am sorry almost he should make such a present to no greater a person; but I am exceeding glad of it and shall study to do him a courtesy for it.

So to my office and wrote a letter to Tom's mistress's mother, to send by Cooke tomorrow. Then came Mr. Moore, thinking to have looked over the business of my Brampton papers against the Court, but my mind was so full of other matters (as it is my nature when I have been a good while from a business that I have almost forgot it, I am loath to come to it again) that I could not set upon it; and so he and I passed the evening away in discourse, and to my lodgings and to bed.

30. We rose; and he about his business and I to my house to look over my workmen. But good God, how I do find myself by yesterday's liberty hard to be brought to fallow business again; but however, I must do it, considering the great sweet and pleasure and content of mind that I have had since I did leave drink and plays and other pleasures and fallowed my business.

So to my office – where we sat till noon, and then I to dinner with Sir W Pen; and while we were at it, coming my wife to the office, and so I sent for her up; and after dinner we took coach and to the Dukes playhouse, where we saw *The Duchesse of Malfy* well performed, but Baterton and Ianthe to admiration.[3] That being done, home again by coach, and my wife's chamber got ready for her to lie in tonight; but my business did call me to my office, so that staying late, I did not lie with her at home but at my lodgings.

Strange to see how easily my mind doth revert to its former practice of loving plays and wine, having given myself a liberty to them both these two days; but this night I have again bound myself to Christmas next, in which I desire God to bless me and preserve me,

1. Shakespeare's comedy, at the Theatre Royal.
2. Of a ship.
3. John Webster's tragedy, in which Thomas Betterton played Bosola and Mary Saunderson ("Ianthe") played the Duchess.

for under God I find it to be the best course that ever I could take to bring myself to mind my business.

I have also made up this evening my monthly ballance; and find that notwithstanding the loss of 30*l* to be paid to the Loyall and necessitous Cavaliers by act of Parliament,[1] yet I am worth about 680*l* – for which the Lord God be praised. My condition at present is this.

I have long been building; and my house, to my great content, is now almost done; but yet not so but that I shall have dirt, which troubles me too – for my wife hath been in the country at Brampton these two months, and is now come home a week or two before the house is ready for her.

My mind is somewhat troubled about my best chamber, which I Question whether I shall be able to keep or no.[2] I am also troubled for my journy which I must needs take suddenly to the Court at Brampton, but most of all for that I am not provided to understand my business, having not minded it a great while; and at the best shall be able but to make a bad matter of it. But God, I hope, will guide all to the best, and I am resolved tomorrow to fall hard to it: I pray God bless me therein, for my father and mother and all our well-doings do depend upon my care therein.

My Lord Sandwich hath lately been in the country, and very civil to my wife; and hath himself spent some pains in drawing a plot of some alteracions in our house there – which I shall fallow as I get money.

As for the office, my late industry hath been such, as I am become as high in reputation as any man there, and good hold I have of Mr. Coventry and Sir G. Carteret – which I am resolved, and it is necessary for me, to maintain by all fair means.

Things are all quiet, but the King poor and no hopes almost of his being otherwise, by which things will go to wrack, especially in the Navy.

The late outing of the presbyter=Clergy, by their not renouncing the Covenant as the act [of] Parliament commands, is the greatest piece of state now in discourse. But for aught I see, they are gone out very peaceably and the people not so much concerned therein as was expected.

My brother Tom is gone out of town this day to make a second

1. An act passed in May to raise funds to support "truly Loyal & Indigent" Cavalier officers, via a levy on office-holders.
2. Mennes had designs on Pepys's best bedroom as recompense for the changes made to his house by Pepys's building works.

journy to his mistress at Banbury – of which I have good expectations – and pray God to bless him therein. My mind, I hope, is settled to fallow my business again, for I find that two days' neglect of business doth give me more discontent in mind then ten times the pleasure thereof can repair again, be it what it will.

OCTOBER.

8. Up, and by water to my Lord Sandwich and was with him a good while in his Chamber; and among other things, to my extraordinary joy he did tell me how much I was beholding to the Duke of Yorke, who did yesterday of his own accord tell him that he did thank him for one person brought into the Navy, naming myself, and much more to my commendation; which is the greatest comfort and encouragement that ever I had in my life, and do owe it all to Mr. Coventry's goodness and ingenuity. I was glad above measure of this.◆

19. *Lords day.* Got me ready in the morning and put on my first new lace-band;[1] and so neat it is, that I am resolved my great expense shall be lace-bands, and it will set off anything else the more. So walk to my brother's, where I met Mr. Cooke; and discoursing with him, do find that he and Tom have promised a joynture of 50*l* to his mistress and say that I did give my consent that she should be joyntured in 30*l* per annum for Sturtlow,[2] and the rest to be made up out of her portion. At which I was stark-mad, and very angry the business should be carried with so much folly, and against my mind and all reason. But I was willing to forbear discovering of it, and did receive Mrs. Butler her mother,[3] and Mr. Lull and his wife, very civil people, very kindly and without the least discontent, and Tom had a good and neat dinner for us. We had little discourse of any business; but leave it to one Mr. Smith on her part,[4] and myself on ours. So we stayed till sermon was done; and I took leave and to see Mr. Moore, who recovers well; and his doctor coming to him, one Dr Merritt, we had some of his very good discourse of Anatomy and other things, very pleasant. By and by I with Mr. Townsend walked in the garden, talking and advising with him about

1. A lace collar.
2. I.e. that land at Stirtloe (bequeathed by Pepys's Uncle Robert) would be used to support Tom's wife should he die first.
3. Elizabeth Butler, the prospective bride's mother.
4. Walter Smith, a scrivener and friend of the bride's family.

Toms business; and he tells me he will speak with Smith, and says I offer fair to give her 30*l* per annum joynture and no more.

Thence, Tom waiting for me, homewards toward my house, talking and schooling him for his folly, and telling him my mind plainly what he hath to trust to if he goes this way to work, for he shall never have her upon the terms they demand, of 50*l*.

He left me, and I to my uncle Wight and there supped; and there was pretty Mrs. Margtt Wight, whom I esteem very pretty and love dearly to look upon her. We were very pleasant, I drolling with my aunt and them. But I am sorry to hear that the news of the selling of Dunkirke is taken so generally ill, as I find it is among the merchants;[1] and other things, as removal of officers at Court, good for worse; and all things else made much worse in their report among people then they are. And this night, I know not upon what ground, the gates of the City ordered to be kept shut and double guards everywhere. So home; and after preparing things against tomorrow for the Duke, to bed.

Endeed, I do find everybody's spirit very full of trouble and the things of the Court and Council very ill taken – so as to be apt to appear in bad colours if there should ever be a beginning of trouble – which God forbid.

22. Up, and carrying my wife and her brother to Covent garden, near their father's new lodging, by coach, I to my Lord Sandwichs; who receives me now more and more kindly, now he sees that I am respected in the world – and is my most noble patron.

Here I stayed and talked about many things with my Lord and Mr. Puvy,[2] being there about Tanger businesses for which the Comission is in taking out.

Thence (after talking with Mr. Cooke, whom I met here, about Mrs. Butler's portion,[3] he doth persist to say that it will be worth 600*l* certain, when he knows as well as I do now, that it is but 400*l*; and so I told him. But he is a fool, and hath made fools of us). So I by water to my brother's and thence to Mr. Smith's, where I was last night; and there by appointment met Mrs. Butler, with whom I plainly discoursed, and she with me. I find she will give but 400*l* and no more, and is not willing to do that without a joynture, which she expects and I will not grant for that portion; and upon the

1. Dunkirk had been sold to the French in a treaty signed this month. The merchants feared (correctly) that it would provide a harbour for privateers.
2. Thomas Povey was Treasurer of Tangier.
3. That is, the dowry of Miss Hobell, Tom's intended bride. Mrs Butler was her mother and chief negotiator.

whole, I do find that Cooke hath made great brags on both sides and so hath abused us both, but know not how to help it – for I perceive she had much greater expectations of Toms house and being than she finds. But however, we did break off the business wholly, but with great love and kindness between her and me. And would have been glad had we known one another's minds sooner, without being misguided by this fellow, to both our shames and trouble. For I find her a very discreet, sober woman; and her daughter, I understand and believe, is a good lady; and if portions did agree, though she finds fault with Toms house and his imperfection in his speech, I believe we should well agree in other matters.[1] After taking a kind farewell, I to Toms and there did give him a full account of this sad news; with which I find he is much troubled, but doth appear to me willing to be guided herein, and apprehends that it is not for his good to do otherwise. And so I do persuade [him] to fallow his business again, and I hope he will. But for Cookes part and Dr Pepys, I shall know them for two fools another time.

Thence, it raining hard, by coach home (being first trimmed here by Benier; who being acquainted with all the players, doth tell me that Baterton is not married to Ianthe as they say;[2] but also that he is a very sober, serious man, and studious and humble, fallowing of his study, and is rich already with what he gets and saves); and there to my office till late, doing a great deal of business and settling my mind in pretty good order as to my business, though at present they are very many. So home and to bed.

This night was buried, as I hear by the bells at Barking church, my poor *Morena* – whose sickness being desperate did kill her poor father; and he being dead for sorrow, she said she could not recover more nor desire to live, but from that time doth languish more and more, and so is now dead and buried.[3]

31. Lay pretty long in bed; and then up and among my workmen – the Carpenters being this day laying of my floor in my dining-room, with whom I stayed a good while; and so to my office and

1. That was the end of this match. Instead of marrying Tom, in 1664 Elizabeth Hobell wed the rector of Alkerton, Oxfordshire, and appears to have had a successful marriage spanning over four decades. Given what Pepys would discover in 1664 about his brother's activities, Mrs Butler made a good call.
2. Thomas Betterton did not marry Mary Saunderson ("Ianthe") until 24 December.
3. "Morena" was Elizabeth Dickons from the neighbouring parish of All Hallows Barking, whom Pepys admired and nicknamed for her dark hair. Her father had died on 3 October.

did a little business, and so home to dinner; and after dinner, all the afternoon with my carpenters, making them lay all my boards but one in my dining-room this day, which I am confident they would have made two good days' work of if I had not been there. And it will be very pleasant. At night to my office and there late doing of my office businesses; and so home to supper and bed.

Thus ends this month. I and my family in good health, but weary heartily of dirt; but now in hopes within two or three weeks to be out of it. My head troubled with much business, but especially my fear of Sir J. Minnes claiming my bed-chamber of me; but I hope now that it is almost over, for I perceive he is fitting his house to go into it the next week. Then my law businesses for Brampton make me mad almost, for that I want time to fallow them; but I must by no means neglect them. I thank God I do save money, though it be but a little; but I hope to find out some jobb or other that I may get a sum by to set me up.

I am now also busy in a discovery for my Lord Sandwich and Sir H. Bennett by Mr. Wade's means, of some of Baxter's money hid in one of his cellars in the tower. If we get it, it may be I may be 10 or 20*l* the better for it.[1]

I thank God I have no crosses, but only much business to trouble my mind with. In all other things, as happy a man as any in the world, for the whole world seems to smile upon me; and if my house were done, that I could diligently fallow my business, I would not doubt to do God and the King, and myself, good service. And all I do impute almost wholly to my late temperance, since my making of my vowes against wine and plays, which keeps me most happily and contentfully to my business – which God continue.

Public matters are full of discontent – what with the sale of Dunkirke – and my Lady Castlemayne and her faction at Court; though I know not what they would have, more then to debauch the King, whom God preserve from it. And then great plots are talked to be discovered, and all the prisons in towne full of ordinary people taken from their meeting-places last Sunday.[2] But for certain, some plot there hath been, though not brought to a head.

1. This was treasure rumoured to have been hidden in the Tower of London by the executed regicide John Barkstead while he was Lieutenant there in the 1650s. Despite enthusiastic digging, nothing was found.
2. Large numbers of Quakers and Baptists were arrested.

NOVEMBER.

12. At my office most of the morning, after I had done among my painters and sent away Mr. Shaw and Hawly,[1] who came to give me a visit this morning. Shaw it seems, is newly remaryed to a rich widow. At noon dined at home with my wife. And by and by, by my wife's appointment comes two young ladies, sisters, acquaintance of my wife's brother's, who are desirous to wait upon some ladies – and proffer their service to my wife. The youngest, endeed, hath a good voice and sings very well, besides other good Qualitys; but I fear hath been bred up with too great liberty for my family, and I fear great inconveniences of expenses and my wife's liberty will fallow, which I must study to avoide till I have a better purse – though I confess the gentlewoman being pretty handsome and singing makes me have a good mind to her.[2]

Anon I took them by coach and carried them to a friend's of theirs in Lincolnes Inne fields, and there I left them. And I to the Temple by appointment to my Cosen Roger Pepys's chamber, where my Uncle Thomas and his son Tho met us, I having hopes that they would have agreed with me to have had ended by my Cosen Roger; but they will have two strangers to be for them, against two others of mine; and so we parted, without doing anything till they two send me the names of their Arbitraters.

Thence I walked home, calling a little in Paul's Churchyard; and I thank God, can read and never buy a book, though I have a great mind to it.◆

So home and to supper and bed. And a little before and after we were in bed, we had much talk and difference between us about my wife's having a woman; which I seemed much angry at that she should go so far in it without consideration and my being consulted with. So to sleep.

13. Up – and begun our discontent again and sorely angered my wife; who endeed doth live very lonely. But I do perceive that it is want of work that doth make her and all other people think of ways

1. Former Exchequer colleagues.
2. Elizabeth wanted the companionship and status afforded by employing a waiting woman – a step up from being accompanied by a maid. The candidate was Miss Gosnell (her first name may have been Winifred).

of spending their time worse; and this I owe to my building, that doth not admit of her undertaking anything of work, because the house hath been and is still so dirty.

I to my office and there sot all the morning, and dined with discontent with my wife at noon; and so to my office, and there this afternoon we had our first meeting upon our Comission for inspecting the chest.[1]◆

And this afternoon my wife in her discontent sent me a letter, which I am in a quandary what to do, whether to read it or not; but I purpose not, but to burn it before her face, that I may put a stop to more of this nature. But I must think of some way, either to find her somebody to keep her company, or to set her to work and by imployment to take up her thoughts and time. After doing what I had to do, I went home to supper. And there was very sullen to my wife, and so went to bed and to sleep (though with much ado, my mind being troubled) without speaking one word to her.

14. She begun to talk in the morning and to be friends, believing all this while that I had read her letter, which I perceive by her discourse was full of good counsel and relating the reason of her desiring a Woman and how little charge she did entend it to be to me. So I begun and argued it so full and plain to her, and she to reason it highly to me to put her away and take one of the Bowyers[2] if I did dislike her, that I did resolve, when the house is ready, she shall try her[3] for a while. The truth is, I having a mind to have her come for her Musique and dancing. So up and I about my painters all the morning; and her brother coming, I did tell him my mind plain, who did assure me that they were, both of the sisters, very humble and very poor, and that she that we are to have would carry herself so.◆

17. To the Duke's today, but he is gone a-hunting. And therefore I to my Lord Sandwichs; and having spoke a little with him about his business, I to Westminster-hall and there stayed long doing many businesses; and so home by the Temple and other places, doing the like. And at home I find my wife dressing by appointment, by her woman that I think is to be. And her other sister being here today with her and my wife's brother, I took Mr. Creede, that came to dine with me, to an ordinary behind the Change, and there

1. A commission to investigate the administration of charitable funds in the Chatham Chest.
2. Friends of the family, living in Westminster.
3. Gosnell.

dined together. And after dinner home and there spent an hour or two till almost dark, talking with my wife and making Mrs. Gosnell sing; and then, there being no coach to be got, by water to White-hall. But Gosnell not being willing to go through bridge,[1] we were forced to land and take water again, and put her and her sister ashore at the Temple. I am mightily pleased with her humour and singing. At White-hall, by appointment Mr. Creede carried my wife and I to the Cockepitt, and we had excellent places and saw the King, Queene, Duke of Monmouth his son, and my Lady Castlemayne and all the fine ladies; and *The Scornfull Lady*,[2] well performed. They had done by 11 a-clock; and it being fine Moone-shine, we took coach and home. But could wake nobody at my house, and so were fain to have my boy get through one of the windows and so opened the door – and called up the maids and went to supper and to bed – my mind being troubled at what my wife tells me, that her woman will not come till she hears from her mother. For I am so fond of her that I am loath now not to have her, though I know it will be a great charge to me, which I ought to avoid; and so I will make it up in other things. So to bed.

27. At my waking, I find the tops of the houses covered with snow, which is a rare sight, that I have not seen these three years.

Up, and put my people to perfect the cleaning of my house, and so to the office – where we sat all the morning till noon; and then we all went to the next house upon Tower hill to see the coming by of the Russia Embassador[3] – for whose reception all the City trained=bands do attend in the streets, and the King's Life-guard, and most of the wealthy citizens in their black velvet coats and gold chains (which remain of their gallantry at the King's coming in); but they stayed so long that we went down again home to dinner. And after I had dined, I heard that they were coming, and so I walked to the Conduict in the *quarrefour*[4] at the end of gracious-street[5] and cornhill; and there (the spouts thereof running, very near me, upon all the people that were under it) I saw them pretty well go by. I could not see the Embassador in his coach – but his attendants in their habitts and fur-caps very handsome comely men, and most of them with Hawkes upon their fists to present to

1. Travelling under London Bridge by boat was a risk due to the narrow channels.
2. A comedy by Beaumont and Fletcher, at the private royal theatre at Whitehall Palace.
3. Three envoys sent by Tsar Alexis.
4. Crossroads.
5. Gracechurch Street.

the King. But Lord, to see the absurd nature of Englishmen, that cannot forbear laughing and jeering at everything that looks strange.

So back and to the office; and there we met and sat till 7 a-clock, making a bargain with Mr. Wood for his Masts of New=England. And then in Mr. Coventry's coach to the Temple; but my Cosen Roger Pepys not being at leisure to speak to me about my business, I presently walked home and to my office till very late, doing business; and so home – where I find my house more and more clean and in order; and hope in a day or two now to be in very good condition there and to my full content – which God grant. So to supper and to bed.

30.◆ Thus ends this month, in great frost.

Myself and family all well, but my mind much disordered about my Uncles law-business, being now in an order of being arbitrated between us, which I wish to God it were done.

I am also somewhat uncertain what to think of my going about to take a woman-servant into my house in the Quality of a Woman for my wife. My wife promises it shall cost me nothing but her meat and wages, and that it shall not be attended with any other expenses; upon which termes I admit of it, for that it will I hope save me money in having my wife go abroad on visitts and other delights. So that I hope the best, but am resolved to alter it if matters prove otherwise then I would have them.

Public matters in an ill condition of discontent against the heighth and vanity of the Court and their bad payments; but that which troubles most is the Clergy, which will never content the City, which is not to be reconciled to Bishopps; the more the pity that differences must still be.

Dunkirke newly sold and the money brought over – of which we hope to get some to pay the Navy – which, by Sir J. Lawson's having dispatched the business in the Straights by making peace with Argier, Tunis and Tripoly, and so his fleet will also shortly come home, will now every day grow less, and so the King's charge be abated – which God send.

DECEMBER.

1. Up and by coach with Sir J. Mennes and Sir W. Batten to Whitehall to the Duke's chamber; where, as is usual, my Lord Sandwich

and all us, after his being ready, to his closet and there discoursed of matters of the Navy. And here Mr. Coventry did do me the great kindness to take notice to the Duke of my pains in making a collection of all Contracts about Masts, which hath been of good use to us. Thence I to my Lord Sandwiches to Mr. Moore to talk a little about business; and then over the parke (where I first in my life, it being a great frost, did see people sliding with their Sckeates, which is a very pretty art)[1] to Mr. Coventry's chamber to St. James's, where we all met to a venison pasty; and were here very merry, Major Norwood being with us, whom they did play upon for his surrendring of Dunkirke.[2]

Here we stayed till 3 or 4 a-clock, and so to the Council chamber, where there met – the Duke of Yorke, Prince Robert, Duke of Albermarle, my Lord Sandwich, Sir Wm. Compton, Mr. Coventry, Sir J. Minnes, Sir R. Ford, Sir W. Rider, my selfe, and Captain Cuttance, as Commissioners for Tanger. And after our Comission was read by Mr. Creede, who I perceive is to be our Secretary, we did fall to discourse of matters. As first, the supplying of them forthwith with victualls; then the Reducing it to make way for the money which upon their reduction is to go to the building of the molde.[3] And so to other matters ordered against next meeting.

This done, we broke up and I to the Cockepitt, with much crouding and waiting, where I saw *The Valiant Cidd* acted – a play I have read with great delight, but is a most dull thing acted (which I never understood before), there being no pleasure in it, though done by Baterton and my Ianthe and another fine wench that is come in the room of Roxalana.[4] Nor did the King or Queene once smile all the whole play, nor any of the company seem to take any pleasure but what was in the greatness and gallantry of the company.

Thence to my Lord's; and Mr. Moore being in bed, I stayed not, but with a link walked home and got thither by 12 a-clock. Knocked up my boy and put myself to bed.

1. Skating was an established pastime in the Netherlands, where skates might have iron-blades rather than the polished bones long used in England. Members of Charles's court seem to have picked up the skill while in exile.
2. Henry Norwood had been Deputy-Governor there.
3. A mole (a stone breakwater) was needed to protect Tangier's harbour from the Atlantic seas and to carry guns to defend the town. This was a major and costly feat of engineering.
4. An English version of Pierre Corneille's *Le Cid*, probably based on Joseph Rutter's translation. This was a performance by the Duke's Company at the private playhouse at Whitehall. The actress who replaced Hester Davenport ("Roxalana") was Mrs Norton.

5. Up, it being a snow and hard frost. And being up, I did call up Sarah, who doth go away today or tomorrow. I paid her her wages and gave her 10*s* myself and my wife 5*s* to give her. For my part, I think never servant and mistress parted upon such foolish terms in the world as they do, only for an opinion in my wife that she is ill-natured, in all other things being a good servant. The wench cried, and I was ready to cry too. But to keep peace, I am content she should go, and the rather, though I say nothing of that, that Jane may come into her place.[1]

This being done, I walked toward Guild-hall, thither being summond by the Comissioners for the Lieutenancy; but they sat not this morning. So meeting in my way W. Swan, I took him to a house thereabout and gave him a morning draught of butterd ale – he telling me still much of his fanatiques stories, as if he were a great zealot, when I know him to be a very rogue. But I do it for discourse and to see how things stand with him and his party; who I perceive have great expectation that God will not bless the Court nor Church as it is now settled, but they must be purifyed. The worst news he tells me is that Mr. Chetwind is dead, my old and most ingenious acquaintance. He is dead worth 3000*l*; which I did not expect, he living so high as he did alway, and neatly. He hath given W. Symons his wife 300*l* and made Will one of his executors.[2]

Thence to the Temple to my counsel and thence to Grays Inne to meet with Mr. Cole, but could not; and so took a turn or two in the garden, being very pleasant with the snow and frost. Thence to my brother's; and there I eat something at dinner and transcribed a copy or two of the state of my Uncles estate which I prepared last night; and so to the Temple church and there walked alone till 4 or 5 a-clock; and then to my Cosen Turner's Chamber and stayed there, up and down from his to Calthrops and Bernards chambers, till so late, that Mr. Cole not coming, we broke up for meeting this night; and so, taking my uncle Thomas homeward with me by coach, talking of our desire to have a peace, I set him down at Gracious-street end; and so I home and there I find Gosnell come, who my wife tells me is like to prove a pretty companion, of which I am glad. So to my office for a little business and then home – my mind having been all this day in most extraordinary trouble and

1. Jane Birch was working as the cookmaid; with Sarah's departure she would be promoted to chambermaid.
2. James Chetwind and Will Symons were government clerks and friends from Pepys's time at the Exchequer.

care for my father, there being so great appearance of my uncles going away with the greatest part of the estate. But in the evening, by Gosnells coming, I do put off these thoughts to entertain myself a little with my wife and her – who sings exceeding well, and I shall take great delight in her. And so merrily to bed.

8. Up; and carrying Gosnell by coach, set her down at Templebarr, she going about business of hers today. By the way she was telling me how Balty did tell her that my wife did go every day in the week to Court and plays, and that she should have liberty of going abroad as often as she pleased, and many other lies; which I am vexed at, and I doubt the wench did come in some expectation of – which troubles me.

So to the Duke and Mr. Coventry, I alone, the rest being at a pay and elsewhere. And alone with Mr. Coventry I did read over our letter to my Lord Treasurer, which I think now is done as well as it can be.[1] Then to my Lord Sandwiches and there spent the rest of the morning in making up my Lord's accounts with Mr. Moore; and then dined with Mr. Moore and Battersby his friend – very well, and merry and good discourse. Then into the parke to see them slide with their Scates, which is very pretty, and so to the Dukes, where the Comittee for Tanger met; and here we sat down all with him at a table and had much good discourse about that business – and is to my great content. That done, and hearing what play it was that is to be acted before the King tonight, I would not stay; but home by coach – where I find my wife troubled about Gosnell, who brings word that her uncle, Justice Jiggins, requires her to come three times a week to him to fallow some business that her mother intrusts her withal, and that unless she may have that leisure given her, he will not have her to take any place – for which we are both troubled, but there is no help for it; and believing it to be a good providence of God to prevent my running behind-hand in the world, I am somewhat contented therewith and shall make my wife so; who, poor wretch, I know will consider of things, though in good earnest, the privacy of her life must need be irke-some to her. So I made Gosnell [sing] and we sat up, looking over the book of Dances[2] till 12 at night, not observing how the time went; and so to prayers and to bed.

9. Lay long with my wife, contenting her about the business of

1. A statement of accounts from the Navy Board.
2. This was a book of country dances, probably by John Playford.

Gosnells going, and I perceive she will be contented as well as myself. And so to the office; and after sitting all the morning in hopes to have had Mr. Coventry dined with me, he was forced to go to White-hall. And so I dined with my own company only, taking Mr. Hater home with me; but he, poor man, was not very well and so could not eat anything. After dinner stayed within all the afternoon, being vexed in my mind about the going away of Sarah this afternoon, who cried mightily, and so was I ready to do, and Jane did also. And then anon went Gosnell away, which did trouble me too, though upon many considerations it is better that I am rid of that charge. Altogether makes my house appear to me very lonely, which troubles me much; and in a melancholly humour I went to the office, and there about business sat till I was called to Sir G. Carteret at the Treasury office about my Lord Treasurer's letter, wherein he puts me to a new trouble to write it over again. So home, and late with Sir J. Mennes at the office, looking over Mr. Creedes accounts; and then home and to supper. And my wife and I melancholy to bed.

25. *Christmas day*. Up pretty early, leaving my wife not well in bed.[1] And with my boy walked, it being a most brave cold and dry frosty morning, and had a pleasant walk to White-hall; where I entended to have received the Comunion with the family,[2] but I came a little too late. So I walked up into the house and spent my time looking over pictures, perticularly the ships in King H the 8ths voyage to Bullen[3] – marking the great difference between their build then and now. By and by down to the Chappell again, where Bishop Morly preached upon the Song of the Angels – "Glory to God on high – on earth peace, and good will towards men."[4] Methought he made but a poor sermon, but long and reprehending the mistaken jollity of the Court for the true joy that shall and ought to be on these days. Perticularized concerning their excess in playes and gameing, saying that he whose office it is to keep the Gamesters in order and within bounds serves but for a second rather in a Duell, meaning the Groome porter.[5] Upon which, it was worth observing how far

1. Elizabeth suffered badly from painful periods, and this was one such occasion.
2. The (lesser) members of the royal household.
3. *The Embarkation of Henry VIII at Dover* shows the fleet leaving for Calais in 1520. It is now at Hampton Court. "Bullen" means Boulogne.
4. A loose recollection of Luke 2.14. George Morley (Bishop of Winchester) was Dean of the Chapel Royal.
5. The Groom-Porter was an officer in the King's Household who supervised and received profits of the gaming allowed there during the twelve days of Christmas. Like the seconds who organized a duel, therefore, he supervised sin.

they are come from taking the Reprehensions of a Bishop seriously, that they all laugh in the chapel when he reflected on their ill actions and courses.

He did much press us to joy in these public days of joy and to Hospitality. But one that stood by whispered in my eare that the Bishop himself doth not spend one groate to the poor himself.

The sermon done, a good Anthemne fallowed, with vialls; and then the King came down to receive the Sacrament, but I stayed not; but calling my boy from my Lord's lodging and giving Sarah some good advice, by my Lord's order, to be Sober and look after the house,[1] I walked home again with great pleasure; and there dined by my wife's bedside with great content, having a mess of brave plum-porridge and a roasted Pullett for dinner; and I sent for a mince-pie abroad, my wife not being well to make any herself yet. After dinner sat talking a good while with her, her [pain] being become less, and then to see Sir W. Penn a little; and so to my office, practising arithmetique alone and making an end of last night's book,[2] with great content, till 11 at night; and so home to supper and to bed.

26. Up. My wife to the making of Christmas-pies all day, being now pretty well again. And I abroad to several places about small businesses; among others, bought a bake=pan in Newgate-market and sent it home; it cost me 16*s*. So to Dr Williams, but he is out of town; then to [Mr. Moore at] the Wardrobe, who is not yet well. Hither came Mr. Battersby; and we falling into a discourse of a new book of Drollery in verse called *Hudebras*, I would needs go find it out; and met with it at the Temple, cost me 2*s*-6*d*.[3] But when I came to read it, it is so silly an abuse of the Presbyter-Knight going to the warrs, that I am ashamed of it; and by and by meeting at Mr. Townsends at dinner, I sold it to him for 18*d*. Here we dined with many Tradesmen that belong to the Wardrobe, but I was weary soon of their company and broke up dinner as soon as I could and away, with the greatest reluctancy and dispute (two or three times, my reason stopping my Sence and I would go back again) within

1. Sandwich's housekeeper, whose drinking concerned her employer.
2. *Trade Revived* (first pub. 1659), a work on improving international commerce. It was by John Bland, a merchant of Pepys's acquaintance.
3. The first part of Samuel Butler's mock-heroic poem *Hudibras* was newly published and would prove a runaway success. It ridiculed Presbyterians through the exploits of Sir Hudibras.

myself, to the Duke's house and saw *The Villaine*[1] – which I ought not to do without my wife, but that my time is now out that I did undertake it for. But Lord, to consider how my natural desire is to pleasure, which God be praised that he hath given me the power by my late oaths to curbe so well as I have done; and will do again, after two or three plays more. Here I was better pleased with the play then I was at first, understanding the design better then I did. Here I saw Gosnell and her sister at a distance, and could have found my heart to have accosted them, but thought it not prudent. But I watched their going out and found that they came, she, her sister and another woman, alone, without any man, and did go over the fields afoote. I find that I have an inclinacion to have her come again, though it is most against my interest, either of profit or content of mind, other then for her singing.◆

Thence home, and find my wife busy among her pies, but angry for some sawcy words that her maid Jane hath given her; which I will not allow of and therefore will give her warning to be gone. As also, we are both displeased for some slight words that Sarah, now at Sir W. Penn's, hath spoke of us; but it is no matter, we shall endeavour to joyne the Lyon's skin to the Foxes tail.[2]

So to my office alone a while, and then home to my study and supper and bed – being also vexed at my boy, for his staying playing abroad when he is sent on errands, so that I have sent him tonight to see whether their country-Carrier[3] be in Towne or no, for I am resolve[d] to keep him no longer.

31. Lay pretty long in bed; and then I up and to Westminster-hall and so to the Swan, sending for Mr. Wm. Bowyer, and there drank my morning's draught and had some of his simple discourse.◆

Thence to a barbers, and so to my wife and at noon took her to Mrs. Pierces by invitation to dinner; where there came Dr. Clerke and his wife and sister and Mr. Knight, chief Chyrurgeon to the King, and his wife. We were pretty merry, the two men being excellent company; but I confess I am wedded from that opinion either of Mrs. Pierces beauty, upon discovery of her naked neck today, being undressed when we came in, or of Mrs. Clerkes genius, which I so much admired, I finding her to be so conceited and

1. A new tragedy by Thomas Porter, performed at the Lincoln's Inn Fields Theatre. Pepys had disliked it on seeing it earlier in the month.
2. "To piece the lion's skin with the fox's tail" was a proverb meaning "where force will not succeed, use cunning". It came from Plutarch's *Moralia* and "Life of Lysander".
3. A carrier service to Gloucestershire, where Wayneman Birch's family lived.

fantaske[1] in her dress this day, and carriage; though the truth is, witty enough.

After dinner, with much ado the Doctor and I got away to fallow our business for a while, he to his patients and I to the Tanger Comittee, where the Duke of Yorke was and we stayed at it a good while; and thence, in order to the dispatch of the boates and provisions for Tanger, away; Mr. Povy in his coach carried Mr. Gauden and I into London to Mr. Blands the merchant, where we stayed discoursing upon the reason of the delay of the going away of those things a great while.[2] Then to eat a dish of Anchoves and drink wine and Syder, and very merry, but above all, pleased to hear Mrs. Bland talk like a merchant in her husband's business very well; and it seems she doth understand it and perform a great deal. Thence merry back, Mr. Povy and I, to White-hall, he carrying me thither on purpose to carry me into the Ball this night before the King. All the way, he talking very ingenuously; and I find him a fine gentleman and one that loves to live nobly and neatly, as I perceive by his discourse of his house, pictures, and horses.

He brought me first to the Duke's chamber, where I saw him and the Duchesse at supper, and thence into the room where the Ball was to be, crammed with fine ladies, the greatest of the Court. By and by comes the King and Queen, the Duke and Duchesse, and all the great ones; and after seating themselfs, the King takes out the Duchess of Yorke, and the Duke the Duchesse of Buckingham, the Duke of Monmouth my Lady Castlemayne, and so other lords other ladies; and they danced the Bransle.[3] After that, the King led a lady a single Coranto;[4] and then the rest of the lords, one after another, other ladies. Very noble it was, and great pleasure to see. Then to Country dances; the King leading the first which he called for; which was – says he, *Cuckolds all a-row*, the old dance of England.[5] Of the ladies that danced, the Duke of Monmouth's mistress and my Lady Castlemayne and a daughter of Sir Harry De Vickes were the best. The manner was, when the King dances, all the ladies in the room, and the Queen herself, stands up; and endeed he dances rarely and much better then the Duke of Yorke.

1. Fantastic, bizarre.
2. Povey was Treasurer of Tangier, while Denis Gauden (the Navy Victualler) and John Bland were involved in supplying Tangier. Bland ran his business with his wife Sarah.
3. A branle was a French dance in a circle or chain, suited to any number of people.
4. Probably a French courante, a solemn and stately dance.
5. The dance and tune were in Playford's popular *The English Dancing Master* (first pub. 1651).

Having stayed here as long as I thought fit, to my infinite content, it being the greatest pleasure I could wish now to see at Court, I went out, leaving them dancing, and to Mrs. Pierces; where I find the company had stayed very long for my coming, but all gone but my wife; so I took her home by coach, and so to my Lord's again. Where, after some supper, to bed – very weary and in a little pain from my riding a little uneasily tonight (for my testicles) in the coach.

Thus ended this year, with great mirth to me and my wife. Our condition being thus – we are at present spending a night or two at my Lord's lodgings at White-hall. Our home at the Navy office – which is and hath a pretty while been in good condition, finished and made very convenient. My purse is worth about 650*l* – besides my goods of all sorts – which yet might have been more but for my late layings-out upon my house and public assessement, and yet would not have been so much if I had not lived a very orderly life all this year, by virtue of the oaths that God put into my heart to take against wine, plays, and other expenses, and to observe for these last twelve months – and which I am now going to renew, I under God oweing my present content thereunto. My family is myself and wife – Wm. my clerk – Jane, my wife's upper-maid; but I think growing proud and negligent upon it, we must part; which troubles me – Susan our cook-maid, a pretty willing wench but no good cook – and Waynman my boy, who I am now turning away for his naughty tricks. We have had from the beginning our healths to this day, very well, blessed be God. Our late mayde Sarah going from us (though put away by us) to live with Sir W. Penn doth trouble me, though I love the wench – so that we do make ourselfs a little strange to him and his family for it, and resolve to do so.

The same we are, for other reasons, to my Lady Batten and hers.

We have lately had it in our thoughts, and I can hardly bring myself off of it since Mrs. Gosnell cannot be with us, to find out another to be in the quality of a Woman to my wife, that can sing or dance. And yet finding it hard to save anything at the year's end as I now live, I think I shall not be such a fool – till I am more warm in my purse; besides my oath of entering into no such expenses till I am worth 1000*l*.

By my last year's diligence in my office, blessed be God, I am come to a good degree of knowledge therein; and am acknowledged so by all the world, even the Duke himself, to whom I have a good accesse, and by that and my being Comissioner with him for Tanger, he takes much notice of me, and I doubt not but by the continuance of the same endeavours I shall in a little time come to be a man much taken notice of in the world – especially, being come to so great an esteem with Mr. Coventry.

The only weight that lies heavy upon my mind is the ending the business with my uncle Thomas about my dead uncles estate, which is very ill on our side; and I fear, when all is done, I must be forced to maintain my father myself, or spare a good deal towards it out of my own purse – which will be a very great pull-backe to me in my fortune. But I must be contented and bring it to an issue one way or other.

Public matters stand thus. The King is bringing, as is said, his family and Navy and all other his charges to a less expense. In the meantime, himself fallowing his pleasures more then with good advice he would do – at least, to be seen to all the world to do so – his dalliance with my Lady Castlemayne being public every day, to his great reproach. And his favouring of none at Court so much as those that are the confidants of his pleasure as Sir H. Bennet and Sir Ch. Barkely[1] – which good God put it into his heart to mend – before he makes himself too much contemned by his people for it.

The Duke of Monmouth is in so great splendour at Court and so dandled by the King, that some doubt, if the King should have no child by the Queene (which there is yet no appearance of), whether he would not be acknowledged for a lawful son. And that there will a difference fallow upon it between the Duke of York – and him – which God prevent.[2]

My Lord Chancellor is threatened by people to be Questioned, the next sitting of the parliament, by some spirits that do not love to see him so great. But certainly he is a good servant to the King.

The Queene Mother is said to keep too great a Court now; and her being married to my Lord St. Albans is commonly talked of, and that they had a daughter between them in France. How true, God knows.[3]

The Bishopps are high[4] and go on without any diffidence in pressing uniformity; and the Presbyters seem silent in it and either

1. Sir Henry Bennet had recently been made Secretary of State and Sir Charles Berkeley made Keeper of the Privy Purse.
2. A very early reference to rumours about Monmouth's legitimacy. In the late 1670s claims that he was legitimate would add fuel to the political crisis over the Duke of York's right, as a Catholic convert, to succeed Charles. In 1685, on James's accession, Monmouth staged a failed rebellion to seize the throne and was executed.
3. The rumours of marriage and a child were untrue.
4. Arrogant.

conform or lay down, though without doubt they expect a turn and would be glad these endeavours of the other Fanatiques would take effect – there having been a plot lately found, for which four have been publicly tried at the old Bayly and hanged.[1]

My Lord Sandwich is still in good esteem, and now keeping his Christmas in the country. And I in good esteem, I think, as any man can be with him.

Mr. Moore is very sickly, and I doubt will hardly get over his late fit of sickness that still hangs on him.

In fine, for the good condition of myself, wife, family and estate, in the great degree that it is, and for the public state of the nation, so quiet as it is, the Lord God be praised.

1. Four men had been executed on the 22nd for plotting an insurrection in London. At their trial the plot was represented as uniting "Fifth Monarchy Men, Anabaptists, Independents, and Fighting Quakers".

1663

JANUARY.

1. Lay with my wife at my Lord's lodgings, where I have been these two nights, till 10 a-clock with great pleasure talking; and then I rose. And to White-hall, where I spent a little time walking among the Courtiers, which I perceive I shall be able to do with great confidence, being now beginning to be pretty well-known among them.

Then to my wife again and dined, Mrs. Sarah with us, in the chamber we lay in. Among other discourse, Mrs. Sarah[1] tells us how the King sups at least four or [five] times every week with my Lady Castlemayne; and most often stays till the morning with her and goes home through the garden all alone privately, and that so as the very Centry's take notice of it and speak of it.

She tells me that about a month ago she quickened[2] at my Lord Gerrards at dinner and cried out that she was undone; and all the lords and men were fain to quit the room, and women called to help her.

In fine, I find that there is nothing almost but bawdry at Court from top to bottom, as if it were fit I could instance, but it is not necessary. Only, they say my Lord Chesterfield, Groom of the Stole to the Queene, is either gone or put away from Court upon the score of his lady's having smitten the Duke of York, so as that he is watched by the Duchesse of Yorke and the lady is retired into the country upon it. How much of this is true, God knows, but it is common talk.

After dinner I did reckon with Mrs. Sarah for what we have eat and drank here, and gave her a crowne; and so took coach and to the Duke's house, where we saw *The Villaine* again;[3] and the more I see it, the more I am offended at my first undervaluing the play, it being very good and pleasant and yet a true and allowable Tragedy. The house was full of Citizens and so the less pleasant, but that I was willing to make an end of my gaddings and to set to my business for all the year again tomorrow. Here we saw the old

1. Sarah was Sandwich's housekeeper. Lady Castlemaine's house in Westminster was next door to Sandwich's.
2. Felt her unborn child begin to move.
3. Thomas Porter's tragedy at the Lincoln's Inn Fields Theatre.

Roxalana[1] in the chief box, in a velvet gowne as the fashion is and very handsome, at which I was glad.

Thence by coach home, where I finde all well. Only, Sir W. Penn they say ill again. So to my office to set down these two or three days' journall and to close the last year therein. And so that being done, home to supper and to bed – with great pleasure talking and discoursing with my wife of our late observations abroad.

8. Up pretty earely and sent my boy to the Carriers with some wine for my father, for to make his feast among his Brampton friends this Christmas – and my Muffe to my mother, sent as from my wife. But before I sent my boy out with them, I beat him for a lie he told me – at which his sister (with whom we have of late been highly displeased, and warned her to be gone) was angry;[2] which vexed me, to see the girl I loved so well, and my wife, should at last turn so much a fool and unthankful to us.

So to the office and there all the morning; and though without and a little against the advice of the officers, did to gratify him send Tho. Hater today towards Portsmouth a day or two before the rest of the clerks, against the pay next week.

Dined at home; and there being the famous new play acted the first time today, which is call[ed] *The Adventures of five houres*, at the Duke's house, being they say made or translated by Collonell Tuke,[3] I did long to see it and so made my wife to get her ready, though we were forced to send for a smith to break open her Trunke, her maid Jane being gone forth with the keyes. And so we went; and though earely, were forced to sit almost out of sight at the end of one of the lower formes, so full was the house. And the play, in one word, is the best, for the variety and the most excellent continuance of the plot to the very end, that ever I saw or think ever shall. And all possible, not only to be done in that time, but in most other respects very admittible and without one word of ribaldry. And the house, by its frequent plaudites, did show their sufficient approbacion. So home, with much ado in an hour getting a coach home; and after writing letters at my office, I went home to supper and to bed – now resolving to set up my rest as to plays till Easter, if not Whitsuntide next, excepting plays at Court.

9. Waking in the morning, my wife I found also awake, and begun

1. Hester Davenport, formerly an actress at this theatre.
2. Jane Birch, sister of Wayneman.
3. An adaptation of the Spanish comedy *Los empeños de seis horas* made by Samuel Tuke.

to speak to me with great trouble and tears; and by degrees, from one discourse to another, at last it appears that Sarah hath told somebody that hath told my wife of my meeting her at my brother's and making her set down by me while she told me stories of my wife, about her giving her Scallop to her brother and other things[1] – which I am much vexed at, for I am sure I never spoke anything of it, nor could anybody tell her but by Sarahs own words. I endeavoured to excuse my silence herein hitherto, by not believing anything she told me; only that of the Scallop, which she herself told me of. At last we were pretty good friends and my wife begun to speak again of the necessity of her keeping somebody to bear her company; for her familiarity with her other servants is it that spoils them all, and other company she hath none (which is too true); and called for Jane to reach her out of her trunk, giving her the keys to that purpose, a bundle of papers; and pulls out a paper, a copy of what, a pretty while since, she had writ in a discontent to me, which I would not read but burned.[2] She now read it, and was so picquant, and wrote in English and most of it true, of the retirednesse of her life and how unpleasant it was, that being writ in English and so in danger of being met with and read by others, I was vexed at it and desired her and then commanded her to teare it – which she desired to be excused it; I forced it from her and tore it, and withal took her other bundle of papers from her and leapt out of the bed and in my shirt clapped them into the pockets of my breeches, that she might not get them from me; and having got on my stockings and breeches and gown, I pulled them out one by one and tore them all before her face, though it went against my heart to do it, she crying and desiring me not to do it. But such was my passion and trouble to see the letters of my love to her, and my Will, wherein I had given her all I have in the world when I went to sea with my Lord Sandwich, to be joyned with a paper of so much disgrace to me and dishonour if it should have been found by anybody. Having tore them all, saving a bond of my uncle Robts. which she hath long had in her hands, and our Marriage=licence and the first letter that ever I sent her when I was her servant,[3] I took up the pieces and carried them into my chamber, and there, after many disputes with myself whether I should burn them or no, and having picked

1. Sarah, the Pepyses' former maid, had gone to work for Sir William Penn. In mid-December 1662 she had warned Pepys about his brother-in-law Balty begging a lace neckerchief and money from Elizabeth.
2. The letter from their fight on 13 Nov. 1662.
3. Suitor.

up the pieces of the paper she read today and of my Will which I tore, I burnt all the rest. And so went out to my office – troubled in mind.

Hither comes Major Tolhurst, one of my old acquaintance in Cromwell's time and sometimes of our clubb,[1] to see me, and I could do no less then carry him to the Miter; and thither having sent for Mr. Beane, a merchant, a neighbour of mine, we sat and talk – Tolhurst telling me the manner of their Collierys in the North. We broke up, and I home to dinner.

And to see my folly, as discontented as I am, when my wife came I could not forbear smiling all dinner, till she begun to speak bad words again; and then I begun to be angry again, and so to my office.

Mr. Bland came in the evening to me hither, and sat talking to me about many things of Merchandize; and I should be very happy in his discourse, durst I confess my ignorance to him, which is not so fit for me to do.

There coming a letter to me from Dr. Pierce the Surgeon, by my desire appointing his and Dr Clerkes coming to dine with me next Monday, I went to my wife and agreed upon matters; and at last, for my honour am forced to make her presently a new Moyre[2] gown to be seen by Mrs. Clerke; which troubles me to part with so much money, but however it sets my wife and I to friends again, though I and she never were so heartily angry in our lives as today almost, and I doubt the heart-burning will not soon over. And the truth is, I am sorry for the tearing of so many poor loving letters of mine from Sea and elsewhere to her.

So to my office again, and there the Scrivener brought me the end of my Manuscript which I am going to get together of things of the Navy – which pleases me much. So home – mighty friends with my wife again, and so to bed.

30. *A solemne Fast for the King's murther.* And we were forced to keep it more then we would have done, having forgot to take any victuals into the house.

I to church in the forenoon, and Mr. Mills made a good sermon upon David's heart smiting him for cutting off the garment of Saule.[3]

1. Jeremiah Tolhurst, now a customs officer in Newcastle active in the coal trade, had been a member of the club of government clerks who met in the late 1650s.
2. Moire: watered silk.
3. 1 Samuel 24.5.

Home and whiled away some of the afternoon at home, talking with my wife. So to my office, and all alone making up my month's accounts; which to my great trouble I find that I am got no further then 640*l* – but I have had great expenses this month. I pray God the next may be a little better, as I hope it will. In the evening my manuscript is brought home, handsomely bound to my full content; and now I think I have a better collection in reference to the Navy, and shall have by the time I have filled it, then any of my predecessors. So home to eat something, such as we have, bread and butter and milk; and so to bed.

FEBRUARY.

1. *Lords day.* Up and to church, where Mr. Mills; a good sermon. And so home and had a good dinner with my wife, with which I was pleased to see it neatly done; and this troubled me, to think of parting with Jane, that is come to be a very good Cooke. After dinner walked to my Lord Sandwich and stayed with him in the chamber talking almost all the afternoon, he being not yet got abroad since his sickness. Many discourses we had; but among others, how Sir R. Bernard is turned out of his Recordership of Huntington by the Comissioners for Regulacion, &c.,[1] at which I am troubled because he thinking it is done by my Lord Sandwich, will act some of his revenge, it is likely, upon me in my business – so that I must cast about me to get some other good counsel to rely upon.

In the evening came Mr. Povey and others to see my Lord; and they gone, my Lord and I and Povey fell to the business of Tanger – as to the victualling, and so broke up; and I, it being a fine frost, my boy lighting me I walked home. And after supper, up to prayers and then alone with my wife and Jane did fall to tell her what I did expect would become of her, since after so long being my servant she hath carried herself so as to make us be willing to put her away; and desired God to bless, but bid her never to let me hear of her what became of her, for that I could never pardon ingratitude.[2] So to bed – my mind much troubled for the poor girl that she leaves us; and yet she not submitting herself for some words she spoke

1. Commissioners for the regulation of corporations were charged with ensuring all local officials were loyal to the crown. Sandwich was a Commissioner for Huntingdon.
2. Jane Birch left the next day.

boldly and yet I believe innocently and out of familiarity to her mistress about six weeks ago, I could not recall my words that she should not stay with me. ⟨This day Creed and I, walking in Whitehall garden, did see the King coming privately from my Lady Castlemayns; which is a poor thing for a Prince to do. And I expressed my sense of it to Creed in termes which I should not have done, but that I believe he is trusty in that point.⟩

3. To the office all the morning; at noon to dinner, where Mr. Creede dined with me – and Mr. Ashwell, with whom after dinner I discoursed concerning his daughter coming to live with us.[1] I find that his daughter will be very fit, I think as any for our turn. But the conditions, I know not what they will be, he leaving it wholly to her, which will be agreed on a while hence when my wife sees her. After an hour's discourse after dinner with them, I to my office again and there about businesses of the office till late; and then I home to supper and to bed.

6. Up and to my office about business, examining people what they could swear against Field; and the whole is, that he hath called us cheating rogues and cheating knaves – for which we hope to be even with him.[2]

Thence to Lincoln Inn fields; and it being too soon to go to dinner, I walked up and down and looked upon the outside of the new Theatre now a-building in Covent garden, which will be very fine;[3] and so to a bookseller's in the Strand and there bought *Hudibras* again,[4] it being certainly some ill humour to be so set against that which all the world cries up to be the example of wit – for which I am resolved once again to read him and see whether I can find it or no. So to Mr. Povys and there find them at dinner and dined there – there being, among others, Mr Williamson, Latin Secretary, who I perceive is a pretty knowing man and a scholar, but it may be thinks himself to be too much so.[5] Thence after dinner to

1. Mary Ashwell was to be Elizabeth's new companion. Her father had worked with Pepys at the Exchequer.
2. In early 1662 Edward Field had accused the Navy Board of failing to act on information he had given about the embezzlement of timber. This led to a series of legal actions, with Field being arrested for slander and in turn suing Navy Board members for false imprisonment.
3. The new Theatre Royal being built for Thomas Killigrew between Drury Lane and Bridges Street.
4. Pepys first purchased Butler's satirical poem on 26 Dec. 1662 and immediately sold it again.
5. Joseph Williamson, under-secretary to Secretary of State Bennet and himself a future Secretary of State.

the Temple to my Cosen Roger Pepys, where met us my uncle Tho. and his son; and after many high demands, we at last came to a kind of agreement upon very hard terms, which are to be prepared in writing against Tuesday next.[1] But by the way, promising them to pay my Cosen Marys Legacys at the time of her Marriage, they afterward told me she was already married, and married very well, so that I must be forced to pay that in some time.

My Cosen Roger was so sensible of our coming to agreement that he could not forbear weeping; and endeed, though it be very hard, yet I am glad to my heart that we are like to end our trouble. So we parted for tonight.

And I to my Lord Sandwich and there stayed, there being a Comittee to sit upon the Contract for the Molle,[2] which I dare say none of us that were there understood; but yet they agreed of things as Mr Cholmly and Sir J Lawson demanded, who are the undertakers;[3] and so I left them to go on to agree, for I understood it not.

So home; and being called by a coachman who had a fare in him, he carried me beyond the Old Exchange and there set down his fare, who would not pay him what was his due because he carried a stranger with him; and so after wrangling, he was fain to be content with *6d.*; and being vexed, the coachman would not carry me home a great while, but set me down there for the other *6d.* But with fair words he was willing to it; and so I came home and to my office, setting business in order; and so home to supper and to bed – my mind being in disorder as to the greatness of this day's business that I have done, but yet glad that my trouble therein is like to be over.

8. *Lords day.* Up; and it being a very great frost, I walked to Whitehall and to my Lord Sandwiches; by the fireside till chapel time and so to chapel, where there preached little Dr. Duport of Cambrige upon Josiahs words, "But I and my house, we will serve the Lord."[4] But though a great scholar, he made the most flat, dead sermon, both for matter and manner of delivery, that ever I heard; and very long beyond his hour, which made it worse.

1. The dispute with Thomas Pepys over Robert Pepys's will was largely resolved by this out-of-court settlement. Thomas Pepys was awarded more land and money than his brother's will had allotted him in return for dropping his legal claims to the rest of the estate. Some matters involving debts due to the estate had yet to be settled.
2. A contract to construct the mole at Tangier.
3. Contractors.
4. James Duport was chaplain to the King. His text was Joshua (not Josiah) 24.15.

Thence with Mr. Creede to the King's-head ordinary, where we dined well; and after dinner Sir Tho. Willis[1] and another stranger and Creede and I fell a-talking – they of the errours and corruptions of the Navy and great expense thereof, not knowing who I was – which at last I did undertake to confute and disabuse them; and they took it very well and I hope it was to good purpose, they being Parliament-men. By and by to my Lord's and with him a good while, talking upon his want of money and ways of his borrowing some, &c. And then by other visitants, I withdrew and away; Creede and I and Captain Ferrers to the parke, and there walked finely, seeing people slide – we talking all the while and Captain Ferrers telling me, among other Court passages – how about a month ago, at a Ball at Court, a child was dropped by one of the ladies in dancing; but nobody knew who, it being taken up by somebody in their handkercher. The next morning all the Ladies of Honour appeared early at Court for their vindication, so that nobody could tell whose this mischance should be. But it seems Mrs. Wells fell sick that afternoon and hath disappeared ever since, so that it is concluded it was her.[2] Another story was how my Lady Castlemayne, a few days since, had Mrs. Stuart to an entertainment, and at night begun a frolique that they two must be married; and married they were, with ring and all other ceremonies of church service, and ribbands and a sack-posset in bed and flinging the stocking.[3] But in the close, it is said that my Lady Castlemayne, who was the bridegroom, rose, and the King came and took her place with pretty Mrs. Stuart. This is said to be very true.[4]◆

19. Up and to my office, where abundance of business all the morning. Dined by my wife's bedside, she not being yet well.[5] We fell out almost upon my discourse of delaying the having of Ashwell come, my wife believing that I have a mind to have Pall; which I have not, though I could wish she did deserve to be had. So to my office, where by and by we sat, this afternoon being the first that we have met upon a great while – our times being changed because of the parliament sitting. Being rose, I to my office till 12

1. Willys had been an MP in the last parliament.
2. Winifred Wells was a Maid of Honour to the Queen.
3. The newly married couple's stockings were flung at them by the wedding party – tradition claimed that hitting the bride or bridegroom was a sign the thrower would soon be married. Sack-posset drink was served to the couple.
4. Frances Stuart was a Maid of Honour to Queen Catherine and, at 15, already a famous beauty. Although reported at this time to have become the King's mistress, she seems to have resisted his advances.
5. She was suffering badly from period pain.

at night, drawing out Copys of the Overcharge of the Navy – one to send to Mr. Coventry early tomorrow. So home and to bed, being weary, sleepy, and my eyes begin to fail me, looking so long by candlelight upon white paper.[1]

This day I read the King's speech to the parliament yesterday; which is very short and not very obliging, but only telling them his desire to have a power of indulging tender consciences, not that he will yield to have any mixture in the uniformity of the Church discipline. And says the same for the papist, but declares against their ever being admitted to have any offices or places of trust in the kingdom – but God knows, too many have.

26. Up, and drinking a draught of wormwood wine with Sir W. Batten at the Steelyard, he and I by water to the parliament-house. He went in and I walked up and down the hall. All the news is the great odds yesterday in the votes between them that are for the indulgence to the papists and presbyters and those that are against it, which did carry it by 200 against 30.[2] And pretty it is to consider how the King would appear to be a stiff Protestant and son of the Church, and yet would appear willing to give a liberty to these people because of his promise at Breda.[3] And yet all the world doth believe that the King would not have this liberty given them at all.

Thence to my Lord's, who I hear hath his ague again, for which I am sorry. And Creed and I to the King's-head ordinary, where much good company – among the rest, a young gallant lately come from France who was full of his French; but methought not very good, but he had enough to make him think himself a wise man a great while. Thence by water from the New Exchange home to the Tower; and so sat at the office and then writing letters till 11 at night.

Troubled this evening that my wife is not come home from Chelsey, whither she is gone to see the Play at the Schoole where Ashwell is.[4] But she came at last, it seems by water, it being cold and

1. This is the first clear reference to the eye condition that would cause Pepys to end his diary, wrongly fearing he was going blind. The exact causes are debated, but he appears to have suffered from longsightedness, astigmatism, and convergence insufficiency.
2. There was no division to vote on this issue. The previous day the House had voted 269 to 30 to debate the King's speech of 18 February concerning the Act of Uniformity.
3. In the Declaration of Breda (April 1660) the King had promised liberty to tender consciences.
4. Mary Ashwell taught the small children at the school.

dark; but came well and tells me she is much pleased with Ashwells acting and carriage, which I am glad of.

So home and to supper and bed.

27. Up and to my office, whither several persons came to me about office business. About 11 a-clock Comissioner Pett and I walked to Chyrurgeons hall (we being all invited thither and promised to dine there), where we were led into the Theatre;[1] and by and by came the Reader, Dr Tearne, with the Maister and Company, in a very handsome manner; and all being settled, he begun his lecture, this being the second upon the Kidnys, Ureters, and yard,[2] which was very fine; and his discourse being ended, we walked into the hall; and there being great store of company we had a fine dinner and good learned company, many Doctors of Physique, and we used with extraordinary great respect.

Among other observables, we drank the King's health out of a gilt cupp given by King Henry the 8th to this Company, with bells hanging at it, which every man is to ring by shaking after he hath drunk up the whole cup. There is also a very excellent piece of the King done by Holben stands up in the hall, with the officers of the Company kneeling to him to receive their charter.[3]

After dinner Dr. Scarborough took some of his friends, and I went along with them, to see the body alone; which we did; he was a lusty fellow, a seaman that was hanged for a robbery. I did touch the dead body with my bare hand; it felt cold, but methought it was a very unpleasant sight.

It seems one Dillon, of a great family, was, after much endeavours to have saved him, hanged with a silken halter this Sessions (of his owne preparing) not for honour only, but it seems, it being saft and slick, it doth slip close and kills, that is, strangles presently; whereas a stiff one doth not come so close together and so the party may live the longer before killed. But all the Doctors at table conclude that there is no pain at all in hanging, for that it doth stop the circulacion of the blood and so stops all sense and motion in an instant.

Thence we went into a private room, where I perceive they prepare the bodies, and there was the Kidnys, Ureters, yard, stones and semenary vessels upon which he read today. And Dr Scarborough,

1. This was a public anatomy lecture held by the Company of Barber-Surgeons at their hall.
2. Penis.
3. *Henry VIII and the Barber-Surgeons* (c.1542), by Hans Holbein the younger.

upon my desire and the company's, did show very clearly the manner of the disease of the stone and the cutting and all other Questions that I could think of, and the manner of the seed, how it comes into the yard, and how the water into the bladder, through the three skinnes or coats, just as poor Dr Jolly[1] had heretofore told me.

Thence, with great satisfaccion to me, back to the Company, where I heard good discourse; and so to the afternoon Lecture upon the heart and lungs, &c. And that being done, we broke up, took leave, and back to the office we two (Sir W. Batten, who dined here also, being gone before).

Here late, and to Sir W. Batten to speak upon some business; where I find Sir J. Mennes pretty well fuddelled I thought. He took me aside to tell me how being at my Lord Chancellors today, my Lord told him that there was a Great Seal passing for Sir W. Penn, through the impossibility of the Comptroller's duty to be performed by one man, to be as it were joynt-controller with him;[2] at which he is stark mad and swears he will give up his place – and doth rail at Sir W. Penn the cruellest; which I made shift to increase as much as I could, but it pleased me heartily to hear him rail against him, so that I do see thoroughly that they are not like to be great friends, for he cries out against him for his house and yard and God knows what. For my part, I do hope, when all is done, that my fallowing my business will keep me secure against all their envys; but to see how the old man doth strut and swear that he understands all his duty as easily as crack a nut; and easier, he told my Lord Chancellor, for his teeth are gone – and that he understands it as well as any man in England; and that he will never leave to Record that he should be said to be unable to do his duty alone; though God knows, he cannot do it no more then a child. All this I am glad to see fall out between them, and myself safe; and yet I hope the King's service will [be] done for all this, for I would not that should be hindered by any of our private differences.

So to my office, and then home to supper and to bed.

1. George Jolliffe, who had attended Pepys after his operation for the stone in 1658 and died shortly afterwards.

2. Mennes was the Comptroller of the Navy, an extremely demanding role in which he was less than competent. This was one of a number of attempts to oust him or diminish his responsibilities.

MARCH. 1662.[1]

5. Rise this morning early only to try, with intentions to begin my last summers course in rising betimes. So to my office a little; and then to Westminster by coach with Sir J. Mennes and Sir W. Batten, in our way talking of Sir W. Penn's business of his patent, which I think I have put a stop to wholly, for Sir J. Mennes swears he will never consent to it.

Here to the Lobby and spoke with my Cosen Rogr., who is going to Cambrige tomorrow. In the hall I do hear that the Catholiques are in great hopes for all this, and do set hard upon the King to get Indulgence. Matters, I hear, are all naught[2] in Ireland; and that the parliament hath voted and the people, that is the papists, do cry out against the Comissioners sent by the King; so that they say the English interest will be lost there.[3] Thence I went to see my Lord Sandwich, who I find very ill; and by his cold being several nights hindered from sleep, he was hardly able to open his eyes, and is very weak and sad upon it – which troubled me much. So after talking with Mr. Cooke,[4] whom I find there, about his folly for looking and troubling me and other friends in getting him a place (that is, Storekeeper of the Navy at Tanger) before there is any such thing, I returned to the hall and thence back with the two knights home again by coach – where I find Mr. Moore got abroad and dined with me; which I was glad to see, he having not been able to go abroad a great while. Then came in Mr. Hawly and dined with us; and after dinner I left them and to the office, where we sat late; and I do find that I shall meet with nothing to oppose my growing great in the office but Sir W. Penn, who is now well again and comes into the office very briscke, and thinks to get up his time that he hath been out of the way by being mighty diligent at the

1. 1662 according to the official calendar in which the new year began on 25 March.
2. Bad.
3. The King had appointed commissioners to a Court of Claims to settle complex disputes arising from the Cromwellian land settlement in Ireland. Catholics understood the Court to be biased against them, while the Irish House of Commons felt the Court was not sympathetic enough to the interests of Protestant settlers. On 10 February the Irish Commons had voted for changes to the Court's procedure, a move that challenged the King's authority.
4. A servant of Sandwich's. Cooke had recently helped Pepys in finding a bride for his brother Tom and been blamed for the failure of those negotiations.

office – which I pray God he may be; but however, I hope by mine to weary him out, for I am resolved to fall to business as hard as I can drive – God giving me health.

At my office late, and so home to supper and to bed.

21. Up betimes and to my office, where busy all the morning. And at noon, after a little dinner, to it again; and by and by, by appointment, our full board met, and Sir Phillip Warwicke and Sir Robt. Long came from my Lord Treasurer to speak with us about the state of the debts of the Navy and how to settle it, so as to begin upon the new Foundacion of 200000*l* per annum which the King is now resolved not to exceed. This discourse done and things put in a way of doing – they went away; and Captain Holmes being called in, he begun his high complaint against his Master, Cooper, and would have him forthwith discharged – which I opposed, not in his defence but for the justice of proceeding, not to condemn a man unheard.[1] Upon [which] we fell from one word to another that we came to very high Termes, such as troubled me, though all and the worst I ever said was that that was insolently and illmannerdly spoken – which he told me it was well it was here that I said it. But all the officers, Sir G. Carteret, Sir J. Mennes, Sir W. Batten, and Sir W. Penn cried shame of it. At last he parted, and we resolved to bring the dispute between him and his Master to a trial next week – wherein I shall not at all concern myself in defence of anything that is unhandsome on the Maister's part, nor willingly suffer him to have any wrong. So we rose and I to my office troubled, though sensible that all the officers are of opinion that he hath carried himself very much unbecoming him.

So wrote letters by the post, and home to supper and to bed.

22. *Lords day.*◆ This day, though I was merry enough, yet I could not get yesterday's quarrel out of my mind and a natural fear of being challenged[2] by Holmes for the words I did give him, though nothing but what did become me as a Principall Officer.

23. Up betimes and to my office. Before noon my wife and I eat something, thinking to have gone abroad together; but in comes Mr. Hunt, who we were forced to stay to dinner; and so while that was got ready, he and I abroad about two or three small business of mine and so back to dinner; and after dinner he went away and my

1. The seaman Richard Cooper taught arithmetic to Pepys, who had rewarded him by making him master of the *Reserve*, captained by Robert Holmes.
2. Challenged to a duel.

wife and I and Ashwell by coach, set my wife down at her mother's and Ashwell at my Lord's, she going to see her father and mother, and I to White-hall, being fearful almost, so poor a spirit I have, of meeting Major Holmes. By and by the Duke comes and we with him about our usual business; and then the Committee for Tanger – where after reading my Lord Rutherfords commission[1] and consented to, Sir R. Ford, Sir W. Rider and I were chosen to bring in some Laws for the Civill government of it; which I am little able to do but am glad to be joined with them, for I shall learn something of them.

Thence to see my Lord Sandwich, and who should I meet at the doore but Major Holmes. He would have gone away, but I told him I would not spoil his visitt and would have gone; but however, we fell to discourse and he did as good as desire excuse for the high words that did pass in his heat the other day, which I was willing enough to close with; and after telling him my mind, we parted – and I left him to speak with my Lord. And I by coach home – where I find Will Howe come home today with my wife and stayed with us all night, staying late up singing songs; and then he and I to bed together in Ashwells bed and she with my wife. This the first time that I ever lay in that room. ⟨This day, Greatorex[2] brought me a very pretty Weather glasse for heat and cold.⟩

24. Lay pretty long, that is, till past 6 a-clock; and then up and W. Howe and I very merry together, till having eat our breakfast, he went away and I to my office. By and by Sir J. Mennes and I to the Victualling Office by appointment to meet several persons upon stating the demands of some people of money from the King.

Here we went into their Bakehouse and saw all the ovens at work – and good bread too, as ever I would desire to eat.

Thence Sir J. Mennes and I homeward, calling at Brownes the Mathematician in the Minnerys with a design of buying Whites ruler to measure timber with, but could not agree on the price.[3] So home and to dinner, and so to my office.

Where we sat anon; and among other things, had Cooper's business tried against Captain Holmes. But I find Cooper a fudling,

1. Andrew Rutherford, Earl of Teviot, was to be the new Governor of Tangier.
2. Ralph Greatorex, mathematical-instrument maker.
3. John Brown, a mathematical-instrument maker, sold an early form of slide rule that could be used to calculate area and volume. Pepys wanted to improve his knowledge of timber measuring to increase his role in the navy's contracts with merchants.

troublesome fellow, though a good artist;[1] and so am contented to have him turned out of his place. Nor did I see reason to say one word against it, though I know what they did against him was with great envy and pride.

So anon broke up, and after writing letters, &c., home to supper and to bed.

25. *Lady day.* Up betimes and to my office, where all the morning. At noon dined and to the Exchange; and thence to the Sun taverne to my Lord Rutherford and dined with him and some other his officers and Scotch gentlemen of fine discourse and educacion. My Lord used me with great respect and discoursed upon his business as with one that he did esteem of. And indeed, I do believe that this guarrison is now likely to come to something under him. ⟨By and by he went away, forgetting to take leave of me, my back being turned looking upon the Aviary, which is there very pretty and the Birds begin to sing well this spring.⟩

Thence home and to my office till night, reading over and consulting upon the book and Ruler that I bought this morning of Browne concerning the Lyne of Numbers, in which I find much pleasure.[2]

This evening came Captain Grove about hiring ships for Tanger.[3] I did hint to him my desire that I could make some lawful profit thereof – which he promises, that he will tell me of all that he gets and that I shall have a share – which I did not demand, but did silently consent to it – and money, I perceive something will be got thereby.

At night Mr. Bland came and sat with me at my office till late, and so I home and to bed. This day being washing-day and my maid Susan ill, or would be thought so, puts my house so out of order that we have no pleasure almost in anything, my wife being troubled thereat for want of a good cook-maid, and moreover I cannot have my dinner tomorrow as I ought in memory of my being cut of the Stone. But I must have it a day or two hence.

1. Practitioner.
2. John Brown's *The Description and Use of the Carpenters-Rule* (1662) contained specific guidance on how to use a slide rule and its logarithmic "line of numbers" to measure timber.
3. Captain Edward Grove wanted to be a shipping agent for the Tangier Committee.

APRILL. 1663.

1. Up betimes and abroad to my brother's; but he being gone out, I went to the Temple to my Cosen Roger Pepys to see and talk with him a little – who tells me that with much ado the parliament doth agree to throw down popery;[1] but he says it is with so much spite and passion and an endeavour of bringing all nonconformists[2] into the same condition, that he is afeared matters will not yet go so well as he could wish.

Thence back to my brother's, in my way meeting Mr. Moore and talking with him about getting me some money; and calling at my brother's, they tell me that my brother is still abroad and that my father is not yet up – at which I wondered, not thinking that he was come, though I expected him, because I looked for him at my house. So I up to his bedside and stayed an hour or two talking with him. Among other things, he tells me how unquiett my mother is grown, that he is not able to live almost with her, if it were not for Pall.

All other matters are as well as upon so hard conditions with my Uncle Tho. we can expect them.

I left him in bed, being very weary – to come to my house tonight or tomorrow when he please; and so I home, calling on the virginall-maker – buying a Rest for myself to tune my Tryangle[3] and taking one of his people along with me to put it in tune once more; by which I learned how to go about it myself for the time to come.

So to dinner, my wife being lazily in bed all this morning. Ashwell and I dined below together, and a pretty girl she is and I hope will give my wife and myself good content, being very humble and active. My Cooke-maid also doth dress my meat very well and neatly.

So to my office all the afternoon till night. And then home – calling at Sir W. Batten, where was Sir J. Mennes and Sir W. Penn – I telling them how by my letter this day from Comissioner Pett,

1. A bill to prevent "the Growth of Popery" was passing through the House of Commons.
2. Protestants who did not worship within the established Church of England.
3. Triangular virginals, a type of keyboard instrument.

I hear that his Stempeece[1] he undertook for for the new ship at Woolwich, which we have been so long to our shame in looking for, doth prove knotty and not fit for service. Lord, how Sir J. Mennes, like a mad coxcomb, did swear and stamp, swearing that Comissioner Pett hath still the old heart against the King that ever he had, and that this was his envy against his brother[2] that was to build that ship – and all the damnable reproaches in the world – at which I was ashamed but said little. But upon the whole, I find him still a fool, led by the nose with stories told by Sir W. Batten, whether with or without reason. So, vexed in my mind to see things ordered so unlike gentlemen or men of reason, I went home and to bed.

3. Waked betimes and talked half an hour with my father, and so I rose and to my office. And about 9 a-clock by water from the Old Swan to White-hall and to Chappell; which being most monstrous full, I could not go into my pew but sat among the Quire. Dr. Creeton the Scotch-man preached a most admirable, good, learned, honest and most severe Sermon, yet Comicall – upon the words of the woman concerning the virgin, "Blessed is the womb that bore thee" (meaning Christ) "and the paps that gave thee suck." And he[3] answered, "Nay; rather is he blessed that heareth the word of God and keeps it."[4]

He railed bitterly ever and anon against John Calvin and his brood, the presbyterians, and against the present terme now in use, of "Tender consciences."[5] He ripped up Hugh Peters (calling him "that execrable Skellum") his preaching and stirring up the maids of the city to bring in their bodkins and thimbles.[6]

Thence going out of White-hall, I met Captain Grove, who did give me a letter directed to myself from himself; I discerned money to be in it and took it, knowing, as I found it to be, the proceed of the place I have got him, to have the taking up of vessells for

1. A principal timber in a ship's bow.
2. Christopher Pett.
3. Jesus.
4. A loose recollection of Luke, 11.27–8. The preacher was Robert Creighton, Dean of Wells and chaplain to the King.
5. A phrase given new currency by its use in Charles's Declaration of Breda (1660). It now meant the scruples of puritan ministers who would not conform to the Act of Uniformity (1662).
6. Peters, the Independent minister, had been the leading preacher of the New Model Army and was known for his begging sermons. Satirists portrayed him calling for silver bodkins and thimbles to fund the parliamentary cause. A "skellum" is a villain.

Tanger. But I did not open it till I came home to my office; and there I broke it open, not looking into it till all the money was out, that I might say I saw no money in the paper if ever I should be Questioned about it. There was a piece in gold and 4*l* in silver.

So home to dinner with my father and wife.◆

4. Up betimes and to my office. By and by to Lumbard-streete by appointment, to meet Mr. Moore; but the business not being ready, I returned to the office, where we sat a while; and being sent for, I returned to him and there signed to some papers in the conveying of some lands morgaged by Sir Rob. Parkehurst in my name to my Lord Sandwich[1] – which I having done, I returned home to dinner.

Whither by and by comes Roger Pepys, Mrs. Turner, her daughter, Joyce Norton and a young lady, a daughter of Collonell Cockes – my uncle Wight – his wife and Mrs. Anne Wight – this being my feast, in lieu of what I should have had a few days ago, for my cutting of the Stone, for which the Lord make me truly thankful.

Very merry before, at, and after dinner, and the more for that my dinner was great and most neatly dressed by our own only mayde. We had a Fricasse of rabbets and chicken – a leg of mutton boiled – three carps in a dish – a great dish of a side of lamb – a dish roasted pigeons – a dish of four lobsters – three tarts – a Lampry pie, a most rare pie – a dish of anchoves – good wine of several sorts; and all things mighty noble and to my great content.

After dinner to Hide parke; my aunt, Mrs. Wight, and I in one Coach, and all the rest of the women in Mrs. Turners – Roger being gone in haste to the parliament about the carrying this business of the papists, in which it seems there is great contest on both sides. And my uncle and father staying together behind. At the parke was the King, and in another coach my Lady Castlemayne, they greeting one another at every Tour.[2] Here about an hour; and so leaving all by the way, we home and find the house as clean as if nothing had been done there today from top to bottom – which made us give the Cooke 12*d* a piece, each of us.

So to my office about writing letters by the post – one to my brother John at Brampton, telling him (hoping to work a good effect by it upon my mother) how melancholly my father is, and bidding him use all means to get my mother to live peaceably and quietly, which I am sure she neither doth nor I fear can ever do –

1. *See* 5 Dec. 1660.
2. In spring and summer members of fashionable society drove in coaches round the "Ring", the internal road in Hyde Park.

but frighting her with his coming down no more and the danger of her condition if he should die, I trust may do good.

So home and to bed.

19. *Easterday.* Up, and this day put on my close-kneed colourd suit; which, with new stockings of that colour, with belt and new gilt-handle sword, is very handsome.

To church alone. And so to dinner, where my father and brother Tom dined with us. And after dinner to church again, my father sitting below in the chancel. After church done (where the young scotch man preaching, I slept all the while) my father and I to see my uncle and aunt Wight; and after a stay of an hour there, my father to my brothers and I home to supper. And after supper fell in discourse of dancing, and I find that Ashwell hath a very fine carriage, which makes my wife almost ashamed of herself to see herself so outdonne; but tomorrow she begins to learn to dance for a month or two.

So to prayers and to bed – my Will being gone with my leave to his father's this day for a day or two, to take physique[1] these holidays.

29. Up betimes, and after having at my office settled some accounts for my Lord Sandwich, I went forth; and taking up my father at my brother's, took coach and towards Chelsey – lighting at an ale-house near the gatehouse at Westminster to drink our morning draught; and so up again and to Chelsey, where we find my Lord all alone at a little table, with one joynt of meat at dinner.[2] We sat down and very merry, talking – and mightily extolling the manner of his retirement and the goodness of his diet; which endeed is so finely dressed, the mistress of the house, Mrs. Becke, having been a woman of good condition heretofore, a merchant's wife, and hath all things most excellently dressed. Among others, her cheeks[3] admirable, and so good that my Lord's words were that they were fit to present to my Lady Castlemaine.◆

Anon I took leave; and coming down, find my father unexpectedly in great pain and desiring for God sake to get him a bed to lie upon; which I did, and W. How and I stayed by him, in so great pain as I never saw, poor wretch, and with that patience, crying only: "Terrible.: terrible pain, God help me, God help me!" – with

1. Medicine.
2. Chelsea, at this time a village outside London, was where Sandwich was staying in order to recover his health.
3. Possibly an error for "cakes".

that mournful voice, that made my heart ake. He desired to rest a little alone, to see whether it would abate; and W. How and I went down and walked in the gardens, which are very fine, and a pretty fountayne, with which I was finely wetted – and up to a banqueting-house with a very fine prospect. And so back to my father, who I find in such pain that I could not bear the sight of it without weeping, never thinking that I should be able to get him from thence; but at last, finding it like to continue, I got him to go to the coach, with great pain; and driving hard, he all the while in a most unsufferable torment (meeting in the way with Captain Ferrer, going to my Lord to tell him that my Lady Jemimah is come to town and that W. Stankes[1] is come with my father's horses), not staying the coach to speak with anybody; but once, in Pauls churchyard, we were forced to stay, the jogging and pain making my father vomit – which it never had done before. At last we got home; and all helping him, we got him to bed presently; and after half an hour's lying in his naked bed (it being a rupture[2] which he is troubled [with] and hath been this 20 years, but never in half the pain and with so great swelling as now, and how this came but by drinking of cold small beer and sitting long upon a low stool and then standing long after it, he cannot tell), his bowells went up again into his belly, being got forth into his cod, as it seems is usual with very many men – after which he was at good ease and so continued – and so fell to sleep and we went down; whither W. Stankes was come with his horses. But it is very pleasant to hear how he rails at the rumbling and ado that is in London over it is in the country, that he cannot endure it.

He supped with us, and very merry. And then he to his lodgings at the Inne with the horses, and so we to bed – I to my father, who is very well again, and both slept very well.

30. Up; and after drinking my morning draught with my father and W. Stankes, I went forth to Sir W. Batten, who is going (to no purpose, as he uses to do) to Chatham upon a Survey.

So to my office, where till towards noon; and then to the Exchange and back home to dinner, where Mr. Hunt, my father, and W. Stankes; but Lord, what a stir Stankes makes with his being crowded in the streets and wearied in walking in London, and would not be woo'd by my wife and Ashwell to go to a play nor to

1. A yeoman of Brampton who looked after John Pepys's property there.
2. Hernia.

White-hall or to see the Lyons,[1] though he was carried in a coach. I never could have thought there had been upon the earth a man so little curious in the world as he is.

At the office all the afternoon till 9 at night; so home – to cards with my father, wife and Ashwell, and so to bed.

MAY.

4. Up betimes, and to setting my Brampton papers in order and looking over my Wardrobe against summer and laying things in order to send to my brothers to alter. By and by took boat, entending to have gone down to Woolwich; but seeing I could not get back time enough to dinner, I returned and home – whither by and by the Dancing Maister[2] came; whom standing by seeing him instructing my wife, when he had done with her he would needs have me try the steps of a *Coranto*; and what with his desire and my wife's importunity, I did begin, and then was obliged to give him entry-money, 10*s* – and am become his Scholler. The truth is, I think it is a thing very useful for any gentleman and sometimes I may have occasion of using it; and though it cost me, which I am heartily sorry it should, besides that I must by my oath give half as much more to the poor,[3] yet I am resolved to get it up some other way; and then it will not be above a month or two in a year. So though it be against my stomach, yet I will try it a little while; if I see it comes to any great inconvenience or charge, I will fling it off.

After I had begun with the steps of half a *coranto*, which I think I shall learn well enough, he went away and we to dinner.◆

8. Up very earely and to my office, there preparing letters to my father, of great import in the settling of our affairs and putting him upon a way [of] good husbandry – I promising him to make out of my own purse him up 50*l* per annum, till either by my Uncle Thomas's death or the fall of the Wardrobe place he be otherwise provided.[4]

That done, I by water to the Strand and there viewed the Queene-Mother's works at Somerset-house; and thence to the new

1. In the Tower of London menagerie.
2. Mr Pembleton.
3. Dancing lessons breached his oaths against unnecessary expense and pleasure, so a fine was due.
4. Pepys wanted his father to have the post of yeoman tailor of the Wardrobe, which was currently occupied.

playhouse, but could not get in to see it; so to visit my Lady Jemimah, who is grown much since I saw her – but lacks mightily to be brought into the fashion of the Court to set her off.

Thence to the Temple and there sat till one a-clock, reading at Playford's in Dr Ushers *Body of Divinity* his discourse of the Scripture;[1] which is as much, I believe, as is anywhere said by any man, but yet there is room to cavill, if a man would use no faith to the tradition of the Church in which he is born; which I think to be as good an argument as most is brought for many things, and it may be for that, among others.

Thence to my brother's, and there took up my wife and Ashwell to the Theatre Royall, being the second day of its being opened.[2] The house is made with extraordinary good contrivance; and yet hath some faults, as the narrowness of the passages in and out of the pit, and the distance from the stage to the boxes, which I am confident cannot hear. But for all other things it is well. Only, above all, the Musique being below, and most of it sounding under the very stage, there is no hearing of the bases at all, nor very well of the trebles, which sure must be mended.[3]

The play was *The Humorous Lieutenant* – a play that hath little good in it, nor much in that very part which, by the King's command, Lacey now acts instead of Clun. In the dance, the Tall Devil's actions was very pretty.[4]

The play being done, we home by water, having been a little ashamed that my wife and woman were in such a pickle, all the ladies being finer and better dressed in the pit then they use I think to be.

To my office to set down this day's passage. And though my oath against going to plays doth not oblige me against this house, because it was not then in being, yet believing that at that time my meaning was against all public houses, I am resolved to deny myself the liberty of two plays at Court which are in arreare to me for the months of March and Aprill; which will more then countervail this

1. James Ussher's *A Body of Divinitie* (first pub. 1645) argued for the superiority of scripture over the church's tradition. Pepys read it at John Playford's bookshop in the Inner Temple.
2. Thomas Killigrew's new playhouse for the King's Company, between Drury Lane and Bridges Street.
3. The musicians were at the front of the stage, where the orchestra pit is situated nowadays. In most Restoration theatres the musicians played in a small gallery above the proscenium arch. Killigrew later moved his musicians to such a gallery.
4. *The Humorous Lieutenant*, a tragicomedy by John Fletcher. John Lacy, one of Charles's favourite comedians, had replaced Walter Clun in the title role. In Act 4 sc. 3 there is a dance of devils.

excess. So that this month of May is the first that I must claim a liberty of going to a Court play, according to my oath.

So home to supper. And at supper comes Pembleton; and afterward we all up to dancing till late, and so broke up and to bed; and they say that I am like to make a dancer.

9. Up betimes and to my office; whither sooner then ordinary comes Mr. Hater,[1] desiring to speak a word to me alone, which I was from the disorder of his countenance amused[2] at; and so the poor man begun telling me that by Providence being the last Lord's day at a meeting of some Friends upon doing of their duties, they were surprized and he carried to the Counter, but afterward released;[3] however, hearing that Sir W. Batten doth hear of [it], he thought it good to give me an account of it, lest it might tend to any prejudice to me. I was extraordinary surprized with it and troubled for him, knowing that now it is out, it is impossible for me to conceal it, or keep him in imployment under me without danger to myself. I cast about all I could and did give him the best advice I could; desiring to know if I should promise that he would not for the time to come commit the same, he told me he desired that I would rather forbear to promise that; for he durst not do it, what[ever] God in His providence shall do with him; and that for my part, he did bless God and thank me for all the love and kindness I have showed him hitherto. I could not, without tears in my eyes, discourse with him further, but at last did pitch upon telling the truth of the whole to Mr. Coventry as soon as I could;[4] and to that end did use means to prevent Sir W. Batten (who came to town last night) from going to that end today, lest he might doe it to Sir G. Carteret or Mr. Coventry before me – which I did prevail, and kept him at the office all the morning.

At noon dined at home with a heavy heart for the poor man. And after dinner went out to my brother's, and thence to Westminster; where at Mr. Jervas my old Barber I did try two or three borders[5] and periwiggs, meaning to wear one; and yet I have no stomach, but that the pains of keeping my hair clean is so great.

1. Thomas Hayter, one of Pepys's clerks in the Navy Office.
2. Puzzled, astonished.
3. That is, Hayter had been arrested for attending a nonconformist religious meeting and taken to the Counter prison.
4. Coventry was a Navy Commissioner and secretary to the Duke of York, thus in a position, if he chose, to help protect Hayter and to ask the Duke to do so. Pepys spoke to him the next day.
5. Locks of hair that covered only the ears and neck; they were fixed to a cap.

He trimmed me; and at last I parted, but my mind was almost altered from my first purpose, from the trouble that I foresee will be in wearing them also. Thence by water home and to the office, where busy late. And so home to supper and bed – with my mind much troubled about T Hater.

15. Up betimes and walked to St. James's; where Mr. Coventry being in bed, I walked in the park, discoursing with the keeper of the Pell Mell[1] who was sweeping of it – who told me of what the earth is mixed that doth floor the Mall, and that over all there is Cockle-shells powdered and spread, to keep it fast; which however, in dry weather turns to dust and deads the ball. Thence to Mr. Coventry; and sitting by his bedside, he did tell me that he sent for me to discourse upon my Lord Sandwiches allowances for his several pays, and what his thoughts are concerning his demands; which he could not take the freedom to do face to face, it being not so proper as by me; and did give me a most friendly and ingenuous account of all, telling me how unsafe at this juncture, while every man's, and his actions perticularly, are descanted upon, it is either for him to put the Duke upon doing or my Lord himself to desire anything extraordinary, especially, the King having been so bountiful already; which the world takes notice of even to some repinings. All which he did desire me to discourse with my Lord of; which I have undertook to do.

We talked also of our office in general; with which he told me that he was nowadays nothing so satisfyed as he was wont to be. I confess I told him things are ordered in that way that we must of necessity break in a little time a-pieces.

After done with him about those things, he told me that for Mr. Hater, the Dukes word was, in short, that he found he had a good servant, an Anabaptist; and unless he did carry himself more to the scandall of the office, he would bear with his opinion till he heard further – which doth please me very much.

Thence walked to Westminster and there up and down in the hall and the parliament-house all the morning. And at noon by coach to my Lord Crews, hearing that my Lord Sandwich did dine there; where I told him what had passed between Mr. Coventry and myself; with which he was contented, though I could perceive not very well pleased.◆

After dinner I went up to Sir Tho. Crew,[2] who lies there not

1. Pall Mall, used for playing the croquet-like game of that name.
2. Sandwich's brother-in-law, an MP from a Presbyterian family.

very well in his head, being troubled with vapours and fits of dizzinesse; and there I sat talking with him all the afternoon, from one discourse to another. The most was upon the unhappy posture of things at this time; that the King doth mind nothing but pleasures and hates the very sight or thoughts of business. That my Lady Castlemayne rules him; who he says hath all the tricks of Aretin[1] that are to be practised to give pleasure – in which he is too able, hav[ing] a large ——;[2] but that which is the unhappiness is that, as the Italian proverb says, *Cazzo dritto non vuolt consiglio.*[3] If any of the Sober counsellors give him good advice and move him in anything that is to his good and honour, the other part, which are his counsellors of pleasure, take him when he [is] with my Lady Castlemayne and in a humour of delight and then persuade him that he ought not to hear or listen to the advice of those old dotards or counsellors that were heretofore his enemies, when God knows it is they that nowadays do most study his honour. It seems the present favourites now are my Lord Bristoll, Duke of Buckingham, Sir H. Bennet, my Lord Ashley, and Sir Ch. Berkely; who among them have cast my Lord Chancellor[4] upon his back, past ever getting up again; there being now little for him to do, and waits at court attending to speak to the King as others do – which I pray God may prove of good effects, for it is feared it will be the same with my Lord Treasurer[5] shortly.◆

Scotland: it seems, for all the news-book tells us every week that they are all so quiet and everything in the Church settled, the old women had like to have killed the other day the Bishop of Galloway, and not half the churches of the whole kingdom conforms.[6]◆

Having thus freely talked with him and of many more things, I took leave; and by coach to St. James's and there told Mr. Coventry what I had done with my Lord, with great satisfaction; and so, well pleased, home – where I find it almost night and my wife and the Dancing Maister alone above, not dancing but walking. Now, so deadly full of jealousy I am, that my heart and head

1. Pietro Aretino (d. 1556) had written descriptive poems to accompany engravings of sexual positions (*I Modi*, "The Postures").
2. The dash is in the diary manuscript.
3. "A straight prick wants no advice".
4. Edward Hyde, Earl of Clarendon.
5. Thomas Wriothesley, Earl of Southampton.
6. The bishops had been restored in Scotland, leading to unrest. In Britain, the Secretary of State's office allowed only two regular newsbook titles. Both had carried the same report in early April that "This country is in all peace and quietness, and most willing to submit to his Majestie in every thing" (*Mercurius Publicus*, 2 April). They had not returned to the topic.

did so cast about and fret, that I could not do any business possibly, but went out to my office; and anon late home again, and ready to chide at everything; and then suddenly to bed and could hardly sleep, yet durst not say anything; but was forced to say that I had bad news from the Duke concerning Tom Hater, as an excuse to my wife – who by my folly hath too much opportunity given her with that man; who is a pretty neat black[1] man, but married. But it is a deadly folly and plague that I bring upon myself to be so jealous; and by giving myself such an occasion, more then my wife desired, of giving her another month's dancing – which however shall be ended as soon as I can possibly. ⟨But I am ashamed to think what a course I did take by lying to see whether my wife did wear drawers today as she used to do, and other things to raise my suspicion of her; but I found no true cause of doing it.⟩

16. Up, with my mind disturbed and with my last night's doubts upon me.

For which I deserve to be beaten, if not really served as I am fearful of being; especially since, God knows, that I do not find honesty enough in my own mind but that upon a small temptation I could be false to her, and therefore ought not to expect more justice from her – but God pardon both my sin and my folly herein.

To my office and there setting all the morning; and at noon dined at home. After dinner comes Pembleton again; and I being out of humour, would not see him, pretending business; but Lord, with what jealousy did I walk up and down my chamber, listening to hear whether they danced or no or what they did; notwithstanding I afterwards knew, and did then believe, that Ashwell was with them. So to my office awhile; and my jealousy still reigning, I went in and, not out of any pleasure but from that only reason, did go up to them to practise; and did make an end of *La Duchesse*,[2] which I think [I] should with a little pains do very well. So broke up and saw him gone.

Then Captain Cocke coming to me to speak about my seeming discourtesy to him in the business of his Hemp, I went to the office with him and there discoursed it largely, and I think to his satisfaction.

Then to my business, writing letters and other things till late at night; and so home to supper and bed. My mind in some better ease – resolving to prevent matters for the time to come as much

1. Dark in hair or complexion.
2. A fashionable courante.

as I can, it being to no purpose to trouble myself for what is past; being occasiond, too, by my own folly.

21. Up; but cannot get up so early as I was wont, nor my mind to business as it should be and used to be before this dancing. However, to my office, where most of the morning talking with Captain Cox of Chatham about his and the whole yard's difference against Mr. Barrow the Storekeeper; wherein I told him my mind clearly, that he would be upheld against the designs of any to ruin him; he being, we all believed but Sir W. Batten his mortal enemy, as good a servant as any the King hath in that yard.

After much good advice and other talk – I home and danced with Pembleton and then the barber trimmed me; and so to dinner – my wife and I having high words about her dancing, to that degree that I did retire and make a vowe to myself, not to oppose her or say anything to dispraise or correct her therein as long as her month lasts, in pain of 2*s*-6*d* for every time; which if God please, I will observe, for this roguish business hath brought us more disquiet then anything hath happened a great while.

After dinner to my office, where late, and then home; and Pembleton being there again, we fell to dance a country dance or two, and so to supper and bed. But being at supper, my wife did say something that caused me to oppose her in; she used the word "Devil," which vexed me; and among other things, I said I would not have her to use that word, upon which she took me up most scornefully; which before Ashwell and the rest of the world, I know not nowadays how to check as I would heretofore, for less then that would have made me strike her. So that I fear, without great discretion, I shall go near to lose too my command over her; and nothing doth it more then giving her this occasion of dancing and other pleasure, whereby her mind is taken up from her business and finds other sweets besides pleasing of me, and so makes her that she begins not at all to take pleasure in me or study to please me as heretofore. But if this month of her dancing were but out (as my first was this night, and I paid off Pembleton for myself), I shall hope with a little pains to bring her to her old wont. This day, Susan that lived with me lately being out of service, and I doubt[1] a simple wench, my wife doth take her for a little time to try her, at least till she goes into the country; which I am yet doubtful whether it will be best for me to send her or no, for fear of her running on in her liberty before I have brought her to her right temper again.

1. Fear.

26. Lay long in bed, talking and pleasing myself with my wife. So up and to my office a while and then home, where I find Pembleton; and by many circumstances I am led to conclude that there is something more then ordinary between my wife and him; which doth so trouble me that I know not, at this very minute that I now write this almost, what either I write or am doing nor how to carry myself to my wife in it, being unwilling to speak of it to her for making of any breach and other inconveniences, nor let it pass for fear of her continuing to offend me and the matter grow worse thereby. So that I am grieved at the very heart, but I am very unwise in being so.

There dined with me Mr. Creed and Captain Grove; and before dinner, I had much discourse in my chamber with Mr. Deane, the Builder of Woolwich, about building of ships. But nothing could get the business out of my head, I fearing that this afternoon, by my wife's sending every[one] abroad and knowing that I must be at the office, she hath appointed him to come. This is my devilish jealousy; which I pray God may be false, but it makes a very hell in my mind; which the God of heaven remove, or I shall be very unhappy. So to the office, where we sat a while.

By and by, my mind being in great trouble, I went home to see how things were; and there I find as I doubted, Mr. Pembleton with my wife and nobody else in the house, which made me almost mad; and going up to chamber, after a turn or two I went out again and called somebody, upon pretence of business, and left him in my little room at the door (it was the Duchman, commander of one of the King's pleasure-boats; who having been beat by one of his men sadly, was come to the office today to complain), telling him I would come again to him to speak with him about his business; so in great trouble and doubt to the office; and Mr. Coventry nor Sir G. Carteret being there, I made a quick end of our business and desired leave to be gone, pretending to go to the Temple, but it was home; and so up to my chamber and, as I think, if they had any intentions of hurt, I did prevent doing anything at that time; but I continued in my chamber vexed and angry till he went away, pretending aloud, that I might hear, that he could not stay, and Mrs. Ashwell not being within they would not dance. And Lord, to see how my jealousy wrought so far, that I went saftly up to see whether any of the beds were out of order or no, which I found not; but that did not content me, but I stayed all the evening walking, and though anon my wife came up to me and would have spoke of business to me, yet I construed it to be but impudence; and though my heart was full, yet I did say nothing, being in a great doubt what to do. So at night suffered them to go all to bed, and late put myself to bed in great discontent, and so to sleep.

27. So I waked by 3 a-clock, my mind being troubled; and so took occasion by making water to wake my wife, and after having lain till past 4 a-clock, seemed going to rise, though I did it only to see what she would do; and so going out of the bed, she took hold of me and would know what ayled me; and after many kind and some cross words, I begun to tax her discretion in yesterday's business, but she quickly told me my owne, knowing well enough that it was my old disease of Jealousy; which I disowned, but to no purpose. After an hour's discourse, sometimes high and sometimes kind, I find very good reason to think that her freedom with him was very great and more then was convenient, but with no evil intent. And so after a while I caressed her and parted seeming friends, but she crying and in a great discontent.◆

So to my office to put things in order there. And by and by comes Pembleton and word is brought me from my wife thereof, that I might come home; so I sent word that I would have her go dance, and I would come presently. So being at a great loss whether I should appear to Pembleton or no, and which would most proclaim my jealousy to him, I at last resolved to go home; and took Tom Hater with me and stayed a good while in my chamber, and there took occasion to tell him how I hear that parliament is putting an act out against all sorts of Conventicles[1] and did give him good counsel, not only in his own behalfe but my own, that if he did hear or know anything that could be said to my prejudice, that he would tell me; for in this wicked age (especially Sir W. Batten being so open to my reproches and Sir J. Mennes, for the neglect of their duty, and so will think themselfs obliged to scandalize me all they can to right themselfs if there shall be any enquiry into the matters of the Navy, as no doubt there will) a man ought to be prepared to answer for himself in all things that can be enquired concerning him.

After much discourse of this nature to him, I sent him away and then went up; and there we danced country dances and single, my wife and I, and my wife paid him off for this month also, and so he is cleared.

After dancing, we took him down to supper and were very merry; and I made myself so and kind to him as much as I could, to prevent his discourse; though I perceive to my trouble that he

1. Religious meetings outside the Church of England.

knows all, and my doty[1] doth me the disgrace to publish it as much as she can. Which I take very ill, and if too much provoked shall witness it to her. After supper and he gone, we to bed.

28. Up this morning; and my wife, I know not for what cause, being against going to Chelsey today, it being a holy day (Ascension day) and I at leisure, it being the first holy-day almost that we have observed since we came to this office – we did give Ashwell leave to go by herself. And I out to several places about business. Among other, to Dr Williams to reckon with him for Physique that my wife hath had for a year or two, coming almost to 4*l*.◆

Home and there find Creede, who dined with us; and after dinner, by water to the Royall Theatre[2] but that was so full they told us we could have no room; and so to the Duke's house and there saw *Hamlett* done, giving us fresh reason never to think enough of Baterton.

Who should we see come upon the Stage but Gosnell, my wife's maid, but she neither spoke, danced nor sung; which I was sorry for. But she becomes the stage very well.[3]◆

29. This day is kept strictly as a holy-day, being the King's Coronacion.[4] We lay long in bed. And it rained very hard, rain and hail almost all the morning. By and by Creed and I abroad and called at several churches; and it is a wonder to see, and by that to guess, the ill temper of the City at this time, either to religion in general or to the King, that in some churches there was hardly ten people in the whole church, and those poor people.

So to a Coffee-house, and there in discourse hear the King of France is likely to be well again.[5]

So home to dinner and out by water to the Royall Theatre, but they not acting today; then to the Dukes house and there saw *The Slighted mayde*,[6] wherein Gosnell acted Peromena, a great part, and did it very well and I believe will do it better and better and prove a good actor.

The play is not very excellent, but is well acted; and in general the actors in all perticulars are better then at the other house.

Thence to the Cocke alehouse; and having there drunk, sent

1. Fool.
2. The Theatre Royal, Drury Lane.
3. Gosnell had been briefly employed as Elizabeth's companion in December 1662.
4. The King's birthday and anniversary of his coronation.
5. Reports that Louis XIV had the "spotted fever" (in this case, measles) had reached Court a few days earlier.
6. A comedy by Sir Robert Stapylton, published in this year.

them with Creede to see the German princesse at the gate house at Westminster;[1] and I to my brother and thence to my uncle Fenners to have seen my aunt James (who hath been long in town and goes away tomorrow, and I not seen her) but did find none of them within, which I was glad of; and so back to my brother's to speak with him, and so home and in my way did take two turns forward and backward through the Fleete ally to see a couple of pretty whores that stood off the doors there; and God forgive me, I could scarce stay myself from going into their houses with them, so apt is my nature to evil, after once, as I have these two days, set upon pleasure again.

So home, and to my office to put down these two days' journalls. Then home again and to supper; and then Creed and I to bed with good discourse, only my mind troubled about my spending my time so badly for these seven or eight days; but I must impute it to the disquiet that my mind hath been in of late about my wife – and for my going these two days to plays, for which I have paid the due forfeit, by money and abating the times of going to plays at Court; which I am now to remember that I have cleared all my times that I am to go to Court Plays to the end of this month, and so June is the first time that I am to begin to reckon.

JUNE.

14. ⟨*Lords day.*⟩ Lay long in bed; and so up and to church. Then to dinner, and Tom dined with me, who I think grows a very thriving man, as he himself tells me.

He tells me that his man John hath got a wife, and for that he entends to part with him, which I am sorry for. And then that Mr. Armiger comes to be a constant lodger at his house, and he says hath money in his purse and will be a good paymaister, but I do much doubt it.

He being gone, I up; and sending my people to church, my wife and I did even our reckonings and have a great deal of serious talk, wherein I took occasion to give her hints of the necessity of our

1. The "German Princess" was really Mary Moders of Canterbury whose exploits had won the public's attention. Posing as a German noblewoman, she had married a clerk, John Carleton, who discovered her ignoble past – including the fact that she was a serial bigamist. She was now in the Gatehouse prison awaiting trial for bigamy (a capital offence). Acquitted in early June, she continued her career as a conwoman, and was hanged in 1673.

saving all we can. I do see great cause every day to curse the time that ever I did give way to the taking of a woman for her, though I could never have had a better, and also the letting of her learn to dance; by both which her mind is so devilishly taken off of her business and minding her occasions, and besides, hath got such an opinion in her of my being jealous, that it is never to be removed I fear, nor hardly my trouble that attends it; but I must have patience.

I did give her 40*s* to carry into the country tomorrow with her, whereof 15*s* is to go for the coach hire for her and Ashwell, there being 20 paid here already in earnest.[1]

In the evening our discourse turned to great content and love, and I hope that after a little forgetting our late differences, and being a while absent one from another, we shall come to agree as well as ever.

So to Sir W. Penn to visit him; and finding him alone, sent for my wife, who is in her riding-suit, to see him; which she hath not done these many months I think. By and by in comes Sir J. Mennes and Sir W. Batten, and so we sat talking; among other things, Sir J. Mennes brought many fine expressions of Chaucer, which he dotes on mightily, and without doubt is a very fine poet.

Sir W. Penn continues lame of the gout, that he cannot rise from his chair; and so after staying an hour with him, we went home and to supper, and so to prayers and bed.

23. Up by 4 a-clock and so to my office. But before I went out, calling, as I have of late done, for my boy's Copy-book, I find that he hath not done his taske, and so I beat him and then went up to fetch my ropes end; but before I got down the boy was gone; I searched the cellar with a Candle, and from top to bottom could not find him high nor low. So to the office; and after an hour or two, by water to the Temple to my Cosen Roger, who I perceive is a deadly high man in the parliament business, and against the Court – showing me how they have computed that the King hath spent, at least hath received, about four Millions of money since he came in.◆

Thence by water home and to the Change. And by and by comes the King and the Queenes by in great state, and the streets full of people. I stood in Mr. [2] Balcone. They dine all at my Lord Mayors – but what he doth for victuals or room for them, I know not.

1. They were going to Brampton for the summer.
2. A blank space in the manuscript.

So home to dinner alone; and there I find that my boy had got out of doors, and came in for his hat and band and so is gone away to his brother.[1] But I do resolve even to let him go for good and all.

So I by and by to the office, and there had a great fray with Sir W. Batten and Sir J. Mennes, who, like an old dotard, is led by the nose by him. It was in Captain Cockes business of hemp, wherein the King is absolutely abused; but I was for peace sake contented to be quiet and to sign to his bill, but in my manner so as to justify myself. And so all was well – but to see what a knave Sir W. Batten is makes my heart ake. So late at my office and then home to supper – and to bed, my man Will not being well.

24. Up before 4 a-clock, and so to my lute an hour and more and then by water, drinking my morning draught alone in an alehouse in Thames-streete, to the Temple; and there, after a little discourse with my cousin Roger about some business, away by water to St. James and there an hour's private discourse with Mr. Coventry – where he told me one thing to my great joy, that in the business of Captain Cockes hemp, disputed before him the other day (Mr. Coventry absent), the Duke did himself tell him since, that Mr. Pepys and he did stand up and carry it against the rest that were there, Sir G. Carteret and Sir W. Batten, which doth please me much, to see that the Duke doth take notice of me.◆

From that, we discoursed of the evil of putting out men of experience in business, as the Chancellor;[2] and from that, to speak of the condition of the King's party at present; who, as the papists, though otherwise fine persons, yet being by law kept for these four score years out of imployment, they are now wholly uncapable of business; and so the Cavalers for 20 years – who, says he, for the most part have either given themselfs over to look after country and family business, and those the best of them, and the rest to debauchery &c.; and that was it that hath made him high against the late bill brought into the House for the making all men incapable of imployment that had served against the King:[3] "Why," says he, "in the sea-service it is impossible to do anything without them, there being not more then three men of the whole King's side that

1. Wayneman Birch's brother worked in London as a groom.
2. Clarendon's relationship with the King was no longer strong and his enemies, encouraged by the Earl of Bristol, were moving against him in parliament.
3. In early May the Commons had made abortive moves towards a law to put all civil and military posts in the hands of men who were "loyal Subjects, and conformable to the Church of *England*".

are fit to command almost;" and those were Captain Allen, Smith and Beech – and it may be Holmes and Utber and Batts might do something.

I desired him to tell me if he thought that I did speak anything that I do against Sir W. Batten or Sir J. Mennes out of ill-will or design. He told me quite the contrary, and that there was reason enough. After a good deal of good and fine discourse, I took leave; and so to my Lord Sandwich's house, where I met my Lord and there did discourse of our office businesses and how the Duke doth show me kindness, though I have endeavoured to displease more or less of my fellow-officers, all but Mr. Coventry and Pett, but it matters not. "Yes," says my Lord, "Sir J. Mennes, who is great with the Chancellor;" I told him the Chancellor I have thought was declining; and however, that the esteem he[1] hath among them is nothing but for a jester or a ballat-maker;[2] at which my Lord laughs and asks me whether I believe he ever could do that well.◆

29. Up betimes and to my office; and by and by to the Temple and there appointed to meet in the evening about my business. And thence I walked home; and up and down the streets is cried mightily the great victory got by the Portugalls against the Spaniards, where 10000 slain, 3 or 4000 taken prisoners, with all the artillery, baggage, money, &c., and Don John of Austria forced to fly with a man or two with him – which is very great news.[3]

Thence home and at my office all the morning, and so dined at home; and then by water to St. James, but no meeting, today being holy-day; but met Mr. Creed in the park, and after a walk or two, discoursing his business, I took leave of him in Westminster-hall, whither we walked; and then came again to the hall and fell in talk with Mrs. Lane[4] and after great talk that she never went abroad with any man as she used heretofore to do, I with one word got her to go with me and to meet me at the further Rhenish wine-house – where I did give her a Lobster and do so towse her and feel her all over, making her believe how fair and good a skin she had; and endeed, she hath a very white thigh and leg, but monstrous fat.

1. Mennes.
2. Mennes's reputation as a raconteur and poet pre-dated the civil wars. From the mid-1650s his burlesque verse and ballads had been printed in miscellanies.
3. The Spanish, under Don Juan of Austria, had invaded Portugal. At the Battle of Ameixial the Portuguese, assisted by British forces, repelled the Spanish.
4. Betty Lane, a linen draper at Westminster Hall. Pepys had known her for years and purchased goods from her. They had had at least one previous sexual encounter.

When weary, I did give over, and somebody having seen some of our dalliance, called aloud in the street, "Sir! why do you kiss the gentlewoman so?" and flung a stone at the window – which vexed me – but I believe they could not see my towsing her; and so we broke up and went out the back way, without being observed I think; and so she towards the hall and I to White-hall, where taking water, I to the temple and thence with my Cosen Roger and Mr. Goldsborough to Gray's-Inne to his counsel, one Mr. Rawworth, a very fine man. Where, it being the Question whether I as Executor should give a warrant to Golsborough in my reconveying her estate[1] back again, the morgage being performed against all acts of the Testator but only my own – my Cosen said he never heard it asked before, and the other that it was always asked and he never heard it denied or scrupled before – so great a distance was there in their opinions, enough to make a man forswear ever having to do with the law. So they agreed to refer it to Serjeant Maynard. And so we broke up, and I by water home from the Temple and there to Sir W. Batten and eat with him, he and his lady and Sir J. Mennes having been below[2] today upon the East India men[3] that are come in; but never tell me so, but that they have been at Woolwich and Deptford and done great deal of business. God help them. So home and up to my lute long; and then after a little Latin chapter with Will,[4] to bed. But I have used of late, since my wife went, to make a bad use of my fancy with whatever woman I have a mind to – which I am ashamed of and shall endeavour to do so no more. And so to sleep.

30.◆ Thus, by God's blessing, end this book of two years.[5] Being in all points in good health, and a good way to thrive and do well. Some money I do and can lay up, but not much; being worth now above 700*l*, besides goods of all Sorts. My wife in the country with Ashwell her woman, with my father. Myself at home with W. Hewre and my cook-maid Hannah, my boy Waynman being lately run away from me.

In my office, my repute and understanding good, especially with the Duke and Mr. Coventry. Only, the rest of the officers do rather envy then love me, I standing in most of their lights, especially Sir

1. Mrs Goldsborough's. This dispute over a mortgage concerned Robert Pepys's estate, of which Pepys was the executor.
2. I.e. downstream from London Bridge.
3. Ships trading with India and South-East Asia.
4. A chapter from the Bible. Pepys was trying to improve Will's Latin.
5. This is the last entry in the second manuscript volume.

W. Batten, whose cheats I do daily oppose, to his great trouble, though he appears mighty kind and willing to keep friendship with mee, while Sir J. Mennes, like a dotard, is led by the nose by him. My wife and I (by my late jealousy, for which I am truly to be blamed) have not that fondness between us which we used and ought to have, and I fear will be lost hereafter if I do not take some course to oblige her and yet preserve my authority. Public matters are in an ill condition – parliament sitting and raising four subsidys for the King, which is but a little, considering his wants; and yet that parted withal with great hardness – they being offended to see so much money go, and no debts of the public paid, but all swallowed by a luxurious Court – which the King, it is believed and hoped, will retrench in a little time, when he comes to see the utmost of the Revenue which shall be settled on him – he expecting to have his 1200000*l* made good to him, which is not yet done by above 150000*l*, as he himself reports to the House.[1]

My differences with my uncle Tho. at a good quiett, blessed be God, and other matters.

The town full of the great overthrow lately given to the Spaniard by the portugall, they being advanced into the very middle of Portugall.

The weather wett for two or three months together, beyond belief; almost not one fair day coming between till this day, which hath been a very pleasant [day], and the first pleasant this summer.

The charge of the Navy entended to be limited to 200000*l* per annum, the ordinary charge of it, and that to be settled upon the Customes.[2]

The King yet greatly taken up with Madam Castlemayne and Mrs. Stewart – which God of Heaven put an end to.

Myself very studious to learn what I can of all things necessary for my place as an officer of the Navy – reading lately what concerns measuring of timber and knowledge of the tides.

I have of late spent much time with Creede, being led to it by his business of his accounts;[3] but I find him a fellow of those designs or reaches, that there is no degree of true friendship to be made with him, and therefore I must cast him off, though he be a very

1. £1,200,000 was the optimistic estimate of the yield of the revenues granted to the King by parliament in 1660; a current yearly shortfall of up to £175,000 had been reported to the Commons in early June 1663.
2. The Navy's peacetime budget was to be funded from customs revenues.
3. John Creed's accounts were from his time as Deputy-Treasurer of Sandwich's fleet in the Mediterranean. The Navy Treasurer had been reluctant to settle these, accusing Creed of corrupt dealings. Pepys had defended him.

understanding man and one that much may be learned of as to cunning and judging of other men. Besides, too, I do perceive more and more that my time of pleasure and idlenesse of any sort must be flung off, to attend the getting of some money and the keeping of my family in order, which I fear by my wife's liberty may be otherwise lost.

JULY. 1663.

1.◆ By water with Sir W. Batten to T[r]inity-house, there to dine with him, which we did; and after dinner we fell in talking, Sir J. Mennes and Mr. Batten[1] and I – Mr. Batten telling us of a late triall of Sir Charles Sydly the other day, before my Lord Chief Justice Foster and the whole Bench – for his debauchery a little while since at Oxford Kates; coming in open day into the Balcone and showed his nakedness – acting all the postures of lust and buggery that could be imagined, and abusing of scripture and, as it were, from thence preaching a Mountebanke sermon from that pulpitt, saying that there he hath to sell such a pouder as should make all the cunts in town run after him – a thousand people standing underneath to see and hear him.[2]

And that being done, he took a glass of wine and washed his prick in it and then drank it off; and then took another and drank the King's health.

It seems my Lord and the rest of the Judges did all of them round give him a most high reproofe – my Lord Chief Justice saying that it was for him and such wicked wretches as he was that God's anger and judgments hung over us – calling him "Sirrah" many times.[3] It's said they have bound him to his good behaviour (there being no law against him for it) in 5000*l*. It being told that my Lord Buckhurst was there, my Lord asked whether it was that Buckhurst that was lately tried for robbery; and when answered "Yes," he asked whether he had so soon forgot his deliverance at that time, and that it would have more become him to have been at his prayers, begging God's forgiveness, then now running into such courses again.[4]

1. William, elder son of Sir William; a barrister.
2. Sedley, a courtier and wit, was on the balcony of a cookhouse in Covent Garden.
3. "Sirrah" was a contemptuous term, marking the addressee as an inferior.
4. Charles Sackville, Lord Buckhurst, had been charged with murder rather than robbery. In February 1662, he and a group of friends killed a tanner, who they claimed was a highwayman. Buckhurst had been pardoned by the King.

Upon this discourse, Sir J. Mennes and Mr. Batten both say that buggery is now almost grown as common among our gallants as in Italy, and that the very pages of the town begin to complain of their masters for it. But blessed be God, I do not to this day know what is the meaning of this sin, nor which is the agent nor which the patient.[1] Thence home; and my clarkes being gone by my leave to see the East India ships that are lately come home, I stayed all alone within my office all the afternoon. This day I hear at dinner that Don John of Austria, since his flight out of Portugall, is dead of his wounds. So there is a great man gone, and a great dispute like to be ended for the crown of Spayne, if the King should have died [be]fore him.[2] I received this morning a letter from my wife, brought by John Goods to town – wherein I find a sad falling-out between my wife and my father and sister and Ashwell, upon my writing to my father to advise pall not to keep Ashwell from her mistress or making any difference between them. Which pall telling to Ashwell and she speaking some words that her mistress heard, caused great difference among them all, which I am sorry from my heart to hear of and I fear will breed ill-blood not to be laid again – so that I fear my wife and I may have some falling-out about it, or at least my father and I; but I shall endeavour to salve up all as well as I can, or send for her out of the country before the time entended – which I would be loath to do.

In the evening by water to my Cosen Roger Pepys's chamber, where he was not come; but I found Dr. John newly come to town, and is well again after his sickness;[3] but Lord, what a simple man he is as to any public matters of state, and talks so sillily. And his Brother, Dr Tom, what the matter is I know not, but he hath taken (as my father told me a good while since) such displeasure, that he would hardly touch his hat to me, and I as little to him.[4]◆

9.◆ Sir W. Batten and I sot a little this afternoon at the office; and then I by water to Deptford and there mustered the yard, purposely (God forgive me) to find out Bagwell, a carpenter whose wife is a pretty woman, that I might have some occasion of knowing him

1. Passive.
2. This story of Don Juan's death was untrue. He was the illegitimate son of Philip IV of Spain and had hopes to succeed his legitimate but much younger half-brother.
3. John Pepys, Fellow of Trinity College, Cambridge, and younger brother of Roger.
4. Pepys's cousin Thomas had reason to be annoyed. He had helped Tom Pepys with the planned match to Elizabeth Hobell – negotiations which Pepys had broken off, describing his cousin in his diary as a "fool". *See* 22 Oct. 1662.

and forcing her to come to the office again – which I did so luckily, that going thence, he and his wife did of themselfs meet me in the way, to thank me for my old kindness; but I spoke little to her, but shall give occasion for her coming to me.[1] Her husband went along with me to show me Sir W. Penn's lodging; which I knew before, but only to have a time of speaking to him and sounding him. So left, and I went in to Sir W. Penn, who continues ill still, and worse I think then before. He tells me my Lady Castlemayne was at Court, for all this talk, this week; which I am glad to hear, but it seems the King is stranger then ordinary to her.

Thence walked home as I use to do; and to bed presently, having taken great cold in my feet by walking in the dirt this day in thin shoes, or some other way – so that I begun to be in pain; and with warm clothes made myself better by morning, but yet in pain.

27.◆ By water to Westminster and there came, most luckily, to the Lords House as the House of Comons were going into the Lords' House, and there I crowded in along with the Speaker – and got to stand close behind him – where he made his speech to the King (who sat with his crown on and robes, and so all the Lords in their robes, a fine sight);[2] wherein he told his Majesty what they have done this parliment, and now offered for his Royall consent. The greatest matters were a Bill for the Lord's Day (which it seems the Lords have lost and so cannot be passed, at which the Commons are displeased)[3] – the bills against Conventicles and papists (but it seems the Lords have not passed them);[4] and giving his Majesty four entire Subsidys; which last, with about twenty smaller acts, were passed.◆

The Speakers speech was far from any Oratory, but was as plain (though good matter) as anything could be and void of elocution.

After the bills passed, the King, sitting in his throne with his speech writ in a paper which he held in his lap and scarce looked

1. William Bagwell was a ship's carpenter. His wife's name is not known, but she may have been Elizabeth, to whom he was married when he wrote his will in 1697.
2. The King had come to the final sitting of this session to prorogue the parliament. Pepys had no right to attend this ceremony, from which the public were supposedly barred. The Speaker was Sir Edward Turnor.
3. The paper for the bill for "the better Observation of the Sabbath" had vanished that morning from the table of the House in suspicious circumstances. The Clerk of the Parliaments reported that it went missing after assorted Lords had "scattered" the bills across the table.
4. Bills against "the unlawful Meetings of Sectaries" and "the Growth of Popery" had reached the Lords but were not passed, despite the Commons' request for them to be expedited.

off of it, I thought, all the time he made his speech to them – giving them thanks for their subsidys, of which, had he not need, he would not have asked or received them – and that need not from extravagancys of his, he was sure, in anything; but the disorders of the times compelling him to be at greater charge then he hoped for the future, ⟨by their care⟩ in their country, he should be. And that for his family expenses and others, he would labour however to retrench in many things convenient, and would have all others to do so too.

He desired that nothing of old faults should be remembered, or severity for the same used to any in the country, it being his desire to have all forgot as well as forgiven. But however, to use all care in suppressing any tumults, &c.; assuring them that the restless spirits of his and their adversarys have great expectations of something to be done this summer.

And promised that though the acts about Conventicles and papists were not ripe for passing this sessions, yet he would take care of himself that neither of them should in this inte[r]vall be encouraged to the endangering of the peace. And that at their next meeting he would himself prepare two bills for them concerning them.

So he concluded, that for the better proceeding of Justice, he did think fit to make this a Sessions, and doth prorogue them to the 16th. of March next.

His speech was very plain, nothing at all of spirit in it, nor spoke with any; but rather on the contrary, imperfectly, repeating many times his words, though he read all – which I was sorry to see, it having not been hard for him to have got all the speech without booke.[1]

So they all went away, the King out of the House at the upper end – he being by and by to go to Tunbrige to the Queene.◆

AUGUST.

7. Up and to my office a little, and then to Browns for my Measuring Rule, which is made, and is certainly the best and the most commodious for carrying in one's pocket and most useful that ever was made, and myself have the honour of being as it were the inventor of this form of it.[2] Here I stayed discoursing an hour with him, and then home. And thither came Dr. Fairbrother to me and

1. I.e. to have memorized it.
2. Having mastered the use of a slide rule, Pepys had commissioned his own design from Brown the mathematical-instrument maker.

we walked a while together in the garden and then abroad into the City, and then we parted for a while and I to my Viall, which I find done and once varnished, and it will please me very well – when it is quite varnisht.

Thence home and to study my new Rule till my head aked cruelly. So by and by to dinner and the Doctor and Mr. Creed came to me.

The Doctors discourse, which (though he be a very good-natured man) is but simple, was some sport to me and Creede, though my head akeing, I took no great pleasure in it.

We parted after dinner, and I walked to Deptford and there found Sir W. Penn; and I fell to measuring of some plank that was serving into the yard; which the people took notice of and the measurer himself was amuzed[1] at, for I did it much more ready then he. And I believe Sir W. Penn would be glad I could have done less, or he more.

By and by he went away, and I stayed walking up and down, discoursing with the officers of the yard of several things; and so walked back again, and on my way young Bagwell and his wife waylayd me to desire my favour about getting him a better ship; which I shall pretend to be willing to do for them, but my mind is to know his wife a little better.

They being parted, I went with Cadbury the mast-maker to view a parcel of good masts which I think it were good to buy and resolve to speak to the board about it.

So home; and my brother John and I up, and I to my Musique and then to discourse with him; and I find him not so thorough a philosopher, at least in Aristotle, as I took him for, he not being able to tell me the definicion of fire nor which of the four Qualitys belonged to each of the four elements.[2]

So to prayers and to bed. Among other things, being much satisfyed in my new Rule.

10. Up, though not so earely this summer as I did all the last, for which I am sorry; and though late, am resolved to get up betimes before the season of rising be quite past. To my office to fit myself to wait on the Duke this day.

By and by, by water to White-hall and so to St. James's and anon

1. Puzzled, astonished.
2. The four elements were earth, water, fire, and air, and their qualities, respectively, dryness, moisture, heat, and cold. John subsequently revealed he had not read Aristotle, but had instead studied Descartes.

called into the Duke's chamber; and being dressed, we were all as usual taken in with him and discoursed of our matters. And that being done, he walked and I in the company with him to Whitehall; and there he took barge for Woolwich, and I up to the Committee of Tanger, where my Lord Sandwich, my Lord Peterborough (whom I have not seen before since his coming back), Sir W Compton, and Mr. Povy – our discourse about supplying my Lord Tiviott[1] with money; wherein I am sorry to see, though they do not care for him, yet they are willing to let him for civility and compliment only, to let him have money, almost without expecting any account of it. But by this means, he being such a cunning fellow as he is, the King is like to pay dear for our Courtiers ceremony. Thence by coach with my Lords Peterborough and Sandwich to my Lord Peterborough's house; and there, after an hour's looking over some fine books of the Italian buildings with fine cuts, and also my Lord Peterborough's bowes and arrows, of which he is a great lover, we sat down to dinner, my Lady coming down to dinner also, and there being Mr. Williamson that belongs to Sir H. Bennett, whom I find a pretty understanding and accomplisht man but a little conceited.

After dinner I took leave and went to Greatorex's,[2] whom I found in his garden and set him to work upon my Ruler, to ingrave an Almanacke and other things upon the brasses of it – which a little before night he did, but the latter part he slubberd over, that I must get him to do it over better or else I shall not fancy my Rule. Which is such a folly that I am come to now, that whereas before my delight was in multitude of books and spending money in that and buying alway of other things, now that I am become a better husband[3] and have left off buying, now my delight is in the neatness of everything, and so cannot be pleased with anything unless it be very neat; which is a strange folly.

Hither came W. Howe[4] about business; and he and I had a great deal of discourse about my Lord Sandwich, and I find by him that my Lord doth dote upon one of the daughters of Mrs. [5] where he lies, so that he spends his time and money upon her. He tells me she is a woman of a very bad fame and very impudent, and hath told my Lord so. Yet for all that, my Lord doth spend all his

1. Governor of Tangier; Peterborough was his predecessor.
2. A mathematical-instrument shop in the Strand.
3. Manager.
4. Will Howe, a clerk in Sandwich's service.
5. Supply "Becke" of Chelsea.

evenings with her, though he be at Court in the daytime. And that the world doth take notice of it. And that Pickering[1] is only there as a blinde, that the world may think that my Lord spends his time with him when he doth worse. And that hence it is that my Lord hath no more mind to go into the country then he hath. in fine, I perceive my Lord is dabling with this wench, for which I am sorry; though I do not wonder at it, being a man amorous enough and now begins to allow himself the liberty that he sees everybody else at Court takes.

Here I am told that my Lord Bristoll is either fled or conceals himself, having been sent for to the King – it is believed to be sent to the tower, but he is gone out of the way.[2]

Yesterday, I am told also that Sir J: Lentall, in Southworke, did apprehend about 100 Quakers and other such people, and hath sent some of them to the gaole at Kingston, its being now the time of the Assizes.

Thence home and examined a piece of Latin of Will's with my brother, and so to prayers and to bed.

This evening I have a letter from my father that says that my wife will come to town this week, at which I wonder she should come without my knowing more of it. But I find they have lived very ill together since she went, and I must use all the brains I have to bring her to any good when she doth come home, which I fear will be hard to do, and do much disquiet me the thoughts of it.

12.◆ By water to my brother's and there I hear my wife is come and gone home, and my father is come to town also, at which I wondered. But I discern it is to give my brother advice about his building,[3] and it may be to pacify me about the differences that have been between my wife and him and my mother at her late being with them – though by and by, he coming to Mr. Holdens (where I was buying a hat), he took no notice to me of anything. I walked with him a little while and left him to lie at that end of the town, and I home – where methinks I find my wife strange, not knowing,

1. Edward (Ned) Pickering, a relative of Sandwich's.
2. In July, George Digby, Earl of Bristol, had made an abortive attempt in the House of Lords to impeach the Earl of Clarendon for high treason. The charges (including orchestrating the sale of Dunkirk to the French) were rejected by the Lords as a breach of legal procedure and as not constituting treason. Charles denounced the charges as a libel on his government and ordered Bristol's arrest. Bristol remained in hiding for several years.
3. Tom was planning building work on his house in Salisbury Court.

I believe, in what temper she could expect me to be in; but I fell to kind words and so we were very kind; only, she could not forbear telling me how she had been used by them and her maid Ashwell in the country; but I find it will be best not to examine it, for I doubt she's in fault too, and therefore I seek to put it off from my hearing; and so to bed and there enjoyed her with great content. And so to sleep.

17. Up; and then fell into discourse, my wife and I, to Ashwell; and much against my Will, I am fain to express a willingness to Ashwell that she should go from us; and yet in my mind I am glad of it, to ease me of the charge. So she is to go to her father this day. And leaving my wife and her talking highly, I went away by coach with Sir J. Mennes and Sir W. Batten to St. James and there attended of course the Duke. And so to White-hall, where I met Mr. Moore and he tells me with great sorrow of my Lord's being debauched, he fears, by this woman at Chelsy; which I am troubled at and resolve to speak to him of it if I can seasonably.

Thence home, where I dined with my wife alone; and after dinner comes our old maid Susan to look for a Gorgett[1] that she says she hath lost by leaving it here; and by many circumstances, it being clear to me that Hannah, our present cook-maid, not only hath it but had it on upon her neck when Susan came in, and shifted it off presently upon her coming in, I did charge her so home with it (having a mind to have her gone from us), that in a huff she told us she would be gone tonight if I would pay her her wages; which I was glad and my wife of, and so fetched her her wages; and though I am doubtful that she may convey some things away with her clothes, my wife searching them, yet we are glad of her being so gone. And so she went away in a quarter of an houre's time – being much amused at this, to have never a maid but Ashwell, that we do not entend to keep, nor a boy; and my wife and I being left for an hour, till my brother came in, alone in the house, I grew very melancholy.◆

But till my house is settled, I do not see that I can mind my business of the office, which grieves me to the heart. But I hope all will over in a little time, and I hope to the best. This day at Mrs. Holdens I find my new Low crowned beaver,[2] according to the present fashion, made; and will be sent home tomorrow.

1. A neckerchief or ornamental collar.
2. Fur hat.

27. Up, after much pleasant talk with my wife and a little that vexes me, for I see that she is confirmed in it that all that I do is by design, and that my very keeping of the house in dirt,[1] and the doing of this and anything else in the house, is but to find her imployment to keep her within and from minding of her pleasure in – which, though I am sorry to see she minds it, is true enough in a great degree.

To my office; and there we sat and despatched much business. Home and dined with my wife well; and then up and made clean my closet of books and had my chamber a third time made very clean, so that it is now in a very fine condition.

Thence down to see some good plank in the River with Sir W. Batten. And back again, it being a very cold day and a cold winde. Home again; and after seeing Sir W. Penn, to my office and there till late doing of business – being mightily incouraged by everybody that I meet withal upon the Change and everywhere else, that I am taken notice of for a man that doth the King's business wholly and well – for which the Lord be praised, for I know no honour I desire more.

Home to supper, where I find my house very clean from top to bottom again, to my great content.◆

31. Up and at my office all the morning, where Sir W. Batten and Sir J. Mennes did pay the short-allowance money to the East India companies,[2] and by the assistance of the City-Marshall and his men did lay hold of two or three of the chief of the companies that were in the mutiny the other day and sent them to prison.[3] I home to dinner; and my wife after dinner going with my brother to see a play, I to my office, where very late doing business; and so home to supper and to bed.

This noon came Jane Gentleman to serve my wife as her chambermaid; I wish she may prove well; she is only thick of hearing, which may be a trouble, but we know not yet, nor is it always so much as at other times.

So ends this month, with my mind pretty well in quiet, and in good disposition of health since my drinking at home of a little

1. The dirt was from joiners re-laying the floors, although the lack of servants cannot have helped.
2. Short-allowance money was paid to compensate crews who had been on restricted rations. These ships had returned from Bombay, granted to Britain as part of Catherine of Braganza's marriage treaty.
3. On 27 August Sir John Mennes had been attacked by sailors angry at their lack of pay. Pepys did not record learning of the attack.

wine with my beer; but nowhere else do I drink any wine at all. My house in a way to be clean again, the Joyners and all having done; but only we lack a Cooke-maid and Jane our chambermaid is but new come to us this day.

The King and Queene and the Court at the Bath. My Lord Sandwich in the country, newly gone, with my doubts concerning him having been debauched by a slut at his lodgings at Chelsy. My brother John with me, but not to my great content, because I do not see him mind his study or give me so good account thereof as I expected.

My Brother ⟨Tom⟩ embarqued in building, and I fear in no good condition for it, for he sent to me to borrow more money, which I shall not lend him.

Myself in good condition in the office, and I hope in a good way of saving of money at home.

SEPTEMBER.

9. Up by break-a-day and then to my Vyall a while, and so to Sir W Warren's by agreement; and after talking and eating something with him, he and I down by water to Woolwich and there I did several businesses and had good discourse. And thence walked to Greenwich; in my way, a little boy overtook us with a fine cup turned out of Lignum vitæ,[1] which the poor child confessed was made in the King's yard by his father, a turner there, and that he doth often do it, and that I might have one and God knows what; which I shall examine. Thence to Sir W. Warren again and there draw up a contract for Masts which he is to sell us. And so home to dinner, finding my poor wife busy.

I after dinner to the office, and then to White-hall to Sir G Carterets, but did not speak with him; and so to Westminster-hall, God forgive me, thinking to meet Mrs. Lane, but she was not there; but here I met with Ned Pickering, with whom I walked three or four hours till evening, he telling me the whole business of my Lord's folly with this Mrs. Becke at Chelsy, of all which I am ashamed to see my Lord so grossly play the beast and fool, to the flinging off of all Honour, friends, servants and every thing and person that is good, and only will have his private lust undisturbed

1. This hard and heavy West Indian wood (much in demand for drinking vessels) was used for ships' pulleys and blocks.

with this common whore – his sitting up, night after night alone, suffering nobody to come to them, and all the day too – casting off Pickering, basely reproaching him with his small estate, which yet is a good one; and other poor courses to obtain privacy beneath his Honour – with his carrying her abroad and playing on his lute under her window, and forty other poor sordid things; which I am grieved to hear, but believe it to no purpose for me to meddle with it; but let him go on till God Almighty and his own conscience and thoughts of his Lady and family do it. So after long discourse, to my full satisfaction but great trouble, I home by water and at my office late; and so to supper to my poor wife, and so to bed – being troubled to think that I shall be forced to go to Brampton the next Court, next week.

14. Up betimes, and my wife's mind and mine holds for her going.[1] So she to get her ready, and I abroad to do the like for myself, and so home; and after setting everything at my office and at home in order, by coach to Bishop-gate – it being a very promising fair day. There at the Dolphin we met my uncle Tho. (and his son-in-Law, which seems a very sober man) and Mr. Moore. So Mr. Moore and my wife set out before, and my uncle and I stayed for his son Thomas,[2] who by a sudden resolution is preparing to go with us, which makes me fear something of mischief which they design to do us. He staying a great while, the old man and I before and about eight mile off his son comes after us, and about six mile further we overtake Mr. Moore and my wife (which makes me mightily consider what a great deal of ground is lost in a little time, when it is to be got up again by another; that is, to go his own ground and the other's too); and so after a little bayte[3] (I paying all the reckonings the whole Journy) at Ware, to Buningford; where my wife, by drinking some cold beer, being hot herself, presently after lighting, begins to be sick and became so pale, and I alone with her in a great chamber there, that I thought she would have died; and so in great horror (and having a great trial of my true love and passion for her) called the maids and mistress of the house; and so with some strong water,[4] and after a little vomitt, she came to be pretty well again; and so to bed, and I having put her to bed with great content – I called in my company and supped in the chamber by her; and

1. Elizabeth was going to Brampton with her husband, where the manorial court was due to consider the will of Pepys's uncle Robert.
2. Thomas Pepys "the turner" (of the several cousin Thomases).
3. A stop for refreshment.
4. Distilled spirits.

being very merry in talk, supped and then parted, and I to bed and lay very well. This day my Cosen Tho dropped his hanger[1] and [it] was lost.

15. Up pretty betimes and rode as far as Godmanchester (Mr. Moore having two falls, once in water and another in dirt) and there light and eat and drunk, being all of us very weary, but especially my uncle and wife. Thence to Brampton to my father's, and there found all well but not sensible how they ought to treat my uncle and his son, at least till the Court bee over; which vexed me. But upon my counsel, they carried it fair to them; and so my father, Cosen Tho, and I up to Hinchingbrooke, where I find my Lord and his company gone to Boughton, which vexed me. But there I find my Lady and the young ladies; and there I alone with my Lady two hours, she carrying me through every part of the house and gardens, which are and will be mighty noble endeed. Here I saw Mrs. Betty Pickering,[2] who is a very well-bred and comely lady, but very fat. Thence, without so much as drinking, home with my father and Cosen (who stayed for me) home and to a good supper, after I had had an hour's talk with my father abroad in the fields; wherein he begin to talk very highly of my promises to him, of giving him the profits of Sturtlow, as if it were nothing that I give him out of my purse, and that he would have me to give this also from myself to my brothers and sisters; I mean, Brampton and all I think. I confess I was angry to hear him talk in that manner, and took him up roundly in it and advised him, if he could not live up[on] 50*l* per annum, which was another part of his discourse, that he would think to come and live at Toms again, where 50*l* per annum will be a good addition to Toms trade; and I think that must be done when all is done. But my father spoke nothing more of it all the time I was in the country, though at that time he seemed to like it well enough. I also spoke with Piggott,[3] too, this evening before I went in to supper, and doubt that I shall meet with some knots in my business tomorrow before I can do it at the Court, but I shall do my best.

After supper my uncle and son to Stankes's to bed (which troubled me), all our father's beds being lent to Hinchingbrooke; and so my wife and I to bed – she very weary.

1. A short sword.
2. Lord and Lady Sandwich's niece.
3. Richard Pigott, a yeoman of Brampton.

16. Up betimes, and with my wife to Hinchingbrooke to see my Lady, she being to go to my Lord this morning; and there I left her. And so back to the Court and heard Sir R. Bernards charges to the Courts Baron and Leete,[1] which took up till noon and was worth hearing; and after putting my business into some way, went home to my father's to dinner. And after dinner to the Court, where Sir Rob and his son came again by and by, and then to our business; and my father and I having given bond to him for the 21*l* Piggott owed him, my uncle Tho. did quietly admit himself and surrender to us the lands first morgaged for our whole debt, and Sir Robts. added to it; which makes it up 209*l*, to be paid in six months.[2]◆

This kept us till night, but am heartily glad it ended so well on my uncles part, he doing that and Priors little house[3] very willingly. So the Court broke up, and my father and Mr. Sheply and I to Gorrums to drink; and then I left them and to the Bull, where my uncle was to hear what he and the people said of our business, and hear nothing but what liked me very well; and so by and by home and to supper, and with my mind in pretty good quiet, to bed.

[Samuel and Elizabeth return to London on 21 September]

24. Up betimes; and after taking leave of my brother John, who went from me to my father's this day, I went forth by water to Sir Ph. Warwickes,[4] where I was with him a pretty while; and in discourse he tells me and made it appear to me that the King cannot be in debt to the Navy at this time 5000*l*.; nay, it is my opinion that Sir G. Carteret doth owe the King money, and yet the whole Navy debt paid.[5] Thence I parted, being doubtful of myself that I have not spoke with the gravity and weight that I ought to do in so great a business. But I rather hope it is my doubtfulness of myself and the haste which he was in, some very great personages waiting for him without while he was with me, that made him willing to be gone. To the office by water; where we sat, doing little now Mr.

1. These manorial courts (civil and criminal respectively) were often held together and in this case Bernard, as the Steward (presiding judge) of both, gave charges to the juries.
2. Pigott owed a mortgage to the heirs of the late Robert Pepys which had been secured on Pigott's lands at Brampton. Thomas Pepys (Robert's heir-at-law) now agreed to the sale of those lands, which would enable Pigott to pay the debt.
3. A contentious sale involving Robert Pepys's estate, now settled.
4. Sir Philip Warwick was secretary to Lord Treasurer Southampton.
5. Pepys believes Carteret, the Navy Treasurer, is inflating the navy's debts. He should be able to pay off the navy's genuine debts with the money awarded and return the surplus to the crown.

Coventry is not here, but only vex myself to see what a sort of coxcombs we are when he is not here to undertake such a business as we do. In the afternoon, telling my wife that I go to Deptford, I went by water to Westminster-hall; and there finding Mrs. Lane, took her over to Lambeth where we were lately, and there did what I would with her but only the main thing, which she would not consent to, for which God be praised; and yet I came so near, that I was provoked to spend.[1] But trust in the Lord I shall never do so again while I live. After, being tired with her company, I landed her at White-hall and so home and at my office writing letters, till 12 at night almost; and then home to supper and bed and there find my poor wife hard at work, which grieved my heart to see that I should abuse so good a wretch, and that it is just with God to make her bad to me for my wronging of her; but I do resolve never to do the like again. So to bed.

27. *Lords day.* Lay chatting with my wife a good while; then up and got me ready, and to church without my man William,[2] whom I have not seen today, nor care; but could be glad to have him put himself far enough out of my favour that he may not wonder to have me put him away. So home to dinner, being a little troubled to see Pembleton look into the church as he used to do, and my wife not being there, to go out again; but I do not discern in my wife the least memory of him.

Dined; and so to my office a little and then to church again, where a drowzy sermon; and so home to spend the evening with my poor wife – consulting about her closet, clothes, and other things. At night to supper, though with little comfort, I finding myself, both head and breast, in great pain; and which troubles me most, my right eare is almost deaf. It is a cold, which God Almighty in justice did give me while I sat lewdly sporting with Mrs. Lane the other day with the broken window in my neck. I went to bed with a posset, being very melancholy in consideration of the loss of my hearing.

OCTOBER.

4. *Lords day.* Up and to church, my house being miserably overflowed with rain last night, which makes me almost mad. At home

1. Ejaculate.
2. Will Hewer, living with Pepys as his manservant and also working as a navy clerk.

to dinner with my wife, and so to talk and to church again; and so home and all the evening most pleasantly passed the time in good discourse of our fortune and family, till supper; and so to bed – in some pain below, through cold got.

⟨⟨*My great fitt of the Collique*⟩⟩[1]

6. Slept pretty well, and my ⟨wife⟩ waked to ring the bell to call up our maids to the washing about 4 a-clock and I was, and she, angry that our bell did not wake them sooner; but I will get a bigger bell. So we to sleep again till 8 a-clock; and then I up in some ease to the office, where we had a full board.◆

At noon, Lewellin coming to me, I took him and Deane, and there met my uncle Thomas and we dined together. But was vexed that it being washing-day, we had no meat dressed; but sent to the cook's and my people had so little wit to send in our meat from abroad in the cook's dishes,[2] which were marked with the name of the Cooke upon them; by which, if they observed anything, they might know it was not my own dinner.

After dinner we broke up, and I by coach, setting down Luellin in Cheapside; and so to White-hall, where at the Committee of Tanger; but Lord, how I was troubled to see my Lord Tiviotts accounts of 10000*l* passed in that manner and wish 1000 times I had not been there.

Thence rise with Sir G. Carteret, and to his lodgings and there discoursed of our frays at the table today, and perticularly of that of the contract and the contract of masts the other day, declaring my fair dealing and so needing not any man's good report of it or word for it, and that I would make it so appear to him if he desired it; which he did, and I will do it.[3]

Thence home by water in great pain, and at my office a while; and thence a little to Sir W. Penn, and so home to bed. And finding myself beginning to be troubled with wind, as I used to be, and with pain in making water, I took a couple of pills that I had by me of Mr. Hollyards.[4]

1. Pepys's fit of colic – symptoms amply described below – lasted until 13 October.
2. The food was brought in from a cookshop.
3. Pepys had drawn up two contracts with William Warren to supply timber for ships, which had been challenged at the Navy Board. Officers of the Board often had their own preferred merchants, who would reward them for assistance in getting contracts agreed.
4. Thomas Hollier, Pepys's surgeon who had operated on him for the stone in 1658 and continued to attend him.

7. They wrought in the morning and I did keep my bed; and my pain continued on me mightily, that I keeped within all day in great pain, and could break no wind nor have any stool after my physic had done working. So in the evening I took coach and to Mr. Hollyards, but he was not at home; and so home again. And whether the coach did me good or no I know not, but having a good fire in my chamber, I begun to break six or seven small and great ⟨⟨8⟩⟩ farts; and so to bed and lay in good ease all night, and pissed pretty well in the morning, but no more wind came as it used to do plentifully, after it once begun, nor any inclination to stool. So, keeping myself warm, to the office; and at noon home to dinner, my pain coming again by breaking no wind nor having any stool; so to Mr. Hollyard and by his direction (he assuring me that it is nothing of the stone, but only my constitution being costive,[1] and that and cold from without breeding and keeping the wind) I took some powder that he did give me in white wine and sat late up, till past 11 at night, with my wife in my chamber, till it had done working; which was so weakly that I could hardly tell whether it did work or no. My maids, being at this time in great dirt toward getting of all my house clean, and weary and having a great deal of work to do therein tomorrow and next day, were gone to bed before my wife and I, who also do lie in our room, more like beasts then Christians; but that it is only in order to having of the house shortly in a cleaner, or rather very clean condition.

Some ease I had so long as this did keep my body loose, and I slept well.

12. Up (though slept well and made some water in the morning [as] I used to do) and a little pain returned to me and some fears; but being forced to go to the Duke at St. James, I took coach, and in my way called on Mr. Hollyard and had his advice to take a glister.[2]◆

So home and to dinner; and thence by coach to the Old Exchange and there cheapened some laces for my wife; and then to Mr.   , the great lace-man in Cheapside, and bought one cost me 4*l*., more by 20*s* then I entended; but when I came to see them, I was resolved to buy one worth wearing with credit. And so to the New Exchange and there put it to making. And so to my Lord's Lodgeings and left my wife; and so I to [the] Comittee of Tanger and then late home with my wife again by coach, beginning to be very well; and yet when I came home and went to try to shit, the

1. Predisposed to constipation.
2. Glyster (or clyster): an enema.

very little straining, which I thought was no strain at all at the present, did by and by bring me some pain for a good while.

Anon, about 8 a-clock, my wife did give me a Clyster which Mr. Hollyard directed, *viz.*, A pinte of strong ale, four ounces of Sugar, and two ounces of butter. It lay while I lay upon the bed above an hour, if not two. And then, thinking it quite lost, I rose; and by and by it begun with my walking to work, and gave me three or four most excellent stools and carried away wind – put me into excellent ease; and taking my usual wallnutt quantity of Electuary[1] at my going into bed, I had about two stools in the night – and pissed well. Voided some wind.

13. And so rose in the morning in perfect good ease, but only strain I put myself to to shit, more then I needed. But continued all the morning well; and in the afternoon had a natural easily and dry Stoole, the first I have had these five days or six, for which God be praised; and so am likely to continue well, observing for the time to come, when any of this pain comes again:

⟨⟨*Rules for my health.*⟩⟩

1. To begin to keep myself warm as I can.
2. Strain as little as ever I can backwards, remembering that my pain will come by and by, though in the very straining I do not feel it.
3. Either by physic forward or by clyster backward, or both ways, to get an easy and plentiful going to stool and breaking of wind.
4. To begin to suspect my health immediately when I begin to become costive and bound, and by all means to keep my body loose, and that to obtain presently after I find myself going to the contrary.

This morning at the office; and at noon with Creede to the Exchange, where much business.◆

Home, and Creede with me to dinner; and after dinner John Cole my old friend[2] came to see and speak with me about a friend. I find him ingenious, but do more and more discern his City pedantry; but however, I will endeavour to have his company now and then, for that he knows much of the temper of the City and is able to acquaint therein as much as most young men – being of large acquaintance, and himself I think somewhat unsatisfied with the present state of things at Court and in the Church.

1. A medicinal salve made with honey or syrup.
2. A school friend; now a London tradesman.

Then to the office and there busy till late; and so home to my wife, with some ease and pleasure that I hope to be able to fallow my business again; which, by God's leave, I am resolved to return to with more and more eagernesse.◆

14. Up and to my office, where all the morning – and part of it Sir J. Mennes spent as he doth everything else, like a fool, reading[1] the Anatomy of the body to me, but so sillily as to the making of me understand anything that I was weary of him. And so I toward the Change and met with Mr. Grant;[2] and he and I to the Coffee-house, where I understand by him that Sir W. Petty and his vessel are coming, and the King entends to go to Portsmouth to meet it.[3] Thence home; and after dinner my wife and I, by Mr. Rawlinsons[4] conduct, to the Jewish Synagogue[5] – where the men and boys in their Vayles,[6] and the women behind a lettice out of sight; and some things stand up, which I believe is their Law, in a press,[7] to which all coming in do bow; and at the putting on their veils do say something, to which others that hear him do cry Amen, and the party doth kiss his veil. Their service all in a singing way, and in Hebrew. And anon their Laws, that they take out of the press, is carried by several men, four or five, several burthens in all, and they do relieve one another, or whether it is that everyone desires to have the carrying of it, I cannot tell. Thus they carried [it] round, round about the room while such a service is singing. And in the end they had a prayer for the King, which they pronounced his name in Portugall; but the prayer, like the rest, in Hebrew. But Lord, to see the disorder, laughing, sporting, and no attention, but confusion in all their service, more like Brutes then people knowing the true God, would make a man forswear ever seeing them more; and endeed, I never did see so much, or could have imagined there had been any

1. Explaining.
2. John Graunt was a Fellow of the Royal Society and a pioneering demographer.
3. William Petty, a Fellow of the Royal Society, was experimenting with designs for a two-hulled or "double bottom" ship. This was a type of catamaran that he believed would be faster than conventional vessels.
4. Daniel Rawlinson, landlord of the Mitre in Fenchurch Street, one of the most elegant London taverns.
5. In Cree Church Lane. Jews had been expelled from England in 1290 and readmitted only in 1656. The Cree Church Lane synagogue was established by Sephardic Jews the following year. Pepys had visited once before in 1659.
6. Prayer shawls.
7. The Ark, containing the Torah.

religion in the whole world so absurdly performed as this.[1] Away thence, with my mind strangely disturbed with them, by coach, and set down my wife in Westminster-hall and I to White-hall, and there [the] Tanger Comittee met; but the Duke and the Affrica Comittee meeting in our room, Sir G. Carteret, Sir W Compton, Mr. Coventry, Sir W. Rider, Cuttance, and myself met in another room, with chairs set in form but no table; and there we had very fine discourses of the business of the fitness to keep Sally,[2] and also of the terms of our King's paying the Portugues that deserted their houses at Tanger[3] – which did much please me; and so to fetch my wife, and so to the New Exchange about her things, and called at Tho: Pepys the Turners and bought some things there; and so home to supper and to bed – after I had been a good while with Sir W. Penn, railing and speaking freely our minds against Sir W. Batten and Sir J. Mennes; but no more then the folly of one and the knavery of the other doth deserve.

17. Up and to my office; and there we sat, a very full board, all the morning upon some accounts of Mr. Gauden's. Here happened something concerning my Will;[4] which Sir W. Batten would fain charge upon him, and I heard him mutter something against him of complaint for his often receiving of people's money to Sir G. Carteret, which displeased me much – but I will be even with him.

Thence to the Dolphin Taverne, and there Mr. Gauden did give us a great dinner. Here we had some discourse of the Queenes being very sick, if not dead, the Duke and Duchesse of York being sent for betimes this morning to come to White-hall to her.[5]

So to my office and there late, doing business; and so home to supper, my house being got mighty clean, to my great content, from top to toe; and so to bed – myself beginning to be in good condition of health also; but only, my laying out so much money upon clothes for myself and wife and her closet troubles me.

19. Waked with a very high winde, and said to my wife, "I pray God

1. Pepys did not realize he was seeing the festival of Simchat Torah (the Rejoicing of the Law) rather than a typical service. Dancing and singing were part of the celebration.
2. Salé, a city south of Tangier, was a stronghold for Moroccan pirates. The British hoped to get control of it.
3. The Portuguese inhabitants who had left Tangier on its transfer to Britain.
4. Will Hewer.
5. She had spotted fever and was dangerously ill for about three weeks.

I hear not of the death of any great person, this wind is so high;" fearing that the Queene might be dead.[1]

So up; and going by coach with Sir W. Batten and Sir J. Mennes to St. James, they tell me that Sir W: Compton, who it is true had been a little sickly for a week or fortnight, but was very well upon Friday at night last at the Tanger Committee with us, was dead – died yesterday[2] – at which I was most exceedingly surprized; he being, and so all the world saying that he was, one of the worthyest men and best officers of State now in England; and so in my conscience he was – of the best temper, valour, abilities of mind, Integrity, birth, fine person, and diligence of any one man he hath left behind him in the three kingdoms; and yet not forty year old, or if so, that is all. I find the sober men of the Court troubled for him; and yet not so as to hinder or lessen their mirth, talking, laughing, and eating, drinking and doing everything else, just as if there was no such thing – which is as good an Instance for me hereafter to judge of Death, both as to the unavoydablenesse, suddenness, and little effect of it upon the spirits of others, let a man be never so high or rich or good; but that all die alike, no more matter being made of the death of one then another; and that even to die well, the prise of it is not considerable in the world, compared to the many in the world that know not nor make anything of it. Nay, perhaps to them (unless to one the like this poor gentleman, which is one of a thousand there, nobody speaking ill of him) that will speak ill of a man.

Coming to St. James's, I hear that the Queene did sleep five hours pretty well tonight, and that she waked and gargled her mouth, and to sleep again – but that her pulse beats fast, beating twenty to the King's or my Lady Suffolkes eleven – but not so strong as it was. It seems she was so ill as to be shaved and pigeons put to her feet,[3] and to have the Extreme unction given her by the priests, who were so long about it that the Doctors were angry. The King, they all say, is most fondly disconsolate for her and weeps by her, which makes her weep; which one this day told me he reckons a good sign, for that it carries away some Rheume from the head.

This morning Captain Allen tells me how the famous Ned Mullins by a slight fall broke his leg at the Ancle, which festered and he had his leg cut off on Saturday, but so ill done, notwithstanding

1. It was a superstition that a severe storm signalled the death of some eminent person.
2. Compton, Master of the Ordinance, died aged 38.
3. A cure for fevers and, as a last resort, used for other illnesses.

all the great Chyrurgeons about the town at the doing of it, that they fear he will not live with it, which is very strange, besides the Torment he was put to with it.[1]

After being a little with the Duke and being invited to dinner to my Lord Barkelys,[2] and so not knowing how to spend our time till noon, Sir W. Batten and I took Coach and to the Coffeehouse in Cornhill; where much talk about the Turkes proceedings[3] and that the plague is got to Amsterdam, brought by a ship from Argier – and it is also carried to Hambrough.[4] The Duke says the King purposes to forbid any ⟨of their⟩ ships coming into the River. The Duke also told us of several Christian Comanders, French, gone over to the Turkes to serve them. And upon enquiry, I find that the King of France doth by this aspire to the Empire, and so to get the Crowne of Spayne also upon the death of the King, which is very probable it seems.[5]

Back to St. James and there dined with my Lord Barkely and his Lady; where Sir G. Carteret, Sir W. Batten and myself, with two Gentlemen more – my Lady and one of the Ladies of Honour to the Duchesse, no handsome woman but a most excellent hand. A fine French dinner; and so we after dinner broke up, and I to Creedes new lodgings in Axe-yard, which I like very well. And so with him to White-hall and walked up and down in the gallerys with good discourse, and anon Mr. Coventry and Povy, sad for the loss of one of our number, we sat down as a Comittee for Tanger and did some business and so broke up, and I down with Mr. Coventry and in his chamber discoursed of businesses of the office and Sir J. Mennes and Sir W. Batten's carriage, which he most ingeniously tells me how they have carried themselfs to him, in forbearing to speak the other day to the Duke what they know they have so largely at other times said to him. And I told him what I am put to about the Bargaine for masts. I perceive he thinks of it all and will remember it.

Thence took up my wife at Mrs. Harpers, where she and Jane

1. Edward Molins was an eminent surgeon at St Thomas's hospital whose patients had included Oliver Cromwell. Molins died on 27 October.
2. John, first Baron Berkeley of Stratton, a Navy Commissioner.
3. To the alarm of Western Europe, an army from the Ottoman Empire had advanced into Hapsburg-ruled Hungary over the summer and now threatened Austria.
4. This is the first mention of the impending plague in the diary. Amsterdam and Hamburg suffered major outbreaks in 1664.
5. Pepys saw Louis XIV as willing to exploit division and weakness among Hapsburg rulers to take control of the Holy Roman Empire and the Spanish Crown. Philip IV of Spain was known to be ill.

was, and so called at the New Exchange for some things for her; and then at Toms went up and saw his house now it is finished; and endeed it is very handsome, but he not within and so home and to my office; and then to supper and to bed.

22. Up and to the office, where we sat till noon, and then I home to dinner; and after dinner, with my wife to her study and there read some more Arithmetique, which she takes with great ease and pleasure. This morning, hearing that the Queene grows worse again, I sent to stop the making of my velvett cloak, till I see whether she lives or dies.[1]

So a little abroad about several businesses, and then home and to my office till night, and then home to supper. Teach my wife, and so to bed.

31. Up and to the office, where we sat all the morning; and at noon home to dinner, where Creed came and dined with me. And after dinner he and I upstairs, and I showed him my velvet cloak and other things of clothes that I have lately bought, which he likes very well; and I took his opinion as to some things of clothes which I purpose to wear, being resolved to go a little handsomer then I have hitherto.

Then to the office, where busy till night; and then to prepare my monthly account, about which I stayed till 10 or 11 a-clock at night; and to my great sorrow, find myself 43*l* worse then I was the last month; which was then 760*l* and now it is but 717*l*. But it hath chiefly arisen from my layings-out in clothes for myself and wife – *viz.*, for her, about 12*l*; and for myself, 55*l* or thereabouts – having made myself a velvet cloak, two new cloth-suits, black, plain both – a new shag-gown, trimmed with gold buttons and twists; and a new hat, and silk top[s] for my legs, and many other things, being resolved henceforward to go like myself. And also two periwigs, one whereof costs me 3*l* and the other 40*s*. I have wore neither yet, but will begin next week, God willing. So that I hope I shall not now need to lay out more money a great while, I having laid out in clothes for myself and wife, and for her closet and other things without, these two months (this and the last), besides household expenses of victuals &c., above 110*l*. But I hope I shall with more comfort labour to get more, and with better successe then when, for want of clothes, I was forced to sneak like a beggar. Having done this, I went home; and after supper to bed, my mind being eased in

1. If the Queen died, Pepys would have to wear mourning.

knowing my condition, though troubled to think that I have been forced to spend so much.

Thus I end this month, worth 717*l* or thereabouts, with a good deal of good goods more then I had and a great deal of new and good clothes.

My greatest trouble and my wife's, is our family; mighty out of order by this fellow Wills corrupting the maids by his idle talk and carriage; which we are going to remove by hastening him out of the house, which his uncle Blackeburne is upon doing. And I am to give him 20*l* per annum towards his maintenance.[1]

The Queen continues light-headed, but in hopes to recover.

The Plague is much in Amsterdam, and we in fears of it here – which God defend.

The Turke goes on mightily in the Emperors dominions, and the princes cannot agree among themselfs how to go against him.[2]

Myself in pretty good health now, after being ill this month for a week together. But cannot yet come to shit well, being so costive, that for this month almost, I have not had a good natural stool; but to this hour am forced to take physic every night, which brings me neither but one stool, and that in the morning as soon as I am up – all the rest of the day very costive.

My father hath been very ill in the country, but I hope better again now.

I am lately come to a conclusion with Tom Trice to pay him 100*l*; which is a great deal of money, but I hope it will save a great deal more.[3]

But thus everything lessens what I have and am like to have; and therefore I must look about me to get something more then just my salary, or else I may resolve to live well and die a beggar.

NOVEMBER.

3. Up and to the office, where busy all the morning; and at noon to the Coffee-house and there heard a long and most passionate discourse between two Doctors of Physique (of which one was Dr. Allen, whom I knew at Cambrige)[4] and a Couple of Apothecarys;

1. Will had to leave his lodgings at Pepys's house, but was not losing his job.
2. The prince-electors of the Holy Roman Empire, meeting at the Diet of Regensburg, had so far failed to agree how to meet the Ottoman threat to Austria.
3. This was an out-of-court settlement over Robert Pepys's estate.
4. Thomas Allen, a fellow at Caius College, 1651–60.

these maintaining Chymistry against their Galenicall physic;[1] and the truth is, one of the Apothecaries, whom they charged most, did speak very prettily; that is, his language and sense good, though perhaps he might not be so knowing a physician as to offer to contest with them. At last they came to some cooler term and broke up. I home; and there Mr. Moore, coming by my appointment, dined with me; and after dinner came Mr. Goldsbrough and we discoursed about the business of his mother, but could come to no agreement in it but parted dissatisfied.[2] By and by comes Chapman the periwig-maker, and [upon] my liking it, without more ado I went up and there he cut off my haire; which went a little to my heart at present to part with it, but it being over and my periwig on, I paid him 3*l* for it; and away went he with my own hair to make up another of; and I by and by, after I had caused all my maids to look upon it and they conclude it to become me, though Jane was mightily troubled for my parting with my own hair and so was Besse – I went abroad to the Coffee-house; and coming back, went to Sir W. Penn and there sat with him and Captain Cocke till late at night, Cocke talking of some of the Roman history very well, he having a good memory. Sir W. Penn observed mightily and discoursed much upon my cutting off my hair, as he doth of everything that concerns me; but it is over, and so I perceive, after a day or two, it will be no great matter.

Home, and there I find my wife and her girl Susan fallen out, and she had struck her and the girl run to Griffen's;[3] but they not receiving nor encouraging of her, I sent for her home and there she fell on her knees and begged pardon; and so I made peace between her mistress and her and so all well again; and a pretty girl she will be, if she doth not get too much head.

To supper and then a little to my viall, and afterward with my wife to her Arithmetique, and so to bed.

9. Up, and find myself very well; and so by coach to White-hall and there met all my fellow-officers; and so to the Duke, where, when we came into his closet, he told us that Mr. Pepys was so altered with his new perriwigg that he did not know him.◆

Thence to Westminster-hall, where I met with Mr. Pierce the

1. Apothecaries prepared and sold Galenic (i.e. plant-based) medicines. Their approach, and that of Galenic physicians, was challenged by followers of Paracelsus and Van Helmont who advocated "chemical" medicines.
2. She owed mortgage payments to Roger Pepys's estate.
3. Will Griffith was doorkeeper at the Navy Office and had recommended the maid Susan.

surgeon;[1] and among other things, he asked me seriously whether I knew anything of my Lord's being out of Favour with the King. And told me that for certain the King doth take mighty notice of my Lord's living obscurely in a corner, not like himself and becoming the honour that he is come to. I was sorry to hear; and the truth is, from my Lord's discourse among his people (which I am told) of the uncertainty of princes favours and his melancholy keeping from Court, I am doubtful of some such thing; but I seemed wholly strange to ⟨him in⟩ it, but will make my use of it.

He told me also how loose the Court is, nobody looking after business but every man his lust and gain; and how the King is now become besotted upon Mrs. Steward, that he gets into corners and will be with her half an hour together, kissing her to the observation of all the world; and she now stays by herself and expects it, as my Lady Castlemayne did use to do; to whom the King, he says, is still kind, so as now and then he goes to have a chat with her as he believes, but with no such fondness as he used to do. But yet it is thought that this new wench is so subtle, that she lets him not do anything more then is safe to her. But yet his doting is so great that Pierce tells me it is verily thought, that if the Queen had died, he would have married her.

◆ And so having taken up something at my wife's tailors, I home by coach and there to my office, whither Shales came and I had much discourse with him about the business of the victualling; and thence in the evening to the Coffee-house and there sat, till by and by, by appointment, Will brought me word that his uncle Blackeburne was ready to speak with me. So I went down to him, and he and I to a taverne hard by; and there I begun to speak to Will friendlily, advising him how to carry himself now he is going from under my roof, without any reflections upon the occasion from whence his removal arose. This his uncle seconded; and after laying down to him his duty to me and what I expect of him, in a discourse of about quarter of an hour or more, we agreed upon his going this week, toward the latter of the week, and dismissed him. And Mr. Blackeburne and I fell to talk of many things; wherein I did speak so freely to him in many things agreeing with his sense, that he was very open to me in all things.

First, in that of Religion, he makes it great matter of prudence for the King and Council to suffer[2] liberty of conscience. And

1. He was surgeon to the Duke of York.
2. Allow.

imputes the loss of Hungary to the Turke from the Emperors denying them this liberty of their religion.[1]

He says that many pious Ministers of the word of God – some thousands of them, do now beg their bread.[2] And told me how highly the present Clergy carry themselfs everywhere, so as that they are hated and laughed at by everybody; among other things, for their excommunicacions, which they send upon the least occasions almost that can be. And I am convinced in my judgment, not only from his discourse but my thoughts in general, that the present clergy will never heartily go down with the generality of the commons of England; they have been so used to liberty and freedom, and they are so acquainted with the pride and debauchery of the present clergy. He did give me many stories of the affronts which the clergy receive in all places of England from the Gentlemen and ordinary persons of the parish.

He doth tell me what the City thinks of Generall Monke, as of a most perfidious man, that hath betrayed everybody, and the King also; who, as he thinks and his party, and so I have heard other good friends of the King say, it might have been better for the King to have had his hands a little bound for the present, then to be forced to bring such a crew of poor people about him, and be liable to satisfy the demands of every one of them.[3]

◆ He tells me that the King, by name, with all his dignities, is prayed for by them that they call Fanatiques, as heartily and powerfully as in any of the other churches that are thought better. And that let the King think what he will, it is them that must help him in the day of Warr – for, as they are the most, so generally they are the most substantiall sort of people, and the soberest.[4] And did desire me to observe it to my Lord Sandwich, among other things, that of all the old army now, you cannot see a man begging about the street. But what? You shall have this Captain turned a shoe-

1. Hungarian Protestants suffered persecution under local Catholic rulers and the Holy Roman Emperor Leopold had failed to intervene. Some Protestant leaders, believing that Ottoman rule would be less harsh, therefore refused to fight the Turks. Robert Blackborne (Secretary to the Admiralty Committee during the Protectorate) was a puritan.
2. The Act of Uniformity and other measures had removed around 2,000 ministers, university fellows, and teachers from office.
3. Blackborne's argument was that if the King at his restoration had accepted limitations on his power – as some Presbyterians had wanted but others (including Monck) had successfully opposed – he would have been protected from such demands.
4. Protestant dissenters were in fact in a minority, but they included many rich merchants.

maker; the lieutenant, a Baker; this, a brewer; that, a haberdasher; this common soldier, a porter; and every man in his apron and frock, &c., as if they never had done anything else – whereas the other[1] go with their belts and swords, swearing and cursing and stealing – running into people's houses, by force oftentimes, to carry away something. And this is the difference between the temper of one and the other; and concludes (and I think with some reason) that the spirits of the old Parliament-soldier[s] are so quiet and contented with God's providences, that the King is safer from any evil meant him by them, a thousand times more then from his own discontented Cavalier[s].◆

From thence we begun to talk of the Navy, and perticularly of Sir W Pen – of whose rise to be a general I had a mind to be informed. He told me he was alway a conceited man and one that would put the best side outward, but that it was his pretence of sanctity that brought him into play.◆ And lastly, tells me that just upon the turn, when Moncke was come from the North to the City and did begin to think of bringing in the King, Pen was then turned Quaker; this he is most certain of. He tells me that Lawson[2] was never counted anything but only a seaman, and a stout man but a false man; and that now he appears the greatest hypocrite in the world – and Pen the same.[3] He tells me that it is much talked of, that the King entends to legitimate the Duke of Monmouth; and that he hath not, nor his friends of his persuasion, had any hopes of getting their consciences at liberty but by God Almighty's turning of the King's heart, which they expect; and are resolved to live and die in quiet hopes of it, but never to repine or act anything more then by prayers towards it. And that not only himself; but all of them have and are willing at any time to take the oaths of Allegiance and Supremacy.

Thus far, and upon many more things, we had discoursed, when some persons in a room hard by begun to sing in three parts very finely, and to play upon a Flagilette so pleasantly, that my discourse afterward was but troublesome and I could not attend it; and so anon considering of a sudden the time a-night, we find it 11 a-clock, which I thought it had not been by two hours, but we were close

1. The cavaliers.
2. John Lawson, a republican and prominent naval officer under the Commonwealth, had been instrumental in restoring the monarchy. He was rewarded with a knighthood and naval commands.
3. Penn was unpopular with Commonwealth men such as Blackborne because of his correspondence with the royalists in the late 1650s.

in talk; and so we rise, he having drunk some wine and I some beer and sugar, and so by a fair moonshine home and to bed. My wife troubled with tooth-ake.◆

12. Lay long in bed; endeed too long, divers people and the officers at the office staying for me – my Cosen Tho. Pepys the Executor being below; and I went to him and stated reckonings about our debt to him for his payments of money to my uncle Tho. heretofore by the Captains[1] order. I did not pay him, but will soon do it if I can.

To the office and there all the morning; where Sir W. Penn, like a coxcomb, was so ready to cross me in a motion I made unawares, for the entering a man at Chatham into the works[2] – wherein I was vexed to see his spleen, but glad to understand it and that it was in no greater a matter, I being not at all concerned here.

To the Change and did several businesses there; and so home with Mr. Moore to dinner – my wife having dined with Mr. Hollyard with her today, he being come to advise about her hollow sore place below in her privities.

After dinner, Mr. Moore and I discoursing of my Lord's negligence in attendance at Court and the discourse the world makes of it, with the too great reason that I believe there is for it, I resolved and took coach to his lodgings, thinking to speak with my Lord about it without more ado. Here I met Mr. How, and he and I largely about it and he very soberly acquainted me how things are with my Lord. That my Lord doth not do anything like himself, but follows his folly and spends his time either at Cards at Court with the ladies, when he is there at all, or else at Chelsy with that slut, to his great disgrace. And endeed, I do see and believe that my Lord doth apprehend that he doth grow less, too, at Court.

Anon my Lord doth come in and I begun to fall in discourse with him; but my heart did misgive me that my Lord would not take it well, and then found him not in a humour to talk; and so after a few ordinary words, my Lord not talking in that manner as he uses to do, I took leave and spent some time with W. Howe again; and told him how I could not do what I had so great a mind and resolution to do, but that I thought it would be as well to do it in writing; which he approves of, and so I took leave of him and by coach home, my mind being full of it and in pain concerning it. So to my office, busy very late, the nights running on faster then one thinks. And so home to supper and to bed.

1. Captain Robert Pepys, Pepys's late uncle.
2. I.e. employing him at Chatham dockyard.

14.◆ This night I think is the first that I have lain without ever a man in my house besides myself since I came to keep any – Will being this night gone to his lodgings. And by the way, I hear today that my boy Waynman hath behaved himself so with Mr. Davis, that they have got him put into a Berbados ship to be sent away; and though he sends to me to get a release for him, I will not, out of love to the boy; for I doubt to keep him here were to bring him to the gallows.[1]

16.◆ In the afternoon to my office and there late; and in the evening Mr. Hollyard came, and he and I about our great work to look upon my wife's malady in her secrets; which he did, and it seems her great conflux of humours heretofore, that did use to swell there, did in breaking leave a hallow;[2] which hath since gone in further and further, till now it is near three inches deep; but as God will have it, it doth not run into the bodyward, but keeps to the outside of the skin, and so he must be forced to cut it open all along; and which my heart I doubt will not serve for me to see done, and yet she will not have anybody else to see it done; no, not her own maids; and therefore I must do it, poor wretch, for her. Tomorrow night he is to do it.

He being gone, I to my office again a little while; and so home to supper and to bed.

17.◆ With Mr. Moore to my office and there I read to him the letter I have writ to send to my Lord, to give him an account how the world, both City and Court, doth talk of him and his living as he doth there, in such a poor and bad house, so much to his disgrace – which Mr. Moore doth conclude so well drawn, that he would not have me by any means to neglect sending it; assuring me, in the best of his judgment, that it cannot but endear me to my Lord, instead of what I fear, of getting his offence; and did offer to take the same words and send them, as from him with his hand, to him – which I am not unwilling should come (if they are at all fit to go) from anybody but myself. And so he being gone, I did take a copy of it to keep by me in shorthand, and sealed them up to send tomorrow by my Will. So home, Mr. Hollyard being come to my wife. And there, she being in bed, he and I alone to look again upon her parts, and there he doth find that though it would not be much

1. It is not known if Wayneman Birch was sent to Barbados as an indentured servant. If so, he was back in London by November 1675 when he married at St George the Martyr, Southwark.
2. Elizabeth suffered from a recurring Bartholin cyst of the labia, now an abscess.

pain, yet she is so fearful, and the thing will be somewhat painful in the tending, which I shall not be able to look after but must require a nurse and people about her; so that upon second thoughts, he believes that a fomentacion[1] will do as well; and though it will be troublesome, yet no pain, and what her maid will be able to do without knowing directly what it is for, but only that it may be for the piles – for though it be nothing but what is very honest, yet my wife is loath to give occasion of discourse concerning it. By this, my mind and my wife's is much eased; for I confess I should have been troubled to have had my wife cut before my face – I could not have borne to have seen it. I had great discourse with him about my disease.[2] He tells me again that I must eat in a morning some loosening grewell; and at night, roasted apples. That I must drink now and then ale with my wine, and eat bread and butter and honey – and rye bread if I can endure it, it being loosening. I must also take once a week a glister of his last prescription; only, honey now and then instead of butter – which things I am now resolved to apply myself to. He being gone, I to my office again to a little business; and then home to supper and to bed – being in a little pain by drinking of cold small beer today, and being in a cold room at the Taverne I believe.

⟨⟨*Physique*⟩⟩

18. Up; and after being ready and done a little business at the office, I and Mr. Hater by water to Redriffe; and so walked to Deptford (where I have not been a very great while) and there paid off the *Milford* in very good order; and all respect showed me in the office, as much as there used to be to any of the rest or the whole board. That done, at noon I took Captain Terne and there coming in by chance Captain Berkely, him also to dinner with me to the Globe. Captain Berkely, who was lately come from Algier, did give us a good account of the place, and how the Bassha[3] there doth live like a prisoner, being at the mercy of the soldiers and officers, so that there is nothing but a great confusion there.

After dinner came Sir Wm Batten, and I left him to pay off another ship and I walked home again, reading of a little book of new poems of Cowly's, given me by his brother.[4] Abraham doth lie, it seems, very sick still; but like to recover.

At my office till late; and then came Mr. Hollyard, so full of

1. The application of warm, soft medicine, sometimes on a heated cloth.
2. Colic.
3. Pasha: the governor.
4. The book was Abraham Cowley's *Verses Written upon Several Occasions* (1663). Cowley's brother Thomas was Clerk of the Cheque at Deptford.

discourse and Latin that I think he hath got a cup, but I do not know; but full of talk he is, in defence of Calvin and Luther. He begun this night the fomentacion to my wife, and I hope it will do well with her. He gone, I to the office again a little, and so to bed.

This morning I sent Will with my great letter of reproof to my Lord Sandwich, who did give it into his own hand.

My Lord.

I do verily hope that neither the manner nor matter of this advice will be condemned by your Lordshipp, when for my defence in the first I shall allege my double attempt (since your return from Hinchingbrooke) of doing it personally, in both of which your Lordships occasions, no doubtfulness of mine prevented me. And that being now fearful of a sudden summons to Portsmouth for the discharge of some ships there, I judge it very unbecoming the duty which (every bit of bread I eat tells me) I owe to your Lordshipp to expose the safety of your Honour to the uncertainty of my return. For the matter (my Lord), it is such as could I in any measure think safe to conceal from, or likely to be discovered to you by any other hand, I should not have dared so far to own what from my heart I believe is false, as to make myself but the relater of others discourse. But, Sir, your Lordships honour being such as I ought to value it to be, and finding both in City and Court that discourses pass to your prejudice, too generally for mine or any man's controlling but your Lordships, I shall (my Lord), without the least greatening or lessening the matter, do my duty in laying it shortly before you.

People of all conditions (my Lord) raise matter of wonder from your Lordships so little appearance at Court – some concluding thence your disfavour there. To which purpose I have had Questions asked me; and endeavouring to put off such insinuacions by asserting the contrary, they have replied that your Lordships living so beneath your Quality, out of the way and declining of Court attendance, hath been more then once discoursed about the King.

Others (my Lord), when the chief Ministers of State, and those most active of the Council have been reckoned up (wherein your Lordship never use to want an eminent place), have said, touching your Lordshipp, that now your turn was served and the King had given you a good estate, you left him to stand or fall as he would. And, perticularly in that of the Navy, have enlarged upon your letting fall all service there.

Another sort (and those the most) insist upon the bad report of the house wherein your Lordship (now observed in perfect health again) continues to sojourne. And by name have charged one of the daughters for a common Courtizan, alleging both places and persons where and with whom she hath been too well known. And how much her wantonness occasions (though unjustly) scandal to your Lordship; and that as well to gratifying of some enemies as to the wounding of more friends, I am not able to tell.

Lastly (my Lord), I find a general coldness in all persons towards your Lordship; such as, from my first dependence on you, I never yet knew. Wherein I shall not offer to interpose any thoughts or advice of mine, well knowing your Lordship needs not any. But, with a most faithful assurance that no person nor papers under Heaven is privy to what I here write, besides myself and this,[1] which I shall be careful to have put into your own hands, I rest confident of your Lordships just construction of my dutiful intents herein, and in all humility take leave.

May it please your Lordship,

Nov. 17. 1663./ Your Lordships most obedient servant,

S.P./

Memorandum. The letter beforegoing was sent sealed up, and enclosed in this that fallows.

My Lord.

If this finds your Lordshipp either not alone or not at leisure, I beg the suspending your opening of the enclosed till you shall be both – (the matter very well bearing such a delay) and in all humility remain.

May it please your Lordshipp

Nov. 17. 1663./ Your Lordships most obedient servant,

S.P./

My servant hath my directions to put this into your Lordships own hand, but not to stay for any answer.

I pray God give a blessing to it. But I confess I am afeared what the consequence may be to me of good or bad, which is according to the ingenuity that he doth receive it with. However, I am satisfied that it will do him good – and that he needs it.

22. *Lords day.* Up pretty early; and having last night bespoke a coach, which failed me this morning, I walked as far as the Temple and there took coach and to my Lord's lodgings; whom I find ready

1. But Pepys had recorded the secret in his diary and read the letter to Moore on 17 November.

to go to chappell. But coming, he begin with a very serious countenance to tell me that he had received my late letter; wherein, first he took notice of my care of him and his honour and did give me thanks for that part of it where I say that from my heart I believe the contrary of what I do there relate to be the discourse of others. But since I entended it not a reproach, but matter of information and for him to make a judgment of it for his practice, it was necessary for me to tell him the persons of whom I have gathered the several perticulars which I there insist on. I would have made excuses in it; but seeing him so earnest in it, I found myself forced to it; and so did tell him Mr. Pierce the surgeon in that of his low living being discoursed of at Court – a maid-servant that I kept that lived at Chelsy school;[1] and also Mr. Pickering, about the report touching the young woman; and also Mr. Hunt in axe-yard, near whom she lodged. I told him the whole City doth discourse concerning his neglect of business; and so I many times asserting my dutiful intention in all this, and he owning his accepting of it as such. That that troubled me most in perticular is that he did there assert the civility of the people of the house and the young gentlewoman, for whose reproach he was sorry. His saying that he was resolved how to live; and that though he was taking a house, meaning to live in another manner, yet it was not to please any people or to stop report, but to please himself (though this I do believe he might say that he might not seem to me to be so much wrought upon by what I have writ); and lastly and most of all, when I spoke of the tenderness that I have used in declaring this to him, there being nobody privy to it, he told me that I must give him leave to except one. I told him that possibly somebody might know of some thoughts of mine, I having borrowed some intelligence in this matter from them, but nobody could say they knew of the thing itself when I writ.[2] This, I confess however, doth trouble me, for that he seemed to speak it as a quick retort; and it must sure be Will Howe, who did not see anything of what I writ, though I told him indeed that I would write; but in this I think there is no great hurt.

I find him, though he cannot but own his opinion of my good intentions, and so he did again and again profess it, that he is troubled in his mind at it; and I confess I think I may have done myself an injury for his good; which, were it to do again and that I believed he would take it no better, I think I should sit quietly,

1. Mary Ashwell.
2. Except, of course, Henry Moore.

without taking any notice of it – for I doubt there is no medium between his taking it very well and very ill.

I could not forbear weeping before him at the latter end; which since I am ashamed of, though I cannot see what he can take it to proceed from but my tenderness and good will to him.

After this discourse was ended, he begun to talk very cheerfully of other things, and I walked with him to White-hall and we discoursed of the pictures in the gallery; which, it may be, he might do out of policy, that the boy might not see any strangeness in him; but I rather think that his mind was somewhat eased, and hope that he will be to me as he was before. But however, I doubt not but when he sees that I fallow my business and become an honour to him, and not to be like to need him or to be a burden to him, and rather able to serve him then to need him, and if he doth continue to fallow business and so come to his right wits again, I do not doubt but he will then consider my faithfulness to him – and esteem me as he ought.

At Chappell I had room in the Privy Seale pew with other gentlemen, and there heard Dr. Killigrew preach;[1] but my mind was so, I know not whether troubled or only full of thoughts of what had passed between my Lord and me, that I could not mind it nor can at this hour remember three words; the Anthemne was good after sermon, being the 51 psalme – made for five voices by one of Captain Cookes[2] boys, a pretty boy – and they say there are four or five of them that can do as much. And here I first perceived that the King is a little Musicall, and kept good time with his hand all along the Anthem.◆

Thence I to the Kings-head ordinary and there dined; good and much company and a good dinner; most of their discourse was about hunting, in a dialect[3] I understand very little.

Thence by coach to our own church; and there, my mind being yet unsettled, I could mind nothing; and after sermon home and there told my wife what had passed; and thence to my office, where doing business only to keep my mind imployed till late; and so home to supper, to prayers and to bed.

1. Henry Killigrew, chaplain to the King.
2. Capt. Henry Cooke, Master of the Children of the Chapel Royal.
3. Jargon.

DECEMBER.

6. *Lords day.* Lay long in bed; and then up and to church alone (which is the greatest trouble that I have, by not having a man or boy to wait on me) and so home to dinner; my wife, it being a cold day and it begin to snow (the first snow we have seen this year), kept her bed till after dinner. And I below by myself looking over my arithmetique books and Timber Rule.

So my wife rise anon, and she and I all the afternoon at Arithmetique; and she is come to do Addicion, Substraccion and Multiplicacion very well – and so I purpose not to trouble her yet with Division, but to begin with the globes to her now.[1]

At night came Captain Grove to discourse with me about Fields business[2] and of other matters. And so he being gone, I to my office and spent an hour or two reading Rushworth;[3] and so to supper home, and to prayers and bed – finding myself by cold to have some pain begin with me, which God defend should encrease.

12.◆ To the Exchange, where I had sent Luellin word I would come to him; and thence brought him home to dinner with me. He told me that W. Symons's wife is dead, for which I am sorry, she being a good woman; and tells me an odde story of her saying before her death, being in good sense, that there stood her uncle Scobell.[4]

Then he begin to tell me that Mr. Deering had been with him to desire him to speak to me that if I would get him off with those goods upon his hands, he would give me 50 peeces. And further, that if I would stand his friend, to help him to the benefitt of his patent as the King's merchant, he could spare me 200*l* per annum out of his profits.[5] I was glad to hear both of these; but answered

1. Pepys planned to teach Elizabeth geography and astronomy using a terrestrial and a celestial globe.
2. On-going legal disputes between Navy Board members and Edward Field. *See* 6 Feb. 1663.
3. John Rushworth's *Historical Collections of Private Passages of State* (1659) offered a political narrative of events from 1618 to 1629, supported by documentation.
4. Henry Scobell's appearance to Margaret Symons was noteworthy because he had died in 1660. Will Symons, like Peter Llewellyn, was a friend from Pepys's time as a clerk during the Commonwealth.
5. Llewellyn was clerk to the merchant Edward Dering, who wanted Pepys's help with selling the navy his surplus of deals. Dering had been appointed "King's Merchant" in 1660.

him no further then that as I would not by anything be bribed to be unjust in my dealings, so I was not so squeemish as not to take people's acknowledgment where I have the good fortune by my pains to do them good and just offices. And so I would not come to be at an agreement with him, but I would labour to do him this service, and to expect his consideration thereof afterward, as he thought fit. So I expect to hear more of it.◆

25. *Christmas.* Lay long, talking pleasantly with my wife; but among other things, she begin, I know not whether by design or chance, to enquire what she should do if I should by an accident die; to which I did give her some slight answer, but shall make good use of it to bring myself to some settlement for her sake, by making a Will as soon as I can.

Up, and to church, where Mr. Mills made an ordinary sermon; and so home and dined with great pleasure with my wife; and all the afternoon, first looking out at window and seeing the boys playing at many several sports in our back-yard by Sir W Pens, which minded me of my own former times; and then I begin to read to my wife upon the globes, with great pleasure and to good purpose, for it will be pleasant to her and to me to have her understand those things.

In the evening to the office, where I stayed late reading Rushworth, which is a most excellent collection of the beginning of the late quarrels in this kingdom. And so home to supper and to bed with good content of mind.

30. Up betimes and by coach to my Lord Sandwich; who I met going out, and he did ask me how his Cosen (my wife) did – the first time he hath done so since his being offended; and in my conscience, he would be glad to be free with me again, but he knows not how to begin. So he went out; and I through the garden to Mr. Coventry, where I saw Mr. Chr. Pett bring him a Modell,[1] and endeed it is a pretty one, for a New Year's gift – but I think the work not better done then mine.

With him by coach to London, with good and friendly discourse of business and against Sir Wm Batten – and his foul dealings. So leaving him at the Guiny-house,[2] I to the Coffee, whither came Mr. Grant and Sir Wm Petty, with whom I talked and so did many,

1. Of a ship.
2. Africa House, headquarters of the Company of Royal Adventurers of England Trading into Africa.

almost all the house there, about his new Vessell;[1] wherein he did give me much satisfaction in every point that I am almost confident she will prove an admirable invencion.

So home to dinner, after been upon the Change a while, and dined with my wife, who took physic today; and so to my office and there all the afternoon till late at night, about office business; and so to supper and to bed.

31. Up and to the office, where we sat all the morning. And among other things, Sir W. Warren came about some contract and there did at the open table, Sir W. Batten not being there, openly defy him and insisted how Sir W. Batten did endeavour to oppose him in everything that he offered. Sir W. Penn took him up for it like a counterfeit rogue, though I know he was as much pleased to hear him talk so as any man there. But upon his speaking, no more was said; but to the business. At noon we broke up, and I to the Change a while and so home again to dinner, my head akeing mightily with being overcharged with business. We had to dinner, my wife and I, a fine Turkey and a mince-pie, and dined in state, poor wretch, she and I; and have thus kept our Christmas together, all alone almost – having not once been out. But tomorrow my vowes are all out as to plays and wine; but I hope I shall not be long before I come to new ones, so much good, and God's blessing, I find to have attended them. Thence to the office and did several businesses and answered several people; but my head akeing and it being my great night of accounts, I went forth, took coach, and to my brother's, but he was not within; and so I back again and sat an hour or two at the Coffee, hearing some simple discourse about Quakers being charmed by a string about their wrists.[2] And so home; and after a little while at my office, I home and supped; and so had a good fire in my chamber and there sat till 4 a-clock in the morning, making up my accounts and writing this last Journall of the year. And first, I bless God I do, after a large expense, even this month by reason of Christmas and some payments to my father and other things extraordinary, find that I am worth in money, besides all my household stuff or anything of Brampton, above 800*l*; whereof, in my Lord Sandwiches hand, 700*l*., and the rest in my hand; so that there is not above 15*l* of all my estate in money at this minute out of my hands and my Lord's – for which the good God be pleased

1. Petty's double-hulled ship.
2. George Fox, a founder of the Quakers, recorded that he was accused in the 1650s of hanging ribbons on people's arms to make them follow him by witchcraft.

to give me a thankful heart and a mind careful to preserve this and encrease it.

I do live at my lodgings in the Navy Office – my family being, besides my wife and I, Jane Gentleman, Besse our excellent good-natured cook-maid, and Susan, a little girl – having neither man nor boy, nor like to have again a good while – living now in most perfect content and quiet and very frugally also. My health pretty good, but only that I have been much troubled with a costivenesse which I am labouring to get away, and have hopes of doing it. At the office I am well, though envied to the devil by Sir W. Batten, who hates me to death but cannot hurt me. The rest either love, or at least do not show otherwise, though I know Sir W. Penn to be a false knave touching me, though he seems fair.

My father and mother well in the country; and at this time, the young ladies of Hinchingbrooke[1] with them, their house having the small-pox in it.

The Queene, after a long and sore sickness, is become well again. And the King minds his mistresses a little too much, [as] if it pleased God. But I hope all things will go well, and in the Navy perticularly; wherein I shall do my duty, whatever comes of it.

The great talk is the designs of the King of France; whether against the Pope or King of Spain nobody knows;[2] but a great and a most promising prince he is, and all the princes of Europe have their eye upon him. My wife's brother come to great unhappiness by the ill-disposition, my wife says, of his wife, and her poverty; which she now professes, after all her husband's pretence of a great portion. But I see none of them; at least, they come not to trouble me.

At present, I am concerned for my Cosen Angier of Cambrige, lately broke in his trade. And this day am sending his son John, a very rogue, to sea.

My brother Tom I know not what to think of, for I cannot hear whether he minds his business or no. And my brother John, at Cambrige with as little hopes of doing good there; for when he was here, he did give me great cause of dissatisfaction with his manner of life. Pall with my father, and God knows what she doth there or what will become of her, for I have not anything yet to spare

1. Sandwich's daughters.
2. Earlier in the year, Louis XIV had broken off diplomatic relations with Pope Alexander VII and seized Avignon from papal control. He had also made claims to the Spanish Netherlands.

her, and she grows now old[1] and must be disposed of one way or other.

The Duchesse of Yorke at this time sick of the Mezles, but is growing well again.

The Turkes very fur entered into Germany,[2] and all that part of the world at a loss what to expect from his proceedings.

Myself, blessed be God, in a good way and design and resolution of sticking to my business to get a little money, with doing the best service I can to the King also – which God continue. So ends the old year.

1. She was 23.
2. Ottoman armies had in fact not entered Austria ("Germany"), but had made gains in Hapsburg-ruled Hungary.

1664

$16\frac{63}{64}$. *JANUARY.*

1. Went to bed between 4 and 5 in the morning with my mind in good temper of satisfaction – and slept till about 8, that many people came to speak with me. Among others, one came with the best New Year's gift that ever I had; namely from Mr. Deering, with a bill of exchange drawn upon himself for the payment of 50*l.* to Mr. Luellin – it being for my use, with a letter of compliment.[1] I am not resolved what or how to do in this business, but I conclude it is an extraordinary good New Year's gift, though I do not take the whole; or if I do, then give some of it to Luellin. By and by comes Captain Allin and his son Jowles and his wife, who continues pretty still. They would have had me set my hand to a certificate for his Loyalty and I know not what, his ability for any imployment.[2] But I did not think it fit, but did give them a pleasing denial – and after sitting with me an hour, they went away. Several others came to me about business; and then, being to dine at my uncle Wights, I went to the Coffee-house (sending my wife by Will) and there stayed talking an hour with Collonell Middleton and others; and among other things, about a very rich widow, young and handsome, of one Sir Nich. Golds, a merchant lately fallen, and of great Courtiers that already look after her. Her husband not dead a week yet. She is reckoned worth 80000*l.*

Thence to my Uncle Wights, where Dr. [3] among others dined, and his wife a seeming proud conceited woman; I know not what to make of her. But the Doctors discourse did please me very well about the disease of the Stone; above all things extolling Turpentine, which he told me how it may be taken in pills with great ease. There was brought to table a hot pie made of a swan I sent them yesterday, given me by Mr. Howe; but we did not eat any of it. But my wife and I rise from table pretending business, and went to the Dukes house, the first play I have been at these six months,

1. This was the money promised to Pepys for helping Dering sell his surplus of deals to the navy (*see* 12 Dec. 1663). He had secured the sale in December.
2. Captain John Allen had until recently been Clerk of the Ropeyard at Chatham; the assistance was for his son-in-law Henry Jowles. Pepys knew Jowles (by the report of Jowles's mother-in-law) as a "coxcomb".
3. Supply "[Alexander] Burnet", a friend of Wight.

according to my last vowe;[1] and here saw the so much cried-up play of *Henry the 8th* – which, though I went with resolution to like it, is so simple a thing, made up of a great many patches, that, besides the shows and processions in it, there is nothing in the world good or well done.[2] Thence, mightily dissatisfied, back at night to my uncle Wights and supped with them; but against my stomach out of the offence the sight of my aunts hands gives me; and ending supper with a mighty laugh (the greatest I have had these many months) at my uncles being out in his grace after meat, we rise and broke up and my wife and I home and to bed – being sleepy since last night.

8.◆ At noon to the Change and there long; and from thence by appointment took Luellin, Mount, and W. Symons and Mr. Pierce the surgeon home to dinner with me, and were merry. But Lord, to hear how W. Symons doth commend [her] and look sadly, and then talk bawdily and merrily, though his wife was dead but the other day, would make a dog laugh. This dinner I did give in further part of kindness to Luellin for his kindness about Deering's fifty pounds which he procured me the other day of him.

We spent all the afternoon together and then they to cards with my wife (who this day put on her Indian blue gown,[3] which is very pretty), where I left them for an hour and to my office and then to them again; and by and by they went away at night and so I again to my office to perfect a letter to Mr. Coventry about Deputy Treasurers; wherein I please myself and hope to give him content and do the King service therein.

So having done, I home and to teach my wife a new lesson in the Globes and to supper and to bed.

We had great pleasure this afternoon, among other things, to talk of our old passages together in Cromwells time. And how W. Symons did make me laugh and wonder today, when he told me how he had made shift to keep in, in good esteem and imployment, through eight governements in one year (the year 1659, which were endeed, and he did name them all)[4] and then failed unhappy in the

1. By an oath on 14 June 1663 (not recorded under that day), Pepys had sworn to attend no more plays until after Christmas.
2. Davenant's revival of Shakespeare's play at the Lincoln's Inn Fields Theatre.
3. A loose gown of Indian style, material, or pattern.
4. Reckoning by the old calendar and counting all changes in executive, there were eight between the Protectorate of Richard Cromwell (ending 22 April 1659) and the reconstituted Council of State (25 February to 1 May 1660). Symons had been an underclerk to the Council of State.

ninth, *viz.* that of the King's coming in. He made good to me the story which Luellin did tell me the other day, of his wife upon her death-bed – how she dreamt of her uncle Scobell and did foretell, from some discourse she had with him, that she should die four days thence and not sooner, and did all along say so and did so.

Upon the Change, a great talk there was of one Mr. Tryan, an old man, a merchant in Lymestreete, robbed last night (his man and maid being gone out after he was a-bed) and gagged and robbed of 1050*l* in money and about 4000*l* in Jewells which he had in his house as security for money. It is believed that his man, by many circumstances, is guilty of confederacy, by their ready going to his secret Till[1] in his desk wherein the key of his cash-chest lay.

10. *Lords day.* Lay in bed with my wife till 10 or 11 a-clock, having been very sleepy all night. So up, and my brother Tom being come to see me, we to dinner – he telling me how Mrs. Turner found herself discontented with her last bad journey, and not well taken by them in the country, they not desiring her coming down nor the burial of Mr. Edw. Pepys's corps there.[2] After dinner, I to the office, where all the afternoon; and at night my wife and I to my Uncle Wight's and there eat some of their swan-pie, which was good, and I invited them to my house to eat a roast swan on Tuesday next; which after I was come home, did make a quarrel between my wife and I, because she had appointed a wash tomorrow. But however, we were friends again quickly. So to bed. All our discourse tonight was about Mr. Tryan's late being robbed and that Collonell Turner (a mad, swearing, confident fellow, well known by all and by me), one much endebted to this man for his very lifelihood, was the man that either did or plotted it; and the money and things are found in his hand and he and his wife now in Newgate for it – of which we are all glad, so very a known rogue he was.[3]

12. Up and to the office, where we sat all the morning; and at noon to the Change awhile and so home – getting things against dinner ready. And anon comes my uncle Wight and my aunt with their Cozen Mary and Robert, and by chance my Uncle Tho. Pepys. We had a good dinner, the chief dish a swan roasted, and that excellent

1. Compartment or drawer for valuables.
2. Edward Pepys, Jane Turner's brother, had died at her London house in December 1663, but been buried at Tattersett, Norfolk.
3. James Turner, self-styled colonel and ex-cavalier, had been a business associate of Tryon. Turner was a noted figure in London thanks to his boastful temper, shady legal dealings, and rumoured crimes (including highway robbery). His life and trial were the subject of multiple pamphlets around this time.

meat. At dinner and all day very merry. After dinner to Cards, where till evening; then to the office a little and to cards again with them – and lost half-a-Crowne. They being gone, my wife did tell me how my Uncle did this day accost her alone and spoke of his hopings she was with child; and kissing her earnestly, told her he should be very glad of it; and from all circumstances, methinks he doth seem to have some intention of good to us, which I shall endeavour to continue more then ever I did yet.[1] So to my office till late and then home to bed – after being at prayers, which is the first time after my late vow to say prayers in my family twice in every week.

16. Up; and having paid some money in the morning to my Uncle Tho. on his yearly annuity – to the office, where we sat all the morning. At noon I to the Change about some pieces-of-eight for Sir J Lawson. And there I hear that Collonell Turner is found guilty of Felony at the Sessions in Mr. Tryan's business, which will save his life.[2] So home and met there James Harper, come to see his kinswoman, our Jane:[3] I made much of him and made him dine with us – he talking after the old simple manner that he used to do. He being gone, I by water to Westminster-hall and there did see Mrs. Lane, and de là, elle and I to the cabaret at the Cloche in the street du roy; and there, after some caresses, je l'ay foutée sous de la chaise deux times, and the last to my great pleasure; mais j'ai grand peur que je l'ay fait faire aussi elle même. Mais after I had done, elle commençait parler as before and I did perceive that je n'avais fait rien de danger à elle. Et avec ça, I came away; and though I did make grand promises à la contraire, nonobstant je ne la verrai pas long time.[4] So by coach home and to my office, where

1. Uncle Wight's intentions were not good, as Pepys would later discover. The nature of the details Elizabeth passed to her husband suggests she may have recognized this earlier than he did.
2. A mistake. Turner had been found guilty of both felony and burglary in Tryon's case. If he had been found guilty of felony alone, he could (as a literate man) have pleaded benefit of clergy, and perhaps have escaped with his life. But burglary was non-clergyable.
3. The chambermaid, Jane Gentleman.
4. This is Pepys's first use of a foreign language when describing his sexual exploits. Translation: "thence, she and I to the tavern at the Bell in King Street; and there, after some caresses, I fucked her under the chair two times, and the last to my great pleasure; but I am much afeared that I made her do [i.e. orgasm] too herself. But after I had done, she began to talk as before and I did perceive that I had done nothing dangerous to her. And with that, I came away; and though I did make great promises to the contrary, notwithstanding I will not see her for a long time." Rather than fearing he has hurt Betty Lane, Pepys's worry appears to be that she enjoyed herself too much, risking pregnancy (*see* 1 Feb. 1664).

Browne of the Minerys brought me an instrument made of a Spyrall line, very pretty for all Questions in Arithmetique almost.[1] But it must be some use that must make me perfect in it.

So home to supper and to bed – with my mind un peu troublé pour ce que j'ai fait today. But I hope it will be la dernière de toute ma vie.[2]

20. Up and by coach to my Lord Sandwiches; and after long staying till his coming down (he not sending for me up, but it may be he did not know I was there), he came down and I walked with him to the Tennis Court, and there left him seeing the King play.◆

Thence by water to my brother's, whom I find not well in bed – sick they think of a consumption. And I fear he is not well; but doth not complain nor desire to take anything. From him I visited Mr. Honiwood,[3] who is lame, and to thank him for his visit to me the other day, but we were both abroad. So to Mr. Comanders[4] in Warwicke-lane to speak to him about drawing up my Will, which he will meet me about in a day or two. So to the Change and walked home thence with Sir Rd. Ford,[5] who told me that Turner is to be hanged tomorrow and with what impudence he hath carried out his trial; but that last night, when he brought him news of his death, he begin to be sober and shed some tears, and he hopes will die a penitent, he having already confessed all the thing; but says it was partly done for a Joco,[6] and partly to get an occasion of obliging the old man by his care in getting him his things again, he having some hopes of being the better by him in his estate at his death.

Home to dinner; and after dinner my wife and I by water (which we have not been together many a day; that is, not since last summer, but the weather is now very warm) and left her at Axe-yard and I to White-hall; and meeting Mr. Pierce, walked with him an hour in the matted gallery. Among other things, he tells me that my Lady Castlemaine is not at all set by by the King, but that he

---

Contemporary medical theories held that both partners had to orgasm (producing seed) for conception to occur.

1. A variety of slide rule consisting of a logarithmic scale marked along a spiral line.
2. "with my mind a little troubled for what I did today, but I hope it will be the last in all my life."
3. Peter Honywood lodged in the house in Salisbury Court once occupied by Pepys's father and now by Tom.
4. A scrivener.
5. Pepys's neighbour was a Sheriff of the City with duties at the Old Bailey where Turner's trial was held.
6. Joco: a joke. This was a very new word in English, first recorded in 1662. "Joke" was a little older (1645).

doth dote upon Mrs. Stuart only – and that to the leaving off all business in the world – and to the open slighting of the Queen. That he values not who sees him or stands by him while he dallies with her openly – and then privately in her chamber below, where the very sentries observe his going in and out – and that so commonly that the Duke or any of the nobles, when they would ask where the King is, they will ordinarily say, "Is the King above or below?" meaning with Mrs. Stuart.

That the King doth not openly disown my Lady Castlemaine, but that she comes to Court; but that my Lord Fitzharding and the Hambletons,[1] and sometimes my Lord Sandwich they say, have their snaps at her. But he says my Lord Sandwich will lead her from her lodgings in the darkest and obscurest manner and leave her at the entrance into the Queens lodgings, that he might be the least observed.

That the Duke of Monmouth the King doth still dote on beyond measure, insomuch that the King only, and the Duke of Yorke and Prince Robt.[2] and the Duke of Monmouth, do now wear deep mourning, that is, long cloaks, for the Duchesse of Savoy; so that he mourns as a Prince of the Blood, while the Duke of Yorke doth no more and all the nobles of the land not so much – which gives great offence, and he says the Duke of Yorke doth consider. But that the Duke of Yorke doth give himself up to business and is like to prove a noble prince; and so endeed I do from my heart think he will.

He says that it is believed, as well as hoped, that care is taken to lay up a hidden treasure of money by the King against a bad day. I pray God it be so. But I should be more glad that the King himself would look after business, which it seems he doth not in the least.

By and by came by Mr. Coventry, and so we broke off, and he and I took a turn or two and so parted; and then my Lord Sandwich came upon me to speak, with whom my business of coming again tonight to this end of the town chiefly was – in order to the seeing in what manner he received me, in order to my inviting him to dinner to my house. But as well in the morning as now, though I did wait upon him home and there offered occasion of talk with him, yet he treats me, though with respect, yet as a stranger, without any

1. The Hamiltons, three brothers. They included Anthony Hamilton who, writing as the Comte de Gramont, later produced a scandalous history of the Stuart court.
2. Rupert.

of the intimacy or friendship which he used to do; and which I fear he will never, through his consciousness of his faults, he ever will again – which I must confess doth trouble me above anything in the world almost, though I neither do need at present or fear to need to be so troubled; nay and more, though I do not think that he would deny me any friendship now if I did need it; but only that he hath not the face to be free with me, but doth look upon me as a remembrancer of his former vanity and an espy upon his present practices. For I perceive that Pickering today is great with him again, and that he hath done a great courtesy for Mr. Pierce the surgeon, to a good value, though both these and none but these did I mention by name to my Lord in the business which hath caused all this difference between my Lord and me.[1] However, I am resolved to forbear my laying out my money upon a dinner till I see him in a better posture,[2] and by grave and humble though high deportment to make him think I do not want him; and that will make him the readier to admit me to his friendship again I believe, the soonest of anything but downright impudence and thrusting myself, as others do, upon him; and imposing upon him which yet I cannot do, nor will not endeavour.

So home, calling with my wife to see my brother again, who was up and walks up and down the house pretty well; but I do think he is in a consumption.

Home – troubled in mind for these passages with my Lord. But am resolved to better my care in my business, to make me stand upon my own legs the better and to lay up as well as to get money; and among other ways, I will have a good fleece out of Creeds coat[3] ere it be long, or I will have a fall.

So to my office and did some business; and then home to supper and to bed – after I had by candlelight shaved myself and cut off all my beard clear,[4] which will make my work a great deal the less in shaving.

21. Up; and after sending my wife to my aunt Wight's to get a place to see Turner hanged, I to the office, where we sat all the morning. And at noon, going to the Change and seeing people flock in that,

1. Sandwich's affair with Betty Becke.
2. Pepys had been considering inviting Sandwich to dine at his house.
3. That is, "a good coat of Creed's fleece": a share of the booty. Creed had profited greatly from dubious accounting practices while Deputy Treasurer to the fleet and Pepys expected a reward for helping to get his accounts passed by the Navy Board.
4. Pepys seems to have had a lightly grown moustache at this time.

I enquired and found that Turner was not yet hanged; and so I went among them to Leadenhall-street at the end of Lyme-street, near where the robbery was done, and to St. Mary Axe, where he lived; and there I got for a shilling to stand upon the wheel of a Cart, in great pain, above an hour before the execution was done – he delaying the time by long discourses and prayers one after another, in hopes of a reprieve; but none came, and at last was flung off the lather[1] in his cloak. A comely-looked man he was, and kept his countenance to the end – I was sorry to see him. It was believed there was at least 12 or 14000 people in the street. So I home all in a sweat, and dined by myself.◆

Thence to the Coffee-house and heard the full of Turner's discourse on the Cart, which was chiefly to clear himself of all things laid to his charge but this fault for which he now suffers, which he confesses. He deplored the condition of his family. But his chief design was to lengthen time, believing still a reprieve would come, though the Sheriffe advised him to expect no such thing, for the King was resolved to grant none. After that, I had good discourse with a pretty young merchant, with mighty content. So to my office and did a little business; and then to my aunt Wights to fetch my wife home, where Dr. Burnett did tell me how poorly the Sheriffes did endeavour to get one Jewell returned by Turner after he was convicted, as a due to them, and not to give to Mr. Tryan the true owner; but ruled against them, to their great dishonour – though they plead it might be another's Jewell for ought they knew and not Tryan's. After supper, home; and my wife tells me mighty stories of my uncles fond and kind discourses to her today, which makes me confident that he hath thoughts of kindness for us, he repeating his desire for her to be with child – for it cannot enter into my head that he should have any unworthy thoughts concerning her. After doing some business at my office, I home to supper, prayers, and to bed.

30. Up, and a sorry sermon of a young fellow I knew at Cambrige. But the day kept solemnly for the King's murther, and I all day within doors making up my Brampton papers; and in the evening Mr. Comander came and we made perfect and signed and sealed my last Will and Testament, which is so to my mind, and I hope to the liking of God Almighty, that I take great joy in myself that it is done, and by that means my mind in a good condition of quiet. At night, to supper and to bed. ⟨This evening, being in an humour

1. Ladder.

of making all things even and clear in the world, I tore some old papers; among others, a Romance which (under the title of *Love a Cheate*) I begun ten year ago at Cambrige; and at this time, reading it over tonight, I liked it very well and wondered a little at myself at my vein at that time when I wrote it, doubting that I cannot do so well now if I would try.⟩

FEBRUARY.

1.◆ To White-hall, where in the Dukes chamber the King came and stayed an hour or two, laughing at Sir W Petty, who was there about his boat, and at Gresham College in general. At which poor Petty was I perceive at some loss, but did argue discreetly and bear the unreasonable follies of the King's objections and other bystanders with great discretion – and offered to take oddes against the King's best boats; but the King would not lay, but cried him down with words only. Gresham College he mightily laughed at for spending time only in weighing of ayre, and doing nothing else since they sat.[1]

Thence to Westminster-hall and there met with diverse people, it being term-time. Among others, I spoke with Mrs. Lane, of whom I doubted[2] to hear something of the effects of our last meeting about a fortnight or three weeks ago, but to my content did not. Here I met with Mr. Pierce, who tells me of several passages at Court; among others, how the King, coming the other day to his Theatre to see *The Indian Queene*[3] (which he commends for a very fine thing), my Lady Castlemaine was in the next box before he came; and leaning over other ladies a while to whisper with the King, she ris out of that box and went into the King's and sat herself on the King's right hand between the King and the Duke of Yorke – which he swears put the King himself, as well as everybody else, out of countenance, and believes that she did it only to show the world that she is not out of favour yet – as was believed.

Thence with Alderman Maynell by his coach to the Change, and there with several people busy; and so home to dinner and took

1. The subjects of mockery were Petty's twin-hulled ship, which had recently arrived in England, and experiments with air pumps by other members of the Royal Society, which met at Gresham College. Pepys often uses "Gresham College" as a synonym for "the Royal Society".
2. Feared.
3. A new heroic drama, in rhyming couplets, by Sir Robert Howard and John Dryden, at the Theatre Royal, Drury Lane.

my wife out immediately to the King's Theatre, it being a new month (and once a month I may go) and there saw *The Indian Queen* acted, which endeed is a most pleasant show and beyond my expectation; the play good but spoiled with the Ryme, which breaks the sense. But above my expectation most, the eldest Marshall did do her part most excellently well as ever I heard woman in my life, but her voice not so sweet as Ianthes – but however, we came home mightily contented.[1] Here we met Mr. Pickering and his mistress, Mrs. Doll. Wilde. He tells me that the business runs high between the Chancellor and my Lord Bristoll against the Parliament.[2] And that my Lord Lauderdale and Cooper[3] open high against the Chancellor – which I am sorry for. In my way home I light and to the Coffee-house, where I heard Lieutenant Collonell Baron[4] tell very good stories of his travels over the high hills in Asia above the Cloudes. How clear the heaven is above them. How thick, like a mist, the way is through the cloud, that wets like a sponge one's clothes. The ground above the clouds all dry and parched, nothing in the world growing, it being only a dry earth. Yet not so hot above as below the clouds. The stars at night most delicate bright and a fine clear blue sky. But cannot see the earth at any time through the clouds, but the clouds look like a world below you.

Thence home and to supper, being hungry; and so to the office, did business, especially about Creed, for whom I am now pretty well fitted – and so home to bed.

This day in Westminster-hall, W. Bowyer told me that his father[5] is dead lately and died by being drowned in the River, coming over in the night; but he says he had not been drinking. He was take with his stick in his hand and cloak over his shoulder, as ruddy as before he died. His horse was taken overnight in the water, hampered in the bridle; but they were so silly as not to look for his master till the next morning that he was found drowned.

2. Up and to the office; where, though Candlemas=day,[6] Mr.

1. Anne Marshall, playing the title role of Zempoalla, was the elder of two sisters who acted in the King's Company. "Ianthe" was Pepys's name for Mary Betterton.
2. The Earl of Bristol had tried and failed to impeach Lord Chancellor Clarendon in the House of Lords in July 1663. He was now making plans for the new parliamentary session.
3. Anthony Ashley Cooper, Lord Ashley (created Earl of Shaftesbury in 1672).
4. Benjamin Baron, a merchant and lieutenant-colonel in the City militia.
5. Robert Bowyer, Pepys's friend with whom Elizabeth had stayed during her husband's trip to the Dutch Republic in 1660.
6. A church festival.

Coventry, Sir W. Penn and I all the morning, the others being at a Survey at Deptford; at noon by coach to the Change with Mr. Coventry. Thence to the Coffee-house with Captain Cocke, who discoursed well of the good effects in some kind of a Duch war and conquest (which I did not consider before but the contrary);[1] that is, that the trade of the world is too little for us two, therefore one must down. Secondly, that though our merchants will not be the better husbands[2] by all this, yet our Wool will bear a better prize by vaunting of our cloths, and by that our tenants will be better able to pay rents and our lands will be more worth, and all our own manufactures – which now the Dutch out-vie us in. ⟨That he thinks the Duch are not in so good a condition as heretofore, because of want of men always, and now from the wars against the Turke more then ever.⟩

Thence to the Change again, and thence off to the Sun taverne with Sir W Warren and with him discoursed long and had good advice and hints from him; and among [other] things, he did give me a pair of gloves for my wife, wrapped up in paper; which I would not open, feeling it hard, but did tell him my wife should thank him, and so went on in discourse. When I came home, Lord, in what pain I was to get my wife out of the room without bidding her go, that I might see what these gloves were; and by and by, she being gone, it proves a pair of white gloves for her and 40 pieces in good gold:[3] which did so cheer my heart that I could eat no victuals almost for dinner for joy to think how God doth bless us every day more and more – and more yet I hope he will upon the encrease of my duty and endeavours. I was at great loss what to do, whether tell my wife of it or no; which I could hardly forbear, but yet I did and will think of it first before I do, for fear of making her think me to be in a better condition or in a better way of getting money then yet I am.

After dinner to the office, where doing infinite of business till past 10 at night to the comfort of my mind; and so home with joy to supper and to bed.◆

3. Up; and after long discourse with my Cosen Tho. Pepys the Executor, I with my wife by coach to Holborne, where I light and she to her father's. I to the Temple and several places and so to the

1. Cocke was a leading member of the Company of Royal Adventurers of England Trading into Africa, which was in direct competition with the Dutch.
2. Managers of their affairs.
3. A reward for Pepys's help to Warren in obtaining navy contracts.

Change, where much business; and then home to dinner alone, and so to the Miter tavern by appointment (and there by chance met with W Howe, come to buy wine for my Lord against his going down to Hinchingbrooke; and I private with him a great while, discoursing of my Lord's strangeness to me; but he answers that I have no reason to think any such thing, but that my Lord is only in general a more reserved man then he was before) to meet Sir W Rider and Mr. Clerke; and there after much ado made an end, giving Mr. Custos 202*l* against Mr Bland; which I endeavoured to bring down but could not, and think it is well enough ended for Mr. Bland for all that.[1] Thence by coach to fetch my wife from her brother's, and find her gone home. Called at Sir Robt. Bernards about surrendering my estate in reversion to the use of my life, which will be done.[2] And at Rog. Pepys, who was gone to bed in pain of a boyle, that he could not sit or stand. So home, where my wife is full of sad stories of her good-natured father and roguish brother, who is going for Holland, and his wife, to be a soldier; and so after a little at the office, to bed. This night late, coming in my coach coming up Ludgate hill, I saw two gallants and their footmen taking a pretty wench which I have much eyed lately, set up shop upon the hill, a seller of ribband and gloves. They seem to drag her by some force, but the wench went and I believe had her turn served; but God forgive me, what thoughts and wishes I had of being in their place.

In Covent-garden tonight, going to fetch home my wife, I stopped at the great Coffee-house there, where I never was before – where Draydon the poet (I knew at Cambrige) and all the wits of the town, and Harris the player and Mr. Hoole of our college;[3] and had I had time then, or could at other times, it will be good coming thither, for there I perceive is very witty and pleasant discourse. But I could not tarry and it was late; they were all ready to go away.

15. Up; and carrying my wife to my Lord's lodgings, left her and I to White-hall to the Duke; where he first put on a periwigg today

1. The merchants Custis and Bland were in dispute over costs due for shipping goods to Tangier that had arrived damaged. Pepys was arbitrator.
2. This was his reversionary interest in the estate of his uncle Robert Pepys. Pepys was arranging the succession to his land but retaining his life income.
3. John Dryden studied at Trinity College, Cambridge, and William Howell, a historian, had been a fellow of Magdalene. Henry Harris acted with the Duke's Company. The coffeehouse was probably the one later known as "Will's", which became famous as a resort for wits.

but methought his hair, cut short in order thereto, did look very prettily of itself before he put on his periwig. Thence to his closet and did our business. And thence Mr. Coventry and I down to his chamber and spent a little time; and so parted and I took my wife homeward, I stopping at the Coffee-house and thence a while to the Change (where great news of the arrivall of two rich ships, the *Greyhound* and another, which they were mightily afeared of and great insurance given);[1] and so home to dinner and after an hour with my wife at her globes, I to the office, where very busy till 11 at night; and so home to supper and to bed.

This afternoon Sir Tho Chamberlin[2] came to the office to me and showed me several letters from the East Indys, showing the heighth that the Dutch are come to there; showing scorn to all the English even in our only Factory[3] there of Surratt, beating several men and hanging the English Standard St. George under the Duch flag in scorn; saying that whatever their masters do or say at home, they will do what they list and will be masters of all the world there, and have so proclaimed themselfs Soveraigne of all the South Seas – which certainly our King cannot endure, if the parliament will give him money. But I doubt and yet do hope they will not yet, till we are more ready for it.

MARCH.

10. Up and to the office, where all the morning doing business. And at noon to the Change and there very busy; and so home to dinner with my wife to a good hog's harslet,[4] a piece of meat I love but have not eat of I think this seven year. And after dinner abroad by coach, set her at Mrs. Hunts and I to White-hall; and at the Privy Seale office enquired and found the Bill[5] come for the Corporacion of the Royall Fishery; whereof the Duke of Yorke is made present Governor and several other very great persons, to the number of 32, made his assistants for their lives: whereof, by my Lord Sandwichs favour, I am one and take it not only as a matter of honour but that

1. These ships had been feared taken by the Turks. Insurance could be paid for while a ship was at sea, with the insurers charging high prices while gambling that the ship would arrive safely.
2. Governor of the East India Company.
3. Trading station.
4. Meat for roasting, especially offal.
5. The royal warrant authorizing the issue of a charter.

that may come to be of profit to me.[1] And so with great content went and called my wife; and so home and to the office, where busy late; and so home to supper, and to bed.

13. *Lords day.* I lay long in bed, talking with my wife; and then up, in great doubt whether I should not go see Mr. Coventry or no, who hath not been well these two or three days; but it being foul weather, I stayed within; and so to my office and there all the morning reading some Common law, to which I will allot a little time now and then, for I much want it. At noon home to dinner; and then after some discourse with my wife, to the office again; and by and by Sir W Pen came to me after sermon and walked with me in the garden, and then one comes to tell me that Anth. and Will Joyce were come to see me;[2] so I in to them and made mighty much of them, and very pleasant we were. And most of their business I find to be to advise about getting some woman to attend my Brother Tom, whom they say is very ill and seems much to want one – to which I agreed, and desired them to get their wifes to enquire out one. By and by they bid me good-night; but immediately as they were gone out of doors comes Mrs. Turner's boy with a note to me, to tell me that my brother Tom was so ill as they feared he could not long live and that it would be fit I should come and see him. So I sent for them back, and they came; and Will Joyce desiring to speak with me alone, I took him up and there he did plainly tell me, to my great astonishment, that my brother is deadly ill and that their chief business of coming was to tell me so; and which is worse, that his disease is the pox,[3] which he hath heretofore got and hath not been cured, but is come to this; and that this is certain, though a secret told his father Fenner[4] by the Doctor which he helped my brother to.

This troubled me mightily; but however, I thought fit to go see him for speech of people's sake,[5] and so walked along with them, and in our way called on my Uncle Fenner (where I have not been this 12 months and more) and advised with him; and then to my brother, who lies in bed talking idle.[6] He could only say that he

1. The Corporation of the Royal Fishery was charged with raising money to improve the fishing industry and so stave off Dutch competition.
2. Anthony and William Joyce were relatives of Pepys on his mother's side: the two brothers had each married sisters, Mary and Kate Fenner, who were Pepys's cousins.
3. Syphilis.
4. Will Joyce's father-in-law, Thomas Fenner.
5. Correctly, "for sake of people's speech".
6. Incoherently, deliriously.

knew me and then fell to other discourse, and his face like a dying man – which Mrs. Turner,[1] who was here, and others conclude he is.

The company being gone, I took the mayde, which seems a very grave and serious woman, and in W. Joyces company did enquire how things are with her master. She told me many things very discreetly and said she had all his papers and books and key of his cutting-house. And showed me a bag which I and Wm: Joyce told, coming to 5*l* 14*s* – which we left with her again.

After giving her good counsel, and the boys, and seeing a nurse there of Mrs. Holden's[2] choosing, I left them and so walked home, greatly troubled to think of my brother's condition and the trouble that would arise to me by his death or continuing sick.

So at home, my mind troubled, to bed.

14. Up, and walked to my brother's, where I find he hath continued talking idle all night and now knows me not – which troubles me mightily. So I walked down and discoursed a great while alone with the mayde, who tells me many passages of her master's practices and how she concludes that he hath run behind-hand a great while and owes money and hath been dunned by several people; among others, by one Cave, both husband and wife, but whether it was for money or something worse she knows not. But there is one Cranburne, I think she called him, in Fleete-lane with whom he hath many times been mighty private, but what their dealings have been she knows not, but believes they were naught.[3] And then his sitting up two Saturday nights, one after another, when all were a-bed, doing something to himself; which she now suspects what it was but did not before. But tells me that he hath been a very bad husband as to spending his time, and hath often told him of it. So that upon the whole, I do find he is, whether he lives or dies, a ruined man. And what trouble will befall me by it, I know not.

Thence to White-hall; and in the Dukes chamber, while he was dressing, two persons of quality that were there did tell his Royal Highness how the other night in Holborne about midnight, being at cards, a link-boy came by and run into the house and told the people the house was a-falling; upon this, the whole family was frighted, concluding that the boy had said that the house was

1. Jane Turner ("Madam Turner"), a relative of Pepys, lived in Salisbury Court, near to Tom.
2. Priscilla Holden (or Holding), wife of a haberdasher who lived near to Tom.
3. Wicked.

a-fire; so they left their cards above, and one would have got out of the balcone, but it was not open; the other went up to fetch down his children that were in bed. So all got clear out of the house; and no sooner so, but the house fell down indeed, from top to bottom. It seems my Lord Southamptons canaille[1] did come too near their foundation and so weakened the house, and down it came – which in every respect is a most extraordinary passage.

By and by into his closet and did our business with him. But I did not speed as I expected, in a business about the manner of buying hemp for this year; which troubled me. But it proceeds only from my pride, that I must need expect everything to be ordered just as I apprehend. Though it was not, I think, from my error, but their not being willing to hear and consider all that I had to propose.

Being broke up, I fallowed my Lord Sandwich and thanked him for his putting me into the Fishery; which I perceive he expected, and cried "Oh!" says he, "in the Fishery you mean. I told you I would remember you in it" – but offered no other discourse; but demanding whether he had any commands for me – methought he cried "No," as if he had no more mind to discourse with me, which still troubles me and hath done all the day, though I think I am a fool for it, in not pursuing my resolution of going handsome in clothes and looking high – for that must do it when all is done with my Lord. Thence by coach with Sir Wm. Batten to the City and his son Castle, who talks mighty highly against Captain Taylor, calling him knave; and I find that the old doting father is led and talks just as the son do, or the son as the father would have him.[2]

Light, and to Mr. Moxons[3] and there saw our office globes in doing, which will be very handsome – but cost money. So to the Coffee-house; and there very fine discourse with Mr. Hill[4] the merchant, a pretty gentile, young, and sober man.

So to the Change and thence home, where my wife and I fell out about my not being willing to have her have her gown laced, but would lay out the same money and more on a plain new one. At this she flounced away in a manner I never saw her, nor which I could ever endure. So I away to the office, though she had dressed

1. Probably the sewer running from old Southampton House, Holborn.
2. The merchant Capt. Taylor was involved in the supply of masts, over which there was currently a dispute. Batten and his son-in-law Castle were supporting the interest of another merchant.
3. Joseph Moxon, mathematical-instrument maker in Cornhill.
4. Thomas Hill, a new friend to whom Pepys would become close.

herself to go see my Lady Sandwich. She by and by in a rage fallows me; and coming to me, tells me in spiteful manner, like a vixen and with a look full of rancour, that she would go buy a new one and lace it and make me pay for it, and then let me burn it if I would after she had done it – and so went away in fury. This vexed me cruelly; but being very busy, I had not hand to give myself up to consult what to do in it. But anon, I suppose after she saw that I did not fallow her, she came again to the office; where I made her stay, being busy with another, half an hour; and her stomach coming down, we were presently friends. And so after my business being over at the office, we out and by coach to my Lady Sandwiches, with whom I left my wife; and I to White-hall, where I met Mr. De Cretz;[1] and after an hour's discourse with him, met with nobody to do other business with, but back again to my Lady and after half an hour's discourse with her, to my brother's, who I find in the same or worse condition. The Doctors give him over and so do all that see him. He talks no sense two words together now. And I confess it made me weep to see that he should not be able when I asked him, to say who I was.

I went to Mrs. Turners, and by her discourse with my brother's Doctor, Mr. Powell, I find that she is full now of the disease which my brother is troubled with, and talks of it mightily; which I am sorry for – there being other company; but methinks it should be for her honour to forbear talking of it. The shame of this very thing, I confess, troubles me as much as anything.

Back to my brother's, and took my wife and carried her to my uncle Fenners and there had much private discourse with him. He tells me the Doctor's thoughts of my brother's little hopes of recovery; and from that, to tell me his thoughts long of my brother's bad husbandry; and from that, to say that he believes he owes a great deal of money – as, to my Cozen Scott, I know not how much – and Dr Tho. Pepys, 30*l*; but that the Doctor confesses that he is paid 20*l* of it. And what with that and what he owes my father and me, I doubt he is in a very sad condition; that if he lives, he will not be able to show his head – which will be a very great shame to me.

After this I went in to my aunt and my wife and Anth. Joyce and his wife, who were by chance there, and drank; and so home, my mind and head troubled, but I hope it will over in a little time, one way or other.

1. Emanuel de Critz, portrait painter.

After doing a little at my office of business, I home to supper and to bed.

From notice that my uncle Fenner did give my father the last week of my brother's condition, my mother is coming up to Towne, which also doth trouble me.

The business between my Lords Chancellor and Bristoll, they say, is hushed up, and the latter gone or going by the King's licence to France.[1]

15. Up and to the office, where we sat all the morning; and at noon comes Madam Turner and her daughter The – her chief errand to tell me that she had got Dr. Wiverly her Doctor to search my brother's mouth, where Mr. Powell says there is an Ulcer; from whence he concludes that he hath had the pox. But the Doctor swears there is not, nor ever was any. And my brother being very sensible, which I was glad to hear, he did talk with him about it; and he did wholly disclaim that ever he had that disease or that ever he said to Powell that he had it – all which did put me into great comfort as to that reproach which was spread against him. So I sent for a barrel of oysters and they dined, and we were very merry, I being willing to be so upon this news. After dinner we took coach and to my brother's; where, contrary to my expectation, he continues as bad or worse, talking idle and now not at all knowing any of us as before. Here we stayed a great while, I going up and down the house looking after things. In the evening Dr. Wiverley came again and I sent for Mr. Powell (the Doctor and I having first by ourselfs searched my brother again at his privities; where he was as clear as ever he was born, and in the Doctor's opinion had been ever so). And we three alone discoursed that business, where the Coxcomb did give us his simple reasons for what he had said; which the Doctor fully confuted and left the fellow, only saying that he should cease to report any such thing and that what he had said was the best of his judgment, from my brother's words and ulcer, as he supposed, in his mouth. I threatened him that I would have satisfaction if I heard any more such discourse. And so good night to them two, giving the Doctor a piece for his fee but the other nothing.

I to my brother again, where Madam Turner and her company, and Mrs. Croxton, my wife, and Mrs. Holding. About 8 a-clock my brother begun to fetch his spittle with more pain and to speak

1. Bristol, who had attempted to impeach Lord Chancellor Clarendon, was not in France, but in hiding in Wimbledon.

as much, but not so distinctly; till at last, the phlegm getting the maistery of him and he beginning as we thought to rattle, I had no mind to see him die, as we thought he presently would, and so withdrew and led Mrs. Turner home. But before I came back, which was in a quarter of an hour, my brother was dead. I went up and found the nurse holding his eyes shut; and he, poor wretch, lying with his chops fallen, a most sad sight and that which put me into a present very great transport of grief and cries. And endeed, it was a most sad sight to see the poor wretch lie now still and dead and pale like a stone. I stayed till he was almost cold, while Mrs. Croxton, Holden, and the rest did strip and lay him out – they observing his corps, as they told me afterwards, to be as clear as any they ever saw. And so this was the end of my poor brother, continuing talking idle and his lips working even to his last, that his phlegm hindered his breathing; and at last his breath broke out, bringing a flood of phlegm and stuff out with it, and so he died.

This evening he talked among other talk a great deal of French, very plain and good; as among others – "*quand un homme boit quand il n'a poynt d'inclinacion a boire il ne luy fait jamais de bien.*"[1] I once begun to tell him something of his condition and asked him whither he thought he should go. He in distracted manner answered me – "Why, whither should I go? there are but two ways. If I go to the bad way, I must give God thanks for it. And if I go the other way, I must give God the more thanks for it; and I hope I have not been so undutiful and unthankful in my life but I hope I shall go that way." This was all the sense, good or bad, I could get of him this day.

I left my wife to see him laid out, and I by coach home, carrying my brother's papers, all I could find, with me. And having wrote a letter to my father, telling him what hath been said, I returned by coach, it being very late and dark, to my brother's. But all being gone, the Corps laid out and my wife at Mrs. Turners, I thither; and there, after an hour's talk, we up to bed – my wife and I in the little blue chamber. And I lay close to my wife, being full of disorder and grief for my brother, that I could not sleep nor wake with
⟨⟨16⟩⟩ satisfaction; at last I slept till 5 or 6 a-clock. And then I rose and up, leaving my wife in bed, and to my brother's, where I set them on cleaning the house. And my wife coming anon to look after things, I up and down to my Cosen Stradwickes and

1. "When a man drinks when he has no inclination to drink he never does himself good."

uncle Fenners about discoursing for the funeral, which I am resolved to put off till Friday next. Thence home and trimmed myself; and then to the Change and told my uncle Wight of my brother's death; and so by coach to my Cosen Turners and there dined very well. But my wife having those[1] upon her today and in great pain, we were forced to rise in some disorder and in Mrs. Turners coach carried her home and put her to bed. Then back again with my Cosen Norton to Mrs. Turners and there stayed a while talking with Dr Pepys,[2] that puppy, whom I had no patience to hear. So I left them, and to my brother's to look after things – and saw the Coffin brought; and by and by Mrs. Holden came and saw him nailed up. Then came W. Joyce to me half-drunk, and much ado I had to tell him the story of my brother's being found clear of what was said, but he would interrupt me by some idle discourse or other, of his crying what a good man and a good speaker[3] my brother was and God knows what. At last, weary of him, I got him away and I to Mrs. Turner's; and there, though my heart is still heavy to think of my poor brother, yet I could give way to my fancy to hear Mrs. The play upon the Harpsicon – though the Musique did not please me neither. Thence to my brother's and found them with my maid Elizabeth, taking an Inventory of the goods of the house; which I was well pleased at, and am much beholding to Mr. Honywoods[4] man in doing of it. His name is Herbert, one that says he knew me when he lived with Sir Samuel Morland[5] – but I have forgot him. So I left them at it and by coach home and to my office, there to do a little business; but God knows, my heart and head is so full of my brother's death and the consequences of it, that I can do very little or understand it.

So home to supper; and after looking over some business in my chamber, to bed to my wife, who continues in bed in some pain still. This day I have a great barrel of Oysters given me by Mr. Barrow, as big as 16 of others, and I took it in the coach with me to Mrs. Turner's and gave them her.

This day the Parliament met again after a long prorogation – but what they have done I have not been in the way to hear.

18. Up betimes and walked to my brother's, where a great while

1. Her period.
2. Thomas Pepys, physician; Pepys's cousin.
3. That is, someone who spoke well of others. Tom had a speech impediment.
4. Peter Honywood lodged with Tom.
5. Pepys's tutor at Cambridge and, like Pepys, a government servant under the Protectorate.

putting things in order against anon.[1] Then to Madam Turners and eat a breakfast there. And so to Wotton my shoemaker and there got a pair of shoes blacked on the soles, against anon for me. So to my brother's, and to the church[2] and with the grave-maker chose a place for my brother to lie in, just under my mother's pew. But to see how a man's tombes are at the mercy of such a fellow, that for 6*d* he would (as his own words were) "I will justle them together but I will make room for him" – speaking of the fullness of the middle Isle where he was to lie. And that he would for my father's sake do my brother that is dead all the civility he can; which was to disturb other corps that are not quite rotten to make room for him. And methought his manner of speaking it was very remarkable – as of a thing that now was in his power to do a man a courtesy or not.

At noon my wife, though in pain, comes; but I being forced to go home, she went back with me – where I dressed myself and so did Besse; and so to my brother's again – whither, though invited as the custom is at 1 or 2 a-clock, they came not till 4 or 5. But at last, one after another they came – many more then I bid; and my reckoning that I bid was 120, but I believe there was nearer 150. Their service was six biscuits a-piece and what they pleased of burnt claret – my Cosen Joyce Norton kept the wine and cakes above – and did give out to them that served, who had white gloves given them. But above all, I am beholden to Mrs. Holding, who was most kind and did take mighty pains, not only in getting the house and everything else ready, but this day in going up and down to see the house filled and served, in order to mine and their great content I think – the men setting by themselfs in some rooms, and women by themselfs in others – very close, but yet room enough. Anon to church, walking out into the street to the Conduict and so across the street, and had a very good company along with the Corps. And being come to the grave as above, Dr. Pierson, the Minister of the parish, did read the service for buriall and so I saw my poor brother laid into the grave; and so all broke up and I and my wife and Madam Turner and her family to my brother's, and by and by fell to a barrell of oysters, Cake, and cheese of Mr. Honiwoods, with him in his chamber and below – being too merry for so late a sad work; but Lord, to see how the world makes nothing of the memory of a man an hour after he is dead. And endeed,

1. For what will happen shortly.
2. St Bride, Fleet Street.

I must blame myself; for though at the sight of him, dead and dying, I had real grief for a while, while he was in my sight, yet presently after and ever since, I have had very little grief endeed for him.

By and by, it beginning to be late, I put things in some order in the house and so took my wife and Besse (who hath done me very good service in cleaning and getting ready everything and serving the wine and things today, and is endeed a most excellent good-natured and faithful wench and I love her mightily) by coach home; and so after being at the office to set down this day's work, home to supper and to bed.

20. *Lords day.* Kept my bed all the morning, having laid a poultice to my cods last night to take down the tumour there which I got yesterday;[1] which it did do, being applied pretty warm and soon after the beginning of the swelling – and the pain was gone also. We lay talking all the while; among other things, of religion, wherein I am sorry so often to hear my wife talk of her being and resolving to die a Catholique; and endeed, a small matter I believe would absolutely turn her, which I am sorry for.[2] Up at noon to dinner; and then to my chamber with a fire till late at night, looking over my brother Tho's papers, sorting of them – among which I find many base letters of my brother John's to him against me and carrying on plots against me to promote Tom's having of his Banbury Mistress,[3] in base slighting terms and in worse of my sister Pall – such as I shall take a convenient time to make my father know, and him also, to his sorrow.

So after supper to bed – our people rising to wash tomorrow.

21. Up; and it snowing this morning a little, which from the mildness of the winter and the weather beginning to be hot and the summer to come on apace is a little strange to us – I did not go abroad, because of my tumour, for fear it shall rise again; but stayed within and by and by my father came, poor man, to me, and my brother John; after much talk and taking them up to my chamber, I did there after some discourse bring in my business of anger with John and did before my father read all his roguish letters; which troubled my father mightily, especially to hear me say what I did,

1. A swelling. Pepys thought crossing his legs had caused it.
2. Elizabeth's immediate family were Protestants but, when living in France aged about 12, she had spent a couple of weeks in a convent.
3. Miss Hobell: the bride projected for Tom before the match was called off by her mother and Pepys.

against my allowing anything for the time to come to him out of my own purse, and other words very severe – while he, like a simple rogue, made very silly and churlish answers to me, not like a man of any goodness or wit – at which I was as much disturbed as the other. And will be as good as my word, in making him to his cost know that I will remember his carriage to me in this perticular the longest day I live. It troubled me to see my poor father so troubled, whose good nature did make him, poor wretch, to yield; I believe to comply with my brother Tom and him in part of their designs, but without any ill intent to me or doubt of me or my good intentions to him or them – though it doth trouble me a little that he should in any manner do it.

They dined with me; and after dinner, abroad with my wife to buy some things for her; and I to the office, where we sat till night; and then after doing some business at my closet, I home and to supper and to bed.

This day the House of Parliament met and the King met them, with the Queene with him – and he made a speech to them; among other things, discoursing largely of the plots abroad against him and the peace of the kingdom. And among other things, that the dissatisfied party had great hopes upon the effect of the act for a Trienniall parliament granted by his father – which he desired them to peruse, and I think repeal.[1] So the House did retire to their own House and did order that act to be read tomorrow before them. And I suppose will be repealed, though I believe much against the will of a good many that sit there.

APRILL.

6. Up and to my office – whither by and by came John Noble, my father's old servant, to speak with me. I smelling the business, took him home; and there all alone he told me how he had been serviceable to my brother Tom in the business of his getting his servant, an ugly jade, Margeret, with child. She was brought to bed in St. Sepulchers parish of two children. One is dead, the other is alive; her name Elizabeth and goes by the name of Taylor, daughter to John Taylor. It seems Tom did a great while trust one Crawly with the business, who daily got money of him; and at last, finding

1. The King said the Triennial Act of 1641, which required parliament to meet every three years, was being used by conspirators who claimed elections were due. The bill was repealed on 5 April 1664.

himself abused, he broke the matter to J. Noble – upon a vow of secrecy. Toms first plot was to go on the other side the water and give a beggar-woman something to take the child. They did once go, but did nothing, J. Noble saying that seven year hence the mother might come to demand the child and force him to produce it, or to be suspected of murther. Then, I think it was, that they consulted and got one Cave, a poor pensioner in St. Brides parish, to take it, giving him 5*l*; he thereby promising to keep it for ever, without more charge to them. The parish hereupon indite the man Cave for bringing this child upon the parish, and by Sir Rd. Browne is sent to the Counter.[1] Cave thence writes to Tom to get him out. Tom answers him in a letter of his own hand, which J Noble showed me, but not signed by him, wherein he speaks of freeing him and getting security for him, but nothing as to the business of the child or anything like it. So that for as much as I could guess, there is nothing therein to my brother's prejudice as to the main point; and therefore I did not labour to tear or take away the paper.

Cave being released, demands 5*l* more to secure my brother for ever against the child. And he was forced to give it him – and took bond of Cave in 100*l*, made at a Scrivener's, one Hudson I think in the Old Bayly, to secure John Taylor and his assigns &c. (in consideration of 10*l* paid him) from all trouble or charge of meat, drink, clothes and breeding of Elizabeth Taylor. And it seems, in the doing of it, J Noble was looked upon as the assigns of this John Taylor. Noble says that he furnished Tom with this money, and is also bound by another bond to pay him 20*s* more this next Easter Monday.[2] But nothing for either sum appears under Toms hand. I told him how I am like to lose a great sum by his death and would not pay any more myself, but I would speak to my father about it against the afternoon. So away he went. And I all the morning in my office busy and at noon home to dinner – mightily oppressed with wind. And after dinner took coach and to Paternoster-Row and there bought a pretty silk for a petticoat for my wife, and thence set her down at the New Exchange; and I leaving the coat at Unthankes,[3] went to White-hall; but the Councell meeting at

1. Cave was charged with illegitimately trying to make the parish responsible for supporting the child and was sent to prison by Browne, a magistrate.
2. Cave has signed a bond that, if he fails to provide for the child, makes him liable to pay £100 to "John Taylor" (aka Tom Pepys) via his agent John Noble. The point was to discourage Cave from further demands and from aiding the parish in any attempts to track down the real father. Noble claims that Pepys owes him the money already paid to Cave.
3. The shop of John Unthank, Elizabeth Pepys's tailor.

Worcester-house, I went thither and there delivered to the Duke of Albemarle a paper touching some Tanger business. And thence to the Change for my wife and walked to my father's,[1] who was packing up some things for the country. I took him up and told him this business of Tom; at which the poor wretch was much troubled and desired me that I would speak with J Noble and do what I could and thought fit in it, without concerning him in it. So I went to Noble and saw the bond that Cave did give and also Toms letter which I mention above. And upon the whole, I think some shame may come but that it will be hard, from anything I see there, to prove the child to be his. Thence to my father and told what I had done and how I had quieted Noble by telling him that though we are resolved to part with no more money out of our own purses, yet if he can make it appear a true debt, that it may be justifiable for us to pay it, we will do our parts to get it paid, and said that I would have it paid before my own debt. So my father and I both a little satisfied, though vexed to think what a rogue my brother was in all respects. I took my wife by coach home; and to my office, where late with Sir Wm. Warren, and so home to supper and to bed.

I heard today that the Dutch have begun with us by granting letters of mart[2] against us. But I believe it not.

13. Though late, past 12, before we went to bed – yet I heard my poor father up;[3] and so I rung up my people and I rose and got something to eat and drink for him; and so abroad – it being a mighty foul day, by coach, setting my father down at Fleetstreet; and I to St. James – where I found Mr. Coventry (the Duke being now come thither for the summer) with a goldsmith, sorting out his old plate to change for new; but Lord, what a deal he hath. I stayed and had two or three hours discourse with him – talking about the disorders of our office, and I largely to tell how things are carried by Sir W. Batten and Sir J. Mennes to my great grief. He seems much concerned also, and for all the King's matters that are done after the same rate everywhere else, and even the Dukes household matters too – generally with corruption, but most endeed with neglect and indifference. I spoke very loud and clear to him my thoughts of Sir J. Mennes and the other, and trust him with the using of them.

1. The Pepys family's house at Salisbury Court, which Tom had taken over from his father.
2. A government licence that allowed the holder to capture the merchant shipping of an enemy state.
3. Pepys's father had come to stay with him the night before.

Then to talk of our business with the Dutch; he tells me fully that he believes it will not come to a warr. For first he showed me a letter from Sir George Downing,[1] his own hand, where he assures him that the Dutch themselfs do not desire but above all things fear it. And that they neither have given letters of Mart against our ships in Guinny, nor doth De Ruyter stay at home with his fleet with an eye to any such thing, but for want of a wind, and is now come out and is going to the Streights.[2]

He tells me also that the most he expects is that upon the merchants' complaints, the parliament will represent them to the King, desiring his securing of his subjects against them. And though perhaps they may not directly see fit, yet even this will be enough to let the Dutch know that the Parliament do not oppose the King; and by that means take away their hopes, which was that the King of England could not get money or do anything towards a war with them. And so thought themselfs free from making any restitution – which by this they will be deceived in.

He tells me also that the Dutch States are in no good order themselfs, differing one with another. And that for certain none but the States of Holland and Zealand will contribute towards a war, the other reckoning themselfs, being inland, not concerned in the profits of war or peace.

But it is pretty to see what he says. That those here that are forward for a war at Court, they are reported in the world to be only designers of getting money into the King's hands. They that elsewhere are for it have a design to trouble the kingdom and to give the fanatics an opportunity of doing hurt. And lastly, those that are against it (as he himself for one is very cold therein) are said to be bribed by the Dutch.

After all this discourse he carried me in his coach, it raining still, to Charing-cross and there put me into another; and I calling my father and brother, carried them to my house to dinner – my wife keeping bed all day, she having those upon her.

All the afternoon at the office with W. Boddam, looking over his perticulars about the Chest of Chatham, which show enough what a knave Commissioner Pett hath been all along, and how Sir W. Batten hath gone on in getting good allowances to himself and others out of the poor's money. Time will show all.

1. Envoy-extraordinary to the Dutch Republic.
2. The straits of Gibraltar; more loosely, the Mediterranean.

So in the evening to see Sir W. Penn and then home to my father to keep him company, he being to go out of town. And up late with him and my brother John, till past 12 at night, to make up papers of Tom's accounts fit to leave with my Cosen Scott. At last we did make an end of them, and so after supper all to bed.

21.◆ To the office; we sat all the afternoon but no sooner sat but news comes my Lady Sandwich was come to see us; so I went out, and running up (her friend however before me) I perceive by my dear Lady's blushing that in my dining-room she was doing something upon the pott; which I also was ashamed of and so fell to some discourse, but without pleasure, through very pity to my Lady. She tells me, and I find true since, that the House this day hath voted that the King be desired to demand right for the wrong done us by the Dutch, and that they will stand by him with their lives and fortunes – which is a very high vote, and more then I expected.[1] What the issue will be, God knows. My Lady, my wife not being at home, did not stay but, poor good woman, went away, I being mightily taken with her dear visitt. And so to the office, where all the afternoon till late; and so to my office and then to supper and to bed – thinking to rise betimes tomorrow.

23. *Coronacion day.* Up; and after doing something at my office, and it being a holiday, no sitting likely to be, I down by water to Sir W Warren's, who hath been ill, and there talked long with him; good discourse, especially about Sir W. Batten's knaveries and his son Castle['s] ill language of me behind my back, saying that I favour my fellow-Traytours[2] – but I shall be even with him. So home and to the Change, where I met with Mr. Coventry – who himself is now full of talk of a Dutch war, for it seems the Lords have concurred in the Commons' vote about it and so the next week it will be presented to the King. Insomuch that he doth desire we would look about to see what stores we lack, and buy what we can. Home to dinner, where I and my wife much troubled about my money that is in my Lord Sandwiches hand, for fear of his going to sea and be killed. But I will get what of it out I can.

All the afternoon, not being well, at my office and there did

1. The Commons had voted to address the King to act against Dutch affronts to the nation's trade, and to defend his rights in Africa, India and elsewhere. They had also pledged financial support. This was a major step towards the Second Anglo-Dutch War (1665–7).
2. Men who, like Pepys, had served the Protectorate governments. Castle probably had William Warren, his competitor for navy contracts, in mind.

much business, my thoughts still running upon a warr and my money.

At night home to supper and to bed.

MAY.

11. Up; and all day, both forenoon and afternoon, at my office, to see it finished by the Joyner and washed and everything in order; and endeed, now my closet is very convenient and pleasant for me. My uncle Wight came to me to my office this afternoon to speak with me about Mr. Maes's business again, and from me went to my house to see my wife; and strange to think that my wife should by and by send for me after he was gone, to tell me that he should begin discourse of her want of children and his also, and how he thought it would be best for him and her to have one between them, and he would give her 500*l* either in money or jewell beforehand and make the child his heyre.[1] He commended her body and discoursed that for all he knew the thing was lawful. She says she did give him a very warm answer, such as he did not excuse himself by saying that he said this in jest but told her that since he saw what her mind was, he would say no more to her of it, and desired her to make no words of it. It seemed he did say all this in a kind of counterfeit laugh; but by all words that passed, which I cannot now so well set down, it is plain to me that he was in good earnest, and that I fear all his kindness is but only his lust to her. What to think of it of a sudden I know not, but I think not to take notice yet of it to him till I have thought better of it. So, with my mind and head a little troubled, I received a letter from Mr. Coventry about a mast for the Dukes Yacht; which, with other business, makes me resolve to go betimes to Woolwich tomorrow. So to supper and to bed.

14. Up, full of pain, I believe by cold got yesterday. To the office, where we sat; and after office, home to dinner, being in extraordinary pain. After dinner, my pain increasing, I was forced to go to bed; and by and by my pain ris to be as great for an hour or two as ever I remember it was in any fit of the stone, both in the lower part of my belly and in my back also. No wind could I break. I took a glister, but it brought away but a little and my heighth of pain fallowed it. At last, after two hours lying

⟨⟨*Sicke.*⟩⟩

1. William Wight, half-brother of Pepys's father, was married but had no living children.

thus in most extraordinary anguish, crying and roaring, I know not whether it was my great sweating that [made] me do it, but upon getting up by chance among my other tumblings, upon my knees in bed, my pain begin to grow less and so continued less and less, till in an hour after I was in very little pain, but could break no wind nor make any water; and so continued and slept well all night.

18. Up and within all the morning, being willing to keep as much as I could within doors. But receiving a very wakening letter from Mr. Coventry about fitting of ships, which speaks something like to be done,[1] I went forth to the office, there to take order in things. And after dinner to White-hall to a Committee of Tanger, but did little. So home again and to Sir W Pen – who, among other things of haste in this new order for ships, is ordered to be gone presently to Portsmouth to look after the work there. I stayed to discourse with him; and so home to supper, where upon a fine couple of pigeons, a good supper. And here I met a pretty Cabinet sent me by Mr. Shales, which I gave my wife – the first of that sort of goods I ever had yet – and very conveniently it comes for her closet. Stayed up late finding out the private boxes,[2] but could not do some of them; and so to bed, afeared that I have been too bold today in venturing in the cold.

This day I begin to drink Butter milke and whey – and I hope to find great good by it.

29. *Sunday. Whitsunday. Kings Birth and Restauracion day.*

Up; and having received a letter last night, desiring it from Mr. Coventry, I walked to St. James; and there he and I did long discourse together of the business of the office and the war with the Dutch and he seemed to argue mightily with the little reason that there is for all this.◆

He doth, as to the effect of the war, tell me clearly that it is not any skill of the Dutch that can hinder our trade if we will, we having so many advantages over them, of Windes, good ports, and men. But it is our pride and the laziness of the merchant.

He seems to think that there may be some Negotiacion which may hinder the war this year: but that he speaks doubtfully, as unwilling, I perceive, to be thought to discourse any such thing.

The main thing he desired to speak with me about was to know whether I do understand my Lord Sandwiches intentions as to

1. Coventry wrote to warn Pepys of an imminent order from the Duke of York, and urging speed because the Dutch were already at sea.
2. The secret drawers. John Shales was navy victualler at Portsmouth.

going to sea with this fleet; saying that the Duke, if he desires it, is most willing to it; but thinking that twelve ships is not a fleet fit for my Lord to be troubled to go out with, he is not willing to offer it him till he hath some intimations of his mind to go or not. He spoke this with very great respect as to my Lord, though methinks it is strange they should not understand one another better at this time then to need another's mediacion.◆

31. Up, and called upon Mr. Hollyard, with whom I advised and shall fall upon some course of doing something for my disease of the wind, which grows upon me every day more and more. Thence to my Lord Sandwiches; and while he was dressing, I below discoursed with Captain Cocke and I think, if I do find it fit to keep a boy at all, I had as good be supplied from him with one as anybody.[1] By and by up to my Lord – and to discourse about his going to sea and the message I had from Mr. Coventry to him. He wonders, as he well may, that this course should be taken, and he every day with the Duke (who nevertheless seems most friendly to him), who hath not yet spoke one word to my Lord of his desire to have him go to sea. My Lord doth tell me clearly that were it not that he, as all other men that were of the parliaments side, are obnoxious to reproach, and so is forced to bear what otherwise he would not, he would never suffer everything ⟨to be⟩ done in the Navy and he never be consulted; and it seems, in the naming of all these commanders for this fleet, he hath never been asked one Question.[2] But we concluded it wholly inconsistent with his Honour not to go [with] this fleet, nor with the reputation which the world hath of his interest at Court; and so he did give me commission to tell Mr. Coventry that he is most willing to receive any commands from the Duke in this fleet, were it less then it is, and that perticularly in this service. With this message I parted; and by coach to the office, where I found Mr. Coventry and told him this. Methinks, I confess, he did not seem so pleased with it as I expected or at least could have wished; and asked me whether I had told my Lord that the Duke doth not expect his going – which I told him I had. But now, whether he means really that the Duke, as he told me the other day, doth think the fleet too small for him to take, or that he would not have him go, I swear I cannot tell. But methinks other ways might have been used to have put him by,

1. Capt. Henry Cooke (Master of the Children of the Chapel Royal) often found employment for his choirboys when their voices broke.
2. Sandwich was Lieutenant-Admiral to the Duke of York.

without going in this manner about it; and so I hope it is out of kindness indeed.

Dined at home; and so to the office, where a great while alone in my office, nobody near, with Bagwell's wife of Deptford; but the woman seems so modest that I durst not offer any courtship to her, though I had it in my mind when I brought her in to me. But am resolved to do her husband a courtesy, for I think he is a man that deserves very well.

So abroad with my wife by coach to St. James, to one Lady Poultny's, where I found my Lord, I doubt at some vain pleasure or other. I did give him a short account of what I had done with Mr. Coventry, and so left him and to my wife again in the coach, and with her to the park; but the Queen being gone by the park to Kensington, we stayed not but straight home and to supper (the first time I have done so this summer); and so to my office doing business, and then to my monthly accounts; where to my great comfort I find myself better then I was still the last month, and now come to 930*l*.

I was told today that upon Sunday night last, being the King's birthday – the King was at my Lady Castlemaine's lodgings (over the hither-gate at Lambert's lodgings) dancing with fiddlers all night almost, and all the world coming by taking notice of it – which I am sorry to hear.

The discourse of the town is only whether a war with Holland or no. And we are preparing for it all we can, which is but little.

Myself subject more then ordinary to pain by winde, which makes me very sad – together with the trouble which at present lies upon me in my father's behalf, rising from the death of my brother – which are many and great. Would to God they were over.

JUNE.

1. Up, having lain long, going to bed very late after the ending my accounts. Being up, Mr. Hollyard came to me; and to my great sorrow, after his great assuring me that I could not possibly have the stone again, he tells me that he doth verily fear that I have it again and hath brought me something to dissolve it – which doth make me very much troubled and pray to God to ease me.

He gone, I down by water to Woolwich and Deptford to look after the despatch of the ships, all the way reading Mr. Spencer's book of Prodigys, which is most ingeniously writ, both for matter and style.[1]

Home at noon and my little girl got me my dinner; and I presently out by water and landed at Somerset-stairs and thence through Coventgarden, where I met with Mr. Southwell (Sir W. Pen's friend), who tells me the very sad newes of my Lord Tiviott's and 19 more commission-officers being killed at Tanger by the Moores, by an ambush of the enemy's upon them while they were surveying their lines; which is very sad, and he says afflicts the King much.[2] Thence to W. Joyces, where by appointment I met my wife (but neither of them at home); and she and I to the King's house and saw *The Silent Woman*;[3] but methought not so well done or so good [a] play as I formerly thought it to be, or else I am nowadays out of humour. Before the play was done, it fell such a storm of Hayle that we in the middle of the pit were fain to rise,[4] and all the house in a disorder; and so my wife and I out and got into a little alehouse and stayed there an hour after the play was done before we could get a coach; which at last we did (and by chance took up Joyce Norton and Mrs. Bowles and set them at home); and so home ourselfs and I a little to my office and so home to supper and to bed.

4. Up and to St. James's by coach (after a good deal of talk before I went forth with J. Noble, who tells me that he will secure us against Cave – that though he knows and can prove it, yet nobody else can prove it to be Tom's child – that the bond was made by one Hudson, a scrivener next to the Fountain tavern in the Old Bailey – that the children were born and christened and entered in the parish-book of St. Sepulchers by the name of Anne and Elizabeth Taylor[5] – and will give us security against Cave if we pay him the money); and there up to the Duke and was with him, giving him an account how matters go. And of the necessity there is of a power to Presse seamen, without which we cannot really raise men for this fleet of twelve sail. Besides that it will assert the King's power of

1. John Spencer's *A Discourse concerning Prodigies* (1663) argued against perceiving comets, apparitions, and other unusual phenomena as signs of God's impending wrath.
2. Teviot (the governor of Tangier) and his force had been attacked on 3 May. Pepys's informant, Robert Southwell, would become a distinguished diplomat and Pepys's friend.
3. Jonson's comedy *Epicœne*.
4. The Theatre Royal was illuminated by a glazed cupola above the pit, but it was not good protection against bad weather.
5. The twins are not in the surviving baptismal register for St Sepulchre, Holborn, but this does not cover most of the relevant period.

pressing, which at present is somewhat doubted, and will make the Dutch believe that we are in earnest.[1]◆

So by coach home and at my office late; and so to supper and to bed – my body, by plenty of breaking of wind, being just now pretty well again, having had a constant akeing in my back these five or six days.◆

14. Up and to the office, where we sat all the morning and had great conflict about the flags again – and am vexed, methought to see my Lord Berkely not satisfied with what I said. But however, I stop the King's being abused by the flag-makers for the present; I do not know how it may end, but I will do my best to preserve it.[2]

So home to dinner; and after dinner by coach to Kensington, in the way overtaking Mr. Laxton the Apothecary with his wife and daughters, very fine young lasses, in a coach. And so both of us to my Lady Sandwich, who hath lain this fortnight here at Deane Hodges.[3]

Much company came hither today, my Lady Carteret &c., Sir Wm. Wheeler and his Lady, and above all Mr. Becke of Chelsy and wife and daughter, my Lord's Mistress – one that hath not one good feature in her face and yet is a fine lady, of a fine Talle[4] and very well carriaged and mighty discreet. I took all the occasion I could to discourse with the young ladies in her company, to give occasion to her to talk; which now and then she did and that mighty finely, and is I perceive a woman of such an ayre, as I wonder the less at my Lord's favour to her, and I dare warrant him she hath brains enough to entangle him. Two or three hours we were in her company, going into Sir H. Finch's garden and seeing the fountayne and singing there with the ladies; and a mighty fine cool place it is, with a great laver of water in the middle, and the bravest place for music I ever heard.

After much mirth, discoursing to the ladies in defence of the city against the country or court, and giving them occasion to invite themselfs tomorrow to me to dinner to my venison pasty, I got their mother's leave and so good-night – very well pleased with my day's work; and above all, that I have seen my Lord's Mistress.

1. A warrant to the Admiral authorizing a press (forced enlistment of men) was issued on 13 June. The King's power to press was questionable on general constitutional grounds and because war had not yet been declared.
2. Probably the dispute (recorded in Pepys's navy papers) in which he criticized the quality of flags supplied by contractors.
3. Thomas Hodges, Dean of Hereford and Vicar of Kensington.
4. Taile: shape.

So home to supper. A little at my office and to bed.

JULY.

1. Up, and within all the morning – first bringing down my Try-angle[1] to my chamber below, having a new frame made proper for it to stand on. By and by comes Dr. Burnett – who assures me that I have an Ulcer either in the Kidnys or Blather; for my water, which he saw yesterday, he is sure the Sediment is not slime gathered by heat, but is a direct pusse. He did write me down some direction what to do for it – but not with the satisfaction I expected. I did give him a piece; with good hopes, however, that his advice will be of use to me – though it is strange Mr. Hollyard should never say one word of this ulcer in all his life to me.

He being gone, I to the Change and thence home to dinner; and so to my office, busy till the evening; and then by agreement came Mr. Hill and Andrew and one Cheswicke, a maister who plays very well upon the Spinette, and we sat singing Psalms till 9 at night, and so broke up with great pleasure; and very good company it is, and I hope I shall now and then have their company. They being gone, I to my office till toward 12 a-clock, and then home and to bed.

Upon the Change this day I saw how uncertain the Temper of the people is – that from our discharging of about 200 that lay idle, having nothing to do upon some of our ships which were ordered to be fitted for service and their works are now done – the town doth talk that the King discharges all his men, 200 yesterday and 800 today, and that now he hath got 100000*l* in his hand, he values not a Dutch warr. But I undeceived a great many, telling them how it is.

10. *Lords day.* Up, and by water towards noon to Somersett-house; and walked to my Lord Sandwiches and there dined with my Lady and the children. And after some ordinary discourse with my Lady, after dinner took our leaves and [my] wife hers, in order to her going to the country tomorrow; but my Lord took not occasion to speak one word of my father or mother about the children at all[2] – which I wonder at, and begin I will not.[3]

1. Triangular virginals.
2. Sandwich's children had stayed at Brampton with Pepys's mother and father the previous winter.
3. Pepys would not mention the topic if Sandwich chose not to.

Here my Lady showed us my Lady Castlemaynes picture, finely done – given my Lord, and a most beautiful picture it is.

Thence with my Lady Jem and Mr. Sidny to St. Gyles church, and there heard a long poor sermon. Thence set them down and in their coach to Kate Joyces christening[1] – where much company – good service of sweetmeats. And after an hour's stay left them and in my Lord's coach, his noble rich coach, home; and there my wife fell to putting things in order against her going tomorrow.[2] And I to read and so to bed – where I not well, and so had no pleasure
⟨⟨11⟩⟩ at all this night with my poor wife. But betimes up this morning; and getting ready, we by coach to Holborne, where at 9 a-clock they set out, and I and my man Will on horse by her to Barnett, a very pleasant day, and there dined with her company, which was very good – a pretty gentlewoman with her that goes but to Huntington, and a neighbour to us in town. Here we stayed two hours and then parted for altogether – and my poor wife I shall soon want, I am sure.

Thence I and Will to see the Wells,[3] half a mile off; and there I drunk three glasses and went and walked, and came back and drunk two more. The woman would have had me drunk three more; but I could not, my belly being full but this wrought very well; and so we rode home round by Kingsland, Hackney, and Mile end, till we were quite weary – and my water working at least seven or eight times upon the road, which pleased me well. And so home, weary; and not being very well, I betimes to bed.

And there fell into a most mighty sweat in the night, about 11 a-clock; and there, knowing what money I have in the house[4] and hearing a noise, I begin to sweat worse and worse, till I melted almost to water. I rung, and could not in half an hour make either of the wenches hear me; and this made me fear the more, lest they might be gag'd; and then I begin to think that there was some design in a stone being flung at the window over our stairs this evening, by which the thiefes meant to try what looking there would [be] after them and know our company. These thoughts and fears I had, and do hence apprehend the fears of all rich men that are covetous and have much money by them. At last Jane[5] rose and then I understand it was only the dog wants a lodging and so

1. A christening for a child of Kate and Anthony Joyce.
2. Elizabeth and her maid Bess were going to Brampton.
3. At Barnet Common.
4. About £1,000.
5. Jane the cookmaid; her surname is not known.

made a noyse. So to bed, but hardly slept; at last did, and so till morning.

13. Up and to my office. At noon (after having at an alehouse hard by discoursed with one Mr. Tyler, a neighbour, and one Captain Sanders about the discovery of some pursers[1] that have sold their provisions), I to my Lord Sandwich, thinking to have dined there; but they not dining at home, I with Captain Ferrers to Mr. Barwell the King's Squire Sadler, where about this time twelvemonth I dined before at a good venison pasty. The like we had now, and very good company, Mr. Tresham and others.

Thence to White-hall to the Fishery, and there did little. So by water home, and there met Lanyon &c. about Tanger matters; and so late to my office and thence home and to bed.

Mr. Moore was with me late, to desire me to come to my Lord Sandwich tomorrow morning; which I shall, but wonder what my business is.

14. My mind being doubtful what the business should be, I rose little after 4 a-clock, and abroad; walked to my Lord's and nobody up, but the porter ris out of bed to me. So I back again to Fleet-street and there bought a little book of law; and thence, hearing a psalm sung, I went into St. Dunstans and there heard prayers read, which it seems is done there every morning at 6 a-clock, a thing I never did do at a chapel, but the College chapel, in all my life.

Thence to my Lord's again; and my Lord being up, was sent for up, and he and I alone: he did begin with a most solemn profession of the same confidence in and love for me that he ever had, and then told me what a misfortune was fallen upon me and him: in me, by a displeasure which my Lord Chancellor did show to him last night against me in the highest and most passionate manner that ever any man did speak, even to the not hearing of anything to be said to him. But he told me that he did say all that could be said for a man as to my faithfullness and duty to his Lordshipp, and did me the greatest right imaginable. And what should the business be but that I should be forward to have the trees in Clarendon-park marked and cut down; which he it seems hath bought of my Lord Albemarle – when God knows I am the most innocent man in the world in it, and did nothing of myself nor knew of his concernment

1. Pursers were ships' officers who kept accounts and oversaw the supply of provisions.

therein, but barely obeyed my Lord Treasurer's warrant for the doing thereof.[1] And said that I did most ungentlemanlike with him, and had justified the rogues in cutting down a tree of his; and that I had sent the veriest fanatique that is in England to mark them,[2] on purpose to nose[3] him – all which, I did assure my Lord, was most utterly false, and nothing like it true – and told my Lord the whole passage. My Lord doth seem most nearly affected with him; partly I believe for me, and partly for himself. So he advised me to wait presently upon my Lord and clear myself in the most perfect manner I could, with all submission and assurance that I am his creature both in this and all other things, and that I do own that all I have is derived through my Lord Sandwich from his Lordshipp. So, full of horror, I went and found him busy in trials of law in his great room;[4] and it being sitting-day, durst not stay, but went to my Lord and told him so – whereupon he directed me to take him after dinner; and so away I home, leaving my Lord mightily concerned for me.

I to the office and there sat busy all the morning. At noon to the Change, and from the Change over with Alsopp and the others to the Popes-head tavern and there stayed a quarter of an hour.◆ So I left them and to my Lord Chancellors; and there coming out after dinner, I accosted him, telling him that I was the unhappy Pepys that hath fallen into his high displeasure, and came to desire him to give me leave to make myself better understood to his Lordshipp – assuring him of my duty and service. He answered me very pleasingly: that he was confident upon the score of my Lord Sandwiches character of me – but that he had reason to think what he did, and desired me to call upon him some evening: I named tonight, and he accepted of it. So with my heart light, I to White-hall, and there, after understanding by a stratagem and yet appearing wholly desirous not to understand Mr. Gaudens price when he desired to show it me – I went down and ordered matters in our tender so well, that

1. The Lord Treasurer was responsible for royal forests. The King had given Clarendon Park in Wiltshire to the Duke of Albemarle but the crown had retained first claim on timber. Lord Chancellor Clarendon had then purchased the estate. Clarendon felt insulted that navy purveyors had marked trees for felling without proper consultation and had not taken timber already felled.
2. Anthony Deane.
3. Affront.
4. Clarendon lived at Worcester House in the Strand. He transacted public business there, including sessions of Chancery.

at the meeting by and by I was ready,[1] with Mr. Gaudens and his,[2] both directed in a letter to me, to give the board their two tenders; but there being none but the Generall Monke and Mr. Coventry and Povy and I, I did not think fit to expose them to view now, but put it off till Saturday – and so with good content rose.

Thence I to the Half-Moone against the Change to acquaint Lanyon and his friends of our proceeding; and thence to my Lord Chancellors and there heard several Tryalls, wherein I perceive my Lord is a most able and ready man. After all done, he himself called, "Come, Mr. Pepys, you and I will take a turn in the garden." So he was led downstairs, having the goute, and there walked with me I think above an hour, talking most friendly yet cunningly. I told him clearly how things were. How ignorant I was of his Lordships concernment in it. How I did not do nor say one word singly; but what was done was the act of the whole Board. He told me by name that he was more angry with Sir G. Carteret then with me, and also with the whole body of the Board. But thinking who it was of the Board that knew him least, he did place his fear upon me. But he finds that he is indebted to none of his friends there. I think I did thoroughly appease him, till he thanked me for my desire and pains to satisfy him. And upon my desiring to be directed who I should of his servants advise with about this business, he told me nobody, but would be glad to hear from me himself. He told me he would not direct me in anything, that it might not be said that the Lord Chancellor did labour to abuse the King or (as I offered) direct the suspending the Report of the Purveyors; but I see what he means, and will make it my work to do him service in it. But Lord, to see how he is incensed against poor Deane, as a fanatic, rogue, and I know not what – and what he did was done in spite to his Lordshipp among all his friends and tenants. He did plainly say that he would not direct me in anything, for he would not put himself into the power of any man to say that he did so and so; but plainly told me as if he would be glad I did something.

Lord, to see how we poor wretches dare not do the King good service for fear of the greatness of these men.

He named Sir G. Carteret and Sir J. Mennes and the rest; and that he was as angry with them all as me.

1. These machinations were over a contract to victual the garrison at Tangier, for which Denis Gauden was bidding. Pepys had arranged with Gauden's competitors, Timothy Alsop and John Lanyon, to support their tender, in hopes to make money by it.
2. Alsop's (or Lanyon's).

But it was pleasant to think that while he was talking to me, comes into the garden Sir G. Carteret, and my Lord avoided speaking with him, and made him and many others stay expecting him, while I walked up and down above an hour I think – and would have me walk with my hat on.[1]

And yet after all this, there hath been so little ground for all this his jealousy of me, that I am sometimes afeared that he doth this only in policy, to bring me to his side by scaring me; or else, which is worse, to try how faithful I would be to the King. But I rather think the former of the two.

I parted with great assurance how I acknowledged all I had to come from his Lordship; which he did not seem to refuse – but with great kindness and respect parted. So I by coach home, calling at my Lord's, but he not within.

At my office late; and so home to eat something, being almost starved for want of eating my dinner today; and so to bed – my head being full of great and many businesses of import to me.

20. Up, and a while to my office. And then home with Mr. Deane, till dinner discoursing upon the business of my Lord Chancellors timber in Clarindon-park and how to make a report therein without offending him; which at last I drew up, and hope it will please him. But I would to God neither I nor he ever had had anything to have done with it.

Dined together with a good pig. And then out by coach to White-hall to the Comittee for Fishing; but nothing done, it being a great day today there, upon drawing at the Lottery of Sir Arth. Slingsby.[2] I got in and stood by the two Queens and the Duchesse of York, and just behind my Lady Castlemayne, whom I do heartily adore; and good sport it was to see how most that did give their ten pounds did go away with a pair of gloves only for their lot, and one gentlewoman, one Mrs. Fish, with the only blanke. And one I stayed to see drew a suit of hangings valued at 430*l*; and they say are well worth the money, or near it. One other suit there is better then that – but very many lots of three and four score pounds. I observed the King and Queens did get but as poor lots as any else. But the wisest man I met with was Mr. Cholmly, who insured as

1. Etiquette required taking one's hat off in the presence of a superior, so Clarendon was showing his respect for Pepys by not requiring this.

2. Lotteries were sometimes granted to individuals as a mark of favour to allow them to raise funds. Slingsby's lottery was presumably a reward for his services as a royalist agent during the interregnum. It was held in the Banqueting Hall, with the prizes including jewels, furnishings, and a coach.

many as would from drawing of the one blanke for 12*d* – in which case there was the whole number of persons to one, which I think was 3 or 400. And so he insured about 200 for 200 shillings, so that he could not have lost if one of them had drawn it – for there was enough to pay the 10*l*; but it happened another drew it, and so he got all the money he took. I left the lottery and went to a play, only a piece of it; which was at the Dukes house, *Worse and Worse* – just the same manner of play, and writ I believe by the same man, as *The Adventures of Five Hours* – very pleasant it was. And I begin to admire Harris more then ever.[1]

Thence to Westminster to see Creed, and he and I took a walk in the park. He is ill, and not able yet to set out after my Lord, but will do tomorrow.[2] So home and late at my office; and so home to bed.

This evening being moonshine, I played a little late upon my flagelette in the garden.

But being at Westminster-hall, I met with great news: that Mrs. Lane is married to one Martin, one that serves Captain Marsh.[3] She is gone abroad with him today, very fine. I must have a bout with her very shortly, to see how she finds marriage.

23. Up, and all the morning at the office. At noon to the Change, where I took occasion to break the business of my Lord Chancellors timber to Mr. Coventry in the best manner I could. He professed to me that till Sir G. Carteret did speak of it at the table after our officers were gone to survey it, he did not know that my Lord Chancellor had anything to do with it. But now he says that he had been told by the Duke that Sir G. Carteret had spoke to him about it, and that he had told the Duke that were he in my Lord Chancellor's case, if he were his father,[4] he would rather fling away the gains of 2 or 3000*l* then have it said that that timber, which should have been the King's if it had continued the Duke of Albemarles, was concealed by us in favour of my Lord Chancellor. "For," says he, "he is a great man, and all such as he, and he himself

1. Henry Harris was a leading actor in the Duke's Company. *Worse and Worse* was an adaptation (now lost) by George Digby, Earl of Bristol, of a Spanish comedy. It was not by the author of *The Adventures of Five Hours*, Samuel Tuke.
2. Sandwich had just set out for Deale, prior to commanding a small fleet in the Channel.
3. Betty Lane, Pepys's mistress, had married Samuel Martin who worked in the Ordnance Office in the Tower.
4. Father-in-law (the Duke of York was married to Clarendon's daughter).

perticularly, have a great many enemies that would be glad of such a advantage against him."

When I told him it was strange that Sir J. Mennes and Sir G. Carteret, that knew my Lord Chancellor's concernment therein, should not at first inform us – he answered me: that for Sir J. Mennes, he is looked upon to be an old good companion, but by nobody at the other end of the town as any man of business; and that my Lord Chancellor, he dares say, never did tell him of it. Only, Sir G. Carteret, he doth believe, must needs know it, for he and Sir J Shaw[1] are the greatest confidants he hath in the world.

So for himself, he said, he would not mince the matter; but was resolved to do what was fit, and stand upon his own legs therein. And that he would speak to the Duke, that he and Sir G. Carteret might be appointed to attend my Lord Chancellor in it.

All this disturbs me mightily; I know not what to say to it, nor how to carry myself therein; for a compliance will discommend me to Mr. Coventry and a discompliance to my Lord Chancellor. But I think to let it alone, or at least meddle in it as little more as I can.

From thence walked toward Westminster; and being in an idle and wanton humour, walked through Fleet-alley, and there stood a most pretty wench at one of the doors.[2] So I took a turn or two; but what by sense of honour and conscience, I would not go in. But much against my will, took coach and away to Westminster-hall, and there light of Mrs. Lane and plotted with her to go over the water; so met at Whites stairs in Channel-row, and over to the old house at Lambeth-marsh and there eat and drank and had my pleasure of her twice – she being the strangest woman in talk, of love to her husband sometimes, and sometimes again she doth not care for him – and yet willing enough to allow me a liberty of doing what I would with her. So spending 5 or 6*s* upon her, I could do what I would; and after an hour's stay and more, back again and set her ashore there again, and I forward to Fleetstreete and called at Fleet-alley, not knowing how to command myself; and went in and there saw what formerly I have been acquainted with, the wickedness of those houses and the forcing a man to present expense. The woman, endeed, is a most lovely woman; but I had no courage to meddle with her, for fear of her not being wholesome, and so counterfeited that I had not money enough. It was pretty to see how cunning that Jade was; would not suffer me to have to do

1. John Shaw held a surveyorship of the royal forests.
2. Fleet Alley had a number of brothels.

in any manner with her after she saw I had no money; but told me then I would not come again, but she now was sure I would come again – though I hope in God I shall not, for though she be one of the prettiest women I ever saw, yet I fear her abusing me.

So desiring God to forgive me for this vanity, I went home, taking some books home from my bookseller and taking his lad home with me, to whom I paid 10*l* for books I have laid up money for and laid out within these three weeks – and shall do no more a great while I hope.

So to my office, writing letters; and then home and to bed, weary of the pleasure I have had today and ashamed to think of it.

26. All the morning at the office. At noon to Anth. Joyces to our gossips dinner;[1] I had sent a dozen and a half of bottles of wine thither and paid my double share besides, which is 18*s*. Very merry we were, and when the women were merry and ris from table, I above with them, ne'er a man but I; I begin discourse of my not getting of children and prayed them to give me their opinions and advice; and they freely and merrily did give me these ten among them. 1. Do not hug my wife too hard nor too much. 2. Eat no late suppers. 3. Drink Juyce of sage. 4. Tent[2] and toast. 5. Wear cool Holland-drawers.[3] 6. Keep stomach warm and back cool. 7. Upon my query whether it was best to do at night or morn, they answered me neither one nor other, but when we have most mind to it. 8. Wife not to go too strait-laced. 9. Myself to drink Mum and sugar. 10. Mrs. Ward did give me to change my plat.[4] The 3rd, 4th, 6th, 7th, and 10th they all did seriously declare and lay much stress upon them, as rules fit to be observed indeed, and especially the last: to lie with our heads where our heels do, or at least to make the bed high at feet and low at head.

Very merry all, as much as I could be in such sorry company.

28. At the office all the morning. Dined, after Change, at home, and then abroad and seeing *The Bondman* upon the posts, I consulted my oaths and find I may go safely this time without breaking it;[5] I went thither, notwithstanding my great desire to have gone to

1. A dinner for godparents (gossips) and others to celebrate the birth of the Joyces' child.
2. Spanish red wine.
3. Drawers made of linen.
4. I.e. tell me to change my position (when lying down).
5. Massinger's *The Bondman* was advertised by playbills stuck up on posts. Pepys's current oath allowed him to go to a play once a month. Although he had seen "a piece of" a play on 20 July, apparently this did not count.

Fleete ally, God forgive me, again. There I saw it acted; it is true, for want of practice they had many of them forgot their parts a little, but Baterton and my poor Ianthe out-do all the world. There is nothing more taking in the world with me then that play.

Thence to Westminster to my barbers; and strange to think how when I found that Jervas himself did intend to bring home my periwig, and not Jane his maid, I did desire not to have it at all, for I had a mind to have her bring it home. I also went to Mr. Blagraves,[1] about speaking to him for his kinswoman to come live with my wife; but they are not come to town, and so I home by coach and to my office, and then to supper and to bed.

My present posture is this. My wife in the country and my maid Besse with her, and all quiet there. I am endeavouring to find a Woman for her to my mind; and above all, one that understands musique, especially singing. I am the willinger to keep one because I am in good hopes to get 2 or 300*l* per annum extraordinary by the business of the victualing of Tanger – and yet Mr. Alsop, my chief hopes, is dead since my looking after it, and now Mr. Lanyon I fear is falling sick too.

I am pretty well in health; only, subject to wind upon any cold, and then immediate and great pains.

All our discourse is of a Dutch war; and I find it is likely to come to it, for they are very high and desire not to compliment us at all as far as I hear, but to send a good fleet to Guinny to oppose us there. My Lord Sandwich newly gone to sea, and I, I think, fallen into his very good opinion again; at least, he did before his going, and by his letter since, show me all manner of respect and confidence.

I am over-Joyed in hopes that upon this month's account I shall find myself worth 1000*l*, besides the rich present of two silver and gilt flagons which Mr. Gauden did give me the other day.[2]

I do now live very prettily at home, being most seriously, quietly, and neatly served by my two maids, Jane and the girl Su – with both of whom I am mightily well pleased.

My greatest trouble is the settling of Brampton estate, that I may know what to expect and how to be able to leave it when I die, so as to be just to my promise to my Uncle Tho. and his son. The next thing is this cursed trouble my Brother Tom is likely to put us to by his death, forcing us to law with his Creditors, among

1. Thomas Blagrave, a court musician.
2. The gift, Pepys suspected, was Gauden's attempt to secure his support in the competition to victual Tangier. Gauden later insisted it was for past services.

others Dr. Tom Pepys, and that with some shame, as trouble. And the last, how to know in what manner, as to saving or spending, my father lives, lest they should run me in debt as one of my uncles executors, and I never the wiser nor better for it. But in all this I hope shortly to be at leisure to consider and inform myself well.

AUGUST.

7. *Lords day.* Lay long, caressing my wife and talking[1] – she telling me sad stories of the ill, improvident, disquiet, and sluttish[2] manner that my father and mother and Pall live in the country; which troubles me mightily and I must seek to remedy it. So up and ready – and my wife also; and then down and I showed my wife, to her great admiration and joy, Mr. Gaudens present of plate, the two Flaggons; which endeed are so noble that I hardly can think that they are yet mine. So blessing God for it, we down to dinner, mighty pleasant; and so up after dinner for a while and I then to White-hall; walked thither – having at home met with a letter of Captain Cooke's, with which he had sent a boy for me to see, whom he did intend to recommend to me. I therefore went, and there met and spoke with him. He gives me great hopes of the boy, which pleases me; and at Chappell I there met Mr. Blagrave, who gives a report of the boy; and he showed me him and I spoke to him, and the boy seems a good willing boy to come to me, and I hope will do well. I am to speak to Mr. Townsend to hasten his clothes for him, and then he is to come.[3] So I walked homeward and met with Mr. Spong;[4] and he with me as far as the Old Exchange, talking of many ingenuous things, Musique, and at last of Glasses, and I find him still the same ingenuous man that ever he was; and doth, among other fine things, tell me that by his Microscope of his own making he doth discover that the wings of a Moth is made just as the feathers of the wing of a bird, and that most plainly and certainly. While we were talking, came by several poor creatures, carried by by Constables for being at a conventicle. They go like lambs, without any resistance. I would to God they would either conform,

1. Elizabeth had returned from Brampton the day before.
2. Slovenly.
3. The boy was Tom Edwards (aged about 19), one of the choristers at the Chapel Royal where Henry Cooke was Master. It was customary for choristers to receive a suit of clothes on leaving the King's service.
4. John Spong, maker of optical instruments.

or be more wise and not be ketched. Thence parted with him, mightily pleased with his company, and away homeward, calling at Dan Rawlinson and supped there with my Uncle Wight; and then home and eat again for form sake with her, and then to prayers and to bed.

14. *Lords day.* After long lying discoursing with my wife, I up; and comes Mr. Holliard to see me, who concurs with me that my pain is nothing but cold in my legs breeding wind, and got only by my using to wear a gowne. And that I am not at all troubled with any ulcer, but my thickness of water comes from my over-heat in my back. He gone, comes Mr. Herbert, Mr. Honiwoods man, and dined with me – a very honest, plain, well-meaning man I think him to be; and by his discourse and manner of life, the true Embleme of an old ordinary serving-man.

After dinner, up to my chamber and made an end of Dr. Powre's book of the Microscope, very fine and to my content;[1] and then my wife and I with great pleasure, but with great difficulty before we could come to find the manner of seeing anything by my Microscope – at last did, with good content, though not so much as I expect when I come to understand it better. By and by comes W. Joyce in his silk suit and cloak lined with velvett. Stayed talking with me, and I very merry at it. He supped with me; but a cunning, crafty fellow he is, and dangerous to displease, for his tongue spares nobody.

After supper I up to read a little, and then to bed.

25.◆ All the morning at the office busy. At noon to the Change; among other things, busy to get a little by the hire of a ship for Tanger. So home to dinner; and after dinner comes Mr. Cooke to see me; it is true he was kind to me at Sea, in carrying messages to and fro to my wife from sea, but I did do him kindnesses too, and therefore I matter not much to compliment or make any regard of his thinking me to slight him, as I do for his folly about my brother Tom's mistress.[2]

After dinner and some talk with him, I to my office, there busy,

⟨⟨Jack Noble⟩⟩ – till by and by Jacke Noble came to me to tell me that he had Cave in prison, and that he

1. Henry Power's *Experimental Philosophy* (1664) began with a section describing objects and creatures when seen through a microscope. These included a flea, seeds, and "Mites in Cheese". It was one of the earliest books on microscopy.

2. Cooke had served with Pepys in the *Naseby* in 1660. He had later bungled the financial negotiations for Tom's match with Elizabeth Hobell. *See* 22 Oct. 1662.

would give me and my father good security that neither we nor any of our family should be troubled with the child[1] – for he could prove that he was fully satisfied for him; and that if the worst came to the worst, the parish must keep it. That Cave did bring the child to his house, but they got it carried back again and that thereupon he put him in prison. When he saw that I would not pay him the money, nor made anything of being secured against the child, he then said that then he must go to law; not himself, but come in as a witness for Cave against us. I could have told him that he could bear witness that Cave is satisfied, or else there is no money due to himself.[2] But I let alone any such discourse, only getting as much out of him as I could. I perceive he is a rogue, and hath enquired into everything and consulted with Dr Pepys.[3] And that he thinks, as Dr. Pepys told him, that my father, if he could, would not pay a farding of the debts. And yet I made him confess that in all his lifetime he never knew my father to be asked for money twice, nay, not once, all the time he lived with him. And that for his own debts, he believed he would do so still; but he meant only for these of Tom.

He said now, that Randall and his wife and the Midwife could prove from my brother's own mouth that the child was his, and that Tom had told them the circumstances of time, upon November the 5 at night, that he got it on her.

I offered him if he would secure my father against being forced to pay the money again, I would pay him; which at first he would do, give his own security; and when I asked more then his own, he told me yes, he would, and those able men, Subsidy men.[4] But when we came by and by to discourse of it again, he would not then do it but said he would take his course and Joyne with Cave and release him; and so we parted.

However, this vexed me, so as I could not be quiet but took Coach to go speak with Mr. Cole;[5] but met him not within, so back, buying a table by the way, and at my office late; and then home to supper and to bed, my mind disordered about this

1. Tom's illegitimate daughter, Elizabeth. Noble was acting as agent in the financial arrangements with her foster-father Cave.
2. According to Noble, the officers of Cave's parish have prevented Cave taking custody of the child (suspecting they will end up supporting her). As Cave failed to keep his bond to care for the baby without further trouble, Noble had him arrested. Noble wants to be paid money due to him, or he will join Cave to sue for money allegedly due to Cave. However, if Cave has not been paid by Noble, Noble has no basis to claim payment from the Pepys family.
3. Pepys's cousin, Dr Thomas Pepys, to whom Tom owed money.
4. Wealthy men, sufficiently well off to be liable for subsidy tax.
5. Pepys's barrister.

roguish business: in everything else, I thank God, well at ease.[1]

27. Up and to the office, where all the morning. At noon to the Change and there almost made my bargain about a ship for Tanger, which will bring me in a little profit with Captain Taylor. Off the Change with Mr Cutler and Sir W Rider to Cutlers house; and there had a very good dinner, and two or three pretty young ladies of their relations there. Thence to my Case=maker for my Stone=case;[2] and had it to my mind, and cost me 24*s* – which is a great deal of money, but it is well done and pleases me. So doing some other small errands, I home and there find my boy Tom Edwards come – sent me by Captain Cooke, having [been] bred in the King's chapel these four years. I purpose to make a clerk of him; and if he deserves well, to do well by him. Spent much of the afternoon to set his chamber in order; and then to the office, leaving him at home. And late at night, after all business was done, I called Will and told him my reason of taking a boy, and that it is of necessity, not out of any unkindness to him, nor should be to his injury. And then talked about his landlord's daughter to come to my wife, and I think it will be.[3] So home and find my boy a very schooleboy that talks inocently and impertinently; but at present it is a sport to us, and in a little time he will leave it. So sent him to bed, he saying that he used to go to bed at 8 a-clock. And then all of us to bed, myself pretty well pleased with my choice of a boy. All the news this day is that the Dutch are with 22 sail of ships of warr crewsing up and down about Ostend; at which we are alarmed. My Lord Sandwich is come back into the Downes with only eight sail, which is or may be a prey to the Dutch, if they knew our weakness and inability to set out any more speedily.

30. Up and to the office, where sat long; and at noon to dinner at home. After dinner comes Mr. Pen to visit me, and stayed an hour talking with me. I perceive something of learning he hath got, but a great deal, if not too much, of the vanity of the French garbe and affected manner of speech and gait – I fear all real profit he hath made of his travel will signify little.[4] So he gone, I to my office and there very busy till late at night; and so home to supper and to bed.

1. Mysteriously, this is the last time Tom's daughter or the financial dispute is mentioned directly in the diary. It is possible that she died, solving Pepys's problem.
2. A case to hold Pepys's bladder stone, removed in 1658.
3. This was Mary Mercer, 17-year-old daughter of William Mercer of St Olave's parish, a merchant.
4. William Penn, future Quaker leader, had been on a tour of Europe and spent time at the Protestant Academy of Saumur, France.

SEPTEMBER.

6. Up and to the office, where we sat all the morning. At noon home to dinner. Then to my office and there waited, thinking to have had Baggwell's wife come to me about business, that I might have talked with her; but she came not. So I to White-hall by coach with Mr. Andrews; and there I got his contract for the victualling of Tanger signed and sealed by us there. So that all that business is well over, and I hope to have made a good business of it – and to receive 100*l* by it the next week – for which God be praised.[1] Thence to W. Joyces and Anthonys to invite them to dinner to meet my aunt James at my house, and the rather because they are all to go down to my father's the next week, and so I would be a little kind to them before they go.

So home, having called upon Doll, our pretty Change woman, for a pair of gloves trimmed with yellow ribbon (to [match the] petticoat she bought yesterday), which costs me 20*s*. But she is so pretty, that, God forgive me, I could not think it too much; which is a strange slavery that I stand in to beauty, that I value nothing near it.

So going home and my coach stopping in Newgate-market over against a poulterer's shop, I took occasion to buy a rabbit; but it proved a deadly old one when I came to eat it – as I did do after an hour's being at my office; and after supper, again there till past 11 at night. And so home and to bed.

⟨⟨Duch.⟩⟩ This day, Mr. Coventry did tell us how the Duke did receive the Dutch Embassador the other day – by telling him that whereas they think us in Jest, he believes that the Prince (Rupert), which goes in this fleet to guinny, will soon tell them that we are in earnest;[2] and that he himself will do the like here in the head of fleet here at home. And that for the Meschants,[3] which he[4] told the Duke there were in England which did hope to

1. Thomas Andrews had replaced the deceased Alsop in the partnership that Pepys supported for the victualling contract (and that had promised to pay him for his help).
2. Both the English and the Dutch were making preparations to send additional forces to West Africa to fight over their possessions there.
3. Villains, i.e. puritan fanatics.
4. The Dutch ambassador, Van Gogh.

do themselfs good by the King's being at war, says he,[1] "the English have ever united all this private differences to attend Forraigne," and that Cromwell, notwithstanding the Meschants in his time (which were the Cavaliers), he did never find them interrupt him in his foreign businesses. And that he did not doubt but to live to see the Dutch as fearful of provoking the English under the government of a King, as he remembers them to have been under that of a Coquin.[2] I writ all this story to my Lord Sandwich tonight into the Downes, it being very good and true, word for word from Mr. Coventry today.

8. Up and to the office, where busy all the morning. At noon dined at home – and I by water down to Woolwich by a gally, and back again in the evening. All haste made in setting out this Guinny fleet, but yet not such as will ever do the King's business if we come to a warr. My [wife] this afternoon, being very well dressed by her new woman, Mary Mercer (a decayed merchant's daughter that our Will helps us to), did go to the christening of Mrs. Mill's the parson's wife's child, where she never was before. After I was come home, Mr. Povey came to me and took me out to supper to Mr. Bland's, who is making now all haste to be gone for Tanger.[3] Here pretty merry, and good discourse; fain to admire the knowledge and experience of Mrs. Bland, who I think as good a merchant as her husband. I went home and there find Mercer, whose person I like well and I think will do well, at least I hope so. So to my office a little and then to bed.

9. Up, and to put things in order against dinner, I out and bought some things; among others, a dozen of Silver Salts.[4] Home and to the office, where some of us met a little; and then home and at noon comes my company – *viz.*, Anth. and Will Joyce and their wifes – my aunt James newly come out of Wales, and my Cosen Sarah Gyles – her husband did not come, and by her I did understand afterward that it was because he was not yet able to pay me the 40*s* she had borrowed a year ago of me. I was as merry as I could, giving them a good dinner; but W. Joyce did so talk, that he made everybody else Dumb, but only laugh at him. I forgot, there was Mr. Harman and his wife. My aunt a very good harmelesse woman. All

1. The Duke of York.
2. Rogue.
3. John Bland, a merchant trading in the Mediterranean, became the first mayor of Tangier in 1668.
4. Saltcellars.

their talk is of her and my two she-Cosen Joyces and Will's little boy Will (who was also here today) [going] down to Brampton to my father's next week – which will be trouble and charge to them; but however, my father and mother desire to see them, and so let them. They eyed mightily my great Cupboard of plate, I this day putting my two Flaggons upon my table;[1] and endeed, it is a fine sight and better then ever I did hope to see of my own. Mercer dined with us at table, this being her first dinner in my house.

After dinner left them and to White-hall, where a small Tanger committee; and so back again home and there my wife and Mercer and Tom and I sat till 11 at night, singing and fiddling; and a great joy it is to see me maister of so much pleasure in my house, that it is, and will be still I hope, a constant pleasure to me to be at home. The girle plays pretty well upon the Harpsicon, but only ordinary tunes; but hath a good hand. Sings a little, but hath a good voyce and eare. My boy, a brave boy, sings finely and is the most pleasant boy at present, while his ignorant boy's tricks last, that ever I saw. So to supper, and with great pleasure to bed.

29. *Michaelmas day.* Up, and to the office, where all the morning. Dined at home and Creed with me. After dinner I to Sir G. Carteret, and with him to his new house he is taking in Broadstreete; and there surveyed all the rooms and bounds in order to the drawing up a lease thereof. And that done, Mr Cutler (his landlord)[2] took me up and down and showed me all his ground and houses, which is extraordinary great, he having bought all the Augustin-fryers; and many many a 1000*l* he hath and will bury there. So home to my business, clearing my papers and preparing my accounts against tomorrow for a monthly and a great Auditt. So to supper and to bed.

Fresh newes came of our beating the Dutch at Guiny quite out of all their castles almost, which will make them quite mad here at home, sure.[3] And Sir G. Carteret did tell me that the King doth joy mightily at it; but asked him laughing, "But," says he, "how shall I do to answer this to the Embassador when he comes?"

Nay, they say that we have beat them out of the New

1. The silver flagons given by Denis Gauden.
2. William Cutler was also a merchant with whom the Navy Board did business.
3. A squadron led by Sir Robert Holmes had attacked Dutch settlements in West Africa. This action, done in the name of protecting English trade, helped provoke the Second Anglo-Dutch War.

Netherlands too[1] – so that we have been doing them mischiefe a great while in several parts of the world, without public knowledge or reason.

Their Fleete for Guinny is now, they say, ready and abroad, and will be going this week.

Coming home tonight, I did go to examine my wife's house-accounts; and finding things that seemed somewhat doubtful, I was angry, though she did make it pretty plain; but confessed that when she doth misse a sum, she doth add something to other things to make it. And upon my being very angry, she doth protest that she will here lay up something for herself to buy her a neckelace with – which madded me and doth still trouble me, for I fear she will forget by degrees the way of living cheap and under a sense of want.

OCTOBER.

1. Up and at the office both forenoon and afternoon, very busy, and with great pleasure in being so. This morning, Mrs. Lane (now Martin) like a foolish woman came to the Hors=shoo hard by, and sent for me while I was at the office to come to speak with her, by a note sealed up – I know, to get me to do something for her husband; but I sent her an answer that I would see her at Westminster. And so I did not go, and she went away, poor soul.

At night home to supper, weary and my eyes sore with writing and reading – and to bed.

We go now on with great Vigour in preparing against the Dutch, who they say will now fall upon us without doubt, upon this high news come of our beating them so wholly in Guiny.

2. *Lords day.* My wife not being well to go to church, I walked with my boy through the City, putting in at several churches; among others, at Bishops-gate, and there saw the picture usually put before the King's book, put up in the church; but very ill painted, though it were a pretty piece to set up in a church.[2] I entended to have seen the Quakers, who they say do meet every Lord's day at

1. New Netherland was a Dutch colony on the east coast of North America. On 27 August the Dutch surrendered the colony's seat of government, New Amsterdam (on Manhattan Island), to a force under Richard Nicholls. It was renamed New York after the Duke of York.
2. The picture (in St Botolph's) was copied from a famous engraving in the *Eikon Basilike*, a collection of writings attributed to Charles I and published after his execution. It showed Charles I spurning his earthly crown for a crown of thorns.

the Mouth at Bishops-gate;[1] but I could see none stirring, nor was it fit to ask for the place. So I walked over Moore-fields, and thence to Clerkenwell church and there (as I wished) sat next pew to the fair Butler, who endeed is a most perfect beauty still.[2] And one I do very much admire myself for my choice of her for a beauty – she having the best lower part of her face that ever I saw all days of my life. After church I walked to my Lady Sandwiches through my Lord Southamptons new buildings in the fields behind Grays Inn; and endeed they are a very great and a noble work. So I dined with my Lady; and the same innocent discourse that we used to have. Only, after dinner, being alone, she asked me my opinion about Creed, whether he would have a wife or no and what he was worth, and proposed Mrs. Wright[3] for him; which she says she heard he was once enquiring after. She desired I would take a good time and manner of proposing it; and I said I would, though I believed he would love nothing but money, and much was not to be expected there she said.

So away back to Clerken-well church, thinking to have got sight of *la belle* Boteler again, but failed; and so after church walked all over the fields home; and there my wife was angry with me for not coming home and for gadding abroad to look after beauties, she told me plainly; so I made all peace, and to supper. This evening came Mrs. Lane (now Martin) with her husband to desire my help about a place for him; it seems poor Mr. Daniel is dead, of the Victualling-Office – a place too good for this puppy to fallow him in – but I did give him the best words I could; and so after drinking a glass of wine, sent them going, but with great kindness. So to supper, prayers, and to bed.

17. Rose very well and not weary, and with Sir W. Batten to St. James's. There did our business. I saw Sir J Lawson since his return from sea first this morning, and hear that my Lord Sandwich is come from Portsmouth to town. Thence I to him; and finding him at my Lord Crews, I went with him home to his house, and much kind discourse. Thence my Lord to Court and I with Creed to the Change. And thence with Sir W Warren to a cook's shop and dined, discoursing and advising him about his great contract he is to make tomorrow. And do every day receive great satisfaction in

1. Pepys seems to have confused the Mouth tavern, Without Bishopsgate, with the Bull and Mouth tavern, Aldersgate Street, where the most important Quaker meeting in the City was held.
2. Frances Butler, sister of a friend.
3. Nan Wright, Lady Sandwich's niece.

his company, and a prospect of just advantage by his friendship. Thence to my office doing some business; but it being very cold, I, for fear of getting cold, went early home to bed – my wife not being come home from my Lady Jemimah, with whom she hath been at a play and at Court today.

20. Up and to the office, where all the morning. At noon my uncle Tho. came; dined with me and received some money of me. Then I to my office, where I took in with me Bagwells wife; and there I caressed her, and find her every day more and more coming, with good words and promise of getting her husband a place, which I will do. So we parted, and I to my Lord Sandwich at his lodgings; and after a little stay, away with Mr. Cholmely to Fleet-street, in the way he telling me that Tanger is like to be in a bad condition with this same Fitzgerald,[1] he being a man of no honour nor presence, nor little honesty, and endeavours to raise the Irish and suppress the English interest there, and offends everybody – and doth nothing that I hear of well – which I am sorry for.

Thence home, by the way taking two silver Tumblers home which I have bought; and so home and there late, busy at my office; and then home to supper and to bed.

24. Up, and in Sir J. Minnes's coach (alone with Mrs. Turner as far as Pater Noster-row, where I set her down) to St. James and there did our business; and I had the good luck to speak what pleased the Duke about our great contract in hand with Sir W Warren against Sir W. Batten, wherein the Duke is very earnest for our contracting.[2]

Thence home to the office till noon; and then dined and to the Change, and off with Sir W Warren for a while, consulting about managing his contract. Thence to a committee at White-hall of Tanger, where I had the good luck to speak something to very good purpose about the Molle at Tanger; which was well received, even by Sir J Lawson and Mr. Cholmly, the undertakers against whose interest I spoke – that I believe I shall be valued for it. Thence into the galleries to talk with my Lord Sandwich; among ⟨other⟩ things, about the Princes[3] writing up to tell us of the danger he and his fleet lies [in] at Portsmouth of receiving affronts from the Dutch –

1. John Fitzgerald, Deputy-Governor of Tangier, had returned there to take charge after the death of Governor Teviot. He was commander of the Irish regiment.
2. A contract for 3,000 loads of timber (150,000 cubic feet), needed for the impending war.
3. Prince Rupert.

which my Lord said he would never have done had he lien there with one ship alone; nor is there any great reason for it, because of the sands. However, the fleet will be ordered to go and lay themselfs up at the Cowes – much beneath the prowesse of the Prince I think, and the honour of the nation, at the first to be found to secure themselfs. My Lord is well pleased to think that if the Duke and the Prince goes, all the blame of any miscarriage will not light on him. And that if anything goes well, he hopes he shall have the share of the glory – for the Prince is by no means well esteemed of by anybody.

Thence home; and though not very well, yet up late about the Fishery business, wherein I hope to give an account how I find the Collections to have been managed – which I did finish to my great content.[1] And so home to supper and to bed.

This day the great Oneale died; I believe, to the content of all the protestant pretenders in Ireland.[2]

NOVEMBER.

13. *Lords day.* The morning to church, where mighty sport to hear our Clerke sing out of tune, though his master sits by him that begins and keeps the tune aloud for the parish.[3]

Dined at home very well. And spent all the afternoon with my wife within doors – and getting a speech out of *Hamlett*, "To bee or not to bee," without book.

In the evening, to sing psalms; and in came Mr. Hill to see me, and then he and I and the boy finely to sing; and so anon broke up after much pleasure. He gone, I to supper and so to prayers and to bed.

14. Up, and with Sir W. Batten to White-hall to the Lords of the Admiralty and there did our business betimes. Thence to Sir Ph. Warwicke about Navy business – and my Lord Ashly; and afterward to my Lord Chancellor, who is very well pleased with

1. Collections had been taken up in churches to support the work of the Corporation for the Royal Fishery in improving the fishing industry. Pepys's report criticized the conduct of the members in charge of the collections.
2. Daniel O'Neill, an extremely rich courtier close to the King, had helped Irish Catholics in their land disputes with Cromwellian settlers ("protestant pretenders").
3. St Olave's had been without an organ since 1644.

me and my carrying of his business.[1] And so to the Change, where mighty busy; and so home to dinner, where Mr. Creed and Moore; and after dinner I to my Lord Treasurers, to Sir Ph. Warwicke there, and then to White-hall to the Duke of Albimarle about Tanger; and then homeward to the Coffee-house to hear news: and it seems the Dutch, as I afterward find by Mr. Coventrys letters, have stopped a ship of masts of Sir W Warrens, coming for us in a Swedes ship; which they will not release upon Sir G Downings[2] claiming her – which appears as the first act of hostility – and is looked upon as so by Mr. Coventry.

The *Elias*, coming from New England (Captain Hill commander), is sunk; only the Captain and a few men saved. She foundered in the sea.

So home, where infinite busy till 12 at night; and so home to supper and to bed.

15. That I might not be too fine for the business I intend this day, I did leave off my fine new cloth suit lined with plush and put on my poor black suit; and after office done (where much business but little done), I to the Change; and thence Bagwell's wife with much ado fallowed me through Moor-fields to a blind[3] alehouse, and there I did caress her and eat and drank, and many hard looks and sithes[4] the poor wretch did give me, and I think verily was troubled at what I did; but at last, after many protestings, by degrees I did arrive at what I would, with great pleasure. Then in the evening, it raining, walked to the town to where she knew where she was; and then I took coach and to White-hall to a Committee of Tanger, where, and everywhere else I thank God, I find myself growing in repute; and so home and late, very late, at business, nobody minding it but myself; and so home to bed – weary and full of thoughts. Businesses grow high between the Dutch and us on every side.

25. Up, and at my office all the morning to prepare an account of the charge we have been put to extraordinary by the Dutch already; and I have brought it to appear 852700*l*; but God knows, this is only a scare to the Parliament, to make them give the more money.

Thence to the Parliament-house and there did give it to Sir Ph. Warwicke, the House being hot upon giving the King a supply of

1. Pepys had managed to placate Clarendon over the navy's claims to timber at Clarendon Park. *See* 14 July 1664.
2. Envoy to the Dutch Republic.
3. Out of the way, obscure.
4. Sighs.

money. And I by coach to the Change and took up Mr. Jenings along with me (my old acquaintance), he telling me the mean manner that Sir Samuel Morland lives near him, in a house he hath bought and laid out money upon; in all, to the value of 1200*l* – but is believed to be a beggar. And so I ever thought he would be.[1]

From the Change, with Mr. Deering and Luellin to the White-horse tavern in Lombard-street – and there dined with them, he giving me a dish of meat, to discourse in order to my serving Deering; which I am already obliged to do, and shall do it – and would be glad he were a man trusty, that I might venture something along with him.[2]

Thence home; and by and by, in the evening, took my wife out by coach, leaving her at Unthankes, while I to White-hall and to Westminster-hall, where I have not been to talk a great while; and there hear that Mrs. Lane and her husband live a sad life together, and he is gone to be a pay-master to a company to Portsmouth to serve at sea. She big with child. Thence I home, calling my wife – and at Sir W. Batten's hear that the House hath given the King 2500000*l* to be paid for this war, only for the Navy, in three years time; which is a joyful thing to all the King's party I see – but was much opposed by Mr. Vaughan and others, that it should be so much.[3] So home and to supper and to bed.

DECEMBER.

10. Lay long; at which I am ashamed, because of so many people's observing it that know not how late I sit up, and for fear of Sir W. Batten's speaking of it to others – he having stayed for me a good while. At the office all the morning, where comes my Lord Brunkard with his patent in his hand and delivered it to Sir J. Mennes and myself, we alone being there – all the day.[4] And at noon I in his coach with him to the Change, where he set me down. A

1. Morland (now a baronet and courtier) had been Pepys's tutor at Magdalene.
2. Pepys had been previously given a generous sum by the merchant Edward Dering in return for assistance with a contract, and he felt he had not reciprocated sufficiently. *See* 12 Dec. 1663 and 1 Jan. 1664.
3. The Royal Aid was the largest grant made to any Stuart government. Its collection was spread over three years. The proposal to make it "only for the Navy" (i.e. to allocate all proceeds to a naval war) was not pursued with this act.
4. William, 2nd Viscount Brouncker, had just been made a Navy Commissioner. He was a mathematician, a ship-designer, and the first President of the Royal Society.

modest civil person he seems to be, but wholly ignorant in the business of the Navy as possible, but I hope to make a friend of him, being a worthy man.

Thence, after hearing the great news of so many Duchmen being brought in to Portsmouth and elsewhere, which it is expected shall either put them upon present revenge or despair, I with Sir W Rider and Cutler to dinner all alone to the Great James – where good discourse, and I hope occasion of getting something hereafter.[1]

After dinner to White-hall to the Fishery, where the Duke was with us.

So home and late at my office, writing many letters; then home to supper and to bed. Yesterday came home, and this night I visited, Sir W Pen, who dissembles great respect and love to me, but I understand him very well.

Major Holmes is come from Guiny and is now at Plymouth, with great wealth they say.[2]

19. Going to bed betimes last night, we waked betimes. And from our people's being forced to take the key to go out to light a candle, I was very angry and begun to find fault with my wife for not commanding her servants as she ought. Thereupon, she giving me some cross answer, I did strike her over her left eye such a blow, as the poor wretch did cry out and was in great pain; but yet her spirit was such as to endeavour to bite and scratch me. But I cogging[3] with her, made her leave crying, and sent for butter and parsley, and friends presently one with another; and I up, vexed at my heart to think what I had done, for she was forced to lay a poultice or something to her eye all day, and is black – and the people of the house observed it.

But I was forced to rise; and up and with Sir J. Mennes to White-hall, and there we waited on the Duke. And among other things, Mr. Coventry took occasion to vindicate himself before the Duke and us, being all there, about the choosing of Taylor for Harwich.[4] Upon which the Duke did clear him, and did tell us that he did expect that after he had named a man, none of us shall then

1. Both men were merchants.
2. Holmes had returned from seizing Dutch settlements in West Africa, bringing captured ships.
3. Wheedling, or flattering cunningly.
4. In November the Admiralty Committee had halted John Taylor's appointment as Navy Commissioner at Harwich because Batten objected that he was a "fanatic". Pepys had sought and received Coventry's support for Taylor.

oppose or find fault with that man. But if we had anything to say, we ought to say it before he had chose him. Sir G. Carteret thought himself concerned, and endeavoured to clear himself. And by and by Sir W. Batten did speak, knowing himself guilty; and did confess that being pressed by the Council, he did say what he did, that he was accounted a fanatique; but did not know that at that time he had been appointed by his Royal Highness – to which the Duke [replied] that it was impossible but he must know that he had appointed him; and so it did appear that the Duke did mean all this while Sir W. Batten. So by and by we parted; and Mr. Coventry did privately tell me that he did this day take this occasion to mention the business, to give the Duke an opportunity of speaking his mind to Sir W. Batten in this business – of which I was heartily glad.

Thence home; and not finding Bagwell's wife as I expected, I to the Change and there walked up and down, and then home; and she being come, I bid her go and stay at Mooregate for me; and after going up to my wife (whose eye is very bad, but she in very good temper to me); and after dinner, I to the place and walked round the fields again and again; but not finding her, I to the Change and there found her waiting for me and took her away and to an alehouse, and there I made much of her; and then away thence and to another, and endeavoured to caress her; but elle ne vouloit pas,[1] which did vex me but I think it was chiefly not having a good easy place to do it upon. So we broke up and parted; and I to the office, where we sat hiring of ships an hour or two; and then to my office and thence (with Captain Taylor home ⟨to my house⟩) to give him instructions and some notice of what, to his great satisfaction, had happened today – which I do because I hope his coming into this office will a little cross Sir W. Batten and may do me good. He gone, I to supper with my wife, very pleasant; and then a little to my office and to bed – my mind, God forgive me, too much running upon what I can faire avec la femme de Bagwell demain – having promised to go to Deptford and à aller à sa maison avec son mari[2] when I come thither.

20. Up and walked to Deptford, where after doing something at the yard, I walked, without being observed, with Bagwell home to his house and there was very kindly used, and the poor people did

1. "she did not want to".
2. "what I can do with Bagwell's wife tomorrow – having promised to go to Deptford and to go to her house with her husband".

get a dinner for me in their fashion – of which I also eat very well. After dinner I found occasion of sending him abroad; and then alone avec elle je tentoy à faire ce que je voudrais, et contre sa force je le faisoy, bien que pas à mon contentment.[1] By and by, he coming back again, I took leave and walked home; and then there to dinner, where Dr. Fayrbrother came to see me, and Luellin; we dined, and I to the office, leaving them – where we sat all the afternoon, and I late at the office. To supper and to the office again very late; then home to bed.

22. Up and betimes to my office and then out to several places. Among others, to Holborne to have spoke with one Mr. Underwood about some English Hemp – he lies against[2] grays Inn. Thereabouts, I to a barbers shop to have my hair cut. And there met with a copy of verses, mightily commended by some gentleman there, of my Lord Mordants in excuse of his going to sea – this late expedition, with the Duke of York. But Lord, they are but sorry things; only, a Lord made them.[3]

Thence to the Change; and there among the merchants, I hear fully the news of our being beaten to dirt at Guiny by De Ruyter with his fleet. The particulars, as much as by Sir G Carteret afterward I heard, I have said in a letter to my Lord Sandwich this day at Portsmouth – it being most wholly to the utter ruine of our Royall Company, and reproach and shame to the whole nation, as well as justification to them, in their doing wrong to no man as to his private [property]; only take whatever is found to belong to the Company, and nothing else.[4]

Dined at the Dolphin, Sir G. Carteret, Sir J. Mennes, Sir W. Batten, and I, with Sir Wm. Boreman and Sir Theoph. Bidulph and others, Commissioners of the Sewers, about our place below to lay masts in.[5]

But coming a little too soon, I out again and took boat down to Redriffe, and just in time, within two minutes, and saw the new Vessell of Sir Wm. Petty's lanched, the King and Duke being there.

1. "with her I tried to do what I would, and against her will [literally 'strength'] I did it, although not to my satisfaction."
2. Dwells opposite.
3. John, 1st Viscount Mordaunt, served briefly as a volunteer in the navy. These verses have not been traced.
4. Beginning in October, Lieutenant-Admiral de Ruyter had seized almost all of the English-held forts on the West African coast, a sharp reversal after Holmes's gains there. This bankrupted the Company of Royal Adventurers of England Trading into Africa.
5. A scheme for a new mast-dock at Deptford.

It swims and looks finely, and I believe will do well. The name I think is *Twilight*,[1] but I do not know certainly, coming away back immediately to dinner – where a great deal of good discourse and Sir G Carterets discourse of this Guinny business, with great displeasure at the loss of our honour there – and doth now confess that that trade brought all these troubles upon us between the Duch and us.

Thence to the office and there sat late; then I to my office and there till 12 at night; and so home to bed, weary.

24. Having sat up all night, to past 2 a-clock this morning, our porter, being appointed, comes and tells us that the Bell-man tells him that the star is seen upon Tower-hill.[2] So I, that had been all night setting in order all my old papers in my chamber, did leave off all; and my boy and I to Tower hill, it being a most fine bright moonshine night and a great frost, but no Comett to be seen; so after running once round the Hill, I and Tom, we home and then to bed.

Rose about 9 a-clock; and then to the office, where sitting all the morning. At noon to the Change to the Coffee-house, and there heard Sir Rd. Ford tell the whole story of our defeat at Guinny – wherein our men are guilty of the most horrid cowardize and perfidiousness, as he says and tells it, that ever Englishmen were. Captain Raynolds, that was the only commander of any of the King's ships there, was shot at by De Ruyter, with a bloody flag flying.[3] He, instead of opposing (which endeed had been to no purpose, but only to maintain honour), did poorly go on board himself to ask what De Ruter would have; and so yielded to whatever Ruyter would desire. The King and Duke are highly vexed at it, it seems, and the business deserves it.

Thence home to dinner and then abroad to buy some things; and among others, to my bookseller's and there saw several books I spoke for, which are finely bound and good books, to my great content.

So home and to my office, where late. This evening, I being informed, did look and saw the Comett, which is now, whether worn away or no I know not, but appears not with a tail; but only is larger and duller then any other star, and is come to rise betimes

1. It was the *Experiment*, the third of Petty's double-hulled ships.
2. This was a non-periodic comet seen across the world in the winter of 1664.
3. Jacob Reynolds commanded the warship *Great Gift* at Cape Verde. A bloody (red) flag signalled readiness for battle.

and to make a great arch, and is gone quite to a new place in the heavens then it was before – but I hope, in a clearer night something more will be seen. So home to bed.

25. *Lords day and Christmas=Day.* Up (my wife's eye being ill still of the blow I did in a passion give her on Monday last) to church alone – where Mr. Mills, a good sermon. To dinner at home, where very pleasant with my wife and family. After dinner, I to Sir W. Batten's and there received so much good usage (as I have of late done) from him and my Lady, obliging me and my wife, according to promise, to come and dine with them tomorrow with our neighbours, that I was in pain all the day, and night too after, to know how to order the business of my wife's not going[1] – and by discourse receive fresh instances of Sir J Minnes's folly in complaining to Sir G. Carteret of Sir W. Batten and me for some family offences; such as my having of a stopcock to keep the water from them – which vexes me, but it would more, but that Sir G. Carteret knows him very well. Thence to the French church;[2] but coming too late, I returned and to Mr. Rawlinson's church, where I heard a good sermon of one that I remember was at Pauls with me, his name Maggett.[3] And very great store of fine women there is in this church, more then I know anywhere else about us.

So home and to my chamber, looking over and setting in order my papers and books; and so to supper, and then to prayers and to bed.

31. At the office all the morning, and after dinner there again; despatched first my letters, and then to my accounts, not of the month but of the whole year also, and was at it till past 12 at night – it being bitter cold; but yet I was well satisfied with my work and, above all, to find myself, by the great blessing of God, worth 1349*l* – by which, as I have spent very largely, so I have laid up above 500*l* this year above what I was worth this day twelvemonth. The Lord make me for ever thankful to his holy name for it.

Thence home to eat a little, and so to bed. As soon as ever the clock struck one, I kissed my wife in the kitchen by the fireside, wishing her a merry New year, observing that I believe I was the

1. An excuse was needed for Elizabeth's non-attendance that did not involve explaining that he had hit her. He subsequently opted for "sickness".
2. The French Protestant Church in Threadneedle Street.
3. Richard Meggot (once a scholar at St Paul's school), Rector of St Olave, Southwark. The church was St Dionis Backchurch.

first proper wisher of it this year, for I did it as soon as ever the clock struck one.

So ends the old year, I bless God with great joy to me; not only from my having made so good a year of profit, as having spent 420*l* and laid up 540*l* and upward.

But I bless God, I never have been in so good plight as to my health in so very cold weather as this is, nor indeed in any hot weather these ten years, as I am at this day and have been these four or five months. But am at a great loss to know whether it be my Hare's foote, or taking every morning of a pill of Turpentine, or my having left off the wearing of a gowne.[1]

My family is my wife, in good health, and happy with her – her woman Mercer, a pretty modest quiet maid – her chambermaid Besse – her cook-maid Jane – the little girle Susan, and my boy which I have had about half a year, Tom Edwards, which I took from the King's Chappell. And a pretty and loving quiet family I have as any man in England.

My credit in the world and my office grows daily, and I am in good esteem with everybody I think.

My troubles of my uncles estate pretty well over. But it comes to be but of little profit to us, my father being much supported by my purse.

But great vexations remain upon my father and me from my Brother Tom's death and ill condition, both to our disgrace and discontent – though no great reason for either.

Public matters are all in a hurry about a Duch warr. Our preparations great. Our provocations against them great; and after all our presumption, we are now afeared as much of them as we lately contemned[2] them.

Everything else in the State quiet, blessed be God. My Lord Sandwich at sea with the fleet at Portsmouth – sending some about to cruise for taking of ships, which we have done to a great number.

This Christmas I judged it fit to look over all my papers and books, and to tear all that I found either boyish or not to be worth keeping, or fit to be seen if it should please God to take me away suddenly. Among others, I found these two or three notes which I thought fit to keep –

1. A hare's foot was worn as a charm against colic. Also to prevent colic, Mr Hollier had advised against gown wearing on 14 Aug. 1664. Dr Burnet had recommended turpentine pills to prevent the stone on 1 Jan. 1664.
2. Scorned, disregarded.

Age of my Grandfather's Children.
Thomas – 1595.
Mary. March. 16. 1597.
Edith. Octob. 11. 1599.
John, (my father). January. 14. 1601./

———

My father and mother marryed at Newington in Surry. Octob. 15. 1626.

———

Theyr Children's ages.[1]

Mary.	July. 24. 1627.	-- *mort.*
Paulina.	Sept. 18. 1628.	-- *mort.*
Esther.	March. 27. 1630.	-- *mort.*
John.	January. 10. 1631.	-- *mort.*
Samuel.	Febr. 23. 1632. ⟨⟨Went to reside in Magd. Coll. Camb., and did put on my gown first. March. 5. 165$\frac{0}{1}$.⟩⟩	
Thomas.	June. 18. 1634.	-- *mort.*
Sarah.	August. 25. 1635.	-- *mort.*
Jacob.	May. 1. 1637.	-- *mort.*
Robert.	Nov. 18. 1638.	-- *mort.*
Paulina.	Octobr. 18. 1640.	
John.	Novemb. 26. 1641.	-- *mort.*

Decembr. 31. 1664./ ◆

1. I.e. the children of Pepys's parents. Pepys added the word "*mort*" (dead) after the close of the diary at least in the case of his brother John, who died in 1677. He did not, however, add it to the name of the younger Paulina, who died in 1689. In the list Pepys uses old-style year-dates.

1665

JANUARY. $166\frac{4}{5}$.

2. Up, and it being a most fine hard frost, I walked a good way toward White-hall; and then being overtaken with Sir W. Penn's coach, went into it, and with him thither and there did our usual business with the Duke. Thence, being forced to pay a great deal of money away in boxes (that is, basons at White-hall),[1] I to my barbers, Gervas's, and there had a little opportunity of speaking with my Jane[2] alone, and did give her something; and of herself she did tell me a place where I might come to her on Sunday next, which I will not fail; but to see how modestly and harmlessly she brought it out was very pretty. Thence to the Swan, and there did sport a good while with Herbert's young kinswoman[3] without hurt though, they being abroad, the old people. Then to the hall, and there agreed with Mrs. Martin, and to her lodgings which she hath now taken to lie in, in Bow streete – pitiful poor things, yet she thinks them pretty; and so they are for her condition I believe, good enough. Here I did ce que je voudrais avec her[4] most freely; and it having cost me 2*s* in wine and cake upon her, I away, sick of her impudence – and by coach to my Lord Brunkers by appointment, in the piazza in Covent-Guarding[5] – where I occasioned much mirth with a ballet I brought with me, made from the seamen at sea to their ladies in town – saying Sir W. Penn, Sir G Ascue, and Sir J Lawson made them.[6] Here a most noble French dinner and banquet, the best I have seen these many a day, and good discourse. Thence to my bookseller's and at his binders saw Hookes book of the Microscope,[7] which is so pretty that I presently bespoke it; and away home to the office, where we met to do something; and then,

1. Christmas or New Year boxes for tips.
2. Jane Welsh, maidservant to Richard Jervas, Pepys's barber. Pepys had admired her for some time, *see* 28 July 1664.
3. Probably, Sarah Udall, servant to William Herbert, the landlord of the Swan, New Palace Yard.
4. "Here I did what I would with her".
5. Covent Garden.
6. A new ballad, "To All You Ladies Now at Land", by Lord Buckhurst. In it, sailors leaving to fight the Dutch beg the muses to "fill our empty Brain" with lines to express their sorrow at parting from their lovers. Penn, Sir George Ayscue, and Sir John Lawson were all naval commanders.
7. Robert Hooke's *Micrographia* (1665) combined detailed description of his observations with lavish illustrations.

though very late, by coach to Sir Ph. Warwickes; but having company with him, could not speak with him. So back again home, where, thinking to be merry, was vexed with my wife's having looked out a letter in Sir Ph. Sidny about jealousy for me to read, which she industriously and maliciously caused me to do;[1] and the truth is, my conscience told me it was most proper for me, and therefore was touched at it; but took no notice of it, but read it out most frankly. But it stuck in my stomach; and moreover, I was vexed to have a dog brought to my house to lime[2] our little bitch, which they make him do in all their sights; which God forgive me, doth stir my Jealousy again, though of itself the thing is a very immodest sight.

However, to Cards with my wife a good while, and then to bed.

9. Up, and walked to White-hall, it being still a brave frost and I in perfect good health, blessed be God. In my way saw a woman that broke her thigh, in her heels slipping up upon the frosty street. To the Duke, and there we did our usual work. Here I saw the Royall Society bring their new book, wherein is nobly writ their Charter and laws, and comes to be signed by the Duke as a Fellow; and all the Fellows' hands are to be entered there and lie as a monument, and the King hath put his, with the word "Founder".[3]

Thence I to Westminster to my barber's and found occasion to see Jane, but in presence of her mistress, and so could not speak to her of her failing me yesterday.[4] And then to the Swan to Herberts girl, and lost time a little with her. And so took coach, and to my Lord Crews[5] and dined with him; who receives me with the greatest respect that could be – telling me that he doth much doubt of the success of this war with Holland; we going about it, he doubts, by the instigation of persons that do not enough apprehend the consequences of the danger of it – and therein I do think with him.

Holmes was this day sent to the tower – but I perceive it is made matter of jest only. But if the Dutch should be our maisters, it may

1. Elizabeth had chosen one of two passages involving letters and jealousy from Sir Philip Sidney's *The Countess of Pembroke's Arcadia* (first published 1593): either the counsellor Philanax's letter to his king in Book 1, or Nico's song in the 3rd Eclogues. Both episodes warn men that possessiveness is self-defeating, since it increases women's curiosity and desire for forbidden pleasures.
2. Impregnate.
3. The Royal Society's charter book contained a copy of their second charter (of 1663), the statutes, and the register of fellows and benefactors.
4. She had not turned up for their meeting, arranged on 2 January.
5. John Crew, Sandwich's father-in-law.

come to be of earnest to him, to be given over to them for a sacrifice, as Sir W. Rawly was.[1]

Thence to White-hall to a Tanger Comittee; where I was accosted and most highly complimented by my Lord Bellasses our new Governor,[2] beyond my expectation or measure I could imagine he would have given any man, as if I were the only person of business that he intended to rely on, and desires my correspondence with him. This I was not only surprized at, but am well pleased with and may make good use of it. Our patent is renewed, and he and my Lord Barkely and Sir Tho. Ingram put in as commissioners. Here some business happened which may bring me some profit.

Thence took coach; and calling my wife at her tailor's (she being come this afternoon to bring her mother some apples, neats[3] tongues and brain) I home, and there at my office late with Sir W Warren and had a great deal of good discourse and counsel from him – which I hope I shall take, being all for my good in my deportment in my office, yet with all honesty.

He gone, I home to supper and to bed.

20. Up and to Westminster, where having spoke with Sir Ph. Warwicke, I to Jervas's and there do find them all in a great disorder about Jane, her mistress telling me secretly that she was sworn not to reveal anything, but she was undone. At last, for all her oath, she told me that she had made herself sure to a fellow that comes to their house that can only fiddle for his living – and did keep him company and had plainly told her that she was sure to him, never to leave him for anybody else. Now they were this day contriving to get her presently[4] to marry one Hayes that was there, and I did seem to persuade her to it, and at last got them to suffer me to advise privately, and by that means had her company and I think shall meet her next Sunday; but I do verily doubt she will be undone in marrying this fellow. But I did give her my advice, and so let her do her pleasure, so I have now and then her company.

Thence to the Swan at noon, and there sent for a bit of meat and dined and had my baiser of the fille of the house there – but

1. Robert Holmes was arrested for his attack on the Dutch in West Africa. He was released and pardoned in March, after the Dutch had declared war. Walter Raleigh had been executed in 1618 after attacking Spanish territory in South America.
2. John Belasyse, 1st Baron Belasyse, had been appointed Governor of Tangier on 4 January.
3. Cattle's.
4. Immediately.

nothing plus.[1] So took coach and to my Lady Sandwiches; and so to my booksellers and there took home Hookes book of Microscopy, a most excellent piece, and of which I am very proud.

So home, and by and by again abroad with my wife about several businesses; and met at the New Exchange, and there to our trouble find our pretty Doll is gone away to live, they say with her father in the country – but I doubt something worse.

So homeward, in my way buying a hare and taking it home – which arose upon my discourse today with Mr. Batten in Westminster-hall – who showed me my mistake, that my haresfoot hath not the joynt to it, and assures me he never had his cholique since he carried it about him. And it is a strange thing how fancy works, for I no sooner almost handled his foot but my belly begin to be loose and to break wind; and whereas I was in some pain yesterday and t'other day, and in fear of more today, I became very well, and so continue.

At home to my office a while, and so to supper – read, and to cards and to bed.

23. Up, and with Sir W. Batten and Sir W. Penn to White-hall; but there finding the Duke gone to his lodgings at St. James's for altogether, his Duchesse being ready to lie-in,[2] we to him and there did our usual business. And here I met the great news, confirmed by the Dukes own relation, by a letter from Captain Allen – first, of our loss of two ships, the *Phœnix* and *Nonesuch*, in the Bay of Gibraltar – then, of his and his seven ships with him, in the Bay of Cales[3] or thereabouts, fight with the 34 Duch Smirna fleet[4] – sinking the *King Salamon*, a ship worth 150000*l* or more, some say 200000*l*, and another, and taking of three merchant-ships. Two of our ships were disabled, by the Duch unfortunately falling against their will against them; the *Advice*, Captain W. Poole, and *Anthelop*, Captain Clerke. The Dutch men-of-warr did little service. Captain Allen did receive many shots at distance before he would fire one gun; which he did not do till he came within pistol-shot of his enemy. The Spaniards on shore at Cales did stand laughing at the Duch, to see them run away and fly to the shore, 34 or thereabouts against 8 Englishmen at most. I do purpose to get the whole relation, if I live, of Captain Allen himself.◆

1. "had my kiss of the girl of the house there – but nothing more".
2. Give birth.
3. Cadiz.
4. A merchant convoy returning from Smyrna (modern-day İzmir in Turkey).

Thence to Jervas's, my mind, God forgive me, running too much after sa fille, but elle[1] not being within, I away by coach to the Change – and thence home to dinner; and finding Mrs. Bagwell waiting at the office after dinner, away elle and I to a cabaret where elle and I have été before; and there I had her company toute l'après-dîner and had mon plein plaisir of elle – but strange, to see how a woman, notwithstanding her greatest pretences of love à son mari and religion, may be vaincue.[2] Thence to the Court of the Turky Company at Sir Andr. Rickard's, to treat about carrying some men of ours to Tanger, and had there a very civil reception, though a denial of the thing, as not practicable with them, and I think so too. So to my office a little; but being minded to make an end of my pleasure today, that I might fallow my business, I did take coach and to Jervas's again, thinking to avoir rencontré Jane; mais elle n'était pas dedans.[3] So I back again and to my office, where I did with great content faire a vow to mind my business and laisser aller les femmes for a month;[4] and am with all my heart glad to find myself able to come to so good a resolution, that thereby I may fallow my business, which, and my honour thereby, lies a-bleeding. So home to supper and to bed.

30. This is solemnly kept as a Fast[5] all over the City; but I kept my house, putting my closett to rights again, having lately put it out of order in removing my books and things in order to being made clean. At this all day, and at night to my office, there to do some business. And being late at it, comes Mercer to me to tell me that my wife was in bed and desired me to come home, for they hear, and have night after night lately heard, noises over their head upon the leads. Now, it is strange to think how, knowing that I have a great sum of money in my house, this puts me into a most mighty affright, that for more then two hours I could not almost tell what to do or say, but feared this and that – and remembered that this evening I saw a woman and two men stand suspiciously in the Entry in the dark; I calling to them, they made me only this answer: the woman said that the men came to see her. But who she was

1. "his girl, but she".
2. "she and I to a tavern, where she and I have been before; and there I had her company all the time after dinner and had my full pleasure of her – but strange, to see how a woman, notwithstanding her greatest pretences of love to her husband and religion, may be vanquished."
3. "thinking to have met Jane; but she was not within."
4. "with great content make a vow to mind my business and to leave off women for a month".
5. For the execution of Charles I.

I could not tell. The truth is, my house is mighty dangerous, having so many ways to be come to, and at my windows over the stairs, to see who goes up and down – but if I escape tonight, I will remedy it. God preserve us this night safe. So at almost 2 a-clock, I home to my house and in great fear to bed, thinking every running of a mouse really a thief – and so to sleep, very brokenly all night long – and found all safe in the morning.

FEBRUARY.

9. Up, and to my office, where all the morning very busy. At noon home to dinner, and then to my office again – where Sir Wm. Petty came, among other things, to tell me that Mr. Barlow is dead; for which, God knows my heart, I could be as sorry as is possible for one to be for a stranger by whose death he gets 100*l* per annum – he being a very honest man.[1] But after having considered that when I come to consider the providence of God, by this means unexpectedly to give me 100*l* a year more in my estate, I have cause to bless God, and do it from the bottom of my heart. So home late at night, after 12 a-clock, and so to bed.

14. *St. Valentine.* This morning comes betimes Dicke Pen[2] to be my wife's valentine, and came to our bedside. By the same token, I had him brought to my side, thinking to have made him kiss me; but he perceived me, and would not. So went to his Valentine – a notable, stout, witty boy. I up, about business; and opening the doore, there was Bagwell's wife, with whom I talked afterwards and there she had the confidence to say that she came with a hope to be time enough to be my Valentine, and so endeed she did – but my oath preserved me from losing any time with her. And so I and my boy abroad by coach to Westminster, where did two or three businesses; and then home to the Change, and did much business there. My Lord Sandwich is, it seems, with his fleet in Alborough bay.[3] So home to dinner, and then to the office, where till 12 almost at night, and then home to supper and to bed.

15. Up, and to my office, where busy all the morning. At noon with Creed to dinner to Trinity-house to dinner, where a very good

1. Thomas Barlow was a former Clerk of the Acts, whose claims on the office Pepys had bought out by an annuity of £100. *See* 17 July 1660.
2. Younger son of Sir William Penn.
3. Aldeburgh Bay, Suffolk.

dinner among the old Sokers[1] – where an extraordinary discourse of the manner of the loss of the *Royall Oake*, coming home from Bantam, upon the rocks of Scilly; many passages therein being very extraordinary – and if I can, I will get it in writing.[2]

Thence with Creed to Gresham College – where I had been by Mr. Povy the last week proposed to be admitted a member; and was this day admitted, by signing a book and being taken by the hand by the Præsident, my Lord Brunkard, and some words of admittance said to me.[3] But it is a most acceptable thing to hear their discourses and see their experiments; which was this day upon the nature of fire, and how it goes out in a place where the ayre is not free, and sooner out where the ayre is exhausted; which they showed by an engine on purpose.[4] After this being done, they to the Crowne tavern behind the Change, and there my Lord and most of the company to a club supper – Sir P. Neale, Sir R. Murrey, Dr. Clerke, Dr. Whistler, Dr. Goddard, and others of most eminent worth. Above all, Mr. Boyle[5] today was at the meeting, and above him Mr. Hooke, who is the most, and promises the least, of any man in the world that ever I saw.[6] Here, excellent discourses till 10 at night, and then home – and to Sir W. Batten, where I hear that Sir Tho Harvy entends to put Mr. Turner out of his house and come in himself, which will be very hard to them.[7] And though I love him not, yet for his family's sake I pity him. So home and to bed.

20. Up, and with Sir J. Mennes to attend the Duke; and then we back again and rode into the beginnings of my Lord Chancellors new house near St. James's,[8] which common people have already called Dunkirke-house, from their opinion of his having a good bribe for the selling of that town. And very noble I believe it will be. Near that is my Lord Berkely beginning another on one side,

1. Old hands (especially at drinking).
2. The ship, an East Indiaman, had been wrecked during a storm on 17–18 January, and the surviving crew took shelter on the tallest rocks. When parts of the ship and cargo washed ashore two days later, boats were sent to pick up the survivors.
3. Pepys was now unanimously elected to the Royal Society.
4. Robert Hooke demonstrated this with an air pump.
5. Robert Boyle, a founder of the Royal Society and one of the most distinguished scientists of the time.
6. Robert Hooke, curator of experiments to the Society and one of its most talented members. His contemporary Richard Waller described his appearance as "pale and lean" and "very crooked".
7. Hervey had been appointed extra Commissioner of the Navy on 30 January. Thomas Turner, Clerk-General to the office, occupied a house next to Pepys's.
8. Clarendon House in Piccadilly.

and Sir J. Denham on the other. Thence I to the House of Lords and spoke with my Lord Bellases; and so to the Change and there did business; and so to the Sun Taverne – having in the morning had some high words with Sir J Lawson about his sending of some bayled goods to Tanger; wherein the truth is, I did not favour him. But being conscious that some of my profit may come out,[1] by some words that fell from him; and to be quiet, I have accommodated it. Here we dined, merry; but my club[2] and the rest come to *7s. 6d*, which was too much. Thence to the office and there found Bagwells wife, whom I directed to go home and I would do her business; which was to write a letter to my Lord Sandwich for her husband's advance into a better ship as there should be occasion – which I did; and by and by did go down by water to Deptford-yard, and then down further and so landed at the lower end of the town; and it being dark, did privately entrer en la maison de la femme de Bagwell, and there I had sa compagnie, though with a great deal of difficulty; néanmoins, enfin je avais ma volonté d'elle.[3] And being sated therewith, I walked home to Redriffe, it being now near 9 a-clock; and there I did drink some strong waters and eat some bread and cheese, and so home – where at my office, my wife comes and tells me that she hath hired a chamber-maid, one of the prettiest maids that ever she saw in her life, and that she is really jealous of me for her – but hath ventured to hire her from month to month. But I think she means merrily. So to supper and to bed.

21. Up, and to the office (having a mighty pain in my forefinger of my left hand, from a strain that it received last night in struggling avec la femme que je mentioned yesterday[4]), where busy till noon; and then, my wife being busy in going with her woman to a hot-house[5] to bath herself, after her long being within doors in the dirt, so that she now pretends to a resolution of being hereafter very clean – how long it will hold, I can guess – I dined with Sir W. Batten and my Lady, they being nowadays very fond of me.

So to the Change, and off of the Change with Mr. Wayth to a cook's shop and there dined again, for discourse with him about

1. I.e. that Pepys's extremely profitable dealings over Tangier business would be exposed.
2. Share of expenses.
3. "did privately enter Bagwell's wife's house, and there I had her company, though with a great deal of difficulty; nevertheless, finally I had my will of her."
4. "with the woman that I mentioned yesterday".
5. A public steam-bath.

Hamaccos[1] and the abuse now practised in tickets,[2] and more like every day to be – also, of the great profit Mr. Fen[3] makes of his place – he being (though he demands but ½ per cent of all he pays, and that is easily computed) but very little pleased with any man that gives him no more.

So to the office; and after office my Lord Brunkerd carried me to Lincoln's Inn fields, and there I with my Lady Sandwich (good lady), talking of innocent discourse of good housewifery and husbands for her daughters, and the luxury and looseness of the times and other such things, till past 10 a-clock at night; and so by coach home, where a little at my office, and so to supper and to bed.

My Lady tells me how my Lord Castlemayne is coming over from France, and is believed will be made friends with his Lady again.

What mad freaks the mayds of Honour at Court have – that Mrs. Jennings, one of the Duchess's maids,[4] the other day dressed herself like an orange-wench and went up and down and cried oranges – till falling down, or by such accident (though in the evening), her fine shoes were discerned and she put to a great deal of shame.

That such as these tricks being ordinary and worse among them, and thereby few will venture upon them for wifes, my Lady Castlemayne will in merriment say that her daughter (not above a year old or two) will be the first mayd in the Court that will be married.

This day my Lord Sandwich writ me word from the Downes that he is like to be in town this week.

23. This day, by the blessing of Almighty God, I have lived 32 years in the world – and am in the best degree of health at this minute that I have been almost in my life-time, and at this time in the best condition of estate that ever I was in; the Lord make me thankful.

Up, and to the office, where busy all the morning. At noon to the Change, where I hear the most horrid and astonishing news that ever was yet told in my memory – that De Ruiter, with his fleet in guinny, hath proceeded to the taking of whatever we have – forts,

1. In March Waith put in a tender for the supply of hammocks.
2. When the navy lacked money it resorted to paying wages "by ticket" rather than with cash. A ticket was a pledge for future payment by the Treasurer of the Navy. Tickets themselves might be accepted as payment by traders (at a discount). The system was open to abuse by clerks, officers, and sailors.
3. John Fenn, Paymaster to the Navy Treasurer.
4. Frances Jennings, maid of honour to the Duchess of York.

goods, ships, and men – and tied our men back to back and thrown them all into the sea – even women and children also. This a Swede or Hamburger is come into the River and tells that he saw the thing done.[1] But Lord, to see the consternation all our merchants are in is observable, and with what fury and revenge they discourse of it – but I fear it will, like other things, in a few days cool among us. But that which I fear most is the reason why he that was so kind to our men at first, should afterward, having let them go, be so cruel when he went further. What I fear is that there he was informed (which he was not before) of some of Holmes's dealings with his countrymen, and so was moved to this fury. God grant it be not so.

But a more dishonourable thing was never suffered by Englishmen, nor a more barbarous done by man, as this by them to us.

Home to dinner, and then to the office, where we sat all the afternoon; and then at night to take my finall leave of Mrs. Bland, who sets out tomorrow for Tanger. And then I back to my office till past 12, and so home to supper and to bed.

25. Up, and to the office, where all the morning. At noon to the Change; where just before I came, the Swede that had told the King and the Duke so boldly this great lie, of the Dutch flinging our men back to back into the sea at Guinny, so perticularly and readily and confidently, was whipped round the Change – he confessing it a lie, and that he did it in hopes to get something. It is said the judges, upon demand, did give it their opinion that the law would judge him to be whipped, to lose his eares, or to have his nose slit – but I do not hear that anything more is to be done to him. They say he is delivered over to the Dutch Embassador to do what he please with him. But the world doth think that there is some design on one side or other, either of the Dutch or French – for it is not likely a fellow would invent such a lie to get money, whereas he might have hoped for a better reward by telling something in behalf of us to please us.

Thence to the Sun Taverne, and there dined with Sir W Warren and Mr. Gifford the merchant.◆ But Lord, to see how full the house is, no room for any company almost to come into it. Thence home to the office, where despatch much business; at night late home and to clean myself with warm water; my wife will have me, because she doth herself; and so to bed.

1. The informant was a Dutchman posing as a Swede, and he alleged that Lieutenant-Admiral de Ruyter killed 1,500 in this way.

28. At the office all the morning. At noon dined at home. After dinner my wife and I to my Lady Batten's, it being the first time my wife hath been there, I think, these two years; but I have a mind in part to take away that strangeness, and so we did, and all very quiet and kind.

Came home; I to the taking my wife's kitchen account at the latter end of the month, and there find *7s* wanting – which did occasion a very high falling out between us; I endeed too eagerly insisting upon so poor a thing, and did give her very provoking words, calling her "beggar" and reproaching her friends;[1] which she took very stomachfully, and reproached me justly with mine; and I confess, being myself, I cannot see what she could have done less. I find she is very cunning, and when she least shows it, hath her wit at work; but it is an ill one, though I think not so bad but with good usage I might well bear with it; and the truth is, I do find that my being over-solicitous and jealous and froward,[2] and ready to reproach her, doth make her worse. However, I find that now and then a little difference doth do no hurt – but too much of it will make her know her force too much. We parted, after many high words, very angry; and I to my office to my month's accounts, and find myself worth 1270*l* – for which the Lord God be praised.

So, at almost 2 a-clock in the morning, I home to supper and to bed.

And so ends this month, with great expectation of the Hollanders coming forth; who are, it seems, very high and rather more ready then we. God give a good issue to it.

MARCH.

1. Up – and this day being the day that, by a promise a great while ago made to my wife, I was to give her 20*l* to lay out in clothes against Easter, she did, notwithstanding last night's falling-out, come to peace with me and I with her, but did boggle mightily at the parting with my money, but at last did give it her; and then she abroad to buy her things, and I to my office, where busy all the morning. At noon I to dinner at Trinity-house – and thence to Gresham College, where, first Mr. Hooke read a second very curious[3] Lecture about the late Comett, among other things, proving

1. Relations.
2. Difficult to please, unreasonable.
3. Ingenious, expert.

very probably that this is the very same Comett that appeared before in the year 1618, and that in such a time probably it will appear again – which is a very new opinion – but all will be in print.[1]

Then to the meeting, where Sir G Carterets two sons, his own and Sir N Slany, were admitted of the Society.[2] And this day I did pay my admission money – 40*s* – to the Society.

Here was very fine discourses – and experiments; but I do lack philosophy enough to understand them, and so cannot remember them. Among others, a very perticular account of the making of the several sorts of bread in France, which is accounted the best place for bread in the world.[3]

So home, where very busy getting an answer to some Questions of Sir Ph. Warwicke touching the expense of the navy; and that being done, I by coach at 8 at night by coach with my wife and Mercer to Sir Ph. and discoursed with him (leaving them in the coach); and then back with them home, and to supper and to bed.

6. Up, and with Sir J. Mennes by coach (it being a most lamentable cold day as any this year) to St. James's, and there did our business with the Duke. Great preparations for his speedy return to sea. I saw him try on his buff coat and hat-piece covered with black velvet. It troubles me more to think of his venture then of anything else in the whole warr.[4] Thence home to dinner – where I saw Besse go away – she having, of all wenches that ever lived with us, received the greatest love and kindness and good clothes, besides wages, and gone away with the greatest ingratitude. I then abroad to look after my Hamaccoes; and so home and there find our new chamber-maid, Mary, come; which instead of handsome, as my wife spoke and still seems to reckon, is a very ordinary wench I think – and therein was mightily disappointed.

To my office, where busy late; and then home to supper and to bed – and was troubled all this night with a pain in my left Testicle, that run up presently into my left Kidny and there kept akeing all night – in great pain.

1. This was the comet Pepys had watched for on 24 Dec. 1664. Hooke was an early proponent of the theory that comets might be periodic, but he was mistaken in thinking this was the same as the comet of 1618. The lecture was printed in the Royal Society's journal *Philosophical Transactions*.
2. I.e. Philip Carteret and Sir Nicholas Slaning, Sir George Carteret's son-in-law.
3. This was a paper read by John Evelyn, soon to become Pepys's good friend.
4. War with the Dutch had been made official in a declaration signed by Charles on 22 Feb. 1665 and proclaimed around London on 4 March, though hostilities had been under way for some time.

7. Up, and was pretty well; but going to the office, and I think it was sitting with my back to the fire, it set me in a great rage again, that I could not continue till past noon at the office, but was forced to go home; nor could sit down to dine, but betook myself to my bed; and being there a while, my pain begun to abate and grow less and less. Anon I went to make water, not dreaming of anything but my testicle, that by some accident I might have bruised as I used to do – but in pissing, there came from me two stones; I could feel them, and caused my water to be looked into, but without any pain to me in going out – which makes me think that it was not a fit of the stone at all; for my pain was asswaged upon my lying down a great while before I went to make water. Anon I made water again very freely and plentifully. I kept my bed in good ease all the evening; then rose and sat up an hour or two; and then to bed and lay till 8 a-clock; and then, though a bitter cold day, yet
⟨⟨8⟩⟩ I rose, and though my pain and tenderness in my testicle remains a little, yet I do verily think that my pain yesterday was nothing else, and therefore I hope my disease of the stone may not return to me, but void itself in pissing; which God grant – but I will consult my physitian.

This morning is brought me to the office the sad news of the *London*, in which Sir J Lawsons men were all bringing her from Chatham to the Hope, and thence he was to go to sea in her – but a little a-this-side the buoy of the Nower, she suddenly blew up.[1] About 24 and a woman that were in the round-house and coach saved; the rest, being above 300, drowned – the ship breaking all in pieces – with 80 pieces of brass ordinance. She lies sunk, with her round-house above water. Sir J Lawson hath a great loss in this, of so many good chosen men, and many relations among them. I went to the Change, where the news taken very much to heart. So home to dinner, and Mr. Moore with me; then I to Gresham College and there saw several pretty experiments; and so home and to my office – and at night, about 11, home to supper and to bed.

17. Up, and to my office; and then with Sir W. Batten to St. James, where many came to take leave, as was expected, of the Duke; but he doth not go till Monday. This night my Lady Wood died of the small-pox, and is much lamented among the great persons for a

1. The *London* was a second-rate, one of the largest ships in the navy.

good-natured woman and a good wife; but for all that, it was ever believed she was as others are.[1]

The Duke did give us some commands, and so broke up, not taking leave of him. But the best piece of newes is that instead of a great many troublesome Lords, the whole business is to be left with the Duke of Albemarle, to act as Admirall in his stead; which is a thing that doth cheer my heart – for the other would have vexed us with attendance, and never done the business.[2]

Thence to the Committee of Tanger, where the Duke a little, and then left us and we stayed – a very great Committee – the Lords Albemarle, Sandwich, Barkely, Fitzharding, Peterborough, ⟨Ashley⟩, Sir Tho. Ingram, Sir G Carteret, and others. The whole business was the stating of Povys accounts;[3] of whom, to say no more, never could man say worse himself nor have worse said of him then was by that company to his face – I mean as to his folly, and very reflecting words to his honesty. Broke up without anything but trouble and shame – only, I got my businesses done, to the signing of two bills for the Contractors and Captain Taylor, and so came away well pleased – and home, taking up my wife at the Change, to dinner. After dinner out again, bringing my wife to her father's again at Charing-cross. And I to the Comittee again, where a new meeting of trouble about Povy, who still makes his business worse and worse; and broke up with most open shame again to him – and high words to him of disgrace, that they would not trust him with any more money till he had given an account of this. So broke up.

Then he took occasion to desire me to step aside, and he and I by water to London together: in the way, of his own accord, proposed to me that he would surrender his place of Treasurer to me, to have half the profit. The thing is new to me; but the more I think, the more I like it, and do put him upon getting it done by the Duke: whether it takes or no, I care not, but I think at present it may have some convenience in it.[4]

Home, and there find my wife come home, and gone to bed not well of a cold got yesterday by water. At the office Bellamy came

1. Mary, wife of Sir Henry Wood, and a dresser to the Queen. Restoration satires refer to her as a procuress and to her husband as a cuckold.
2. The "troublesome Lords" were privy councillors who had acted in the Admiral's absence during the campaign of the previous year.
3. Thomas Povey was Treasurer of Tangier.
4. The Duke of York supported Pepys and within three days the Tangier Committee agreed to make him their Treasurer. He was formally appointed on 20 April 1665.

to me again, and I am in hopes something may be got by his business. So late home to supper and bed.

22. Up, and to Mr. Povy's about our business, and thence I to see Sir Ph. Warwicke, but could not meet with him. So to Mr. Coventry, whose profession of love and esteem for me to myself was so large and free, that I never could expect or wish for more, nor could have it from any man in England that I should value it more. Thence to Mr. Povys, and with Creed to the Change and to my house; but it being washing-day, dined not at home, but took him (I being invited) to Mr. Hublands the merchant, where Sir W Petty and abundance of most ingenious men, owners and freighters of the *Experiment*, now going with her two bodies to sea.[1] Most excellent discourse. Among others, Sir Wm. Petty did tell me that in good earnest, he hath in his will left such parts of his estate to him that could invent such and such things – as among others, that could discover truly the way of milk coming into the breasts of a woman – and he that could invent proper Characters to express to another the mixture of relishes and tastes. And says that to him that invents gold, he gives nothing for the Philosopher's stone;[2] "for," says he, "they that find out that will be able to pay themselfs – but," says he, "by this means it is better then to give to a lecture.[3] For here my executors, that must part with this, will be sure to be well convinced of the invention before they do part with their money."

After dinner Mr. Hill took me with Mrs. Hubland, who is a fine gentlewoman – into another room, and there made her sing; which she doth very well – to my great content.

Then to Gresham College and there did see a kitlin killed almost quite (but that we could not quite kill her) with sucking away the Ayre out of a Receiver wherein she was put – and then the ayre being let in upon her, revives her immediately. Nay, and this ayre is to be made by putting together a Liquor and some body that firments – the steam of that doth do the work.[4]

Thence home, and thence to White-hall, where the House full

1. Petty's twin-hulled ship *Experiment* was shortly after wrecked in a storm. Pepys's host, James Houblon jun., was one of a family of merchants trading in the Mediterranean. He became Pepys's closest friend.
2. The means of transmuting base metals into gold.
3. To fund a lectureship at an institution such as Gresham College.
4. An experiment devised to find a way of breathing under water. A kitten was placed in an air pump and deprived of air. "Steam" of aquafortis (fumes of nitric acid) was then released to see if this would serve as a new kind of breathable air. (It did not – but the animal later revived when placed in open air.)

of the Dukes going tomorrow; and thence to St. James, wherein these things fell out:

1 I saw the Duke. Kissed his hand. And had his most kind expressions of his value and opinion of me, which comforted me above all things in the world.

2 The like from Mr. Coventry, most heartily and affectionately.

3 Saw, among other fine ladies, Mrs. Middleton, a very great beauty I never knew or heard of before;[1]

4 I saw Waller the Poet,[2] whom I never saw before.

So, very late, by coach home with W Pen, who was there.

To supper and to bed – with my heart at rest and my head very busy, thinking of my several matters now on foot – the new comfort of my old Navy business, and the new one of my imployment on Tanger.

APRILL.

6. At the office, sat all the morning – where in the absence of Sir W. Batten, Sir G. Carteret, being angry about the business of tickets, spoke of Sir W. Batten for speaking some words about the signing of tickets,[3] and called Sir W. Batten in his discourse at the table to us (the clerks being withdrawn) "shitten fellow" – which vexed me.

At noon to the Change and there set my business, of Lighters[4] buying for the King, to Sir W. Warren, and I think he will do it for me to very good advantage – at which I am mightily rejoiced. Home; and after a mouthful of dinner, to the office, where till 6 a-clock; and then to White-hall and there with Sir G. Carteret and my Lord Brunkerd attended the Duke of Albemarle about the business of money.

I also went to Jervas's my barber for my periwig that was mending there. And there do hear that Jane is quite undone – taking that idle fellow for her husband, yet not married, and lay with him several weeks that had another wife and child – and she is now going into Ireland.

1. Jane, wife of Charles Myddelton and later mistress of the Duke of York.
2. Edmund Waller, known for his panegyrics.
3. Signing was part of the process to authenticate tickets for pay due to seamen. Carteret was the Navy Treasurer.
4. Boats used for unloading ships or transporting goods.

So called my wife at the Change, and home and at my office, writing letters till one a-clock in the morning, that I was ready to fall down asleep again. Great talks of a new Comett – and it is certain one doth now appear, as bright as the late one at the best; but I have not seen it myself.

12. Up, and to White-hall to a Committee of Tanger; where contrary to all expectation, my Lord Ashly, being vexed with Poveys accounts, did propose it as necessary that Povy should be still continued Treasurer of Tanger till he had made up his account – and with such arguments as I confess I was not prepared to answer – but by putting off of that discourse; and so I think brought it right again, but it troubled me so all the day after, and night too, that I was not quiet, though I think it is doubtful whether I shall be much the worse for it or no, if it should come to be so.

Dined at home; and thence to White-hall again (where I lose most of my time nowadays, to my great trouble, charge, and loss of time and benefit) and there, after the Council rose, Sir G Carteret, my Lord Brunkard, Sir Tho. Harvy, and myself down to my Lord Treasurer's chamber to him and the Chancellor and the Duke of Albemarle. And there I did give them a large account of the charge of the Navy, and want of money. But strange, to see how they held up their hands, crying, "What shall we do?" Says my Lord Treasurer,[1] "Why, what means all this, Mr. Pepys? This is true, you say, but what would you have me to do? I have given all I can for my life. Why will not people lend their money? Why will they not trust the King as well as Oliver? Why do our prizes come to nothing, that yielded so much heretofore?" And this was all we could get, and went away without other answer. Which is one of the saddest things, that at such a time as this, with the greatest action on foot that ever was in England, nothing should be minded, but let things go on of themselfs – do as well as they can.

So home, vexed. And going to my Lady Battens, there found a great many women with her in her chamber, merry – my Lady Pen and her daughter, among others; where my Lady Pen flung me down upon the bed, and herself and others, one after another, upon me, and very merry we were; and thence I home and called my wife with my Lady Pen to supper, and very merry as I could be, being vexed as I was.

So home to bed.

1. Thomas Wriothesley, Earl of Southampton.

30. *Lords day.* Up, and to my office alone all the morning, making up my monthly accounts; which though it hath been very intricate, and very great disbursements and receipts and odd reckonings, yet I differed not from the truth – *viz.*, between my first computing what my profit ought to be, and then what my cash and debts do really make me worth, not above 10*s* – which is very much, and I do much value myself upon that account. And herein, I with great joy find myself to have gained this month above 100*l* clear; and in the whole, to be worth above 1400*l* – the greatest sum I ever yet was worth.

Thence home to dinner and there find poor Mr. Spong[1] walking at my door; where he had knocked, and being told I was at the office, stood modestly there walking, because of disturbing me; which methinks was one of the most modest acts (of a man that hath no need of being so to me) that ever I knew in my life.

He dined with me; and then after dinner, to my closet, where abundance of mighty pretty discourse; wherein, in a word, I find him the man of the world that hath of his own ingenuity obtained the most in most things, being withal no scholler. He gone, I took boat and down to Woolwich and Deptford; and made it late home, and so to supper and to bed.

Thus I end this month: in great content as to my estate and gettings. In much trouble as to the pains I have taken and the rubs I expect yet to meet with about the business of Tanger. The fleet, with about 106 ships, upon the coast of Holland, in sight of the Dutch within the Texell.[2] Great fears of the Sickenesse here in the City, it being said that two or three houses are already shut up. God preserve us all.[3]

MAY.

13. Up, and all day in some little grutchings of pain, as I use to have – from Winde – arising, I think, from my fasting so long and want

1. John Spong, maker of optical instruments.
2. I.e. behind Texel island, off the coast of Holland – a safe anchorage where Dutch ships could gather.
3. When plague was suspected in a household its members were confined inside as a quarantine measure. This is the first of Pepys's entries on the "Great Plague" in London, which reached its height in September 1665. In an average year the peak number of burials per week was 350; during the plague the highest figure was over 8,000 per week. During 1665 there were over 97,000 burials recorded in the metropolitan area, representing perhaps 17% of the population.

of exercise – and I think, going so hot in clothes, the weather being hot and I in the same clothes I wore all winter.

To the Change after office, and received my Wach from the watch-maker; and a very fine [one] it is – given me by Briggs the Scrivener.

Home to dinner; and then I abroad to the Atturny Generall about advice upon the act for Land Carriage[1] – which he desired not to give me before I had received the King's and Council's order therein. Going home, bespoke the King's *works*; will cost me 50*s* I believe.[2] So home, and late at my office. But Lord, to see how much of my old folly and childishnesse hangs upon me still, that I cannot forbear carrying my watch in my hand in the coach all this afternoon, and seeing what a-clock it is 100 times. And am apt to think with myself: how could I be so long without one – though I remember since, I had one and found it a trouble, and resolved to carry one no more about me while I lived.

So home to supper and to bed – being troubled at a letter from Mr. Cholmly from Tanger,[3] wherein he doth advise me how people are at work to overthrow our victualling business; by which I shall lose 300*l* per annum. I am much obliged to him for this secret kindness, and concerned to repay it him in his own concernments and look after this.

24. Up by 4 a-clock in the morning; and with W Hewer there till 12 without intermission, putting some papers in order. Thence to the coffee-house with Creed, where I have not been a great while – where all the news is of the Dutch being gone out – and of the plague growing upon us in this town and of remedies against it; some saying one thing, some another.

So home to dinner; and after dinner Creed and I to Colvells, thinking to show him all the respect we could, by obliging him in carrying him five tallies of 5000*l*, to secure him for so much credit he hath formerly given Povy to Tanger.[4] But he, like a impertinent fool, cavills at it, the most ignorantly that ever I heard man in my

1. An act of 1662 that provided land transport for the navy's timber.
2. *Eikon Basilike*, a collection of spiritual and biographical writings attributed to Charles I. First published immediately after the King's execution in early 1649, it proved tremendously effective as propaganda. Pepys bought a 1662 edition.
3. Hugh Cholmley, the engineer in charge of building the mole at Tangier.
4. John Colvill was a goldsmith-banker. Pepys, as the new Treasurer to the Tangier Committee, and John Creed, as Secretary to the Committee, were trying to get a loan to cover Tangier costs. As security for a previous loan they offered tallies, wooden sticks that the Exchequer issued as pledges to pay from public funds.

life. At last Mr. Viner[1] by chance comes, who I find a very moderate man, but could not persuade the fool to reason; but I brought away the tallies again, and so, vexed, to my office, where late, and then home to my supper and to bed.

26. Up at 4 a-clock, and all the morning in my office with W. Hewer, finishing my papers that were so long out of order. And at noon to my bookseller's and there bespoke a book or two; and so home to dinner, where Creed dined with me; and he and I afterward to Alderman Backewell's[2] to try him about supplying us with money – which he denied at first, and last also, saving that he spoke a little fairer at the end then before. But the truth is, I do fear I shall have a great deal of trouble in getting of money. Thence home; and in the evening by water to the Duke of Albemarle, whom I found mightily off the hooks that the ships are not gone out of the River; which vexed me to see, insomuch that I am afeared that we must expect some change or addition of new officers brought upon us, so that I must from this time forward resolve to make myself appear eminently serviceable in attending at my office duly, and nowhere else; which makes me wish with all my heart that I had never anything to do with this business of Tanger. After a while at my office, home to supper, vexed, and to bed.

28. *Lords day.* By water to the Duke of Albemarle – where I hear that Nixon is condemned to be shot to death for his Cowardize by a council of war.[3] Went to chapel and heard a little Musique and there met with Creed, and with him a little while walking and to Wilkinsons for me to drink, being troubled with Winde; and at noon to Sir Ph. Warwicke's to dinner, where abundance of company came in unexpectedly. And here I saw one pretty piece of household stuff; as the company encreaseth, to put a larger leaf upon an Ovall table. After dinner much good discourse with Sir Phillip, who I find, I think, a most pious good man, and a professor of a philosiphicall manner of life and principles like Epictetus, whom he cites in many things.[4] Thence to my Lady Sandwiches, where to my shame I had not been a great while before. Here, upon my telling her a story of my Lord of Rochester's running away on Friday night last with Mrs. Mallet, the great beauty and fortune of

1. Robert Vyner, goldsmith-banker.
2. Edward Backwell, the most powerful goldsmith-banker in London.
3. Capt. Nixon had been court-martialled for fleeing from two Dutch privateers off the coast of Cornwall.
4. Pepys was also an admirer of the Greek philosopher Epictetus, *see* 9 Sept. 1662.

the North,[1] who had supped at White-hall with Mrs. Stewart and was going home to her lodgings with her grandfather, my Lord Haly, by coach, and was at Charing-cross seized on by both horse and foot-men and forcibly taken from him, and put into a coach with six horses and two women provided to receive her, and carried away. Upon immediate pursuit, my Lord of Rochester (for whom the King had spoke to the lady often, but with no success) was taken at Uxbridge; but the lady is not yet heard of, and the King mighty angry and the Lord sent to the Tower. Hereupon, my Lady did confess to me, as a great secret, her being concerned in this story – for if this match breaks between my Lord Rochester and her, then, by the consent of all her friends, my Lord Hinchingbrooke[2] stands fair, and is invited for her. She is worth, and will be at her mother's death (who keeps but a little from her), 2500*l* per annum. Pray God give a good success to it. But my poor Lady, who is afeared of the sickness and resolved to be gone into the country, is forced to stay in town a day or two or three about it, to see the event of it. Thence home, and to see my Lady Pen – where my wife and I were shown a fine rarity: of fishes kept in a glass of water, that will live so for ever; and finely marked they are, being foreign.[3] So to supper at home and to bed – after many people being with me about business – among others, the two Bellamys about their old debt due to them from the King for their victualling business – out of which I hope to get some money.

JUNE.

3.◆ All this day, by all people upon the River and almost everywhere else hereabout, were heard the Guns, our two fleets for certain being engaged; which was confirmed by letters from Harwich, but nothing perticular;[4] and all our hearts full of concernment for the Duke, and I perticularly for my Lord Sandwich and Mr. Coventry after his Royal Highness.[5]

1. Correctly, the West. Elizabeth Malet was a wealthy Somerset heiress and grand-daughter of Lord Hawley. She eventually married John Wilmot, 2nd Earl of Rochester, in 1667.
2. Lady Sandwich's eldest son.
3. Possibly paradise fish from South-East Asia.
4. This was the sound of the Battle of Lowestoft.
5. The Duke of York, as Lord High Admiral, was commanding the fleet, with Coventry as his Secretary. Sandwich was in command of a squadron.

6. Waked in the morning at 4 a-clock with great pain to piss and great pain in pissing, by having, I think, drank too great a draught of cold drink before going to bed – but by and by to sleep again; and then rose and to the office, where very busy all the morning. And at noon to dinner with Sir G. Carteret to his house, with all our Board, where a good pasty and brave discourse. But our great fears was some fresh news of the fleet, but not from the fleet, all being said to be well and beaten the Dutch; but I do not give much belief to it, and endeed, the news came from Sir W Batten at Harwich, and writ so simply that we all made good mirth of it. Thence to the office, where upon Sir G Carteret's accounts, to my great vexation, there being nothing done by the Controller to right the King therein. I then to my office and wrote letters all the afternoon; and in the evening by coach to Sir P Warwickes about my Tanger business, to get money; and so to my Lady Sandwiches, who, poor lady, expects every hour to hear of my Lord; but in the best temper, neither confident nor troubled with fear, that I ever did see in my life. She tells me my Lord Rochester is now declaredly out of hopes of Mrs. Mallett, and now she is to receive notice in a day or two how the King stands enclined to the giving leave for my Lord Hinchingbrooke to look after her; and that being done, to bring it to an end shortly. Thence by coach home, and to my office a little; and so, before 12 a-clock, home to bed.

7. This morning my wife and mother rose about 2 a-clock, and with Mercer, Mary, the boy and W Hewer, as they had designed, took boat and down to refresh themselfs on the water to Gravesend. I lay till 7 a-clock; then up, and to the office upon Sir G Carteret's accounts again – where very busy. Thence abroad and to the Change, no news of certainty being yet come from the Fleete. Thence to the Dolphin Taverne, where Sir J. Mennes, Lord Brunkard, Sir Tho Harvy and myself dined upon Sir G Careteret's charge – and very merry we were, Sir Tho Harvy being a very drolle. Thence to the office; and meeting Creed, away with him to my Lord Treasurer's, there thinking to have met the goldsmiths, or at White-hall; but did not, and so appointed another time for my Lord to speak to them to advance us some money. Thence, it being the hottest day that ever I felt in my life, and it is confessed so by all other people the hottest they ever knew in England in the beginning of June – we to the New Exchange and there drunk whey; with much entreaty, getting it for our money, and would not be entreated to let us have one glasse more. So took water, and to Fox

hall[1] to the Spring-garden and there walked an hour or two with great pleasure, saving our minds ill at ease concerning the fleet and my Lord Sandwich, that we have no news of them, and ill reports run up and down of his being killed, but without ground. Here stayed, pleasantly walking and spending but 6*d*, till 9 at night; and then by water to White-hall, and there I stopped to hear news of the fleet, but none come, which is strange; and so by water home – where, weary with walking and with the mighty heat of the weather, and for my wife's not coming home – I staying walking in the garden till 12 at night, when it begun to Lighten[2] exceedingly through the greatness of the heat. Then, despairing of her coming home, I to bed.

This day, much against my Will, I did in Drury-lane see two or three houses marked with a red cross upon the doors, and "Lord have mercy upon us" writ there – which was a sad sight to me, being the first of that kind that to my remembrance I ever saw.[3] It put me into an ill conception of myself and my smell, so that I was forced to buy some roll=tobacco to smell to and chaw – which took away the apprehension.[4]

8. About 5 a-clock my wife came home, it having lightened all night hard, and one great shower of rain. She came and lay upon the bed. I up, and to the office, where all the morning. I alone at home to dinner, my wife, mother, and Mercer dining at W. Joyces, I giving her a caution to go round by the Half-Moone to his house, because of the plague. I to my Lord Treasurer's, by appointment of Sir Tho. Ingram's, to meet the goldsmiths – where I met with the great news, at last newly come, brought by Bab May[5] from the Duke of Yorke, that we have totally routed the Dutch. That the Duke himself, the Prince, my Lord Sandwich, and Mr. Coventry are all well. Which did put me into such a joy, that I forgot almost all other thoughts. The perticulars I shall set down by and by. By and by comes Alderman Maynell and Mr. Viner, and there my Lord Treasurer did intreat them to furnish me with money upon my tallies – Sir Ph. Warwicke, before my Lord, declaring the King's changing of the hand from Mr. Povy to me, whom he called a very sober person and

1. Vauxhall.
2. To flash with lightning.
3. These were the official signs of a house under quarantine for plague.
4. One contemporary theory held that plague spread via miasma (poison air), which was discernible by a bad smell. Tobacco was seen as medicinal and its smoke was used to counteract infected air.
5. Baptist May, courtier and servant to the Duke of York.

one whom the Lord Treasurer would own in all things that I should concern myself with them in the business of money. They did at present declare they could not part with money at present. My Lord did press them very hard – and I hope, upon their considering, we shall get some of them.

Thence with great Joy to the Cockepitt – where the Duke of Albemarle, like a man out of himself with content, new told me all; and by and by comes a letter from Mr. Coventry's own hand to him; which he never opened (which was a strange thing), but did give it me to open and read, and consider what was fit for our office to do in it and leave the letter with Sir W Clerke – which, upon such a time and occasion, was a strange piece of indifference, hardly pardonable. I copied out the letter, and did also take minutes out of Sir W Clerkes other letters; and the sum of the news is:

Victory over the Dutch. June. 3. 1665./[1]

This day they engaged – the Dutch neglecting greatly the opportunity of the wind they had of us – by which they lost the benefit of their fire-ships.

The Earl of Falmouth, Muskery, and Mr. Rd. Boyle killed on board the Dukes ship, the *Royall Charles*, with one shot.[2] Their blood and brains flying in the Duke's face – and the head of Mr. Boyle striking down the Duke, as some say.

Earle of Marlbrough, Portland, Rere-[A]dmirall Sansum (to Prince Rupert) killed, and Captain Kirby and Ableson. Sir Jo. Lawson wounded on the knee – hath had some bones taken out, and is likely to be well again.[3] Upon receiving the hurt, he sent to the Duke for another to command the *Royall Oake*. The Duke sent Jordan out of the *St. George*, who did brave things in her. Captain Jer. Smith of the *Mary* was second to the Duke, and stepped between him and Captain Seaton of the *Urania* (76 guns and 400 men),[4] who had sworn to board the Duke. Killed him, 200 men, and took the ship. Himself losing 99 men, and never an officer saved but himself and Lieutenant. His maister endeed is saved, with his leg cut off.

Admirall Opdam blown up. Trump killed, and said by Holmes. All the rest of their Admiralls, as they say, but Everson (whom they

1. The Battle of Lowestoft, the principal encounter of the year's campaign.
2. These three nobles – the Earl of Falmouth, Viscount Muskerry, and Richard Boyle, son of the Earl of Burlington – were killed by a chain-shot.
3. Gangrene, however, set in and he died on 25 June.
4. Capt. Centen of the *Oranje*, a Dutch warship.

dare not trust for his affection to the Prince of Orange) are killed.[1] We have taken and sunk, as is believed, about 24 of their best ships. Killed and taken near 8 or 10000 men;[2] and lost, we think, not above 700. A great victory, never known in the world. They are all fled; some 43 got into the Texell and others elsewhere, and we in pursuit of the rest.

Thence, with my heart full of Joy, home, and to my office a little; then to my Lady Pen's, where they are all joyed and not a little puffed up at the good success of their father; and good service endeed is said to have been done by him.[3]

Had a great bonfire at the gate; and I with my Lady Pens people and others to Mrs. Turner's great room,[4] and then down into the street. I did give the boys 4*s* among them – and mighty merry; so home to bed – with my heart at great rest and quiet, saving that the consideration of the victory is too great for me presently to comprehend.

9. Lay long in bed, my head akeing with too much thoughts, I think, last night. Up, and to White-hall and my Lord Treasurer's to Sir Ph. Warwicke about Tanger business; and in my way met with Mr. Moore, who eases me in one point wherein I was troubled – which was, that I heard of nothing said or done by my Lord Sandwich. But he tells me that Mr. Cowling, my Lord Chamberlain's Secretary, did hear the King say that my Lord Sandwich had done nobly and worthily.

The King, it seems, is much troubled at the fall of my Lord of Falmouth.[5] But I do not meet with any man else that so much as wishes him alive again, the world conceiving him a man of too much pleasure to do the King any good or offer any good office to him. But I hear of all hands, that he is confessed to have been a man of great Honour, that did show it in this his going with the Duke, the most that ever any man did.

Home, where my people busy to make ready a supper against night for some guests, in lieu of my Stonefeast.[6]

1. Of the Dutch flag-officers, Obdam (the commander-in-chief) and two others were killed but no more. Vice-Admiral Tromp survived.
2. The Dutch had lost seventeen ships, with around 5,000 casualties.
3. Sir William Penn, an experienced officer, had been the Duke of York's adviser on the *Royal Charles*.
4. Elizabeth Turner, a neighbour at the Navy Office.
5. Charles Berkeley, created Earl of Falmouth shortly before his death, had been one of the King's favourites.
6. The anniversary of Pepys's successful operation was 26 March, but in 1665 this clashed with Easter Sunday so the usual celebratory dinner had not taken place.

At noon eat a small dinner at home; and so abroad to buy several things; and among others, with my Taylor to buy a silk suit; which, though I made one lately, yet I do for joy of the good news we have lately had of our victory over the Dutch, which makes me willing to spare myself something extraordinary in clothes; and after long resolution of having nothing but black, I did buy a coloured silk Ferrandin.[1] So to the Old Exchange, and there at my pretty seamstress's bought a pair of stockings of her husband; and so home, where by and by comes Mr. Honiwood and Mrs. Wilde and Roger Pepys – and after long time spent, Mrs. Turner, The, and Joyce.[2] We had a very good venison pasty – this being, endeed, instead of my Stonefeast the last March – and very merry we were; and the more I know, the more I like Mr. Honiwoods conversation. So after a good supper, they parted, walking to the Change for a coach, and I with them to see them there. So home and to bed – glad it was over.

10. Lay long in bed; and then up and at the office all the morning. At noon dined at home, and then to the office, busy all the afternoon. In the evening home to supper, and there to my great trouble hear that the plague is come into the City (though it hath these three or four weeks since its beginning been wholly out of the City); but where should it begin but in my good friend and neighbour's, Dr. Burnett in Fanchurch-street – which in both points troubles me mightily.[3]

To the office to finish my letters, and then home to bed – being troubled at the sickness, and my head filled also with other business enough, and perticularly how to put my things and estate in order, in case it should please God to call me away – which God dispose of to his own glory.

23. Up, and to Whitehall to a Committee for Tanger, where his Royal Highness was. Our great design was to state to them the true condition of this commission for want of money, the want whereof was so great as to need some sudden help; and it was with some content resolved to see it supplied, and means proposed toward the doing of it.

At this Committee, unknown to me, comes my Lord of

1. Farandine: cloth of silk mixed with wool or hair.
2. Honywood was a lodger at Pepys's old home in Salisbury Court and "Mrs Wilde" was probably his niece. The rest were Pepys's relatives.
3. The physician Alexander Burnet had advised Pepys on preventing bladder stones.

Sandwich, who it seems came to town last night. After the Committee was up, my Lord Sandwich did take me aside, and we walked an hour alone together in the robe-chamber, the door shut – telling me how much the Duke and Mr. Coventry did, both in the fleet and here, make of him, and that in some opposition to the Prince;[1] and as a more private passage, he told me that he hath been with them both when they have made sport of the Prince and laughed at him. Yet that all the discourse of the town, and the printed relation, should not give him one word of honour, my Lord thinks mighty strange – he assuring me that though by accident the Prince was in the Van[2] the beginning of the fight for the first pass, yet all the rest of the day my Lord was in the Van, and continued so.[3] That notwithstanding all this noise of the Prince, he hath hardly a shot in his side, nor a man killed – whereas he hath above 30 in her hull, and not one mast whole nor yard – but the most battered ship of the fleet, and lost most men, saving Captain Smith of the *Mary*. That the most the Duke did was almost out of gun-shot. But that endeed, the Duke did come up to my Lord's rescue, after he had a great while fought with four of them. How poorly Sir John Lawson performed, notwithstanding all that that was said of him; and how his ship turned out of the way, while Sir J. Lawson himself was upon the deck, to the endangering of the whole fleet. It therefore troubles my Lord that Mr. Coventry should not mention a word of him in his relation. I did in answer offer that I was sure the relation was not compiled by Mr. Coventry, but by Lestrange out of several letters, as I could witness. And that Mr. Coventry's letter that he did give the Duke of Albimarle did give him as much right as the Prince – for I myself read it first and then copied it out, which I have promised to show my Lord – with which he was something satisfied.[4]

From that discourse, my Lord did begin to tell me how much he was concerned to dispose of his children, and would have my advice and help; and propounded to match my Lady Jemimah to

1. Rupert.
2. The foremost position.
3. Sandwich had led his squadron in a decisive attack on the centre of the Dutch fleet and his ship had taken heavy damage. Yet he had been mentioned only briefly in the two official printed accounts of the battle.
4. Roger L'Estrange, surveyor of the press and government journalist, had licensed both official pamphlets on the battle. As Sandwich and Coventry were two of Pepys's principal supporters, Pepys was anxious that Coventry not be blamed for the reporting.

Sir G Careterets eldest son[1] – which I approved of, and did undertake the speaking with him about it as from myself; which my Lord liked. So parted, with my head full of care about this business.

Thence home to the Change, and so to dinner. And thence by coach to Mr. Povys; whence by appointment with him and Creed to one Mr. Finch, one of the Comissioners for the Excize, to be informed about some things of the Excize, in order to our settling matters therein better for us for our Tanger matters. I find him a very discreet, grave person. Thence, well satisfied, I and Creed to Mr. Fox at Whitehall to speak with him about the same matter; and having some pretty satisfaction from him also, he and I took boat and to Fox hall, where we spent two or three hours, talking of several matters very soberly, and contentfully to me – which, with the ayre and pleasure of the garden, was a great refreshment to me, and methinks that which we ought to Joy ourselfs in. Thence back to White hall, where we parted; and I to find my Lord to receive his further direction about his proposal this morning – wherein I did [agree] that I should first, by another hand, break my intentions to Sir G Carteret. I pitched upon Dr Clerke, which my Lord liked – and so I endeavoured, but in vain, to find him out tonight. So home by hackney-coach; which is become a very dangerous passage nowadays, the sickness encreasing mightily. And to bed.

24. *Midsummer Day.* Up very betimes, by 6, and at Dr. Clerkes at Westminster by 7 of the clock, having over-night by a note acquainted him with my intention of coming. And there I, in the best manner I could, broke my errand about a match between Sir G Carter[e]ts eldest son and my Lord Sandwiches eldest daughter – which he (as I knew he would) took with great content; and we both agreed that my Lord and he, being both men relating to the sea – under a kind aspect of His Majesty – already good friends, and both virtuous and good families, their allyance might be of good use to us. And he did undertake to find out Sir George this morning, and put the business in execution. So being both well pleased with the proposition, I saw his neece there and made her sing me two or three songs, very prettily; and so home to the office – where to my great trouble, I found Mr. Coventry and the board met before I came. I excused my late coming, by having been upon the River about office business. So to business all the morning. At noon

1. A marriage between Philip Carteret (aged 22) and the Earl's eldest daughter (aged 19) promised political advantages for both families. Sir George Carteret, besides being Treasurer of the Navy, was a wealthy and influential courtier.

Captain Ferrers and Mr. Moore dined with me; the former of them, the first time I saw him since his coming from sea – who doth give me the best account in general, and as good an account of the perticular service of the Prince and my Lord of Sandwich in the late sea fight that I could desire. After dinner they parted. So I to Whitehall, where I with Creed and Povy attended my Lord Treasurer, and did prevail with him to let us have an assignment for 15 or 20000*l*, which I hope will do our business for Tanger. So to Dr. Clerke, and there find that he hath broke the business to Sir G Carteret and that he takes the thing mighty well. Thence I to Sir G. Carteret at his Chamber, and in the best manner I could, and most obligingly, moved that business; he received it with great respect and content and thanks to me, and promised that he would do what he could possibly for his son, to render him fit for my Lord's daughter. And showed great kindness to me, and sense of my kindness to him herein. Sir Wm. Pen told me this day that Mr. Coventry is to be sworn a Privy Counsellor – at which my soul is glad. So home and to my letters by the post, and so home – to supper and bed.

28. Sir J Minnes carried me ⟨and my wife⟩ to White-hall; and thence, his coach along with my wife where she would. Thereafter attending the Duke to discourse of the Navy. We did not kiss his hand; nor do I think, for all their pretence of going away tomorrow – yet I believe they will not go for good and all.[1] But I did take my leave of Sir Wm. Coventry, who it seems was knighted and sworn a Privy Councillor two days since – who with his old kindness treated me, and I believe I shall ever find a noble friend.

Thence by water to Blackfriars, and so to Paul's churchyard and bespoke several books, and so home and there dined – my man William giving me a lobster, sent him by my old maid Sarah.

This morning I met with Sir G. Carteret, who tells me how all things proceed between my Lord Sandwich and himself to full content, and both sides depend upon having the match finished presently. And professed great kindness to me, and said that now we were something akinned. I am mightily, both with respect to myself and much more of my Lord's family, glad of this alliance.

After dinner to White-hall, thinking to speak with my Lord

1. The court was to leave Whitehall because of the plague and, despite Pepys's predictions, removals began the next day. The court moved several times during the summer, remaining at Oxford between late September and late January. It did not return to Whitehall again until 1 Feb. 1666.

Ashly, but failed; and I whiled away some time in Westminster hall against he did come – in my way observing several plague-houses in Kings-street and the Palace. Here I hear Mrs. Martin is gone out of town, and that her husband, an idle fellow, is since come out of France, as he pretends; but I believe not that he hath been. I was fearful of going to any house, but I did to the Swan; and thence to White-hall, giving the waterman a shilling, because a young fellow and belonging to the *Plymouth*.

Thence by coach to several places, and so home and all the evening with Sir J. Minnes and all the women of the house (excepting my Lady Batten) late in the garden, chatting. At 12 a-clock home to supper and to bed.

My Lord Sandwich is gone toward the sea today, it being a sudden resolution – having taken no leave of him.

30. Up, and to White-hall to the Duke of Albemarle, who I find at Secretary Bennets, there being now no other great statesman, I think, but my Lord Chancellor in town.[1] I received several commands from them; among others, to provide some bread and cheese for the garrison at Guernsy; which they promised to see me paid for.

So to the Change, and home to dinner. In the afternoon, I down to Woolwich and after me, my wife and Mercer, whom I led to Mr. Sheldens to see his house; and I find it a very pretty place for them to be at.[2] So I back again, walking both forward and backward, and left my wife to come by water. I straight to Whitehall late, to Secretary Bennets to give him an account of the business I received from him today; and there stayed, weary and sleepy, till past 12 at night. Then writ my mind to him; and so back by water, and in the dark and against tide shot the bridge, groping with their pole for the way; which troubled me before I got through. So home about one or two a-clock in the morning – my family at a great loss what was become of me. To supper and to bed.

Thus this book of two years ends. Myself and family in good health, consisting of myself and wife – Mercer, her woman – Mary, Alce and Su, our maids; and Tom, my boy. In a sickly time, of the plague growing on. Having upon my hands the troublesome care of the Treasury of Tanger, with great sums drawn upon me and

1. Albemarle remained as the government's chief representative in the metropolis during the plague. He was based at the Cockpit in Whitehall Palace, where Pepys reported to him regularly.
2. William Sheldon was Clerk of the Cheque at Woolwich. The plan was for Elizabeth and Mary Mercer to stay at his house during the plague.

nothing to pay them with. Also, the business of the office great. Consideration of removing my wife to Woolwich. She lately busy in learning to paint, with great pleasure and successe. All other things well; especially a new interest I am making, by a match in hand between the eldest son of Sir G Carteret and my Lady Jemimah Mountagu. The Duke of York gone down to the fleet; but, all suppose, not with intent to stay there – as it is not fit, all men conceive, he should.

FINIS.[1]

JULY. 1665.

14.◆ I by water to Sir G. Carteret, and there find my Lady Sandwich and her buying things for my Lady Jem's wedding. And my Lady Jem is beyond expectation come to Dagenhams,[2] where Mr. Carteret is to go to visit her tomorrow; and my proposal of waiting on him, he being to go alone to all persons strangers to him, was well accepted and so I go with him. But Lord, to see how kind my Lady Carteret is to her – sends her most rich Jewells, and provides bedding and things of all sorts most richly for her – which makes my Lady and me out of our wits almost, to see the kindness she treats us all with – as if they would buy the young lady.

Thence away home; and foreseeing my being abroad two days, did sit up late, making of letters ready against tomorrow and other things; and so to bed – to be up betimes by the help of a larumwach,[3] which by chance I borrowed of my watchmaker today while my own is mending.

15. Up, and after all business done at the office, though late, I to Deptford. But before I went out of the office, saw there young Bagwells wife returned; but could not stay to speak to her, though I had a great mind to it. And also another great lady, as to fine clothes, did attend there to have a ticket signed; which I did do, taking her through the garden to my office, where I signed it and had a salute of her; and so I away by boat to Redriffe, and thence walked; and after dinner, at Sir G. Carteret, where they stayed till almost 3 a-clock for me; and anon took boat, Mr. Carteret and I,

1. End of the third manuscript volume.
2. Dagenhams, Essex, the home of Lady Anne Wright, Lady Jemima Mountagu's aunt.
3. Alarm-watch.

to the ferry-place at Greenwich and there stayed an hour, after crossing the water to and again to get our coach and horses over, and by and by set out and so toward Dagenham. But Lord, what silly discourse we had by the way as to matter of love-matters, he being the most awkerd man I ever I met withal in my life as to that business. Thither we came by time it begin to be dark, and were kindly received by my Lady Wright and my Lord Crew; and to discourse they went, my Lord discoursing with him, asking of him questions of Travell, which he answered well enough in a few words. But nothing to the lady from him at all. To supper, and after supper to talk again, he yet taking no notice of the lady. My Lord would have had me have consented to leaving the young people together tonight to begin their amours, his staying being but to be little. But I advised against it, lest the lady might be too much surprized. So they led him up to his chamber, where I stayed a little to know how he liked the lady; which he told me he did mightily, but Lord, in the dullest insipid manner that ever lover did. So I bid him good-night, and down to prayers with my Lord Crew's family. And after prayers, my Lord and Lady Wright and I to consult what to do; and it was agreed at last to have them go to church together as the family used to do, though his lameness was a great objection against it; but at last my Lady Jem sent me word by my Lady Wright that it would be better to do just as they used to do before his coming, and therefore she desired to go to church – which was yielded then to.

16. *Lords day.* I up, having lain with Mr. Moore in the Chaplins chamber. And having trimmed myself, down to Mr. Carteret; and he being ready, we down and walked in the gallery an hour or two, it being a most noble and pretty house that ever for the bigness I saw. Here I taught him what to do; to take the lady alway by the hand to lead her; and telling him that I would find opportunity to leave them two together, he should make these and these compliments, and also take a time to do the like to my Lord Crew and Lady Wright. After I had instructed him, which he thanked me for, owning that he needed my teaching him, my Lord Crew came down and family, the young lady among the rest; and so by coaches to church, four mile off – where a pretty good sermon – and a declaration of penitence of a man that had undergone the Church censure for his wicked life.

Thence back again by coach – Mr. Carteret having not had the confidence to take his lady once by the hand, coming or going;

which I told him of when we came home, and he will hereafter do it. So to dinner. My Lord excellent discourse. Then to walk in the gallery and to sit down. By and by my Lady Wright and I go out (and then my Lord Crew, he not by design); and lastly my Lady Crew came out and left the young people together. And a little pretty daughter of my Lady Wright's most innocently came out afterward, and shut the door to, as if she had done it, poor child, by inspiration – which made us without have good sport to laugh at.

They together an hour; and by and by church-time, whither he led her into the coach and into the church; and so at church all the afternoon. Several handsome ladies at church – but it was most extraordinary hot that ever I knew it.

So home again and to walk in the gardens, where we left the young couple a second time; and my Lady Wright and I to walk together, who to my trouble tells me that my Lady Jem must have something done to her body by Scott before she can be married,[1] and therefore care must be had to send him – also, that some more new clothes must of necessity be made her, which, and other things, I took care of.

Anon to supper, and excellent discourse and dispute between my Lord Crew and the Chaplin, who is a good Scholler but a nonconformist.

Here this evening I spoke with Mrs. Carter, my old acquaintance that hath lived with my Lady these twelve or thirteen years, the sum of all whose discourse, and others for her, is that I would get her [a] good husband; which I have promised, but know not when I shall perform.

After Mr. Carteret carried to his chamber, we to prayers again and then to bed.

17. Up, all of us, and to Billiards – my Lady Wright, Mr. Carter[e]t, myself and everybody. By and by the young couple left together. Anon to dinner, and after dinner Mr. Carteret took my advice about giving to the servants, and I led him to give 10*l* among them, which he did by leaving it to the chief manservant, Mr. Medows, to do for him. Before we went, I took my Lady Jem apart and would know how she liked this gentleman and whether she was under any difficulty concerning him. She blushed and hid her face awhile, but at last I forced her to tell me; she answered that she could readily

1. Jemima Mountagu suffered from a malformed neck; Scott was her medical practitioner.

obey what her father and mother had done – which was all she could say or I expect.

So anon took leave and for London. But Lord, to see, among other things, how all these great people here are afeared of London, being doubtful of anything that comes from thence or that hath lately been there, that I was forced to say that I lived wholly at Woolwich.

In our way Mr. Carteret did give me mighty thanks for my care and pains for him, and is mightily pleased – though the truth is, my Lady Jem hath carried herself with mighty discretion and gravity, not being forward at all in any degree but mighty serious in her answers to him, as by what he says and I observed, I collect.[1]◆

20. Up in a boat, among other people, to the Tower, and there to the office, where we sat all the morning. So down to Deptford and there dined; and after dinner saw my Lady Sandwich and Mr. Carteret and his two sisters over the water, going to Dagenhams, and my Lady Carteret toward Cranburne. So all the company broke up in most extraordinary joy – wherein I am mighty contented that I have had the good fortune to be so instrumental, and I think it will be of good use to me. So walked to Redriffe, where I hear the sickness is, and endeed is scattered almost everywhere – there dying 1089 of the plague this week. My Lady Carteret did this day give me a bottle of plague-water [to take] home with me. So home to write letters late, and then home to bed, where I have not lain these three or four nights.[2] I received yesterday a letter from my Lord Sandwich, giving me thanks for my care about their marriage business and desiring it to be despatched, that no disappointment may happen therein – which I will help on all I can. This afternoon I waited on the Duke of Albemarle; and so to Mrs. Crofts, where I found and saluted[3] Mrs. Burrows, who is a very pretty woman for a mother of so many children. But Lord, to see how the plague spreads; it being now all over Kings-street, at the Axe and the next door to it, and in other places.

29. Up betimes.[4] And after viewing some of wife's pictures, which now she is come to do very finely, to my great satisfaction, beyond what I could ever look for – I went away; and by water to the office, where nobody to meet me, but busy all the morning. At noon to

1. Deduce.
2. He had been staying with the Carterets at Deptford.
3. Greeted with a kiss.
4. He had spent a night at Woolwich, visiting Elizabeth in her lodgings.

dinner, where I hear that my Will is come in thither and laid down upon my bed, ill of the head-ake; which put me into extraordinary fear, and I studied all I could to get him out of the house, and set my people to work to do it without discouraging him. And myself went forth to the Old Exchange to pay my fair Batelier[1] for some linen, and took leave of her, they breaking up shop for a while. And so by coach to Kate Joyces, and there used all the vehemence and Rhetorique I could to get her husband to let her go down to Brampton, but I could not prevail with him – he urging some simple reasons, but most that of profit, minding the house – and the distance, if either of them should be ill. However, I did my best, and more then I had a mind to do, but that I saw him so resolved against it – while she was mightily troubled at it. At last he yielded she should go to Winsor to some friends there. So I took my leave of them, believing that it is great odds that we ever all see one another again – for I dare not go any more to that end of the town.

So home, and to writing of letters hard; and then at night home and fell to my Tanger Papers – till late; and then to bed – in some ease of mind that Will is gone to his lodging and that he is likely to do well, it being only the head-ake.

30. *Lord's day.* Up, and in my nightgown, cap, and neckcloth, undressed all day long; lost not a minute, but in my chamber setting my Tanger accounts to rights, which I did by night, to my very heart's content; not only that it is done, but I find everything right and even beyond what, after so long neglecting them, I did hope for. The Lord of Heaven be praised for it.

Will was with me today and is very well again. It was a sad noise to hear our Bell[2] to toll and ring so often today, either for deaths or burials; I think five or six times.

At night, weary with the day's work but full of joy at my having done it – I to bed, being to rise betimes tomorrow to go to the wedding at Dagenhams.

So to bed – fearing I have got some cold sitting in my loose garment all this day.

31. Up, and very betimes, by 6 a-clock, at Deptford; and there find Sir G. Carteret and my Lady ready to go[3] – I being in my new

1. Mary Batelier, linen draper at the Royal Exchange and a neighbour.
2. The bell of St Olave, Hart Street.
3. To the wedding of Philip Carteret and Jemima Mountagu at Dagenhams.

coloured-silk suit and coat, trimmed with gold buttons and gold broad lace round my hands, very rich and fine. By water to the Ferry, where, when we came, no coach there – and tide of ebb so far spent as the horse-boat could not get off on the other side the river to bring away the coach. So we were fain to stay there in the unlucky Isle of Doggs – in a chill place, the morning cool and wind fresh, above two if not three hours, to our great discontent. Yet being upon a pleasant errand, and seeing that could not be helped, we did bear it very patiently; and it was worth my observing, I thought as ever anything, to see how upon these two scores, Sir G. Carteret, the most passionate man in the world and that was in greatest haste to be gone, did bear with it, and very pleasant all the while, at least not troubled much so as to fret and storm at it.

Anon the coach comes – in the meantime there coming a citizen thither with his horse to go over, that told us he did come from Islington this morning, and that Proctor the vintener of the Miter in Woodstreet, and his son, is dead this morning there – of the plague. He having laid out abundance of money there – and was the greatest vintener for some time in London for great entertainments.

We fearing the canonicall hour would be past before we got thither, did with a great deal of unwillingness send away the Licence and wedding-ring.[1] So that when we came, though we drove hard with six horses, yet we found them gone from home; and going toward the church, met them coming from church – which troubled us. But however, that trouble was soon over – hearing it was well done – they being both in their old Cloaths. My Lord Crew giving her – there being three coach-fulls of them. The young lady mighty sad, which troubled me; but yet I think it was only her gravity, in a little greater degree then usual. All saluted her, but I did not till my Lady ⟨Sandwich⟩ did ask me whether I had not saluted her or no. So to dinner, and very merry we were; but yet in such a Sober way as never almost any wedding was in so great families – but it was much better. After dinner, company divided, some to cards – others to talk. My Lady Sandwich and I up to settle accounts and pay her some money – and mighty kind she is to me, and would fain have had me gone down for company with her to Hinchingbrooke – but for my life I cannot.

1. Weddings had to take place between the canonical hours of 8 a.m. and noon. A marriage licence allowed a couple to marry without banns and away from their parishes of residence.

At night to supper, and so to talk and, which methought was the most extraordinary thing, all of us to prayers as usual, and the young Bride and bridegroom too. And so after prayers, Soberly to bed; only, I got into the bridegroom's chamber while he undressed himself, and there was very merry – till he was called to the bride's chamber and into bed they went. I kissed the bride in bed, and so the curtaines drawne with the greatest gravity that could be, and so good-night.

But the modesty and gravity of this business was so decent, that it was to me, endeed, ten times more delightful then if it had been twenty times more merry and Joviall.

Whereas I feared I must have sat up all night, we did here all get good beds – and I lay in the same I did before, with Mr. Brisband,[1] who is a good scholar and sober man; and we lay in bed, getting him to give me an account of Rome, which is the most delightful talk a man can have of any traveller. And so to sleep – my eyes much troubled already with the change of my drink.

Thus I ended this month with the greatest joy that ever I did any in my life, because I have spent the greatest part of it with abundance of joy and honour, and pleasant Journys and brave entertainments, and without cost of money. And at last live to see that business ended with great content on all sides.◆

Thus we end this month, as I said, after the greatest glut of content that ever I had; only, under some difficulty because of the plague, which grows mightily upon us, the last week being about 1700 or 1800 of the plague.

My Lord Sandwich, at sea with a fleet of about 100 sail to the Norward, expect De Ruyter or the Duch East-India fleet.

My Lord Hinchingbrooke coming over from France, and will meet his sister at Scott's hall.

Myself having obliged both these families in this business very much, as both my Lady and Sir G. Carteret and his Lady do confess exceedingly; and the latter two also now call me Cosen, which I am glad of.

So God preserve us all friends long, and continue health among us.

1. John Brisbane, Deputy-Treasurer to the Fleet.

AUGUST.

2. Up, it being a public fast, as being the first Wednesday of the month, for the plague. I within-doors all day,[1] and upon my month's accounts late – and there to my great joy settled almost all my private matters of money in my books clearly; and allowing myself several sums which I had hitherto not reckoned myself sure of, because I would not be over-sure of anything, though with reason enough I might do it, I did find myself really worth 1900*l* – for which the great God of heaven and earth be praised. At night to the office to write a few letters, and so home to bed, after fitting myself for tomorrow's Journy.

3. Up, and betimes to Deptford to Sir G. Carteret's; where not liking the horse which had been hired by Mr. Uthwayt for me, I did desire Sir G. Carteret to let me ride his new 40*l* horse; which he did and so I left my hacquenee[2] behind. And so after staying a good while in their bedchamber while they were dressing themselfs, discoursing merrily, I parted and to the Ferry, where I was forced to stay a great while before I could get my horse brought over. And then mounted and rode very finely to Dagenham's – all the way, people, Citizens, walking to and again to enquire how the plague is in the City this week by the Bill – which by chance at Greenwich I had heard was 2010 of the plague, and 3000 and odd of all diseases; but methought it was a sad question to be so often asked me.[3] Coming to Dagenham's, I there met our company coming out of the house, having stayed as long as they could for me. So I let them go a little before, and went and took leave of my Lady Sandwich – good woman, who seems very sensible of my service and this late business – and having her directions in some things; among others, to get Sir G. Carteret and my Lord to settle the portion and what Sir G. Carteret is to settle into land as soon as may be; she not liking that it should lie long undone, for fear of death on either side. So took leave of her, and then down to the buttery and eat a piece of cold venison-pie and drank and took some bread and cheese in my

1. He had returned to Seething Lane on 1 August.
2. Hackney: a hired horse or riding horse.
3. The weekly bills of mortality recorded deaths in the parishes in the London area, along with the causes as determined by parish officials.

hand; and so mounted after them, Mr. Marr very kindly staying to lead me the way. By and by met my Lord Crew returning, after having accompanied them a little way. And so after them, Mr. Marr telling me by the way how a maid-servant of Mr. John Wrights (who lives thereabouts), falling sick of the plague, she was removed to an out-house, and a nurse appointed to look to her – who being once absent, the maid got out of the house at the window and run away. The nurse coming and knocking, and having no answer, believed she was dead, and went and told Mr. Wright so; who, and his lady, were in great strait what to do to get her buried. At last resolved to go to Burntwood hard by, being in that parish, and there get people to do it – but they would not; so he went home full of trouble, and in the way met the wench walking over the Common, which frighted him worse then before. And was forced to send people to take her; which he did, and they got one of the pest Coaches and put her into it to carry her to a pest-house. And passing in a narrow lane, Sir Anthony Browne, with his brother and some friends in the coach, met this coach with the Curtains drawn close. The brother being a young man, and believing there might be some lady in it that would not be seen, and the way being narrow, he thrust his head out of his own into her coach to look, and there saw somebody look very ill, and in a sick dress and stunk mightily; which the coachman also cried out upon. And presently they came up to some people that stood looking after it; and told our gallants that it was a maid of Mr. Wrights carried away sick of the plague – which put the young gentleman into a fright had almost cost him his life, but is now well again.

I, overtaking our young people, light and into the coach to them, where mighty merry all the way. And anon came to the Blockehouse over against Gravesend,[1] where we stayed a great while – in a little drinking-house – sent back our coaches to Dagenhams. I by and by, by boat to Gravesend, where no news of Sir G. Carteret come yet. So back again and fetched them all over but the two saddle-horses that were to go with us, which could not be brought over in the horse-boat, the wind and tide being against us, without towing. So we had some difference with some watermen, who would not tow them over under 20*s* – whereupon I swore to send one of them to sea, and will do it. Anon some others come to me and did it for ten. By and by comes Sir G. Carteret, and so we set out for Chatham – in my way overtaking some company, wherein

1. Tilbury fort.

was a lady, very pretty, riding single, her husband in company with her. We fell into talk, and I read a copy of verses which her husband showed me, and he discommended but the lady commended; and I read them so as to make the husband turn to commend them. By and by he and I fall into acquaintance, having known me formerly at the Exchequer; his name is Nokes, over against Bow Church; he was servant to Alderman Dashwood. We promised to meet if ever we came both to London again. And at parting I had a fair salute on horseback in Rochester streets of the lady – and so parted.

Came to Chatham mighty merry. And anon to supper, it being near 9 a-clock ere we came thither. My Lady Carteret came thither, in a coach by herself, before us. Great mind they have to buy a little hacquenee that I rode on from Gravesend, for a woman's horse. Mighty merry; and after supper, all being withdrawn, Sir G. Carteret did take an opportunity to speak with much value and kindness to me, which is of great joy to me. So anon to bed – Mr. Brisband and I together, to my content.

10.◆ By and by to the office, where we sat all the morning, in great trouble to see the Bill this week rise so high, to above 4000 in all, and of them, about 3000 of the plague. And an odd story of Alderman Bences stumbling at night over a dead Corps in the street; and going home and telling his wife, she at the fright, being with child, falls sick and died of the plague. We sat late; and then by invitation My Lord Brouncker, Sir J. Mennes, Sir W. Batten, and I to Sir G Smith's to dinner, where very good company and good cheer. Captain Cocke was there, and Jacke Fenn – but to our great wonder, Alderman Bence; and tells us that not a word of all this is true, and others said so too. But by his own story, his wife hath been ill, and he fain to leave his house and comes not to her – which continued a trouble to me all the time I was there.

Thence to the office; and after writing letters, home to draw over anew my Will, which I had bound myself by oath to despatch by tomorrow night, the town growing so unhealthy that a man cannot depend upon living two days to an end. So having done something of it, I to bed.

15. Up by 4 a-clock and walked to Greenwich, where called at Captain Cockes and to his chamber, he being in bed – where something put my last night's dream into my head, which I think is the best that ever was dreamed – which was, that I had my Lady Castlemayne in my armes and was admitted to use all the dalliance I desired with her, and then dreamed that this could not be awake

but that it was only a dream. But that since it was a dream and that I took so much real pleasure in it, what a happy thing it would be, if when we are in our graves (as Shakespeere resembles it), we could dream, and dream but such dreams as this[1] – that then we should not need to be so fearful of death as we are this plague-time.◆

I by water to the Duke of Albemarle, with whom I spoke a great deal in private with him, they being designed to send a fleet of ships privately to the Streights. No news yet from our Fleete, which is much wondered at; but the Duke says for certain, Guns have been heard to the Norward very much.

It was dark before I could get home; and so land at churchyard-stairs, where to my great trouble I met a dead Corps, of the plague, in the narrow ally, just bringing down a little pair of stairs – but I thank God I was not much disturbed at it. However, I shall beware of being late abroad again.[2]

25. Up betimes to the office, and there, as well as all the afternoon (saving a little dinner time, all alone) till late at night, writing letters and doing business, that I may get beforehand with my business again, which hath run behind a great while; and then home to supper and to bed.

This day I am told that Dr. Burnett my physician is this morning dead of the plague – which is strange, his man dying so long ago, and his house this month open again.[3] Now himself dead – poor unfortunate man.

30. Up betimes, and to my business of settling my house and papers; and then abroad and met with Hadly our Clerke,[4] who upon my asking how the plague goes, he told me it encreases much, and much in our parish: "For," says he, "there died nine this week, though I have returned but six" – which is a very ill practice, and makes me think it is so in other places, and therefore the plague much greater then people take it to be.

Thence, as I entended, to Sir R Viner's,[5] and there found not

1. Hamlet's soliloquy, Act 3 sc. 1.
2. The City's regulations to control infection required burials to occur between sundown and sunrise.
3. Burnet's house had been one of the first in the City to be quarantined. *See* 10 June 1665.
4. James Hadley, parish clerk of St Olave, Hart Street. Parish clerks sent burial figures to the Company of Parish Clerks, which were used to compile the bills of mortality.
5. Robert Vyner, recently knighted goldsmith-banker, who had loaned money for Tangier.

Mr. Lewes ready for me; so I went forth and walked toward Moorefields to see (God forgive my presumption) whether I could see any dead Corps going to the grave; but as God would have it, did not. But Lord, how everybody's looks and discourse in the street is of death and nothing else, and few people going up and down, that the town is like a place distressed – and forsaken. After one turn there, back to Viners and there found my business ready for me and evened all reckonings with them to this day, to my great content. So home; and all day, till very late at night, setting my Tanger and private accounts in order, which I did in both – and in the latter, to my great joy do find myself yet in the much best condition that ever I was in – finding myself worth 2180*l* and odd, besides plate and goods which I value at 250*l* more – which is a very great blessing to me. The Lord make me thankful. ⟨And of this, at this day above 1800*l* in cash in my house, which speaks but little out of my hands in desperate condition. But this is very troublesome to have in my house at this time.⟩

So late to bed, well pleased with my accounts, but weary of being so long at them.

31. Up, and after putting several things in order to my removal to Woolwich,[1] the plague having a great encrease this week beyond all expectation, of almost 2000 – making the general Bill 7000, odd 100, and the plague above 6000 – I down by appointment to Greenwich to our office, where I did some business, and there dined with our company and Sir W Boreman and Sir The Bidulph at Mr. Boreman's, where a good venison pasty. And after a good merry dinner, I to my office and there late, writing letters; and then to Woolwich by water, where pleasant with my wife and people; and after supper, to bed.

Thus this month ends, with great sadness upon the public through the greatness of the plague, everywhere through the Kingdom almost. Every day sadder and sadder news of its encrease. In the City died this week 7496; and of them, 6102 of the plague. But it is feared that the true number of the dead this week is near 10000 – partly from the poor that cannot be taken notice of through the greatness of the number, and partly from the Quakers and others that will not have any bell ring for them.[2]

1. He was going to stay at Woolwich where Elizabeth was already living. The Navy Office had just relocated from Seething Lane to Greenwich Palace.
2. Nonconformists and Catholics buried outside Church of England burial grounds were not included in the bills of mortality.

Our fleet gone out to find the Dutch, we having about 100 sail in our fleet, and in them, the *Soveraigne* one; so that it is a better fleet then the former with the Duke was. All our fear is that the Dutch should be got in before them – which would be a very great sorrow to the public, and to me perticularly, for my Lord Sandwichs sake.[1] A great deal of money being spent, and the Kingdom not in a condition to spare, nor a parliament, without much difficulty, to meet to give more. And to that, to have it said "What hath been done by our late fleets?"

As to myself, I am very well; only, in fear of the plague, and as much of an Ague, by being forced to go early and late to Woolwich, and my family to lie there continually.

My late gettings have been very great, to my great content, and am likely to have yet a few more profitable jobbs in a little while – for which, Tanger and Sir W Warren I am wholly obliged to.

SEPTEMBER.

3. *Lords day.* Up, and put on my colourd silk suit, very fine, and my new periwigg, bought a good while since, but darst not wear it because the plague was in Westminster when I bought it. And it is a wonder what will be the fashion after the plague is done as to periwigs, for nobody will dare to buy any haire for fear of the infection – that it had been cut off of the heads of people dead of the plague.

Before church-time comes Mr. Hill (Mr. Andrews failing because he was to receive the sacrament), and to church, where a sorry dull parson; and so home and most excellent company with Mr. Hill, and discourse of Musique. I took my Lady Pen home and her daughter Peg, and merry we were, and after dinner I made my wife show them her pictures, which did mad pegg Pen who learns of the same man – and cannot do so well. After dinner left them, and I by water to Greenwich, where much ado to be suffered to come into the town because of the sickness, for fear I should come from London – till I told them who I was. So up to the church, where at the door I find Captain Cocke in my Lord Brunkers coach, and he came out and walked with me in the churchyard till the church was done. Talking of the ill-government of our Kingdom, nobody setting to heart the business of the Kingdom, but

1. Sandwich was in sole command of the English fleet. His priority was to intercept merchant convoys returning to the Dutch Republic and seize prizes to finance the war.

everybody minding their perticular profit or pleasures, the King himself minding nothing but his ease – and so we let things go to wrack. This arose upon considering what we shall do for money when the fleet comes in, and more if the fleet should not meet with the Dutch, which will put a disgrace upon the King's actions, so as the Parliament and Kingdom will have the less mind to give more money. Besides, so bad an account of the last money, we fear, will be given; not half of it being spent, as it ought to be, upon the Navy.[1] Besides, it is said that at this day our Lord Treasurer cannot tell what the profits of Chimny money is;[2] what it comes to per annum – nor looks whether that or any other part of the Revenue be duly gathered as it ought – the very money that should pay the City the 200000*l* they lent the King being all gathered and in the hands of the Receiver, and hath been long, and yet not brought up to pay the City, whereas we are coming to borrow 4 or 500000*l* more of the City – which will never be lent as is to be feared.

Church being done, my Lord Brouncker, Sir J. Mennes, and I up to the Vestry at the desire of the Justices of the Peace, Sir Th Bidolph and Sir W Boreman and Alderman Hooker – in order to the doing something for the keeping of the plague from growing; but Lord, to consider the madness of people of the town, who will (because they are forbid) come in Crowds along with the dead Corps to see them buried.[3] But we agreed on some orders for the prevention thereof. Among other stories, one was very passionate methought – of a complaint brought against a man in the town for taking a child from London from an infected house. Alderman Hooker told us it was the child of a very able citizen in Gracious-street, a saddler, who had buried all the rest of his children of the plague; and himself and wife now being shut up, and in despair of escaping, did desire only to save the life of this little child; and so prevailed to have it received stark-naked into the arms of a friend, who brought it (having put it into new fresh clothes) to Grenwich; where, upon hearing the story, we did agree it should be ⟨permitted to be⟩ received and kept in the town. Thence with my Lord Brouncker to Captain Cockes, where we mighty merry, and supped; and very late, I by water to Woolwich, in great appre-

1. Money collected from the Royal Aid Act, passed earlier in the year.
2. The Hearth Tax levied from 1662 onwards.
3. Orders published by the Lord Mayor forbade people assembling for burials in London. The principal officers of the navy were entitled to act as magistrates for all counties in which naval dockyards were situated.

hensions of an Ague. Here was my Lord Brouncker's lady of pleasure, who I perceive goes everywhere with him, and he I find is obliged to carry her and make all the Courtship to her that can be.[1]

10. *Lords day.* Walked home, being forced thereto by one of my watermen falling sick yesterday; and it was God's great mercy I did not go by water with them yesterday, for he fell sick on Saturday night and it is to be feared of the plague. So I sent him away to London with his fellow.

But another boat came to me this morning, whom I sent to Blackewall for Mr. Andrews; I walked to Woolwich, and there find Mr. Hill, and he and I all the morning at Musique and a song he hath set, of three parts; methinks very good. Anon comes Mr. Andrews, though it be a very ill day. And so after dinner we to Musique and sang till about 4 or 5 a-clock, it blowing very hard, and now and then raining – and, wind and tide being against us, Andrews and I took leave and walked to Greenwich – my wife before I came out telling me the ill news that she hears, that her father is very ill; and then I told her I feared of the plague, for that the house is shut up. And so, she much troubled, she did desire me to send them something, and I said I would, and will do so.[2]

But before I came out, there happened news to come to me by an expresse from Mr. Coventry, telling me the most happy news of my Lord Sandwiches meeting with part of the Dutch; his taking two of their East India ships and six or seven others, and very good prize – and that he is in search of the rest of the fleet, which he hopes to find upon the Well bancke – with the loss only of the *Hector*, poor Captain Cuttle. This news doth so overjoy me, that I know not what to say enough to express it; but the better to do it, I did walk to Greenwich; and there sending away Mr. Andrews, I to Captain Cocke's, where I find my Lord Brouncker and his mistress and Sir J. Mennes – where we supped (there was also Sir W Doyly and Mr. Eveling);[3] but the receipt of this news did put us all into such an extasy of joy, that it inspired into Sir J. Mennes and Mr. Eveling such a spirit of mirth, that in all my life I never met with

1. This was Abigail Williams, Brouncker's partner until his death in 1684.
2. He did so two days later, when Elizabeth pressed him. After this, there are no further reports of her father's condition in the diary, but he recovered.
3. John Evelyn, of Sayes Court near Deptford, was a Commissioner for the Sick and Wounded, as were Doyly and Cocke. Evelyn's work during the war introduced him to Pepys and began a friendship that lasted until Pepys's death. Evelyn's diary, kept for much of his life, is a valued source on the later seventeenth century.

so merry a two hours as our company this night was. Among other humours, Mr. Eveling's repeating of some verses made up of nothing but the various acceptations of May and Can,[1] and doing it so aptly, upon occasion of something of that nature, and so fast, did make us all die almost with laughing, and did so stop the mouth of Sir J. Mennes in the middle of all his mirth (and in a thing agreeing with his own manner of Genius) that I never saw any man so outdone in all my life; and Sir J. Mennes's mirth too, to see himself out-done, was the crown of all our mirth.

In this humour we sat till about 10 at night; and so my Lord and his mistress home, and we to bed – it being one of the times of my life wherein I was the fullest of true sense of joy.

14. Up, and walked to Greenwich and there fitted myself in several businesses to go to London, where I have not been now a pretty while. But before I went from the office, news is brought by word of mouth that letters are now just now brought from the Fleete of our taking a great many more of the Dutch fleet – in which I did never more plainly see my command of my temper, in my not admitting myself to receive any kind of joy from it till I had heard the certainty of it. And therefore went by water directly to the Duke of Albemarle, where I find a letter of the 12th from Soldbay, from my Lord Sandwich, of the fleet's meeting with about 18 more of the Dutch fleet and his taking of most of them; and the messenger says they had taken three after the letter was wrote and sealed; which being 21, and the 14 took the other day, is 45 sail[2] – some of which are good, and others rich ships – which is so great a cause of joy in us all, that my Lord and everybody is highly joyed thereat. And having taken a copy of my Lord's letter, I away back again to the Bear at the Bridge-foot, being full of wind and out of order, and there called for a biscuit and a piece of cheese and gill of sack

1. "Acceptations" means "accepted meanings". Evelyn was performing this tongue-twister:

"I think indeed that whoso May & Can
Can never May, for May must Can obey
Yet for that May & Can, May will as man
For May may Will, tho his Will can not May."
or thus.
"I grant indeed that whoso May & Can
May Can & Will, for May does Can obey
But whoso Can & Will may Will as man
For man may Will, tho his Will never May."
(British Library, MS Add. 18220).

2. The action took place off the Dutch coast on 9 September. The total of captured ships was less than Pepys reports.

– being forced to walk over the Bridge toward the Change, and the plague being all thereabouts. Here my news was highly welcome, and I did wonder to see the Change so full, I believe 200 people; but not a man or merchant of any fashion, but plain men all. And Lord, to see how I did endeavour all I could to talk with as few as I could, there being now no observation of shutting up of houses infected, that to be sure we do converse and meet with people that have the plague upon them. I to Sir Rob. Viners, where my main business was about settling the business of Debusty's 5000*l* tallies – which I did for the present to enable me to have some money.[1] And so home, buying some things for my wife in the way. So home and put up several things to carry to Woolwich – and upon serious thoughts, I am advised by W Griffin[2] to let my money and plate rest there, as being as safe as any place, nobody imagining, that people would leave money in their houses now, when all their families are gone. So for the present, that being my opinion, I did leave them there still. But Lord, to see the trouble that it puts a man to to keep safe what with pain a man hath been getting together; and there is good reason for it. Down to the office, and there wrote letters to and again about this good news of our victory, and so by water home late –

Where when I came home, I spent some thoughts upon the occurrences of this day, giving matter for as much content on one hand and melancholy on another as any day in all my life – for the first, the finding of my money and plate and all safe at London ⟨and speeding in my business of money this day⟩ – the hearing of this good news, to such excess after so great a despair of my Lord's doing anything this year – adding to that, the decrease of 500 and more, which is the first decrease we have yet had in the sickness since it begun – and great hopes that the next week it will be greater. Then on the other side – my finding that though the Bill in general is abated, yet the City within the walls is encreased and likely to continue so ⟨and is close to our house there⟩ – my meeting dead corps's of the plague, carried to be buried close to me at noonday through the City in Fanchurch-street – to see a person sick of the sores carried close by me by Grace-church in a hackney-coach – my finding the Angell tavern at the lower end of Tower-hill shut up; and more then that, the alehouse at the Tower-stairs; and more then that, that the person was then dying of the plague when I was last there,

1. Debussy was a provisions merchant, and this was presumably Tangier business.
2. Doorkeeper of the Navy Office at Seething Lane.

a little while ago at night, to write a short letter there, and I overheard the mistress of the house sadly saying to her husband somebody was very ill, but did not think it was of the plague – to hear that poor Payne my water[man] hath buried a child and is dying himself – to hear that ⟨a labourer I sent but the other day to Dagenhams to know how they did there is dead of the plague; and that⟩ one of my own watermen, that carried me daily, fell sick as soon as he had landed me on Friday morning last, when I had been all night upon the water (and I believed he did get his infection that day at Brainford) is now dead of the plague – to hear ⟨that Captain Lambert and Cuttle are killed in the taking these ships and⟩ that Mr. Sidny Mountagu is sick of a desperate fever at my Lady Carteret's at Scott's hall – to hear that Mr. Lewes hath another daughter sick – and lastly, that both my servants, W Hewers and Tom Edwards, have lost their fathers, both in St. Sepulcher's parish, of the plague this week – doth put me into great apprehensions of melancholy, and with good reason. But I put off the thoughts of sadness as much as I can; and the rather to keep my wife in good heart, and family also. After supper (having eat nothing all this day) upon a fine Tench of Mr. Sheldens taking, we to bed.

20. Called up by Captain Cocke (who was last night put into great trouble upon his boy's being rather worse then better, upon which he removed him out of his house to his stable), who told me that to my comfort his boy was now as well as ever he was in his life.

So I up; and after being trimmed (the first time I have been touched by a barber these 12 months I think and more), went to Sir J. Mennes, where I find all out of order still, they having not seen one another;[1] till by and by Sir J. Mennes and Sir W. Batten met to go into my Lord Brouncker's coach, and so we four to Lambeth, and thence to the Duke of Albemarle to inform him what we have done as to the fleet, which is very little, and to receive his direction. But Lord, what a sad time it is, to see no boats upon the River – and grass grow all up and down Whitehall-court – and nobody but poor wretches in the streets. And which is worst of all, the Duke showed us the number of the plague this week, brought in the last night from the Lord Mayor – that it is encreased about 600 more then the last, which is quite contrary to all our hopes and expectations from the coldness of the late season: for the whole general number is 8297; and of them, the plague 7165 – which is more in

1. Sir John Mennes was in lodgings at Greenwich. Sir William and Lady Batten were visiting him but there had been a falling out.

the whole, by above 50, then the biggest Bill yet[1] – which is very grievous to us all. ◆

23. Up, and to my Lord Sandwich[2] – who did advise alone with me how far he might trust Captain Cocke in the business of the prize goods – my Lord telling me that he hath taken into his hands 2 or 3000*l* value of them.[3] It being a good way, he says, to get money, and afterward to get the King's allowance thereof – it being easier, he observes, to keep money when got of the King, then to get it when it is too late. I advised him not to trust Cocke too far. And did thereupon offer him ready money for a thousand pound or two, which he listens to and doth agree to – which is great joy to me, hoping thereby to get something.[4]

Thence by coaches to Lambeth, his Lordshipp and all our office, and Mr. Eveling, to the Duke of Albemarle – where after the compliment with my Lord, very kind, we sat down to consult of the disposing and supporting of the fleet with victuals and money, and for the sick men and prisoners. And I did propose the taking out some goods out of the prizes, to the value of 10000*l*; which was accorded to, and an order drawn up and signed by the Duke and my Lord, done in the best manner I can and referred to my Lord Brouncker and Sir J. Mennes.[5] But what inconveniences may arise from it I do not yet see, but fear there may be many. ◆

OCTOBER.

1. *Lords day.* Called up about 4 of the clock, and so dressed myself; and so on board the *Bezan*,[6] and there finding all my company asleep, I would not wake them; but it beginning to be break of day, I did stay upon the Decke walking and then into the Maisters

1. The week of 12–19 September was to prove the worst of the whole plague period.
2. He had returned from sea and was making a short visit to Greenwich.
3. Sandwich had captured two Dutch East Indiamen on 3 September. Unwisely, he violated naval procedures for the distribution of prize-goods by allowing his flag-officers to take part of the rich cargo immediately. He also took his share. Captain Cocke was helping to manage removal of these goods. Sandwich's pre-emptive "breaking bulk" caused a scandal, especially given that money from prizes was badly needed to fund the war. The ensuing allegations of corruption were a major factor in Sandwich's decline in status towards the end of this year.
4. Pepys intended to purchase part of the East India goods and sell them on at a profit.
5. Brouncker and Mennes were supervising the unloading of the captured ships.
6. He was going on a day's visit to Lord Sandwich and the fleet at the Nore.

Cabbin and there leaned[1] and slept a little; and so at last was wakened by Captain Cockes calling of me, and so I turned out, and then to chat and talk and laugh, and mighty merry. We spent most of the morning talking, and reading of *The Seige of Rhodes*,[2] which is certainly (the more I read it the more I think so) the best poem that ever was wrote. We breakfasted betimes and came to the fleet about 2 of the clock in the afternoon, having a fine day and a fine winde. My Lord received us mighty kindly; and after discourse with us in general, left us to our business, and he to his officers, having called a council of Warr. We in the meantime settling of papers with Mr. Pierce[3] and everybody else, and by and by with Captain Cuttance. Anon called down to my Lord, and there with him till supper, talking and discourse. Among other things, to my great joy he did assure me that he had wrote to the King and Duke about these prize-goods, and told me that they did approve of what he had done and that he would own what he had done, and would have me to tell all the world so; and did under his hand give Cocke and me his Certificate of our bargains, and giving us full power of disposal of what we have so bought.[4] This doth ease my mind of all my fear, and makes my heart lighter by 100*lb* then it was before. He did discourse to us of the Dutch fleet being abroad, 85 of them still, and are now at the Texell he believes, in expectation of our Eastland ships coming home with masts and hemp, and our loaden Hambrough ships going to Hambrough.[5] He discoursed against them that would have us yield to no conditions but conquest over the Dutch, and seems to believe that the Dutch will call for the protection of the King of France and come under his power – which were to be wished they might be brought to do under ours, by fair means; and to that end would have all Dutchmen and families that would come hither and settled, to be declared Denizens. And my Lord did whisper to me alone, that things here must break in pieces, nobody minding anything, but every man his own business of profit or pleasure, and the King some little designs of his own; and that certainly the Kingdom could not stand in this condition long – which I fear and believe is very true.

So to supper, and there my Lord the kindest man to me before

1. Lay down.
2. Sir William Davenant's operatic drama.
3. The papers concerned prize-goods. Andrew Pearse was a purser.
4. The surviving certificate shows Pepys had bought spices, silks and other goods worth over £1,000.
5. These were ships trading with Scandinavia and the Baltic States, and with Hamburg.

all the table, talking of me to my advantage, and with tenderness too, that it overjoyed me. So after supper Captain Cocke and I and Temple on board the *Bezan*, and there to Cards for a while, and then to read again in *Rhodes* and so to sleep.[1] But Lord, the mirth which it caused to me to be waked in the night by their Snoaring round about me – I did laugh till I was ready to burst, and waked one of the two companions of Temple, who could not a good while tell where he was, that he heard one laugh so, till he recollected himself and I told him what it was at; and so to sleep again, they still Snoaring.

4.◆ This night comes Sir George Smith to see me at the office, and tells me how the plague is decreased this week 740, for which God be praised – but that it encreases at our end of the town still. And says how the towne is full of Captain Cocke's being in some ill condition about prize-goods, his goods being taken from him and I know not what; but though this troubles me to have it said, and that it was likely to be a business in Parliament, yet I am not much concerned at it, for he would have wrote to me, sure, about it.

Being come home to my wife at our lodging, I did go to bed, and left my wife and her people to laugh and dance, and I to sleep.

5. Lay long in bed, talking; among other things, talking of my sister Pall, and my wife of herself is very willing that I should give her 400*l* to her portion – and would have her married as soon as we could; but this great sickness-time doth make it unfit to send for her up.

I abroad to the office, and thence to the Duke of Albemarle, all my way reading a book of Mr. Evelins translating, and sending me as a present, about directions of gathering a Library, but the book is above my reach, but his epistle to my Lord Chancellor is a very fine piece.[2] When I came to the Duke, it was about the victuallers business, to put it into other hands, or more hands – which I do advise in, but I hope to do myself a jobb of work in it.[3] So I walked through Westminster to my old house, the Swan, and there did pass

1. The yacht carried them back to land overnight.
2. Evelyn's *Instructions concerning Erecting of a Library* (1661) was a translation of Gabriel Naudé's French work aimed at extremely wealthy, aristocratic collectors. Evelyn's translation was dedicated to the Earl of Clarendon.
3. There had been serious failures in navy supplies during the war. The merchant Denis Gauden was in sole charge of navy victualling. Needing a quick wartime solution, Pepys recommended the appointment of a new Surveyor-General who would gather reports on supplies in each port and oversee Gauden's work. In the meantime, he looked for merchants to be partners with Gauden.

some time with Sarah; and so down by water to Deptford and there to my Valentine's;[1] round about and next door on every side is the plague, but I did not value it but there did what I would con ella;[2] and so away to Mr. Evelings to discourse of our confounded business of prisoners and sick and wounded seamen, wherein he and we are so much put out of order. And here he showed me his gardens, which are, for variety of Ever=greens and hedge of Holly, the finest things I ever saw in my life. Thence in his coach to Greenwich, and there to my office, all the way having fine discourse of Trees and the nature of vegetables. And so to write letters I very late, to Sir W Coventry, of great concernment; and so to my last night's lodging, but my wife is gone home to Woolwich.

The Bill, blessed be God, is less this week by 740 of what it was the last week. Being come to my lodging,[3] I got something to eat, having eat little all the day, and so to bed – having this night renewed my promises of observing my vowes as I used to do, for I find that since I left them off, my minde is run a'wool-gathering and neglected my business.

7. Up, and to the office along with Mr. Childe, whom I sent for to discourse about the victualling business; who will not come into partenership (no more will Captain Beckford) but I do find him a mighty understanding man, and one I will keep a knowledge of. Did business, though not much, at the office, because of the horrible Crowd and lamentable moan of the poor seamen that lie starving in the streets for lack of money – which doth trouble and perplex me to the heart. And more at noon, when we were to go through them; for then a whole hundred of them fallowed us – some cursing, some swearing, and some praying to us.

And that that made me more troubled, was a letter come this noon from the Duke of Albemarle, signifying the Duch to be in sight, with 80 sail, yesterday morning off of Soldbay, coming right into the bay; God knows what they will and may do to us, we having no force abroad able to oppose them, but to be sacrifized to them. Here came Sir Wm. Rider to me, whom I sent for about the victualling business also; but he neither will not come into partenership, but desires to be of the Commission, if there be one. Thence back the back-way to my office, where very late, very busy – but most of

1. Mrs Bagwell. *See* 14 Feb. 1665.
2. "with her".
3. In addition to lodgings at Woolwich for Elizabeth, Pepys was now maintaining lodgings for himself at Greenwich, near the relocated Navy Office.

all when at night comes two waggons from Rochester with more goods from Captain Cocke; and in housing them at Mr. Tookers lodgings, comes two of the Custome-house to seize them, and did seize them, but I showed them my Transire. However, after some heat and angry words, we locked them up, and sealed up the key and did give it to the constable to keep till Monday – and so parted.[1] But Lord, to think how the poor constable came to me in the dark, going home: "Sir," says he, "I have the Key, and if you would have me do any service for you, send for me betimes tomorrow morning and I will do what you would have me." Whether the fellow doth this out of kindness or knavery, I cannot tell, but it is pretty to observe.

Talking with him in the highway, comes close by the bearers with a dead corps of the plague; but Lord, to see what custom is, that I am come almost to ⟨think⟩ nothing of it.

So to my lodging, and there with Mr. Hater and Will ending a business of the state of the last six months' charge of the Navy, which we bring to 1000000*l* and above – and I think we do not enlarge much in it, if anything. So to bed.

11.◆ Against tide and in the dark and very cold weather, to Woolwich, where we had appointed to keep the night merrily; and so, by Captain Cockes coach, had brought a very pretty child (a daughter of one Mrs. Tookers, next door to my lodging), and so she and a daughter and kinsman of Mr. Petts made up a fine company at my lodgings at Woolwich, where my wife and Mercer and Mrs. Barbara danced, and mighty merry we were, but especially at Mercer's dancing a Jigg, which she does the best I ever did see, having the most natural way of it and keeps time the most perfectly I ever did see. This night is kept, in lieu of yesterday, for my wedding-day of Ten Yeares – for which God be praised – being now in an extreme good condition of health and estate and honour, and a way of getting more money – though at this hour under some discomposure, rather then dammage, about some prize-goods that I have bought of the Fleete in partenership with Captain Cocke – and for the discourse about the world concerning my Lord Sandwich, that he hath done a thing so bad; and indeed it must needs have been a very rash act. And the rather, because of a parliament now newly met to give money and will have some account of what hath already

1. A transire was a warrant permitting merchandise to pass customs. The arguments with customs officials about the prize-goods continued for much of this month.

been spent – besides the precedent for a General to take what prizes he pleases – and the giving a pretence to take away much more then he entended, and all will lie upon him. And not giving to all the Commanders, as well as the Flags,[1] he displeases all them – and offends even some of them, thinking others to be better served then themselfs. And lastly, puts himself out of a power of begging anything again a great while of the King. Having danced my people as long as I saw fit to sit up, I to bed, and left them to do what they would. I forgot that we had W Hewer there and Tom – and Golding, my barber at Greenwich, for our fiddler, to whom I did give x*s*.

19. Up, and to my accounts again, and stated them very clear and fair; and at noon dined at my lodgings, with Mr. Hater and W. Hewer at table with me – I being come to an agreement yesterday with my landlady for 6*l* per month for so many rooms for myself; them and my wife, and maid when she shall come – and to pay besides for my Dyet.[2] After dinner I did give them my accounts and letters to write, against I went to the Duke of Albemarle this evening – which I did; and among other things, spoke to him for my wife's brother Balty to be of his guard, which he kindly answered that he should. My business of the victualling goes on as I would have it; and now my head is full how to make some profit of it to myself or people. To that end, when I came home, I wrote a letter to Mr. Coventry, offering myself to be the Surveyor Generall, and am apt to think he will assist me in it; but I do not set my heart much on it, though it would be a good help. So back to my office, and there till past one before I could get all these letters and papers copied out, which vexed me. But so sent them away without hopes of saving the post, and so to my lodging to bed.

25. Up, and to my Lord Sandwiches,[3] where several commanders, of whom I took the state of all their ships, and of all could find not above four capable of going out – the truth is, the want of victuals being the whole overthrow of this year, both at sea and now at the Noure here and Portsmouth, where all the fleet lies. By and by comes down my Lord, and then he and I an hour together alone upon private discourse. He tells me that Mr. Coventry and he are not reconcilable, but declared enemies; the only occasion of it, he tells me, being his ill-usage from him about the first Fight, wherein

1. Flag-officers.
2. The agreement was with Mrs Clerke, his landlady at Greenwich.
3. Sandwich was making a short visit to Greenwich.

he had no right done him[1] (which methinks is a poor occasion, for in my conscience, that was no design of Coventry's); but however, when I asked my Lord whether it were not best, though with some condescensions, to be friends with him, he told me it was not possible, and so I stopped. He tells me, as very private, that there are great factions at the Court between the King's party and the Duke of Yorkes, and that the King (which is a strange difficulty) doth favour my Lord in opposition to the Duke's party. That my Lord Chancellor being, to be sure, the patron of the Duke's, it is a mystery whence it should be that Mr. Coventry is looked upon by him[2] as an enemy to him. That if he[3] had a mind himself to be out of this imployment, as Mr. Coventry he believes wishes (and himself, and I do, doth encline to wish it also in many respects), yet he believes he shall not be able because of the King, who will keep him in on purpose in opposition to the other party. That Prince Rupert and he are all possible friends in the world. That Coventry hath aggravated this business of the prizes, though never so great plundering in the world as while the Duke and he were at sea.[4]◆

After dinner my Lord by a Ketch down to Erith, where the *Bezan* was – it blowing these last two days, and now both night and day very hard Southwardly – so that it hath certainly drove the Duch off the coast.

My Lord being gone, I to the office and there find Captain Ferrer, who tells me his wife is come to town to see him, having not seen him since fifteen ⟨weeks⟩ ago, at his first going to sea last. She is now at a Taverne and stays all night, so I was obliged to give him my house and chamber to lie in, which he, with great modesty and after much force, took; and so I got Mr. Evelings coach to carry her thither, and the coach coming back, I with Mr. Eveling to Deptford, where a little while with him doing a little business; and so in his coach back again to my lodgings, and there sat with Mrs. Ferrer two hours, and with my little girle, Mrs. Fran. Tooker,[5] and very pleasant: anon the Captain comes, and then to supper, very

1. Sandwich felt his importance in the Battle of Lowestoft had not been publicly recognized. *See* 23 June 1665.
2. Lord Chancellor Clarendon. Clarendon was the Duke of York's father-in-law and Coventry the Duke's secretary, so Clarendon's hostility to someone of the same "party" was surprising.
3. Sandwich.
4. In summer 1665, when both the Duke and Coventry were on the *Royal Charles*. These allegations of plundering appear baseless.
5. Daughter of Pepys's neighbour at his Greenwich lodgings.

merry; and so I led them to bed. And so to bed myself – having seen my pretty little girl home first, at the next door.

27. Up, and after some pleasant discourse with my wife, I out, leaving her and Mrs. Ferrers there; and I to Captain Cocke's, there to do some business; and then away with Cocke in his coach through Kent-street, a miserable, wretched, poor place, people sitting sick and muffled up with plasters[1] at every four or five door. So to the Change, and thence I by water to the Duke of Albemarle; and there much company, but I stayed and dined, and he makes mighty much of me; and here he tells us the Dutch are gone, and have lost above 160 cables and anchors through the last foul weather. Here he proposed to me from Mr. Coventry (as I had desired of Mr. Coventry) that I should be Surveyor Generall of the victualling business, which I accepted. But endeed, the terms in which Mr. Coventry proposes it for me are the most obliging that ever I could expect from any man, and more – it saying me to be the fittest man in England, and that he is sure, if I will undertake it, I will perform it – and that it will be also a very desirable thing that I might have this encouragement, my encouragement in the Navy alone being in no wise proportionable to my pains or deserts. This, added to the letter I had three days since from Mr. Southerne, signifying that the Duke of Yorke had in his master's absence opened my letter and commanded him to tell me that he did approve of my being the Surveyor general, doth make me joyful beyond myself, that I cannot express it; to see that as I do take pains, so God blesses me and hath sent me masters that do observe that I take pains. ◆

NOVEMBER.

1. Lay very long in bed, discoursing with Mr. Hill[2] of most things of a man's life, and how little merit doth prevail in the world, but only favour – and that for myself, chance without merit brought me in, and that diligence only keeps me so, and will, living as I do among so many lazy people, that the diligent man becomes necessary, that they cannot do anything without him. And so told him of my late business of the victualling and what cares I am in to keep myself, having to do with people of so different factions at Court,

1. Dressings to treat plague sores.
2. Thomas Hill, friend and merchant, had stayed the night at Greenwich after a party.

and yet must be fair with them all – which was very pleasant discourse for me to tell, as well, as he seemed to take it, for him to hear.◆

5. *Lords day.* Up, and after being trimmed, by boate to the Cockepitt, where I heard the Duke of Albemarle's chaplain make a simple sermon. Among other things, reproaching the imperfection of humane learning, he cried – "All our physicians can't tell what an ague is, and all our Arithmetique is not able to number the days of a man" – which, God knows, is not the fault of arithmetique, but that our understandings reach not that thing.

To dinner, where a great deal of silly discourse. But the worst is, I hear that the plague encreases much at Lambeth, St. Martins, and Westminster, and fear it will all over the City. Thence I to the Swan, there thinking to have seen Sarah, but she was at church; and so by water to Deptford, and there made a visit to Mr. Evelings, who, among other things, showed me most excellent painting in little – in distemper, Indian Incke – water colours – graveing; and above all, the whole secret of Mezzo Tinto and the manner of it, which is very pretty, and good things done with it.[1] He read to me very much also of his discourse he hath been many years and now is about, about Guardenage; which will be a most noble and pleasant piece.[2] He read me part of a play or two of his making, very good, but not as he conceits them, I think, to be. He showed me his *Hortus hyemalis*; leaves laid up in a book of several plants, kept dry, which preserve Colour however, and look very finely, better than any herball.[3] In fine, a most excellent person he is, and must be allowed a little for a little conceitedness; but he may well be so, being a man so much above others. He read me, though with too much gusto, some little poems of his own, that were not transcendent, yet one or two very pretty Epigrams: among others, of a lady looking in at a grate and being pecked at by an Eagle that was there.[4]

Here comes in in the middle of our discourse, Captain Cocke, as drunk as a dog, but could stand and talk and laugh. He did so

1. Evelyn had published a work on engraving, *Sculptura* (1662). This celebrated Prince Rupert's discoveries in the new process of mezzotinting and contained the first example of a mezzotint produced in a book.
2. Evelyn's *Elysium Britannicum* ("British Elysium") on gardening was begun c.1657 but never finished.
3. *Hortus hyemalis* ("Winter Garden") was a large volume of plants collected by Evelyn while in Padua in 1645.
4. "Celia Afraid of an Eagle" is in a manuscript volume of Evelyn's verse.

joy himself in a brave woman that he had been with all the afternoon, and who should it be but my Lady Robinson.[1] But very troublesome he is with his noise and talk and laughing, though very pleasant.

With him in his coach to Mr. Glanvills, where he sat with Mrs. Penington and myself a good while, talking of this fine woman again, and then went away.[2] Then the lady and I to very serious discourse; and among other things, of what a bonny lass my Lady Robinson is, who is reported to be kind to the prisoners, and hath said to Sir G. Smith, who is her great Chrony: "Look, there is a pretty man; I could be contented to break a commandment with him" – and such loose expressions she will have often.

After an hour's talk, we to bed – the lady mightily troubled about a little pretty bitch she hath, which is very sick and will eat nothing. And the jest was, I could hear her in her chamber bemoaning the bitch; and by and by taking her to bed with her, the bitch pissed ⟨and shit⟩ abed, and she was fain to rise and had coals out of my chamber to dry the bed again. This night, I had a letter that Sir G Carteret would be in town tomorrow, which did much surprize me.

13. Up, and to my office, where busy all the morning; and at noon to Captain Cockes to dinner as we had appointed, in order to settle our business of accounts. But here came in an Alderman, a merchant, a very merry man, and we dined; and he being gone – after dinner Cocke and I walked into the garden and there, after a little discourse, he did undertake under his hand to secure me in 500*l* profit for my share of the profit of what we bought of the prize-goods; we agreed upon the terms, which were easier on my side then I expected; and so, with extraordinary inward joy, we part till the evening.[3] So I to the office, and among other business, prepared a deed for him to sign and seal to me about our agreement, which at night I got him to come and sign and seal. And so he and I to Glanvills, and there he and I sat talking and playing with Mrs. Penington, whom we found undressed in her smock and petticoats by the fireside; and there we drank and laughed, and she willingly suffered me to put my hand in her bosom very wantonly, and keep it

1. Wife of the Lieutenant of the Tower; Pepys knew her husband.
2. Pepys was staying temporarily with William Glanville at Greenwich. Judith Penington, daughter of a puritan former Lord Mayor, was another visitor.
3. This proved a smart move on Pepys's part. By selling his goods to Cocke, he helped ensure he would not be a principal target in official enquiries into the fate of the prize-goods. The consequences of the scandal continued to follow Sandwich and others for years.

there long – which methought was very strange, and I looked upon myself as a man mightily deceived in a lady, for I could not have thought she could have suffered it, by her former discourse with me – so modest she seemed, and I know not what. We stayed here late; and so home, after he and I had walked till past midnight, a bright moonshine, clear, cool night, before his door by the water; and so I home after one of the clock.

22. Up, and by water to the Duke of Albemarle and there did some little business – but most to show myself, and mightily I am yet in his and Lord Cravens books; and thence to the Swan and there drank, and so down to the bridge, and so to the Change, where spoke with many people and about a great deal of business, which kept me late. I heard this day that Mr. Harrington is not dead of the plague as we believed; at which I was very glad – but most of all to hear that the plague is come very low; that is, the whole under 1000 and the plague 600 and odd – and great hopes of a further decrease, because of this day's being a very exceeding hard frost – and continues freezing. This day the first of the *Oxford Gazettes* came out, which is very pretty, full of news, and no folly in it – wrote by Williamson.[1] Fear that our Hambrough ships at last cannot go, because of the great frost which we believe it is there. Nor are our ships cleared at the Pillow,[2] which will keep them there too, all this winter I fear.

From the Change, which is pretty full again, I to my house and there took some things, and so by water to my lodging at Greenwich and dined; and then to the office a while and at night home to my lodgings, and took T Willson and T Hater with me and there spent the evening till midnight, discoursing and settling of our Victualling business, that thereby I might draw up instructions for the Surveyours, and that we might be doing something to earne our money. This done, I late to bed. Among other things, it pleased me to have it demonstrated that a purser without professed cheating is a professed loser, twice as much as he gets.

1. Joseph Williamson oversaw the newsbook, which was at first written by Pepys's acquaintance Henry Muddiman (*see* 9 Jan. 1660). When the court returned from Oxford to London in February 1666, the newsbook became *The London Gazette*. From September 1666 until after the end of the diary it was the only English newsbook available.
2. Pillau, a Baltic port.

DECEMBER.

6. Up betimes, it being Fast day,[1] and by water to the Duke of Albemarle, who came to town from Oxford last night. He is mighty brisk, and very kind to me and asks my advice principally in everything. He surprizes me with the news that my Lord Sandwich goes Embassador to Spayne speedily – though I know not whence this arises, yet I am heartily glad of it.[2] He did give me several directions what to do; and so I home by water again, and to church a little, thinking to have met Mrs. Pierce in order to our meeting at night.[3] But she not there, I home – and dined; and comes presently by appointment my wife. I spent the afternoon upon a song of Solyman's words to Roxolana that I have set;[4] and so with my wife walked, and Mercer, to Mrs. Pierces, where Captain Rolt and Mrs. Knipp,[5] Mr. Coleman and his wife, and Laneare,[6] Mrs. Worship, and her singing daughter met; and by and by unexpectedly comes Mr. Pierce from Oxford. Here the best company for Musique I ever was in in my life, and wish I could live and die in it, both for music and the face of Mrs. Pierce and my wife and Knipp, who is pretty enough, but the most excellent mad-hum[ou]rd thing; and sings the noblest that ever I heard in my life, and Rolt with her, some things together most excellently – I spent the night in an ectasy almost; and having invited them to my house a day or two hence, we broke up – Pierce having told me that he is told how the King hath done my Lord Sandwich all the right imaginable, by showing him his countenance before all the world on every occasion, to remove thoughts of discontent – and that he is to go Embassador;

1. For the plague.
2. Sandwich was to be sent to Spain as ambassador-extraordinary to obtain a badly needed commercial treaty. This was, on the face of it, a prestigious appointment but by the end of the month Pepys recognized it as a ploy to get Sandwich out of the way until the scandal over the prize-goods died down.
3. That is, to make arrangements for the evening's gathering.
4. The passage was that beginning "Beauty retire" from Davenant's *The Siege of Rhodes*, Part 2, Act 4. The song has become Pepys's best-known composition. He holds the manuscript of it in his 1666 portrait by John Hayls.
5. Elizabeth (or possibly Mary) Knepp was an actress in the King's Company. She became a friend of Pepys and, to a lesser extent, of Elizabeth.
6. Edward Coleman (a singer in the King's Musick) and his wife Catherine had both sung in the first version of Davenant's *The Siege of Rhodes* in 1656. Nicholas Lanier was Master of the King's Musick.

and that the Duke of Yorke is made Generall of all forces by land and sea, and the Duke of Albemarle Lieutenant-Generall; whether the two latter alterations be so true or no, he knows not, but he is told so[1] – but my Lord is in full favour with the King. So all home and to bed.

25. *Christmas Day.* To church in the morning, and there saw a wedding in the church, which I have not seen many a day, and the young people so merry one with another; and strange, to see what delight we married people have to see these poor fools decoyed into our condition, every man and wife gazing and smiling at them. Here I saw again my beauty Lethulier.[2] Thence to my Lord Brouncker by invitation, and dined there – and so home to my lodgings to settle myself to look over and settle my papers, both of my accounts private and those of Tanger, which I have let go so long that it were impossible for any soul, had I died, to understand them or ever come to any good end in them. I hope God will never suffer me to come to that disorder again.

31. *Lords day.* All the morning in my chamber, writing fair the state of my Tanger accounts, and so dined at home. In the afternoon to the Duke of Albemarle, and thence back again by water, and so to my chamber to finish the entry of my accounts and to think of the business I am next to do, which is the stating my thoughts and putting in order my collections about the business of Pursers, to see where the fault of our present constitution relating to them lies, and what to propose to mend it. And upon this late, and, with my head full of this business, to bed.

Thus ends this year, to my great joy, in this manner: –

I have raised my estate from 1300*l* in this year to 4400*l*. I have got myself greater interest, I think, by my diligence; and my imployments encreased by that of Treasurer for Tanger and Surveyor of the Victuals.

It is true we have gone through great melancholy because of the great plague, and I put to great charges by it, by keeping my family long at Woolwich, and myself and another part of my family, my clerks, at my charge at Greenwich, and a maid at London. But I hope the King will give us some satisfaction for that. But now the plague is abated almost to nothing, and I entending to get to

1. The rumours about York and Albemarle were not true.
2. Anne Lethieulier, a "fat brown beauty" from Pepys's home parish of St Olave. The church on this occasion was St Alfege, Greenwich.

London as fast as I can, my family, that is, my wife and maids, having been there these two or three weeks.[1] The Duch war goes on very ill, by reason of lack of money; having none to hope for, all being put into disorder by a new Act that is made as an experiment to bring Credit to the Exchequer, for goods and money to be advanced upon the credit of that Act.[2] I have never lived so merrily (besides that I never got so much) as I have done this plague-time, by my Lord Brouncker's and Captain Cocke's good company, and the acquaintance of Mrs. Knipp, Coleman and her husband, and Mr. Laneare; and great store of dancings we have had at my cost (which I was willing to indulge myself and wife) at my lodgings. The great evil of this year, and the only one endeed, is the fall of my Lord of Sandwich, whose mistake about the Prizes hath undone him, I believe, as to interest at Court; though sent (for a little palliateing it) Imbassador into Spayne, which he is now fitting himself for. But the Duke of Albemarle goes with the Prince to sea this next year, and my Lord very meanly spoken of; and endeed, his miscarriage about the prize-goods is not to be excused, to suffer a company of rogues to go away with ten times as much as himself, and the blame of all to be deservedly laid upon him.

My whole family hath been well all this while, and all my friends I know of, saving my aunt Bell, who is dead, and some children of my Cosen Sarah's, of the plague. But many of such as I know very well, dead. Yet to our great joy, the town fills apace, and shops begin to be open again. Pray God continue the plague's decrease – for that keeps the Court away from the place of business, and so all goes to wrack as to public matters, they at this distance not thinking of it.

1. Keen to be home, Elizabeth had returned in the first week of December after the bill of mortality for 21–28 November showed a sharp drop to 333 deaths from plague.
2. The Act for an Additional Aid specified that the sums it raised would be for war purposes. It allowed for supplies and money to be advanced to the government on credit, with regular interest payments.

1666

JANUARY. 166$\frac{5}{6}$.

1. *New yeare's Day.* Called up by 5 a-clock by my order by Mr. Tooker, who wrote, while I dictated to him, my business of the Pursers, and so without eating or drinking till 3 in the afternoon, and then to my great content finished it.[1] So to dinner, Gibson and he and I – and then to Copying it over, Mr. Gibson reading and I writing, and went a good way in it till interrupted by Sir W Warren's coming, of whom I alway learn something or other, his discourse being very good, and his brains also. He being gone, we to our business again, and wrote more of it fair; and then late to bed.

5. I, with my Lord Brouncker and Mrs. Williams, by coach with four horses to London, to my Lord's house in Covent Guarden. But Lord, what staring to see a nobleman's coach come to town – and porters everywhere bow to us, and such begging of beggars. And a delightful thing it is to see the town full of people again, as now it is, and shops begin to open, though in many places, seven or eight together, and more, all shut; but yet the town is full compared with what it used to be – I mean the City-end, for Covent Gu[a]rden and Westminster are yet very empty of people, no Court nor gentry being there.[2]◆

7. *Lords day.* Up, and being trimmed, I was invited by Captain Cocke; so I left my wife,[3] having a mind to some discourse with him, and dined with him. He tells me of new difficulties about his goods,[4] which troubles me and I fear they will be great. He tells me too, what I hear everywhere, how the town talks of my Lord Craven being to come into Sir G. Carteret's place; but sure it cannot be true.[5] But I do fear those two families, his and my Lord Sandwiches, are quite broken – and I must now stand upon my own legs.

Thence to my lodging; and considering how I am hindered by company there to do anything among my papers, I did resolve to go away today, rather than stay to no purpose till tomorrow; and so

1. This was Pepys's report on methods for holding pursers to account over wages and victuals. His proposals were largely adopted by the Navy Board.
2. The court did not return to Whitehall until 1 February.
3. Elizabeth was visiting Pepys at his Greenwich lodgings.
4. The contested prize-goods.
5. It was not true.

got all my things packed up – and spent half an hour with W. How about his papers of accounts for contingencies and my Lord's accounts,[1] and so took leave of my landlady and daughters, having paid dear for what time I have spent there; but yet, having beeen quiet and in health, I am very well contented therewith. So with my wife and Mercer took boat, and away home. But in the evening, before I went, comes Mrs. Knipp just to speak with me privately, to excuse her not coming to me yesterday, complaining how like a devil her husband treats her, but will be with us in town a week hence; and so I kissed her and parted.

Being come home, my wife and I to look over our house, and consider of laying out a little money to hang our bedchamber better then it is; and so resolved to go and buy something tomorrow; and so after supper, with great joy in my heart for my coming once again hither, to bed.[2]

25. Up, and to the office. At noon home to dinner. So abroad to the Duke of Albemarle and K. Joyces and her husband, with whom I talked a great deal about Pall's business; and told them what portion I would give her, and they do mightily like of it and will proceed further in speaking with Harman, who hath already been spoke to about it, as from them only; and he is mighty glad of it, but doubts it may be an offence to me if I should know of it; so thinks that it doth come only from Joyce, which I like the better.[3] So I do believe the business will go on, and I desire it were over. I to the office then, where I did much business and set my people to work against furnishing me to go to Hampton Court, where the King and Duke will be on Sunday next. It is now certain that the King of France hath publicly declared war against us, and God knows how little fit we are for it.[4] At night comes Sir W. Warren, and he and I into the garden and talked over all our businesses. He gives me good advice, not to imbark into trade (as I have had it in my thoughts about ⟨Collonell⟩ Norwood) so as to be seen to mind it, for it will do me hurt, and draw my mind off from my business and imbroil my estate too soon. So to the office business, and I find him as cunning a man

1. Howe was Deputy-Treasurer of Sandwich's fleet in 1665.
2. From this day Pepys was back home at Seething Lane after three months in Greenwich lodgings. The Navy Office also returned from Greenwich to Seething Lane.
3. Philip Harman, an upholsterer, was one of several husbands suggested for Pepys's sister Paulina in this year. Kate and Anthony Joyce, cousins of Pepys, were acting as go-betweens.
4. War was declared on 16 January (26 January New Style), after Louis resolved to act on an existing defence treaty with the Dutch.

in all points as ever I met with in my life; and mighty merry we were in the discourse of our own tricks. So about 10 a-clock at night, I home and stayed with him there, settling my Tanger=Boates business, and talking and laughing at the folly of some of our neighbours of this office, till 2 in the morning; and so to bed.

27. Up very betimes to finish my letter and write it fair to Mr. Gawden, it being to demand several queries in the present state of the victualling, partly to the King's [advantage], and partly to give him occasion to say something relating to the want of money on his own behalf.[1] This done, I to the office – where all the morning. At noon, after a bit of dinner, back to the office, and there fitting myself in all points to give an account to the Duke and Mr. Covent[r]y in all things and in my Tanger businesses, till 3 a-clock in the morning; and so to bed, and up again about 6. *Lords day.*

⟨⟨28.⟩⟩ And being dressed in my velvet coat and plain Cravatt, took a hackney-coach provided ready for me by 8 a-clock; and so to my Lord Brouncker with all my papers. And there took his coach with four horses and away towards Hampton Court, having a great deal of good discourse with him – perticularly about his coming to lie at the office; which I went further in inviting him to then I intended, having not yet well considered whether it will be convenient for me or no to have him here so near us. And then of getting Mr. Eveling or Sir Robt. Murry into the Navy in the room of Sir Tho. Harvy.[2] At Branford I light, having need to shit; and went into an Inne doore that stood open, found the house of office, and used it, but saw no people: only after I was in the house, heard a great dog bark and so was afeared how I should get safe back again, and therefore drew my sword and scabbard out of my belt to have ready in my hand – but did not need to use it, but got safe into the coach again. But lost my belt by that shift, not missing it till I came to Hampton Court. At the Wicke found Sir J. Mennes and Sir W. Batten at a lodging provided for us by our Messenger, and there a good dinner ready. After dinner took coach, and to Court, where we find the King and Duke and Lords all in council; so we walked up and down – there being none of the ladies come, and so much the more business I hope will be done. The Council being up, out comes the King, and I kissed his hand and he grasped me very kindly by the hand. The Duke also, I kissed his; and he mighty

1. Gauden was responsible for navy victualling with Pepys overseeing his work.
2. Hervey had recently been appointed a Navy Commissioner. Pepys wanted someone more capable.

kind, and Sir W Coventry. I found my Lord Sandwich there, poor man, I saw, with a melancholy face and suffers his beard to grow on his upper lip more then usual. I took him a little aside, to know when I should wait on him, and where; he told me, and that it would be best to meet at his lodgings, without being seen to walk together – which I liked very well; and Lord, to see in what difficulty I stand, that I dare not walk with Sir W. Coventry for fear my Lord or Sir G. Carteret should see me; nor with any of them, for fear Sir W. Coventry should.[1] After changing a few words with Sir W. Coventry, who assures me of his respect and love to me and his concernment for my health in all this sickness – I went down into one of the Courts and there met the King and Duke; and the Duke called me to him – and the King came to me of himself and told me: "Mr. Pepys," says he, "I do give you thanks for your good service all this year, and I assure you I am very sensible of it." And the Duke of Yorke did tell me with pleasure that he had read over my discourse about Pursers and would have it ordered in my way, and so fell from one discourse to another; I walked with them quite out of the Court into the fields, and then back and to my Lord Sandwich's chamber, where I find him very melancholy and not well satisfied, I perceive, with my carriage to Sir G. Carteret; but I did satisfy him, and made him confess to me that I have a very hard game to play; and told me that he was sorry to see it, and the inconveniences which likely may fall upon me with him. But for all that, I am not much afeared, if I can but keep out of harm's way, in not being found too much concerned in my Lord's or Sir G. Carteret's matters; and that I will not be if I can help it. He hath got over his business of the prizes so far as to have a Privy Seale passed for all that was in his distribucion to the officers, which I am heartily glad of; and for the rest, he must be answerable for what he is proved to have. But for his pardon for anything else, he thinks it not seasonable to ask it, and not useful to him; because that will not stop a Parliaments mouth, and for the King, he is sure enough of him. I did ask him whether he was sure of the interest and friendship of any great Ministers of State, and he told me yes. As we were going further, in comes my Lord Mandeville, so we were forced to break off; and I away and to Sir W Coventry's chamber, where he not come in; but I find Sir W Pen, and he and I to

1. Relations had deteriorated between, on the one side, Sandwich and Carteret, and on the other, Coventry, over matters such as war-reporting, the prize-goods affair, and navy finances. All three were men whom Pepys counted as allies or patrons.

discourse. I find him very much out of humour, so that I do not think matters go very well with him, and I am glad of it. He and I staying till late, and Sir W. Coventry not coming in (being shut up close all the afternoon with the Duke of Albemarle), we took boat and by water to Kingstone; and so to our Lodgeings, where a good supper and merry; only, I sleepy, and therefore after supper I slunk away from the rest to bed, and lay very well and slept soundly – my mind being in a great delirium, between joy for what the King and Duke have said to me and Sir W. Coventry – and trouble for my Lord Sandwiches concernments and how hard it will be for me to preserve myself from feeling thereof.

30. Lay long, till Mr. Gawden was gone out,[1] being to take a little journy. Up, and Creed and I some good discourse, but with some trouble for the state of my Lord's matters. After walking a turn or two in the garden, and bid good-morrow to Mr. Gauden's sons and sent my service to the ladies, I took coach after Mr. Gawden's; and home, finding the town keeping the day solemly, it being the day of the King's Murther;[2] and they being at church, I presently into the church, thinking to see Mrs. Lethulier or Batelier, but did not – and a dull sermon of our young Lecturer to boot. This is the first time I have been in this church[3] since I left London for the plague; and it frighted me indeed to go through the church, more then I thought it could have done, to see so [many] graves lie so high upon the churchyard, where people have been buried of the plague. I was much troubled at it, and do not think to go through it again a good while. So home to my wife, whom I find not well in bed; and it seems hath not been well these two days. She rose, and we to dinner. After dinner up to my chamber, where she entertained me with what she hath lately bought of clothes for herself, and Damaske, linen, and other things for the house. I did give her a serious account how matters stand with me, of favour with the King and Duke, and of danger in reference to my Lord's and Sir G. Carteret's falls, and the dissatisfaction I have heard the Duke of Albemarle hath acknowledged to somebody; among other things, against my Lord Sandwich, that he did bring me into the Navy against his desire and endeavour for another, which was

1. Pepys was staying at Gauden's house at Clapham on his way back from Hampton Court.
2. The anniversary of Charles I's execution.
3. St Olave, Hart Street.

our doting fool Turner.[1] Thence, from one discourse to another, and looking over ⟨my⟩ house and other things, I spent the day at home; and at night betimes to bed.◆

FEBRUARY.

4. *Lords day.* And my wife and I the first time together at church since the plague, and now only because of Mr. Mills[2] his coming home to preach his first sermon, expecting a great excuse for his leaving the parish before anybody went, and now staying till all are come home; but he made but a very poor and short excuse, and a bad sermon. It was a frost, and had snowed last night, which covered the graves in the churchyard, so I was the less afeared for going through. Here I had the content to see my noble Mrs. Lethulier; and so home to dinner, and all the afternoon at my Journall till supper, it being a long while behindhand. At supper my wife tells me that W. Joyce hath been with her this evening, the first time since the plague – and tells her my aunt James is lately dead of the stone, and what she had hath given to his and his brother's wife and my cousin Sarah. So after supper to work again, and late to bed.

19. Up, and by coach to my Lord Sandwiches, but he was gone out. So I to White-hall, and there waited on the Duke of Yorke with some of the rest of our brethren; and thence back again to my Lord's to see my Lord Hinchingbrooke, which I did, and I am mightily out of countenance, in my great expectation of him by others' report;[3] though he is endeed a pretty Gentleman, yet nothing what I took him for methinks, either as to person, or discourse discovered to me – but I must try him more before I go too far in censuring. Thence to the Exchequer from office to office, to set my business of my tallies in doing, and there all the morning. So at noon by coach to St. Paul's churchyard to my bookseller's, and there bespoke a few more books, to bring all I have lately bought to 10*l*. Here I am told for certain, what I have heard once or twice already, of a Jew in town, that in the name of the rest doth offer to give any man 10*l*, to be paid 100*l* if a certain person now at Smirna be within

1. Thomas Turner, currently clerk to the Comptroller of the Navy, and Pepys's neighbour.
2. Daniel Milles, Rector of St Olave's.
3. Hinchingbrooke, Sandwich's eldest son, had been abroad in France and Italy between 1661 and August 1665.

these two years owned by all the princes of the East, and perticularly the Grand Segnor, as the King of the world, in the same manner we do the King of England here, and that this man is the true Messiah.[1] One named a friend of his that had received ten pieces in gold upon this score, and says that the Jew hath disposed of 1100*l* in this manner – which is very strange; and certainly this year of 1666 will be a year of great action, but what the consequence of it will be, God knows.[2]

Thence to the Change, and from my stationer's thereabouts carried home by coach two books of Ogilbys, his *Æsop* and *Coronacion*, which fell to my lot at his lottery; cost me 4*l*, besides the binding.[3] So home.

I find my wife gone out to Hales her painter's, and I after a little dinner do fallow her, and there do find him at work, and with great content I do see it will be a very rare picture.[4] Left her there, and I to my Lord Treasurer's, where Sir G. Carteret and Sir J. Mennes met me; and before my Lord Treasurer and Duke of Albemarle, the state of our Navy debts was laid open, being very great, and their want of money to answer them openly professed – there being but 1500000*l* to answer a certain expense and debt of 2300000*l*.

Thence walked with Fenn down to White-hall, and there saw the Queene at Cards with many ladies, but none of our beauties were there. But glad I was to see the Queen so well, who looks prettily – and methinks hath more life then before, since it is confessed of all that she miscarryed lately – Dr. Clerke telling me yesterday at White-hall that he had the membranes and other vessels in his hands which she voided, and were perfect as ever woman's was that bore a child.

Thence, hoping to find my Lord Sandwich, away by coach to my Lord Chancellors, but missed him; and so home and to office, and then to supper and my Journall, and to bed.

1. Sabbatai Zevi of Smyrna claimed to be the Jewish Messiah and his fame had spread around Europe. Later this year, when threatened with execution, he converted to Islam.
2. 1666 prompted fear and millenarianism because it contained '666', the number of the Beast from Revelation.
3. The publisher John Ogilby ran lotteries to dispose of his stock. Pepys had won two expensive works, *The Fables of Aesop Paraphras'd in Verse* (1665) and *The Entertainment of … Charles II, in his Passage through the City of London to his Coronation* (1662).
4. John Hayls had been hired to paint a portrait of Elizabeth. The original portrait is lost, but the companion piece of her husband survives as the most famous of Pepys's portraits.

23. Up betimes, and out of doors by 6 of the clock and walked (W How with me) to my Lord Sandwiches, who did lie the last night at his house in Lincolns Inne-fields – it being fine walking in the morning, and the streets full of people again. There I stayed, and the house full of people come to take leave of my Lord, who this day goes out of Towne upon his Embassy towards Spayne. And I was glad to find Sir W. Coventry to come, though I know it is only a piece of Courtshipp. I had much discourse with my Lord, he telling me how fully he leaves the King his friend, and the large discourse he had with him the other day, and how he desired to have the business of the prizes examined before he went, and that he yielded to it and it is done, as far as concerns himself, to the full, and the Lords Commissioners for Prizes did reprehend all the Informers in what related to his Lordshipp – which I am glad of in many respects. But we could not make an end of discourse, so I promised to wait upon [him] on Sunday at Cranborne.[1] And took leave, and away thence to Mr. Hales's (with Mr. Hill and two of the Houblons, who came thither to speak with me) and there saw my wife's picture, which pleases me well; but Mr. Hills picture never a whit so well as it did before it was finished, which troubled me – and I begin to doubt the picture of my Lady Peters my wife's takes her posture from, and which is an excellent picture, is not of his making, it is so master-like.[2]

I set them down at the Change, and I home to the office, and at noon dined at home, and to the office again. Anon comes Mrs. Knipp to see my wife, who is gone out; so I fain to entertain her, and took her out by coach to look my wife at Mrs. Pierces and Unthankes, but find her not; so back again, and then my wife comes home, having been buying of things. And at home I spent all the night talking with this baggage and teaching her my song of *Beauty retire*,[3] which she sings and makes go most rarely, and a very fine song it seems to be. She also entertained me with repeating many of her own and others' parts of the playhouse, which she doth most excellently; and tells me the whole practices of the play-house and players, and is in every respect most excellent company. So I supped, and was merry at home all the evening, and the rather it being my Birthday, 33 years – for which God be praised that I am in so good a condition of health and state and everything else as

1. Carteret's residence at Cranbourne Lodge, near Windsor.
2. Elizabeth was posing as St Catherine, having admired Hayls's portrait of Lady Petre in the same pose.
3. Pepys's setting of a passage from Davenant's *The Siege of Rhodes*, Part 2.

I am, beyond expectation in all. So she to Mrs. Turner's to lie, and we to bed – mightily pleased to find myself in condition to have these people come about me, and to be able to entertain them and have the pleasure of their qualities, then which no man can have more in this world.

25. *Lords day.* My wife up between 3 and 4 of the clock in the morning to dress herself, and I about 5, and were all ready to take coach, she and I and Mercer, a little past 5; but to our trouble, the coach did not come till 6. Then, with our coach of four horses I hire on purpose, and Lashmore to ride by, we through the City, it being clear day, to Branford, and so to Windsor (Captain Ferrer overtaking us at Kensington, being to go with us) and here drank; and so through, making no stay, to Cranborne about 11 a-clock, and found my Lord and the ladies at a sermon in the house – which being ended, we to them; and all the company glad to see us, and mighty merry to dinner. Here was my Lord, and Lord Hinchingbrooke and Mr. Sidny – Sir Ch. Herbert and Mr. Carteret – my Lady Carteret, my Lady Jemimah, and Lady Slaning. After dinner to talk to and again, and then to walk in the Parke, my Lord and I alone, talking upon these heads – first, he hath left his business of the prizes as well as is possible for him, having cleared himself before the Commissioners by the King's commands, so that nothing or little is to be feared from that point – he goes fully assured, he tells me, of the King's favour. That upon occasion I may know, I desired to know his friends I may trust to. He tells me, but that he[1] is not yet in England but continues this summer in Ireland, my Lord Orrery is his father almost in affection. He tells me, my Lord of Suffolke – Lord Arlington – Archbishop of Canterbury – Lord Treasurer – Mr. Atturny Mountagu – (Sir Tho. Clifford in the House of Commons), Sir G Carteret, and some others I cannot presently remember, are friends that I may rely on for him. ◆

He told me it would not be necessary for him to tell me his debts, because he thinks I know them so well.

He tells me that for the match propounded of Mrs. Mallet for my Lord Hinchingbrooke,[2] it hath been lately off, and now her friends bring it on again, and an overture hath been made to him by a servant of hers to compass the thing without consent of friends, she herself having a respect to my Lord's family, but my Lord will not listen to it but in a way of honour.

1. Lord Orrery, Lord President of Munster.
2. *See* 28 May 1665.

The Duke hath for this week or two been very kind to him, more then lately, and so others; which he thinks is a good sign of fair weather again.

He says the Archbishop of Canterbury hath been very kind to him, and hath plainly said to him that he and all the world knows the difference between his judgment and brains and the Duke of Albema[r]les – and then calls my Lady Duchess the veriest slut and drudge, and the foulest word that can be spoke of a woman almost.[1]

My Lord having walked an hour with me talking thus, and going in, and my Lady Carteret not suffering me to go back again tonight, my Lord to walk again with me about some of this and other discourse; and then in a-doors and to talk, he alone with my Lady Carteret, and I with the young ladies and gentlemen, who played on the guittarr and mighty merry, and anon to supper; and then my Lord going away to write, the young gentlemen to flinging of cushions and other mad sports. At this late, till towards 12 at night; and then being sleepy, I and my wife in a passage-room to bed, and slept not very well, because of noise.

26. Called up about 5 in the morning, and my Lord upp and took coach a little after 6, very kindly, of me and the whole company. Then I in, and my wife up and to visit my Lady Slaning in her bed, and there sat three hours, with Lady Jemimah with us, talking and laughing. And by and by my Lady Carteret comes, and she and I to talk – I glad to please her, in discourse of Sir G. Carteret, that all will do well with him, which she is much pleased with, having had great noises and fears about his well-doing – and I fear hath doubted that I have not been a friend to him. But cries out against my Lady Castlemayne, that makes the King neglect his business; and seems much to fear that all will go to wrack, and I fear with great reason. Exclaims against the Duke of Albemarle, and more the Duchess, for a filthy woman, as endeed she is.

Here stayed till 9 a-clock almost, and then took coach, with so much love and kindness from my Lady Carteret, Lady Jemimah, and Lady Slaning, that it joys my heart (and when I consider the manner of my going hither, with a coach and four horses, and servants and a woman with us, and coming hither, being so much made of, and used with that state, and then going to Windsor[2] and

1. Albemarle's wife Anne had been a seamstress, so he was seen to have married well below his rank. Their marriage occurred at a point when it was not certain Anne's first husband was actually dead. Commentators noted she was not "cleanly".
2. A stop on their journey home.

being shown all that we were there, and had wherewith to give everybody something for their pains, and then going home, and all in fine weather, and no fears nor cares upon me, I do think myself obliged to think myself happy, and do look upon myself at this time in the happiest occasion a man can be; and whereas we take pains in expectation of future comfort and ease, I have taught myself to reflect upon myself at present as happy and enjoy myself in that consideration, and not only please myself with thoughts of future wealth, and forget the pleasures we at present enjoy).◆

MARCH.

7. Up betimes and to St. James's, thinking Mr. Coventry had lain there, but he doth not, but at White-hall; so thither I went, and had as good a time as heart could wish; and after an hour in his chamber about public business, he and I walked up; and the Duke being gone abroad, we walked an hour in the Matted Gallery, he of himself beginning to discourse of the unhappy differences between him and my Lord of Sandwich, and from the beginning to the end did run through all passages wherein my Lord hath at any time gathered any dissatisfaction, and cleared himself to me most honourably; and in truth, I do believe he doth as he says. I did afterward purge myself of all partiality in the business of Sir G. Carteret (whose story Sir W. Coventry did also run over), that I do mind the King's interest notwithstanding my relation to him; all which he declares he firmly believes, and assures me he hath the same kindness and opinion of me as ever. And when I said I was jealous[1] of myself, that having now come to such an income as I am by his favour, I should not be found to do as much service as might deserve it, he did assure me he thinks it not too much for me, but thinks I deserve it as much as any man in England. All this discourse did cheer my heart, and sets me right again, after a good deal of melancholy, out of fears of his disinclination to me upon the differences with my Lord Sandwich and Sir G. Carteret; but I am satisfied thoroughly, and so went away quite another man, and by the grace of God will never lose it again by my folly in not visiting and writing to him as I used heretofore to do.◆

9. Up, and being ready, to the Cockepitt – to make a visit to the Duke of Albemarle; and to my great joy find him the same man

1. Mistrustful, fearful.

to me that heretofore, which I was in great doubt of through my negligence in not visiting of him a great while; and having now set all to rights there, I am in mighty ease in my mind, and I think shall never suffer matters to run so far backward again, as I have done of late with reference to my neglecting him and Sir W. Coventry.

Thence by water down to Deptford, where I met my Lord Brouncker and Sir W. Batten by agreement, and to measuring Mr. Castles new third-rate ship, which is to be called the *Defyance.* And here I had my end, in saving the King some money and getting myself some experience in knowing how they do measure ships. Thence I left them and walked to Redriffe, and there taking water, was overtaken by them in their boat, and so they would have me in with them to Castle's house, where my Lady Batten and Madame Williams were, and there dined and a deal of doings. I had a good dinner, and counterfeit mirth and pleasure with them, but had but little, thinking how I neglected my business. Anon all home to Sir W. Batten's, and there, Mrs. Knipp coming, we did spend the even-[ing] together very merry, she and I singing; and God forgive me, I do still see that my nature is not to be quite conquered, but will esteem pleasure above all things; though, yet in the middle of it, it hath reluctancy after my business, which is neglected by my fallowing my pleasure. However, music and women I cannot but give way to, whatever my business is. They being gone, I to the office a while, and so home to supper and to bed.

17. Up, and to finish my Journall, which I had not sense enough the last night to make an end of[1] – and thence to the office, where very busy all the morning. At noon home to dinner, and presently with my wife out to Hales's, where I am still infinitely pleased with my wife's picture. I paid him 14*l* for it, and 25*s* for the frame, and I think it not a whit too dear for so good a picture. It is not yet quite finished and dry, so as to be fit to bring home yet. This day I begun to sit, and he will make me, I think, a very fine picture. He promises it shall be as good as my wife's, and I sit to have it full of shadows, and do almost break my neck looking over my shoulder to make the posture for him to work by.[2] Thence home and to the office;

1. Because he had been too exhausted.
2. The portrait by John Hayls, now in the National Portrait Gallery, shows Pepys wearing an Indian gown hired for the occasion, holding his music for "Beauty Retire", and turning sideways to look out at the viewer. It was completed in late April 1666.

and so home, having a great cold, and so my wife and Mrs. Barbary[1] have very great ones – we are at a loss how we all come by it together. So to bed, drinking butter-ale.[2] This day my W. Hewers comes from Portsmouth – and gives me an instance of another piece of knaveries of Sir W. Penn, who wrote to Comissioner Middleton that it was my negligence the other day he was not acquainted, as the Board directed, with our clerks coming down to the pay. But I need no new arguments to teach me that he is a false rogue to me, and all the world besides.

25. *Lady day and Sunday.* Up, and to my chamber, in my gown all the morning, about settling my papers there. At noon to dinner, where my wife's brother, whom I sent for to offer making him a muster-master and send to sea; which the poor man likes well of and will go, and it will be a good preferment to him – only hazardous. I hope he will prove a good discreet man.

After dinner, to my papers and Tanger accounts again till supper, and after supper, again to them; but by my mixing them, I know not how, my private and public accounts, it makes me mad to see how hard it is to bring them to be understood; and my head is confounded, that though I did swear to sit up till one a-clock upon them, yet I fear it will be to no purpose, for I cannot understand what I do or have been doing of them today.

29. All the morning hard at the office. At noon dined, and then out to Lumbard-street to look after the getting in of some money that is lodged there of mine in Viner's hands, I having no mind to have it lie there longer. So back again and to the office, where, and at home, about public and private business and accounts till past 12 at night, and so to bed. This day poor Jane, my old little Jane,[3] came to us again, to my wife's and my great content; and we hope to take mighty pleasure in her, she having all the marks and qualities of a good and loving and honest servant – she coming by force away from the other place where she hath lived ever since she went from us, and at our desire – her late mistress having used all the stratagems she could to keep her.

1. Barbara Sheldon, a friend from Elizabeth's stay at Woolwich, was visiting for a couple of weeks.
2. Hot butter-ale was a cold remedy.
3. Jane Birch, the Pepyses' servant, who had last worked from them in February 1663.

APRILL.

5. Up, and before office time to Lumbard-street; and there at Viner's was shown the silver plates made for Captain Cocke to present my Lord Brouncker; and I chose a dozen of the same weight to be bespoke for myself, which he told me yesterday he would give me on the same occasion.[1] To the office, where the falseness and impertinencies of Sir W Pen would make a man mad to think of. At noon would have avoided, but could not, dining with my Lord Brouncker and his mistress with Captain Cocke at the Sun tavern in Fish-street; where a good dinner, but the woman doth tire me. And endeed, to see how simply my Lord Brouncker (who is otherwise a wise man) doth proceed at the table[2] in serving of Cocke, without any means of understanding in his proposal or defence when opposed, would make a man think him a fool.

After dinner home, where I find my wife hath on a sudden, upon notice of a coach going away tomorrow, taken a resolution of going in it to Brampton – we having lately thought it fit for her to go, to satisfy herself and me in the nature of the fellow that is there proposed to my sister. So she to fit herself for her journy, and I to the office all the afternoon till late; and so home, and late putting notes to *It is decreed, nor shall thy fate*, &c.,[3] and then to bed.

The plague this week is to our great grief increased 9 this week, though decreased a few in the total.[4] And this increase runs through many parishes, which makes us much fear the next year.

11. To White-hall, having first set my people to work about setting my rails upon the leads of my wife's closet, a thing I have long designed, but never had a fit opportunity till now.[5] After having done with the Duke of Yorke, I to Hales's, where there was nothing found to be done more to my picture but the Musique; which now pleases me mightily, it being painted true. Thence home; and after dinner to Gresham College, where a great deal of do and formality

1. A "gift" to Pepys and Brouncker for assistance with Cocke's navy business.
2. The office-table, not the dining table.
3. The words are Catiline's first soliloquy in Jonson's play of that name (Act 1, sc. 1).
4. I.e. in the last bill of mortality the number of plague deaths had increased, although deaths from all diseases had decreased.
5. Railings were put on the flat space on the roof above Elizabeth's private chamber to allow it to better function as a walkway.

in choosing of the Council and Officers. I had three votes to be of the Council – who am but a stranger, nor expected any.[1] So my Lord Brouncker being continued President, I home, where I find to my great content my rails up upon my leads. To the office and did a little business, and then home and did a great Jobb at my Tanger accounts – which I find are mighty apt to run into confusion – my head also being too full of other businesses and pleasures. This noon Bagwell's wife came to me to the office, after her being long at Portsmouth. After supper, and past 12 at night, to bed.

15. *Easter day.* Up, and by water to Westminster to the Swan to lay down my cloak, and there found Sarah alone; with whom after I had stayed awhile, I to White-hall chapel; and there coming late, could hear nothing of the Bishop of London's sermon; so walked into the park to the Queen's chapel and there heard a good deal of their mass and some of their Musique, which is not so contemptible, I think, as our people would make it, it pleasing me very well – and indeed, better then the Anthemne I heard afterward at White-hall at my coming back.

I stayed till the King went down to receive the Sacrament; and stood in his Closett with a great many others and there saw him receive it – which I did never see the manner of before. But do see very little difference between the degree of the ceremonies used by our people in the administration thereof and that in the Roman church, saving that methought our chapel was not so fine, nor the manner of doing it so glorious, as it was in the Queenes chapel.

Thence walked to Mr. Pierce's and there dined, I alone with him and her and their children. Very good company, and good discourse, they being able to tell me all the businesses of the Court – the Amours and the mad doings that are there – how for certain, Mrs. Steward doth do everything now with the King that a mistress should do – and that the King hath many bastard children that are known and owned, besides the Duke of Monmouth. After a great deal of this discourse – I walked thence into the park, with her little boy James with me, who is the wittiest boy, and the best company in the world. And so back again through White-hall both coming and going. And people did generally take him to be my boy – and some would ask me.

Thence home to Mr. Pierce again; and he being gone forth, she and I and the children out by coach to Kensington, to where we were the other day, and with great pleasure stayed till night; and

1. A meeting of the Royal Society. Pepys was first elected to its Council in 1672.

were mighty late getting home, the horses tiring and stopping at every twenty steps. By the way we discoursed of Mrs. Clerke,[1] who she says is grown mighty high, fine, and proud. But tells me an odd story, how Captain Rolt did see her the other day accost a gentleman in Westminster-hall and went with him; and he dogged them to Moore fields to a little blind bawdy house, and there stayed watching three hours and they came not out; so could stay no longer, but left them there. And he is sure it was she, he knowing her well and describing her very clothes to Mrs. Pierce, which she knows are what she wears.

Seeing them well at home – I homeward; but the horses at Ludgate-hill made a final stop, so there I lighted and with a link, it being about 10 a-clock, walked home. And after singing a psalm or two, and supped, to bed.

19. Lay long in bed; so to the office, where all the morning. At noon dined with Sir W Warren at the Pope's-head. So back to the office, and there met with the Comissioners of the Ordnance, where Sir W Pen, being almost drunk, vexed me, and the more because Mr. Chichly observed it with me – and it was a disparagement to the office.

They gone, I to my office. Anon comes home my wife from Brampton – not looked for till Saturday; which will hinder me of a little pleasure, but I am glad of her coming. She tells me Palls business with Ensum is like to go on;[2] but I must give, and she consents to it, another 100*l.* She says she doubts[3] my father is in want of money, for rents come in mighty slowly. My mother grows very impatient and troublesome, and my father mighty infirm, through his old distemper – which all together makes me mighty thoughtful. Having heard all this, and bid her welcome, I to the office, where late; and so home, and after a little more talk with my wife, she to bed and I after her.

23. Being mighty weary last night, lay long this morning then up and to the office, where Sir W. Batten, Lord Brouncker, and I met; and toward noon took coach – and to White-hall, where I had the opportunity to take leave of the Prince, and again of the Duke of Albemarle – and saw them kiss the King's hand and the Duke's. And much content endeed there seems to be in all people at their

1. Wife to Pepys's friend Dr Clarke, royal physician.
2. Robert Ensum, living near Brampton, was a prospective husband for Paulina Pepys.
3. Suspects.

going to sea, and promise themselfs much good from them.[1] This morning the House of parliament have met, only to Adjourne again till winter. The plague I hear encreases in the town much, and exceedingly in the country everywhere.

Thence walked to Westminster-hall; and after a little stay there, there being nothing now left to keep me there, Betty Howlett being gone,[2] I took coach and away home, in my way asking in two or three places the worth of pearl – I being now come to the time that I have long ago promised my wife a necklace.

Dined at home, and took Balty with me to Hales's to show him his sister's picture; and thence to Westminster, and there I to the Swan and drank; and so back again alone to Hales and there met my wife and Mercer – Mrs. Pierce being sitting, and two or three idle people of her acquaintance more standing by. Her picture doth come on well. So stayed till she had done, and then set her down at home; and my wife and I and the girl by coach to Islington, and there eat and drank in the coach; and so home and there find a girl, sent at my desire by Mrs. Michell of Westminster-hall to be my girl under the cook-maid, Susan; but I am a little dissatisfied that the girl, though young, is taller and bigger then Su, and will not I fear be under her command; which will trouble me, and the more because she is recommended by a friend that I would not have any unkindness with. But my wife doth like very well of her.

So to my accounts and Journall at my chamber – there being bonefires in the street, for being St. George's day and the King's Coronation and the day of the Prince and Duke's going to sea. So having done my business, to bed.

28. Up and to the office. At noon dined at home. After dinner abroad with my wife to Hales's to see only our pictures and Mrs. Pierce's, which I do not think so fine as I might have expected it. My wife to her father's to carry him some ruling work[3] which I have advised her to let him do; it will get him some money. She also is to look out again for another little girl, the last we had being also gone home, the very same day she came. She was also to look after a necklace of pearl, which she is mighty busy about, I being contented to lay out 80*l* in one for her.

1. Prince Rupert and the Duke of Albemarle were in joint command of this year's fleet.
2. Betty, whom Pepys affectionately called his "second wife", was the daughter of a shopkeeper at Westminster Hall. She had just married Michael Mitchell, son of Pepys's bookseller there, Ann Mitchell.
3. Work ruling lines on papers.

I home to my business. By and by comes my wife, and presently after that, tide serving, Balty took leave of us, going to sea, and upon very good terms, to be muster-maister of a squadron, which will be worth 100*l* this year to him, besides keeping him the benefit of his pay in the guard.[1]

He gone, I very busy all the afternoon till night – among other things, writing a letter to my brother John, the first I have done since my being angry with him;[2] and that so sharp a one too, that I was sorry almost to send it when I had wrote it; but it is preparative to my being kind to him, and sending for him up hither when he hath passed his degree of Maister in Arts. So home to supper and to bed.

MAY.

1. Up, and all the morning at the office. At noon my Cosen Tho. Pepys did come to me to consult about the business of his being a Justice of the Peace, which he is much against; and among other reasons, tells me as a confidence that he is not free to exercise punishment according to the act against Quakers and other people, for religion. Nor doth he understand Latin, and so is not capable of the place as formerly, now all warrants do run in Latin. Nor is he in Kent, though he be of Deptford parish, his house standing in Surry.[3] However, I did bring him to encline toward it if he be pressed to take it. I do think it may be some repute to me to have my kinsman in commission there – especially if he behave himself to content in the country.

He gone, and my wife gone abroad, I out also, to and fro to see and be seen; among others, to find out in Thames-street where Betty Howlett is come to live, being married to Mrs. Michells son – which I did about the Old Swan, but did not think fit to go thither or see them. Thence by water to Redriffe, reading a new French book my Lord Brouncker did give me today, *L'histoire amoureuse*

1. Pepys this day wrote to recommend Balty to John Harman, Rear-Admiral of the Blue Squadron. Balty already held a position in Albemarle's guards.
2. They had fallen out after their brother Tom's death. *See* 21 March 1664. John was studying at Cambridge.
3. Thomas Pepys ("the Executor") objected to being made a magistrate as he felt unable to impose the Conventicle Act (1664) against nonconformists; he could not read warrants in Latin (which during the Interregnum had been in English); and he had been called to serve by the wrong county. There is no record of his being put on the commission.

des Gaules, being a pretty Libell against the amours of the Court of France.[1] I walked up and down Deptford-yard, where I had not been since I came from living at Greenwich – which is some months. There I met with Mr. Castle and was forced against my will to have his company back with me. So we walked and drank at the Halfway-house, and so to his house, where I drank a cup of Syder; and so home – where I find Mr. Norbury, newly come to town, come to see us. After he gone, my wife tells me the ill News that our Su is sick, and gone to bed with great pain in her head and back – which troubles us all. However, we to bed, expecting what tomorrow would produce. She hath, we conceive, wrought a little too much, having neither maid nor girl to help her.

3. Up, and all the morning at the office. At noon home, and contrary to my expectation find my little girl Su worse then she was, which troubled me; and the more to see my wife minding her painting, and not thinking of her house business (this being the first day of her beginning the second time to paint). This together made me froward, that I was angry with my wife and would not have Browne[2] to think to dine at my table with me always, being desirous to have my house to myself, without a stranger and a Mechanique[3] to be privy to all my concernments. Upon this my wife and I had a little disagreement, but it ended by and by. And then to send up and down for a nurse to take the girle home, and would have given anything; I offered to the only one that we could get 20*s* per week, and we to find clothes and bedding and physic. And would have given 30*s* as demanded, but desired an hour or two's time.

So I away by water to Westminster and there sent for the girl's mother to Westminster-hall to me; she came, and undertakes to get her daughter a lodging and nurse at next door to her, though she dare not, for the parish sake (whose sexton her husband is), to [take] her into her own house.[4] Thence home, calling at my bookseller's and other trifling places, three or four, and so home. And in the evening the mother came, and with a nurse she hath got, who demanded, and I did agree at, x*s* per week to take her. And so she away – and my house mighty uncouth, having so few in it, and we

1. A scandal chronicle by Roger de Rabutin, Comte de Bussy, first published in 1665.
2. Alexander Browne, Elizabeth's drawing master.
3. A man with a manual occupation (not a gentleman).
4. The fear, of course, was that Su had the plague. As a sexton's duties included burials, plague in his household or a quarantine would be especially damaging to the parish.

shall want a servant or two by it. And the truth is, my heart was a little sad all the afternoon, and jealous of myself. But she went, and we all glad of it.[1] And so a little to the office; and so to home to supper and to bed.

9.◆ By coach to Mrs. Pierces, thinking to have gone to Hales's; but she was not ready, so away home and to dinner. And after dinner out by coach to Lovett's to have forwarded what I have doing there, but find him and his pretty wife gone to my house – to show me something.[2] So away to my Lord Treasurer's; and thence to Pierces, where I find Knipp and I took them to Hales's to see our pictures finished; which are very pretty, but I like not hers half so well as I thought at first, it being not so like, nor so well painted as I expected or as mine and my wife's are. Thence with them to Cornehill to call and choose a chimney-piece[3] for Pierce's closet; and so home, where my wife in mighty pain, and mightily vexed at my being abroad with these women – and when they were gone, called them "whores" and I know not what; which vexed me, having been so innocent with them. So I with them to Mrs. Turner's and there sat with them a while; anon my wife sends for me; I come, and what was it but to scold at me, and she would go abroad to take the ayre presently, that she would. So I left my company and went with her to Bow, but was vexed and spoke not one word to her all the way, going nor coming – or being come home; but went up straight to bed. Half an hour after (she in the coach leaning on me, as being desirous to be friends), she comes up, mighty sick with a fit of the Cholique and in mighty pain, and calls for me out of the bed; I rose and held her; she prays me to forgive her, and in mighty pain we put her to bed – where the pain ceased by and by; and so had some sparagus to our beds-side for supper, and very kindly afterward to sleep, and good friends in the morning.

29. *King's Birth and Restauracion day.* Waked with the ringing of the bells all over the town. So up before 5 a-clock, and to the office, where we met; and I all the morning with great trouble upon my spirit to think how I should come off in the afternoon when Sir W. Coventry did go to the Victualling Office to see the state of matters there. And methought, by his doing of it without speaking to me,

1. Su proved not to have plague and she was back working for Pepys nine days later.
2. Lovett was a varnisher, now employed on Pepys's project of varnishing paper on one side to produce a smooth, white surface for writing. The invention did not prosper.
3. A picture over a fireplace, or the ornamental structure around a fireplace.

and only with Sir W. Penn, it must be of design to find my negligence. However, at noon I did, upon a small invitation of Sir W Pen's go and dine with Sir W. Coventry at his office, where great good cheer – and many pleasant stories of Sir W. Coventry, but I had no pleasure in them. However, I had last night and this morning made myself a little able to report how matters were – and did readily go with them after dinner to the Victualling Office; and there beyond belief did acquit myself very well, to full content; so that, beyond expectation, I got over this second rub in this business;[1] and if ever I fall on it again, I deserve to be undone.

Being broke up there, I with a merry heart home to my office; and thither my wife comes to me to tell me that if I would see the handsomest woman in England, I shall come home presently; and who should it be but the pretty lady of our parish that did heretofore sit on the other side of our church over against our gallery, that is since married. She, with Mrs. Anne Jones, one of this parish that dances finely, and Mrs. [2] sister did come to see her this afternoon. And so I home, and there found Creed also come to me; so there I spent most of the afternoon with them; and endeed, she is a pretty black woman – her name, Mrs. Horesely. But Lord, to see how my nature could not refrain from the temptation, but I must invite them to go to Fox hall to Spring Garden, though I had freshly received minutes of a great deal of extraordinary business. However, I could not help it; but sent them before with Creed, and I did some of my business, and so after them and find them there in an Arbour; and had met with Mrs. Pierce and some company with her. So here I spent 20*s* upon them, and were pretty merry. Among other things, had a fellow that imitated all manner of birds and dogs and hogs with his voice, which was mighty pleasant. Stayed here till night; then set Mrs. Pierce in at the New Exchange, and ourselfs took coach and so set Mrs. Horsly home, and then home ourselfs, but with great trouble in the streets by bonefires, it being the King's birthday and day of restoration; but Lord, to see the difference, how many there was on the other side, and so few our, the City side of Temple, would make one wonder the difference between the temper of one sort of people and the other – and the difference among all, between what they do now, and what it was the night when Monke came into the City[3] – such a night as

1. The "first rub" had been an awkward meeting with Coventry over victualling earlier in the month.
2. There is no blank in the manuscript but a name appears to be missing.
3. *See* 11 Feb. 1660.

that I never think to see again, nor think it can be. ⟨After I came home, I was till one in the morning with Captain Cocke drawing up a contract with him, intended to be offered to the Duke tomorrow – which if it proceeds, he promises me 500*l*.⟩

31. Waked very betimes in the morning by extraordinary Thunder and rain, which did keep me sleeping and waking till very late; and it being a holiday, and my eye very sore, and myself having had very little sleep for a good while till 9 a-clock – and so up, and so saw all my family up, and my father and sister (who is a pretty good-bodied woman and not over-thicke, as I thought she would have been; but full of Freckles and not handsome in face); and so I out by water among the ships, and to Deptford and Blackewall about business; and so home and to dinner with my father and sister and family, mighty pleasant all of us – and among other things, with a Sparrow that our Mercer hath brought up now for three weeks, which is so tame, that [it] flies up and down and upon the table and eats and pecks, and doth everything so pleasantly, that we are mightily pleased with it.

After dinner I to my papers and accounts of this month, to set all straight – it being a public fast-day, appointed to pray for the good success of the fleet. But it is a pretty thing to consider how little a matter they make of this keeping of a fast, that it was not so much as declared time enough to be read in the churches the last Sunday – but ordered by proclamation since – I suppose upon some sudden news of the Duch being come out.

To my accounts and settled them clear; but to my grief, find myself poorer then I was the last by near 20*l* – by reason of my being forced to return 50*l* to Downing the smith which he had presented me with.[1] However, I am well contented, finding myself yet to be worth 5200*l*.

Having done – to supper with my father – and then to finish the writing fair of my accounts; and so to bed.◆

Thus ends this month, with my mind oppressed by my defect in my duty of the victualling, which lies upon me as a burden till I get myself into a better posture therein, and hinders me and casts down my courage in everything else that belongs to me – and the jealousy I have of Sir W. Coventry's being displeased with me about it. But I hope in a little time to remedy all.

1. Downing was an anchor-smith who had paid Pepys to help him to a navy appointment, but then been unable to take up the post, meaning Pepys felt honour bound to return the payment.

As to public business: by late tidings of the French Fleete being come to Rochell (how true, though, I know not), our fleet is Divided; Prince Rupert being gone with about 30 ships to the Westward; as is conceived, to meet the French, to hinder their coming to join with the Duch.[1]

My Lord Duke of Albemarle lies in the Downes with the rest, and intends presently to sail to the Gunfleete.

JUNE.

2. Up, and to the office, where certain news is brought us of a letter come to the King this morning from the Duke of Albemarle, dated yesterday at 11 a-clock as they were sailing to the Gunfleet, that they were in sight of the Duch Fleete and were fitting themselfs to fight them – so that they are, ere this, certainly engaged; besides, several do averr they heard the guns all yesterday in the afternoon. This put us at the board into a Tosse.

Presently comes orders for our sending away to the fleet a recruite of 200 soldiers. So I rose from the table, and to the Victualling Office and thence upon the river among several vessels, to consider of the sending them away; and lastly down to Greenwich and there appointed two Yachts to be ready for them – and did order the soldiers to march to Blackewall. Having set all things in order against the next Flood,[2] I went on shore with Captain Erwin at Greenwich and into the parke and there we could hear the guns from the Fleete most plainly. Thence he and I to the King's-head and there bespoke a dish of steaks for our dinner about 4 a-clock. While that was doing, we walked to the water-side, and there seeing the King and Duke come down in their barge to Greenwich-house, I to them and did give them an account what I was doing. They went up to the park to hear the guns of the fleet go off. All our hopes now is that Prince Rupert with his fleet is coming back and will be with the fleet this noon – a message being sent to him to that purpose on Wednesday last. And a return is come from him this morning, that he did intend to sail from St. Ellens point about

1. This division of the English fleet was crucial in the Four Days Battle in early June. The main French fleet was not in fact at La Rochelle, but at Lisbon. On 1 June, two days after Prince Rupert's ships had gone west to try to meet the French, Albemarle sighted the Dutch battle fleet off the North Foreland, Kent. He had 56 ships and the Dutch 86, but nonetheless chose to attack. After days of heavy fighting, Rupert's fleet of 24 joined the battle on the evening of 3 June.
2. The incoming tide.

4 in the afternoon on Wednesday,[1] which was yesterday; which gives us great hopes, the wind being very fair, that he is with them this noon; and the fresh going-off of the guns makes us believe the same.

After dinner, having nothing else to do till flood, I went and saw Mrs. Daniel – to whom I did not tell that the fleets were engaged, because of her husband, who is in the *Royal Charles.* Very pleasant with her half an hour, and so away, and down to Blackewall and there saw the soldiers (who were by this time gotten most of them drunk) shipped off. But Lord, to see how the poor fellows kissed their wifes and sweethearts in that simple manner at their going off, and shouted and let off their guns, was strange sport.

In the evening came up the River the *Katharine* Yacht, Captain Fazeby, who hath brought over my Lord of Alesbury and Sir Thom. Liddall (with a very pretty daughter, and in a pretty travelling-dress) from Flanders, who saw the Duch fleet on Thursdy and ran from them; but from that hour to this hath not heard one gun, nor any news of any fight.

Having put the soldiers on board, I home and wrote what I had to write by the post; and so home to supper and to bed, it being late.

3. *Lords day* ⟨*Whitsunday*⟩. Up and by water to White-hall; and there met with Mr. Coventry, who tells me the only news from the fleet is brought by Captain Elliott of the *Portland*, which, by being run on board by the *Guernsey*, was disabled from staying abroad – so is come in to Albrough. That he saw one of the ⟨Duch⟩ great ships blown up, and three on fire. That they begun to fight on Friday. And at his coming into port, could make another ship of the King's coming in, which he judged to be the *Rupert.* That he knows of no other hurt to our ships.

With this good news, I home by water again, and to church in the sermon time and with great joy told it my fellows in the pew. So home after church-time to dinner. And after dinner my father, wife, sister, and Mercer by water to Woolwich, while I walked by land and saw the Exchange as full of people, and hath been all this noon, as of any other day, only for news.[2]

I to St. Margaret's Westminster, and there saw at church my pretty Betty Michell. And thence to the Abbey, and so to Mrs. Martin and there did what je voudrais avec her, both devante and

1. Correctly, Friday.
2. The Royal Exchange was not open for trading on Sundays.

backward, which is also muy bon plazer.[1] So by and by he[2] came in; and after some discourse with him, I away to White-hall and there met with this bad news farther: that the Prince came to Dover but at 10 a-clock last night, and there heard nothing of a fight – so that we are defeated of all our hopes of his help to the fleet. It is also reported by some victuallers that the Duke of Albemarle and Homes their flags were shot down, and both fain to come to Anchor to renew their Rigging and sails.

A letter is also come this afternoon from Harman in the *Henery* (which is she was taken by Elliott for the *Rupert*), that being fallen into the body of the Duch fleet, he made his way through them, was set on by three fireships, one after another – got two of them off and disabled the third – was set on fire himself; upon which many of his men leaped into the sea and perished; among others, the Parson first – hath lost above 100 men and a good many wounded (God knows what is become of Balty);[3] and at last quenched his own fire and got to Albrough – being, as all say, the greatest hazard that ever any ship scaped, and as bravely managed by him. The mast of the third fireship fell into their ship on Fire and hurt Harman's leg, which makes him lame now, but not dangerous.

I to Sir G. Carteret, who told me there hath been great bad management in all this; that the King's orders that went on Friday for calling back the Prince, was sent but by the ordinary post on Wednesdy, and came to the Prince his hands but on Friday. And then instead of sailing presently,[4] he stays till 4 in the evening; and that which is worst of all – the *Hampshire*, laden with merchants money come from the Streights, set out with or but just before the fleet and was in the Downes by 5 of the clock yesterday morning – and the Prince with his fleet came to Dover but at 10 of the clock at night. This is hard to [be] answered, if it be true.[5]

This puts great astonishment into the King and Duke and

1. "there did what I would with her, both in front and backward, which is also very good pleasure."
2. Mrs Martin's husband.
3. Elizabeth's brother was serving under John Harman in the *Henry*.
4. Immediately.
5. These charges led to one of the most hard-fought controversies of the war and became part of the Commons enquiry into naval miscarriages. When Rupert's recall order was sent, it was not known that battle was imminent. Coventry had drawn up the order late on Wednesday 30 May and, after trouble obtaining a courier, sent it by express post before 1 a.m. Rupert's fleet, off the Isle of Wight, received it at 10 a.m. on Friday 1 June. Rupert did not sail until 4 p.m. because the tides were unfavourable.

Court, everybody being out of countenance. So meeting Creed, he and I by coach to Hide parke alone to talk of these things, and do bless God that my Lord Sandwich was not here at this time – to be concerned in a business like to be so misfortunate.

It was a pleasant thing to consider how fearful I was of being seen with Creed all this afternoon, for fear of people's thinking that by our relation to my Lord Sandwich we should be making ill constructions of the Prince's failure. But God knows, I am heartily sorry, for the sake of the whole nation; though if it were not for that, it would not be amisse to have these high blades find some check to their presumption – and their disparaging of so good men.

Thence set him down in Common Guarden, and so home by the Change; which is full of people still, and all talk highly of the failure of the Prince in not making more haste after his instructions did come, and of our managements herein, not giving it sooner and with more care and oftener thence.

After supper, to bed.

4. Up, and with Sir Jo. Minnes and Sir W Pen to White-hall in the latter's coach – where when we came, we find the Duke at St. James's, whither he is lately gone to lodge. So walking through the park, we saw hundreds of people listening at the Gravell-pits, and to and again in the park to hear the guns. And I saw a letter, dated last night, from Strowd, Governor of Dover Castle, which says that the Prince came thither the night before with his fleet. But that for the guns which we writ that we heard, it is only a mistake for Thunder; and so far as to yesterday, it is a miraculous thing that we all Friday and Saturday and yesterday did hear everywhere most plainly the guns go off, and yet at Deale and Dover, to last night, they did not hear one word of a fight, nor think they heard one gun. This, added to what I have set down before the other day about the *Katharine*,[1] makes room for a great dispute in Philosophy: how we should hear it and not they, the same wind that brought it to us being the same that should bring it to them. But so it is.

Major Halsey, however (he was sent down on purpose to hear news), did bring news this morning that he did see the Prince and his fleet at 9 of the clock yesterday morning, four or five leagues to sea behind the Goodwin. So that by the hearing of the guns this morning, we conclude he is come to the fleet.

After Wayting upon the Duke, Sir W. Penn (who was com-

1. On 2 June.

manded to go to rights[1] by water down to Harwich to despatch away all the ships he can) and I home, drinking two bottles of Cocke ale in the street, in his new fine coach, and so home – where no sooner come, but news is brought me of a couple of men come to speak with me from the fleet. So I down, and who should it be but Mr. Daniel,[2] all muffled up, and his face as black as the chimney and covered with dirt, pitch and tar, and powder, and muffled with dirty clouts and his right eye stopped with Okum.[3] He is come last night at 5 a-clock from the fleet, with a comrade of his that hath endangered another eye. They were set on shore at Harwich this morning at 2 a-clock in a ketch, with about twenty more wounded men from the *Royall Charles.*

They being able to ride, took post[4] about 3 this morning and was here between 11 and 12. I went presently into the coach with them, and carried them to Sumersett-house stairs and there took water (all the world gazing upon us and concluding it to be news from the fleet; and everybody's face appeared expecting of news) to the Privy-stairs and left them at Mr. Coventry's lodging (he, though, not being there); and so I into the park to the King, and told him my Lord Generall was well the last night at 5 o'clock, and the Prince come with his fleet and joyned with his about 7. The King was mightily pleased with this news and so took me by the hand and talked a little of it – I giving him the best account I could; and then he bid me to fetch the two seamen to him – he walking into the house. So I went and fetched the seamen into the Vane-room to him, and there he heard the whole account.

The Fight.

How we found the Duch fleet at anchor on Friday, half-seas-over, between Dunkirke and Oastend, and made them let slip their Anchors – they about 90, and we less then 60. We fought them and put them to the run, till they met with about 16 sail of fresh ships and so bore up again. The fight continued till night, and then again the next morning from 5 till 7 at night – and so too, yesterday morning they begun again, and continued till about 4 a-clock – they chasing us for the most part of Saturday and yesterday; we fleeing

1. Directly.
2. Samuel Daniel, a lieutenant on the *Royal Charles*; known to Pepys because he was the son-in-law of Mrs Clerke, his landlady in Greenwich during the plague.
3. Oakum: hemp fibres, used to dress wounds.
4. Employed post-horses (for speed).

from them. The Duke[1] himself, then those people, were put into the ketch, and by and by spied the Prince's fleet coming – upon which, De Ruyter[2] called a little council (being in chase at this time of us); and thereupon their fleet divided into two squadrons, 40 in one and about 30 in the other (the fleet being at first about 90, but by one accident or other supposed to be lessened to about 70); the bigger to fallow the Duke, the less to meet the Prince. But the Prince came up with the Generalls fleet, and the Dutch came together again and bore toward their own coast – and we with them. And now, what the consequence of this day will be, that we [hear] them fighting, we know not. The Duke was forced to come to Anchor on Friday, having lost his sails and rigging. No perticular person spoken of to be hurt but Sir W Clerke, who hath lost his leg, and bore it bravely. The Duke himself had a little hurt in his thigh, but signified little.

The King did pull out of his pocket about twenty pieces in gold, and did give it Daniel for himself and his companion. And so parted, mightily pleased with the account he did give him of the fight and the success it ended with – of the Prince's coming – though it seems the Duke did give way again and again. The King did give order for care to be had of Mr. Daniel and his companion; and so we parted from him, and then met the Duke and gave him the same account; and so broke up, and I left them going to the surgeon's; and I myself by water to the Change, and to several people did give account of the business; and so home about 4 a-clock to dinner and was followed by several people home, to be told the news, and good news it is. God send we may hear a good issue of this day's business.

After I had eat something, I walked to Gressham College, where I heard my Lord Bruncker was; and there got a promise of the receipt of the fine Varnish – which I shall be glad to have. Thence back with Mr. Hooke to my house, and there lent some of my tables of navall matters, the names of rigging and the timbers about a ship – in order to Dr. Wilkins's book coming out about the Universall Language.[3]

Thence (he being gone) to the Crowne behind the Change, and

1. Albemarle; also referred to as "the Generall".
2. Michiel de Ruyter, Commander-in-Chief of the Dutch fleet.
3. John Wilkins's *Essay towards a Real Character, and a Philosophical Language* was published in 1668. To aid accurate communication and international commerce, Wilkins proposed a new language founded on a systematic classification of knowledge.

there supped at the Clubb with my Lord Bruncker, Sir G. Ent, and others of Gresham College. And all our discourse is of this fight at sea; and all are doubtful of the success, and conclude all had been lost if the Prince had not come in – they having chased us the greatest part of Saturdy and Sunday.

Thence with my Lord Brouncker and Creed by coach to Whitehall – where fresh letters are come from Harwich – where the *Glocester*, Captain Clerke, is come in. And says that on Sunday night, upon coming in of the Prince, the Duch did fly. But all this day they have been fighting; therefore, they did face again, to be sure. Captain Bacon of the *Bristoll* is killed. They cry up Jenings of the *Ruby* and Saunders of the *Sweepstakes*. They condemn mightily Sir Tho. Teddiman for a Coward, but with what reason, time must show.

Having heard all this, Creed and I walked into the park till 9 or 10 at night, it being fine moonshine – discoursing of the unhappiness[1] of our fleet. What it would have been if the Prince had not come in. How much the Duke hath failed of what he was so presumptuous of. How little we deserve of God Almighty to give us better fortune. How much this excuse[s] all that was imputed to my Lord Sandwich; and how much more he is a man fit to be trusted with all these matters then these that now command, who act by nor with any advice,[2] but rashly and without any order. How bad we are at intelligence, that should give the Prince no sooner notice of anything, but let him come to Dover without notice of any fight, or where the fleet were, or anything else; nor give the Duke any notice that he might depend upon the Prince's reserve. And lastly, of how good use all may be to check our pride and presumption in adventuring upon hazards upon unequal force, against a people that can fight, it seems now, as well as we, and that will not be discouraged by any losses, but that they will rise again.

Thence by water home, and to supper (my father, wife, and sister having been at Islington today at Pitts's) and to bed.

5. Up, and to the office, where all the morning – expecting every hour more news of the fleet and the issue of yesterday's fight, but nothing came. At noon, though I should have dined with my Lord Mayor and Aldermen at an entertainment of Comissioner Taylors,

1. Unluckiness.
2. Pepys appears to intend "who neither act by nor with any advice" (i.e. they act without counsel or forethought).

yet, it being a time of expectation of the success of[1] the fleet, I did not go – but dined at home; and after dinner by water down to Depford (and Woolwich, where I had not been since I lodged there, and methinks the place is grown natural to me), and thence down to Longreach, calling on all the ships in the way, seeing their condition for sailing and what they want. Home about 11 of the clock; and so eat a bit and to bed – having received no manner of news this day but of the *Raynbows* being put in from the fleet, maimed as the other ships are – and some say that Sir W Clerke is dead of his leg being cut off.

6. Up betimes, and vexed with my people for having a key taken out of one of the chamber doors – and nobody knew where it was. As also with my boy for not being ready as soon as I, though I called him, whereupon I boxed him soundly. And then to my business at the office and at the Victualling Office; and thence by water to St. James's ⟨(whither he[2] is now gone)⟩, it being a ⟨monthly⟩ Fast day for the Plague. There we all met and did our business as usual with the Duke; and among other things, had Captain Cockes proposal of East Country goods read, brought by my Lord Bruncker; which I make use of but as a monkey doth the cat's foot.[3] Sir W. Coventry did much oppose it, and it's ⟨likely it⟩ will not do – so away goes my hopes of 500*l*.

Thence after the Duke into the park, walking through to White-hall; and there everybody listening for guns, but none heard; and every creature is now overjoyed and conclude, upon very good grounds, that the Duch are beaten, because we have heard no guns nor no news of our fleet. By and by, walking a little further, Sir Ph. Frowde did meet the Duke with an express to Sir W. Coventry (who was by) from Captain Taylor, the Storekeeper at Harwich; being the narration of Captain Hayward of the *Dunkirke*; who gives a very serious account how upon Monday the two fleets [were] fighting all day till 7 at night, and then the whole fleet of Duch did betake themselfs to a very plain flight and never looked back again. That Sir Chr. Mings is wounded in the leg. That the Generall is well. That it is conceived reasonably that of all the Dutch fleet, which, with what recruits they had, came to 100 sail, there is not above 50 got home – and of them, few, if any, of their

1. Outcome for.
2. The Duke of York.
3. In one of Aesop's fables, a monkey uses a cat's paw to get chestnuts out of a fire and avoid being injured himself. Pepys is using Brouncker as his instrument in securing Cocke's contract for Baltic goods, for which he expects a reward.

flags.[1] And that little Captain Bell in one of the fireships did at the end of the day fire a ship of 70 guns.

We were all so overtaken with this good news that the Duke ran with it to the King, who was gone to chapel; and there all the Court was in a hubbub, being rejoiced over head and ears in this good news.

Away go I by coach to the New Exchange and there did spread this good news a little, though I find it had broken out before. And so home to our own church, it being the common fast-day; and it was just before sermon, but Lord, how all the people in the church stared upon me to see me whisper to Sir Jo Minnes and my Lady Pen. Anon I saw people stirring and whispering below, and by and by comes up the Sexton ⟨from⟩ my Lady Ford to tell me the news (which I had brought), being now sent into the church by Sir W Batten – in writing, and handed from pew to pew. But that which pleased me as much as the news, was to have the fair Mrs. Middleton at our church, who indeed is a very beautiful lady. Here after sermon comes to our office 40 people almost, of all sorts and qualities, to hear the news; which I took great delight to tell them. Then home and found my wife at dinner, not knowing of my being at church. And after dinner my father and she out to Hales's, where my father is to begin to sit today for his picture, which I have a desire to have. I all the afternoon at home doing some business, drawing up of my vows for the rest of the year to Christmas. But Lord, to see in what a condition of happiness I am, if I could but keep myself so; but my love of pleasure is such, that my very soul is angry with itself for my vanity in so doing. Anon took coach and to Hales's; but he was gone out, and my father and wife gone. So I to Lovetts, and there to my trouble saw plainly that my project of varnish'd books will not take – it not keeping colour, nor being able to take polishing upon a single paper. Thence home, and my father and wife not coming in, I proceeded with my coach to take a little ayre as far as Bow all alone, and there turned back and home. But before I got home, the Bonefires were lighted all the town over; and I going through Crouched-Friars, seeing Mercer at her mother's gate, stopped and light, and into her mother's (the first time I ever was there) and find all my people, father and all, at a very fine supper at W Hewers's lodging; very neatly, and to my great pleasure. After supper into his chamber, which is mighty fine, with pictures and everything else very curious – which pleased me exceedingly.

1. Flagships.

Thence to the gate, with the Women all about me; and Mrs. Mercer's son had provided a great many Serpents,[1] and so I made the women all fire some serpents. By and by comes our fair neighbour Mrs. Turner, and two neighbour's daughters, Mrs. Tite; the elder of which, a long red-nosed silly jade; the younger, a pretty black girl, and the merriest sprightly jade that ever I saw. With them idled away the whole night, till 12 at night, at the bonefire in the streets – some of the people thereabouts going about with Musquets, and did give me two or three volleys of their Musquetts, I giving them a crown to drink; and so home – mightily pleased with this happy day's news; and the more because confirmed by Sir Daniel Harvy, who was in the whole fight with the Generall, and tells that there appear but 36 in all of the Duch fleet left at the end of the voyage when they run home. The joy of the City was this night exceeding great.

7. Up betimes, and to my office about business (Sir W. Coventry having sent me word that he is gone down to the fleet to see how matters stand, and to be back again speedily), and with the same expectation of congratulating ourselfs with the victory that I had yesterday. But my Lord Brouncker and Sir T. Harvey, that came from Court, tell me quite contrary news, which astonishes me. That is to say, that we are beaten – lost many ships and good commanders – have not taken one ship of the enemy's, and so can only report ourselfs a victory; nor is it certain that we were left maisters of the field. But above all, that the *Prince* run on shore upon the Galoper, and there stuck[2] – was endeavoured to be fetched off by the Duch but could not, and so they burned her – and Sir G Ascue is taken prisoner and carried into Holland. This news doth much trouble me, and the thoughts of the ill-consequences of it, and the pride and presumption that brought us to it.

At noon to the Change, and there find the discourse of town, and their countenances, much changed – but yet not very plain. So home to dinner all alone, my father and people being gone all to Woolwich to see the launching of the new ship, the *Greenwich*, built by Chr. Pett – I left alone with little Mrs. Tooker, whom I kept with me in my chamber all the afternoon, and did what I would with her.[3]

1. A type of firework.
2. On the evening of 3 June, the *Royal Prince*, a first-rate which many considered the best in the navy, ran aground on the Galloper sandbank in the Thames estuary.
3. Daughter of Pepys's neighbour at Greenwich; described as a "child" and "little girle". *See* 11 and 25 Oct. 1665.

By and by comes Mr. Wayth to me; and discoursing of our ill success, he tells me plainly, from Captain Pages own mouth (who hath lost his arm in the fight), that the Duch did pursue us two hours before they left us; and then they suffered us to go on homewards, and they retreated toward their coast – which is very sad news.

Then to my office, and anon to White-hall late, to the Duke of York to see what commands he hath and to pray a meeting tomorrow for Tanger in behalf of Mr. Yeabsly – which I did do, and do find the Duke much damped in his discourse touching the late fight, and all the Court talk sadly of it. The Duke did give me several letters he had received from the fleet and Sir W. Coventry and Sir W. Penn, who are gone down thither for me to pick out some works to be done for the setting out the fleet again; and so I took them home with me, and was drawing out an Abstract of them till midnight. And as to news, I do find great reason to think that we are beaten in every respect, and that we are the losers. The *Prince* upon the Galloper, where both the *Royall Charles* and *Royall Katharine*, had come twice aground, but got off. The *Essex* carried into Holland. The *Swiftsure* misseing (Sir Wm Barkely) ever since the beginning of the fight. Captains Bacon, Tearne, Wood, Mootham, Whitty, and Coppin Slayne.[1] The Duke of Albemarle writes that he never fought with worse officers in his life, not above 20 of them behaving themselfs like men. Sir Wm. Clerke[2] lost his leg, and in two days died. ⟨The *Loyall George*, *Seven Oakes*, and *Swiftsure* are still missing, having never, as the Generall writes himself, engaged with them.⟩

It was as great an alteration to find myself required to write a sad letter, instead of a triumphant one, to my Lady Sandwich this night, as ever on any occasion I had in my life.

So late home, and to bed.

8. Up very betimes, and to attend the Duke of Yorke by order, all of us – to report to him what the works are that are required of us and to divide among us, wherein I have taken a very good share, and more then I can perform I doubt.

Thence to the Exchequer about some Tanger businesses; and then home, where to my very great joy I find Balty come home without any hurt, after the utmost imaginable danger he hath gone

1. The English command took heavy losses: two vice-admirals (Sir William Berkeley and Sir Christopher Myngs) and ten captains died during or after the fight.
2. Secretary-at-War and Albemarle's right-hand man.

through in the *Henery*, being upon the Quarter-deck with Harman all the time; and for which ⟨service⟩ Harman, I heard this day, commended most seriously, and most eminently by the Duke of Yorke. As also, the Duke did do most utmost right to Sir Tho. Teddiman, of whom a scandal was raised, but without cause, he having behaved himself most eminently brave all the whole fight, and to extraordinary great service and purpose, having given Trump[1] himself such a broadside as was hardly ever given to any ship.

Mings is shot through the face and into the shoulder, where the bullet is lodged.[2] Young Holmes[3] is also ill-wounded, and Utber in the *Rupert*.

Balty tells me the case of the *Henery*, and it was endeed most extraordinary sad and desperate.

After dinner Balty and I to my office, and there talked a great deal of this fight; and I am mightily pleased in him, and have great content in and hopes of his doing well.

Thence out to White-hall to a Committee for Tanger, but it met not. But Lord, to see how melancholy the Court is under the thoughts of this last overthrow (for so it is), instead of a victory so much and so unreasonably expected.

Thence, the Committee not meeting, Creed and I down the River as low as Sir W Warren's; with whom I did motion a business that may be of profit to me, about buying some lighters to send down to the fleet, wherein he will assist me.

So back again, he and I talking of the last ill-management of this fight, and of the ill-management of fighting at all against so great a force, bigger then ours. And so to the office, where we parted – but with this satisfaction, that we hear the *Swiftsure*, Sir W Barkely, is come in safe to the Nowre after her being absent ever since the beginning of the fight, wherein she did not appear at all from beginning to end. But wherever she hath been, they say she is arrived there well; which I pray God, however, may be true.[4]

At the office late doing business; and so home to supper and to bed.

13.◆ With Balty to Hales's by coach (it being the seventh day from my making my last oaths, and by them I am at liberty to dispense

1. Lieutenant-Admiral Cornelis Tromp, commanding the Dutch rear squadron.
2. Sir Christopher Myngs died within a couple of days.
3. John Holmes, younger brother of naval officer Sir Robert Holmes.
4. It was not true. Berkeley had been killed and the *Swiftsure* captured by the Dutch.

with any of my oaths every seventh day, after I had for the six days before-going performed all my vows).[1]

Here I find my father's picture begun; and I think so much to my content, that it joys my very heart to think that I should have his picture so well done – who, besides that he is my father, and a man that loves me and hath ever done so – is also at this day one of the most careful and innocent men in the world.

Thence with mighty content homeward; and in my way, at the Stockes, did buy a couple of lobsters, and so home to dinner.

Where I find my wife and father had dined, and were going out to Hales's to sit there. So Balty and I alone to dinner; and in the middle of my grace, praying for a blessing upon (these his good creatures), my mind fell upon my Lobsters – upon which I cried "Cuds zookes!" And Balty looked upon me like a man at a loss what I meant, thinking at first that I meant only that I had said the grace after meat, instead of that before meat; but then I cried, "What is become of my lobsters?", whereupon he run out of doors to overtake the coach, but could not, and so came back again, and mighty merry at dinner to think of my Surprize. After dinner to the Excize office by appointment, and there find my Lord Bellasyse and the Commissioners; and by and by the whole company came to dispute the business of our running so far behind-hand there, and did come to a good issue in it – that is to say, to resolve upon having the debt due to us[2] and the household and the Guards from the Excize stated, and so we shall come to know the worst of our condition and endeavour for some help from my Lord Treasurer.

Thence home, and put off Balty; and so (being invited) to Sir Chr. Mings's Funerall, but find them gone to church. However, I into the church[3] (which is a fair large church, and a great Chappell), and there heard the service and stayed till they buried him, and then out. And there met with Sir W. Coventry (who was there out of great generosity, and no person of quality there but he) and went with him into his Coach; and being in it with him, there happened this extraordinary case – one of the most Romantique[4] that ever I heard of in my life, and could not have believed but that I did see it – which was this.

About a Dozen able, lusty, proper men came to the coach-side

1. This midday coach trip to a portrait artist was apparently against recent vows curtailing his "love of pleasure". *See* 6 June 1666.
2. The Tangier commissioners.
3. St Mary, Whitechapel.
4. Resembling a story of extraordinary adventure.

with tears in their eyes, and one of them, that spoke for the rest, begun and says to Sir W. Coventry – "We are here a Dozen of us that have long known and loved and served our dead commander, Sir Chr. Mings, and have now done the last office of laying him in the ground. We would be glad we had any other to offer after him, and in revenge of him – all we have is our lives. If you will please to get his Royal Highness to give us a Fireshipp among us all, here is a Dozen of us, out of all which choose you one to be commander, and the rest of us, whoever he is, will serve him, and, if possible, do that that shall show our memory of our dead commander and our revenge."[1] Sir W. Coventry was herewith much moved (as well as I, who could hardly abstain from weeping) and took their names; and so parted, telling me that he would move his Royal Highness as in a thing very extraordinary (what was done thereon, see the next day in this book),[2] and so we parted.

The truth is, Sir Chr. Mings was a very stout man, and a man of great parts and most excellent tongue among ordinary men; and as Sir W. Coventry says, could have been the most useful man in the world at such a pinch of time as this. He was come into great renowne here at home, and more abroad, in the West Indys. He had brought his family into a way of being great. But dying at this time, his memory and name (his father being always, and at this day, a Shoomaker, and his mother a Hoymans[3] daughter, of which he was used frequently to boast) will be quite forgot in a few months, as if he had never been, nor any of his name be the better by it – he having not had time to coll[ect] any estate; but is dead poor rather then rich.

So we left the church and crowd, and I home (being set down on Tower hill) and there did a little business, and then in the evening went down by water to Deptford, it being very late. And there I stayed out as much time as I could and then took boat again homeward. But the officers being gone in, returned and walked to Mrs. Bagwell's house; and there (it being by this time pretty dark and past 10 a-clock) went into her house and did what I would. But I was not a little fearful of what she told me but now; which is, that her servant was dead of the plague – that her coming to me yesterday was the first day of her coming forth, and that she had new-whitened the house all below stairs, but that above stairs they are not so fit for me to go up to, they being not so. So I parted thence

1. Service in fireships was the most dangerous of all naval duties.
2. Unfortunately, there is no further mention of this episode in the diary.
3. Master of a small vessel.

with a very good will, but very civil; and away to the waterside and sent for a pint of sack, and so home, drank what I would and gave the waterman the rest, and so adieu. Home about 12 at night, and so to bed – finding most of my people gone to bed.

In my way home I called on a fisherman and bought three Eeles, which cost me 3*s*.

24. *Sunday. Midsummer Day.*

Up, but, being weary the last night, not so soon as I intended. Then being dressed, I down by water to Deptford and there did a great deal of business, being in a mighty hurry – Sir W. Coventry writing to me that there was some thoughts that the Duch fleet were out or coming out. Business being done, in providing for the carrying down of some provisions to the fleet, I away back home. And after dinner, by water to White-hall and there waited, till the Council rose, in the boarden gallery.◆

By and by the Council rises, and Sir W. Coventry comes out and he and I went aside and discoursed of much business of the Navy; and afterwards took his coach and to Hide parke, he and I alone. There we had much talk. First, he started a discourse of a talk he hears about the town, which, says he, is a very bad one, and fit to be suppressed if we knew how: which is the comparing of the success of the last year[1] with that of this, saying that that was good and that bad. I was as sparing in speaking as I could, being jealous of him, and myself also,[2] but wished it could be stopped; but said I doubted it could not, otherwise then by the fleet's being abroad again, and so finding other work for men's minds and discourse. Then to discourse of himself, saying that he heard that he was under the lash of people's discourse about the Princes not having notice of the Dutch being out and for him to come back again, nor the Duke of Albemarle notice that the Prince was sent for back again. To which, he told me very perticularly how careful he was, the very same night that it was to resolve to send for the Prince back, to cause orders to be writ; and waked the Duke,[3] who was then in bed, to sign them; and that they went by express that very night, being the Wednesdy night before the Fight, which begun on the Friday; and that, for sending them by the post express and not by gentlemen on purpose, he made a sport of it, and said, "I knew

1. The Battle of Lowestoft; *see* 8 June 1665.
2. Pepys was wary because he recognized Coventry was not just seeking his opinions, but sounding out his allegiances. Sandwich had been absent at the recent defeat, but present and effective at the Battle of Lowestoft.
3. The Duke of York.

none to send it with but would at least have lost more time in fitting themselfs out then any diligence of theirs beyond that that the ordinary post would have recovered."

I told him that this was not so much the towne-talk as the reason of dividing the Fleete. To this, he told me he ought not to say much; but did assure me in general, that the proposition did first come from the Fleete; and the resolution not being prosecuted with orders so soon as the Generall[1] thought fit, the Generall did send Sir Edwd Spragge up on purpose for them; and that there was nothing in the whole business which was not done with the full consent and advice of the Duke of Albemarle. But he did adde (though as the Catholiques call *le Secret de la Messe*)[2] that Sir Edwd. Spragge, who had even in Sir Chr. Mings's time put in to be the great favourite of the Prince, but much more now had a mind to be the great man with him, and to that end had a mind to have the Prince at a distance from the Duke of Albemarle, that they might be doing something alone, did, as he believed, put on this business of dividing the fleet, and that thence it came.

He tells me, as to the business of Intelligence, the want whereof the world did complain much of, that for that it was not his business, and as he was therefore to have no share in the blame, so he would not meddle to lay it anywhere else.

That De Ruyter was ordered by the States[3] not to make it his business to come into much danger, but to preserve himself, as much as was fit, out of harm's way, to be able to direct the fleet.

He doth, I perceive, with some violence forbear saying anything to the reproach of the Duke of Albemarle, but, contrarily, speaks much of his courage; but I do as plainly see that he doth not like the Duke of Albemarle's proceedings, but, contrarily, is displeased therewith. And he doth plainly diminish the commanders put in by the Duke, and doth lessen the miscarriages of any that have been removed by him.

He concurs with me that the next bout will be a Fatall one to one side or other; because if we be beaten, we shall not be able to set out our fleet again.

He doth confess, with me, that the hearts of our Seamen are much saddened – and for that reason, among others, wishes Sir Chr. Mings alive, who might inspire courage and spirit into them.

1. Albemarle.
2. The secret of the mass is a prayer said by the celebrant in a low voice.
3. The States General, the representative assembly of the Dutch Republic.

Speaking of Holmes,[1] how great a man he is, and that he doth for the present, and hath done all this voyage, kept himself in good order and within bounds – "But," says he, "a Catt will be a Catt still; and some time or other, out his humour must break again."

He doth not dis=owne but that the dividing of the fleet, upon the presumptions that was then had (which I suppose was the French fleet being come this way), was a good resolution.

Having had all this discourse, he and I back to White-hall; and there I left him (being [in] a little doubt whether I had behaved myself in my discourse with the policy and circumspection which ought to be used to so great a courtier as he is and so wise and factious a man) and by water home; and so after supper, to bed.

JULY.

1. *Sunday.* Up betimes and to the office, receiving letters, two or three one after another, from Sir W. Coventry, and sent as many to him – being full of variety of business and hurry; but among the chiefest, is the getting of these pressed men out of the City down the River to the fleet.

While I was hard at it, comes Sir W Pen to town, which I little expected, having invited my Lady and her daughter Pegg to dine with me today – which at noon they did, and Sir W. Penn with them, and pretty merry we were. And though I do not love him, yet I find it necessary to keep in with him – his good service at Sherenesse in getting out the fleet being much taken notice of, and reported to the King and Duke even from the Prince and Duke of Albemarle themselfs, and made the most of to me and them by Sir W. Coventry. Therefore, I think it discretion, great and necessary discretion, to keep in with him.

After dinner to the office again, where busy; and then down to Deptford to the yard, thinking to have seen Bagwell's wife, whose husband is gone yesterday back to the fleet; but I did not see her, so missed what I went for; and so back and to the Tower several times about the business of the pressed men, and late at it, till 12 at night, shipping of them. But Lord, how some poor women did cry, and in my life I never did see such natural expression of passion as I did here – in some women's bewailing themselfs, and running to

1. Sir Robert Holmes, a skilled commander but arrogant and prone to exceeding orders.

every parcel of men that were brought, one after another, to look for their husbands, and wept over every vessel that went off, thinking they might be there, and looking after the ship as far as ever they could by moone-light – that it grieved me to the heart to hear them. Besides, to see poor patient labouring men and housekeepers, leaving poor wifes and families, taken up on a sudden by strangers, was very hard; and that without press-money, but forced against all law to be gone. It is a great tyranny. Having done this, I to the Lieutenant of the Tower and bade him good-night, and so away home and to bed.

6. Up, and after doing some business at my office, abroad to Lumbardstreete about the getting of a good sum of money; thence home, in preparation for my having some good sum in my hands, for fear of a trouble in the State, that I may not have all I have in the world out of my hands and so be left a beggar.[1] Having put that in a way, I home to the office; and so to the Tower about shipping of some more pressed-men – and that done, away to Broadstreete to Sir G. Carteret, who is at a pay of Tickets all alone. And I believe not less then 1000 people in the streets. But it is a pretty thing to observe, that both there and everywhere else a man shall see many women nowadays of mean sort in the streets, but no men; men being so afeared of the press.

I dined with Sir G. Carteret; and after dinner had much discourse about our public business, and he doth seem to fear every day more and more what I do, which is a general confusion in the State. Plainly answering me to the question, Who is it that the weight of the Warr depends? that it is only Sir W Coventry.

He tells me too, that the Duke of Albemarle is dissatisfied, and that the Duchesse doth curse Coventry as the man that betrayed her husband to the sea[2] – though I believe that it is not so.

Thence to Lumberdstreete, and received 2000*l* and carried it home – whereof, 1000*l* in gold, the greatest quantity, not only that I ever had of gold, but that ever I saw together; and is not much above half a 100lb bag full – but is much weightier. This I do for security sake, and convenience of carriage – though it costs me above 70*l* the change of it, at 18½*d* per peece.

That being at home, I there met with a letter from Bab Allen to

1. Lombard Street was famous for its goldsmiths. Pepys's banker Sir Robert Vyner had premises there.
2. The Duchess had been opposed from the first to her husband's appointment as joint commander of the fleet. Coventry was not responsible for this.

invite me to be godfather to her boy with Mrs. Williams; which I consented to, but know not the time when it is to be.[1]

Thence down to the Old Swan, calling at Michells, he not being within; and there I did steal a kiss or two of her,[2] and staying a little longer, he came in, and her father, whom I carried to Westminster, my business being thither; and so back again home, and very busy all the evening; at night, a song in the garden and to bed.

10. Up, and to the office, where busy all the morning sitting. And there presented Sir W. Coventry with my little book made up of Lovetts varnished paper, which he and the whole board liked very well. At noon home to dinner, and then to the office, the yard being very full of women (I believe above 300) coming to get money for their husbands and friends that are prisoners in Holland; and they lay clamouring and swearing, and cursing us, that my wife and I were afeared to send a venison-pasty that we have for supper tonight to the cook's to be baked, for fear of their offering violence to it – but it went, and no hurt done. Then I took an opportunity, when they were all gone into the fore=yard, and slipped into the office and there busy all the afternoon. But by and by the women got into the garden, and came all to my closet window and there tormented me; and I confess, their cries were so sad for money, and laying down the condition of their families and their husbands, and what they have done and suffered for the King, and how ill they are used by us, and how well the Duch are used here by the allowance of their masters, and what their husbands are offered to serve the Duch abroad, that I do most heartily pity them, and was ready to cry to hear them – but cannot help them; however, when the rest was gone, I did call one to me, that I heard complain only and pity her husband, and did give her some money; and she blessed me and went away.

Anon, my business at the office being done, I to the Tower to speak with Sir Jo Robinson[3] about business – principally, the bad condition of the pressed men for want of clothes, as it is represented from the fleet; and so to provide them shirts and stockings and drawers. Having done with him about that, I home, and there find

1. "Bab Allen" was Pepys's nickname for Mrs Knepp, due to her excellent singing of the tragic ballad "Barbary Allen". The burial of her son Samuel was recorded on 16 July at St Paul, Covent Garden, but not his christening – he may have been too ill for this to take place as planned.
2. Betty Mitchell (née Howlett).
3. The Lieutenant of the Tower.

my wife and the two Mrs. Bateliers[1] walking in the garden; I with them till almost 9 at night, and then they and we, and Mrs. Mercer the mother and her daughter Anne, and our Mercer to supper, to a good venison-pasty and other good things, and had a good supper and very merry – Mrs. Bateliers being both very good-humoured. We sang and talked, and then led them home; and there they made us drink, and among other things, did show us in Cages some Birds brought from about Bourdeaux, that are all fat; and examining one of them, they are so, almost all fat. Their name is ,[2] which are brought over to the King for him to eat, and endeed are excellent things.

We parted from them, and so home to bed, it being very late; and to bed.

23. Up and to my chamber, doing several things there of moment. And then comes Simpson the Joyner, and he and I with great pains contriving presses to put my books up in; they now growing numerous, and lying one upon another on my chairs, I lose the use, to avoid the trouble of removing them when I would open a book.[3]

Thence out to the Excise Office about business, and then homewards; met Colvill, who tells me he hath 1000*l* ready for me upon a tally[4] – which pleases me, and yet I know not now what to do with it, having already as much money as is fit for me to have in the house. But I will have it. I did also meet Alderman Backewell, who tells me of the hard usage he now finds from Mr. Fen, in not getting him a bill or two paid – now that he can be no more useful to him. Telling me that what by his being abroad and Shaws death, he hath lost the Ball;[5] but that he doubts not to come to give a Kicke at it still, and then he shall be wiser and keep it while he hath it. But he says he hath a good maister, the King, who will not suffer him to be undone, as other[wise] he must have been; and I believe him.

So home and to dinner, where I confess, reflecting upon the ease and plenty that I live in, of money, goods, servants, honour,

1. Neighbours; daughters of a wine merchant.
2. Possibly "ortolans".
3. The two bookcases he now had made survive in Magdalene College, Cambridge. Thomas Simpson was Master-Joiner at Deptford and Woolwich shipyards.
4. John Colville, goldsmith-banker, offered a loan for Tangier secured on an Exchequer tally.
5. Backwell, a goldsmith-banker, was one of the government's main sources of credit. He had been in Antwerp in summer 1665 when his principal assistant Shaw died, crippling his business. John Fenn was Paymaster to the Navy Treasurer, now neglectful of Backwell's interests.

everything, I could not but with hearty thanks to Almighty God ejaculate my thanks to Him while I was at dinner, to myself.

After dinner to the office, and there till 5 or 6 a-clock, and then by coach to St. James and there with Sir W. Coventry and Sir G Downing to take the ayre in the park – all full of expectation of the fleet's engagement, but it is not yet. ◆

25. Up betimes to write fair my last night's paper for the Duke;[1] and so along with Sir W. Batten by hackney-coach to St. James – where the Duke is go[ne] abroad with the King to the park, but anon came back to White-hall; and so we, after an hour's waiting, walked thither (I having desired Sir W. Coventry in his chamber to read over my paper about the victualling, which he approves of, and I am glad I showed it him first; it makes it the less necessary to show it the Duke at all, if I find it best to let it alone); at White-hall we find [the Court] gone to chapel, it being St. James's day. And by and by, while they are at chapel and we waiting chapel being done, comes people out of the parke, telling us that the guns are heard plain. And so everybody to the park, and by and by, the chapel done, and the King and Duke into the bowling-green and upon the leads (whither I went) and there the guns were plain to be heard (though it was pretty to hear how confident some would be in the lowdnesse of the guns, when it was as much as ever I could do to hear them): by and by the King to dinner, and I waited there his dining; but Lord, how little I should be pleased, I think, to have so many people crowding about me. And among other things, it astonished me to see my Lord Barkeshire, waiting at table and serving the King drink, in that dirty pickle as I never saw man in my life. Here I met Mr. Williams,[2] who in serious discourse told me he did hope well of this fight, because of the equality of force, or rather our having the advantage in number, and also because we did not go about it with that presumption that we did heretofore – when, he told me, he did before the last fight look upon us by our pride fated to be overcome.

He would have me to dine where he was invited to dine, at the backe stayres. So after the King's meat was taken away, we thither, but he could not stay; but left me there among two or three of the King's servants, where we dined with the meat that came from his table; which was most excellent, with most brave drink, cooled in Ice (which at this hot time was welcome); and I, drinking no wine,

1. On the state of navy victualling.
2. Probably Vincent Williams, Groom of the Great Chamber.

had Metheglin[1] for the King's own drinking, which did please me mightily.

Thence, having dined mighty nobly, I away to Mrs. Martin's new lodgings, where I find her, and was with her alone; but Lord, how big she is already.[2] She is, at least seems, in mighty trouble for her husband at sea, when I am sure she cares not for him, and I would not undeceive her, though I know his ship is one of those that is not gone, but left behind without men.[3]

Thence to White-hall again to hear news, but found none; so back toward Westminster, and there met Mrs. Burroughs,[4] whom I had a mind to meet, but being undressed[5] did appear a mighty ordinary woman. Thence by water home, and out again by coach to Lovetts to see my Crucifix, which is not done.[6] So to White-hall again to have met Sir G. Carteret, but he is gone abroad; so back homewards, and seeing Mr. Spong, took him up; and he and I to Reeves the glass-maker's[7] and did see several glasses, and had pretty discourse with him; and so away and set down Mr. Spong in London, and so home, and with my wife late, twatling at my Lady Penns; and so home to supper and to bed.

I did this afternoon call at my woman that ruled my paper to bespeak a Musique Card,[8] and there did kiss Nan.

No news tonight from the fleet how matters go yet.

29. *Lords day.* Up and all the morning in my chamber, making up my accounts in my book with my father and brother, and stating them. Towards noon, before sermon was done at church, comes news by a letter to Sir W. Batten (to my hand) of the late fight – which I sent to his house, he at church: but Lord, with what impatience I stayed till sermon was done, to know the issue of the fight, with a thousand hopes and fears and thoughts about the consequences of either. At last sermon is done and he came home, and the bells immediately rung as soon as the church was done; but coming to Sir W. Batten to know the news, his letter said nothing of it – but all the town is full of a victory.[9] By and by, a letter from Sir W. Coventry tells me that we have the victory. Beat them into

1. Mead with herbs and spices.
2. She was about five months pregnant.
3. Pepys had recently found Samuel Martin a place as a purser.
4. Elizabeth Burrows, widow of a naval lieutenant.
5. I.e. in ordinary clothes.
6. Lovett was varnishing a picture of the Passion of Jesus.
7. Richard Reeve, like John Spong, was an optical-instrument maker.
8. Perhaps a card used for composition.
9. This was the St James's Day Fight of 25 July.

the Weelings.[1] Had taken two of their great ships, but by the orders of the Generals they are burned – this being methought but a poor result after the fighting of two so great fleets; and four days having no tidings of them, I was still impatient – but could know no more; so away home to dinner, where Mr. Spong and Reeves dined with me by invitation. After dinner to our business of my Microscope, to be shown some of the observables of that; and then down to my office to look in a dark room with my glasses and Tube, and most excellently things appeared indeed, beyond imagination. This was our work all the afternoon, trying the several glasses and several objects; among others, one of my plats,[2] where the lines appeared so very plain, that it is not possible to think how plain it was done.

Thence, satisfied exceedingly with all this, we home, and to discourse many pretty things; and so stayed out the afternoon till it begun to be dark and then they away, and I to Sir W. Batten, where the Lieutenant of the Tower was, and Sir J. Mennes; and the news, I fear, is nor more [nor] less then what I had heard before. Only, that our Blue Squadron, it seems, was pursued the most of the time, having more ships, a great many, then its number allotted to her share. Young Seamour is killed, the only captain slain.[3] The *Resolution* burned; but, as they say, most of her [men] and commander saved. This is all; only, we keep the sea; which denotes a victory, or at least that we are not beaten. But no great matters to brag on, God knows.[4] So home to supper and to bed.

AUGUST.

14. *Thankesgiving day.*[5] Up, and comes Mr. Foly[6] and his man with a box of great variety of Carpenters and Joyners tooles which I had bespoke, to me, which please me mightily, but I will have more. Then I abroad down to the Old Swan, and there I called and kissed Betty Michell and would have got her to go with me to Westminster, but I find her a little colder then she used to be methought, which did a little molest me. So I away, not pleased, and to White-

1. The Weilings: the channels south-west of Flushing.
2. Maps or engravings.
3. Four more captains were killed.
4. Although the Dutch had been forced to retreat, the English had missed a chance to inflict a heavy defeat.
5. A celebration in London for the victory of 25 July.
6. Robert Foley, ironmonger to the Navy.

hall, where I find them[1] at Chappell.◆ So to the chapel, and heard a piece of the Dean of Westminsters sermon and a special good Anthemne before the king after sermon. And then home by coach with Captain Cocke – who is in pain about his Hemp, of which he says he hath bought great quantities, and would gladly be upon good terms with us for it – wherein I promise to assist him. So we light at the Change, where after a small turn or two, taking no pleasure nowadays to be there, because of answering questions that would be asked there which I cannot answer.[2] So home and dined. And after dinner with my wife and Mercer to the Beare=garden, where I have not been I think of many years, and saw some good sport of the bull's tossing of the dogs – one into the very boxes. But it is a very rude and nasty pleasure. We had a great many hectors in the same box with us ⟨(and one, very fine, went into the pit and played his dog for a wager, which was a strange sport for a gentleman)⟩, where they drank wine, and drank Mercer's health first, which I pledged with my hat off. And who should be in the house but Mr. Pierce the surgeon, who saw us and spoke to us. Thence home, well enough satisfied however with the variety of this afternoon's exercise; and so I to my chamber, till in the evening our company came to supper we had invited to a venison pasty – Mr. Batelier[3] and his sister Mary, Mrs. Mercer – her daughter Anne, Mr. Le Brun, and W Hewers. And so we supped, and very merry. And then about 9 a-clock to Mrs. Mercers gate, where the fire and boys expected us and her son had provided abundance of Serpents and rockets; and there mighty merry (my Lady Pen and Pegg going thither with us ⟨and Nan Wright⟩) till about 12 at night, flinging our fireworks and burning one another and the people over the way. And at last, our businesses being most spent – we into Mrs. Mercers, and there mighty merry, smutting one another with Candlegresse and soot, till most of us were like devils; and that being done, then we broke up and to my house, and there I made them drink; and upstairs we went, and then fell into dancing (W Batelier dancing well) and dressing, him and I and one Mr. Banister (who with his wife came over also with us) like women; and Mercer put on a suit of Toms, like a boy, and mighty mirth we had, and Mercer danced a Jigg, and Nan Wright and my wife and Pegg Pen put on periwigs. Thus we spent till 3 or 4 in the morning, mighty merry; and then parted and to bed.

1. The court.
2. Questions about navy finances and the conduct of the war.
3. William Batelier, neighbour and wine merchant.

15. Mighty sleepy; slept till past 8 of the clock, and was called up by a letter from Sir W. Coventry; which, among other things, tells me how we have burned 160 ships of the enemy within the Fly.[1] I up, and with all possible haste, and in pain for fear of coming late, it being our day of attending the Duke of York, to St. James's, where they are full of the perticulars – how they are generally good merchant-ships, some of them laden, and supposed rich ships. We spent five fireships upon them. We landed on the Schelling (Sir Ph. Howard with some men, and Holmes I think with others, about 1000 in all), and burned a town – and so came away. By and by the Duke of York with his books showed us the very place and manner – and that it was not our design or expectation to have done this, but only to have landed on the Fly and burned some of their stores; but being come in, we spied these ships, and with our longboats one by one fired them, our ships running all aground, it being so shoal water. We were led to this by, it seems, a Renegado Captain of the Hollanders, who found himself ill-used by De Ruyter for his good service, and so came over to us; and hath done us good service, so that now we trust him, and he himself did go on this expedition. The service is very great – and our joys as great for it. All is, it will make the Duke of Albemarle in repute again I doubt – though there be nothing of his in this. But Lord, to see what success doth, whether with or without reason, and making a man seem wise, notwithstanding never so late demonstration of the profoundest folly in the world.[2]◆

22. Up and by coach with 100*l* to the Exchequer to pay fees there. There left it, and I to St. James's and there with the Duke of York. I had opportunity of much talk with Sir W. Penn today (he being newly come from the fleet); and he doth much undervalue the honour that is given to the conduct of the late business of Holmes in burning the ships and town, saying it was a great thing endeed, and of great profit to us, in being of great loss to the enemy; but that it was wholly a business of chance, and no conduct imployed in it. I find Sir W. Penn doth hold up his head at this time higher then ever he did in his life. I perceive he doth look after Sir J. Mennes's

1. This raid ("Holmes's Bonfire") took place on 9–10 August. The English intended to burn Dutch naval stores on the island of Vlieland. Sir Robert Holmes's squadron sailed into the Fly (the channel between Vlieland and Terschelling), discovered many merchant ships gathered there, and burnt over 100 of them. The next day the English plundered the village of Westterschelling on Terschelling.
2. Pepys was deeply critical of Albemarle's management of the Four Days Battle and the St James's Day Fight.

place[1] if he dies; and though I love him not, nor do desire to have him in, yet I do think him the ablest man in England for it.

To the Chequer, and there received my tallies and paid my fees in good order. And so home, and there find Mrs. Knipp and my wife going to dinner. She tells me my song of *Beauty Retire* is mightily cried up – which I am not a little proud of; and do think I have done *It is Decreed*[2] better, but I have not finished it. My Closet is doing by Upholsters, which I am pleased with, but fear my purple will be too sad for that melancholy room.

After dinner and doing something at the office, I with my wife, Knepp, and Mercer by coach to Moore fields and there saw *Polichinelle*,[3] which pleases me mightily; and here I saw our Mary, our last chamber-maid, who is gone from Mrs. Pierce's it seems. Then carried Knipp home, calling at the Cocke ale-house at the door and drank. And so home and there find Reeves; and so up to look upon the Starrs, and do like my glass very well and did even with him for it, and a little perspective and the Lanthorne that shows tricks[4] – all together costing me 9*l* 5*s*. So to bed, he lying at our house.

26. *Lords day*. Up betimes, and to the finishing the setting things in order in my new closet out of my old; which I did thoroughly by the time sermon was done at church – to my exceeding joy; only, I was a little disturbed with news my Lord Bruncker brought me, that we are to attend the King at White-hall this afternoon, and that it is about a complaint from the Generals[5] against us.

Sir W. Penn dined by invitation with me, his Lady and daughter being gone into the country. We very merry. After dinner we parted, and I to my office, whither I sent for Mr. Lewes[6] and instructed myself fully in the business of the victualling, to enable me to answer in that matter; and then Sir W. Penn and I by coach to White-hall and there stayed till the King and Cabinet was met in the green Chamber, and then were called in; and there the King begun with me, to hear how the victualls of the fleet stood; I did in a long discourse tell him and the rest (the Duke of York, Lord

1. Comptroller of the Navy.
2. His setting of a soliloquy from Jonson's *Catiline*.
3. He had seen Italian puppet plays before but this is his first direct mention of Polichinello, one of the ancestors of the English "Punch". His diary contains the first records of a version of Mr Punch in England.
4. The "perspective" was probably a small telescope. The "lanthorne" was an early magic lantern, which projected images from glass slides onto a wall.
5. Prince Rupert and the Duke of Albemarle, in command of the fleet.
6. Thomas Lewis, Clerk of the Issues in the Victualling Office.

Chancellor, Lord Treasurer, both the Secretarys,[1] Sir G. Carteret, and Sir W. Coventry) how it stood; wherein they seemed satisfied, but press mightily for more supplies; and the letter of the Generals, which was read, did lay their not going, or too soon returning from the Duch coast, this next bout, to the want of victuals.[2] Then they proceeded to the enquiry after the fireships; and did all very superficially – and without any severity at all. But however, I was in pain, after we came out, to know how I had done – and hear, well enough. But however, it shall be a caution to me to prepare myself against a day of inquisition.

Being come out, I met with Mr Moore; and he and I an hour together in the gallery – telling me how far they are gone in getting my Lord's pardon, so as the Chancellor is prepared in it. And Sir H. Bennet doth promote it, and the warrant for the King's signing is drawn.[3] The business between my Lord Hinchingbrooke and Mrs. Mallet is quite broke off, he attending her at Tunbridge, and she declaring her affections to be settled – and he not being fully pleased with the vanity and liberty of her carriage.[4] He told me how my Lord hath drawn a bill of exchange from Spain of 1200*l*, and would have me supplied him with 500*l* of it; but I avoided it – being not willing to imbark myself in money there where I see things going to ruine.◆

Thence Sir W. Penn and I to Islington, and there drank at the Katherine Wheele; and so down the nearest way home, where there was no kind of pleasure at all. Being come home, hear that Sir J. Mennes hath had a very bad fit all this day. And a Hickup do take him, which is a very bad sign – which troubled me truly. So home to supper a little, and then to bed.

SEPTEMBER.

2. *Lords day.* Some of our maids sitting up late last night to get things ready against our feast today, Jane called us up, about 3 in

1. The Secretaries of State, Arlington and Morice.
2. The fleet had been on reduced rations since 2 August and the Dutch fleet was now known to be out, so the lack of victuals was pressing. Pepys's victualling organization was affected by factors including lack of money and bad weather.
3. This was a pardon to Sandwich for the prize-goods affair.
4. Elizabeth Malet married the Earl of Rochester the following year.

the morning, to tell us of a great fire they saw in the City.[1] So I rose, and slipped on my nightgown[2] and went to her window, and thought it to be on the back side of Markelane at the furthest; but being unused to such fires as fallowed, I thought it far enough off, and so went to bed again and to sleep. About 7 rose again to dress myself, and there looked out at the window and saw the fire not so much as it was, and further off. So to my closet to set things to rights after yesterday's cleaning. By and by Jane comes and tells me that she hears that above 300 houses have been burned down tonight by the fire we saw, and that it was now burning down all Fishstreet by London Bridge. So I made myself ready presently, and walked to the Tower and there got up upon one of the high places, Sir J Robinsons little son going up with me; and there I did see the houses at that end of the bridge all on fire, and an infinite great fire on this and the other side the end of the bridge – which, among other people, did trouble me for poor little Michell and our Sarah on the Bridge. So down, with my heart full of trouble, to the Lieutenant of the Tower, who tells me that it begun this morning in the King's bakers[3] house in Pudding-lane, and that it hath burned down St. Magnes Church and most part of Fishstreete already. So I down to the water-side and there got a boat and through bridge, and there saw a lamentable fire. Poor Michells house,[4] as far as the Old Swan, already burned that way and the fire running further, that in a very little time it got as far as the Stillyard while I was there.[5] Everybody endeavouring to remove their goods, and flinging into the River or bringing them into lighters[6] that lay off. Poor people staying in their houses as long as till the very fire

1. The start of the Great Fire of London. It began about 1 a.m. at a baker's in Pudding Lane, near London Bridge in the east of the City. This was less than 450m south-west of Pepys's home. Over five days the wind drove the fire westwards, destroying about 85% of the City of London. The fire also travelled slowly eastwards. By Wednesday it was perilously close to Pepys's home and office in Seething Lane, held off only by desperate fire-fighting measures. On Thursday 6th the worst was over. Only eight deaths were directly attributed to the fire, but 13,200 houses were burnt and upwards of 65,000 people made homeless. The buildings destroyed included St Paul's Cathedral, the Royal Exchange, the Guildhall, and eighty-seven churches. Although the fire had begun accidentally, Londoners suspected a plot by Catholics, the French, or the Dutch. The city ruins remained hazardous for months.
2. Dressing gown.
3. Thomas Farriner.
4. Michael and Betty Mitchell's house, in Thames Street near Old Swan Lane.
5. The Stillyard (or Steelyard) was about 300m west of London Bridge, on the Thames.
6. Boats used to transport goods.

touched them, and then running into boats or clambering from one pair of stair by the water-side to another. And among other things, the poor pigeons I perceive were loath to leave their houses, but hovered about the windows and balconies till they were some of them burned, their wings, and fell down.

Having stayed, and in an hour's time seen the fire rage every way, and nobody to my sight endeavouring to quench it, but to remove their goods and leave all to the fire; and having seen it get as far as the Steeleyard, and the wind mighty high and driving it into the city, and everything, after so long a drougth, proving combustible, even the very stones of churches, and among other things, the poor steeple by which pretty Mrs. [1] lives, and whereof my old school-fellow Elborough is parson, taken fire in the very top and there burned till it fall down – I to White-hall with a gentleman with me who desired to go off from the Tower to see the fire in my boat – to White-hall, and there up to the King's closet in the chapel, where people came about me and I did give them an account dismayed them all; and word was carried in to the King, so I was called for and did tell the King and Duke of York what I saw, and that unless his Majesty did command houses to be pulled down, nothing could stop the fire.[2] They seemed much troubled, and the King commanded me to go to my Lord Mayor from him and command him to spare no houses but to pull down before the fire every way. The Duke of York bid me tell him that if he would have any more soldiers, he shall; and so did my Lord Arlington afterward, as a great secret. Here meeting with Captain Cocke, I in his coach, which he lent me, and Creed with me, to Pauls; and there walked along Watling-street as well as I could, every creature coming away loaden with goods to save – and here and there sick people carried away in beds. Extraordinary good goods carried in carts and on backs. At last met my Lord Mayor[3] in Canning Streete, like a man spent, with a hankercher about his neck. To the King's message, he cried like a fainting woman, "Lord, what can I do? I am spent! People will not obey me. I have been pull[ing] down houses. But the fire overtakes us faster then we can do it." That he needed no more soldiers; and that for himself, he must go and refresh himself, having been up all night. So he left me, and I him, and walked home – seeing people all almost distracted and no manner of means used to quench the fire. The houses too, so

1. Supply "Horsley". The church was St Laurence Pountney.
2. Pulling down houses created a firebreak, if the debris could be removed in time.
3. Sir Thomas Bludworth.

very thick thereabouts, and full of matter for burning, as pitch and tar, in Thames-street – and warehouses of oyle and wines and Brandy and other things. Here I saw Mr. Isaccke Houblon, that handsome man – prettily dressed and dirty at his door at Dowgate, receiving some of his brothers things whose houses were on fire; and as he says, have been removed twice already, and he doubts (as it soon proved) that they must be in a little time removed from his house also – which was a sad consideration. And to see the churches all filling with goods, by people who themselfs should have been quietly there at this time.

By this time it was about 12 a-clock, and so home and there find my guests, which was Mr. Wood and his wife, Barbary Shelden, and also Mr. Moone – she mighty fine, and her husband, for aught I see, a likely man.[1] But Mr. Moones design and mine, which was to look over my closet and please him with the sight thereof, which he hath long desired, was wholly disappointed, for we were in great trouble and disturbance at this fire, not knowing what to think of it. However, we had an extraordinary good dinner, and as merry as at this time we could be.

While at dinner, Mrs. Batelier came to enquire after Mr. Woolfe and Stanes (who it seems are related to them), whose houses in Fishstreet are all burned, and they in a sad condition. She would not stay in the fright.

As soon as dined, I and Moone away and walked through the City, the streets full of nothing but people and horses and carts loaden with goods, ready to run over one another, and removing goods from one burned house to another – they now removing out of Canning-street (which received goods in the morning) into Lumbard Streete and further;[2] and among others, I now saw my little goldsmith Stokes receiving some friend's goods, whose house itself was burned the day after. We parted at Pauls, he home and I to Pauls-Wharf, where I had appointed a boat to attend me; and took in Mr. Carcasse and his brother, whom I met in the street, and carried them below and above bridge, to and again, to see the fire, which was now got further, both below and above, and no likelihood of stopping it. Met with the King and Duke of York in their Barge, and with them to Queen-Hith and there called Sir Rd.

1. Barbara Sheldon, a friend from Woolwich, had recently married Robert Wood, son of William Wood, a timber merchant with whom Pepys dealt. Pepys had met Joshua Moone, secretary to Lord Belasyse, through his Tangier work.
2. Cannon Street ran west–east, about 250m north of London Bridge; Lombard Street was a further 150m north.

Browne to them.[1] Their order was only to pull down houses apace, and so below bridge at the water-side; but little was or could be done, the fire coming upon them so fast. Good hopes there was of stopping it at the Three Cranes above, and at Buttolphs-Wharf below bridge, if care be used; but the wind carries it into the City, so as we know not by the water-side what it doth there. River full of lighter[s] and boats taking in goods, and good goods swimming in the water; and only, I observed that hardly one lighter or boat in three that had the goods of a house in, but there was a pair of virginalls[2] in it. Having seen as much as I could now, I away to Whitehall by appointment, and there walked to St. James's Park, and there met my wife and Creed and Wood and his wife and walked to my boat, and there upon the water again, and to the fire up and down, it still increasing and the wind great. So near the fire as we could for smoke; and all over the Thames, with one's face in the wind you were almost burned with a shower of Firedrops – this is very true – so as houses were burned by these drops and flakes of fire, three or four, nay five or six houses, one from another. When we could endure no more upon the water, we to a little alehouse on the Bankside over against the Three Cranes, and there stayed till it was dark almost and saw the fire grow; and as it grow darker, appeared more and more, and in Corners and upon steeples and between churches and houses, as far as we could see up the hill of the City, in a most horrid malicious bloody flame, not like the fine flame of an ordinary fire. Barbary[3] and her husband away before us. We stayed till, it being darkish, we saw the fire as only one entire arch of fire from this to the other side the bridge, and in a bow up the hill, for an arch of above a mile long. It made me weep to see it. The churches, houses, and all on fire and flaming at once, and a horrid noise the flames made, and the cracking of houses at their ruine. So home with a sad heart, and there find everybody discoursing and lamenting the fire; and poor Tom Hater[4] came with some few of his goods saved out of his house, which is burned upon Fish-street hill. I invited him to lie at my house, and did receive his goods: but was deceived in his lying there, the noise coming every moment of the growth of the Fire, so as we were forced to begin to pack up our own goods and prepare for their removal. And did by

1. Alderman of the nearby Langbourn ward, Justice of the Peace, and a major-general in the City militia.
2. A keyboard instrument.
3. Barbara Wood.
4. Pepys's clerk in the Navy Office.

Moone-shine (it being brave, dry, and moonshine and warm weather) carry much of my goods into the garden, and Mr. Hater and I did remove my money and Iron-chests into my cellar – as thinking that the safest place. And got my bags of gold into my office ready to carry away, and my chief papers of accounts also there, and my tallies into a box by themselfs. So great was our fear, as Sir W. Batten had carts come out of the country to fetch away his goods this night. We did put Mr. Hater, poor man, to bed a little; but he got but very little rest, so much noise being in my house, taking down of goods.

3. About 4 a-clock in the morning, my Lady Batten sent me a cart to carry away all my money and plate and best things to Sir W Riders at Bednall greene;[1] which I did, riding myself in my night-gown in the Cart; and Lord, to see how the streets and the high-ways are crowded with people, running and riding and getting of carts at any rate to fetch away thing[s]. I find Sir W Rider tired with being called up all night and receiving things from several friends. His house full of goods – and much of Sir W. Batten and Sir W. Penn's. I am eased at my heart to have my treasure so well secured. Then home with much ado to find a way. Nor any sleep all this night to me nor my poor wife. But then, and all this day, she and I and all my people labouring to get away the rest of our things, and did get Mr. Tooker[2] to get me a lighter to take them in, and we did carry them (myself some) over Tower-hill, which was by this time full of people's goods, bringing their goods thither. And down to the lighter, which lay at the next quay above the Tower-dock. And here was my neighbour's wife, Mrs. ,[3] with her pretty child and some few of her things, which I did willingly give way to be saved with mine. But there was no passing with anything through the postern, the crowd was so great.

The Duke of York came this day by the office and spoke to us, and did ride with his guard up and down the City to keep all quiet (he being now General, and having the care of all).[4]

This day, Mercer[5] being not at home, but against her mistress order gone to her mother's, and my wife going thither to speak with

1. The merchant William Rider had a country house at Bethnal Green, north-east of the City. The precious items Pepys sent to safety included his diary (*see* 8 Sept. 1666).
2. River agent to the Navy Board.
3. (Hester) Buckworth, wife of a merchant. Her son John was nearly 4.
4. The Duke of York had this day been put in charge of fire-fighting.
5. Mary Mercer, Elizabeth's paid companion.

W. Hewer, met her there and was angry; and her mother saying that she was not a prentice girl, to ask leave every time she goes abroad, my wife with good reason was angry, and when she came home, bid her be gone again. And so she went away, which troubled me; but yet less then it would, because of the condition we are in fear of coming into in a little time, of being less able to keep one in her quality. At night, lay down a little upon a quilt of W. Hewer in the office (all my own things being packed up or gone); and after me, my poor wife did the like – we having fed upon the remains of yesterday's dinner, having no fire nor dishes, nor any opportunity of dressing anything.

4. Up by break of day to get away the remainder of my things, which I did by a lighter at the Iron-gate; and my hands so few, that it was the afternoon before we could get them all away.

Sir W. Penn and I to Tower-street, and there met the fire Burning three or four doors beyond Mr. Howells;[1] whose goods, poor man (his trayes and dishes, Shovells &c., were flung all along Tower-street in the kennels,[2] and people working therewith from one end to the other), the fire coming on in that narrow street, on both sides, with infinite fury. Sir W. Batten, not knowing how to remove his wind,[3] did dig a pit in the garden and laid it in there; and I took the opportunity of laying all the papers of my office that I could not otherwise dispose of. And in the evening Sir W. Penn and I did dig another and put our wine in it, and I my parmazan cheese[4] as well as my wine and some other things.

The Duke of York was at the office this day at Sir W. Penn's, but I happened not to be within. This afternoon, sitting melancholy with Sir W. Penn in our garden and thinking of the certain burning of this office without extraordinary means, I did propose for the sending up of all our workmen from Woolwich and Deptford yards (none whereof yet appeared), and to write to Sir W. Coventry to have the Duke of York's permission to pull down houses rather then lose this office, which would much hinder the King's business. So Sir W. Penn he went down this night, in order to the sending them up tomorrow morning; and I wrote to Sir W. Coventry about the business, but received no answer.

This night Mrs. Turner[5] (who, poor woman, was removing her

1. Richard Howell, turner to the Navy Board.
2. Drainage gutters.
3. Wine.
4. An expensive delicacy.
5. Elizabeth Turner, neighbour; the wife of Thomas, a navy clerk.

goods all this day – good goods, into the garden, and knew not how to dispose of them) – and her husband supped with my wife and I at night in the office, upon a shoulder of mutton from the cook's, without any napkin or anything, in a sad manner but were merry. Only, now and then walking into the garden and saw how horridly the sky looks, all on a fire in the night, was enough to put us out of our wits; and endeed it was extremely dreadfull – for it looks just as if it was at us, and the whole heaven on fire. I after supper walked in the dark down to Tower-street, and there saw it all on fire at the Trinity house on that side and the Dolphin tavern on this side, which was very near us – and the fire with extraordinary vehemence. Now begins the practice of blowing up of houses in Tower-street, those next the Tower, which at first did frighten people more then anything;[1] but it stop[ped] the fire where it was done – it bringing down the houses to the ground in the same places they stood, and then it was easy to quench what little fire was in it, though it kindled nothing almost. W. Hewer this day went to see how his mother did, and comes late home, but telling us how he hath been forced to remove her to Islington, her house in pye=Corner being burned. So that it is got so far that way and all the Old Bayly, and was running down to Fleetestreete. And Pauls is burned, and all Cheapside. I wrote to my father this night; but the post-house being burned, the letter could not go.

5. I lay down in the office again upon W. Hewer's quilt, being mighty weary and sore in my feet with going till I was hardly able to stand. About 2 in the morning my wife calls me up and tells of new Cryes of "Fyre!" – it being come to Barkeing Church,[2] which is the bottom of our lane. I up; and finding it so, resolved presently to take her away; and did, and took my gold (which was about 2350*l*), W. Hewer, and Jane down by Poundy's boat to Woolwich. But Lord, what a sad sight it was by moonlight to see the whole City almost on fire – that you might see it plain at Woolwich, as if you were by it. There when I came, I find the gates[3] shut, but no guard kept at all; which troubled me, because of discourses now begun that there is plot in it and that the French had done it. I got the gates open, and to Mr. Shelden's,[4] where I locked up my gold

1. This was done to protect the Tower of London. The Tower usually held gunpowder stores, though as the fire approached these had been removed.
2. All Hallows Barking, about 150m from the navy buildings.
3. Of the dockyard.
4. Clerk of the Cheque at Woolwich and Elizabeth's host during the plague. She now appears to have stayed there until 13 September.

and charged my wife and W. Hewer never to leave the room without one of them in it night nor day. So back again, by the way seeing my goods well in the lighters at Deptford and watched well by people. Home, and whereas I expected to have seen our house on fire, it being now about 7 a-clock, it was not. But to the Fyre, and there find greater hopes then I expected; for my confidence of finding our office on fire was such, that I durst not ask anybody how it was with us, till I came and saw it not burned. But going to the fire, I find, by the blowing up of houses and the great help given by the workmen out of the King's yards, sent up by Sir W. Penn, there is a good stop given to it, as well at Marke-lane end as ours – it having only burned the Dyall of Barkeing Church, and part of the porch, and was there quenched. I up to the top of Barkeing steeple, and there saw the saddest sight of desolation that I ever saw. Everywhere great fires. Oyle-cellars and brimstone and other things burning. I became afeared to stay there long; and therefore down again as fast as I could, the fire being spread as far as I could see it, and to Sir W. Penn's and there eat a piece of cold meat, having eaten nothing since Sunday but the remains of Sunday's dinner.

Here I met with Mr. Young and Whistler;[1] and having removed all my things, and received good hopes that the fire at our end is stopped, they and I walked into the town and find Fanchurch-street, Gracious-street, and Lumbard-street all in dust. The Exchange a sad sight, nothing standing there of all the statues or pillars but Sir Tho. Gresham's[2] picture in the corner. Walked into Moore-fields (our feet ready to burn, walking through the town among the hot coles) and find that full of people, and poor wretches carrying their goods there, and everybody keeping his goods together by themselfs (and a great blessing it is to them that it is fair weather for them to keep abroad night and day); drank there, and paid twopence for a plain penny loaf.

Thence homeward, having passed through Cheapside and Newgate-market, all burned – and seen Anthony Joyces house in fire. And took up (which I keep by me) a piece of glass of Mercer's chapel[3] in the street, where much more was, so melted and buckled with the heat of the fire, like parchment. I also did see a poor Catt taken out of a hole in the chimney joyning to the wall of the Exchange, with the hair all burned off the body and yet alive. So home at night, and find there good hopes of saving our office – but

1. Flagmakers for the navy.
2. Gresham (d. 1579) was the founder of the Royal Exchange.
3. The Mercers' Company chapel on Cheapside.

great endeavours of watching all night and having men ready; and so we lodged them in the office, and had drink and bread and cheese for them. And I lay down and slept a good night about midnight – though when I rose, I hear that there had been a great alarme of French and Duch being risen – which proved nothing. But it is a strange thing to see how long this time did look since Sunday, having been alway full of variety of actions, and little sleep, that it looked like a week or more. And I had forgot almost the day of the week.

6. Up about 5 a-clock, and there met Mr Gawden at the gate of the office (I entending to go out, as I used every now and then to do, to see how the fire is) to call our men to Bishopps-gate, where no fire had yet been near, and there is now one broke out – which did give great grounds to people, and to me too, to think that there is some kind of plott in this (on which many by this time have been taken, and it hath been dangerous for any stranger to walk in the streets);[1] but I went with the men and we did put it out in a little time, so that that was well again. It was pretty to see how hard the women did work in the cannells[2] sweeping of water; but then they would scold for drink and be as drunk as devils. I saw good Butts of sugar broke open in the street, and people go and take handfuls out and put into beer and drink it. And now all being pretty well, I took boat and over to Southwarke, and took boat on the other side the bridge and so to Westminster, thinking to Shift[3] myself, being all in dirt from top to bottom. But could not there find any place to buy a Shirt or pair of gloves, Westminster-hall being full of people's goods – those in Westminster having removed all their goods, and the Exchequer money put into vessels to carry to Nonsuch. But to the Swan, and there was trimmed. And then to Whitehall, but saw nobody, and so home. A sad sight to see how the River looks – no houses nor church near it to the Temple – where it stopped.[4] At home did go with Sir W. Batten and our neighbour Knightly (who, with one more, was the only man of any fashion left in all the neighbourhood hereabouts, they all removing their goods and leaving their houses to the mercy of the fire) to Sir R. Ford's, and there dined, in an earthen platter a fried breast of

1. There were multiple reports of crowds attacking foreigners and individuals they deemed suspicious.
2. Drainage gutters.
3. Change.
4. In the west the fire was stopped partway down Fleet Street, burning some of the Temple area but not the Temple church.

mutton, a great many of us. But very merry; and endeed as good a meal, though as ugly a one, as ever I had in my life. Thence down to Deptford, and there with great satisfaction landed all my goods at Sir G Carteret's,[1] safe, and nothing missed I could see, or hurt. This being done to my great content, I home; and to Sir W. Batten's, and there with Sir R. Ford, Mr Knightly, and one Withers, a professed lying rogue, supped well; and mighty merry and our fears over. From them to the office and there slept, with the office full of labourers, who talked and slept and walked all night long there. But strange it was to see Cloathworkers-hall on fire these three days and nights in one body of Flame – it being the cellar, full of Oyle.

7. Up by 5 a-clock and, blessed be God, find all well, and by water to Paul's wharfe. Walked thence and saw all the town burned, and a miserable sight of Pauls church, with all the roofs fallen and the body of the Quire fallen into St Fayths[2] – Paul's school[3] also – Ludgate – Fleet street – my father's house, and the church, and a good part of the Temple the like. So to Creeds lodging near the New Exchange, and there find him laid down upon a bed – the house all unfurnished, there being fears of the fire's coming to them. There borrowed a shirt of him – and washed. To Sir W. Coventry at St. James's, who lay without Curtains, having removed all his goods – as the King at White-hall and everybody had done and was doing. He hopes we shall have no public distractions upon this fire, which is what everybody fears – because of the talk of the French having a hand in it. And it is a proper time for discontents – but all men's minds are full of care to protect themselfs and save their goods. The Militia is in armes everywhere. Our Fleetes, he tells me, have been in sight one of another, and most unhappily by Fowle weather were parted, to our great loss, as in reason they do conclude – the Duch being come out only to make a show and please their people; but in very bad condition as to stores, victuals, and men. They are at Bullen,[4] and our fleet come to St. Ellens.[5] We have got nothing, but have lost one ship, but he knows not what.

Thence to the Swan and there drank; and so home and find all well. My Lord Brouncker at Sir W. Batten's, and tells us the

1. He had an official residence there, as Navy Treasurer.
2. "St-Faith's-under-St-Pauls" was the popular name for the crypt under the choir of the cathedral.
3. Pepys's own school.
4. Boulogne, France.
5. St Helen's Road, off the Isle of Wight.

Generall is sent for up to come to advise with the King about business at this juncture, and to keep all quiet – which is great honour to him, but I am sure is but a piece of dissimulation.[1] So home and did give order for my house to be made clean; and then down to Woolwich and there find all well. Dined, and Mrs. Markeham came to see my wife. So I up again, and calling at Deptford for some things of W. Hewer, he being with me; and then home and spent the evening with Sir R. Ford, Mr. Knightly, and Sir W. Penn at Sir W. Batten's. This day our Merchants first met at Gresham College, which by proclamation is to be their Exchange.[2] Strange to hear what is bid for houses all up and down here – a friend of Sir W Riders having 150*l* for what he used to let for 40*l* per annum. Much dispute where the Custome-house shall be; thereby the growth of the City again to be foreseen. My Lord Treasurer, they say, and others, would have it at the other end of the town. I home late to Sir W. Penn, who did give me a bed – but without curtains or hangings, all being down. So here I went the first time[3] into a naked bed, only my drawers on – and did sleep pretty well; but still, both sleeping and waking, had a fear of fire in my heart, that I took little rest. People do all the world over cry out of the simplicity of my Lord Mayor in general, and more perticularly in this business of the fire, laying it all upon him. A proclamation is come out for markets to be kept at Leaden hall and Mile=end greene and several other places about the town, and Tower hill, and all churches to be set open to receive poor people.

8. Up, and with Sir W. Batten and Sir W. Penn by water to Whitehall, and they to St. James's. I stopped with Sir G Carteret, to desire him to go with us and to enquire after money. But the first he cannot do, and the other as little, or says, "When can we get any, or what shall we do for it?" He, it seems, is imployed in the correspondence between the City and the King every day, in settling of things. I find him full of trouble to think how things will go. I left him, and to St. James's, where we met first at Sir W. Coventry's chamber and there did what business we can without any books. Our discourse, as everything else, was confused. The fleet is at

1. The Duke of Albemarle was summoned from Plymouth. Rather than it being a ploy, his presence was genuinely wanted as he was much respected by the London public.
2. The Royal Exchange – the bourse and many of the shops – relocated to the buildings of Gresham's College, a short walk away from its old site. This remained "the Exchange" until after the end of the diary. It also doubled as the Guildhall.
3. I.e. since the fire.

Portsmouth, there staying a wind to carry them to the Downes or toward Bullen, where they say the Dutch fleete is gone and stays. We concluded upon private meetings for a while, not having any money to satisfy any people that may come to us. I bought two eeles upon the Thames, cost me *6s.*[1] Thence with Sir W. Batten to the Cockpit, whither the Duke of Albemarle is come. It seems the King holds him so necessary at this time, that he hath sent for him and will keep ⟨him⟩ here. Endeed, his interest in the City, being acquainted, and his care in keeping things quiet, is reckoned that wherein he will be very serviceable. We to him. He is courted in appearance by everybody. He very kind to us. I perceive he lays by all business of the fleet at present and minds the City, and is now hastening to Gresham-College to discourse with the Aldermen. Sir W. Batten and I home (where met by my Brother John, come to town to see how things are with us). And then presently he with me to Gresham-College – where infinite of people; partly through novelty to see the new place, and partly to find out and hear what is become one man of another. I met with many people undone, and more that have extraordinary great losses. People speaking their thoughts variously about the beginning of the fire and the rebuilding of the City. Then to Sir W. Batten and took my brother with me, and there dined with a great company of neighbours, and much good discourse; among others, of the low spirits of some rich men in the City, in sparing any encouragement to the poor people that wrought for the saving their houses. Among others, Alderman Starling, a very rich man, without children, the fire at next door to him in our Lane – after our men had saved his house, did give *2s 6d* among 30 of them, and did quarrel with some that would remove the rubbish out of the way of the fire, saying that they came to steal. Sir W. Coventry told me of another this morning in Holborne, which he showed the King – that when it was offered to stop the fire near his house for such a reward, that came but to *2s 6d* a man among the neighbours, he would give but *18d.* Thence to Bednall-green by coach, my brother with me, and saw all well there and fetched away my Journall-book to enter for five days past; and then back to the office, where I find Bagwells wife and her husband come home. Agreed to come [to] their house tomorrow, I sending him away back to his ship today. To the office, and late writing letters; and then to Sir W. Penn, my brother lying with me, and Sir W. Penn gone down to rest himself at Woolwich. But I was much

1. Three times what he had paid on 13 June: the fire had raised prices.

frighted, and kept awake in my bed, by some noise I heard a great while below-stairs and the boys not coming up to me when I knocked. It was by their discovery of people stealing of some neighbours' wine that lay in vessels in the street. So to sleep. And all well all night.

9. *Sunday.* Up, and was trimmed, and sent my brother to Woolwich to my wife to dine with her. I to church, where our parson made a melancholy but good sermon – and many, and most, in the church cried, especially the women. The church mighty full, but few of fashion, and most strangers. I walked to Bednall-green; and there dined well, but a bad venison pasty, at Sir W Rider's. Good people they are, and good discourse. And his daughter Middleton, a fine woman and discreet.[1] Thence home, and to church again, and there preached Deane Harding;[2] but methinks a bad poor sermon, though proper for the time – nor eloquent, in saying at this time that the City is reduced from a large Folio to a Decimo tertio.[3] So to my office, there to write down my journall and take leave of my brother, whom I sent back this afternoon, though rainy – which it hath not done a good while before. But I had no room nor convenience for him here till my house is fitted; but I was very kind to him, and do take very well of him his journey. I did give him 40*s* for his pocket; and so he being gone, and it presently rayning, I was troubled for him, though it is good for the Fyre. Anon to Sir W. Penn to bed, and made my boy Tom to read me asleep.

10. All the morning clearing our cellars and breaking in pieces all my old Lumber, to make room and to prevent fire. And then to Sir W. Batten and dined, and there hear that Sir W Rider says that the town is full of the report of the wealth that is in his house, and would be glad that his friends would provide for the safety of their goods there. This made me get a cart; and thither, and there brought my money all away – took a hackney-coach myself (the hackney-coaches now standing at Allgate); much wealth endeed there is at his house. Blessed be God, I got all mine well thence and lodged it in my office; but vexed to have all the world see it – and

1. Discerning.
2. Nathaniel Hardy, Dean of Rochester.
3. I.e. from a large work to a small one – it was supposed to be a mathematically accurate comparison. The published version of the sermon described the City as a "Folio abridged almost to an Octavo, there being, as is probably computed, scarce a sixth part remaining within the Walls". "Decimo tertio" is not a standard book format, so either Pepys misremembered or Hardy revised in response to booklovers' criticisms of his ineloquence.

with Sir W. Batten, who would have taken away my hands[1] before they were stowed. But by and by comes Brother Balty from sea, which I was glad of; and so got him and Mr. Tooker and the boy to watch with them all in the office all night, while I, upon Janes coming, went down to my wife; calling at Deptford, intending to Bagwell, but did not ouvrir la porta como yo did expect.[2] So down late to Woolwich, and there find my wife out of humour and indifferent, as she uses upon her having much liberty abroad.

12. Up and with Sir W. Batten [and] Sir W. Penn to St James's by water, and there did our usual business with the Duke of York. Thence I to Westminster, and there speak with Michell and Howlett, who tell me how their poor young ones are going to Shadwell.[3] The latter told me of the unkindness of that young man to his wife; which is now over, and I have promised to appear a counsellor to him. I am glad she is like to be so near again. Thence to Martin, and there did tout ce que je voudrais avec her,[4] and drank, and away by water home and to dinner, Balty and his wife there. After dinner I took him down with me to Deptford; and there, by the *Bezan*, loaded above half my goods and sent them away. So we back home, and then I found occasion to return in the dark, and to Bagwell and there nudo in lecto con ella did do all that I desired; but though I did intend para aver demorado con ella toda la night, yet when I had done ce que je voudrais, I did hate both ella and la cosa; and taking occasion from the uncertainty of su marido's return esta noche, did me levar;[5] and so away home late to Sir W. Penn (Balty and his wife lying at my house); and there in the same simple humour, I found Sir W. Penn, and so late to bed.

13. Up, and downe to Tower wharfe; and there with Balty and labourers from Deptford did get my goods housed well at home. So down to Deptford again to fetch the rest, and there eat a bit of dinner at the Globe, and with the maister of the *Bezan* with me, while the labourers went to dinner. Here I hear that this poor town doth bury still of the plague seven or eight in a day. So to Sir G.

1. Workers.
2. "did not open the door as I did expect."
3. Michael Mitchell and his wife Betty had been burnt out of Thames Street. Their parents were shopkeepers in Westminster Hall.
4. "all that I would with her" ("her" being Betty Martin).
5. "there naked in bed with her did do all that I desired; but though I did intend to have stayed with her all night, yet when I had done what I would, I did hate both her and the thing; and taking occasion from the uncertainty of her husband's return this night, did rise".

Carteret's to work; and there did, to my great content, shipp off into the *Bezan* all the rest of my goods, saving my pictures and fine things, that I will bring home in wherrys when my house is fit to receive them. And so home and unloaden them by carts and hands before night, to my exceeding satisfaction; and so after supper to bed in my house, the first time I have lain there; and lay with my wife in my old closet upon the ground, and Balty and his wife in the best chamber upon the ground also.

19. Up, and with Sir W. Penn by coach to St. James's, and there did our usual business before the Duke of York; which signified little, our business being only complaints of lack of money.◆ Thence home and dined, and to Deptford and got all my pictures put into wherries, and my other fine things, and landed them all very well, and brought them home and got Symson[1] to set them up all tonight; and he gone, I and the boy to finish and set up my books and everything else in my house, till 2 in the morning, and then to bed. But mightily troubled, and even in my sleep, at my missing four or five of my biggest books – Speed's Chronicle – and maps, and the two parts of Waggoner, and a book of Cards;[2] which I suppose I have put up with too much care, that I have forgot where they are, for sure they are not stole. Two little pictures of sea and ships, and a little gilt frame belonging to my platt[3] of the River I want; but my books do heartily trouble me. Most of my gilt frames are hurt, which also troubles me; but most my books. This day I put on two shirts, the first time this year, and do grow well upon it; so that my disease is nothing but wind.

21. Up, and mightily pleased with the setting of my books the last night in order; and that which did please me most of all, is that W. Hewer tells me that upon enquiry, he doth find that Sir W. Penn hath a hamper more then his own, which he took for a hamper of bottles of wine, and are books in it. I was impatient to see it, but they were carried into a wine-cellar, and the boy is abroad with him at the House, where the Parliament meet today, and the King to be with them. At noon, after dinner, I sent for Harry, and he tells me it is so, and brought me by and by my hamper of books, to my great

1. Thomas Simpson, navy joiner.
2. The books were John Speed's *History of Great Britaine* (1650), his *Prospect of the Most Famous Parts of the World* (1631), and Waghenaer's *Mariners Mirrour* (1588) – all still in the Pepys Library at Magdalene College, Cambridge. The "cards" were probably sea-charts.
3. Map or engraving.

joy, with the same books I missed, and three more great ones and no more – I did give him 5*s* for his pains; and so home with great joy, and to the setting some of them right; but could not finish it, but away by coach to the other end of the town, leaving my wife at the Change. But neither came time enough to the Council to speak with the Duke of York nor with Sir G. Carteret; and so called my wife and paid for some things she bought, and so home, and there, after a little doing at the office about our accounts, which now draw near the time they should be ready, the House having order[ed] Sir G. Carteret, upon his offering them to bring them in on Saturday next – I home; and there with great pleasure very late, new setting all my books; and now I am in as good condition as I desire to be in all worldly respects, the Lord of heaven make me thankful and continue me therein. So to bed. This day I had new stairs of main timber put to my cellar going into the yard.

26. Up, and with Sir J. Mennes to St. James's; where, everybody going to the House, I away by coach to Westminster hall; and after a few turns, and hearing that our accounts came into the House but today, being hindered yesterday by other business, I away by coach home, taking up my wife and calling at Bennet's, our late mercer, who is come into Covent-garden to a fine house looking down upon the Exchange;[1] and I perceive many Londoners every day come, and Mr. Pierce[2] hath let his wife's closet, and the little blind bed-chamber, and a garret to a silk-man for 50*l* fine and 30*l* per annum, and 40*l* per annum more for dieting the master and two prentices. So home, not agreeing for silk for a petticoat for her which she desired; but home to dinner, and then back to White-hall, leaving my wife by the way to buy her petticoat of Bennet; and I to White-hall, waiting all the day on the Duke of York to move the King for getting Lanyon some money at Plymouth, out of some oyle-prizes brought in thither – but could get nothing done.[3] But here by Mr. Dugdale[4] I hear the great loss of books in St. Pauls churchyard, and at their hall also – which they value at about 150000*l*; some booksellers being wholly undone; and among others,

1. The New Exchange, a fashionable shopping emporium on the Strand.
2. James Pearse lived in Bedford Street, Covent Garden.
3. Lanyon was the naval agent at Plymouth. Pepys hoped to use the oil from two captured Greenland ships to pay off some of the navy's debts.
4. John, son of the herald and antiquarian William Dugdale.

they say, my poor Kirton.[1] And Mr. Crumlum,[2] all his books and household stuff burned; they trusting to St. Fayths, and the roof of the church falling, broke the Arch down into the lower church, and so all the goods burned – a very great loss. His father hath lost above 1000*l* in books – one book newly-printed, a discourse it seems of Courts.[3] Here I had the hap to see my Lady Denham;[4] and at night went into the drawing-room and saw several fine ladies; among others, Castlemayne, but chiefly Denham again, and the Duke of York taking her aside and talking to her in the sight of all the world, all alone; which was strange – and what also I did not like. Here I met with good Mr. Eveling, who cries out against it and calls it bichering, for the Duke of York talks a little to her, and then she goes away and then he fallows her again, like a dog. He observes that none of the nobility came out of the country at all to help the King or comfort him or prevent commotions at this fire, but do as if the King were nobody; nor ne'er a priest comes to give the King and Court good counsel or to comfort the poor people that suffer; but all is dead – nothing of good in any of their minds. He bemoans it, and says he fears more ruin hangs over our heads. Thence away by coach and called away my wife at Unthankes,[5] where she tells me she hath bought a gown of 15*s* per yard; the same, before her face, my Lady Castlemaine this day bought also – which I seemed vexed for; though I do not grudge it her, but to encline her to have Mercer again – which I believe I shall do, but the girl, I heare, hath no mind to come to us again – which vexes me. Being come home, I to Sir W. Batten, and there hear our business was tendered to the House today and a Committee of the whole House chosen to examine our accounts, and a great many hot-spurs enquiring into it – and likely to give us much trouble and blame, and perhaps (which I am afeared of) will find faults enow[6] to demand better

1. The Stationers' Hall and St Faith's (the crypt under St Paul's) had been used for storage by the booksellers hoping to save their wares. Joshua Kirton was Pepys's main bookseller before the fire.
2. Samuel Cromleholme, High Master of St Paul's School. The loss of his fine library shortened his life according to fellow collector John Bagford.
3. William Dugdale had lost editions of several works to the fire, including most copies of his *Origines Juridiciales* (1666), a history of law courts.
4. The Duke of York's mistress.
5. Elizabeth's tailor at Charing Cross.
6. Enough.

officers.[1] This I truly fear. Thence away with Sir W. Penn, who was there; and he and I walked in the garden by moonlight, and he proposes his and my looking out into Scotland about timber, and to use Pett there; for timber will be a good commodity this time of building the City. And I like the motion, and doubt not that we may do good in it.[2] We did also discourse about our Privateer, and hope well of that also, without much hazard, as, if God blesses us, I hope we shall do pretty well toward getting a penny.[3] I was mightily pleased with our discourse; and so parted, and to the office to finish my Journall for three or four days; and so home to supper and to bed. Our fleet abroad, and the Duch too, for all we know. The weather very bad; and under the command of an unlucky man I fear. God bless him and the fleet under him.

OCTOBER.

2. Up, and am sent for to Sir G. Carteret; and to him, and there he tells me how our lists are referred to a sub-committee to consider and examine, and that I am ordered to be there this afternoon.[4] So I away thence to my new bookbinders to see my books gilding in the backs, and then to Westminster-hall to the House and spoke with Sir W. Coventry, where he told me I must attend the committee in the afternoon, and received some hints of more work to do.◆ And I into the committee-chamber before the committee sat, and there heard Birch discourse highly and understandingly about the Navy business and a proposal made heretofore to farm the Navy.[5] But W. Coventry did abundantly answer him – and is a most excellent person. By and by the committee met, and I walked out; and anon they rose and called me in, and appointed me to attend a

1. A Commons select committee was to examine the accounts of the Navy, Treasury, and Ordnance Office. Over the next few years Pepys would find himself repeatedly called to defend the Navy Board as committees scrutinized its wartime finances and decision-making.
2. Nothing came of this proposal. Phineas Pett was in Scotland on the Navy Board's business.
3. At the end of this month a Dutch prize, the *Flying Greyhound*, was lent for free to Pepys, Batten, and Penn as a privateer, initially on condition that it be restored to the King's service in the spring.
4. A parliamentary subcommittee to scrutinize the navy's accounts wanted to examine lists of ships in wartime service.
5. Col. John Birch MP was an expert on naval administration. "Farming" involved private individuals providing a service (such as equipping navy vessels) for a fixed sum, while keeping any profits.

committee of them tomorrow at the office to examine our lists. This put me into a mighty fear and trouble, they doing it in a very ill humour methought. So I away, and called on my Lord Brouncker to desire him to be there tomorrow. And so home, having taken up my wife at Unthankes – full of trouble in mind to think what I shall be obliged to answer, that am neither fully fit, nor in any measure concerned to take the shame and trouble of this office upon me; but only from the inability and folly of the Controller[1] occasions it. When come home, I to Sir W. Penn to his boy for my book, and there find he hath it not, but delivered it to the doorkeeper of the committee for me. This, added to my former disquiet, made me stark mad, considering all the nakedness of the office lay open in papers within those Covers. I could not tell in the world what to do, but was mad on all sides; and that which made me worse, Captain Cocke was there, and he did so swear and curse at the boy that told me. So Cocke, Griffin, and the boy with me – they to find out the housekeeper of the Parliament, Hughes, while I to Sir W. Coventry, but could hear nothing of it there; but coming to our Rendezvous at the Swan tavern in Kings-street, I find they have found the housekeeper, and the book simply locked up in the Court. So I stayed and drank, and rewarded the doorkeeper and away home, my heart lighter by all this; but to bed very sad notwithstanding, in fear of what will happen tomorrow upon their coming.

3. Waked betimes, mightily troubled in mind, and in the most true trouble that I ever was in my life, saving in that business last year of the East India prizes. So up, and with Mr. Hayter and W. Hewer and Gibson to consider of our business and books and papers necessary for this examination; and by and by, by 8 a-clock, comes Birch the first, with the list and books of accounts delivered in. He calls me to work, and there he and I begin; when by and by comes Garraway, the first time I ever saw him, and Sir W Thomson and Mr. Boscawen.[2] They to it, and I did make shift to answer them better then I expected. Sir W. Batten, Lord Brouncker, W. Penn came in, but presently went out; and J. Mennes came in, and said two or three words from the purpose but to do hurt; and so away he went also – and left me all the morning with them alone, to stand or fall. At noon W. Batten comes to them to invite them (though

1. Sir John Mennes.
2. The MPs in this subcommittee were William Garraway, William Thomson, and Edward Boscawen.

fast-day) to dinner – which they did, and good company they were, but especially Garraway. Here I have news brought me of my father's com[ing] to town, and I presently to him. Glad to see him, poor man, he being come unexpected to see us and the City. I could not stay with him, but after dinner to work again, only the committee and I, till dark night; and by that time they cast up all the lists and found out what the medium of men was borne all the war, of all sorts – and ended with good peace and much seeming satisfaction; but I find them wise and reserved, and instructed to hit all our blots – as, among others, that we reckon the ships full manned from the beginning. They gone, and my heart eased of a great deal of fear and pain, and reckoning myself to come off with victory, because not overcome in anything or much foiled, I away to Sir W. Coventry's chamber, but he not within; then to White-hall and there among the ladies, and saw my Lady Castlemaine never looked so ill, nor Mrs. Stewart neither, as in this plain natural dress; I was not pleased with either of them. Away, not finding W. Coventry; and so home, and there find my father and my brother come to town – my father without my expectation; but glad I am to see him. And so to supper with him, and to work again at the office; then home to set up all my Folio books, which are come home gilt on the backs, very handsome to the eye; and then at midnight to bed. This night W. Penn told me W. Batten swears he will have nothing to do with the privateer if his son do not go Lieutenant; which angers me and him, but we will be even with him one way or other.

11. Up, and discoursed with my father of my sending some money for safety into the country, for I am in pain what to do with what I have. I did give him money, poor man, and he overjoyed. So left him, and to the office, where nothing but sad evidences of ruine coming on us for want of money. So home to dinner, which was a very good dinner, my father, brother, wife and I; and then to the office again, where I was all the afternoon till very late, busy; and then home to supper and to bed.

⟨⟨*Memorandum.*⟩⟩[1] I had taken my Journall during the fire and the disorders fallowing in loose papers until this very day, and could not get time to enter them in my book till January 18 in the morning, having made my eyes sore by frequent attempts this winter to do it. But now it is done, for

1. This note is crowded into the bottom of a page, having been written on or after 18 Jan. 1667.

which I thank God, and pray never the like occasion may happen.

19. Up, and by coach to my Lord Ashlys,[1] and thence (he being gone out) to the Exchequer chamber, and there find him and my Lord Bellasses about my Lord Bellasses' accounts – which was the business I went upon. This was soon ended, and then I with Creed back home to my house, and there he and I did even accounts for salary.[2] And by that time dinner was ready, and merry at dinner and then abroad to Povy's,[3] who continues as much confounded in all his businesses as ever he was; and would have had me paid money as like a fool as himself, which I troubled him in refusing, but I did persist in it. After a little more discourse, I left them and to Whitehall, where I met with Sir Rob. Viner, who told me a little of what in going home I had seen; also, a little of the disorder and mutiny among the seamen at the Treasurer's office[4] – which did trouble me then and all this day since, considering how many more seamen will come to town every day, and no money for them – a Parliament sitting – and the Exchange close by, and an enemy to hear of and laugh at it.

Viner too, and Backewell, were sent for this afternoon and was before the King and his Cabinet about money; they declaring they would advance no more – it being discourse in the House of Parliament for the King to issue out his privy-seals to them to command them to trust him,[5] which gives them reason to decline trusting. But more money they are persuaded to lend, but so little, that (with horrour I speak it) coming after the Council was up, with Sir G. Carteret, Sir W. Coventry, Lord Brouncker, and myself, I did lay the state of our condition before the Duke of York. That the fleet could not go out without several things it wanted and we could not have without money – perticularly broom and reed, which we had promised the man Swan to help him to 200*l* of his debt,[6] and a few other small sum[s] of 200*l* a-piece to some others. And that I do foresee the Duke of York would call us to an account why the fleet is not abroad, and we cannot answer otherwise then our want of money. And that endeed we do not do the King any service now,

1. Sir Anthony Ashley Cooper (later Lord Shaftesbury), Chancellor of the Exchequer.
2. For Pepys's salary as Treasurer of Tangier and Creed's as Secretary.
3. Thomas Povey, former Treasurer of Tangier who had resigned in favour of Pepys. They had an arrangement to split profits from the post.
4. The Navy Treasurer's Office in Broad Street.
5. I.e. writs for forced loans.
6. Broom and reed were used in fireships as combustible materials and for cleaning ships' hulls. Humphrey Swan supplied these to the navy.

but do rather abuse and betray his service, by being there and seeming to do something while we do not. Sir G. Carteret asked me (just in these words, for in this and all the rest I set down the very words for memory sake, if there should be occasion) whether 50 or 60*l* would do us any good; and when I told him the very broomman must have 200*l*, he held up his eyes as if we had asked a million. Sir W. Coventry told the Duke of York plainly, he did rather desire to have his commission called in then serve in so ill a place, where he cannot do the King service; and I did concur in saying the same. This was all very plain, and the Duke of York did confess that he did not see how we could do anything without a present supply of 20000*l*, and that he would speak to the King next council-day, and I promised to wait on him to put him in mind of it. This I set down for my future justification, if need be. And so we broke up, and all parted – Sir W. Coventry being not very well, but I believe made much worse by this night's sad discourse.

So I home by coach, considering what the consequence of all this must be in a little time – nothing but distraction and confusion – which makes me wish with all my heart that I were well and quietly settled with what little I have got, at Brampton, where I might live peaceably and study and pray for the good of the King and my country.

Home, and to Sir W. Batten, where I saw my Lady, who is now come downstairs after a great sickness. Sir W. Batten was at the pay today, and tells me how rude the men were; but did go away quietly, being promised pay on Wednesday next. God send us money for it.

So to the office, and then to supper and to bed.

Among other things proposed in the House today to give the King in lieu of Chimnys, there was the bringing up of Sealed=paper, such as Sir J. Mennes showed me tonight at Sir W. Batten's is used in Spayne, and brings the King a great revenue.[1] But it shows what shifts we are put to, too much.

27. Up, and there comes to see me my Lord Bellasses, which was a great honour. He tells me great news, yet but what I suspected: that Vernatty is fled, and so hath cheated him and twenty more; but most of all, I doubt, Mr. Povy.[2]

1. The scheme suggested here was to replace the hearth tax with a form of stamp duty. In Spain the crown charged for specially marked paper, use of which was mandatory for legal contracts.
2. Philibert Vernatti was Muster-Master and Treasurer of the Tangier garrison.

Thence to talk about public business; he tells me how the two Houses begin to be troublesome, the Lords to have quarrels one with another, my Lord Duke of Buckingham having said to the Lord Chancellor (who is against the passing of the Bill for prohibiting the bring[ing] over of Irish Cattle), that whoever was against the Bill was there led to it by an Irish Interest or an Irish understanding, which is as much as to say he is a fool.[1] This bred heat from my Lord Chancellor, and something he[2] said did offend my Lord of Ossory (my Lord Duke of Ormond's son),[3] and they two had hard words; upon which the latter sends a challenge to the former – of which the former complains to the House, and so the business is to be heard on Monday next.[4]

Then as to the Commons; some ugly Knifes, like poignards to stob people with, about 2 or 300 of them were brought in yesterday to the House, found in one of the houses rubbish that was burnt, and said to be the house of a Catholique.[5] This, and several letters out of the country, saying how high the Catholiques are everywhere and bold in the owning their religion, have made the Commons mad; and they presently voted that the King be desired to put all Catholiques out of imployment, and other high things[6] – while the business of money hangs in the hedge. So that upon the whole, God knows we are in a sad condition like to be – these being the very beginnings of the late troubles.[7] He gone, I at the office all the morning. At noon home to dinner, where Mrs. Pierce and her boy and Knipp – who sings as well, and is the best company in the world – dined with us, and infinite mirth. The playhouses begin to play next week.[8]

Toward evening I took them out to the New Exchange, and there my wife bought things, and I did give each of them a pair of

1. Proponents of the bill believed a ban on importing Irish cattle would raise the value of English cattle. Opponents feared high prices for consumers and damage to the business of fattening Irish cattle in England.
2. Buckingham.
3. Born and raised in Ireland, and a member of the Irish House of Lords.
4. Both men were briefly imprisoned by the Lords until they apologized to the House.
5. John Milward MP wrote that just two daggers were brought into the House as samples.
6. The Commons asked the King to banish priests and Jesuits, to enforce recusancy laws, and to require all officers (civil and military) to take the oaths of allegiance and supremacy or be dismissed.
7. I.e. like the start of the civil wars, when the Commons was similarly enflamed against "popery" and the crown was in desperate need of money.
8. Regular performances had been suspended since June 1665 because of the plague.

Jesimy[1] plain gloves and another of white. Here Knipp and I walked up and down to see handsome faces, and did see several. Then carried each of them home, and with great pleasure and content home myself; where, having writ several letters, I home; and there, upon some serious discourse between my wife and I about that business, I called to us my brother, and there broke to him our design to send him into the country with some part of our money; and so did seriously discourse the whole thing, and then away to supper and to bed. I pray God give a blessing to our resolution, for I do much fear we shall meet with speedy distractions for want of money.

31.◆ And thus ends the month – with an ill aspect. The business of the Navy standing wholly still. No credit. No goods sold us. Nobody will trust. All we have to do at the office is to hear complaints for want of money. The Duke of York himself, for now three weeks, seems to rest satisfied that we can do nothing without money, and that all must stand still till the King gets money – which the Parliament have been a great while about, but are so dissatisfied with the King's management, and his giving himself up to pleasures, and not minding the calling to account any of his officers – and they observe so much the expense of the war, and yet that after we have made it the most we can, it doth not amount to what they have given the King for the Warr, that they are backward of giving any more. However, 1800000*l* they have voted, but the way of gathering it hath taken up more time then is fit to be now lost.[2] The seamen grow very rude, and everything out of order – commanders having no power over their seamen, but the seamen do what they please. Few stay on board, but all coming running up hither to town; and nobody can with justice blame them, we owing them so much money, and their families must starve if we do not give them money or they procure upon their tickets from some people that will trust them.[3] A great folly is observed by all people, in the King's giving leave to so many merchantmen to go abroad this winter, and some upon voyages where it is impossible they should be back again by the spring; and the rest will be doubtful, but yet we let them go.[4] What the reason of state is, nobody can tell, but all condemn it. The Prince and Duke of Albemarle have got no great credit by this

1. Jasmine: yellow-coloured or jasmine-perfumed.
2. The Commons had resolved on 12 October to investigate how to supply the King with £1,800,000 but they had yet to reach conclusions.
3. I.e. use their tickets, showing navy wages due to them, to get credit.
4. The concern was that the ships and men would not be available for service against the Dutch.

year's service, our losses, both of reputation and ships, having been greater then is thought have ever been suffered in all ages put together before – being beat home and fleeing home the first fight, and then losing so many ships then and since upon the sands, and some falling into the enemy's hands, and not one taken this year but the *Ruby*, French prize, now at the end of the year, by the Frenchmen's mistake in running upon us.[1]

Great folly in both Houses of Parliament, several persons falling together by the eares; among others, in the House of Lords, the Duke of Buckingham and my Lord Ossory. Such is our case, that everybody fears an invasion the next year; and for my part, I do methinks foresee some great unhappiness coming upon us, and do provide for it by laying by something against a rainy day – dividing what I have and laying it in several places – but with all faithfulness to the King in all respects – my grief only being that the King doth not look after his business himself, and thereby will be undone, both himself and his nations – it being not yet, I believe, too late, if he would apply himself to it, to save all and conquer the Duch; but while he and the Duke of York mind their pleasure as they do, and nothing else, we must be beaten.

So late, with my mind in good condition of quiet after the settling all my accounts, and to bed.

NOVEMBER.

4. *Lords day.* Comes my Taylors man in the morning and brings my vest home, and coat to wear with it,[2] and belt and silver-hilted sword. So I rose and dressed myself, and I like myself mightily in it, and so doth my wife. Then being dressed, to church; and after church pulled my Lady Pen and Mrs. Markeham into my house to dinner; and Sir J. Mennes, he got Mrs. Pegg along with him. I had a good dinner for them, and very merry. And after dinner to the waterside, and so, it being very cold, to White-hall, and was mighty fearful of an ague (my vest being new and thin, and the Coate cut not to meet before upon my breast). Here I waited in the gallery till the Council was up; and among others, did speak with Mr. Cooling, my Lord Chamberlain's secretary – who tells me my

1. This was the only warship captured, rather than the only prize captured.
2. Worn under a loose-fitting coat, the "vest" was a collarless garment reaching to the knee. This new fashion had been introduced by the King in October as a conscious rejection of French style.

Lord-Generall[1] is become mighty low in all people's opinion, and that he hath received several slurs from the King and Duke of York. That people at Court do see the difference between his and the Prince's management and my Lord Sandwiches. That this business which he is put upon, of crying out against the Catholiques and turning them out of all imployment, will undo him when he comes to turn out the officers out of the army – and this is a thing of his own seeking. That he is grown a drunken sot, and drinks with nobody but Troutbecke,[2] whom nobody else will keep company with – of whom he told me this story: That once, the Duke of Albemarle in his drink taking notice as of a wonder that Nan Hide should ever come to be Duchess of Yorke – "Nay," says Troutbecke, "ne'er wonder at that; for if you will give me another bottle of wine, I will tell you as great, if not greater, a miracle." And what was that but that "Our Dirty Besse" (meaning his Duchesse) should come to be Duchesse of Albemarle.[3] Here we parted, and so by and by the Council rose, and out comes Sir G. Carteret and Sir W. Coventry and they and my Lord Brouncker and I went to Sir G. Carteret's lodgings, there to discourse about some money demanded by Sir W Warren; and having done that, broke up – and Sir G. Carteret and I alone together a while, where he shows me a long letter, all in cipher, from my Lord Sandwich to him. The contents he hath not yet found out – but he tells me that my Lord is not sent for home, as several people have enquired after of me. He spoke something reflecting upon me in the business of pursers: that their present bad behaviour is but what he did foresee and had convinced me of; and yet when it came last year to be argued before the Duke of York, I turned and said as the rest said. I answered nothing to it, but let it go. And so to other discourse of the ill state of things, of which all people are full of sorrow and observation; and so parted, and then by water (landing in Southwarke) home to the Tower; and so home, and there begun to read Potters discourse upon 666,[4] which pleases me mightily; and then broke off, and to supper and to bed.

1. Albemarle.
2. John Troutbeck, surgeon to Albemarle's troop of Life Guards.
3. Anne Hyde had married the heir to the throne when her father was a mere knight (before he was made Earl of Clarendon). The Duchess of Albemarle had been a married seamstress when she met George Monck, who was then a prisoner in the Tower.
4. Francis Potter's *An Interpretation of the Number 666* (1642). It used mathematics to interpret the "Number of the Beast" from Revelation in support of the Protestant belief that the Pope was Antichrist.

5. A holiday – lay long; then up and to the office, where vexed to meet with people come from the fleet at the Nore, where so many ships are laid up and few going abroad; and yet Sir Tho. Allen hath sent up some Lieutenants with warrants to press men for a few ships to go out this winter, while every day thousands appear here, to our great trouble and affright, here every day before our office and the ticket office, and no Captain able to command one man aboard.◆

Thence to my Lord Crews, and there dined and mightily made of, having not, to my shame, been there in eight months before. Here my Lord and Sir Tho. Crew, Mr. John, and Dr Crew – and two strangers. ⟨The⟩ best family in the world for goodness and sobriety. Here, beyond my expectation, I met my Lord Hinchingbrooke, who is come to town two days since from Hinchingbrooke, and brought his sister and brother Carteret with him – who are at Sir G. Carteret's. After dinner I and Sir Tho Crew went aside to discourse of public matters, and do find by him that all the country gentlemen are publicly jealous of the Courtiers in the Parliament, and that they do doubt everything that they propose.◆

He doth, from what he hath heard at the Committee for examining the burning of the City, conclude it as a thing certain, that it was done by plot – it being proved by many witnesses that endeavours were made in several places to encrease the fire, and that both in city and country it was bragged by several papists that upon such a day or in such a time we should find the hottest weather that ever was in England, and words of plainer sense.[1] But my Lord Crew was discoursing at table how the Judges have determined in that case whether the Landlords or the Tenants (who are in their leases all of them generally tied to maintain and uphold their houses) shall bear the loss of the fire. And they say that ⟨Tenants⟩ should, against all Casualtys of fire beginning either in their own or in their neighbour's; but where it is done by an Enemy, they are not to do it. And this was by an enemy, there having been one Convict and hanged upon this very score – which is an excellent Salvo for the Tenants, and for which I am glad – because of my father's house.[2]◆

1. The Commons committee appointed to investigate the fire reported back in January 1667, citing witnesses who alleged Catholics had foreknowledge of the disaster. Crew was not a member of the committee.
2. Under normal circumstances leaseholders had to rebuild destroyed property. However, Robert Hubert, a Frenchman, had been executed in October for starting the fire (although it later emerged he was at sea when it began). As Britain was at war with France, the conviction allowed the fire damage to be classed as enemy action, exempting tenants from responsibility. Pepys's father leased his house in Salisbury Court.

9. Up and to the office, where did a good deal of business. And then at noon to the Exchange and to my little goldsmith's, whose wife is very pretty and modest, that ever I saw any. Upon the Change, where I have seldom of late been, I find all people mightily at a loss what to expect, but confusion and fears in every man's head and heart. Whether war or peace, all fear the event will be bad. Thence home and with my brother to dinner, my wife being dressing herself against night. After dinner I to my closet all the afternoon, till the porter brought my vest back from the Taylors, and then to dress myself very fine, about 4 or 5 a-clock; and by that time comes Mr. Batelier and Mercer,[1] and away by coach to Mrs. Pierces by appointment, where we find good company – a fair lady, my Lady Prettyman – Mrs. Corbet – Knipp. And for men, Captain Downing[2] – Mr. Lloyd, Sir W. Coventry's clerk – and one Mr. Tripp, who dances well. After some trifling discourse, we to dancing and very good sport, and mightily pleased I was with the company. After our first bout of dancing, Knipp and I to sing, and Mercer and Captain Downing (who loves and understands music) would by all means have my song of *Beauty Retire* – which Knipp hath spread abroad, and he extols it above anything he ever heard. And without flattery, I think it is good in its kind. This being done, and going to dance again, comes news that White-hall was on fire – and presently more perticulars, that the Horse guard was on fire.[3] And so we run up to the garret and find it so, a horrid great fire – and by and by we saw and heard part of it blown up with powder. The ladies begun presently to be afeared – one fell into fits. The whole town in an Alarme. Drums beat and trumpets, and the guards everywhere spread – running up and down in the street. And I begun to have mighty apprehensions how things might be at home, and so was in mighty pain to get home; and that that encreased all is that we are in expectation (from common fame) this night or tomorrow to have a Massacre – by the having so many fires one after another – as that in the City. And at the same time begun in Westminster by the Palace, but put out – and since in Southworke, to the burning down some houses; and now this, doth make all people conclude there is something extraordinary in it, but nobody knows what. By and by comes news that the fire is

1. Will Batelier, wine merchant, and Mary Mercer, formerly Elizabeth's paid companion.
2. Probably Capt. John Downing, soldier and client of Albemarle.
3. An accidental fire started between 7 and 8 p.m. in the Horse Guard House, but was put out by 10 p.m.

slackened; so then we were a little cheered up again, and to supper and pretty merry. But above all, there comes in that Dumb boy[1] that I knew in Olivers time, who is mightily acquainted here and with Downing; and he made strange signs of the fire, and how the King was abroad, and many things they understood but I could not – which I wondering at, and discoursing with Downing about it, "Why," says [he], "it is only a little use, and you will understand him and make him understand you, with as much ease as may be." So I prayed him to tell[2] him that I was afeared that my coach would be gone, and that he should go down and steal one of the seats out of the coach and keep it, and that would make the coachman to stay. He did this, so that the Dumb boy did go down, and like a cunning rogue went into the coach, pretending to sleep; and by and by fell to his work, but finds the seats nailed to the coach; so he did all he could, but could not do it; however, stayed there and stayed the coach, till the coachman's patience was quite spent, and beat the dumb boy by force, and so went away. So the Dumb boy came up and told him all the story, which they below did see all that passed and knew it to be true. After supper another dance or two, and then news that the fire is as great as ever, which put us all to our wit's end, and I mightily [eager] to go home; but the coach being gone, and it being about 10 at night and rainy dirty weather, I knew not what to do but to walk out with Mr. Batelier, myself resolving to go home on foot and leave the women there. And so did; but at the Savoy got a coach and came back and took up the women; and so (having by people come from the fire understood that the fire was overcome, and all well) we merrily parted, and home. Stopped by several guards and Constables quite through the town (round the wall as we went), all being in armes. We got well home; and in the way I did con mi mano tocar la jambe de Mercer sa chair. Elle retirait sa jambe modestement, but I did tocar sa peau with my naked hand. And the truth is, la fille hath something that is assez jolie.[3] Being come home, we to Cards till 2 in the morning; and drinking lamb's-wool,[4] to bed.

22. Up, and to the office, where we sat all the morning. And my

1. "Dumb" means mute – the boy was deaf. What follows is one of the earliest detailed accounts of a signed conversation in Britain.
2. Pepys originally wrote "bid him by signs go down".
3. "I did with my hand touch the leg of Mercer her flesh. She withdrew her leg modestly, but I did touch her skin with my naked hand. And the truth is, the girl hath something that is quite pretty."
4. Hot ale with apples and spices.

Lord Brouncker did show me Holler's new print of the City, with a pretty representation of that part which is burnt, very fine endeed. And tells me that he was yesterday sworn the King's servant,[1] and that the King hath commanded him to go on with his great map of the City which he was upon before the City was burned, like Gombout of Paris;[2] which I am glad of.

At noon home to dinner, where my wife and I fell out, I being displeased with her cutting away a lace hankercher so wide about the neck, down to her breasts almost, out of a belief, but without reason, that it is the fashion. Here we did give one another the lie too much, but were presently friends; and then I to my office, where very late and did much business; and then home, and there find Mr. Batelier – and did sup and play at Cards awhile. But he tells me the news how the King of France hath, in defiance to the King of England, caused all his footmen to be put into Vests, and that the noblemen of France will do the like;[3] which, if true, is the greatest indignity ever done by one prince to another, and would incite a stone to be revenged; and I hope our King will, if it be so as he tells me it is – being told by one that came over from Paris with my Lady Fanshaw (who is come over with the dead body of her husband)[4] and that saw it before he came away. This makes me mighty merry, it being an ingenious kind of affront; but yet makes me angry to see that the King of England is become so little as to have that affront offered him.

So I left my people at Cards, and to my chamber to read, and then to bed. Batelier did bring us some oysters tonight, and some bottles of new French wine of this year, mighty good – but I drank but little.

This noon Bagwell's wife was with me at the office, and I did what I would; and at night came Mrs. Burroughs,[5] and appointed to meet upon the next holiday and go abroad together.

1. Wenceslaus Hollar's map was published as *A Map or Groundplott of the Citty of London . . . The Blanke Space Signifying the Burnt Part*. He was sworn in as King's Scenographer.
2. Jacques Gomboust had published a large map of Paris in 1652.
3. This unconfirmed story concerned Louis's revenge for Charles's new anti-French fashion.
4. Sir Richard Fanshawe, Ambassador to Spain, had died in Madrid.
5. Elizabeth Burrows, widow of a naval lieutenant, had recently allowed Pepys's sexual advances.

DECEMBER.

1. Up and to the office, where we sat all the morning. At home to dinner, and then abroad, walking to the Old Swan, and in my way did see a cellar in Tower streete in a very fresh Fire, the late great winds having blown it up; it seemed to be only of Loggwood, that hath kept the fire all this while in it. Going further, I met my late Lord Mayor ⟨Bludworth⟩, under whom the City was burned, and went with him by water to White-hall. But Lord, the silly talk that this fellow had – only, how ready he would be to part with all his estate in these difficult times to advance the King's service, and complaining that now (as everybody did lately in the Fire) everybody endeavours to save himself and let the whole perish – but a very weak man he seems to be. I left him at White-hall, he giving 6*d* towards the boat, and I to Westminster-hall, where I was again defeated in my expectation of Burroughs – however, I was not much sorry for it; but by coach home in the evening, calling at Faythornes and buying three of my Lady Castlemaynes heads, printed this day; which endeed is, as to the head, I think a very fine picture, and like her.[1] I did this afternoon get Mrs. Michell to let me only have a sight of a pamphlett lately printed, but suppressed and much called after, called *The Catholiques Apology*,[2] lamenting the severity of the Parliament against them – and comparing it with the lenity of other princes to protestants. Giving old and late instances of their Loyalty to their princes, whatever is objected against them. And excusing their disquiets in Queen Elizabeths time, for that it was impossible for them to think her a lawful queen, if Queene Mary, who had been owned as such, were so; one being the daughter of the true, and the other of a false wife – and that of the Gunpowder Treason, by saying that it was only the practice of some of us, if not the King, to trapan some of their religion into it, it never being defended by the generality of their Church, nor endeed known by them. And ends with a large Catalogue in red Letters,

1. William Faithorne's engraving of Lady Castlemaine was based on a portrait by Peter Lely.
2. *The Humble Apology* [i.e. defence] *of the English Catholicks* had been suppressed by the King's order on 28 November. The bookseller Ann Mitchell would not risk selling the work but let Pepys, a good friend, have a look. Government investigations soon identified the author as the Earl of Castlemaine, husband of the King's mistress.

of the Catholiques which have lost their lives in the quarrel of the late King and this. The thing is very well writ endeed. So home to my letters, and then to my supper and to bed.

19.◆ The Lieutenant of the Tower took me with him and would have me to the Tower to dinner; where I dined – at the head of his table next his lady – who is comely, and seeming sober and stately, but very proud and very cunning, or I am mistaken – and wanton too.[1]◆ But a strange conceited, vain man he is, that ever I met withal, in his own praise – as I have heretofore observed of him. Thence home, and upon Tower hill saw about 3 or 400 seamen get together; and one, standing upon a pile of bricks, made his sign with his handkercher upon his stick, and called all the rest to him, and several shouts they gave. This made me afeared, so I got home as fast as I could – and hearing of no present hurt, did go to Sir Robt. Viners about my plate again;[2] and coming home, do hear of 1000 seamen said in the streets to be in armes. So in great fear home, expecting to find a tumult about our house, and was doubtful of my riches there – but I thank God, I found all well. But by and by Sir W. Batten and Sir R Ford do tell me that the seamen have been at some prisons to release some seamen, and that the Duke of Albemarle is in armes, and all the Guards at the other end of the town; and the Duke of Albemarle is gone with some forces to Wapping to quell the seamen – which is a thing of infinite disgrace to us.[3]

I sat long, talking with them. And among other things, Sir R. Ford[4] did make me understand how the House of Commons is a beast not to be understood – it being impossible to know beforehand the success almost of any small plain thing – there being so many to think and speak to any business, and they of so uncertain minds and interests and passions.

He did tell me, and so did Sir W. Batten, how Sir Allen Brodericke and Sir Allen Apsly did come drunk the other day into the House, and did both speak for half an hour together, and could not be either laughed or pulled or bid to sit down and hold their peace – to the great contempt of the King's servants and cause – which I am aggrieved at with all my heart.

1. Anne, wife of Sir John Robinson. For her reputation, *see* 5 Nov. 1665.
2. The silver plate from Vyner, a goldsmith, was Captain Cocke's gift for Pepys's help with a hemp contract.
3. Six hundred seamen had broken into Newgate prison to rescue some of their fellows sent there for discontented words.
4. MP and merchant.

We were full in discourse of the sad state of our times. And the horrid shame brought on the King's service by the just clamours of the poor seamen. And that we must be undone in a little time.

Home, full of trouble on these considerations. And among other things, I to my chamber and there to ticket a good part of my books, in order to the Numbring of them – for my easy finding them to read, as I have occasion.[1]

So to supper and to bed – with my heart full of trouble.

24. Up and to the office, where Lord Brouncker, J. Mennes, W. Penn, and myself met; and there I did use my notes I took on Saturday night about tickets,[2] and did come to a good settlement in that business of that office, if it be kept to – this morning being a meeting on purpose. At noon, to prevent my Lord Brouncker's dining here, I walked as if upon business with him (it being frost and dry) as far as Paul's, and so back again through the City by Yildhall,[3] observing the ruines thereabouts, till I did truly lose myself; and so home to dinner. I do truly find that I have overwrought my eyes, so that now they are become weak and apt to be tired, and all excess of light makes them sore, so that now, to the candlelight I am forced to sit by, adding the Snow upon the ground all day, my eyes are very bad, and will be worse if not helped; so my Lord Brouncker doth advise me, as a certain cure, to use Greene Spectacles, which I will do. So to dinner, where Mercer with us, and very merry. After dinner, she goes and fetches a little son of Mr. Buckeworths, the whitest-haired and of the most spirit that ever I saw in my life – for discourse of all kind, and so ready and to the purpose, not above four year old. Thence to Sir Robt. Viners and there paid for the plate I have bought, to the value of 94*l*, with the 100*l* Captain Cocke did give me to that purpose, and received the rest in money. I this evening did buy me a pair of green spectacles, to see whether they will help my eyes or no. So to the Change, and went to the Upper Change, which is almost as good as the old one; only, shops are but on one side. Then home to the office and did business till my eyes begun to be bad; and so home to supper (my people busy making mince-pies) and so to bed. No news yet of our Gottenburgh fleet; which makes [me] have some fears, it being of mighty concernment to have our supply of masts safe. I met with Mr. Cade

1. This was work towards the first of Pepys's library catalogues, pasting paper "tickets" on the book spines.
2. The tickets given to seamen in lieu of cash payment.
3. Guildhall (the spelling reflects a common pronunciation).

tonight, my stationer, and he tells me that he hears for certain that the Queene-Mother is about and hath near finished a peace with France; which, as a Presbyterian, he doth not like, but seems to fear it will be a means to introduce Popery.[1]

25. *Christmas day.* Lay pretty long in bed. And then rise, leaving my wife desirous to sleep, having sat up till 4 this morning seeing her maids make mince-pies. I to church, where our parson Mills made a good sermon. Then home, and dined well on some good ribbs of beef roasted and mince pies; only my wife, brother, and Barker,[2] and plenty of good wine of my own; and my heart full of true joy and thanks to God Almighty for the goodness of my condition at this day. After dinner I begun to teach my wife and Barker my song, *It is decreed* – which pleases me mightily, as now I have Mr. Hinxton's bass.[3] Then out, and walked alone on foot to Temple, it being a fine frost, thinking to have seen a play all alone; but there missing of any Bills,[4] concluded there was none; and so back home, and there with my brother, reducing the names of all my books to an Alphabet,[5] which kept us till 7 or 8 at night; and then to supper, W. Hewer with us, and pretty merry; and then to my chamber to enter this day's journal only, and then to bed – my head a little thoughtful how [to] behave myself in the business of the victualling, which I think will be prudence to offer my service in doing something in passing the pursers' accounts – thereby to serve the King – get honour to myself, and confirm me in my place in the victualling, which at present hath not work enough to deserve my wages.

31. Rising this day with a full design to mind nothing else but to make up my accounts for the year past, I did take money and walk forth to several places in the town, as far as the New Exchange, to pay all my debts, it being still a very great frost and good walking. I stayed at the Fleece tavern in Covent-garden, while my boy Tom went to W. Joyces to pay what I owed for candles there. Thence to the New Exchange to clear my wife's score; and so going back

1. Henrietta Maria, who was living in France, had tried to mediate in the war. In the autumn Charles had begun to make secret moves towards a peace, although in December official negotiations had yet to start.
2. Elizabeth's new paid companion, replacing Mary Mercer who had been dismissed on 3 September. Barker stayed till May 1667.
3. Pepys had written the voice-line, but had recently turned to John Hingston, a court musician, to supply the bass.
4. Playbills advertising performances, posted up in the streets.
5. An alphabetical catalogue.

again, I met Doll Lane (Mrs. Martin's sister) with another young woman of the Hall, one Scott, and took them to the Half-Moon tavern and there drank some burned wine with them, without more pleasure; and so away home by coach, and there to dinner and then to my accounts, wherein at last I find them clear and right; but to my great discontent, do find that my gettings this year have been 573*l* less then my last – it being this year in all, but 2986*l*; whereas the last I got 3560*l*. And then again, my spendings this year have exceeded my spendings the last, by 644 – my whole spendings last year being but 509*l*; whereas this year it appears I have spent 1154*l* – which is a sum not fit to be said that ever I should spend in one year, before I am maister of a better estate then I am. Yet, blessed be God, and I pray God make me thankful for it, I do find myself worth in money, all good, above 6200*l*; which is above 1800*l* more then I was the last year. This, I trust in God, will make me thankful for what I have, and careful to make up by care next year what by my negligence and prodigality I have lost and spent this year.

The doing of this and entering it fair, with the sorting of all my expenses to see how and in what points I have exceeded, did make it late work, till my eyes became very sore and ill; and then did give over, and supper and to bed.

Thus ends this year of public wonder and mischief to this nation – and therefore generally wished by all people to have an end. Myself and family well, having four maids and one clerk, Tom, in my house; and my brother now with me, to spend time in order to his preferment.[1] Our healths all well; only, my eyes, with over-working them, are sore as soon as candlelight comes to them, and not else. Public matters in a most sad condition. Seamen discouraged for want of pay, and are become not to be governed. Nor, as matters are now, can any fleet go out next year. Our enemies, French and Duch, great, and grow more, by our poverty. The Parliament backward in raising, because jealous of the spending of the money. The City less and less likely to be built again, everybody settling elsewhere, and nobody encouraged to trade. A sad, vicious, negligent Court, and all sober men there fearful of the ruin of the whole Kingdom this next year – from which, good God deliver us. One thing I reckon remarkable in my own condition is that I am come to abound in good plate, so as at all entertainments to be served wholly with silver plates, having two dozen and a half.

1. John, having finished his MA and entered holy orders, was now seeking employment.

1667

JANUARY. 166$\frac{6}{7}$.

4. Up; and seeing things put in order for a dinner at my house today, I to the office awhile; and about noon home, and there saw all things in good order. Anon comes our company – my Lord Brouncker – Sir W. Penn, his Lady, and Peg and her servant, Mr. Lowder[1] – my Lady Batten – Sir W. Batten being forced to dine at Sir R Ford's, being invited – Mr. Turner and his wife. Here I had good room for ten, and no more would my table have held well had Sir J. Mennes (who was fallen lame) and his sister and niece and Sir W. Batten come, which was a great content to me to be without them. I did make them all gaze to see themselfs served so nobly in plate; and a neat dinner endeed, though but of seven dishes. Mighty merry I was and made them all – and they mightily pleased. My Lord Brouncker went away after dinner to the Ticket Office, the rest stayed; only my Lady Batten home, her ague-fit coming on her at table. The rest merry, and to cards and then to sing and talk; and at night to sup and then to cards; and last of all, to have a flagon of Ale and apples, drunk out of a wood Cupp as a Christmas draught, made all merry; and they full of admiration at my plate, perticularly my flagons (which endeed are noble); and so late home, all with great mirth and satisfaction to them as I thought, and to myself to see all I have and do so much out-do, for neatness and plenty, anything done by any of them. They gone, I to bed much pleased. And do observe Mr. Lowder to be a pretty gentleman – and I think too good for Peg. And by the way, Peg Penn seems mightily to be kind to me, and I believe by her father's advice, who is also himself so – but I believe not a little troubled to see my plenty; and was much troubled to hear the song I sung – *The new Droll* – it touching him home.[2] So to bed.

11. Up, being troubled at my being found abed a-days by all sorts of people – I having got a trick of sitting up later then I need, never supping, or very seldom, before 12 at night. Then to the office; there

1. Peg Penn was being courted by Anthony Lowther, a Yorkshire gentleman.
2. Probably the song "The old Rowndhead. And the new turncoate", the first line of which describes it as "A new droll". It mocks the roundhead for hypocritically feigning godliness under the Commonwealth, before he adopts all the trappings of a cavalier to gain preferment under Charles. This fits Pepys's view of Penn (Bodleian Library, MS Rawl. Poet 84).

busy all the morning; and among other things, comes Sir W. Warren and talked with me a good while; whose discourse I love, he being a very wise man and full of good counsel, and his own practices for wisdom much to be observed. And among other things, he tells me how he is fallen in with my Lord Brouncker, who hath promised him most perticular inward friendship, and yet not to appear at the board to do so. And he told me how my Lord Brouncker should take notice of the two flagons he saw at my house at dinner at my late feast, and merrily (yet I know enviously) said I could not come honestly by them.[1] This I am glad to hear, though vexed to see his ignoble soul. But I shall beware of him; and yet it is fit he should see I am no mean fellow but can live in the world and have something. At noon home to dinner; and then to the office with my people and very busy, and did despatch to my great satisfaction abundance of business, and do resolve by the grace of God to stick to it till I have cleared my hand of most things wherein I am in arrear in public and private matters. At night home to supper and to bed. ⟨This day, ill news of my father's being very ill of his old grief, the Rupture,[2] which troubles me.⟩

18. Up, and most of the morning finishing my entry of my Journall during the late fire out of loose papers into this book, which did please me mightily when done, I writing till my eyes were almost blind therewith to make end of it. Then all the rest of the morning, and after a mouthful of dinner, all the afternoon in my closet till night, sorting all my papers which have lain unsorted for all the time we were at Greenwich during the plague. Which did please me also – I drawing on to put my office into a good posture, though much is behind.◆

At night, I by appointment home, where W. Batelier and his sister Mary, and the two Mercers,[3] to play at cards and sup; and did cut our great cake lately given us by Russell[4] – a very good one. Here very merry, late.

Sir W Pen told me this night how the King did make them a very sharp speech in the House of Lords today, saying that he did expect to have had more Bills. That he purposes to prorogue them on Monday come sennit. That whereas they have unjustly conceived some jealou[s]ys of his making a peace, he declares he knows

1. The silver and gilt flagons had been given by Denis Gauden, the Navy Victualler, for services rendered. *See* 28 July 1664.
2. Hernia.
3. Mary Mercer (Elizabeth's former companion) and her sister Anne.
4. John Russell, master ropemaker at Woolwich Yard.

of no such thing or treaty.[1] And so left them – but with so little effect, that as soon as come into the House, Sir W Coventry moving that now the King hath declared his intention of proroguing them, it would be loss of time to go on with the thing they were upon when they were called to the King, which was the calling over the Defaults of members appearing in the House;[2] for that before any person could now come or be brought to town, the House would be up. Yet the faction did desire to delay time, and contend so as to come to a division[3] of the House; where, however, it was carried by a few voices that the debate should be laid by. But this shows that they are not pleased, or that they have any awe over them from the King's displeasure.

The company being gone, to bed.

20. *Lords day.* Up betimes and down to the Old Swan; there called on Michell and his wife, which in her night linen appeared as pretty almost as ever to my thinking I saw woman. Here I drank some burned brandy. And they showed me their house which, poor people, they have built, and it is very pretty.[4] I invited them to dine with me; and so away to White-hall to Sir W. Coventry, with whom I have not been alone a good while. And very kind he is. And tells me how the business is now ordered, by order of council, for my Lord Brouncker to assist Sir J. Mennes in all matters of accounts relating to the Treasurer and Sir W. Penn in all matters relating to the victuallers' and pursers' accounts – which I am very glad of, and the more for that I think it will not do me any hurt at all.[5] Other discourse; much especially about the heat the House was in yesterday about the ill management of the Navy; which I was sorry to hear, though I think they were well answered both by Sir G. Carteret and W. Coventry, as he informs me the substance of their speeches. Having done with him, I home, mightily satisfied with my being with him; and coming home, I to church, and there beyond expectation find our seat and all the church crammed by twice as many people as used to be; and to my great joy find Mr.

1. It was true that official negotiations had not begun with France or the Dutch Republic, but soundings had been made to both. The Commons were wary of granting Charles money for the war, fearing he would dismiss parliament, make peace, and keep the money – so he could not afford to acknowledge negotiations.
2. I.e. members failing to attend without authorized excuse.
3. A vote, with MPs leaving to stand in separate lobbies according to their choice.
4. Michael and Betty Mitchell's strong-water house (for the sale of spirits) had burned in the Great Fire. This was a temporary structure on the same site.
5. Mennes was Comptroller of the Navy, an onerous job. His colleagues had been seeking to lessen his responsibilities since 1663.

Frampton[1] in the pulpit. So to my great joy I hear him preach, and I think the best sermon, for goodness – oratory – without affectation or study – that ever I heard in my life. The truth is, he preaches the most like an Apostle that ever I heard man. And was much the best time that ever I spent in my life at church. His text, *Ecclesiastes* 11, verse 8th – the words – "But if a man live many years and rejoice in them all, yet let him remember the days of darkness, which shall be many. All that cometh is vanity."

He done, I home; and there Michell and his wife and we dined, and mighty merry; I mightily taken, more and more, with her. After dinner, I with my brother away by water to White-hall and there walked in the park. And a little to my Lord Chancellors, where the King and Cabinet met, and there met Mr. Brisband, with whom good discourse; to White-hall towards night, and there he did lend me the *Third Advice to a paynter*, a bitter Satyr upon the service of the Duke of Albemarle the last year. I took it home with me and will copy it, having the former – being also mightily pleased with it.[2]

So after reading it, I to Sir W. Penn to discourse a little with him about the business of our prizes;[3] and so home to supper and to bed.

23.◆ To the New Exchange, there to take up my wife and Mercer, and to Temple Barr to my ordinary and had a dish of meat for them, they having not dined; and thence to the King's House and there saw *The Humerous Lieutenant* – a silly play, I think – only the spirit in it, that grows very Tall and then sinks again to nothing, having two heads treading upon one, and then Knipps singing, did please us.[4] Here, in a box above, we spied Mrs. Pierce; and going out, they called us, and so we stayed for them and Knipp took us all in and brought to us Nelly,[5] a most pretty woman, who acted the great part, Cœlia, today very fine, and did it pretty well; I kissed her and so did my wife, and a mighty pretty soul she is. We also saw Mrs.

1. Robert Frampton, a celebrated preacher and later Bishop of Gloucester.
2. John Brisbane, a naval official, supplied a manuscript copy of *The Third Advice to a Painter*, now widely attributed to Andrew Marvell. It satirized the conduct of the Four Days Battle in June 1666. Pepys already owned Marvell's *Second Advice* on the Battle of Lowestoft.
3. Ships seized by the *Flying Greyhound*, the privateer part-owned by Pepys and Penn.
4. A tragicomedy by John Fletcher at the Theatre Royal. In Act 4 sc. 3 a magician conjures up a spirit.
5. Nell Gwyn, one of the most talented actresses of the Restoration. This was the first time Pepys had met her. In the late 1660s she became the King's mistress.

Hall, which is my little Roman-nose black girl that is mighty pretty: she is usually called Betty. Knipp made us stay in a box and see the dancing preparatory to tomorrow for *The Goblins*,[1] a play of Suckelings not acted these 25 years, which was pretty; and so away thence, pleased with this sight also, and especially kissing of Nell; we away, Mr. Pierce and I on foot to his house, the women by coach. In our way we find the Guards of Horse in the street, and hear the occasion to be news that the Seamen are in a mutiny, which put me into a great fright.◆ And when I came home, hear of no disturbance there of the seamen, but that one of them being arrested today, others do go and rescue him. So to the office a little, and then home to supper and to my chamber a while, and then to bed.

26. Up, and at the office sat all the morning – where among other things, I did the first unkind [thing] that ever I did design to Sir W. Warren. But I did it now to some purpose, to make him sensible how little any friendship shall avail him if he wants mine. I perceive he doth nowadays court much my Lord Brouncker's favour, who never did any man much courtesy at the Board, nor ever will be able – at least, so much as myself. Besides, my Lord would do him a kindness in concurrence with me; but he would have the danger of the thing to be done lie upon me, if there be any danger in it (in drawing up a letter to Sir W. Warren's advantage); which I do not like, nor will endure. I was, I confess, very angry, and will venture the loss of Sir W. Warren's kindnesses rather then he shall have any man's friendship in greater esteem then mine.

At noon home to dinner; and after dinner to the office again and there all the afternoon. And at night poor Mrs. Turner came and walked in the garden for my advice about her husband and her, relating to my Lord Brouncker's late proceedings with them;[2] and I do give her the best I can, but yet can lay asides some ends of my own in what advice I do give her. So she being gone, I to make an end of my letters; and so home to supper and to bed – Balty lodging here with my brother, he being newly returned from mustering in the River.

31.◆ Thus the month ends. Myself in very good health, and content of mind in my family.[3] All our heads full in the office at this dividing of the Controller's duty, so that I am in some doubt how it may

1. A comedy by John Suckling.
2. Brouncker had laid claim to the lodgings used at the Navy Office by Elizabeth and Thomas Turner.
3. Household.

prove to intrench upon my benefits; but it cannot be much. The Parliament upon breaking up – having given the King money with much ado and great heats, and neither side pleased, neither King nor them. The imperfection of the Pole Bill, which must be mended before they rise, there being several horrible oversights to the prejudice of the King, is a certain sign of the care anybody hath of the King's business.[1] Prince Rupert very ill, and to be trepan'd on Saturday next.[2] Nobody knows who commands the fleet next year, or endeed whether we shall have a fleet or no. Great preparations in Holland and France. And the French have lately taken Antego from us, which vexes us.[3] I am in a little care, through my at last putting a great deal of money out of my hands again into the King's, upon tallies for Tanger; but the interest which I wholly lost while in my trunk is a temptation while things look safe, as they do in some measure for six months I think, and I would venture but little longer.

FEBRUARY.

3. *Lords day.* Up, and with Sir W. Batten and W. Penn by coach to White-hall; and there to Sir W. Coventry's chamber and there stayed till he was ready – talking; and among other things, of the Princes being trepanned, which was in doing just as we passed through the Stone Gallery, we asking at the door of his lodgings and were told so. We are all full of wishes for the good success – though I dare say but few do really concern ourselfs for him in our hearts. Up to the Duke of York, and with him did our business we come about; and among other things, resolve upon a meeting at the office tomorrow morning, Sir W. Coventry to be there to determine of all things necessary for the setting of Sir W. Penn to work in his victualling business. This did awake in me some thoughts of what might in discourse fall out touching my imployment – and did give me some apprehension of trouble. Having done here, and after our laying our necessities for money open to the Duke of York, but nothing obtained concerning it – we parted; and I with others

1. This day the Commons agreed several amendments to the Poll Bill, needed to raise funds for the crown and the war.
2. He needed an operation for a longstanding head wound, received on a Flanders campaign in the 1640s. His enemies alleged the illness was syphilis.
3. The French took Antigua in the Caribbean in November 1666. It was restored to Britain in the Treaty of Breda in 1667.

into the House and there hear that the work is done to the Prince in a few minutes, without any pain at all to him, he not knowing when it was done. It was performed by Moulins.[1] Having cut the outward table,[2] as they call it, they find the inner all corrupted, so as it came out without any force; and their fear is that the whole inside of his head is corrupted like that – which doth yet make them afeared of him; but no ill accident appeared in the doing of the thing, but all with all imaginable success; as Sir Alexander Frazier[3] did tell me himself; I asking him, who is very kind to me. I to the Chapel a little; but hearing nothing, did take a turn into the park, and then back to Chapel and heard a very good Anthemne to my heart's delight; and then to Sir G. Carteret's to dinner, and before dinner did walk with him alone a good while and from him hear our case likely, for all these acts, to be bad for money; which troubles me, the year spending so fast. And he tells me that he believes the Duke of York will go to sea with the fleet – which I am sorry for in respect to his person, but yet there is no person in condition to command the fleet, now the captains are grown so great, but him – it being impossible for anybody else but him to command any order or discipline among them. He tells me there is nothing at all in the late discourse about my Lord Sandwich and the French Embassadors meeting and contending for the way; which I wonder at, to see the confidence of report without any ground.[4] By and by to dinner, where very good company. Among other discourse, we talked much of Nostradamus his prophecy of these times and the burning of the City of London, some of whose verses are put into Bookers Almanac this year.[5] And Sir G. Carteret did tell a story, how at his death he did make the town swear that he should never be dug up, or his tomb opened, after he was buried; but they did after 60 years do it, and upon his breast they found a plate of brasse, saying what a wicked and unfaithful people the people of that place were, who after so many vows should disturb and open him such a day and year and hour – which if true, is very

1. James Molins, Surgeon to St Thomas's and St Bartholomew's hospitals.
2. The tables are two dense bony layers of the skull.
3. Physician to the King.
4. A few days before a rumour had spread that Sandwich's and the French Ambassador's entourages had come to blows in Madrid, killing two Englishmen and twenty-five Frenchmen.
5. John Booker in his almanac for 1667, *Telescopium Uranicum*, reported that in 1555 Nostradamus had predicted the Great Fire. He quoted Nostradamus's cryptic lines on London being burnt by thunder "de Vingt trois les Six" (interpretable as "three times twenty, and six" – in "66").

strange. Then we fell to talk of the burning of the City; and my Lady Carteret herself did tell us how abundance of pieces of burnt papers were cast by the wind as far as Cranborne;[1] and among others, she took up one, or had one brought her to see, which was a little bit of paper that had been printed, wherein there remained no more nor less then these words: *Time is; it is done*. After dinner I went and took a turn into the park, and then took boat and away home.◆

7. Lay long with pleasure with my wife; and then up and to the office, where all the morning; then home to dinner, and before dinner I went into my green dining room; and there talking with my brother upon matters relating to his Journy to Brampton tomorrow and giving him good counsel about spending that time which he shall stay in the country with my father, I looking another way, I heard him fall down, and turned my head and he was fallen down all along upon the ground, dead – which did put me into a great fright; and to see my brotherly love, I did presently lift him up from [the] ground, he being as pale as death. And being upon his legs, he did presently come to himself, and said he had something come into his stomach, very hot; he knew not what it was, nor ever had such a fit before. I never was so frighted but once, when my wife was ill at Ware upon the road.[2] And I did continue trembling a good while, and ready to weep to see him, he continuing mighty pale all dinner, and melancholy, that I was loath to let him take his journey tomorrow. But begun to be pretty well; and after dinner my wife and Barker[3] fell to singing, which pleased me pretty well, my wife taking mighty pains and pride that she shall come to trill; and endeed, I think she will. So to the office and there all the afternoon late doing business; and then home and find my brother pretty well. So to write a letter to my Lady Sandwich for him to carry, I having not writ to her a great while. Then to supper and so to bed. I did this night give him 20*s* for books and as much for his pocket, and 15*s* to carry him down. And so to bed. Poor fellow, he is so melancholy and withal, my wife says, harmless,[4] that I begin to love him, and would be loath he should not do well.

8. This morning my brother John came up to my bedside and took

1. George Carteret's official residence near Windsor, about 23 miles from the City of London.
2. *See* 14 Sept. 1663.
3. Elizabeth's paid companion.
4. Innocent, inoffensive.

his leave of us, going this day to Brampton. My wife loves him mightily, as one that is pretty harmless; and I do begin to fancy him from yesterday's accident, it troubling me to think I should be left without a brother or son, which is the first time that ever I had thoughts of that kind in my life. He gone, I up and to the office, where we sat upon the Victualler's accounts all the morning. At noon Lord Brouncker, W. Batten, W. Penn and myself to the Sun in Leadenhall-street to dinner, where an exceeding good dinner and good discourse. Sir W. Batten comes this morning from the House, where the King hath prorogued this Parliament to October next – I am glad they are up. The Bill for Accounts was not offered, the party being willing to let it fall – but the King did tell them he expected it.[1] They are parted with great heart-burnings, one party against the other. Pray God bring them hereafter together in better temper.◆

14.◆ H. Cholmly[2] and I to the Temple and there walked in the dark in the walks, talking of news; and he surprizes me with the certain news that the King did last night in council declare his being in Treaty with the Dutch. That they had sent him a very civil letter, declaring that if nobody but themselfs were concerned, they would not dispute the place of treaty but leave it to his choice; but that being obliged to satisfy therein a prince of equal quality with himself,[3] they must except any place in England or Spain. And so the King hath chosen The Hague, and thither hath chose my Lord Hollis and Harry Coventry to go Embassadors to treat; which is so mean a thing as all the world will believe that we do go to beg a peace of them, whatever we pretend;[4] and it seems all our Court are mightily for a peace, taking this [to] be the time to make one, while the King hath money, that he may save something of what the Parliament hath given him to put him out of debt, so as he may need the help of no more Parliaments as to the point of money. But our debt is so great, and expense daily so encreased, that I believe little of the money will be saved between this and the making of the peace up. But that which troubles me most is that we have chosen a

1. The Lords and Commons had failed to agree on the scope of a bill for the examination of accounts related to the war, so it was abandoned.
2. Sir Hugh Cholmley, First Gentleman-Usher to the Queen and known to Pepys through his Tangier work.
3. Louis XIV.
4. Negotiating on enemy soil was normally a sign of weakness. The location was later changed to Breda, also in the Dutch Republic. The ambassadors were Denzil Holles and Henry Coventry (brother of William). Negotiations began in mid-May between Britain, the Dutch Republic, France, and Denmark.

son of Secretary Morris, a boy never used to any business, to go Secretary to the Embassy;[1] which shows how little we are sensible of the weight of the business upon us. God therefore give a good end to it, for I doubt it; and yet do much more doubt the issue of our continuing the war, for we are in no wise fit for it. And yet it troubles me to think what Sir H. Cholmly says, that he believes they will not give us any reparation for what we have suffered by the warr, nor put us into any better condition then what we were in before the war, for that will be shameful for us. Thence parted with him and home through the dark over the ruins by coach, with my sword drawn, to my office, where despatched some business; and so home to my chamber and to supper and to bed.

This morning came up to my wife's bedside, I being up dressing myself, little Will Mercer[2] to be her Valentine; and brought her name writ upon blue paper in gold letters, done by himself, very pretty – and we were both well pleased with it. But I am also this year my wife's Valentine, and it will cost me 5*l* – but that I must have laid out if we had not been Valentines. So to bed.

15.◆ Home and to dinner, where I hear Pegg Pen is married this day privately;[3] no friends but two or three relations on his side and hers – borrowed many things of my kitchen for dressing their dinner. So after dinner I to the office and there busy and did much business, and late at it. Mrs. Turner came to me to hear how matters went; I told her of our getting rent for a house for her. She did give me account of this wedding today, its being private being imputed to its being just before Lent, and so vain to make new clothes till Easter, that they might see the fashions as they are like to be this summer – which is reason good enough. She tells me she hears he gives 4500*l* or 4000*l* with her. They are gone to bed – so I wish them much sport, and home to supper and to bed. They own the treaty for a peace publicly at Court, and the Commissioners providing themselfs to go over as soon as a passe comes for them.

16. Up and to the office, where all the morning. Among other things, great heat we were all in on one side or other in the examining witnesses against Mr. Carcasse about his buying of tickets, and a cunning knave I do believe he is and will appear, though I have

1. Nicholas, youngest son of Secretary of State William Morice.
2. Mary Mercer's brother and a neighbour, aged 17.
3. She married Anthony Lowther. The licence gives her age as 15 and his as 24.

thought otherwise heretofore.[1] At noon home to dinner and there find Mr. Andrews and Pierce and Hollyard, and they dined with us and merry; but we did rise soon for saving of my wife's seeing a new play this afternoon, and so away by coach and left her at Mrs. Pierces; myself to the Excise Office about business, and thence to the Temple to walk a little only, and then to Westminster to pass away time till anon. And here I went to Mrs. Martin's to thank her for her oysters and there yo did hazer tout ce que je would con her, and she grown la plus bold moher of the orbis – so that I was almost defessus of the pleasure que ego was used para tener with ella.[2]

Thence away to my Lord Bruncker's, and there was Sir Rob. Murray,[3] whom I never understood so well as now by this opportunity of discourse; he is a most excellent man of reason and learning, and understands the doctrine of Musique and everything else I could discourse of very finely. Here came Mr. Hooke, Sir George Ent, Dr. Wren,[4] and many others; and by and by the music, that is to say, Seignor Vincentio,[5] who is the maister Composer, and six more, where of two Eunuches (so tall, that Sir T. Harvy said well that he believes they did grow large by being gelt, as our Oxen do) and one woman, very well dressed and handsome enough but would not be kissed, as Mr. Killigrew, who brought the company in, did acquaint us.[6] They sent two Harpsicons before; and by and by, after tuning them, they begun; and I confess, very good music they made; that is, the composition exceeding good, but yet not at all more pleasing to me then what I have heard in English by Mrs. Knipp, Captain Cooke and others. Nor do I dote of the Eunuchs; they sing endeed pretty high and have a mellow kind of sound, but yet I have been as well satisfied with several women's voices, and men also, as Crispe of the Wardrobe. The woman sung well, but that which distinguishes all is this: that in singing, the words are

1. James Carkesse, a clerk in the Ticket Office and a client of Brouncker, was also accused of taking bribes. He continued to trouble Pepys, making repeated appearances in the diary. Dismissed in March, Carkesse petitioned the King, who ordered an enquiry by a committee of council. Their report was in his favour and he was reinstated. In 1679, after being sent to a madhouse, he wrote a book of verse in which he blamed Pepys for his struggles over the past thirteen years.
2. "I did do all that I would with her, and she grown the most bold woman of the world – so that I was almost weary of the pleasure that I was used to having with her."
3. Moray was, like Brouncker, a founder member of the Royal Society.
4. Robert Hooke, Ent and Christopher Wren were all founder members of the Royal Society.
5. Vincenzo Albrici of the King's Italian musicians.
6. Probably Leonora Albrici, Vincenzo's sister. Thomas Killigrew, manager of the Theatre Royal, was the organizer.

to be considered and how they are fitted with notes, and then the common accent of the country is to be known and understood by the hearer, or he will never be a good judge of the vocall music of another country. So that I was not taken with this at all, neither understanding the first nor by practice reconciled to the latter, so that their motions and risings and fallings, though it may be pleasing to an Italian or one that understands that tongue, yet to me it did not; but do from my heart believe that I could set words in English, and make music of them, more agreeable to any Englishman's eare (the most judicious) then any Italian music set for the voice and performed before the same man, unless he be acquainted with the Italian accent of speech. The composition as to the Musique part was exceeding good, and their justness in keeping time by practice much before any that we have, unless it be a good band of practised fiddlers. So away; here being Captain Cocke, with him stole away, leaving them at it, in his coach; and to Mrs. Pierces, where I took up my wife and there find that Mrs. Pierce's little girl is my Valentine, she having drawn me[1] – which I was not sorry for, it easing me of something more that I must have given to others. But here I do first observe the fashion of drawing of Motto's as well as names; so that Pierce, who drew my wife, did draw also a motto, and this girl drew another for me. What mine was I have forgot; but my wife's was (*Most virtuous and most fair*); which, as it may be used, or an Anagram made upon each name, might be very pretty. Thence with Cocke and my wife; set him at home, and then we home. To the office and there did a little business, troubled that I have so much been hindered by matters of pleasure from my business; but I shall recover it I hope in a little time. So home and to supper, not at all smitten with the music tonight, which I did expect should have been so extraordinary, Tom Killigrew crying it up, and so all the world, above all things in the world; and so to bed. One wonder I observed today: that there was no Musique in the morning to call up our new-married people; which is very mean methinks, and is as if they had married like dog and bitch.

25. Lay long in bed, talking with pleasure with my poor wife how she used to make coal fires and wash my foul clothes with her own hand for me, poor wretch, in our little room at my Lord Sandwiches; for which I ought for ever to love and admire her, and do, and persuade myself she would do the same thing again if God

1. In this custom, names of prospective valentines were written on slips of paper and drawn in a lottery.

should reduce us to it. So up, and by coach abroad to the Duke of Albemarle's about sending soldiers down to some ships; and so home, calling at a belt-makers to mend my belt, and so home and to dinner, where pleasant with my wife; and then to the office, where mighty busy all the day, saving going forth to the Change to pay for some things and on other occasions; and at my goldsmith's did observe the King's new Medall, where in little there is Mrs. Stewards face, as well done as ever I saw anything in my whole life I think – and a pretty thing it is that he should choose her face to represent Britannia by.[1] So at the office late very busy, and much business with great joy despatched; and so home to supper and to bed.

28. Up, and there comes to me Drumbleby[2] with a flagelette made to suit with my former, and brings me one Greeting, a master to teach my wife. I agree by the whole with him, to teach her to take out any lesson of herself for 4*l*. She was not ready to begin today, but doth tomorrow. So I to the office, where my Lord Brouncker and I only, all the morning, and did business. At noon to the Exchange and to Sir Rob. Viner's about settling my accounts there. So back home and to dinner, where Mr. Holliard[3] dined with us – and pleasant company he is. I love his company and he secures me against ever having the stone again. He gives it me as his opinion that the City will never be built again together as is expected while any restraint is laid upon them. He hath been a great loser, and would be a builder again; but he says he knows not what restrictions there will be, so as it is unsafe for him to begin.[4] He gone, I to the office and there busy till night, doing much business; then home and to my accounts; wherein, beyond expectation, I succeeded so well as to settle them very clear and plain, though by borrowing of monies this month to pay D Gawden and chopping and changing with my Tanger money, they were become somewhat intricate. And blessed be God, upon the evening my accounts, I do appear 6800*l* creditor. This done, I to supper about 12 at night, and so to bed – the weather for three or four days being come to be exceeding cold again, as any time this year.

I did within these six days see smoke still remaining of the late

1. The medal known as "The Peace of Breda", engraved by John Roettier. Frances Stuart was widely believed to be the King's mistress.
2. A flageolet (wind-instrument) maker.
3. Thomas Hollier, surgeon.
4. The new Rebuilding Act had left many crucial decisions, such as the width of streets, to be determined by the King and City.

fire in the City; and it is strange to think how to this very day I cannot sleep a-night without great terrors of fire; and this very night could not sleep till almost 2 in the morning through thoughts of fire.

Thus this month is ended with great content of mind to me – thriving in my estate, and my matters in my offices going pretty well as to myself. This afternoon Mr. Gawden was with me, and tells me more then I knew before: that he hath orders to get all the victuals he can to Plymouth and the Western ports and other outports, and some to Scotland; so that we do entend to keep but a flying fleet this year;[1] which it may be may preserve us a year longer, but the end of it must be ruin.

Sir J. Mennes this night tells me that he hears for certain that ballads are made of us in Holland for begging of a peace; which I expected, but am vexed at. So ends this month, with nothing of weight upon my mind but for my father and mother, who are both ill and have been so for some weeks – whom God help, but I do fear my poor father will hardly be ever thoroughly well again.[2]

MARCH. 166$\frac{6}{7}$.

2. Up, and to the office, where sitting all the morning; and among other things, did agree upon a distribution of 30000*l* and odd, which is the only sum we hear of like to come out of all the Poll Bill for the use of this office for buying of goods. I did herein some few courtesies for perticular friends I wished well to, and for the King's services also – and was therefore well pleased with what was done. Sir W Pen this day did bring an order from the Duke of York for our receiving from him a small vessel for a fireship and taking away a better of the King's for it, it being expressed for his great service to the King.[3] This I am glad of; not for his sake, but that it will give me a better ground, I believe, to ask something for myself of this kind; which I was fearful to begin. This doth make Sir W. Penn the most fond to me that can be. I suppose it is this: lest it

1. To save money and with peace moves under way, Charles and his advisers made the fateful decision not to prepare a battle fleet but instead to send out squadrons of smaller, faster ships.
2. End of the fourth manuscript volume.
3. Penn was turning over a ship to the Navy Board for use as a fireship and, as a reward for his wartime service, getting a better ship from the King in return.

should find any opposition from me; but I will not oppose, but promote it.

After dinner with my wife to the King's house, to see *The Mayden Queene*, a new play of Dryden's mightily commended for the regularity of it[1] and the strain and wit; and the truth is, there is a comical part done by Nell, which is Florimell, that I never can hope ever to see the like done again by man or woman. The King and Duke of York was at the play; but so great performance of a comical part was never, I believe, in the world before as Nell doth this, both as a mad girle and then, most and best of all, when she comes in like a young gallant; and hath the motions and carriage of a spark the most that ever I saw any man have.[2] It makes me, I confess, admire her. Thence home and to the office, where busy a while; and then home to read the lives of Henry the 5th and 6th, very fine, in Speede;[3] and so to bed. This day I did pay a bill of 50*l* from my father, it being so much out of my own purse given to pay my Uncle Robert's legacy to my aunt Perkins's child.

3.◆ I walked into the park, it being a fine but very cold day, and there took two or three turns the length of the Pell Mell. And there I met Serjeant Barcroft, who was sent for the Duke of Buckingham to have brought him prisoner to the Towre.[4] He came to town this day; and brings word that being overtaken and outridd by the Duchess of Buckingham, within a few miles of the Duke's house of Westthorp he believes, she got thither about a quarter of an hour before him and so had time to consider – so that when he came, the doors were kept shut against him. The next day, coming with officers of the neighbour market-town to force open the doors, they were open for him, but the Duke of Buckingham gone; so he took horse presently, and heard upon the road that the Duke of Buckingham was gone before him for London; so that he believes he is this day also come to town before him – but no news is yet heard of him. This is all he brings. Thence to my Lord Chancellor; and there meeting Sir H. Cholmly, he and I walked in my Lord's garden and talked, among other things, of the treaty; and he says there will

1. I.e. it followed neoclassical rules regarding drama's place, action, and time.
2. In Dryden's *Secret-Love, or The Maiden-Queen*, first acted this year at the Theatre Royal, Florimell impersonates a rakish gentleman in order to win her lover's mistresses away from him.
3. John Speed's *The History of Great Britaine*.
4. John Barcroft was sergeant-at-arms to the King. Since 1666 Buckingham had led a fierce parliamentary attack on the government, charging them with inefficiency and corruption in the conduct of the war.

certainly be a peace, but I cannot believe it. He tells me that the Duke of Buckingham his crimes, as far as he knows, is his being of a Caball with some discontented persons of the late House of Commons, and opposing the desires of the King in all his matters in the House – and endeavouring to become popular – and advising how the Commons' House should proceed, and how he would order the House of Lords – and that he hath been endeavouring to have the King's nativity calculated; which was done, and the fellow now in the Tower about it – which itself hath heretofore, as he says, been held treason, and people died for it – but by the Statute of Treasons, in Queen Mary's times and since, it hath been left out.[1] He tells me that this silly Lord hath provoked, by his ill-carriage, the Duke of York, my Lord Chancellor, and all the great persons, and therefore most likely will die. He tells me too, many practices of treachery against this King; as betraying him in Scotland and giving Oliver an account of the King's private councils;[2] which the King knows very well and yet hath pardoned him.

Here I passed away a little time more, talking with him and Creed, whom I met there; and so away, Creed walking with me to White-hall; and there I took water, and staying at Michells to drink, I home and there to read very good things in Fullers *Church History* and *Worthies*,[3] and so to supper; and after supper had much good discourse with W. Hewers, who supped with us, about the Ticket Office and the knaveries and extortions every day used there; and perticularly of the business of Mr. Carcasse, whom I fear I shall find a very rogue. So parted with him, and then to bed.

8.◆ To Westminster hall, where I saw Mr. Martin[4] the purser come through with a picture in his hand which he had bought, and observed how all the people of the Hall did fleer and laugh upon him, crying, "There is plenty grown up on a sudden!" and the truth is, I was a little troubled that my favour should fall on so vain a fellow as he; and the more because methought the people do gaze

1. John Heydon, an astrologer and associate of Buckingham, had been arrested; among his papers was an unsigned letter ordering him to cast the King's nativity. This had never been treasonable as such, though it might come within the terms of "compassing or imagining" the death of the monarch, which was treasonable. The charge was a pretext used by Buckingham's enemies for their own purposes.
2. Buckingham's intrigues in Scotland in 1650–1 had been with Argyll (leader of a rival royalist faction) rather than Cromwell.
3. Thomas Fuller's *Church-History of Britain* (1656) and his *History of the Worthies of England* (1662).
4. Husband of Pepys's mistress Betty Martin, whom Pepys had helped to his navy job.

upon me as the man that had raised him, and as if they guessed whence my kindness to him springs.

So thence to White-hall, where I find all met at the Duke of York's chamber; and by and by the Duke of York comes and Carcasse is called in, and I read the depositions and his answers, and he added with great confidence and good words, even almost to persuasion, what to say; and my Lord Brouncker, like a very silly solicitor,[1] argued against me and us all for him; and being asked first by the Duke of York his opinion, did give it for his[2] being excused. I next did answer the contrary very plainly; and had in this dispute (which vexed and will never be forgot by my Lord) many occasions of speaking severely, and did, against his bad practices. Commissioner Pett, like a fawning rogue, sided with my Lord Brouncker, but to no purpose; and W. Penn, like a cunning rogue, spoke mighty indifferently and said nothing in all the fray, like a knave as he is. But W. Batten spoke home, and did come off himself by the Duke's kindness very well; and then Sir G. Carteret and Sir W. Coventry, and the Duke of York himself, flatly as I said; and so he was declared unfit to continue in, and therefore to be presently discharged the office; which among other good effects, I hope will make my Lord Brouncker not altogether so high – when he shall consider he hath had such a public foyle[3] as this is.◆

9. Up, and to the office, where sat all the morning busy. At noon home to dinner, where Mrs. Pierce did continue with us, and her boy (who I still find every day more and more witty beyond his age) and did dine with us; and by and by comes in her husband and a brother-in-law of his, a parson, one of the tallest biggest men that ever I saw in my life. So to the office, where a meeting extraordinary about settling the number and wages of my Lord Brouncker's clerks for his new work upon the Treasurer's accounts;[4] but this did put us upon running into the business of yesterday about Carcasse, wherein I perceive he is most dissatisfied with me; and I am not sorry for it, having all the world but him of my side therein, for it will let him know another time that he is not to expect our submitting to him in everything, as I think he did heretofore expect. He did speak many severe words to me and I returned as many to him, so that I do think there cannot for a great while be any right peace

1. Agent or pleader.
2. Carkesse. For his offences *see* 16 Feb. 1667.
3. Defeat.
4. He had been appointed to assist Mennes, the Comptroller. *See* 20 Jan. 1667.

between us – and I care not a fart for it; but however, I must look about me and mind my business, for I perceive by his threats and inquiries he is and will endeavour to find out something against me or mine. Breaking up here somewhat brokenly, I home and carried Mrs. Pierce and wife to the New Exchange, and there did give her and myself a pair of gloves and then set her down at home; and so back again straight home and there to do business; and then to Sir W. Batten, where W. Penn and others, and mighty merry; only, I have got a great cold, and the scolding this day at the office with my Lord Brouncker hath made it worse, that I am not able to speak. But Lord, to see how kind Sir W. Batten and his Lady are to me upon this business of my standing by W. Batten against Carcasse; and I am glad of it. Captain Cocke, who was here tonight, did tell us that he is certain that yesterday a proclamation was voted at the Council touching the proclaiming of my Lord Duke of Buckingham a Traytor, and that it will be out on Monday.[1] So home late and drank some buttered ale, and so to bed and to sleep. This cold did most certainly come by my staying a little too long bare-legged yesterday morning when I rose while I looked out fresh socks and thread stockings, yesterday's having in the night, lying near the window, been covered with Snow within the window, which made me I durst not put them on.

22.◆ Landing at the Tower tonight, I met on Tower hill with Captain Cocke and spent half an hour walking in the dusk of the evening with him, talking of the sorrowful condition we are in. That we must be ruined if the Parliament do not come and chastize us. That we are resolved to make a peace whatever it cost. That the King is disobliging the Parliament in this interval all that may be, yet his money is gone and he must have more; and they likely not to give it without a great deal of do. God knows what the issue of it will be. But the considering that the Duke of York, instead of being at sea as Admirall, is now going from port to port, as he is at this day at Harwich and was the other day with the King at Sheernesse and hath ordered at Portsmouth how Fortificacions shall be made to oppose the enemy in case of invasion, is to us a sad consideration and a shameful to the nation, especially after so many proud vaunts as we have made against the Dutch; and all from the folly of the Duke of Albemarle, who made nothing of beating them; and Sir

1. The proclamation accused Buckingham of trying to raise mutiny and sedition and of resisting arrest. Buckingham had gone into hiding.

John Lawson,[1] he always declared that we never did fail to beat them with lesser numbers then theirs – which did so prevail with the King as to throw us into this war.

23. At the office all the morning, where Sir W. Penn came, being returned from Chatham from considering the means of fortifying the River Medway, by a chain at the stakes and ships laid there, with guns to keep the enemy from coming up to burn our ships – all our care now being [to] fortify ourselfs against their invading us. At noon home to dinner, and then to the office all the afternoon again – where Mr. Moore came, who tells me that there is now no doubt made of a peace being agreed on, the King having declared this week in council that they would treat at Bredagh.[2] He gone, I to my office, where busy late; and so to supper and to bed – vexed with our maid Luce, our cook-maid, who is a good drudging servant in everything else and pleases us, but that she will be drunk, and hath been so last night and all this day, that she could not make clean the house – my fear is only fire.

25. *Lady day.* Up, and with Sir W. Batten and W. Penn by coach to Exeter-house to our lawyers to have consulted about our trial tomorrow,[3] but missed them; so parted and W. Penn and I to Mr. Povy's about a little business of W. Penn's; where we went over Mr. Povy's house, which lies in the same good condition as ever, which is most extraordinary fine; and he was now at work with a cabinet-maker, making of a new inlaid table. Having seen his house, we away (having in our way thither called at Mr. Lilly's,[4] who was working; and endeed, his pictures are without doubt much beyond Mr. Hales's, I think I may say I am convinced); but a mighty proud man he is, and full of state. So home and to the office; and by and by to dinner, a poor dinner, my wife and I, at Sir W. Penn's; and then he and I before to Exeter-house, where did not stay; but to the King's playhouse, and by and by comes Mr. Lowder and his wife and mine and into a box forsooth, neither of them being dressed, which I was almost ashamed of – Sir W. Penn and I in the pit; and here saw *The Mayden Queene* again; which endeed, the more I see the more I like, and is an excellent play, and so done by

1. Vice-Admiral, killed in the Battle of Lowestoft in 1665.
2. Breda in the Dutch Republic.
3. A trial at the court of the Admiralty, concerning the fate of a Swedish ship that had been captured by the privateer owned by Pepys, Batten, and Penn. They were awarded some of the prize but the verdict was appealed.
4. Peter Lely.

Nell her merry part, as cannot be better done in Nature I think. Thence home, and there I find letters from my brother which tell me that yesterday, when he wrote, my mother did rattle in the throat, so as they did expect every moment her death, which though I have a good while expected, did much surprize me; yet was obliged to sup at Sir W. Penn's, and my wife; and there counterfeited some little mirth, but my heart was sad; and so home after supper and to bed, and much troubled in my sleep with dreams of my being crying by my mother's bedside, laying my head over hers and crying, she almost dead and dying, and so waked; but which is strange, methought she had hair on her face, and not the same kind of face as my mother really has; but yet did not consider that, but did weep over her as my mother – whose soul God have mercy of.

26. Up, with a sad heart in reference to my mother, of whose death I do undoubtedly expect to hear the next post, if not of my father's also, who, by his pain as well as his grief for her, is very ill. But on my own behalf, I have cause to be joyful this day, as being my usual feast-day for my being cut of the stone this day nine years; and through God's blessing am at this day and have long been in as good condition of health as ever I was in my life, or any man in England is, God make me thankful for it. But the condition I am in in reference to my mother makes it unfit for me to keep my usual feast, unless it should please God to send her well (which I despair wholly of); and then I will make amends for it by observing another day in its room. So to the office, and at the office all the morning, where I had an opportunity to speak to Sir Jo. Harman about my desire to have my brother Balty go again with him to sea as he did the last year; which he doth seem not only contented, but pleased with – which I was glad of.◆

27.◆ So I home, and there up to my wife in our chamber; and there received from my brother the news of my mother's dying on Monday, about 5 or 6 a-clock in the afternoon, and that the last time she spoke of her children was on Friday last, and her last words was, "God bless my poor Sam!" The reading hereof did set me a-weeping heartily; and so, weeping to myself a while and my wife also to herself – I then spoke to my wife, recollecting myself, and endeed having some thoughts how much better, both for her and us, it is then it might have been had she outlived my father and me or my happy present condition in the world, she being helpless, I was the sooner at ease in my mind; and then found it necessary to go abroad with my wife to look after the providing mourning to send into the country, some tomorrow and more against Sundy, for my family, being resolved to put myself and wife, and Barker and Jane, W Hewers and Tom, in mourning; and my two under-maids, to give them hoods and scarfs and gloves. So to my tailor's and up and down; and then home and to my office a little; and then to supper and to bed – my heart sad and afflicted, though my judgment at ease.

31. *Lords day.* Up; and my tailor's boy brings my mourning clothes home, and my wife's, hers and Barker's; but they go not to church this morning. I to church, and with my mourning, very handsome, and new periwig make a great show. After church, home to dinner, and there came Betty Michell and her husband; I do and shall love her; but, poor wretch, she is now almost ready to lie down.[1] After dinner, Balty (who dined also with us) and I with Sir J. Mennes in his coach to White-hall, but did nothing; but by water to Strand bridge and thence walked to my Lord Treasurer's, where the King, Duke of York, and the Caball,[2] and much company without; and a fine day. Anon comes out from the Caball my Lord Hollis and Mr. H. Coventry, who it is conceived have received their instructions from the King this day; they being to begin their journey towards their treaty at Bredagh speedily, their passes being come. Here I saw the Lady Northumberland and her daughter-in-law (my Lord Treasurer's daughter), my Lady Piercy, a beautiful lady endeed. So away back by water; and left Balty at White-hall, and I to Mrs. Martin and there haze todo which yo would hazer con her;[3] and so by coach home and there to my chamber; and then to supper and bed – having not had time to make up my accounts of this month at this very day, but will in a day or two and pay my forfeit for not doing it, though business hath most hindered me.[4]

The month shuts up, only with great desires of peace in all of us, and a belief that we shall have a peace in most people, if a peace can be had on any terms, for there is a necessity of it; for we cannot go on with the war, and our maisters are afeared to come to depend upon the good will of the Parliament any more as I do hear.

1. She gave birth in late April.
2. "The Cabal" meant select members of Charles's privy council, loosely equivalent to a cabinet.
3. "there did all which I would do with her".
4. His vows now apparently included one to review his accounts at the end of each month. A fine was due to the poor box.

APRILL.

6. Up, and betimes in the morning down to the Tower wharfe, there to attend the shipping of soldiers to go down to man some ships going out; and pretty to see how merrily some and most go and how sad others, the leave they take of their friends, and the tears that some wifes and others' wenches shed to part with them: a pretty mixture. So to the office, having stayed as long as I could, and there sat all the morning; and then home at noon to dinner; and then abroad, Balty with me, and to White-hall by water to Sir G. Carteret about Balty's 1500*l* contingent money for the fleet to the West Indys;[1] and so away with him to the Exchange and mercers and drapers, up and down, to pay all my scores occasioned by this mourning for my mother – and emptied a 50*l* bag; and it was a joy to me to see that I am able to part with such a sum without much inconvenience – at least, without any trouble of mind. So [to] Captain Cocke's to meet Fenn to talk about this money for Balty; and there Cocke tells me that he is confident there will be a peace, whatever terms be asked us; and he confides that it will take, because the French and Dutch will be jealous one of another which shall give the best terms, lest the other should make the peace with us alone, to the ruin of the third – which is our best defence, this jealousy, for aught I at present see. So home and there very late, very busy; and then home to supper and to bed – the people having got their house very clean against Mondy dinner.[2]

15. Lay long in bed – and by and by called up by Sir H. Chumbly, who tells me that my Lord Middleton is for certain chosen Governor of Tanger; a man of moderate understanding, not covetous, but a soldier-of-fortune and poor.[3] Here comes Mr. Sanchy with an impertinent business to me of a ticket, which I put off. But by and by comes Dr Childe[4] by appointment, and sat with me all the morning, making me Bases and inward parts to several songs that I desired of him – to my great content. Then dined and then abroad

1. Balty St Michel was going as Deputy-Treasurer with John Harman's fleet.
2. A dinner on Easter Monday.
3. John Middleton, 1st Earl of Middleton. Pepys did not yet realize that he was famous as a royalist leader of the Scottish army during the civil wars. Middleton did not sail for Tangier until September 1669.
4. William Child, one of the King's musicians and an organist at the Chapel Royal.

by coach, and I set him down at Hatton Guarden and I to the King's house by chance, where a new play; so full as I never saw it, I forced to stand all the while close to the very door, till I took cold, and many people went away for want of room. The King and Queen and Duke of York and Duchesse there and all the Court, and Sir W. Coventry. The play called *The Change of Crownes*, a play of Ned Howard's, the best that I ever saw at that House, being a great play and serious; only, Lacy did act the country gentleman come up to Court, who doth abuse the Court with all the imaginable wit and plainness, about selling of places and doing everything for money.[1] The play took very much. Thence I to my new bookseller's and there bought Hookers *Policy*, the new edition, and Dugdale's history of the Inns of Court, of which there was but a few saved out of the Fire – and Playfords new ketch-book, that hath a great many new fooleries in it.[2] Then home; a little at the office, and then to supper and to bed, mightily pleased with the new play.

20. Up, with much pain in my eare and palate. To the office, out of humour all the morning. At noon dined; and with my wife to the King's house, but there found the bill torn down and no play acted; and so being in the humour to see one, went to the Duke of York's house and there saw *The Witts* again; which likes me better then it did the other day, having much wit in it.[3] Here met with Rolt,[4] who tells me the reason of no play today at the King's house – that Lacy had been committed to the porter's lodge[5] for his acting his part in the late new play; and that being thence released, he came to the King's house and there met with Ned Howard, the poet of the play, who congratulated his release; upon which, Lacy cursed him as that it was the fault of his nonsensical play that was the cause of his ill usage; Mr. Howard did give him some reply, to which Lacy [answered] him that he was more a fool then a poet; upon which Howard did give him a blow on the face with his glove; on

1. John Lacy played Asinello in Edward Howard's tragicomedy. The character sells his estate, assuming he can obtain preferment at court by bribery. Lacy reportedly added some of his own jokes to the satire.
2. His new bookseller was John Starkey in Fleet Street, the Great Fire having destroyed the bookshops in St Paul's Churchyard. He purchased Richard Hooker's *Of the Lawes of Ecclesiastical Politie* (1666), William Dugdale's *Origines Juridiciales* (1666) and John Playford's musical collection *Catch that Catch Can* (1667).
3. A comedy by William Davenant, showing at the Lincolns Inn Fields Theatre. Pepys had seen it earlier in the week.
4. Captain Edward Rolt, formerly an army officer under Cromwell; he was friendly with several actors.
5. At the gatehouse at Whitehall Palace; it served as a prison.

which Lacy, having a cane in his hand, did give him a blow over the pate. Here, Rolt and others that discoursed of it in the pit this afternoon did wonder that Howard did not run him through, he being too mean a fellow to fight with – but Howard did not do anything but complain to the King of it; so the whole House is silenced – and the gentry seem to rejoice much at it, the House being become too insolent. Here was many fine ladies this afternoon at this House as I have at any time seen; and so after the play, I home and there wrote to my father; and then to walk in the garden with my wife, resolving by the grace of God to see no more plays till Whitsuntide, I having now seen a play every day this week, till I have neglected my business, and that I am ashamed of, being found so much absent – the Duke of York and Sir W. Coventry having been out of town at Portsmouth did the more imbolden me thereto. So home; and having brought home with me from Fanchurch-street a hundred of sparrowgrass,[1] cost 18*d*, we had them and a little bit of salmon which my wife had a mind to, cost 3*s*; so to supper, and my pain being somewhat better in my throat, we to bed.

26. Up, and by coach with W. Batten and W. Penn to White-hall and there saw the Duke of Albemarle, who is not well and doth grow crazy.[2] Thence I to St. James's, there to meet Sir G. Carteret, and did, and Lord Berkely, to get them (as we would have done the Duke of Albemarle) to the meeting of the Lords of Appeale in the business of one of our prizes.[3] With them to the meeting of the Guinny Company, and there stayed; and went with Lord Berkely. While I was waiting for him in the Matted Gallery, a young man was most finely working in Indian Inke the great picture of the King and Queen sitting, by van Dike, and did it very finely.[4] Thence to Westminster-hall to hear our cause, but did not come before them today; so went down and walked below in the Hall and there met with Ned Pickering,[5] who tells me the ill news of his nephew Gilbert ⟨who is turned a very rogue⟩. And then I took a turn with Mr. Eveling, with whom walked two hours, till almost one of the clock – talking of the badness of the Government, where nothing but wickedness, and wicked men and women command the King.

1. Asparagus.
2. Infirm.
3. A Swedish ship captured by Pepys, Batten, and Penn's privateer. The Swedes were contesting the decision of the Admiralty Court that had given much of the cargo to Pepys and his partners.
4. A portrait of Charles I and Henrietta Maria (c.1632) by Anthony van Dyck.
5. Sandwich's relative.

That it is not in his nature to gainsay anything that relates to his pleasures. That much of it arises from the sickliness of our Ministers of State,[1] who cannot be about him as the idle companions are, and therefore give way to the young rogues; and then from the negligence of the Clergy, that a Bishop shall never be seen about him, as the King of France hath always.◆ He tells me the King of France hath his Maistresses, but laughs at the foolery of our King, that makes his bastards princes, and loses his revenue upon them – and makes his mistresses his maisters. And the King of France did never grant Lavaliere anything to bestow on others; and gives a little subsistence, but no more, to his bastards.[2] He told me the whole story of Mrs. Stewarts going away from Court, he knowing her well and believes her, to her leaving the Court, to be as virtuous as any woman in the world;[3] and told me, from a Lord that she told it to but yesterday with her own mouth, and a sober man, that when the Duke of Richmond did make love to her,[4] she did ask the King and he did the like also; and that the King did not deny it; and told this Lord that she was come to that pass as to resolve to have married any gentleman of 1500*l* a year that would have had her in honour – for it was come to that pass, that she could not longer continue at Court without prostituting herself to the King, whom she had so long kept off, though he had liberty more then any other had, or he ought to have, as to dalliance. She told this Lord that she had reflected upon the occasions she [had] given the world to think her a bad woman, and that she had no way but to marry and leave the Court, rather in this way of discontent then otherwise – that the world might see that she sought not anything but her honour; and that she will never come to live at Court, more then when she comes to town to come to kiss the Queen her mistress's hand; and hopes, though she hath little reason to hope, she can please her Lord so as to reclaim him, that they may yet live comfortably in the country on his estate. She told this Lord that all the jewels she ever had given her at Court, or any other presents (more then the King's allowance of 700*l* per annum out of the Privy-purse for her clothes) was: at her first coming, the King did give her a necklace of pearl of about 1100*l*; and afterward, about seven months since,

1. Clarendon and Southampton, the elder statesmen in the King's service.
2. Louise de La Vallière was Louis XIV's principal mistress until 1667. At this time Louis had yet to legitimate any children by her or award them titles.
3. Frances Stuart (widely reputed to be Charles's mistress) had eloped from court and married the Duke of Richmond at the end of March.
4. Court her.

when the King had hopes to have obtained some courtesy of her, the King did give her some jewels, I have forgot what, and I think a pair of pendants. The Duke of York, being once her Valentine, did give her a jewell of about 800*l*; and my Lord Mandeville, her valentine this year, a ring of about 300*l*; and the King of France, who would have had her mother (who he says is one of the most cunning women in the world) to have let her stay in France, saying that he loved her not as a mistress but as one that he could marry as well as any lady in France, and that if she might stay, for the honour of his Court he would take care she should not repent. But her mother, by command of the Queene-mother, thought rather to bring her into England, and the King of France did give her a Jewell; so that Mr. Eveling believes she may be worth in jewells about 6000*l*, and that that is all that she hath in the world – and a worthy woman, and in this hath done as great an act of honour as ever was done by woman. That now the Countesse Castlemayne doth carry all before her; and among other arguments to prove Mrs. Stewart to have been honest to the last, he says that the King's keeping in still with my Lady Castlemaine doth show it, for he never was known to keep two mistresses in his life – and would never have kept to her had he prevailed anything with Mrs. Steward. She is gone yesterday with her Lord to Cobham.[1]◆ After having this long discourse, we parted about one of the clock; and so away by water home, calling on Michell, whose wife and girl is pretty well; and I home and to dinner, and after dinner with Sir W. Batten to White-hall, there to attend the Duke of York before council, where we all met at his closet and there did the little business we had; and here he did tell us how the King of France is intent upon his design against Flanders, and hath drawn up a remonstrance of the cause of the war, and appointed the 20th of the next month for his Rendezvouz, and himself to depart for the Campagne the 30th – so that this we are in hopes will keep him in imployment.[2] Turin[3] is to be his Generall. Here was Carcasse's business unexpectedly moved by him, but what was done therein appears in my account of his case in writing by itself. Certain news of the Dutch being abroad on our coast with 24 great ships.[4] This

1. Cobham Hall, Richmond's house near Gravesend.
2. Louis XIV laid claim to large parts of the Spanish Netherlands. This was the prelude to the War of Devolution (1667–8), which began in May.
3. The Vicomte de Turenne.
4. This was a diversionary fleet. The Dutch plan for this year was to attack British shipping in the Thames, and their main fleet left the Dutch coast for that purpose on 4 June.

done, Sir W. Batten and I back again to London; and in the way met my Lady Newcastle,[1] going with her coaches and footmen all in velvet; herself (whom I never saw before) as I have heard her often described (for all the town-talk is nowadays of her extravagancies), with her velvet-cap, her hair about her ears, many black patches because of pimples about her mouth, naked necked, without anything about it, and a black juste-au-corps;[2] she seemed to me a very comely woman – but I hope to see more of her on May-day. My mind is mightily of late upon a coach. At home to the office, where late, spending all the evening upon entering in long-hand our late passages with Carcasse for memory sake; and so home, in great pain in my back by the uneasiness of Sir W. Batten's coach driving hard this afternoon over the stones to prevent coming too late. So at night to supper in great pain, and to bed, where lay in great pain, not able to turn myself all night.

MAY.

1. Up, it being a fine day; and after doing a little business in my chamber, I left my wife to go abroad with W. Hewer and his mother in a hackney-coach incognit[3] to the park, while I abroad to the Excize Office first, and there met the Cofferer and Sir St. Fox about our money matters there, wherein we agreed; and so to discourse of my Lord Treasurer,[4] who is a little better then he was of the stone, having rested a little this night. I there did acquaint them with my knowledge of that disease, which I believe will be told my Lord Treasurer. Thence to Westminster, in the way meeting many milk-maids with their garlands upon their pails, dancing with a fiddler before them, and saw pretty Nelly[5] standing at her lodgings door in Drury-lane in her smock-sleeves and bodice, looking upon one – she seemed a mighty pretty creature. To the Hall and there walked a while, it being term; and thence home to the Rose and there had Doll Lane vener para me; but it was in a lugar mighty ouvert, so as we no poda hazer algo; so parted and then met again at the Swan, where for la misma reason we no pode hazer, but put

1. Margaret Cavendish, Duchess of Newcastle, writer and philosopher.
2. A close-fitting long coat.
3. I.e. in a closed coach.
4. The Earl of Southampton.
5. Nell Gwyn.

off to recontrar anon,[1] which I only used as a put-off; and so parted and to my Lord Crew's, where I found them at dinner; and among others, Mrs. Bocket, which I have not seen a long time, and two little dirty children, and she as idle a prating, impertinent woman as ever she was. After dinner my Lord took me alone, walked with me, giving me an account of the meeting of the Commissioners for Accounts, whereof he is one.[2]◆ Then to talk of my Lord Sandwich, whom my Lord Crew hath a great desire might get to be Lord Treasurer if the present Lord should die, as it's believed he will in a little time – and thinks he can have no competitor but my Lord Arlington, who it is given out desires [it]. But my Lord thinks it is not so, for that the being Secretary doth keep him a great[er] interest with the King then the other would do – at least, doth believe that if my Lord would surrender him his Wardrobe place, it would be a temptation to Arlington to assist my Lord in getting the Treasurer['s].[3] I did object to my Lord that it would be no place of content nor safety, nor honour for my Lord – the State being so indigent as it is and the [King] so irregular, and those about him, that my Lord must be forced to part with anything to answer his warrants; and that therefore I do believe the King had rather have a man that may be one of his vicious cabal, then a sober man that will mind the public, that so they may sit at cards and dispose of the revenue of the kingdom. This my Lord was moved at, and said he did not indeed know how to answer it, and bid me think of it and so said he himself would also do. He doth mightily cry out of the bad management of our monies, the King having had so much given him; and yet when the Parliament do find that the King should have 900000*l* in his purse by the best account of issues they have yet seen, yet we should report in the Navy a debt due from the King of 900000*l*;[4] which I did confess I doubted was true in the first, and knew to be true in the last, and did believe that there was

1. "had Doll Lane come to me; but it was in a place mighty open, so as we could not do anything; so parted and then met again at the Swan where for the same reason we could not do [it], but put off to meet anon".
2. A short-lived committee appointed by the King to examine accounts related to the war.
3. Lord Crew thinks Sandwich should seek to be Lord Treasurer. Rumour has it that Arlington, the Secretary of State, desires to be Lord Treasurer himself, but Crew doubts this because Arlington's current position is of more influence with the King. Crew believes if Sandwich surrendered his place as Master of the King's Wardrobe, Arlington would be inclined to support his bid to be Lord Treasurer. Pepys goes on to tell Crew his reservations about Sandwich's taking up that post.
4. This was the figure the navy had reported owing in September 1666.

some great miscarriages in it; which he owned to believe also, saying that at this rate it is not in the power of the kingdom to make a war nor answer the King's wants. Thence away to the King's playhouse by agreement; met Sir W. Penn and saw *Love in a Maze*;[1] but a sorry play, only Lacy's clowne's part, which he did most admirably endeed; and I am glad to find the rogue at liberty again. Here was but little, and that ordinary company. We sat at the upper bench next the boxes; and I find it doth pretty well – and hath the advantage of seeing and hearing the great people, which may be pleasant when there is good store. Now was only Prince Rupert and my Lord Lauderdale, and my Lord ,[2] (the naming of whom puts me in mind of my seeing at Sir Robt. Viner's[3] two or three great silver flagons made with inscriptions, as gifts of the King to such and such persons of quality as did stay in town the late great plague for the keeping things in order in the town; which is a handsome thing); but here was neither Hart, Nell, nor Knepp; therefore the play was not likely to please me. Thence Sir W. Penn and I in his coach, Tiburne way, into the park; where a horrid dust and number of coaches, without pleasure or order.[4] That which we and almost all went for was to see my Lady Newcastle; which we could not, she being fallowed and crowded upon by coaches all the way she went, that nobody could come near her; only, I could see she was in a large black coach, adorned with silver instead of gold, and so with the curtains and everything black and white, and herself in her cap; but other parts I could not make. But that which I did see and wonder at, with reason, was to find Pegg Penn in a new coach, with only her husband's pretty sister with her, both patched and very fine, and in much the finest coach in the park and I think that ever I did see, one or other, for neatness and richness in gold and everything that is noble – my Lady Castlemaine, the King, my Lord St. Albans, nor Mr. Germin have so neat a coach that ever I saw – and Lord, to have them have this, and nothing else that is correspondent, is to me one of the most ridiculous sights that ever I did see, though her present dress was well enough; but to live in the condition they do at home, and be abroad in this coach, astonishes me. When we had spent half an hour in the park, we went out again, weary of the dust and despairing of seeing my Lady Newcastle; and so back the same way and

1. A comedy by James Shirley.
2. Probably Lord Craven, who been active in London during the plague.
3. The King's goldsmith.
4. Parading in coaches in Hyde Park was a May Day tradition.

to St. Jones's,[1] thinking to have met my Lady Newcastle before she got home; but we staying by the way to drink, she got home a little before us, so we lost our labours; and then home, where we find the two young ladies come home and their patches[2] off (I suppose Sir W. Penn doth not allow of them in his sight) and going out of town tonight, though late, to Walthamstow. So to talk a little at Sir W. Batten's, and then home to supper, where I find Mrs. Hewer and her son, who have been abroad with my wife in the park; and so after supper to read and then to bed.◆

15. ⟨⟨This morning my wife had some things brought home by a new woman of the ⟨New⟩ Exchange, one Mrs. Smith, which she would have me see for her fine hand; and endeed, it is a fine hand and the woman I have observed is a mighty pretty-looked woman.⟩⟩ Up, and with Sir W. Batten and J. Mennes to St. James's, and stopped at Temple Barr for Sir J. Mennes to go into the Devil tavern to shit, he having drunk whey and his belly wrought. Being come, we up to the Duke of York's chamber; who when ready, we to our usual business, and being very glad that we all that signed it, that is, Sir J. Mennes, W. Batten, W. Penn and myself, and then Sir G. Carteret and W. Coventry, Brouncker, and T. Harvy, and the officers of the Ordinance, Sir J. Duncombe and Mr. Chichely – I presented our report about Carcasse to the Duke of York, and did afterwards read it, with that success that the Duke of York was for punishing him, not only with turning him out of the office but what other punishment he could; which nobody did forward, and so he escaped only with giving security to secure the King against double tickets[3] of his, and other things that he might have wronged the King or subject in before his dismission. Yet Lord, to see how our silly Lord Brouncker would have stirred to have justified this rogue, though to the reproach of all us that have signed; which I shall never forget to have been a most malicious or a most silly act, and I do think it is as much the latter as the other, for none but a fool could have done as this silly Lord hath done in this business.◆ News still that my Lord Treasurer is so ill as not to be any man of this world;[4] and it is said that the Treasury shall be managed by commission. I would to God Sir G. Carteret or my Lord Sandwich be in it – but the latter is the more fit for it. This day, going to

1. St John's, Clerkenwell. The Duchess's London house was in Clerkenwell Close.
2. Fashionable black patches, worn on the face.
3. The fraudulent issue of two tickets pledging payment to the same seaman.
4. Lord Treasurer Southampton died of a bladder stone the next day.

White-hall, Sir W. Batten did tell me strange stories of Sir W. Penn: how he is already ashamed of that fine coach which his son-in-law and daughter have made; and endeed, it is one of the most ridiculous things for people of their low, mean fashion to make such a coach that ever I saw. He tells me how his people comes, as they do to mine every day, to borrow one thing or other; and that his Lady hath been forced to sell some coals (in the late dear time) only to enable her to pay money that she hath borrowed of Griffin to defray her family expense – which is a strange story for a rogue that spends so much money on clothes and other occasions himself as he doth. But that which is most strange, he tells me that Sir W. Penn doth not give 6000*l*, as is usually [supposed], with his daughter to him; and that Mr. Lowder is come to use the Tubb; that is, to bathe and sweat himself, and that his lady is come to use the Tubb too; which he takes to be that he hath and hath given her the pox,[1] but I hope it is not so – "but," says Sir W. Batten, "this is a fair Joynture that he hath made her;" meaning by that, the costs [of] the having of a Bath.

22. Up and by water to White-hall to Sir G. Carteret, who tells me now for certain how the Commission for the Treasury is disposed of: *viz.*, to Duke of Albemarle, Lord Ashly, Sir W. Coventry, Sir Jo. Duncum, and Sir Tho. Clifford; at which he says all the whole Court is disturbed, it having been once concluded otherwise, into the other hands◆; but all of a sudden the King's choice was changed, and these are to be the men; the first of which is only for a puppet to give honour to the rest.[2] He doth presage that these men will make it their business to find faults in the management of the late Lord Treasurer and in discouraging the banquiers;[3] but I am (whatever I in compliance do say to him) of another mind, and my heart is very glad of it; for I do expect they will do much good, and that it is the happiest thing that hath appeared to me for the good of the nation since the King came in. Thence to St. James's and up to the Duke of York; and there in his chamber Sir W. Coventry did of himself take notice of this business of the Treasury, wherein he is in the Commission, and desired that I would be thinking of anything fit for him to be acquainted with for the lessening of charge and bettering of our credit; and what our

1. Sweating was a common treatment for syphilis.
2. False rumours had circulated that the Lord Chancellor and the Secretaries of State would be among the Commissioners. With the exception of Albemarle, the new appointments were men known for their administrative skills.
3. Bankers.

expense hath been since the King's coming home, which he believes will be one of the first things they shall enquire into – which I promised him; and from time to time, which he desires, give him an account of what I can think of worthy his knowledge. I am mighty glad of this opportunity of professing my joy to him in what choices the King hath made, and the hopes I have that it will save the kingdom from perishing, and how it doth encourage me to take pains again, after my having through despair neglected it: which he told me of himself that it was so with him; that he had given himself up to more ease then ever he expected; and that his opinion of matters was so bad, that there was no public imployment in the kingdom should have been accepted by him but this which the King hath now given him; and therein he is glad, in hopes of the service he may do therein – and in my conscience he will.◆

26. *Lords day.* Up sooner then usual on Sundays, and to walk, it being exceeding hot all night (so as this night I begin to leave off my waistcoat[1] this year) and this morning; and so to walk in the garden till toward church time, when my wife and I to church; where several strangers of good condition came to our pew, where the pew was full. At noon dined at home, where little Michell came, and his wife, who continues mighty pretty. After dinner, I by water alone to Westminster, where not finding Mrs. Martin within, did go toward the parish church and in the way did overtake her, who resolved to go into the church with her that she was going with (Mrs. Hargrave, the little crooked woman, the vintner's wife of the Dog) and then go out again; and so I to the church; and seeing her return, did go to go out again myself, but met with Mr. Howlett, who offering me a pew in the gallery, I had no excuse but up with him I must go, and there, much against my will, stayed out the whole church in pain, while she expected me at home; but I did entertain myself with my perspective glass[2] up and down the church, by which I had the great pleasure of seeing and gazing a great many very fine women; and what with that and sleeping, I passed away the time till sermon was done; and then to Mrs. Martin and there stayed with her an hour or two, and there did what jo[3] would with her. And after having been here so long, I away to my boat, and up with it as far as Barne Elmes, reading of Mr. Eveling's late new book against Solitude, in which I do not find

1. Warm undergarment.
2. Telescope.
3. "I".

much excess of good matter, though it be pretty for a by-discourse.[1] I walked the length of the Elmes, and with great pleasure saw some gallant ladies and people, come with their bottles and basket[s] and chairs and form[s][2] to sup under the trees by the waterside, which was mighty pleasant. I to boat again and to my book; and having done that, I took another book, Mr. Boyles of Colours, and there read where I left,[3] finding many fine things worthy observation. And so landed at the Old Swan and so home, where I find my poor father newly come out of an unexpected fit of his pain, that they feared he would have died. They had sent for me to White-hall and all up and down, and for Mr. Holliard also, who did come. But W Hewers being here did I think do the business, in getting my father's bowel, that was fallen down, into his body again. And that which made me the more sensible of it was that he this morning did show me the place where his bowels did use to fall down and swell, which did trouble me to see. But above all things, the poor man's patience under it, and his good heart and humour as soon as he was out of it, did so work upon me, that my heart was sad to think of his condition; but do hope that a way will be found by a steele truss to relieve him. By and by to supper, all our discourse about Brampton, and my intentions to build there if I could be free of my engagement to my Uncle Tho and his son, that they may not have what I have built, against my will, to them, whether I will or no, in case of my and my brothers being without heirs males[4] – which is the true reason why I am against laying out money upon that place, together with my fear of some inconvenience by being so near Hinchingbrooke; being obliged to be a servant to that family,[5] and subject to what expenses they shall cost me, and to have all that I shall buy or do esteemed as got by the death of my Uncle; when endeed, what I have from him is not worth naming. After supper, I to read and then to bed.

29.◆ My wife comes home from Woolwich but did not dine with me, going to dress herself against night to go to Mrs. Pierces to be merry, where we are to have Knipp and Harris and other good

1. John Evelyn's *Publick Employment and an Active Life Prefer'd to Solitude* (1667). "By-discourse" meant a subsidiary or minor piece.
2. Benches.
3. Robert Boyle's *Experiments and Considerations touching Colours* (1664), which Pepys read from where he had left off previously.
4. Under an agreement made in February 1663, if Pepys had no male heirs he was required to leave the land he had inherited from his Uncle Robert to Thomas Pepys and his son.
5. The Earl of Sandwich's family.

people. I at my accounts all the afternoon, being a little lost in them as to reckonings of interest. Anon comes down my wife, dress[ed] in her second mourning,[1] with her black moyre waistcoat and short petticoat, laced with silver lace so basely that I could not endure to see her, and with laced lining, which is too soon; so that I was horrid angry and went out of doors to the office, and there stayed and would not go to our intended meeting, which vexed me to the blood; and my wife sent twice or thrice to me to direct her any way to dress her but to put on her cloth gown, which she would not venture, which made me mad; and so in the evening to my chamber, vexed, and to my accounts, which I ended to my great content, and did make amends for the loss of our mirth this night by getting this done, which otherwise I fear I should not have done a good while else. So to bed.

30. Up, and to the office, where all the morning. At noon dined at home; being, without any words, friends with my wife, though last night I was very angry, and do think I did give her as much cause to be angry with me. After dinner I walked to Arundell-house,[2] the way very dusty (the day of meeting of the Society being changed from Wednesday to Thursday; which I knew not before because the Wednesday is a Council-day and several of the Council are of the Society, and would come but for their attending the King at Council); where I find much company, endeed very much company, in expectation of the Duchesse of Newcastle, who had desired to be invited to the Society, and was, after much debate pro and con, it seems many being against it, and we do believe the town will be full of ballets[3] of it. Anon comes the Duchesse, with her women attending her; among others, that Ferrabosco[4] of whom so much talk is, that her lady would bid her show her face and kill the gallants. She is endeed black and hath good black little eyes, but otherwise but a very ordinary woman I do think; but they say sings well. The Duchesse hath been a good comely woman; but her dress so antic and her deportment so unordinary, that I do not like her at all, nor did I hear her say anything that was worth hearing, but that

1. The stage after full mourning, when trimming or new accessories could be added to black mourning clothes. The family were in mourning for Pepys's mother, who had died in March.
2. Arundel House, in the Strand, was where the Royal Society met after the Great Fire. Gresham College, their pre-fire venue, had been taken over for use as the Royal Exchange and Guildhall.
3. Ballads.
4. One of a family of court musicians, her identity is unknown.

she was full of admiration, all admiration. Several fine experiments were shown her of Colours, Loadstones, Microscope, and of liquors: among others, of one that did while she was there turn a piece of roasted mutton into pure blood[1] – which was very rare – here was Mr. Moore of Cambrige, whom I had not seen before,[2] and I was glad to see him – as also a very pretty black[3] boy that run up and down the room, somebody's child in Arundell-house. After they had shown her many experiments, and she cried still she was "full of admiration," she departed, being led out and in by several Lords that were there; among others, Lord George Barkely and the Earl of Carlisle and a very pretty young man, the Duke of Somersett.

She gone, I by coach home and there busy at my letters till night; and then with my wife in the evening, singing with her in the garden with great pleasure. And so home to supper and to bed.

JUNE.

1. Up; and there comes to me Mr. Commander, whom I imploy about hiring of some ground behind the office for the building of me a stable and Coach-house, for I do find it necessary for me, both in respect to honour and the profit of it also (my expense in hackney-coaches being now so great) to keep a coach, and therefore will do it. Having given him some instructions about it, I to the office, where we sat all the morning – where we have news that our peace with Spaine as to trade is wholly concluded, and we are to furnish him with some men for Flanders against the French;[4] how that will agree with the French, I know not, but they say that he also hath liberty to get what men he pleases out of England. But for the Spaniard, I hear that my Lord Castlehaven is raising a Regiment of 4000 men, which he is to command there, and several young gentlemen are going over in commands with him. And they say the Duke of Monmouth[5] is going over only as a Travailer, not to engage on either side but only to see the Campagne – which will be becoming him much more then to live whoreing and rogueing

1. An experiment that dissolved meat in sulphuric acid. It did not produce "pure blood".
2. Henry Moore, a highly influential philosopher and theologian.
3. Dark in hair or complexion.
4. Sandwich, as ambassador-extraordinary to Madrid, had agreed a commercial treaty but nothing regarding military assistance.
5. Charles's illegitimate son, aged 18.

of it here, as he now does. After dinner to the office, where after a little nap I fell to business and did very much, with infinite joy to myself, as it always is to me when I have despatched much business; and therefore it troubles me to see how hard it is for me to settle to it sometimes, when my mind is upon pleasure. So home late to supper and to bed.

4. Up and to the office; and there busy all the morning putting in order the answering the great letter sent to the office by the new Commissioners of the Treasury, who demand an account from the King's coming in to this day; which we shall do in the best manner we can. At noon home to dinner; and after dinner comes Mr. Commander to me and tells me after all, that I cannot have a lease of the ground for my coach-house and stable till a suit in law be ended about the end of the old stable now standing, which they and I would have pulled down to make a better way for a coach. I am a little sorry that I cannot presently have it, because I am pretty full in my mind of keeping a coach; but yet when I think on it again, the Dutch and French both at sea and we poor, and still out of order, I know not yet what turns there may be, and besides, I am in danger of parting with one of my places (which relates to the Victualling, that brings me by accident in 800*l* a year; that is, 300*l* from the King and 500*l* from D. Gawden), I ought to be well contented to forbear awhile, and therefore am contented. To the office all the afternoon, where I despatched much business to my great content; and then home in the evening, and there to sing and pipe with my wife; and that being done, she fell all of a sudden to discourse about her clothes and my humours in not suffering her to wear them as she pleases, and grew to high words between us. But I fell to read a book (Boyle's *Hydrostatickes*)[1] aloud in my chamber and let her talk till she was tired, and vexed that I would not hear her; and so become friends and to bed together, the first night after four or five that she hath lain from me by reason of a great cold she had got.

8. Up and to the office, where all the news this morning is that the Duch are come with a fleet of 80 sail to Harwich, and that guns were heard plain by Sir W Rider's people at Bednall Greene all yesterday noon. So to the office we all, and sat all the morning; and then home to dinner – where our dinner, a ham of French Bacon boiled with pigeons – an excellent dish. Here dined with us only

1. Robert Boyle's *Hydrostatical Paradoxes* (1666) on his experiments in fluid pressure.

W Hewers and his mother. After dinner to the office again, where busy till night; and then home and to read a little and then to bed. The news is confirmed that the Dutch are off of Harwich, but had done nothing last night. The King hath sent down my Lord of Oxford to raise the country there; and all the Westerne Barges are taken up to make a bridge over river about the Hope, for horse to cross the river if there be occasion.

9. *Lords day.* Up and by water to White-hall; and so walked to St. James's, where I hear that the Duke of Cambrige,[1] who was given over long since by the Doctors, is now likely to recover; for which God be praised. To Sir W. Coventry and there talked with him a great while; and mighty glad I was of my good fortune to visit him, for it keeps in my acquaintance with him, and the world sees it and reckons my interest accordingly. In comes my Lord Berkely, who is going down to Harwich also to look after the Militia there; and there is also the Duke of Monmouth, and with him a great many young Hectors, the Lord Chesterfield, my Lord Mandevill, and others; but to little purpose, I fear, but to debauch the country-women thereabouts.◆ Being come home, I find an order come for the getting some fireships presently to annoy the Dutch, who are in the King's Channel[2] and expected up higher. So W. Batten and W. Penn being come this evening from their country houses to town, we did issue orders about it; and then home to supper and to bed.

10. Up; and news brought us that the Dutch are come up as high as the Nore,[3] and more pressing orders for fireships. W. Batten, W. Penn and I to St. James, where the Duke of York gone this morning betimes to send away some men down to Chatham. So we three to White-hall and met Sir W. Coventry, who presses all the possible for fireships; so we three to the office presently, and thither comes Sir Fr. Hollis,[4] who is to command them all in some exploits he is to do with them on the enemy in the river. So we all down to Deptford and pitch upon ships and set men at work; but Lord, to see how backwardly things move at this pinch, notwithstanding that by the enemy's being now come up as high as almost the

1. Infant son of the Duke of York.
2. In the Thames estuary, south of Harwich.
3. Near the mouths of the rivers Thames and Medway.
4. Sir Frescheville Holles, captain of the *Cambridge*, had been put in command of the fireships in the river and given warrants to press men.

Hope,[1] Sir J. Mennes (who was gone down to pay some ships there) hath sent up the money; and so we are possessed of money to [do] what we will with. Yet partly ourselfs, being used to be idle and in despair, and partly people, that have been used to be deceived by us as to money, won't believe us; and we know not, though we have it, how almost to promise it; and our wants such, and men out of the way, that it is an admirable thing to consider how much the King suffers, and how necessary it is in a State to keep the King's service always in a good posture and credit. Here I eat a bit; and then in the afternoon took boat and down to Greenwich, where I find the stairs full of people, there being a great Riding[2] there today for a man, the constable of the town, whose wife beat him. Here I was with much ado fain to press two water-men to make me a galley; and so to Woolwich to give order for the despatch of a ship I have taken under my care to see despatched; and orders being so given, I, under pretence to fetch up the ship, which lay at Grays (the *Golden hand*), did do that in my way; and went down to Gravesend, where I find the Duke of Albemarle just come, with a great many idle lords and gentlemen with their pistols and fooleries, and the Bulworke[3] not able to have stood half an hour had they come up; but the Dutch are fallen down from the Hope and Shell haven as low as the Sheernesse, and we do plainly at this time hear the guns play. Yet I do not find the Duke of Albemarle entends to go thither, but stays here tonight and hath (though the Dutch are gone) ordered our frigates to be brought in a line between the two block-houses[4] – which I took then to be a ridiculous thing. So I away into the town and took a Captain or two of our ships (who did give me an account of the proceedings of the Dutch fleet in the river) to the tavern and there we eat and drank; and I find the town had removed most of their goods out of the town, for fear of the Duch coming up to them; and Sir Jo. Griffen[5] [told me] that last night there was not twelve men to be got in the town to defend it – which the master of the house tells me is not true; but that the men of the town did entend to stay, though they did endeed, and so had he (at the Ship), removed their goods. Thence went off to an Ostend man-of-war, just now come up, who met the Dutch fleet, who took three ships that he came convoying hither from him – says they are as

1. The Hope Reach, part of the River Thames east of Tilbury.
2. A mock-procession to humiliate one or both of a misbehaving couple.
3. The defences of Gravesend.
4. Artillery fortifications at Gravesend.
5. Sir John Griffith, in charge of the blockhouses at Gravesend.

low as the Nore or thereabouts. So I homeward, as long as it was light reading Mr. Boyles book of *Hydrostatickes*, which is a most excellent book as ever I read; and I will take much pains to understand him through if I can, the doctrine being very useful. When it grew too dark to read, I lay down and took a nap, it being a most excellent fine evening; and about one a-clock got home, and after having wrote to Sir W. Coventry an account of what I had done and seen (which is entered in my letter-book), I to bed.

11. Up, and more letters still from Sir W. Coventry about more fireships; and so W. Batten and I to the office, where Brouncker came to us; who is just now going to Chatham upon a desire of Commissioner Pett's,[1] who is in a very fearful stink for fear of the Dutch, and desires help for God and the King and kingdom's sake. So Brouncker goes down, and Sir J. Mennes also, from Gravesend. This morning Pett writes us word that Sherenesse is lost last night, after two or three hours dispute – the enemy hath possessed himself of the place;[2] which is very sad and puts us into great fears of Chatham.[3] Sir W. Batten and I down by water to Deptford, and there Sir W. Penn and we did consider of several matters relating to the despatch of the Fireshipps; and so W. Batten and I home again – and there to dinner, my wife and father having dined. And after dinner, by W. Hewer's lucky advice, went to Mr. Fenn[4] and did get him to pay me above 400*l* of my Wages, and W. Hewer received it for me and brought it home this night. Thence, I meeting Mr. Moore, went toward the other end of the town by coach; and spying Mercer in the street, I took leave of Moore and light and fallowed her; and at Pauls overtook her and walked with her through the dusty street almost to home; and there in Lumbard-street met The Turner[5] in coach, who had been at my house to see us, being to go out of town tomorrow to the Northward, and so I promised to see her tomorrow; and then home and there to our business, hiring some fireships and receiving every hour almost letters from Sir W. Coventry, calling for more Fireshipps – and an order from Council to enable us to take any man's ships; and Sir

1. Peter Pett, Navy Commissioner at Chatham.
2. Sheerness was a new navy dockyard on the Isle of Sheppey, at the mouth of the Medway. Its fortifications were unfinished when the Dutch attacked.
3. The warships of the fleet were laid up Chatham on the River Medway. Although Chatham was fortified, the ships were not crewed for action and were highly vulnerable.
4. Paymaster to the Navy Treasurer.
5. Theophila Turner, a relative.

W. Coventry in his letter to us says he doth not doubt but at this time (under an Invasion, as he owns it to be) the King may by law take any man's goods. At this business late, and then home, where a great deal of serious talk with my wife about the sad state we are in, and especially from the beating-up of drums this night for the train-bands,[1] upon pain of death to appear in arms tomorrow morning, with bullet and powder and money to supply themselfs with victuals for a fortnight – which, considering the soldiers drawn out to Chatham and elsewhere, looks as if they had a design to ruin the City and give it up to be undone – which I hear makes the sober citizens to think very sadly of things. So to bed after supper, ill in my mind. ⟨This afternoon Mrs. Williams sent to me to speak with her, which I did, only about news. I had not spoke with her many a day before by reason of Carcasse's business.[2]⟩

12. Up very betimes to our business at the office, there hiring of more fireships; and at it close all the morning. At noon home, and Sir W. Penn dined with us. By and by, after dinner, my wife out by coach to see her mother; and I in another (being afeared at this busy time to be seen with a woman in a coach, as if I were idle) toward The Turners; but met Sir W. Coventry's boy, and there in his letter find that the Dutch had made no motion since their taking Sheresse; and the Duke of Albemarle writes that all is safe as to the great ships against any assault – the boom and Chaine being so fortified;[3] which put my heart into great joy.

When I came to Sir W. Coventry's chamber, I find him abroad; but his clerk Powell doth tell me that ill news is come to Court of the Dutch breaking the Chaine at Chatham, which struck me to the heart, and to White-hall to hear the truth of it; and there, going up the park stairs, I did hear some lackeys speaking of sad news come to Court, saying that hardly anybody in the court but doth look as if they cried; and would not go into the house for fear of being seen, but slunk out and got into a coach, and to The Turner to Sir W Turner's, where I met Roger Pepys, newly come out of the country (he and I talked aside a little, he offering a match for Pall, one Barnes, of whom we shall talk more the next time; his father married a Pepys). In discourse, he told me further that his grandfather, my great grandfather, had 800*l* per annum in Queen

1. The City militia.
2. Her partner, Brouncker, supported Carkesse, the clerk of the Ticket Office charged with corruption. Pepys did not.
3. An iron chain across the Medway protected ships anchored at Chatham from enemy vessels.

Elizabeth's time in the very town of Cottenham – and that we did certainly come out of Scotland with the Abbot of Crowland. More talk I had, and shall have more with him, but my mind is so sad and head full of this ill news, that I cannot now set it down. A short visit here, my wife coming to me, and took leave of The; and so home, where all our hearts do now ake; for the news is true, that the Dutch have broke the Chain and burned our ships, and perticularly the *Royall Charles*; other perticulars I know not, but most sad to be sure.[1] And the truth is, I do fear so much that the whole kingdom is undone, that I do this night resolve to study with my father and wife what to do with the little that I have in money by me, for I give all the rest that I have in the King's hands for Tanger for lost. So God help us, and God knows what disorders we may fall into and whether any violence on this office, or perhaps some severity on our persons, as being reckoned by the silly people, or perhaps may by policy of State be thought fit to be condemned by the King and Duke of York, and so put to trouble; though God knows I have in my own person done my full duty, I am sure. So having with much ado finished my business at the office, I home to consider with my father and wife of things; and then to supper and to bed with a heavy heart. The manner of my advising this night with my father was: I took him and my wife up to her chamber, and shut the door and there told them the sad state of the times; how we are like to be all undone – that I do fear some violence will be offered to this office, where all I have in the world is. And resolved upon sending it away – sometimes into the country, sometimes my father to lie in town and have the gold with him at Sarah Giles's;[2] and with that resolution went to bed – full of fear and fright; hardly slept all night.

13. No sooner up but hear the sad news confirmed, of the *Royall Charles* being taken by them and now in fitting by them (which Pett should have carried up higher by our several orders, and deserves therefore to be hanged for not doing it) and burning several others, and that another fleet is come up into the Hope; upon which news the King and Duke of York have been below[3] since 4 a-clock in the morning, to command the sinking of ships at Barking Creeke and

1. The *Royal Charles* was a first-rate, one of the principal ships of the navy. It was captured, not burnt, and towed away in triumph on the 14th. The Dutch fleet's daring raid on the Medway remains one of the greatest humiliations for the English navy.
2. A poor cousin of Pepys's on his mother's side, probably living in Whitechapel.
3. Downstream from London Bridge.

other places, to stop their coming up higher; which put me into such a fear that I presently resolved of my father's and wife's going into the country; and at two hours' warning they did go by the coach this day – with about 1300*l* in gold in their night-bag; pray God give them good passage and good care to hide it when they come home, but my heart is full of fear. They gone, I continued in frights and fear what to do with the rest. W. Hewer hath been at the banquiers and hath got 500*l* out of Backewell's hands of his own money; but they are so called upon that they will be all broke, hundreds coming to them for money – and their answer is, "It is payable at twenty days; when the days are out, we will pay you;" and those that are not so, they make tell over their money, and make their bags false on purpose to give cause to retell it and so spend time; I cannot have my 200 pieces of gold again for silver, all being bought up last night that were to be had – and sold for 24 and 25*s* a-piece. So I must keep the silver by me, which sometimes I think to fling into the house of office[1] – and then again, know not how I shall come by it if we be made to leave the office. Every minute some[one] or other calls for this order or that order; and so I forced to be at the office most of the day about the fireships which are to be suddenly fitted out; and it's a most strange thing that we hear nothing from any of my Brethren at Chatham; so that we are wholly in the dark, various being the reports of what is done there – insomuch, that I sent ⟨Mr.⟩ Clapham express thither to see how matters go. I did about noon resolve to send Mr. Gibson[2] away after my wife with another 1000 pieces, under colour of an express to Sir Jer: Smith, who is, as I hear, with some ships at Newcastle; which I did really send to him, and may possibly prove of good use to the King; for it is possible, in the hurry of business they may not think of it at Court, and the charge of express is not considerable to the King. So though I entend Gibson no further then to Huntington, yet I direct him to send the packet forward. My business the most of the afternoon is listening to everybody that comes to the office, what news, which is variously related, some better, some worse, but nothing certain. The King and Duke of York up and down all the day here and there; some time on Tower-hill, where the City Militia was; where the King did make a speech to them that they should venture themselfs no further then he would himself. I also sent (my mind being in pain) Saunders after my wife and father, to overtake

1. The privy.
2. Richard Gibson, navy clerk.

them at their night's lodging to see how matters go with them. In the evening I sent for my cousin Sarah and her husband; who came and I did deliver them my chest of writings about Brampton, and my brother Tom's papers and my Journalls, which I value much[1] – and did send my two silver flagons to Kate Joyce's: that so, being scattered what I have, something might be saved. I have also made a girdle, by which with some trouble I do carry about me 300*l* in gold about my body, that I may not be without something in case I should be surprized; for I think, in any nation but ours, people that appear (for we are not endeed so) so faulty as we would have their throats cut. In the evening comes Mr. Pelling[2] and several others to the office, and tell me that never were people so dejected as they are in the City all over at this day, and do talk most loudly, even treason; as, that we are bought and sold, that we are betrayed by the papists and others about the King – cry out that the Office of the Ordinance hath been so backward as no powder to have been at Chatham nor Upner Castle till such a time, and the carriages all broken – that Legg is a papist[3] – that Upner, the old good castle built by Queen Elizabeth, should be lately slighted[4] – that the ships at Chatham should not be carried up higher. They look upon us as lost; and remove their families and rich goods in the City and do think verily that the French, being come down with his army to Dunkirke, it is to invade us – and that we shall be invaded. Mr. Clerke the solicitor comes to me about business, and tells me that he hears that the King hath chosen Mr. Pierpoint and Vaughan of the West privy councillors – that my Lord Chancellor was affronted in the Hall this day by people telling him of his Dunkirke house[5] – and that there are Regiments ordered to be got together, whereof to be commanders my Lord Fairfax, Ingolsby, Bethell, Norton, and Birch and other presbyterians; and that Dr. Bates will have liberty to preach.[6] Now whether this be true or not, I know not; but do think that nothing but this will unite us together. Late at night comes Mr. Hudson the cooper, my neighbour, and tells me that he came from Chatham this evening at 5 a clock and saw this

1. Sarah Giles was entrusted with papers relating to Robert Pepys's legacy, the estate of Pepys's brother Tom, and the diary volumes.
2. John Pelling, an apothecary from the nearby parish of All Hallows Staining.
3. William Legge, Lieutenant-General of the Ordnance, was wrongly suspected of being secretly Catholic.
4. Upnor Fort protected Chatham. Its garrison had been reduced in 1666.
5. Clarendon's new-built house, allegedly paid for with French bribes in return for the sale of Dunkirk in 1662.
6. Dr William Bates, a Presbyterian.

afternoon the *Royall James*, *Oake*, and *London* burnt by the enemy with their fireships; that two or three men-of-war came up with them, and made no more of Upner castle's shooting then of a fly – that these ships lay below Upner Castle (but therein I conceive he is in an error) – that the Dutch are fitting out the *Royall Charles* – that we shot so far as from the yard thither, so that the shot did no good, for the bullets grazed on the water – that Upner played hard with their guns at first, but slowly afterward, either from the men being beat off or their powder spent. But we hear that the fleet in the Hope is not come up any higher the last flood. And Sir W. Batten tells me that ships are provided to sink in the River about Woolwich, that will prevent their coming up higher if they should attempt it. I made my will also this day, and did give all I had equally between my father and wife – and left copies of it in ⟨each of⟩ Mr. Hater and W. Hewer's hands, who both witnessed the will; and so to supper and then to bed; and slept pretty well, but yet often waking.

14. Up, and to the office; where Mr. Fryer comes and tells me that there are several Frenchmen and Flemish ships in the River, with passes from the Duke of York for carrying of prisoners, that ought to be parted from the rest of the ships and their powder taken, lest they do fire themselfs when the enemy comes and so spoil us; which is good advice I think, and will give notice of it – and did so. But it is pretty odd to see how everybody, even at this high time of danger, puts business off of their own hands. He says that he told this to the Lieutenant of the Tower (to whom I for the same reason was directing him to go) and the Lieutenant of the Tower bade him come to us, for he had nothing to do with it – and yesterday comes Captain Crow off one of the fireships and told me that the officers of the Ordinance would deliver his gunner's materials but not compound them, but that we must do it; whereupon I was forced to write to them about it – and one that like a great many comes to me this morning. By and by comes Mr. Willson and, by direction of his, a man of Mr. Gawden's who came from Chatham last night and saw the three ships burnt, they lying all dry, and boats going from the men-of-war and fire them. But that that he tells me of worst consequence is that he himself (I think he said) did hear many Englishmen on board the Dutch ships, speaking to one another in English, and that they did cry and say, "We did heretofore fight for tickets; now we fight for Dollers!"[1] and did ask how

1. Rix-dollars: Dutch silver coins.

such and such a one did, and would commend themselfs to them – which is a sad consideration. And Mr. Lewes (who was present at this fellow's discourse to me) did tell me that he is told that when they took the *Royall Charles*, they said that they had their tickets signed (and showed some) and that now they came to have them paid, and would have them paid before they parted. And several seamen came this morning to me to tell me that if I would get their tickets paid, they would go and do all they could against the Dutch; but otherwise they would not venture being killed and lose all they have already fought for – so that I was forced to try what I could do to get them paid. This man tells me that the ships burnt last night did lie above Upner Castle over against the Docke; and the boats came from the ships of war and burnt them – all which is very sad; and maisters of ships that we are now taking up do keep from their ships all their stores, or as much as they can, so that we can despatch them – having not time to appraise them nor secure their payment. Only, some little money we have, which we are fain to pay the men we have with every night, or they will not work. And endeed, the hearts as well as affections of the seamen are turned away; and in the open streets in wapping, and up and down, the wifes have cried publicly, "This comes of your not paying our husbands; and now your work is undone, or done by hands that understand it not;" and Sir W. Batten told me that he was himself affronted with a woman in language of this kind himself on tower-hill publicly yesterday; and we are fain to bear it – and to keep one at the office-door to let no idle people in, for fear of firing of the office and doing us mischief. The City is troubled at their[1] being put upon duty: summoned one hour and discharged two hours after and then again summoned two hours after that, to their great charge as well as trouble; and Pelling the pothecary tells me the world says all over that less charge then what the kingdom is put to, of one kind or other, by this business, would have set out all our great ships. It is said they did in open streets yesterday, at Westminster, cry, "A Parliament! a Parliament!"; and do believe it will cost blood to answer for these miscarriages. We do not hear that the Duch are come to Gravesend, which is a wonder; but a wonderful ⟨thing⟩ it is that to this day we have not one word yet from Brouncker or P. Pett or J. Mennes of anything at Chatham; the people that come hither to hear how things go make me ashamed to be found unable to answer them, for I am left alone

1. The militia.

here at the office; and the truth is, I am glad my station is to be here – near my own home and out of danger, yet in a place of doing the King good service. I have this morning good news from Gibson; three letters, from three several stages, that he was safe last night as far as Royston at between 9 and 10 at night. The dismay that is upon us all in the business of the kingdom and Navy at this day, is not to be expressed otherwise then by the condition the citizens were in when the City was on fire, nobody knowing which way to turn themselfs, while everything concurred to greaten the fire; as here, the easterly gale and spring-tides, for coming up both rivers and enabling them to break the chain. D. Gawden did tell me yesterday that the day before at the Council, they were ready to fall together by the ears at the council-table, arraigning one another of being guilty of the counsel that brought us into this misery, by laying up all the great ships. Mr. Hater tells me at noon that some rude people have been, as he hears, at my Lord Chancellor's, where they have cut down the trees before his house and broke his windows; and a Gibbet either set up before or painted upon his gate, and these words writ – "Three sights to be seen; Dunkirke, Tanger, and a barren Queen."[1] It gives great matter of talk that it is said there is at this hour in the Exchequer as much money as is ready to break down the floor. This arises, I believe, from Sir G. Downing's late talk of the greatness of the sum lying there of people's money that they would not fetch away, which he showed me and a great many others. Most people that I speak with are in doubt how we shall do to secure our seamen from running over to the Duch; which is a sad but very true consideration at this day. At noon am told that my Lord Duke of Albemarle is made Lord High Constable; the meaning whereof at this time I know not, nor whether it be true or no. Dined, and Mr. Hater and W. Hewer with me; where they do speak very sorrowfully of the posture of the times, and how people do cry out in the streets of their being bought and sold; and both they and everybody that come to me do tell me that people make nothing of talking treason in the streets openly: as, that we are bought and sold and governed by Papists and that we are betrayed by people about the King and shall be delivered up to the French, and I know not what. At dinner we discoursed of Tom of the Wood, a fellow that lives like a Hermit near Woolwich,

1. Clarendon was accused of having sold Dunkirk to the French and of acquiring a useless colony in Tangier. He had also allegedly arranged for Charles to marry a barren Queen so that the throne would pass to the Duke of York, who was married to his daughter.

who as they say (and Mr. Bodham, they tell me, affirms that he was by at the Justice's when some did accuse him there for it) [did] foretell the burning of the City, now says that a greater desolation is at hand. Thence we read and laughed at Lillys prophecies this month – in his almanac this year.[1] So to the office after dinner; and thither comes Mr. Pierce, who tells me his condition: how he cannot get his money (about 500*l*, which he says is a very great part of what he hath for his family and children) out of Viner's hand – and endeed, it is to be feared that this will wholly undo the banquiers. He says he knows nothing of the late affronts to my Lord Chancellors house as is said, nor hears of the Duke of Albemarle's being made High Constable; but says that they are in great distraction at White-hall – and that everywhere people do speak high against Sir W. Coventry; but he agrees with me that he is the best Minister of State the King hath, and so from my heart I believe. At night came home Sir W. Batten and W. Penn, who only can tell me that they have placed guns at Woolwich and Deptford and sunk some ships below Woolwich and Blackwall, and are in hopes that they will stop the enemy's coming up. But strange our confusion; that among them that are sunk they have gone and sunk without consideration the *Franckin*, one of the King's ships, with stores to a very considerable value, that hath been long loaden for supply of the ships and the new ship at Bristoll, and much wanted there – and nobody will own that they directed it, but do lay it on Sir W Rider; they speak also of another ship, loaden to the value of 80000*l*, sunk with the goods in her, or at least was mightily contended for by him, and a foreign ship that had the faith of the nation for her security; this Sir R. Ford tells us. And it is too plain a truth, that both here and at Chatham the ships that we have sunk have many, and the first of them, been ships completely fitted for fireships at great charge. But most strange, the backwardness and disorder of all people, especially the King's people in pay, to do any work (Sir W. Penn tells me), all crying out for money. And it was so at Chatham, that this night comes an order from Sir W. Coventry to stop the pay of the wages of that Yard, the Duke of Albemarle having related that not above three of 1100 in pay there did attend to do any work there. This evening, having sent a messenger to Chatham on purpose, we have received

1. William Lilly, in his *Merlini Anglici Ephemeris* (1667), had forecast for June 1667 "a most strange and unusual loss at Sea [for the Dutch], if they shall dare to fight His Majesties Forces ... Strange news out of *Holland*, as if all were in an uproar; we believe they are now in a sad and fearful condition".

a dull[1] letter from my Lord Brouncker and P. Pett how matters have gone there this week; but not so much, or so perticular as we knew it by common talk before, and as true. I doubt they will be found to have been but slow men in this business; and they say the Duke of Albemarle did tell my Lord Brouncker to his face that his discharging of the great ships there was the cause of all this; and I am told that it is become common talk against my Lord Brouncker, but in that he is to be justified, for he did it by verball order from Sir W. Coventry, and with good intent; and was to good purpose, whatever the success be, for the men would have but spent the King so much the more in wages, and yet not attended on board to have done the King any service [and as an evidence of that just now, being the 15th day in the morning that I am writing yesterday's passages, one is with me, Jacob Bryan, purser of the *Princesse*, who confesses to me that he hath above 180 men borne at this day in victuals and wages on that ship lying at Chatham, being lately brought in thither; of which 180 there was not above five appeared to do the King any service at this late business. And this morning also, some of the *Cambriges* men came up from Portsmouth by order from Sir Fre. Hollis, who boasted to us the other day that he had sent for 50, and would be hanged if 100 did not come up, that would do as much as twice the number of other men: I say some of them, instead of being at work at Deptford where they were intended, do come to the office this morning to demand the payment of their tickets, for otherwise they would, they said, do no more work; and are, as I understand from everybody that have do with them, the most debauched, damning, swearing rogues that ever were in the Navy, just like their profane commander].[2] So to W. Batten's to sit and talk a little; and then home to my flagelette, my heart being at pretty good ease by a letter from my wife, brought by Saunders, that my father and wife got well last night to their Inne and out again this morning, and Gibson's being got safe to Caxton[3] at 12 last night. So to a supper, and then to bed. No news today of any motion of the enemy, either upwards towards Chatham or this way.[4]

19. Up and to the office, where all the morning busy with Fist[5]

1. Spiritless, sluggish.
2. The brackets (square altered from round) are Pepys's.
3. Near Cambridge.
4. The Dutch withdrew from the Medway on the 14th, but continued to blockade the Thames until late July.
5. Clerk to Sir William Batten.

again, beginning early to overtake my business in my letters, which for a post or two have by the late and present troubles been interrupted. At noon comes Sir W. Batten and W. Penn, and we to W. Penn's house and there discoursed of business an hour; and by and by comes an order from Sir R. Browne, commanding me this afternoon to attend the Council-board with all my books and papers touching the Medway. I was ready [to fear] some mischief to myself, though that that appears most reasonable is that it is to inform them about Comissioner Pett.[1] I eat a little bit in haste at W. Batten's without much comfort, being fearful, though I show it not; and to my office and did get up some papers and find out the most material letters and orders in our books. And so took coach and to the Council-chamber lobby, where I met Mr. Eveling, who doth miserably decry our follies that brings all this misery upon us. While we were discoursing over our public misfortunes, I am called in to a large committee of the Council: present, the Duke of Albemarle, Anglesy, Arlington, Ashly, Carteret, Duncomb, Coventry, Ingram, Clifford, Lauderdale, Morice, Manchester, Craven, Carlisle, Bridgewater; and after Sir W. Coventry's telling them what orders his Royal Highness had made for the safety of the Medway, I told them to great full content what we had done, and showed them our letters. Then was P. Pett call[ed] in with the Lieutenant of the Tower. He is in his old clothes, and looked most sillily. His charge was chiefly the not carrying up of the great ships, and the using of the boats in carrying away his goods; in which he answered very sillily – though his faults to me seem only great omissions. Lord Arlington and Coventry very severe against him; the former saying that if he was not guilty, the world would think them all guilty. The latter urged that there must be some fault, and that the Admiral[2] must be found to have done his part. I did say an unhappy word, which I was sorry for, when he complained of want of oares for the boats; and there was it seems enough, and good enough to carry away all the boats with from the King's occasions. He said he used never a boat till they were all gone but one – and that was to carry away things of great value, and those were his models of ships; which when the Council, some of them, had said they wished that the Dutch had had them instead of the King's ships, he answered he did believe the Dutch would have made more advantage of the models then of the ships, and the King

1. Peter Pett, as Commissioner at Chatham, had been arrested and sent to the Tower on 17 June.
2. The Duke of York.

have had greater loss thereby.[1] This they all laughed at. After having heard him for an hour or more, they bid him withdraw, I all this while showing him no respect, but rather against him; for which God forgive me, for I mean no hurt to him, but only find that these Lords are upon their own purgation, and it is necessary I should be so in behalf of the office. He being gone, they caused Sir Rd. Browne to read over his minutes; and then my Lord Arlington moved that they might be put into my hands to put into form, I being more acquainted with such business; and they were so. So I away back with my books and papers; and when I got into the Court, it was pretty to see how people gazed upon me – that I thought myself obliged to salute people and to smile, lest they should think I was a prisoner too; but afterward I found the most did take me to be there to bear evidence against P. Pett. But my fear was such, at my going in, of the success[2] of the day, that at my going in I did think fit to give T. Hater (whom I took with me to wait the event) my closet-key and directions where to find 500*l* and more in silver and gold, and my tallies, to remove in case of any misfortune to me. Thence to Sir G. Carteret's to take my leave of my Lady Jem, who is going into the country tomorrow; but she being now at prayers with my Lady and family, and hearing here by Yorke the carrier that my wife was coming to town, I did make haste home to see her, that she might not find me abroad, it being the first minute I have been abroad since yesterday was sennit.[3] It is pretty to see how strange it is to be abroad to see people, as it used to be after a month or two's absence; and I have brought myself so to it, that I have no great mind to be abroad – which I could not have believed of myself. I got home; and after being there a little, she came, and two of her fellow-travellers with her, with whom we drunk – a couple of merchant-like men I think, but have friends in our country. They being gone, I and my wife to talk; who did give me so bad an account of her and my father's method in burying of our gold, that made me mad – and she herself is not pleased with it, she believing that my sister knows of it. My father and she did it on Sunday when they were gone to church, in open daylight in the midst of the garden, where for aught they knew, many eyes might see them; which put me into such trouble, that I was almost mad about it, and presently cast about how to have it back again to

1. Models of warships could reveal advances in design and a ship's vulnerabilities.
2. Outcome.
3. Sennight: a week (here "a week ago yesterday").

secure it here, the times being a little better now; at least, at White-hall they seem as if they were – but one way or other, I am resolved to free them from the place if I can get them. Such was my trouble at this, that I fell out with my wife; that though new come to town, I did not sup with her nor speak to her tonight, but to bed and sleep.

25.◆ Busy all the afternoon at the office. Towards night, I with Mr. Kinaston to White-hall about a Tanger Order, but lost our labour; only met Sir H Cholmly there, and he tells me great news: that this day in Council, the King hath declared that he will call his Parliament in 30 days – which is the best news I have heard a great while, and will, if anything, save the Kingdom. How the King came to be advised to this, I know not; but he tells me that it was against the Duke of York's mind flatly, who did rather advise the King to raise money as he pleased; and against the Chancellors, who told the King that Queen Elizabeth did do all her business in 88 without calling a Parliament, and so might he do for anything he saw; but blessed be God, it is done, and pray God it may hold, though some of us must surely go to the pot, for all must be flung up to them or nothing will be done. So back home, and my wife down the water; I sent her with Mrs. Hewers and her son, W. Hewers, to see the sunk ships, while I stayed at the office; and in the evening was visited by Mr. Roberts, the merchant by us, about the getting him a ship cleared from serving the King as a man-of-war, which I will endeavour to do. So home to supper and to bed.

JULY.

3.◆ To the office – where to do a little business; and then by water to White-hall (calling at Michells in my way, but the rogue would not invite me in, I having a mind para ver his wife[1]); and there to the Council-chamber to deliver a letter to their Lordships about the state of the six merchantmen which we have been so long fitting out.[2] When I came, the King and the whole tableful of Lords were hearing of a pitiful cause of a complaint of an old man, with a great gray beard, against his son, for not allowing himself something to live on; and at last came to the ordering the son to allow his father

1. "to see his wife". The last two words are in garbled shorthand. In this example, and until the end of the diary, Pepys often obscures the sense in passages with erotic content by inserting extra shorthand letters. These letters are excluded from the transcription.
2. The merchantmen had been acquired in June to fit out as battleships.

10*l* a year. This cause lasted them near two hours; which methinks, at this time to be the work of the Council-board of England, is a scandalous thing, and methought Sir W. Coventry to me did own as much. Here I find all the news is the enemy's landing 3000 men near Harwich, and attacquing Langnerfort and being beat off thence with our great guns, killing some of their men and they leaving their lathers[1] behind them; but we had no Horse in the way on Suffolke side, otherwise we might have galled their Foot.[2] The Duke of York is gone down thither this day, while the Generall[3] sat sleeping this afternoon at the Council-table.◆ Thence I to Westminster-hall and there hear how they talk against the present management of things, and against Sir W. Coventry for his bringing in of new commanders and casting out the old seamen; which I did endeavour to rectify Mr. Michell and them in, letting them know that he hath opposed it all his life, the most of any man in England. After a deal of this bibble babble, I to Mrs. Martins and there she was gone in before; but when I came, contrary to my expectation, I find her all in trouble, and what was it for but that I have got her with child, for those do not venir[4] upon her as they should have done; and is in exceeding grief, and swears that the child is mine; which I do not believe, but yet do comfort her that either it can[not] be so; or if it be, that I will take care to send for her husband, though I do hardly see how I can be sure of that, the ship being at sea and as far as Scotland; but however, I must do it, and shall find some way or other of doing it, though it doth trouble me not a little. Thence, not pleased, away to White-hall to Mr. Williamson and by and by my Lord Arlington about Mr. Lanyon's business;[5] and it is pretty to see how Mr. Williamson did altogether excuse himself that my business was not done, and when I came to my Lord and told him my business, – "Why," says my Lord, "it hath [been] done, and the King signed it several days ago;" and so it was, and was in Mr. Williamson's hand, which made us both laugh; and I in innocent mirth, I remember, said, "It is pretty to see in what a condition we are, that all our matters nowadays are undone we know not how, and done we know not when." He laughed at it, but I have since reflected on it and find it a severe

1. Ladders.
2. On 2 June the Dutch assaulted Landguard Fort, as a prelude to a planned attack on Harwich. They were repulsed by infantry and local militia forces.
3. Albemarle.
4. "come".
5. This concerned a payment due for Tangier victualling.

speech, as it might be taken by a chief minister of state, as endeed Mr. Williamson is, for he is endeed the Secretary.[1] But we fell to other pleasant talk, and a fine gentleman he is; and so gave him 5*l* for his fee, and away home and to Sir W. Batten's to talk a little; and then to the office to do a little business, and so home to supper and to read myself asleep, and then to bed.

6. Up and to the office, where some of us sat busy all the morning. At noon home to dinner, whither Creed came to dine with us and brings the first word I hear of the news of a peace, the King having letters come to him this noon, signifying that it is concluded on and that Mr. Coventry[2] is upon his way, coming over for the King's ratification. The news was so good and sudden, that I went with great joy to W. Batten and then to W. Penn to tell it them; and so home to dinner, mighty merry and light at my heart only on this ground, that a continuing of the war must undo us, and so, though peace may do the like, if we do not make good use of it to reform ourselfs and get up money, yet there is an opportunity for us to save ourselfs – at least, for my own perticular, we shall continue well till I can get my money into my hands, and then I will shift for myself. After dinner away, leaving Creed there, by coach to Westminster, where to the Swan and drank; and then to the Hall and there talked a little, with great joy of the peace; and then to Mrs. Martins, where I met with the good news que esta no es con child ⟨she having de estos upon her⟩[3] – the fear of which, which she did give me the other day, had troubled me much. My joy in this made me send for wine, and thither came her sister and Mrs. Cragg and I stayed a good while there. But here happened the best instance of a woman's falseness in the world; that her sister Doll, who went for a bottle of wine, did come home all blubbering and swearing against one Captain Vandena, a Dutchman of the Rhenish wine-house, that pulled her into a stable by the Dog tavern and there did tumble her and toss her; calling him all the rogues and toads in the world, when she knows that ella[4] hath suffered me to do anything with her a hundred times. Thence with joyful heart to White-hall to ask Mr.

1. Joseph Williamson was Arlington's principal secretary. He did not himself become Secretary of State until 1674.
2. Henry Coventry, ambassador at the peace negotiations at Breda.
3. "news that this one [i.e. she] is not with child ⟨she having these [i.e. 'those', her period] upon her⟩". As with two examples here, Pepys's usage of Spanish pronouns beginning "es", "est" and "ell" frequently presents transcription and translation issues. He will opt for one such word, while the context and his usual forms of expression indicate he means another of them.
4. "she".

Williamson the news; who told me that Mr. Coventry is coming over with a project of a peace; which, if the States agree to and our King, when their ministers on both sides have showed it them, we shall agree, and that is all; but the King I hear doth give it out plain that the peace is concluded. Thence by coach home and there wrote a few letters; and then to consult with my wife about going to Epsum tomorrow, sometimes designing to go and then again not; and at last it grew late and I bethought myself of business to imploy me at home tomorrow, and so I did not go. This afternoon I met with Mr. Rolt, who tells me that he is going Cornett under Collonell Ingoldsby, being his old acquaintance, and Ingoldsby hath a troop now from under the King; and I think it is a handsome way for him. But it was an ominous thing methought, just as he was bidding me his last Adieu, his nose fell a-bleeding, which run in my mind a pretty while after. This afternoon Sir Alex. Frazier,[1] who was of counsel for Sir Jo. Minnes and had given him over for a dead man, said to me at White-hall: "What," says he, "Sir Jo. Minnes is dead." I told him no, but that there is hopes of his life.[2] Methought he looked very sillily after it, and went his way. Late home to supper, a little troubled at my not going to Epsum tomorrow as I had resolved, especially having the Duke of York and W. Coventry out of town; but it was my own fault, and at last my judgment to stay; and so after supper, to bed. ⟨This day, with great satisfaction I hear that my Lady Jemimah is brought to bed at Hinchingbrooke of a boy.⟩[3]

9. Up pretty betimes and to the office, where busy till office time; and then we sat, but nothing to do but receive clamours about money. This day my Lord Anglesy, our new Treasurer, came the first time to the Board, and there sat with us till noon;[4] and I do perceive he is a very notable man and understanding, and will do things regular and understand them himself, not trust Fenn[5] as Sir G. Carteret did, and will solicit soundly for money; which I do fear was Sir G. Carteret's fault, that he did not do that enough, considering the age we live in, that nothing will do but by solicitation

1. Physician to the King.
2. Mennes, who had been ill since late June, recovered and lived till 1671.
3. George Carteret, later first Baron Carteret.
4. Arthur Annesley, Earl of Anglesey, became Treasurer of the Navy, replacing Sir George Carteret. Carteret took up Anglesey's former position as Vice-Treasurer of Ireland. Both men were under attack and hoped (in vain) to save themselves by switching offices.
5. Paymaster to the Navy Treasure, whom Pepys suspected of malpractices.

– though never so good for the King or Kingdom; and a bad business well solicited shall for peace sake speed, when a good one shall not. But I do confess I do think it a very bold act of him to take upon him the place of Treasurer of the Navy at this time; but when I consider that a regular accountant never ought to fear anything, nor have reason, I then do cease to wonder. At noon home to dinner and to play on the flagelette with my wife; and then to the office, where very busy, close at my office till late at night; at night walked and sang with my wife in the garden, and so home to supper and to bed. This evening news comes for certain that the Dutch are with their fleet before Dover, and that it is expected they will attempt something there. The business of the peace is quite dashed again, so as now it is doubtful whether the King will condescend to what the Dutch demand, it being so near the Parliament, it being a thing that will, it may be, recommend him to them when they shall find that the not having of a peace lies on his side, by denying some of their demands.◆

14. *Lords day.* Up, and my wife, a little before 4, and to make us ready; and by and by Mrs. Turner[1] came to us by agreement, and she and I stayed talking below while my wife dressed herself; which vexed me that she was so long about it, keeping us till past 5 a-clock before she was ready. She ready, and taking some bottles of wine and beer and some cold Fowle with us into the Coach, we took coach and four horses which I had provided last night, and so away – a very fine day; and so towards Epsum, talking all the way pleasantly, and perticularly of the pride and ignorance of Mrs. Lowther in having of her train carried up.[2] The country very fine; only, the way very dusty. We got to Epsum by 8 a-clock to the Well, where much company; and there we light and I drank the water; they did not, but do go about and walk a little among the women, but I did drink four pints and had some very good stools by it. Here I met with divers of our town; among others, with several of the tradesmen of our office, but did talk but little with them, it growing hot in the sun; and so we took coach again and to the Towne to the King's Head, where our coachman carried us; and there had an ill room for us to go into, but the best in the house that was not taken up; here we called for drink and bespoke dinner. And hear that my Lord Buckhurst and Nelly is lodged at the next house, and Sir Ch. Sidly with them, and keep a

1. Elizabeth Turner, neighbour.
2. Peg Lowther's (née Penn) latest social sin was having a page carry her train.

merry house.[1] Poor girl, I pity her; but more the loss of her at the King's House. Here I saw Gilsthrop, Sir W. Batten's clerk that hath been long sick; he looks like a dying man, with a consumption[2] got, as is believed, by the pox; but God knows that, but the man is in a sad condition, though he finds himself much better since his coming thither he says. W Hewers rode with us, and I left him and the women, and myself walked to church, where few people (contrary to what I expected) and none I knew but all the Houblons brothers; and them after sermon I did salute and walk with towards my Inne, which was in their way to their lodgings. They came last night to see their elder brother, who stays here at the waters, and away tomorrow. James[3] did tell me that I was the only happy man of the Navy; of whom, he says, during all this freedom the people have taken of speaking treason, he hath not heard one bad word of me – which is a great joy to me, for I hear the same of others; but do know that I have deserved as well as most. We parted, to meet anon; and I to my women into a better room, which the people of the house borrowed for us; and there to dinner, a good dinner, and were merry; and Pendleton[4] came to us, who happened to be in the house, and there talked and were merry. After dinner, he gone, we all lay down after dinner (the day being wonderful hot) to sleep, and each of us took a good nap and then rose; and Tom Willson came to see me and sat and talked an hour, and I perceive he hath been much acquainted with Dr. Fuller (Tom) and Dr. Pierson and several of the great Cavalier parsons during the late troubles;[5] and I was glad to hear him talk of them, which he did very ingeniously, and very much of Dr. Fullers art of memory, which he did tell me several instances of. By and by he parted, and we took coach and to take the ayre, there being a fine breeze abroad; and I went and carried them to the Well and there filled some bottles of water to carry home with me. And there talked with the two women that farm the well of the lord of the manor, Mr. Eveling (who with his lady and also my Lord George Berkely's lady, and their fine daughter that the King of France liked so well and did dance so rich in Jewells before the King at the Ball I was at, at our Court last

1. Nell Gwynn had (temporarily) left acting with the King's Company to become Buckhurst's mistress. Sir Charles Sedley was a courtier and playwright.
2. A wasting disease.
3. James Houblon, a merchant and later one of Pepys's closest friends.
4. Elizabeth's former dancing master (and former cause of Pepys's intense jealousy).
5. Wilson was a Navy Office clerk. Thomas Fuller, the historian, and John Pearson had both been preachers in London during the 1650s.

Winter, and also their son, a Knight of the Bath, were at church this morning), at 12*l* per annum.[1] Here W. Hewer's horse broke loose, and we had the sport to see him taken again. Then I carried them to see my Cosen Pepys's house;[2] and light and walked round about it, and they like it (as endeed it deserves) very well, and is a pretty place; and then I walked them to the wood hard by and there got them in in the thickets, till they had lost themselfs and I could not find the way into any of the walks in the wood, which endeed are very pleasant if I could have found them. At last got out of the wood again; and I, by leaping down the little bank coming out of the wood, did sprain my right foot, which brought me great present pain; but presently, with walking, it went away for the present, and so the women and W. Hewer and I walked upon the Downes, where a flock of sheep was, and the most pleasant and innocent sight that ever I saw in my life; we find a shepheard and his little boy reading, far from any houses or sight of people, the Bible to him. So I made the boy read to me, which he did with the forced Tone that children do usually read, that was mighty pretty; and then I did give him something and went to the father and talked with him; and I find he had been a servant in my Cosen Pepys's house, and told me what was become of their old servants. He did content himself mightily in my liking his boy's reading and did bless God for him, the most like one of the old Patriarchs that ever I saw in my life, and it brought those thoughts of the old age of the world in my mind for two or three days after. We took notice of his woolen knit stockings of two colours mixed, and of his shoes shod with Iron shoes, both at the toe and heels, and with great nails in the soles of his feet, which was mighty pretty; and taking notice of them, "Why," says the poor man, "the Downes, you see, are full of stones, and we are fain to shoe ourselfs thus; and these," says he, "will make the stones fly till they sing before me." I did give the poor man something, for which he was mighty thankful, and I tried to cast stones with his Horne Crooke. He values his dog mightily, that would turn a sheep any way which he would have him when he goes to fold them. Told me there was about 18 Scoare sheep in his flock, and that he hath 4*s* a week the year round for keeping of them. So we parted thence, with mighty pleasure in the discourse we had with this poor man; and Mrs. Turner, in the common fields here, did gather one of the prettiest nosegays that ever I saw in my

1. Richard Evelyn, brother of John Evelyn, lived at Woodcote Park. The family of Lord Berkeley lived nearby.
2. The house of John Pepys at Ashtead.

life. So to our coach, and through Mr. Minnes's wood and looked upon Mr. Eveling's house;[1] and so over the common and through Epsum towne to our Inne, in the way stopping a poor woman with her milk-pail and in one of my gilt Tumblers did drink our bellyfuls of milk, better then any Creame; and so to our Inne and there had a dish of creame, but it was sour and so had no pleasure in it; and so paid our reckoning and took coach, it being about 7 at night, and passed and saw the people walking with their wifes and children to take the ayre; and we set out for home, the sun by and by going down, and we in the cool of the evening all the way with much pleasure home, talking and pleasing ourselfs with the pleasure of this day's work; and Mrs. Turner mightily pleased with my resolution, which I tell her is never to keep a country-house, but to keep a coach and with my wife on the Saturday and to go sometimes for a day to this place and then quite to another place; and there is more variety, and as little charge and no trouble, as there is in a country-house. Anon it grew dark, and as it grew dark we had the pleasure to see several Glow wormes, which was mighty pretty. But my foot begins more and more to pain me; which Mrs. Turner, by keeping her warm hand upon it, did much ease; but so that when we came home, which was just at 11 at night, I was not able to walk from the lane's end to my house without being helped, which did trouble me; and therefore to bed presently; but thanks be to God, found that I had not been missed nor any business happened in my absence; so to bed and there had a cere-cloth[2] laid to my foot; and lay alone,
⟨⟨15⟩⟩ but in great pain all night long, so as I was not able to go
today to wait on the Duke of York with my fellows; but was forced in bed to write the perticulars for their discourse there, and kept my bed all day; and anon comes Mrs. Turner and new-dressed my foot, and did it so, that I was at much ease presently and so continued all day, so as I slept much and well in the daytime and in the evening rose and eat something. Where our poor Jane very sad for the death of her poor brother,[3] who hath left a wife and two small children. I did give her 20*s* in money, and what wine she needed for the burying him. After supper I was willing to go to bed to ease my foot again; which I did, and slept well all night ⟨this
⟨⟨16⟩⟩ evening came to see me Pelling[4] and we did sing together;
and he sings well endeed⟩ and in the morning I was able to

1. Richard Evelyn's house.
2. Cloth covered with wax and medicines.
3. Jane Birch's older brother Will.
4. John Pelling, local apothecary.

put on a wide shoe on that foot; and to the office without much pain and there sat all the morning. At noon home to dinner, where Creed to discourse of our Tanger business, which stands very bad in the business of money – and therefore we expect to have a committee called soon, and to acquaint them, among other things, with the order come to me for the not paying of any more pensions. We dined together; and after dinner, I to the office and there very late, very busy, doing much business endeed; and so with great comfort home to supper, and so to bed to ease my foot, which toward night begun to ake.

17. Up, and to my chamber to set down my Journall of Sunday last with much pleasure; and my foot being pretty well, but yet I am forced to limp. Then by coach; set my wife down at the New Exchange, and I to White-hall to the Treasury-chamber, but to little purpose; so to Mr. Burges,[1] to as little.◆

Home and to dinner; and by and by comes Mr. Pierce, who is interested in the *Panther*, for some advice;[2] and then comes Creed, and he and I spent the whole afternoon, till 8 at night, walking and talking of sundry things, public and private, in the garden; but most of all, of the unhappy state of this nation at this time by the negligence of the King and his Council. The Duke of Buckingham is it seems set at Liberty,[3] without any further charge against him or other clearing of him, but let to go out; which is one of the strangest instances of the fool's play with which all public things are done in this age that is to be apprehended. And it is said that when he was charged with making himself popular (as endeed he is, for many of the discontented Parliament, Sir Robt. Howard and Sir Tho. Meres and others, did attend at the Council-chamber when he was examined), he should answer that whoever was committed to prison by my Lord Chancellor or my Lord Arlington could not want being popular. But it is worth considering the ill state a Minister of State is in under such a prince as ours is; for undoubtedly, neither of those two great men would have been so fierce against the Duke of Buckingham at the Council-table the other day had they [not] been assured of the King's good liking and supporting them therein; whereas, perhaps at the desire of my Lady

1. Of the Exchequer.
2. James Pearse was part-owner of the privateer the *Panther*, which had been seizing prizes in consort with the privateer part-owned by Pepys.
3. Buckingham had been in the Tower since late June, when he had finally surrendered to the King after several months evading arrest for sedition. For his disgrace, *see* 3 March 1667.

Castlemayne (who I suppose hath at last overcome the King), the Duke of Buckingham is well received again, and now these men delivered up to the interest he can make for his revenge. He told me over the story of Mrs. Stewart, much after the manner which I was told it long since and have entered it in this book, told me by Mr. Eveling.[1] Only, he says it is verily believed that the King did never intend to marry her to any but himself, and that the Duke of York and Lord Chancellor were jealous of it; and that Mrs. Stewart might be got with child by the King or somebody else, and the King own a marriage before his contract (for it is but a contract, as he tells me, to this day) with the Queene, and so wipe their noses of the Crown; and that therefore the Duke of York and Chancellor did do all they could to forward the match with my Lord Duke of Richmond, that she might be married out of the way. But above all, it is a worthy part that this good lady hath acted. Thus we talked till night and then parted; and so I to my office and did business, and so home to supper and there find my sister Michell come from Lee[2] to see us; but doth tattle so much of the late business of the Duch coming thither, that I was weary of it. Yet it is worth remembering what she says: that she hath heard both seamen and soldiers swear they would rather serve the Dutch then the King, for they should be better used. She saw the *Royal Charles* brought into the River by them, and how they shot off their great guns for joy when they got her out of Chatham River.[3] I would not forget that this very day, when we have nothing to do almost but five merchantmen to man in the River, which have now been about it some weeks, I was asked at Westminster what the matter was that there was such ado kept in pressing of men, as it seems there is thereabouts at this day. So after supper, we all to bed. My foot very well again, I thank God.

29. Up, and with Sir W. Batten to St. James's to Sir W. Coventry's chamber; where among other things, he came to me and told me that he had received my yesterday's letters and that we concurred very well in our notions; and that as to my place which I had offered to resign of the Victualling, he had drawn up a letter at the same time, for the Duke of York's signing for the like places in general raised during this war, and that he had done me right to the Duke

1. *See* 26 April 1667.
2. Ester St Michel, wife of Balty, had come from Leigh-on-Sea, Essex.
3. The captured *Royal Charles* was taken to the Dutch Republic. The ship's stern-piece remains on display in the Rijksmuseum, Amsterdam.

of York, to let him know that I had of my own accord offered to resign mine.[1] The letter doth bid us to do all things, perticularizing several, for the laying up of the ships and easing the King of charge; so that the war is now professedly over.◆

The Duke of York being ready, we into his closet; but being in haste to go to the Parliament House, could not stay, so we parted and to Westminster-hall, where the Hall full of people to see the issue of the day, the King being to come to speak to the House today. One thing extraordinary was this day, a man, a Quaker, came naked through the Hall, only very civilly tied about the privities to avoid scandal, and with a chafing-dish of fire and brimstone burning upon his head did pass through the Hall, crying, "Repent! Repent!"[2] I up to the Painted Chamber, thinking to have got in to have heard the King's speech, but upon second thoughts did not think it would be worth the crowd, and so went down again into the Hall and there walked with several; among others, my Lord Rutherford, who is come out of Scotland, and I hope I may get some advantage by it in reference to the business of the interest of the great sum of money I paid him long since without interest – but I did not now move him in it;[3] but presently comes down the House of Commons, the King having made them a very short and no pleasing speech to them at all, not at all giving them thanks for their readiness to come up to town at this busy time; but told them that he did think he should have had occasion for them, but had none and therefore did dismiss them to look after their own occasions till October;[4] and that he did wonder any should offer to bring in a suspicion that he intended to rule by an army or otherwise then by the laws of the land, which he promised them he would not; and so bade them go home and settle the minds of the country in that perticular; and only added that he hath had made a peace, which he did believe they would find reasonable and a good peace, but did give them none of the perticulars thereof. Thus, they are dismissed again, to their general great distaste, I believe the greatest that ever

1. Pepys offered to resign his position as Surveyor-General of the Victualling, since it was a wartime appointment and peace was near. Coventry, as the Duke's secretary, had prepared a letter to the Navy Board for the Duke to sign, on the ending of other wartime appointments.
2. Solomon Eccles, known for making similarly spectacular calls to repentance during the plague and at fairs.
3. Lord Rutherford was heir to the late Earl of Teviot who had been Governor of Tangier 1663–4. Pepys had helped the family with their Tangier accounts and hoped to profit from it.
4. He prorogued parliament until 10 October.

Parliament was, to see themselfs so fooled and the nation in certain condition of ruin, while the King, they see, is only governed by his lust and women and rogues about him. The Speaker, they found, was kept from coming in the morning to the House on purpose, till after the King was come to the House of Lords, for fear they should be doing anything in the House of Commons to the further dissatisfaction of the King and his courtiers. They do all give up the kingdom for lost that I speak of, and do hear what the King says, how he and the Duke of York do do what they can to get up an army, that they may need no more Parliaments. And how my Lady Castlemayne hath, before the late breach between her and the King,[1] said to the King that he must rule by an Army or all would be lost. And that Bab May[2] hath given the like advice to the King to crush the English gentlemen, saying that 300*l* a year was enough for any man but them that lived at Court. I am told that many petitions were provided for the Parliament, complaining of the wrongs they have received from the Court and courtiers in City and Country, if the Parliament had but sat; and I do perceive they all do resolve to have a good account of the money spent before ever they give a farding more; and the whole Kingdom is everywhere sensible of their being abused, insomuch that they forced their Parliament-men to come up to sit; and my Cousin Roger told me that (but that was in mirth) he believed, if he had not come up he should have had his house burned. The kingdom never in so troubled a condition in this world as now; nobody pleased with the peace, and yet nobody daring to wish for the continuance of the war, it being plain that nothing doth nor can thrive under us.◆

AUGUST.

1. Up, and all the morning at the office. At noon my wife and I dined at Sir W Pen's, only with Mrs. Turner and her husband, on a damned venison pasty that stunk like a devil; however, I did not know it till dinner was done. We had nothing but only this and a leg of mutton and a pullet or two. Mrs. Markeham was here, with her great belly. I was very merry; and after dinner, upon a motion of the women, I was got to go to a play with them, the first I have seen since before the Duch coming upon our Coast; and so to the

1. She had fallen out with the King over her support for the Duke of Buckingham and, reportedly, over Charles's refusal to acknowledge the child she was carrying.
2. Baptist May, Keeper of the Privy Purse.

King's House to see *The Custome of the Country.*[1] The house mighty empty – more than ever I saw it – and an ill play. After the play, we into the House and spoke with Knepp, who went abroad with us by coach to the Neat-houses[2] in the way to Chelsy; and there in a box in a tree we sat and sang and talked and eat – my wife out of humour, as she always is when this woman is by. So after it was dark, we home; set Knepp down at home, who told us the story how Nell is gone from the King's House and is kept by my Lord Buckhurst. Then we home, the gates of the City shut, it being so late; and at Newgate we find them in trouble, some thiefs having this night broke open prison. So we through and home; and our coachman was fain to drive hard from two or three fellows, which he said were rogues, that he met at the end of Blowblather-street, next Cheapside. So set Mrs. Turner home, and then we home and I to the office a little; and so home and to bed, my wife in an ill Humour still.

16. Up, and at the office all the morning; and so at noon to dinner. And after dinner, my wife and I to the Duke's playhouse, where we saw the new play acted yesterday, *The Feign Innocence or Sir Martin Marr=all*, a play made by my Lord Duke of Newcastle, but as everybody says corrected by Dryden.[3] It is the most entire piece of Mirth, a complete Farce from one end to the other, that certainly was ever writ. I never laughed so in all my life; I laughed till my head [ached] all the evening and night with my laughing, and at very good wit therein, not fooling. The house full, and in all things of mighty content to me. Thence to the New Exchange with my wife, where at my bookseller's I saw the *History of the Royall Society*, which I believe is a fine book and I have bespoke one in quires.[4] So home, and I to the office a little; and so to my chamber and read the history of 88 in Speede, in order to my seeing the play thereof acted tomorrow at the King's House.[5] So to supper, in some pain by the sudden change of the weather cold and my drinking of cold drink; which I must I fear begin to leave off, though I shall try it

1. A comedy by John Fletcher and Philip Massinger.
2. Houses of entertainment on the riverbank opposite Vauxhall.
3. *Sir Martin Mar-all, or The Feign'd Innocence*, first performed on 15 August, became one of the Duke's Company's most successful comedies. Newcastle appears to have adapted from French two plays by Philippe Quinault and Molière, with Dryden making further changes.
4. Thomas Sprat's history had just been published; Pepys ordered one unbound.
5. He read John Speed's *History of Great Britaine* on the attempted Spanish invasion in 1588. He was preparing to see a version of Thomas Heywood's *If You Know Not Me You Know No Body, or The Troubles of Queen Elizabeth*, first acted c.1605.

as long as I can without much pain. But I find myself to be full of wind, and my anus to be knit together, as it is always with cold. Everybody wonders that we have no news from Bredah of the ratification of the peace, and do suspect that there is some stop in it. So to bed.

19. Up and at the office all the morning, very busy. Towards noon, I to Westminster about some tallies at the Exchequer and then straight home again and dined; and then to sing with my wife with great content; and then I to the office again, where busy. And then out and took coach and to the Duke of York's House all alone, and there saw *Sir Martin Marr-all* again, though I saw him but two days since, and do find it the most comical play that ever I saw in my life. As soon as the play done, I home and there busy till night; and then comes Mr. Moore[1] to me, only to discourse with me about some general things touching the badness of the times, how ill they look; and he doth agree with most people that I meet with, that we shall fall into a commonwealth in a few years, whether we will or no; for the charge of a Monarchy is such as the Kingdom cannot be brought to bear willingly, nor are things managed so well nowadays under [it] as it was heretofore. He says everybody doth think that there is something extraordinary that keeps us so long from the news of the peace being ratified – which the King and the Duke of York have expected these six days. He gone, my wife and I and Mrs. Turner walked in the garden a good while, till 9 at night, and then parted; and I home to supper and to read a little (which I cannot refrain, though I have all the reason in the world to favour my eyes, which every day grow worse and worse by over-useing them) and then to bed.

24. *St. Bartholomew's day.* This morning was proclaimed the peace between us and the States of the United Provinces, and also of the King of France and Denmarke, and in the afternoon the proclamations were printed and came out. And at night the bells rung, but no bonfires that I hear of anywhere, partly from the dearness of firing but principally from the little content most people have in the peace.[2]

All the morning at the office. At noon dined, and Creed with

1. Henry Moore, Sandwich's man of business.
2. The peace of Breda, made up of treaties between the several warring parties, was signed on 21 July 1667 (31 July New Style). The lack of celebration stemmed from the sense that the King had been compelled to make peace, with much lost and little gained.

me, at home. After dinner, we to a play and there saw *The Cardinall* at the King's House, wherewith I am mightily pleased; but above all with Becke Marshall.[1] But it is pretty to observe how I look up and down for and did espy Knepp; but durst not own it to my wife that I saw her, for fear of angering her, who doth not like my kindness to her – and so I was forced not to take notice of her. And so homeward, leaving Creed at the Temple: and my belly now full with Plays, that I do entend to bind myself to see no more till Michaelmas. So with my wife to Mile end and there drank of Bides ale,[2] and so home; most of our discourse about our keeping a coach the next year, which pleases my wife mightily; and if I continue as able as now, it will save us money.

This day came a letter from the Duke of York to the Board, to invite us, which is as much as to fright us, into the lending the King money;[3] which is a poor thing and most dishonourable – and shows in what a case we are at the end of the war to our neighbours. And the King doth now declare publicly to give 10 per cent to all lenders; which makes some think that the Dutch themselfs will send over money and lend it upon our public faith, the Act of Parliament. So home and to my office; wrote a little and then home to supper and to bed.

26. Up; and Greeting came and I reckoned with him for his teaching of my wife and me upon the Flagielette to this day, and so paid him off, having as much as he can teach us. Then to the office, where we sat upon a perticular business all the morning, and my Lord Anglesey with us; who, and my Lord Brouncker, do bring us news how my Lord Chancellors seal is to be taken away from him today.[4] The thing is so great and sudden to me, that it put me into a very great admiration what should be the meaning of it; and they do not own that they know what it should be. But this is certain: that the King did resolve it on Saturday, and did yesterday send the Duke of Albemarle (the only man fit for those works) to him for his purse; to which the Chancellor answered that he received it from the King, and would deliver it to the King's own hand, and so civilly returned the Duke of Albemarle without it; and this

1. Rebecca Marshall acted in James Shirley's tragedy.
2. Alderman John Bide (d. 1665) had been a brewer of note.
3. The letter asked for a list of names and sums so that the Duke could give the King an account of their zeal for his service.
4. The great seal, held in a ceremonial purse, was the Lord Chancellor's symbol of office. Clarendon, who had defeated previous attempts to deprive him of office, now fell dramatically from the King's favour.

morning my Lord Chancellor is to be with the King, to come to an end in that business. After sitting, we rose; and my wife being gone abroad with Mrs. Turner to her washing at the whitster's,[1] I dined at Sir W. Batten, where Mr. Boreman was, who came from White-hall; who tells us that he saw my Lord Chancellor come in his coach with some of his men, without his Seal, to White-hall to his chamber; and thither the King and Duke of York came, and stayed together alone an hour or more. And it is said that the King doth say that he will have the Parliament meet, and that it will prevent much trouble by having of him out of their envy, by his place being taken away – for that all their envy will be at him. It is said also that my Lord Chancellor answers that he desires he may be brought to his trial if he have done anything to lose his office; and that he will be willing, and is most desirous, to lose that and his head both together. Upon what terms they parted nobody knows; but the Chancellor looked sad he says. Then in comes Sir Rd. Ford and says he hears that there is nobody more presses to reconcile the King and Chancellor then the Duke of Albemarle and Duke of Buckingham; the latter of which is very strange, not only that he who was so lately his enemy should do it, but that this man, that but the other day was in danger of losing his own head, should so soon come to be a mediator for others. It shows a wise government. They all say that he is but a poor man, not worth above 3000*l* a year in land, but this I cannot believe; and all do blame him for having built so great a house, till he had got a better estate.[2] Having dined, Sir J. Mennes and I to White-hall, where we could be informed in no more then we were told before, nobody knowing the result of the meeting but that the matter is suspended. So I walked to the King's playhouse, there to meet Sir W. Penn; and we saw *The Surprizall*,[3] a very mean play I thought, or else it was because I was out of humour and but very little company in the house. But there Sir W. Penn and I had a great deal of discourse with Mall,[4] who tells us that Nell is already left by my Lord Buckhurst, and that he makes sport of her and swears she hath had all she could get of him; and Hart,[5] her great admirer, now hates her; and that she is very poor and hath lost my Lady Castlemayne, who was her great friend,

1. Specialists in bleaching clothes.
2. Clarendon's house at Piccadilly had drawn public ire as a result of the belief it was funded by French bribes.
3. A comedy by Sir Robert Howard, first acted in 1662.
4. Mary Meggs, orange-seller at the Theatre Royal.
5. Charles Hart, the leading actor at the Theatre Royal.

also. But she is come to the House, but is neglected by them all.

Thence with Sir W. Penn home, and I to my office, where late about business; and then home to supper and so to bed.

31. At the office all the morning – where by Sir W. Penn I do hear that the Seal was fetched away to the King yesterday from the Lord Chancellor, by Secretary Morrice – which puts me into a great horror, to have it done after so much debate and confidence that it would not be done at last.◆ After having wrote my letters at the office in the afternoon, I in the evening to White-hall to see how matters go; and there I met with Mr. Ball of the Excise-Office and he tells me that the Seal is delivered to Sir Orlando Bridgeman, the man of the whole nation that is the best spoken of and will please most people;[1] and therefore I am mighty glad of it. He was then at my Lord Arlington's, whither I went, expecting to see him come out; but stayed so long, and Sir W. Coventry coming thither, whom I had not a mind should see me there idle upon a post-night,[2] I went home without seeing him; but he is there with his Seal in his hand. So I home; took up my wife, whom I left at Unthankes, and so home; and after signing my letters, to bed.

This day, being dissatisfied with my wife's learning so few songs of Goodgroome, I did come to a new bargain with him, to teach her songs at so much, *viz.*, 10*s* a song; which he accepts of and will teach her.

SEPTEMBER.

2. This day is kept in the City as a public fast for the fire this day twelve months. But I was not at church, being commanded with the rest to attend the Duke of York; and therefore with Sir J. Mennes to St. James's, where we had much business before the Duke of York; and observed all things to be very kind between the Duke of York and W. Coventry, which did mightily joy me. When we had done, Sir W. Coventry called me down with him to his chamber and there told me that he is leaving the Duke of York's service, which I was amazed at; but he tells me that it is not with the least unkindness on the Duke of York's side, though he expects

1. Bridgeman (Chief Justice of the Common Pleas) now became Lord Keeper, an inferior office to that of Chancellor which Clarendon had held.
2. It was a Saturday, one of the three nights a week that post left London for all parts of the kingdom.

(and I told him he was in the right) it will be interpreted otherwise, because done just at this time.[1] "But," says he, "I did desire it a good while since, and the Duke of York did with much entreaty grant it, desiring that I would say nothing of it, that he might have time and liberty to choose his successor without being importuned for others whom he should not like" – and that he hath chosen Mr. Wren;[2] which I am glad of, he being a very ingenious man, and so W. Coventry says of him, though he knows him little; but perticularly commends him for the book he writ in answer to Harrington's *Oceana*, which for that reason I intend to buy.[3] He tells me the true reason is that he being a man not willing to undertake more business then he can go through, and being desirous to have his whole time to spend upon the business of the Treasury and a little for his own ease, he did desire this of the Duke of York. He assures me that the kindness with which he goes away from the Duke of York is one of the greatest joys that ever he had in the world. I used some freedom with him, telling him how the world hath discourse of his having offended the Duke of York about the late business of the Chancellor; he doth not deny it, but says that perhaps the Duke of York might have some reason for it, he opposing him in a thing wherein he was so earnest;[4] but tells me that notwithstanding all that, the Duke of York doth not now, nor can blame him – for he tells me that he was the man that did propose the removal of the Chancellor; and that he did still persist in it, and at this day publicly owns it and is glad of it; but that the Duke of York knows that he did first speak of it to the Duke of York, before he spoke to any mortal creature besides, which was fair dealing; and that the Duke of York was then of the same mind with him and did speak of it to the King, though since, for reasons best known to himself, he was afterward altered. I did then desire to know what was the great matter that grounded his desire of the Chancellor's removal; he told me many things not fit to be spoken, and yet not anything of his being unfaithful to the King; but, *instar omnium*,[5] he told me that while he was so great at the Council-board and in the administration of matters, there was no room for anybody to propose any

1. Coventry had resigned his post as secretary to the Duke of York. This followed hard on the fall of Clarendon (the Duke's father-in-law), of whom Coventry was a known opponent.
2. Matthew Wren, cousin of Christopher Wren, had been Clarendon's secretary.
3. Wren had written two replies to James Harrington's republican treatise *Oceana* (1656), only one of which, *Monarchy Asserted* (1659), appeared under his name.
4. Coventry had opposed the Duke of York's defence of Clarendon.
5. A specimen of the whole.

remedy to what was amiss or to compass anything, though never so good for the Kingdom, unless approved of by the Chancellor, he managing all things with that greatness which now will be removed, that the King may have the benefit of others' advice.◆

Thence home and took my wife out to Mile-end-green and there drank; and so home, having a very fine evening. Then home, and I to Sir W. Batten and W. Penn and there discoursed of Sir W. Coventry's leaving the Duke of York and Mr. Wren's succeeding him; they told me both seriously, that they had long cut me out for Secretary to the Duke of York if ever W. Coventry left him; which, agreeing with what I have heard from other hands heretofore, doth make me not only think that something of that kind hath been thought on, but doth comfort me to see that the world hath such an esteem of my qualities as to think me fit for any such thing – though I am glad with all my heart that I am not so, for it would never please me to be forced to the attendance that that would require, and leave my wife and family to themselfs, as I must do in such a case; thinking myself now in the best place that ever man was in to please his own mind in, and therefore I will take care to preserve it. So to bed, my cold remaining, though not so much, upon me. ⟨This day, Nell, an old tall maid, came to live with us, a cook maid recommended by Mr. Batelier.⟩

11. Up, and with Mr. Gawden to the Exchequer. By the way he tells me this day he is to be answered whether he must hold Sheriffe or no – for he would not hold unless he may keep it at his office, which is out of the City (and so my Lord Mayor must come with his sword down whenever he comes thither), which he doth because he cannot get a house fit for him in the City, or else he will fine for it.[1] Among others that they have in nomination for Sheriffe, one is little Chaplin, who was his servant and a very young man to undergo that place, but as the City is now, there is no great honour nor joy to be had in being a public officer. At the Exchequer I looked after my business; and when done, went home to the Change and there bought a case of knifes for dinner and a dish of fruit of 5*s* and bespoke other things, and then home; and here I find all things in good order, and a good dinner towards. Anon comes Sir W. Batten and his Lady, and Mr. Griffith their Ward, and Sir

1. I.e. pay a fine and so avoid the burden of office. Denis Gauden did in fact serve as sheriff in 1667. His office (that of the Navy Victualler) was in Middlesex. The Lord Mayor was attended by a sword-bearer who normally carried his sword upright.

W. Penn and his Lady, and Mrs. Louther (who is grown, either through pride or want of manners, a fool, having not a word to say almost all dinner; and as a further mark of a beggarly proud fool, hath a bracelet of diamonds and rubies about her wrist and a six-penny necklace about her neck and not one good rag of clothes upon her back); and Sir Jo Chichly[1] in their company – and Mrs. Turner. Here I had an extraordinary good and handsome dinner for them, better then any of them deserve or understand (saving Sir Jo. Chichly and Mrs. Turner); and not much mirth, only what I by discourse made, and that against my genius.[2] After dinner I took occasion to break up the company – as soon as I could, and all parted. Sir W. Batten and I by water to White-hall, there to speak with the Commissioners of the Treasury, who are mighty earnest for our hastening all that may be the paying-off of the seamen now there is money, and are considering many other things for easing of charge; which I am glad of, but vexed to see that J. Duncomb should be so pressing in it, as if none of us had like care with him. Having done there, I by coach to the Duke of York's playhouse and there saw part of *The Ungratefull Lovers*;[3] and sat by Beck Marshall, who is very handsome near-hand. Here I met Mrs. Turner and my wife as we agreed, and together home; and there my wife and I part of the night at the Flagilette, which she plays now anything upon almost, at first sight and in good time. But here came Mr. Moore and sat and discoursed with me of public matters; the sum of which is that he doth doubt that there is more at the bottom then the removal of the Chancellor; that is, he doth verily believe that the King doth resolve to declare the Duke of Monmouth legitimate – and that we shall soon see it. This I do not think the Duke of York will endure without blows;[4] but his poverty, and being lessened by having the Chancellor fallen and W. Coventry gone from him, will disable him from being able to do anything almost, he being himself almost lost in the esteem of people; and will be more and more, unless my Lord Chancellor (who is already begun to be pitied by some people, and to be better thought of then was expected) doth recover himself in Parliament. He would seem to fear that this difference about the Crowne (if there be nothing else) will undo us. He doth say that it is very true, that my

1. Sir John Chicheley, naval captain during the recent war.
2. Spirit.
3. No play of this title is known. Pepys may mean *The Unfortunate Lovers*, by Sir William Davenant, licensed in 1638 and in the Duke's Company's repertoire.
4. It would deprive the Duke of York of his place as heir presumptive.

Lord[1] did lately make some stop of some grants of 2000*l* a year to my Lord Grandison, which was only in his name for the use of my Lady Castlemayn's children; and that this did incense her, and she did speak very scornful words and sent a scornful message to him about it. He gone after supper, I to bed – being mightily pleased with my wife's playing so well upon the flagelette, and I am resolved she shall learn to play upon some instrument – for though her eare be bad, yet I see she will attain anything to be done by her hand.

27. Up and to the office, where very busy all the morning. While I was busy at the office, my wife sends for me to come to home, and what was it but to see the pretty girl which she is taking to wait upon her; and though she seems not altogether so great a beauty as she had before told me, yet endeed she is mighty pretty; and so pretty, that I find I shall be too much pleased with it, and therefore could be contented as to my judgment, though not to my passion, that she might not come, lest I may be found too much minding her, to the discontent of my wife.[2] She is to come next week. She seems by her discourse to be grave beyond her bigness and age, and exceeding well-bred as to her deportment, having been a scholar in a school at Bow these seven or eight year. To the office again, my [mind] running on this pretty girl; and there till noon, when Creed and Sheres[3] come and dined with me; and we had a great deal of pretty discourse of the ceremoniousness of the Spaniards. ◆ That my Lord Sandwich wears a beard[4] now, turned up in the Spanish manner. But that which pleases me most endeed, is that the peace which he hath made with Spain is now printed here, and is acknowledged by all the merchants to be the best peace that ever England had with them;[5] and it appears that the King thinks it so, for this is printed before the Ratification is gone over; whereas that with France and Holland was not in a good while after, till Copys came over of it ⟨in English⟩ out of Holland and France, that it was a reproach not to have it printed here. This I am mighty glad of; and is the first and only piece of good news, or thing fit to be owned, that this nation hath done several years.

After dinner, I to the office; and they gone and anon, comes

1. Lord Chancellor Clarendon.
2. This was Deborah Willet, aged 16. Pepys's forecast proved only too accurate.
3. Henry Sheeres, who had been with Sandwich in Spain, had just returned with a copy of the Anglo-Spanish treaty for ratification by the King.
4. Moustache.
5. The treaty was the greatest achievement of Sandwich's embassy; welcomed by both sides, it remained unaltered for nearly thirty years.

Pelling, and he and I to Greys Inne-fields, thinking to have heard Mrs. Knight[1] sing at her lodgings by a friend's means of his; but we came too late, so must try another time. So lost our labour, and I by coach home and there to my chamber and did a great deal of good business about my Tanger accounts; and so with pleasure discoursing with my wife of our Journy shortly to Brampton, and of this little girle, which endeed runs in my head and pleases me mightily, though I dare not own it; and so to supper and to bed.

OCTOBER.

5. Up, and to the office and there all the morning, none but my Lord Anglesy and myself. But much surprized with the news of the death of Sir W. Batten, who died this morning, having been but two days sick. Sir W. Penn and I did despatch a letter this morning to Sir W. Coventry to recommend Colonel Middleton, who we think a most honest and understanding man, and fit for that place.[2] Sir G. Carteret did also come this morning, and walked with me in the garden and concluded not to concern or have any advice made to Sir W. Coventry in behalf of my Lord Sandwiches business;[3] so I do rest satisfied, though I do think they are all mad, that they will judge Sir W. Coventry an enemy, when he is endeed no such man to anybody, but is severe and just, as he ought to be, where he sees things ill done. At noon home, and by coach to Temple-bar to a India shop and there bought a gown and Shash, which cost me 26*s*. And so she and Willett away to the Change, and I to my Lord Crew and there met my Lord Hinchingbrooke and Lady Jemimah, and there dined with them and my Lord – where pretty merry. And after dinner, my Lord Crew and Hinchingbrooke and myself went aside to discourse about my Lord Sandwiches business, which is in a very ill state for want of money; and so parted, and I to my tailors and there took up my wife and Willet, who stayed there for me, and to the Duke of York's playhouse; but the House so full, it being a new play *The Coffee-House*,[4] that we could not get in, and so to the King's House; and there going in, met

1. Mary Knight, probably the best-known soprano of her day.
2. Thomas Middleton, who had done excellent service as Navy Commissioner at Portsmouth, was appointed Surveyor of the Navy and took up his duties in December.
3. Sandwich had spent thousands of pounds on embassy to Madrid, and needed either a new supply of money or to be recalled home.
4. *Tarugo's Wiles, or The Coffee House*, a comedy by Thomas St Serfe.

with Knipp and she took us up into the Tireing-rooms and to the women's Shift,[1] where Nell was dressing herself and was all unready; and is very pretty, prettier then I thought; and so walked all up and down the House above, and then below into the Scene-room,[2] and there sat down and she gave us fruit; and here I read the Qu's to Knepp while she answered me, through all her part of *Flora's Figarys*, which was acted today.[3] But Lord, to see how they were both painted would make a man mad – and did make me loath them – and what base company of men comes among them, and how lewdly they talk – and how poor the men are in clothes, and yet what a show they make on the stage by candle-light, is very observable. But to see how Nell cursed for having so few people in the pit was pretty, the other House carrying away all the people at the new play, and is said nowadays to have generally most company, as being better players. By and by into the pit and there saw the play; which is pretty good, but my belly was full of what I had seen in the House; and so after the play done, away home and there to the writing my letters; and so home to supper and to bed.

7. Up betimes, and did do several things towards the settling all matters, both of house and office, in order for my journey this day; and did leave my chief care, and the key of my closet, with Mr. Hater, with direction what papers to secure in case of fire or other accident; and so about 9 a-clock, I and my wife and Willett set out in a coach I have hired, with four horses, and W. Hewer and Murford[4] rode by us on horseback; and so, my wife and she in their morning gowns, very handsome and pretty and to my great liking, we set out; and so out at Allgate and so to the Greenman and so on to Enfield, in our way seeing Mr. Louther and his lady in a coach going to Walthamstow, and he told us that he would overtake us at night, he being to go that way. So we to Enfield and there bayted,[5] it being but a foul, bad day; and there Louther and Mr. Burford, an acquaintance of his, did overtake us, and there drank and eat together; and by and by we parted, we going before them; and very merry, my wife and girl and [I], talking and telling tales and singing; and before night did come to Bishop=stafford, where Louther and his friend did meet us again and carried us to the

1. Dressing-room.
2. Space used for storage or preparation of scenery.
3. *Flora's Vagaries*, a comedy by Richard Rhodes, first acted 1663. Nell Gwyn played the wild Flora and Knepp was the more conventional Otrante.
4. Will Murford, Navy Office messenger.
5. Stopped for refreshment.

Raynedeere, where Mrs. Aynsworth (who lived heretofore at Cambrige and whom I knew better then they think for, doth live[1] – it was the woman that, among other things, was great with my Cosen Barmston of Cottenham, and did use to sing to him and did teach me *Full forty times over*, a very lewd song[2]) doth live, a woman they are very well acquainted with, and is here what she was at Cambrige, and all the goodfellows of the country come hither. Louther and his friend stayed and drank and then went further this night, but here we stayed and supped and lodged. But as soon as they were gone and my supper getting ready, I fell to write my letter to my Lord Sandwich, which I could not finish before my coming from London; so did finish it to my good content, and a good letter, telling him the present state of all matters; and did get a man to promise to carry it tomorrow morning to be there at my house by noon, and I paid him well for it. So that being done and my mind at ease, we to supper and so to bed, my wife and I in one bed and the girl in another in the same room. And lay very well, but there was so much tearing[3] company in the house, that we could not see my landlady, so I had no opportunity of renewing my old acquaintance with her. But here we slept very well.

8. Up pretty betimes, though not so soon as we entended, by reason of Murford's not rising and then not knowing how to open our door; which, and some other pleasant simplicities of the fellow, did give occasion to us to call him Sir Martin Marr=all; and W Hewers being his helper and counsellor, we did call him all this journey, Mr. Warner, which did give us good occasion of mirth now and then.[4] At last rose, and up and broke our fast, and then took coach and away; and at Newport did call on Mr. Louther, and he and his friend and the maister of the house, their friend where they were (a gentleman), did presently get a-horseback and overtook us, and went with us to Audly end and did go along with us all over the house and garden; and mighty merry we were. The house

1. Elizabeth Aynsworth had been banished from Cambridge by the university authorities for being a bawd. She settled at the Reindeer Inn in Bishop's Stortford.
2. An innuendo-laden song comparing obtaining sex from reluctant women to siege warfare. Sample lyric: "There's a breach ready made, which still open hath bin / And thousands of thoughts to betray it within, / If you once come to storme her, you're sure to get in / Then stand off not coldly, / But venter on boldly, / With weapon in hand," etc. It was first published in *Wit and Drollery* (1656).
3. Boisterous, drunken.
4. Sir Martin Mar-all, the title character in Pepys's favourite comedy, is continually saved from the consequences of his foolishness by his servant Warner.

endeed doth appear very fine, but not so fine as it hath heretofore to me.◆ Here we parted with Louther and his friends, and away to Cambrige, it being foul, rainy weather; and there did take up at the Rose, for the sake of Mrs. Dorothy Drawwater, the vintener's daughter, which is mentioned in the play of *Sir Martin Marr=all.*[1] Here we had a good chamber and bespoke a good supper; and then I took my wife and W. Hewer and Willett (it holding up a little) and showed them Trinity College and St. Johns Library, and went to King's College chapel to see the outside of it only, and so to our Inne; and with much pleasure did this, they walking in their pretty morning gowns, very handsome, and I proud to find myself in condition to do this; and so home to our lodging, and there by and by to supper with much good sport, talking with the drawers concerning matters of the town and persons whom I remember; and so after supper to cards and then to bed, lying, I in one bed and my wife and girl in another in the same room; and very merry talking together and mightily pleased both of us with the girl. Saunders, the only[2] Viallin in my time, is I hear dead of the plague in the late plague there.

[They arrive at Brampton]

10. Waked in the morning with great pain I, of the Collique, by cold taken yesterday, I believe with going up and down in my shirt; but with rubbing my belly, keeping of it warm, I did at last come to some ease, and rose; and up to walk up and down the garden with my father, to talk of all our concernments – about a husband for my sister, whereof there is at present no appearance. But we must endeavour to find her one now, for she grows old and ugly. Then for my brother; and resolve he shall stay here this winter, and then I will either send him to Cambridge for a year, till I get him some church promotion, or send him to sea as a chaplain – where he may study and earn his living. Then walked round about our Greene to see whether, in case I cannot buy out my uncle Tho. and his son's right in this house, that I can buy another place as good thereabouts to build on, and I do not see that I can; but this, with new building, may be made an excellent pretty thing, and I resolve

1. In Act 5 of Dryden's *Sir Martin Mar-all*, there is a fleeting reference to "Dorothy, Daughter to one Draw-water, a Vintner at the Rose". Dryden and Pepys had studied at Cambridge together.
2. Best.

to look after it as soon as I can and Goody Gorrum dies.[1] By this time it was almost noon, and then my father and I and wife and Willett abroad by coach round the Towne of Brampton to observe any other place as good as ours, and find none; and so back with great pleasure and thence went all of us, my sister and brother and W. Hewer, to dinner to Hinchingbrooke, where we had a good plain country dinner, but most kindly used; and here dined the Minister of Brampton and his wife, who is reported a very good, but poor man. Here I spent alone with my Lady,[2] after dinner, the most of the afternoon; and anon the two Twins were sent for ⟨from Schoole at Mr. Taylors⟩ to come to see me;[3] and I took them into the garden and there in one of the Summer-houses did examine them; and do find them so well advanced in their learning, that I was amazed at it, they repeating a whole Ode without book out of Horace, and did give me a very good account of anything almost, and did make me very readily very good Latin and did give me good account of their Greek grammer, beyond all possible expectation; and so grave and manly as I never saw, I confess, nor could have believed – so that they will be fit to go to Cambridge in two years at most. They are but little, but very like one another; and well-looked children. Then in to my Lady again, and stayed till it was almost night again; and then took leave for a great while again, but with extraordinary kindness from my Lady, who looks upon me like one of her own family and interest. So thence, my wife and people [by] the highway, and I walked over the park with Mr. Sheply and through the grove, which is mighty pretty as is imaginable; and so over their drawbridge to Nun's Bridge and so to my father's, and there sat and drank and talked a little and then parted; and he being gone, and what company there was, my father and I with a dark lantern, it being now night, into the guarden with my wife and there went about our great work to dig up my gold.[4] But Lord, what a tosse I was for some time in, that they could not justly tell where it was, that I begun heartily to sweat and be angry that they should not agree better upon the place, and at last to fear that it was gone; but by and by, poking with a spit, we found it, and then begun with

1. By Robert Pepys's will, ownership of Widow Gorham's alehouse at Brampton would on her death pass to Pepys's father and then to him.
2. Lady Sandwich.
3. Oliver and John (aged 12), sons of Sandwich, who were studying at Huntingdon Grammar School.
4. The money taken from London by Elizabeth, Pepys's father, and Gibson (a navy clerk) during the Dutch invasion scare. Elizabeth and Pepys's father had buried it together. *See* 13 and 19 June 1667.

a spudd[1] to lift up the ground; but good God, to see how sillily they did it, not half a foot under ground and in the sight of the world from a hundred places if anybody by accident were near-hand, and within sight of a neighbour's window and their hearing also, being close by; only, my father says that he saw them all gone to church before he begun the work when he laid the money, but that doth not excuse it to me; but I was out of my wits almost, and the more from that upon my lifting up the earth with the spud, I did discern that I scattered the pieces of gold round about the ground among the grass and loose earth; and taking up the Iron head-pieces[2] wherein they were put, I perceive the earth was got among the gold and wet, so that the bags were all rotten, all the notes, that I could not tell what in the world to say to it, not knowing how to judge what was wanting or what had been lost by Gibson in his coming down; which, all put together, did make me mad; and at last was forced to take up the head-pieces, dirt and all, and as many of the scattered pieces as I could with the dirt discern by the candlelight, and carry them up into my brother's chamber and there lock them up till I had eat a little supper; and then all people going to bed, W. Hewer and I did all alone, with several pales of water and basins, at last wash the dirt off of the pieces and parted the pieces and the dirt, and then begun to tell; and by a note which I had of the value of the whole (in my pocket) do find that there was short above 100 pieces, which did make me mad; and considering that the neighbour's house was so near, that we could not suppose we could speak one to another in the garden at the place where the gold lay (especially by my father being deaf) but they must know what we had been doing on, I feared that they might in the night come and gather some pieces and prevent us the next morning; so W. Hewer and I out again about midnight (for it was now grown so late) and there by candlelight did make shift to gather 45 pieces more – and so in and to cleanse them, and by this time it was past 2 in the morning; and so to bed, with my mind pretty quiet to think that I have recovered so many. And then to bed, and I lay in the trundle-bed, the girl being gone to bed to my wife. And there lay in some disquiet all night, telling of the clock till it was daylight; and then rose

⟨⟨11⟩⟩ and called W. Hewer, and he and I, with pails and a Sive, did lock ourselfs into the garden and there gather all the earth about the place into pails, and then Sive those pails in one of

1. A narrow, sharp spade.
2. Helmets.

the summer-houses (just as they do for Dyamonds in other parts of the world); and there to our great content did with much trouble by 9 a-clock, and by that time we emptied several pails and could not find one, we did make the last night's 45 up 79; so that we are come to about 20 or 30 of what I think the true number should be, and perhaps within less; and of them I may reasonably think that Mr. Gibson might lose some, so that I am pretty well satisfied that my loss is not great and do bless God that it is so well; and do leave my father to make a second examination of the dirt – which he promises he will do; and poor man, is mightily troubled for this accident. But I declared myself very well satisfied, and so endeed I am and my mind at rest in it, it being but an accident which is unusual; and so gives me some kind of content to remember how painful it is sometimes to keep money, as well as to get it, and how doubtful I was how to keep it all night and how to secure it to London. And so got all my gold put up in bags; and so having the last night wrote to my Lady Sandwich to lend me John Bowles to go along with me my Journy, not telling her the reason, but it was only to secure my gold, we to breakfast; and then about 10 a-clock took coach, my wife and I, and Willett and W. Hewer, and Murford and Bowles (whom my Lady lent me), and my brother John on horseback; and with these four I thought myself pretty safe. But before we went out, the Huntington music came to me and played, and it was better then that of Cambridge. Here I took leave of my father, and did give my sister 20*s*. She cried at my going; but whether it was at her unwillingness for my going or any unkindness of my wife's or no, I know not; but God forgive me, I take her to be so cunning and ill-natured that I have no great love for her; but only, is my sister and must be provided for. My gold, I put into a basket and set under one of the seats; and so my work every quarter of an hour was to look to see whether all was well, and did ride in great fear all the day; but it was a pleasant day and good company, and I mightily contented. Mr. Sheply saw me beyond St. Neotts and there parted, and we straight to Stevenage, through Baldock lanes, which are already very bad. And at Stevenage we came well before night, and all safe; and there with great care I got the gold up to the chamber, my wife carrying one bag and the girl another and W. Hewer the rest in the basket, and set it all under a bed in our chamber; and then sat down to talk and were very pleasant, satisfying myself; among ⟨other⟩ things from Jo. Bowles, in some terms of Hunting and about deere, bucks, and does; and so anon to supper, and very merry we were and a good supper; and after supper to bed. Brecocke[1] alive still, and the best Host I know almost.

12. Up, and eat our breakfast and set out about 9 a-clock; and so to Barnett, where we stayed and baited (the weather very good all day and yesterday) and by 5 a-clock got home, where I find all well; and did bring my gold, to my heart's content, very safe home, having not this day carried it in a basket but in our hands: the girl took care of one and my wife another bag, and I the rest – I being afeared of the bottom of the coach, lest it should break; and therefore was at more ease in my mind then I was yesterday. At home do find that Sir W. Batten's buriall was today; carried from hence with a hundred or two of coaches to Walthamstow and there buried. Here I hear by Mr. Pierce the surgeon, and then by Mr. Lewes and also by Mr. Hater, that the Parliament hath met on Thursday last and adjourned to Monday next. The King did make them a very kind speech, promising them to leave all to them to do, and call to account what and whom they pleased;[2] and declared by my Lord Keeper how many gracious acts he had done since he saw them; among others, disbanding the army, and putting all papists out of imployment, and displacing persons that had managed their business ill[3] – that the Parliament is mightily pleased with the King's speech, and voted giving him thanks for what he said and hath done; and among other things, would by name thank him for displacing my Lord Chancellor, for which a great many did speak in the House, but was opposed by some, and perticularly Harry Coventry, who got that it should be put to a committee to consider what perticulars to mention in their thanks to the King, saying that it was too soon to give thanks for the displacing of a man, before they knew or had examined what was the cause of his displacing. And so it rested; but this doth show that they are and will be very high. And Mr. Pierce doth tell me that he fears, and doth hear, that it hath been said among them that they will move for the calling my Lord Sandwich home, to bring him to account – which doth trouble me mightily; but I trust it will not be so. Anon comes home Sir W. Penn from the buriall, and he and I to walk in the garden, where he did confirm the most of this news; and so to talk of our perticular concernments; and among the rest, he says that my Lady

1. Richard Bowcocke, landlord of the Swan Inn.
2. The speech pledged to allow parliament to examine expenditure during the war. The words were those of Lord Keeper Bridgeman, on behalf of the King.
3. These particulars were not in the Lord Keeper's speech, but featured in the Commons' address of thanks that was now being drawn up.

Batten and her children-in-law[1] are all broke in pieces, and that there is but 800*l* found in the world of money, and is in great doubt what we shall do toward the doing ourselfs right with them about the prize-money.[2] This troubles me, but we will fall to work upon that next week close. Then he tells me he did deliver my petition[3] into the hands of Sir W. Coventry, who did take it with great kindness and promised to present it to the Duke of York, and that himself hath since seen the Duke of York, but it was in haste, and thinks the Duke of York did tell him that the thing was done; but he is confident that either it is or will be done. This doth please me mightily. So after a little talk more, I away home to supper with Jo. Bowles and brother and wife (who I perceive is already a little jealous of my being fond of Willett, but I will avoid giving her any cause to continue in that mind, as much as possible); and before that, did go with Sir W. Penn to my Lady Batten, whom I had not seen since she was a widow; which she took unkindly but I did excuse it. And the house being full of company and of several factions, she against the children and they against one another and her, I away and home to supper; and after supper to bed.

20. *Lords day.* Up, and put on my new Tunique of velvett, which is very plain, but good. This morning is brought to me an order for the presenting the committee of Parliament[4] tomorrow with a list of the commanders and ships' names of all the fleets set out since the war, and perticularly of those ships which were divided from the fleet with Prince Rupert;[5] which gives me occasion to see that they are busy after that business – and I am glad of it. So I alone to church and then home, and there Mr. Deane[6] comes and dines with me by appointment; and both at and after dinner, he and I spent all the day till it was dark in discourse of business of the Navy and the ground of the many miscarriages; wherein he doth inform me in many more then I knew, and I had desired him to put them in writing; and many endeed they are, and good ones. And also we discoursed of the business of shipping, and he hath promised me a

1. Step-children.
2. Pepys had sold Batten his share of the prize recently taken by their privateer and Batten died in debt to him.
3. The petition asked that Pepys be granted, as a war bounty, a ship seized from the Dutch. It was successful.
4. The Commons Committee on Miscarriages, set up to enquire into the conduct of the war campaigns.
5. The controversial division of the fleet that had preceded the Four Days Battle in June 1666.
6. Anthony Deane, Master-Shipwright at Harwich dockyard.

Draught of the ship he is now building – wherein I am mightily pleased. This afternoon comes to me Captain O Bryan,[1] about a ship that the King hath given him, and he and I to talk of the Parliament and he tells me that the business of the Duke of York's slackening sail in the first fight, at the beginning of the war,[2] is brought into Question, and Sir W Pen and Captain Cox is to appear tomorrow about it. And is thought will at last be laid upon Mr. Brouncker's bringing orders from the Duke of York (which the Duke of York doth not own) to Captain Cox to do it; but it seems they do resent this very highly, and are mad in going through all businesses where they can lay any fault.[3] I am glad to hear that in the world I am as kindly spoke of as anybody; for, for aught I see, there is bloody work like to be, Sir W. Coventry having been forced to produce a letter in Parliament wherein the Duke of Albemarle did from Sherenesse write in what good posture all things were at Chatham, and that the Chain was so well placed that he feared no attempt of the enemy. So that, among ⟨other⟩ things, I see everybody is upon his own defence, and spares not to blame another to defend himself; and the same course I shall take. But God knows where it will end. He gone and Deane, I to my chamber for a while, and then comes Pelling the apothecary to see us and sat and supped with me (my wife being gone to bed sick of the Cholique); and then I to bed after supper. Pelling tells me that my Lady Duchesse Albemarle was at Mrs. Turner's this afternoon (she being ill) and did there publicly talk of business and of our Office, and that she believed that I was safe and had done well; and so, I thank God, I hear everybody speaks of me, and endeed, I think without vanity I may expect to be profited rather then injured by this enquiry which the Parliament makes into business.

22. Slept but ill all the last part of the night, for fear of this day's success in Parliament; therefore up, and all of us all the morning close, till almost 2 a-clock, collecting all we had to say and had done from the beginning touching the safety of the River Medway and Chatham; and having done this and put it into order, we away, I

1. Charles O'Brien, courtier and gentleman-captain.
2. The Battle of Lowestoft, 3 June 1665.
3. On the night of 3–4 June 1665, the English fleet, in pursuit of the Dutch, lost touch with the enemy. Henry Brouncker, an officer in the Duke of York's household and brother to Lord Brouncker, was generally held responsible. In his anxiety to protect the Duke's life, he had taken an order to John Cox, sailing-master of the *Royal Charles*, to slacken sail and falsely represented it as coming from the Duke. Penn was also on the *Royal Charles* as the Duke's adviser.

not having time to eat my dinner; and so all in my Lord Brouncker's coach (that is to say, Brouncker, W. Penn, T. Harvy, and myself), talking of the other great matter with which they charge us, that is, of discharging men by ticket, in order to our defence in case that should be asked. We came to the Parliament-door; and there, after a little waiting till the Committee was sat, we were, the House being very full, called in (Sir W. Penn went in and sat as a Member; and my Lord Brouncker would not at first go in, expecting to have a chair set for him, and his brother[1] had long bid him not go in till he was called for; but after a few words I had occasion to mention him, and so he was called in, but without any more chair or respect paid him then myself); and so Brouncker and T. Harvy and I were there to answer, and I had a chair brought for me to lean my books upon; and so did give them such an account, in a series, of the whole business that had passed the office touching the matter, and so answered all Questions given me about it, that I did not perceive but they were fully satisfied with me and the business as to our Office;[2] and then Comissioner Pett (who was by at all my discourse, and this held till within an hour after candlelight, for I had candles brought in to read my papers by) was to answer for himself, we having lodged all matters with him for execution. But Lord, what a tumultuous thing this committee is, for all the reputation they have of a great council, is a strange consideration; there being as impertinent[3] Questions, and as disorderly proposed, as any man could make. But Comissioner Pett, of all men living, did make the weakest defence for himself; nothing to the purpose nor to satisfaction nor certain, but sometimes one thing and sometimes another, sometimes for himself and sometimes against him; and his greatest failure was (that I observed) from his not considering whether the Question propounded was his part to answer to or no, and the thing to be done was his work to do – the want of which distinction will overthrow him; for he concerns himself in giving an account of the disposal of the boats, which he had no reason at all to do, or take any blame upon him for them.[4] He charged the not carrying up of

1. Henry Brouncker MP.
2. The Navy Board disclaimed immediate responsibility. They argued that after 3 Dec. 1666 Commissioner Pett had been responsible, by the Duke's order, for the defence of Chatham, and that the defences of Sheerness were the responsibility of the Ordnance Office.
3. Irrelevant.
4. Sir Edward Spragge, the officer commanding the ships in the river, had charge of the boats.

the *Charles*[1] upon the Tuesdy, to the Duke of Albemarle; but I see the House is mighty favourable to the Duke of Albemarle and would give little way to it. And something of want of armes he spoke, which Sir J Duncomb answered with great imperiousness and earnestness; but for all that, I do see the House is resolved to be better satisfied in the business of the unreadiness of Sherenesse, and want of armes and ammunition there and everywhere; and all their officers[2] were here today attending, but only one called in about armes for boats to answer Comissioner Pett. None of my Brethren said anything but myself; only two or three silly words my Lord Brouncker gave, in answer to one Question about the number of men there in the King's yard at that time.

At last the House dismissed us, and shortly after did adjourne the debate till Friday next; and my Cosen Pepys did come out and joy me in my acquitting myself so well, and so did several others, and my fellow-officers all very briske to see themselfs so well acquitted – which makes me a little proud, but yet not secure but we may yet meet with a back-blow which we see not.

So, with our hearts very light, Sir W. Penn and I in his coach home, it being now near 8 a-clock; and so to the office and did a little business by the post, and so home, hungry, and eat a good supper and so, with my mind well at ease, to bed – my wife not very well of those.[3]

31.◆ I to Westminster, and there at the lobby do hear by Comissioner Pett to my great amazement that he is in worse condition then before, by the coming in of the Duke of Albemarle's and Prince Rupert's narratives[4] this day; wherein the former doth most severely lay matters upon him, so as the House this day have I think ordered him to the Tower again, or something like it; so that the poor man is likely to be overthrown I doubt, right or wrong, so infinite fond they are of anything the Duke of Albemarle says or writes to them. I did then go down, and there met with Collonell Reemes[5] and Cosen Rogr. Pepys; and there they do tell me how the Duke of Albemarle and the Prince have lay blame on a great many;

1. I.e. the failure to move the *Royal Charles* to safety upriver, well above the defensive chain.
2. I.e. Officers of the Ordnance.
3. Her period.
4. Two memoranda on the miscarriages of the war, principally on the shortage of supplies, the division of the fleet (June 1666), and the Medway disaster (June 1667).
5. Col. Bullen Reymes MP, Pepys's colleague on the Fishery Corporation and Tangier Committee.

and perticularly on our office in general, and perticularly for want of provisions, wherein I shall come to be questioned again in that business myself; which doth trouble me. But my Cosen Pepys and I had much discourse alone, and he doth bewail the constitution of this House and says that there is a direct Caball and faction, as much as is possible, between them for and those against the Chancellor, and so in other factions, that there is nothing almost done honestly and with integrity; only, some few he says there are that do keep out of all plot and combinations, and, when their time comes, will speak and see right done if possible; and that he himself is looked upon to be a man that will be of no faction, and so they do shun to make him – and I am glad of it. He tells me that he thanks God he never knew what it was to be tempted to be a knave in his life, till he did come into the House of Commons, where there is nothing done but by passion and faction and private interest. Reemes did tell me of a fellow last night (one Kelsy, a commander of a fireship, who complained for want of his money paid him) did say that he did see one of the Commissioners of the Navy bring in three wagon-loads of prize-goods into Greenwich one night, but that the House did take no notice of it, nor enquire; but this is me, and I must expect to be called to account and answer what I did as well as I can.[1] So thence away home; and in Holborne, going round, it being dark, I espied Sir D. Gawden's coach, and so went out of mine into his and there had opportunity to talk of the business of victuals, which the Duke of Albemarle and Prince did complain that they were in want of the last year; but we do conclude we shall be able to show the quite contrary of that; only, it troubles me that we must come to contend with these great persons, which will overrun us. So with some disquiet in my mind on this account, I home; and there comes Mr. Yeabsly,[2] and he and I to even some accounts, wherein I shall be a gainer about 200*l*; which is a seasonable profit, for I have got nothing a great while. And he being gone, I to bed.

NOVEMBER.

4. Up betimes, and by water with Sir R. Ford (who is going to the Parliament) to Westminster; and there landing at the New

1. It was a delivery for Capt. Cocke and Pepys. *See* 7 Oct. 1665.
2. Victualler to the Tangier garrison.

Exchange stairs, I to Sir W. Coventry and there he read over to me the Prince and the Duke of Albemarle's Narratives; wherein they are very severe against him and our office, but W. Coventry doth contemn them; only, that their persons and qualities are great, and so I do perceive is afeared of them, though he will not confess it. But he doth say that if he can get out of these Bryers, he will never trouble himself with Princes nor Dukes again. He finds several things in their Narratives which are both inconsistent and foolish, as well as untrue; especially as to what the Duke of Albemarle avers of his knowing of the enemy's being abroad sooner then he says it, which W. Coventry will show his own letter against him for. I confess I do see so much, that were I but well possessed of what I should have in the world, I think I could willingly retreat and trouble myself no more with it.

Thence home, and there met Sir H. Cholmly[1] and he and I to the Excise Office to see what tallies are paying; and thence back to the Old Exchange, by the way talking of news, and he owning Sir W. Coventry in his opinion to be one of the worthiest men in the nation – as I do really think he is. He tells me he doth think really that they will cut off my Lord Chancellor's head, the Chancellor at this day showing as much pride as is possible to those few that venture their fortunes by coming to see him; and that the Duke of York is troubled much, knowing that those that fling down the Chancellor cannot stop there, but will do something to him to prevent his having it in his power hereafter to revenge himself and father-in-law upon them. And this, Sir H. Cholmly fears may be by divorcing the Queen and getting another, or declaring the Duke of Monmouth legitimate – which God forbid. He tells me he doth verily believe that there will come in an Impeachment of high treason against my Lord of Ormond; among other things, for ordering the quartering of soldiers in Ireland on free quarter, which it seems is high treason in that country and was one of the things that lost the Lord Strafford his head, and the law is not yet repealed[2] – which he says was a mighty oversight of him not to have repealed (which he might with ease have done) or have justified himself by an act.

From the Exchange I took coach and went to Turlington the great spectacle-maker for advice; who dissuades me from useing

1. Engineer of the mole at Tangier and First Gentleman-Usher to the Queen.
2. Ormond was Clarendon's principal ally in government. He was not impeached, but was removed from his office as Lord-Lieutenant of Ireland. The charges against Strafford in 1641 had included illegal quartering of troops.

old spectacles, but rather young ones.[1] And doth tell me that nothing can wrong them more then for me to use reading-glasses – which do magnify much.

Thence home and there dined, and then abroad and left my wife and Willett at her tailor's; and I to White-hall, where the Comissioners of Treasury do not sit, and therefore I to Westminster to the hall; and there meeting with Collonell Reames, I did very happily by him get Copys of the Prince and Duke of Albemarle's Narratives which they did deliver the other day to the House; of which I am mighty glad, both for my present information and for my future satisfaction. So back by coach and took up my wife, and away home and there in my chamber all the evening among my papers and my accounts of Tanger, to my great satisfaction; and so to supper and to bed.

7. Up, and at the office hard all the morning; and at noon resolve with Sir W. Penn to go see *The Tempest*, an old play of Shakespeares, acted here the first day.[2] And so my wife and girl and W. Hewer by themselfs, and Sir W. Penn and I afterward by ourselfs, and forced to sit in the side Balcone over against the Musique-room at the Dukes-House, close by my Lady Dorsett and a great many great ones: the house mighty full, the King and Court there, and the most innocent play that ever I saw, and a curious piece of Musique in an Echo of half-sentences, the Echo repeating the former half while the man goes on to the latter, which is mighty pretty.[3] The play no great wit; but yet good, above ordinary plays. Thence home with W. Penn, and there all mightily pleased with the play; and so to supper and to bed, after having done at the office.

9. Up and to my workmen, who are at work close again, and I at the office all the morning and there do hear by a messenger that Roger Pepys would speak with me; so before the office up, I to Westminster and there find the House very busy, and like to be so all day, about my Lord Chancellors impeachment, whether treason or not; where everybody is mighty busy.[4] I spoke with my Cosen Roger, whose business was only to give me notice that Carcasse

1. John Turlington's shop was in Cornhill. He advised using concave lenses, suitable for young people suffering from shortsightedness.
2. An adaptation of Shakespeare's play by Sir William Davenant and John Dryden (they later adapted it into an opera).
3. Ferdinand's song (echoed by Ariel) in Act 3, set by John Banister.
4. In the process of impeachment, the Commons determined the charges and the accused would then be tried by the Lords.

hath been before the Committee, and to warn me of it;[1] which is a great courtesy in him to do, and I desire him to continue to do so. This business of this fellow, though it be a foolish thing, yet it troubles me; and I do plainly see my weakness, that I am not a man able to go through trouble as other men are, but that I should be a miserable man if I should meet with adversity – which God keep me from. He desirous to get back into the House, he having his notes in his hands, the lawyers being now speaking to the point of whether treason or not treason, the Article of advising the King to break up the Parliament and to govern by the sword.[2] Thence I down to the Hall and there met Mr. King, the Parliament-man for Harwich; and there he did show and let me take a copy of all the Articles against my Lord Chancellor, and what members they were that undertook to bring witnesses to make them good – of which I was mighty glad; and so away home to dinner and to my workmen; and in the afternoon out to get Simpson the joyner to come to work at my office; and so back home and to my letters by the post tonight, and there by W. Penn do hear that this Article was over-voted in the House, not to be a ground of Impeachment of Treason – at which I was glad, being willing to have no blood spilt if I could help it. So home to supper; and glad that the dirty bricklayers' work of my office is done, I home to supper and to bed.

10. *Lords day.* Mighty cold; and with my wife to church, where a lazy sermon; but here was my Lady Batten in her mourning at church – but I took no notice of her. At noon comes Michell and his wife to dine with us, and pretty merry; I glad to see her still. After dinner Sir W. Penn and I to White-hall to speak with Sir W. Coventry; and there, beyond all we looked for, do hear that the Duke of York hath got and is full of the small-pox. And so we to his lodgings and there find most of the family going to St. James's and the gallery doors locked up, that nobody might pass to nor fro – and a sad house there is, I am sure; I am sad to consider the effects of his death if he should miscarry. But Dr. Frazier tells me that he is in as good condition as a man can be in his case. They appeared last night – it seems he was let blood on Friday. Thence, not finding

1. Carkesse, the clerk of the Ticket Office dismissed by the Navy Board for corruption, was appearing before the Committee investigating the miscarriages of the war.
2. There were seventeen charges in all. The first alleged that Clarendon had advised the King to dissolve the current parliament in favour of government by a standing army. Others included advising the sale of Dunkirk to the French and betraying secrets to the enemy during the war.

W. Coventry and going back again home, we met him coming with the Lord Keeper; and so returned and spoke with him in Whitehall garden two or three turns, advising with him what we should do about Carcasse's bringing his matter into the committee of Parliament. And he told us that the counsel he hath too late learned, is to spring nothing in the House nor offer anything but just what is drawne out of a man – that this is the best way of dealing with a Parliament; and that he hath paid dear, and knows not how much more he may pay, for not knowing it sooner, when he did unnecessarily produce the Duke of Albemarle's letter about Chatham;[1] which if demanded, would have come out with all the advantages in the world to W. Coventry; but as he brought it out himself, hath drawn much evil upon him. After some talk of this kind, we back home; and there I to my chamber, busy all the evening; and then to supper and to bed – my head running all night upon our businesses in Parliament and what examinations we are likely to go under before they have done with us, which troubles me more then it should a wise man, and a man the best able to defend himself, I believe, of our whole office, or any other I am apt to think.

12. Up, and to the office, where sat all the morning and there hear that the Duke of York doth yet do very well with his small-pox; pray God he may continue to do so. This morning also, to my astonishment, I hear that yesterday my Lord Chancellor, to another of his Articles, that of betraying the King's counsels to his enemies, is voted to have matter against him for an impeachment of high Treason, and that this day the impeachment is to be carried up to the House of Lords – which is very high and I am troubled at it – for God knows what will fallow, since they that do this must do more, to secure themselfs against any that will revenge this – if it ever come in their power. At noon home to dinner; and then to my office and there saw everything finished, so as my papers are all in order again and my office ⟨twice⟩ as pleasant as ever it was, having a noble window in my closet and another in my office, to my great content. And so did business late, and then home to supper and to bed.

21. Up, and to the office, where all the morning; and at noon home, where my wife not very well, but is to go to Mr. Mills's[2] child's

1. Coventry had told the Commons about Albemarle's letter to the King, prior to the Dutch attack on Chatham, which reported that the warships there were well protected. *See* 20 Oct. 1667.
2. Daniel Milles, Rector of Pepys's parish.

christening, where she is godmother, Sir J. Mennes and Sir R. Brookes her companions. I left her after dinner (my clerks dining with me) to go with Sir J. Mennes, and I to the office, where did much business till after candlelight; and then, my eyes beginning to fail me, I out and took coach and to Arundell-house, where the meeting of Gresham College was broke up; but there meeting Creed, I with him to the tavern in St. Clements churchyard, where was Deane Wilkins, Dr. Whistler, Dr. Floyd, a divine, admitted, I perceive, this day, and other brave men;[1] and there among other things of news, I do hear that upon the reading of the House of Commons' reasons of the manner of their proceedings in the business of my Lord Chancellor,[2] the reasons were so bad, that my Lord Bristoll himself did declare that he would not stand to what he had, and did still, advise the Lords to concurr to, upon any of the reasons of the House of Commons; but if it was put to the question whether it should be done on their reasons, he would be against them. And endeed, it seems the reasons, however they came to escape the House of Commons (which shows how slightly the greatest matters are done in this world, and even in Parliaments), were none of them of strength, but the principle of them untrue; they saying that where any man is brought before a Judge accused of Treason in general, without specifying the perticular, the Judge doth there constantly, and is obliged to commit him.[3] Whereas the question being put by the Lords to my Lord Keeper, he said the quite contrary was true.[4] And in the sixth Article (I will get a copy of them if I can) there are two or three things strangely asserted, to the diminishing of the King's power as is said; at least, things that heretofore would not have been heard of.[5] But then the question being put among the Lords, as my Lord Bristoll advised: whether upon the whole matter and reasons that had been laid before them, they would

1. An informal gathering of Royal Society Fellows and their friends. John Wilkins, Dean of Ripon, and Daniel Whistler, a physician, were Fellows. "Dr Floyd" was presumably William Lloyd (later Bishop of Worcester), a friend of Wilkins, but he was never admitted to the Royal Society.
2. The Lords had refused to have Clarendon taken into custody for treason since the Commons had not specified the charges; in response the Commons sent a list of reasons why the Lords was required to act on a general treason charge.
3. The argument rested on the contention that in treason trials speed was essential.
4. The Lord Keeper, Orlando Bridgeman, was also a leading judge.
5. The sixth article of the Commons' reasons stated that proceedings in inferior courts between the King and the subject were "bounded and limited by the Discretion of the Parliament", with "Parliament" defined as "the whole Publick, comprehending the King, Lords, and Commons, (for the King's Presence is supposed in the Lords House)".

commit my Lord Clarenden, it was carried five to one against it, there being but three Bishops against him, of which Cosens and Dr. Reynolds were two, and I know not the third. This made the opposite Lords, as Bristoll and Buckingham, so mad, that they declared and protested against it, speaking very broad that there was mutiny and rebellion in the heart of the Lords, and that they desired they might enter their dissents,[1] which they did do in great fury. So that upon the Lords sending to the Commons, as I am told, to have a conference for them to give their answer to the Commons' reasons, the Commons did desire a free conference; but the Lords do deny it, and the reason is that they hold not the Commons any Court, but that themselfs only are a Court, and the chief court of Judicature, and therefore are not to dispute the laws and method of their own Court with them that are none; and so will not submit so much as to have their power disputed.[2] And it is conceived that much of this eagerness among the Lords doth arise from the fear some of them have, that they may be dealt with in the same manner themselfs, and therefore to stand upon it now. It seems my Lord Clarenden hath, as is said and believed, had his coach and horses several times in his coach, ready to carry him to the Tower, expecting a message to that purpose – but by this means his case is like to be laid by. From this we fall to other discourse, and very good. Among the rest, they discourse of a man that is a little frantic (that hath been a kind of minister, Dr. Wilkins saying that he hath read for him in his church) that is poor and a debauched man, that the College have hired for 20*s* to have some of the blood of a Sheep let into his body; and it is to be done on Saturday next.[3] They purpose to let in about twelve ounces, which they compute is what will be let in in a minutes time by a watch. They differ in the opinion they have of the effects of it; some think that it may have a good effect upon him as a frantic man, by cooling his blood; others, that it will not have any effect at all. But the man is a healthy man, and by this means will be able to give an account what alteration, if any, he doth find in himself, and so may be usefull. On this occasion Dr. Whistler told a pretty story related by Muffett, a good author, of Dr. Cayus that built Key's-College: that being very old and lived

1. In the Journal of the House of Lords.
2. A free conference between Lords and Commons would have allowed the Commons to raise this constitutional issue. The Lords did eventually agree to grant a free conference on 28 November.
3. The subject of the Royal Society's experiment was Arthur Coga. He held a BA from Cambridge, reportedly in divinity. The description of him as "a little frantic" meant he displayed signs of frenzy or madness.

only at that time upon woman's milk, he, while he fed upon the milk of a angry fretful woman, was so himself; and then being advised to take of a good-natured patient woman, he did become so, beyond the common temper of his age.[1] Thus much nutriment, they observed, might do. Their discourse was very fine; and if I should be put out of my office, I do take great content in the liberty I shall be at of frequenting these gentlemen's companies. Broke up thence and home, and there to my wife in her chamber, who is not well (of those); and there she tells me great stories of the gossiping women of the parish, what this and what that woman was; and among the rest, how Mrs. Hollworthy is the veriest confident bragging gossip of them all, which I should not have believed – but that Sir R. Brookes, her partner,[2] was mighty civil to her and taken with her and what not. My eyes being bad, I spent the evening with her in her chamber, talking and inventing a Cypher[3] to put on a piece of plate which I must give, better then ordinary, to the parson's child; and so to bed, and through my wife's illness had a bad night of it, and she a worse, poor wretch.

29. Waked about 7 a-clock this morning with a noise I supposed I heard near our chamber, of knocking, which by and by increased, and I more awake, could distinguish it better; I then waked my wife and both of us wondered at it, and lay so a great while, while that encreased; and at last heard it plainer, knocking as if it were breaking down a window for people to get out – and then removing of stools and chairs, and plainly by and by going up and down our stairs. We lay both of us afeared; yet I would have rose, but my wife would not let me; besides, I could not do it without making noise; and we did both conclude that thiefs were in the house, but wondered what our people did, whom we thought either killed or afeared as we were. Thus we lay till the clock struck 8, and high day. At last I removed my gown and slippers safely to the other side the bed over my wife, and there safely rose and put on my gown and breeches, and then with a firebrand in my hand safely opened the door, and saw nor heard anything. Then (with fear, I confess) went to the maid's chamber-door, and all quiet and safe. Called Jane up, and went down safely and opened my chamber, where all

1. A story told in Thomas Moffet's *Healths Improvement* (1655) about John Caius (d. 1573), founder of Gonville and Caius College, Cambridge. Breast milk was considered a product of the blood, so the story was relevant to the wider discussion.
2. Elizabeth's partner as a godparent.
3. A device of interlinked initials.

well. Then more freely about, and to the kitchen, where the cook-maid up and all safe. So up again, and when Jane came and we demanded whether she heard no noise, she said, "Yes, and was afeared," but rose with the other maid and found nothing, but heard a noise in the great stack of chimneys that goes from Sir J. Mennes's through our house; and so we sent, and their chimneys have been swept this morning, and the noise was that and nothing else. It is one of the most extraordinary accidents in my life, and gives ground to think of Don Quixot's adventures how people may be surprized[1] – and the more from an accident last night, that our young gibb-cat[2] did leap down our stairs from top to bottom at two leaps and frighted us, that we could not tell well whether it was the cat or a spirit, and do sometimes think this morning that the house might be haunted. Glad to have this so well over, and endeed really glad in my mind, for I was much afeared. I dressed myself, and to the office both forenoon and afternoon, mighty hard putting papers and things in order to my extraordinary satisfaction, and consulting my clerks in many things, who are infinite helps to my memory and reasons of things. And so, being weary and my eyes akeing, having overwrought them today reading so much short-hand, I home and there to supper, it being late, and to bed. This morning Sir W. Penn and I did walk together a good while, and he tells me that the Houses are not likely to agree after their free conference yesterday, and he fears what may fallow.

30. Up and to the office, where all the morning, and then by coach to Arundell-house to the elections of Officers[3] for the next year; where I was near being chosen of the Council, but am glad I was not, for I could not have attended; though above all things, I could wish it, and do take it as a mighty respect to have been named there. The company great and elections long; and then to Cary-house, a house now of entertainment, next my Lord Ashly's; and there, where I have heretofore heard Common-Prayer in the time of Dr. Mossum,[4] we after two hours' stay, sitting at the table with our nap-kins open, had our dinners brought; but badly done. But here was

1. In Cervantes's *Don Quixote*, the would-be hero is frightened at night by the sound of terrible blows. In daylight he manages to marshal his courage, only to discover the noise is that of fulling mills beating cloth. The Pepys Library contains three versions of *Don Quixote*, including a 1662 edition in Spanish.
2. A cat that has been castrated.
3. Of the Royal Society.
4. Dr Robert Mossom had conducted services there at the end of the Interregnum using the illegal Book of Common Prayer.

good company, I choosing to sit next Dr. Wilkins, Sir George Ent, and others whom I value. And there talked of several things; among others, Dr. Wilkins, talking of the universall speech, of which he hath a book coming out,[1] did first inform me how man was certainly made for society, he being of all creatures the least armed for defence; and of all creatures in the world, the young ones are not able to do anything to help themselfs, nor can find the dug without being put to it, but would die if the mother did not help it. And he says were it not for speech, man would be a very mean creature. Much of this good discourse we had. But here above all, I was pleased to see the person who had his blood taken out. He speaks well, and did this day give the Society a relation thereof in Latin, saying that he finds himself much better since, and as a new man. But he is cracked a little in his head, though he speaks very reasonably and very well. He had but 20*s* for his suffering it, and is to have the same again tried upon him – the first sound man that ever had it tried on him in England, and but one that we hear of in France, which was a porter hired by the virtuosi.[2] Here all the afternoon till within night. Then I took coach and to the Exchange, where I was to meet my wife, but she was gone home; and so I to Westminster-hall and there took a turn or two; but meeting nobody to discourse with, returned to Cary-house and there stayed a little and saw a pretty deception of the sight, by a glass with water poured into it, with a stick standing up with three balls of wax upon it, one distant from the other – how these balls did seem double and disappear one after another, mighty pretty.[3] Here Mr. Carcasse[4] did come to me, and brought first Mr. Colwall our Treasurer and then Dr. Wilkins to engage me to be his friend; and himself asking forgiveness and desiring my friendship, saying that the Council have now ordered him to be free to return to the office to be imployed. I promised him my friendship, and am glad of this occasion, having desired it; for there is nobody's ill tongue that I fear like his – being a malicious and cunning bold fellow. Thence, paying our shot, 6*s* apiece, I home and there to the office and wrote my letters; and then home, my eyes very sore with yesterday's work. And so home and tried to make a piece by my eare and viall to "*I wonder what*

1. *Essay towards a Real Character, and a Philosophical Language* (1668).
2. In Paris in June 1667 Jean-Baptiste Denis had carried out a similar experiment on a sedan-chair carrier, which was reported in learned journals. It was not Denis's first transfusion of sheep's blood into a human subject. "Virtuosi" means learned men.
3. An experiment in refraction.
4. Troublesome navy clerk and a Fellow of the Royal Society.

the grave, &c";[1] and so to supper and to bed – where frighted a good while, and my wife, again with noises; and my wife did rise twice, but I think it was Sir J. Mennes's people again, late cleaning their house, for it was past one a-clock in the morning before we could fall to sleep; and so slept – but I perceive well what the care of money and treasure in a man's house is to a man that fears to lose it.

My Lord Anglesy told me this day that he did believe the House of Commons would the next week yield to the Lords. But speaking with others this day, they conclude they will not, but that rather the King will accommodate it by committing my Lord Clarendon himself: I remember what Mr. Evelin said: that he did believe we should soon see ourselfs fall into a Commonwealth again. Joseph Williamson[2] I find mighty kind still, but close, not daring to say anything almost that touches upon news or state of affairs.

DECEMBER.

3.◆ At noon home to dinner and busy all the afternoon; and at night home and there met W. Batelier, who tells me the first great news, that my Lord Chancellor is fled this day.[3] By and by to Sir W. Penn's, where Sir R Ford, and he and I met with Mr. Young and Lewes about our accounts with my Lady Batten – which prove troublesome and I doubt will prove to our loss. But here I hear the whole, that my Lord Chancellor is gone and left a paper behind him for the House of Lords, telling them the reason of his retiring, complaining of a design for his ruin. But the paper I must get; only, the thing at present is great and will put the King and Commons to some new counsels certainly. So home to supper and to bed.

Sir W. Penn I find in much trouble this evening, having been called to the committee this afternoon about the business of prizes.[4]

6. Up, and with Sir J. Mennes to the Duke of York, the first time that I have seen or we waited on him since his sickness; and blessed be God, he is not at all the worse for the smallpox, but is only a

1. Abraham Cowley's poem "Resolved to Love", first published in *The Mistresse* (1647). It begins "I Wonder what the Grave and Wise / Thinke of all us that Love".
2. Williamson worked for Secretary of State Arlington, who was at risk during the current crisis.
3. Clarendon had fled to France on 30 November.
4. The prize-goods affair, in which Penn had been one of Sandwich's advisers. Penn was impeached in 1668 but proceedings stalled in the House of Lords.

little weak yet. We did much business with him – and so parted. My Lord Anglesy told me how my Lord Northampton brought in a Bill into the House of Lords yesterday, under the name of *A Bill for the honour and privilege of the House, and mercy to my Lord Clarendon* – which he told me he opposed, saying that he was a man accused of treason by the House of Commons, and mercy was not proper for him, having not been tried yet, and so no mercy needful for him. However, the Duke of Buckingham did, and others, desire the Bill might be read; and it was for banishing my Lord Clarendon from all his Majesty's dominions and that it should be treason to have him found in any of them. The thing is only a thing of vanity and to insult over him; which is mighty poor I think, and so doth everybody else, and ended in nothing I think.

By and by home with Sir J. Mennes, who tells me that my Lord Clarendon did go away in a Custom house boat and is now at Callis: upon [whom], I confess, nothing seems to hang more heavy then his leaving of this unfortunate paper behind him, that hath angered both Houses and hath I think reconciled them in that which otherwise would have broke them in pieces; so that I do hence, and from Sir W. Coventry's late example and doctrine to me,[1] learn that on these sorts of occasions there is nothing like silence – it being seldom any wrong to a man to say nothing, but for the most part it is to say anything. This day, in coming home, Sir J. Mennes told me a pretty story of Sir Lewes Dives, whom I saw this morning speaking with him; that having escaped once out of prison through a house of office, and another time in woman's apparel and leaping over a broad canal, a soldier in roguery put his hand towards her belly, and swore, says he, "This is a strong Jade, but I never felt a cunt with a handle to it before."[2] He told me also a story of my Lord Cottington: who wanting a son, entended to make his Nephew his heir, a country boy, but did alter his mind upon the boy's being persuaded by another young heir (in roguery) to Crow like a cock at my Lord's table, much company being there and the boy having a great trick at doing that perfectly – my Lord bade them take away that fool from the table, and so gave over the thoughts of making him his heir from this piece of folly.◆

21. At the office all the morning, and at noon home to dinner with

1. *See* 10 Nov. 1667.
2. Sir Lewis Dyve had been a royalist soldier. The first of these escapes, the day after Charles I's execution, had been from prison in Whitehall, down a privy, and into the Thames.

my clerks and Creed; who among other things, all alone after dinner, talking of the times, he tells me that the Nonconformists are mighty high and their meetings frequented and connived at; and they do expect to have their day now soon, for my Lord of Buckingham is a declared friend to them, and even to the Quakers, who had very good words the other day from the King himself; and which is more, the Archbishop of Canterbury is called no more to the Caball (nor, by the way, Sir W. Coventry; which I am sorry for, the Caball at present being, as he says, the King and Duke of Buckingham and Lord Keeper, Albemarle and Privy Seale),[1] the Bishops differing from the King in the late business in the House of Lords[2] having caused this and what is like to fallow, for everybody is encouraged nowadays to speak and even to print (as I have one of them) as bad things against them as ever in the year 1640; which is a strange change. He gone, I to the office, where busy till late at night; and then home to sit with my wife, who is a little better and her cheek aswaged.[3] I read to her out of the *History of Algiers*,[4] which is mighty pretty reading – and did discourse alone about my sister Pall's match which is now on foot with one Jackson, another nephew of Mr. Phillips's, to whom the former hath left his estate.[5] And so to supper and then to bed.

24. Up, and all the morning at the office; and at noon with my clerks to dinner and then to the office again, busy at the office till 6 at night; and then by coach to St. James's, it being now about 6 at night, my design being to see the Ceremonys, this night being the Eve of Christmas, at the Queen's Chapel. But it being not begun, I to Westminster hall and there stayed and walked; and then to the Swan and there drank and talked, and did besar a little Frank;[6] and so to White-hall and sent my coach round, and I through the park to chapel, where I got in up almost to the rail

1. The Lord Keeper was Sir Orlando Bridgeman and the Privy Seal Lord Robartes. All the ministers named here had Presbyterian sympathies.
2. Clarendon's impeachment, which the bishops in the Lords had overwhelmingly opposed.
3. She had a dental abscess.
4. Emanuel D'Aranda's *History of Algiers and its Slavery* (1666), translated from French by John Davies. It was full of anecdotes about the author's time as a slave in Algiers.
5. Paulina married John Jackson of Ellington, near Brampton, in February 1668. Like a previous suitor, Robert Ensum, he was a nephew of Lewis Phillips. Ensum, who died in 1666, had left part of his estate to Jackson. "Former" here means "former suitor".
6. "Besar" (Spanish) means "kiss". "Frank" was Frances Udall, a serving maid at the Swan.

and with a great deal of patience, stayed from 9 at night to 2 in the morning in a very great Crowd; and there expected, but found nothing extraordinary, there being nothing but a high Masse. The Queen was there and some ladies. But Lord, what an odde thing it was for me to be in a crowd of people, here a footman, there a beggar, here a fine lady, there a zealous poor papist, and here a Protestant, two or three together, come to see the show. I was afeared of my pocket being picked very much. But here I did make myself to do la cosa by mere imagination, mirando a jolie mosa[1] and with my eyes open, which I never did before – and God forgive me for it, it being in the chapel. Their music very good endeed, but their service I confess too frivolous, that there can be no zeal go along with it; and I do find by them themselfs, that they do run over their beads with one hand, and point and play and talk and make signs with the other, in the midst of their Messe. But all things very rich and beautiful. And I see the papists had the wit, most of them, to bring cushions to kneel on; which I wanted, and was mightily troubled to kneel. All being done, and I sorry for my coming, missing of what I expected; which was to have had a child borne and dressed there and a great deal of do, but we broke up and nothing like it done; and there I left people receiving the sacrament, and the Queen gone, and ladies; only my [Lady] Castlemayne, who looks prettily in her night-clothes. And so took my coach, which waited, and away through Covent-garden to set down two gentlemen and a lady, who came thither to see also and did make mighty mirth in their talk of the folly of this religion; and so I stopped, having set them down, and drank some burnt wine at the Rose tavern door, while the constables came and two or three Bell-men went by, it
⟨⟨25⟩⟩ being a fine light moonshine morning; and so home round the City and stopped and dropped money at five or six places, which I was the willinger to do, it being Christmas-day; and so home and there find wife in bed, and Jane and the maids making pyes, and so I to bed and slept well; and rose about 9, and to church and there heard a dull sermon of Mr. Mills, but a great many fine people at church, and so home; wife and girl and I alone at dinner, a good Christmas dinner; and all the afternoon at home, my wife reading to me the history of the Drummer, of Mr. Monpesson, which is a strange story of spirits, and worth

1. "to do the thing [i.e. orgasm] by mere imagination, looking at a pretty girl".

reading indeed.[1] In the evening comes Mr. Pelling, and he sat and supped with us; and very good company, he reciting to us many copies of good verses of Dr. Wilde, who writ *Iter Boreale*;[2] and so to bed – my boy being gone with W. Hewer and Mr. Hater to Mr. Gibsons in the country to dinner, and lie there all night.

29. *Lords day.* Up, and at my chamber all the day, both morning and afternoon (only, a little at dinner with my wife alone) upon the settling of my Tanger accounts, towards the evening of all reckonings now against the new year; and here I do see the great folly of letting things go long unevened, it being very hard for me, and dangerous to state, after things are gone out of memory, and much more would be so should I have died in this time and my accounts come to other hands to understand, which would never be. At night comes Mrs. Turner to see us; and there, among other talk, she tells me that Mr. Will Pen, who is lately come over from Ireland, is a Quaker again, or some very melancholy thing; that he cares for no company, nor comes into any – which is a pleasant thing, after his being abroad so long – and his father such a hypocritical rogue, and at this time an atheist.[3] She gone, I to my very great content do find my accounts to come very even and naturally; and so to supper and to bed.

30. Up before day and by coach to Westminster; and there first to Sir H. Cholmly, and there I did to my great content deliver him up his little several papers for sums of money paid him, and took his regular receipts upon his orders, wherein I am safe. Thence to White-hall and there to visit Sir G. Carteret, and there was with him a great while and my Lady and they seem in very good humour; but by and by Sir G. Carteret and I all alone, and there we did talk of the ruinous condition we are in, the King being going to put out of the Council so many able men, such as my Lord Anglesy, Ashly, Hollis, Secretary Morrice (to bring in Mr. Trevor) and the

1. In the early 1660s John Mompesson's house at Tidworth was plagued by seemingly supernatural occurrences, including the beating of a drum by invisible forces. The account Samuel and Elizabeth read, in Joseph Glanvill's *A Blow at Modern Sadducism* (1668), argued that this was evidence for the reality of witchcraft.
2. Robert Wild's most popular poem, *Iter Boreale* (1660), was written in praise of General Monck and the restoration of the monarchy.
3. William Penn, future Quaker leader, had attended a Quaker meeting while living in Ireland and his conversion dates from around this time. The situation was amusing ("pleasant") partly because travel was supposed to improve sociability. This was also a sharp contrast with the "affected" French manners that Penn had shown after studying on the continent (*see* 30 Aug. 1664).

Archbishop of Canterbury and my Lord Bridgewater.[1] He tells me that this is true; only, the Duke of York doth endeavour to hinder it, and that the Duke of York himself did tell him so. That the King and the Duke of York do not in company disagree, but are friendly; but that there is a core in their hearts, he doubts, which is not to be easily removed – for these men do suffer only for their constancy to the Chancellor, or at least [for being] against the King's will against him. That they do now all they can to vilify the Clergy, and do accuse Rochester (Dolben),[2] of his being given to boys and of his putting his hand into a gentleman (who now comes to bear evidence against him) his codpiece while they were at table together. And so do raise scandals, all that is possible, against other of the Bishops. He doth suggest that something is intended for the Duke of Monmouth, and it may be against the Queene also. That we are in no manner sure against an invasion the next year. That the Duke of Buckingham doth rule all now; and the Duke of York comes endeed to the Caball but signifies little there. That this new faction doth not endure, nor the King, Sir W. Coventry; but yet that he is so usefull that they cannot be without him, but that he is not now called to the Caball. That my Lord of Buckingham, Bristoll, and Arlington do seem to agree in these things; but that they do not in their hearts trust one another, but do drive several ways, all of them. In short, he doth bless himself that he is no more concerned in matters now and the hopes he hath of being at liberty, when his accounts are over, to retire into the country. That he doth give over the Kingdom for wholly lost. So after some other little discourse, I away; and meeting Mr. Cooling,[3] I with him by coach to the Wardrobe, where I never was since the Fire, in Hatton-garden, but did not light; and he tells me he fears that my Lord Sandwich will suffer much by Mr. Townsends' being untrue to him, he being now unable to give the Commissioners of the Treasury an account of his money received, by many thousands of pounds – which I am troubled for.[4]

Thence to the Old Exchange together, he telling me that he believes there will be no such turning out of great men as is talked of, but that it is only to fright people – but I do fear there may be

1. None of these men was in fact dismissed.
2. John Dolben, Bishop of Rochester.
3. Richard Coling, Secretary to the Lord Chamberlain and a friend.
4. Sandwich was Master of the Great Wardrobe and Thomas Townshend his deputy. The Wardrobe was now being reorganized and Townshend's practices were under investigation.

such a thing doing. He doth mightily inveigh against the folly of the King to bring his matters to wrack thus, and that we must all be undone without help.◆

31.◆ Thus ends the year, with great happiness to myself and family as to health and good condition in the world, blessed be God for it; only, with great trouble to my mind in reference to the public, there being little hopes left but that the whole nation must in a very little time be lost, either by troubles at home, the Parliament being dissatisfied and the King led into unsettled counsels by some about him, himself considering little – and divisions growing between the King and Duke of York; or else by foreign invasion, to which we must submit, if any at this bad point of time should come upon us; which the King of France is well able to do. These thoughts, and some cares upon me concerning my standing in this office when the committee of Parliament shall come to examine our Navy matters, which they will now shortly do. I pray God they may do the Kingdom service therein, as they will have sufficient opportunity of doing it.

1668

JANUARY.

1. Up, and all the morning in my chamber making up some accounts against this beginning of the new year; and so about noon abroad with my wife, who was to dine with W. Hewer and Willett at Mrs. Pierce's; but I had no mind to be with them, for I do clearly find that my wife is troubled at my friendship with her and Knepp, and so dined with my Lord Crew, with whom was Mr. Browne, Clerk of the House of Lords, and Mr. John Crew. Here was mighty good discourse, as there is alway; and among other things, my Lord Crew did turn to a place in the *Life of Sir Ph. Sidny*, wrote by Sir Fulke Grevill, which doth foretell the present condition of this nation in relation to the Dutch, to the very degree of a prophecy; and is so remarkable that I am resolved to buy one of them, it being quite through a good discourse.[1] Here they did talk much of the present cheapness of Corne, even to a miracle; so as their farmers can pay no rent, but do fling up their lands – and would pay in corne; but (which I did observe to my Lord, and he liked well of it) our gentry are grown so ignorant in everything of good husbandry, that they know not how to bestow this corn; which, did they understand but a little trade, they would be able to joyne together, and know what markets there are abroad and send it thither, and thereby ease their tenants and be able to pay themselfs. They did talk much of the disgrace the Archbishop is fallen under with the King, and the rest of the Bishops also. Thence I after dinner to the Duke of York's playhouse, and there saw *Sir Martin Marrall*, which I have seen so often; and yet am mightily pleased with it and think it mighty witty, and the fullest of proper matter for mirth that ever was writ.[2] And I do clearly see that they do improve in their acting of it. Here a mighty company of citizens, prentices and others; and it makes me observe that when I begin first to be able to bestow a play on myself, I do not remember that I saw so many by half of the ordinary prentices and mean people in the pit, at 2*s*-6*d* apiece, as now;

1. Sir Fulke Greville's *Life of the Renowned Sir Philip Sidney* (1652) discussed the threat posed by an ambitious Spanish monarch, which in the Elizabethan period had driven the English and the Dutch together. Now, facing an ambitious French monarch's attack on the Spanish Netherlands, the English and the Dutch were again uniting (the alliance between them being concluded in this month). Pepys acquired a copy of Greville's work a few days later.
2. For the play, *see* 16 Aug. 1667.

I going for several years no higher then the 12*d*, and then the 18*d* places,[1] and though I strained hard to go in then when I did – so much the vanity and prodigality of the age is to be observed in this perticular. Thence I to White-hall, and there walked up and down the House a while and do hear nothing of anything done further in this business of the change of Privy-counsellors. Only, I hear that Sir G. Savill, one of the Parliament committee of nine for examining the accounts, is by the King made a Lord, the Lord Hallifax; which I believe will displease the Parliament.[2] By and by I met with Mr. Brisban;[3] and having it in my mind this Christmas to (do what I never can remember that I did) go to see the manner of the gaming at the Groome porter's[4] (I having in my coming from the playhouse stepped into the two Temple-halls,[5] and there saw the dirty prentices and idle people playing – wherein I was mistaken in thinking to have seen gentlemen of quality playing there, as I think it was when I was a little child, that one of my father's servants, John Bassum I think, carried me in his armes thither), I did tell him of it and he did lead me thither; where after staying an hour, they begin to play at about 8 at night – where to see how differently one man took his losing from another, one cursing and swearing, and another only muttering and grumbling to himself, a third without any appearing discontent at all – to see how the dice will run good luck in one hand for half an hour together – and another have no good luck at all. To see how easily here, where they play nothing but guinnys, 100*l* is won or lost. To see two or three gentlemen come in there drunk, and putting their stock of gold together – one 22 pieces, the second 4, and the third 5 pieces; and these to play one with another, and forget how much each of them brought, but he that brought the 22 think that he brought no more then the rest. To see the different humours of gamesters to change

1. The prices (in shillings 1*s* and 1*s* 6*d*) were for the upper gallery and middle gallery respectively.
2. The new committee (later known as the Brooke House committee) was empowered by a recent act of parliament to investigate the finances of the Anglo-Dutch war. Pepys often calls them the "Commissioners for Accounts". The Commons had selected commissioners who were not members of the English Lords or Commons, so Savile's peerage complicated this arrangement. In the coming months, Pepys dealt with both the "Commissioners for Accounts" and the separate Commons Committee on the Miscarriages of the War.
3. John Brisbane, naval official.
4. A court official at Whitehall Palace who supervised the gaming allowed there during the twelve days of Christmas.
5. The Halls of the Inner and Middle Temple, which allowed gaming over Christmas.

their luck when it is bad – how ceremonious they are as to call for new dice – to shift their places – to alter their manner of throwing; and that with great industry, as if there was anything in it. To see how some old gamesters, that have no money now to spend as formerly, do come and sit and look on; as among others, Sir Lewes Dives, who was here and hath been a great gamester in his time. To hear their cursing and damning to no purpose; as one man, being to throw a seven if he could and failing to do it after a great many throws, cried he would be damned if ever he flung seven more while he lived, his despair of throwing it being so great, while others did it as their luck served, almost every throw. To see how persons of the best quality do here sit down and play with people of any, though meaner; and to see how people in ordinary clothes shall come hither and play away 100, or 2 or 300 guinnys, without any kind of difficulty. And lastly, to see the formality of the Groomeporter, who is their judge of all disputes in play and all quarrels that may arise therein; and how his under-officers are there to observe true play at each table and to give new dice, is a consideration I never could have thought had been in the world, had I not now seen it. And mighty glad I am that I did see it; and it may be will find another evening, before Christmas be over, to see it again; when I may stay later, for their heat of play begins not till about 11 or 12 a-clock; which did give me another pretty observation, of a man that did win mighty fast when I was there: I think he won 100*l* at single pieces in a little time; while all the rest envied him his good fortune, he cursed it, saying, "A pox on it that it should come so earely upon me! For this fortune two hours hence would be worth something to me; but then, God damn me, I shall have no such luck." This kind of profane, mad entertainment they give themselfs. And so I having enough for once, refusing to venture, though Brisband pressed me hard and tempted me with saying that no man was ever known to lose the first time, the devil being too cunning to discourage a gamester; and he offered me also to lend me ten pieces to venture, but I did refuse and so went away – and took coach and home about 9 or 10 at night; where, not finding my wife come home, I took the same coach again; and leaving my watch behind for fear of robbing, I did go back and to Mr. Pierce's, thinking they might not have broken up yet, but there I find my wife newly gone; and not going out of my coach, spoke only to Mr. Pierce in his nightgown in the street; and so away back again home, and there to supper with my wife and to talk about their dancing and doings at Mrs. Pierce's today; and so to bed.

10. Up, and with Sir Denis Gawden, who called me to White-hall; and there to wait on the Duke of York with the rest of my brethren, which we did a little in the King's green room while the King was in Council; and in this room we found my Lord Bristoll walking alone; which wondering at, while the Council was sitting, I was answered that, as being a Catholique, he could not be of the Council; which I did not consider before. After, broke up and walked a turn or two with Lord Brouncker, talking about the times; and he tells me that he thinks, and so doth everybody else, that the great business of putting out some of the Council, to make room for some of the Parliament men to gratify and wheadle them, is over – thinking that it might do more hurt then good, and not obtain much upon the Parliament neither. This morning there was a Persian in the country dress, with a Turban, waiting to kiss the King's hand in the Vane-room against he came out; it was a comely man as to features, and his dress methinks very comely. Thence in Sir W. Penn's coach alone (he going with Sir D. Gawden) to my new bookseller, Martin's; and there did meet with Fournier, the Frenchman that hath wrote of the Sea=Navigation, and I could not but buy him;[1] and also bespoke an excellent book which I met with there, of China.[2] The truth is, I have bought a great many books lately, to a great value; but I think to ⟨buy⟩ no more till Christmas next, and these that I have will so fill my two presses,[3] that I must be forced to give away some to make room for them, it being my design to have no more at any time for my proper Library then to fill them. Thence home and to the Exchange, there to do a little business; where I find everybody concerned whether we shall have out a fleet this next year or no, they talking of a peace concluded between France and Spayne, so that the King of France will have nothing to do with his Army unless he comes to us. But I do not see in the world how we shall be able to set out a fleet, for want of money to buy stores and pay men, for neither of which we shall be any more trusted. So home to dinner, and there with my wife and Deb to the King's House to see *Aglaura*,[4] which hath been always mightily cried up; and so I went with mighty expectation, but do find nothing extraordinary in it at all, and but hardly good in any

1. Pepys means he met with the book, not its author Georges Fournier (d. 1652). Fournier's *Hydrographie* covered a variety of sea-matters, from naval architecture to the tides. Pepys's new bookseller was John Martin near Temple Bar.
2. Probably Athanasius Kircher's lavishly illustrated *China monumentis* (1667).
3. Bookcases.
4. A tragicomedy by Sir John Suckling, first performed in 1638.

degree. So home, and thither comes to us W. Batelier and sat with us all the evening, and to Cards and supper, passing the evening pretty pleasantly; and so late at night parted, and so to bed.◆

This day I received a letter from my father and another from my Cosen Roger Pepys, who have had a view of Jackson's[1] evidences of his estate and do mightily like of the man and his condition and estate, and do advise me to accept of the match for my sister and to finish it as soon as I can; and he doth it so as I confess I am contented to have it done, and so give her her portion; and so I shall be eased of one care how to provide for her. And do in many respects think that it may be a match proper enough to have her married there, and to one that may look after my concernments if my father should die and I continue where I am. And there[fore] I am well pleased with it. And so to bed.

17. Up, and by coach to White-hall to attend the Council there; and here I met, first by Mr. Castle the shipwright whom I met there, and then from the whole House, all the discourse of the Duell yesterday between the Duke of Buckingham, Holmes, and one Jenkins on one side, and my Lord of Shrewsbury, Sir Jo. Talbot, and one Bernard Howard, on the other side; and all about my Lady Shrewsbury, who is a whore and is at this time, and hath for a great while been, a whore to the Duke of Buckingham; and so her husband challenged him, and they met yesterday in a close near Barne Elmes and there fought; and my Lord Shrewsbury is run through the body from the right breast through the shoulder, and Sir Jo. Talbot all along up one of his arms, and Jenkins killed upon the place, and the rest all in a little measure wounded.[2] This will make the world think that the King hath good councillors about him, when the Duke of Buckingham, the greatest man about him, is a fellow of no more sobriety then to fight about a whore. And this may prove a very bad accident to the Duke of Buckingham, but that my Lady Castlemaine doth rule all at this time as much as ever she did, and she will, it is believed, keep all matters well with the Duke of Buckingham;[3] though this is a time that the King will be very backward, I suppose, to appear in such a business. And it is pretty to hear how that the King had some notice of this challenge

1. John Jackson of Ellington.
2. This was perhaps the most notorious duel of the period. Buckingham and Shrewsbury were both pardoned by the King. Shrewsbury died two months later, possibly of his wounds.
3. Castlemaine was Buckingham's cousin and, at this point, his ally.

a week or two ago, and did give it to my Lord Generall[1] to confine the Duke, or take security that he should not do any such thing as fight; and the Generall trusted to the King that he, sending for him, would do it, and the King trusted to the Generall; and so between both, as everything else of the greatest moment doth, doth fall between two stools. The whole House full of nothing but the talk of this business; and it is said that my Lord Shrewsbury's case is to be feared, that he may die too, and that may make it much the worse for the Duke of Buckingham; and I shall not be much sorry for it, that we may have some soberer man come in his room to assist in the government. Here I waited till the Council rose and talked the while with Creed, who tells me of Mr. Harry Howards giving the Royall Society a piece of ground next to his house to build a College on, which is a most generous Act.[2] And he tells me he is a very fine person, and understands and speaks well; and no rigid papist neither, but one that would not have a protestant servant leave his religion, which he was going to do, thinking to recommend himself to his maister by it – saying that he had rather have an honest protestant then a knavish catholique. I was not called into the Council; and therefore home, first informing myself that my Lord Hinchingbrook ⟨hath⟩ been married this week to my Lord Burlington's daughter;[3] so that that great business is over, and I mighty glad of it – though I am not satisfied that I have not a favour[4] sent me – as I see Atturny Mountagu and the vice-chamberlain have. But I am mighty glad that the thing is done. So home, and there alone with my wife and Deb to dinner; and after dinner comes Betty Turner, and I carried them to the New Exchange; and thence I to Whitehall and did a little business at the Treasury, and so called them there and so home and to Cards and supper; and her mother came and sat at Cards with us till past 12 at night, and then broke up and to bed, after entering my journall, which made it one before I went to bed.

20. Up, and all the morning at the office very busy; and at noon by coach to Westminster to the Chequer about a warrant for Tanger money. In my way, both coming and going, I did stop at Drumbleby's the pipe-maker, there to advise about the making of a flagelette

1. Albemarle.
2. Henry Howard was second son of the Earl of Arundel. The building scheme was eventually abandoned.
3. Sandwich's eldest son married Lady Anne Boyle.
4. A ribbon or other token given to wedding guests and to friends who did not attend.

to go low and saft; and he doth show me a way which doth do, and also a fashion of having two pipes of the same note fastened together, so as I can play of one and then echo it upon the other; which is mighty pretty. So to my Lord Crew's to dinner, where we hear all the good news of our making a league now with Holland against the French power coming over them or us,[1] which is the first good act that hath been done a great while, and done secretly and with great seeming wisdom; and is certainly good for us at this time, while we are in no condition to resist the French if he should come over hither; and then a little time of peace will give us time to lay up something; which these Commissioners of the Treasury are doing, and the world doth begin to see that they will do the King's work for him if he will let them.◆

It seems there is great presumption that there will be a Toleration granted;[2] so that the presbyters do hold up their heads, but they will hardly trust the King or the Parliament where to yield to them – though most of the sober party be for some kind of allowance to be given them. Thence and home, and then to the Change in the evening; and there Mr. Cade told me how my Lord Gerard is likely to meet with trouble the next sitting of Parliament, about   being set in the pillory; and I am glad of it.[3] And it is mighty acceptable to the world to hear that among other reductions, the King doth reduce his Guards; which doth please mightily. So to my bookbinder's with my boy, and there did stay late to see two or three things done that I had a mind to see done; among other, my Tanger papers of accounts; and so home to supper and to bed.

21. Up, and while at the office comes news from Kate Joyce[4] that if I would see her hus[band] alive, I must come presently; so after the office was up, I to him, and W. Hewer with me, and find him in his sick bed (I never was at their house, this Inne, before), very sensible in discourse and thankful for my kindnesses to him; but his

1. Signed on the 13th (23rd New Style) and quickly broadened into the Triple Alliance between Britain, the Dutch Republic, and Sweden.
2. Since the fall of Clarendon, the government had encouraged discussion of schemes to allow Presbyterians and other nonconformists greater religious liberty.
3. William Carr (the name missing in this sentence) had been put in the pillory by the House of Lords for libel after he published allegations that Lord Gerard was corrupt.
4. A cousin of Pepys and wife to Anthony Joyce. Once very wealthy, the couple had suffered heavy losses in the Great Fire and, by late 1666, had taken up innkeeping. Their substantial inn was the Red Lion in Grub Street, Cripplegate.

breath rattled in his throate and they did lay pigeons to his feet while I was in the house;[1] and all despair of him, and with good reason. But the sorrow is that it seems on Thursday last he went sober and quiet out of doors in the morning to Islington, and behind one of the Inns, the White Lion, did fling himself into a pond – was spied by a poor woman and got out by some people binding up Hay in a barn there, and set on his head and got to life; and known by a woman coming that way, and so his wife and friends[2] sent for. He confessed his doing the thing, being led by the Devil; and doth declare his reason to be his trouble that he found in having forgot to serve God as he ought since he came to this new imployment; and I believe that, and the sense of his great loss by the fire, did bring him to it, and so everybody concludes. He stayed there all that night, and came home by coach next morning; and there grew sick, and worse and worse to this day. I stayed a while among the friends that were there; and they being now in fear that the goods and estate would be seized on, though he lived all this while, because of his endeavouring to drown himself,[3] my cousin did endeavour to remove what she could of plate out of the house, and desired me to take her flagons; which I was glad of, and did take them away with me, in great fear all the way of being seized; though there was no reason for it, he not being dead; but yet so fearful I was. So home and there eat my dinner, and busy all the afternoon, and troubled at this business. In the evening, with Sir D Gawden to Guild hall to advise with the Towne Clerke about the practice of the City and nation in this case, and he thinks it cannot be found Selfe-murder; but if it be, it will fall, all the estate, to the King. So we parted, and I to my cousin's again; where I no sooner came but news was brought down from his chamber that he was departed. So at their entreaty I presently took coach and to White-hall, and there find W. Coventry and he carried me to the King, the Duke of York being with him, and there told my story which I had told him; and the King without more ado granted that if it was found [self-murder] the estate should be to the widow and children. I presently to each Secretary's office and there left Caveats,[4] and so away back again to my cousin's – leaving a Chimny

1. A remedy of last resort.
2. Relatives.
3. The property of suicides was forfeit to the crown.
4. Notifications to the Secretary of States' Offices that no warrant was to be issued that would give Anthony Joyce's estate to anyone other than his widow and her children.

on fire at White-hall in the King's closet, but no danger. And so when I came thither, I found her all in sorrow, but she and the rest mightily pleased with my doing this for them; and endeed, it was a very great courtesy, for people are looking out for the estate, and the Coroner will be sent to and a jury called to examine his death. This being well done, to my and their great joy, I home and there to my office; and so to supper and to bed.

FEBRUARY.

5. Up, and I to Captain Cockes, where he and I did discourse of our business that we are to go about to the Comissioners of Accounts, about our prizes.[1] And having resolved to conceal nothing but confess the truth, the truth being likely to do us most good, we parted; and I to White-hall, where missing of the Commissioners of the Treasury, I to the Commissioners of Accounts, where I was forced to stay two hours I believe before I was called in; and when came in, did take an oath to declare the truth to what they should ask me (which is a great power, I doubt more then the Act doth, or as some say can, give them: to force a man to swear against himself);[2] and so they fell to enquire about the business of prize-goods, wherein I did answer them as well as I could answer them, to everything the just truth, keeping myself to that. I do perceive at last that that they did lay most like a fault to me was that I did buy goods upon my Lord Sandwiches declaring that it was with the King's allowance, and my believing it without seeing the King's allowance – which is a thing I will own, and doubt not to justify myself in. That that vexed me most was their having some watermen by to witness my saying that they were rogues, that they had betrayed my goods; which was upon some discontent with one of the watermen that I imployed at Greenwich, who I did think did discover[3] the goods sent from Rochester to the Custome-house officer[4] – but this can do me no great harm. They were inquisitive into the meanest particulars, and had had great information; but I think that it can do me no hurt, at the worst more then to make me refund, if it must

1. In autumn 1665, Pepys and Cocke had both purchased Dutch prize-goods that Sandwich had distributed in violation of procedure. Pepys had sold his share to Cocke for £500 when scandal loomed.
2. They had been given statutory powers to compel witnesses to answer questions.
3. Disclose.
4. For this strife with Customs, *see* 7 Oct. 1665.

be known, what profit I did make of my agreement with Captain Cocke. And yet though this be all, yet I do find so poor a spirit within me, that it makes me almost out of my wits, and puts me to so much pain that I cannot think of anything, nor do anything but vex and fret and imagine myself undone – so that I am ashamed of myself to myself, and do fear what would become of me if any real affliction should come upon me.◆

7. Up, and to the office to the getting of my books in order to carry to the Commissioners of Accounts this morning. This being done, I away, first to Westminster-hall and there met my Cosen Rogr. Pepys by his desire (the first time I have seen him since his coming to town, the Parliament meeting yesterday and adjurned to Monday next); and here he tells me that Mr. Jackson, my sister's servant,[1] is come to town and hath this day suffered a Recovery on his estate, in order to the making her a settlement.◆ Thence I to the Comissioners of Accounts and there presented my books, and was made to sit down and used with much respect, otherwise then the other day when I came to them as a Criminall about the business of the prizes. I sat here with them a great while, while my books were inventoried.◆ I find these gentlemen to sit all day and only eat a bit of bread at noon and a glass of wine; and are resolved to go through their business with great severity and method. Thence I about 2 a-clock to Wesminster-hall by appointment, and there met my cousin Roger again and Mr. Jackson, who is a plain young man, handsome enough for her; one of no education nor discourse, but of few words, and one altogether that I think will please me well enough. My cousin hath got me to give the od sixth, 100*l*,[2] presently, which I intended to keep to the birth of the first child: and let it go, I shall be eased of that care; and so after little talk we parted, resolving to dine all together at my house tomorrow. So there parted, my mind pretty well satisfied with this plain fellow for my sister, though I shall I see have no pleasure nor content in him, as if he had been a man of breeding and parts like Cumberland.[3] And to the Swan I, and there sent for a bit of meat and eat and drank; and so to White-hall to the Duke of York's chamber, where I find him and ⟨my⟩ fellows at their usual meeting, discoursing about securing the Medway this year; which is to shut the door

1. Suitor.
2. Pepys was to settle £600 on his sister at her marriage.
3. Richard Cumberland was an old college friend of Pepys whom he had once considered as a potential husband for Pall.

after the horse is stole – however, it is good. Having done here, my Lord Brouncker and W. Penn and I, and with us Sir Arnold Breames, to the King's playhouse, and there saw a piece of *Love in a Maze*,[1] a dull, silly play I think; and after the play, home with W. Penn and his son Lowther, whom we met there. And there home, and sat most of the evening with my wife and Mr. Pelling talking, my head being full of business of one kind or other, and most such as doth not please me. And so to supper and to bed.

8. Up and to the office, where sat all day; and at noon home and there find Cosen Roger and Jackson by appointment come to dine with me, and Creed – and very merry; only, Jackson hath few words, and like him never the worse for it. ◆ We had a great deal of good discourse at table; and after dinner we four men took coach, and they set me down at the Old Exchange and they home, having discoursed nothing today with cousin or Jackson about our business. I to Captain Cocke's and there discoursed over our business of prizes; and I think I shall go near to state the matter so as to secure myself without wrong to him, doing nor saying anything but the very truth. Thence away to the Strand to my bookseller's, and there stayed an hour and bought that idle, roguish book, *L'escholle des Filles*;[2] which I have bought in plain binding (avoiding the buying of it better bound) because I resolve, as soon as I have read it, to burn it, that it may not stand in the list of books, nor among them, to disgrace them if it should be found. Thence home, and busy late at the office; and then home to supper and to bed. My wife well pleased with my sister's match, and designing how to be merry at their marriage. And I am well at ease in my mind to think that that care will be over. This night, calling at the Temple at the Auditors,[3] his man told me that he heard that my account must be brought to the view of the Commissioners of Tanger before it can be passed; which though I know no hurt in it, yet it troubled me, lest there should be any or any designed by them who put this into the head of the Auditor; I suppose Auditor Beale or Creed, because they saw me carrying my account another way then by them.

9. *Lords day.* Up, and at my chamber all the morning and the office, doing business and also reading a little of *L'escolle des Filles*, which is a mighty lewd book, but yet not amiss for a sober man once to

1. *The Changes, or Love in a Maze*, a comedy by James Shirley, first performed 1632.
2. *L'École des filles* (first published 1655) consisted of two "educative" dialogues between female characters on the delights of sex.
3. An Exchequer official, John Wood.

read over to inform himself in the villainy of the world. At noon home to dinner, where by appointment Mr. Pelling came, and with him three friends: Wallington that sings the good bass, and one Rogers, and a gentleman, a young man, his name Tempest, who sings very well endeed and understands anything in the world at first sight.[1] After dinner, we into our dining-room and there to singing all the afternoon (by the way, I must remember that Pegg Pen was brought to bed yesterday of a girl; and among other things, if I have not already set it down, that hardly ever was remembered such a season for the smallpox as these last two months have been, people being seen all up and down the streets, newly come out after the smallpox): but though they sang fine things, yet I must confess that I did take no pleasure in it, or very little, because I understood not the words; and with the rests that the words are set, there is no sense nor understanding in them, though they be English – which makes us weary of singing in that manner, it being but a worse sort of instrumental music. We sang till almost night, and drank my good store of wine; and then they parted and I to my chamber, where I did read through *L'escholle des Filles*; a lewd book, but what doth me no wrong to read for information sake (but it did hazer my prick para stand all the while, and una vez to decharger);[2] and after I had done it, I burned it, that it might not be among my books to my shame; and so at night to supper and then to bed.

10.◆ To Westminster-hall, where the Hall mighty full; and among other things, the House begins to sit today, and the King came. But before the King's coming, the House of Commons met; and upon information given them of a Bill intended to be brought in, as common report said, for Comprehension,[3] they did mightily and generally inveigh against it, and did vote that the King should be desired by the House, and the message delivered by the Privy-counsellors of the House, that the laws against breakers of the Act of Uniformity should be put in execution. And it was moved in the House that

1. Pepys's friend John Pelling and these men were all members of a local "Musick Society", according to the publisher John Playford. Playford dedicated his collection of rounds, *Catch as Catch Can* (1667), to them as regular users of his music.
2. "(but it did make my prick to stand all the while, and once to spend)". The verb "décharger" is used in *L'École des filles* to mean male and female orgasm, so the book's instructional uses may have included expanding Pepys's erotic French vocabulary.
3. Several proposals had been drafted to allow Presbyterian clergy to be comprehended within the Church of England and to give greater liberty of worship to other nonconformists. The intention was to reverse elements of the divisive Act of Uniformity (1662).

if any people had a mind to bring any new laws into the House about religion, they might come as a proposer of new laws did in Athens, with ropes about their necks.[1] By and by the King comes to the Lords' House and there tells them of his league with Holland – and the necessity of a fleet, and his debts and therefore want of money; and his desire that they would think of some way to bring in all his protestant subjects to a right understanding and peace one with another, meaning the Bill of Comprehension. The Commons coming to their House, it was moved that the vote passed this morning might be suspended, because of the King's speech, till the House was full and called over two days hence; but it was denied, so furious they are against this Bill; and thereby a great blow either given to the King and presbyters; or, which is the rather of the two, to the House itself, by denying a thing desired by the King and so much desired by much the greater part of the nation. Whatever the consequence be, if the King be a man of any stomach and heat, all do believe that he will resent this vote.

Thence with Creed home to my house to dinner, where I met with Mr. Jackson and find my wife angry with Deb, which vexes me. After dinner by coach away to Westminster, taking up a friend of Mr. Jacksons, a young lawyer; and parting with Creed at White-hall, they and I to Westminster-hall; and there met Roger Pepys and with him to his chamber and there read over and agreed upon the deed of Settlement to our minds: my sister to have 600*l* presently and she to be joyntured in 60*l* per annum – wherein I am very well satisfied.◆

11. At the office all the morning, where comes a damned summons to attend the Committee of Miscarriges today; which makes me mad that I should by my place become the hackney[2] of this Office, in perpetual trouble and vexation, that need it least. At noon home to dinner, where little pleasure, my head being split almost with the variety of troubles upon me at this time and cares. And after dinner by coach to Westminster-hall and sent my wife and Deb to see *Mustapha* acted.[3] Here I brought a book to the Committee, and do find them, and perticularly Sir Tho. Clerges, mighty hot in the

1. The motion has not been traced. It appears to be a muddled reference to Demosthenes' *Against Timocrates*, in which he warned the Athenians against allowing dangerous changes to their laws. He instanced the city of Locri, where a legislator proposing a new law would wear a rope around his neck and be strangled if his measure was rejected.
2. Workhorse, drudge.
3. A tragedy by Roger Boyle, Earl of Orrery, first performed in 1665.

business of tickets; which makes me mad, to see them bite at the stone and not at the hand that flings it.◆

This morning, my wife in bed told me the story of our Tom and Jane;[1] how the rogue did first demand her consent to love and marry him and then, with pretence of displeasing me, did slight her; but both he and she have confessed the matter to her, and she hath charged him to go on with his love to her and be true to her, and so I think the business will go on; which, for my love to her because she is in love with him, I am pleased with, but otherwise I think she will have no good bargain of it; at least, if I should not do well in my place. But if I do stand, I do entend to give her 50*l* in money and do them all the good I can in my way.

18. Up by break of day, and walked down to the Old Swan, where I find little Michell building, his Booth[2] being taken down and a foundation laid for a new house, so that that street is like to be a very fine place. I drank, but did not see Betty. And so to Charing-cross stairs, and thence walked to Sir W. Coventry and talked with him; who tells me how he hath been prosecuted, and how he is yet well come off in the business of the dividing of the fleet and the sending of the letter.[3]◆ I will remember what in mirth he said to me this morning when upon this discourse he said, if ever there was another Dutch war, they should not find a Secretary; "Nor," said I, "a Clerk of the Acts, for I see the reward of it; and thanked God I have enough of my own to buy me a good book and a good fiddle, and I have a good wife;" – "Why," says he, "I have enough to buy me a good book, and shall not need a fiddle,[4] because I have never a one of your good wifes." I understand by him that we are likely to have our business of tickets voted a miscarriage;[5] but cannot tell me what that will signify, more then that he thinks they will report them to the King and there leave them. But I doubt[6] they will do more.◆

1. Tom Edwards, Pepys's servant, and Jane Birch, the household's long-serving maid.
2. A temporary structure put up after the Great Fire. Michael and Betty Mitchell sold spirits.
3. The Committee on Miscarriages had recently reported to the Commons after investigating the division of the fleet prior to the Four Days Battle and the late arrival of Prince Rupert's ships to the fight. Coventry had despatched the letter recalling Rupert.
4. "Fiddle" in the seventeenth century served for assorted sexual innuendos; here the main sense is "penis".
5. The report by the Committee on Miscarriages particularly criticized the discharging of whole ships by ticket and the disorderly payment of tickets.
6. Fear.

I to the Hall and there met Sir W Pen; and he and I to the Beare in Drury-lane, an excellent ordinary after the French manner, but of Englishmen, and there had a little fricasse, our dinner coming to 8*s*; which was mighty pretty, to my great content; and thence he and I to the King's House, and there in one of the upper boxes saw *Flora's vagarys*,[1] which is a very silly play; and the more, I being out of humour, being at a play without my wife and she ill at home, and having no desire also to be seen and therefore could not look about me. Thence to the Temple and there we parted; and I to see Kate Joyce, where I find her and her friends in great ease of mind, the Jury having this day given in their verdict that her husband died of a Feaver. Some opposition there was, the foreman pressing them to declare the cause of the Feaver, thinking thereby to obstruct it; but they did adhere to their verdict and would give no reason. And so all trouble is now over, and she's safe in her estate, which I am mighty glad of; and so took leave and home and up to my wife, not owning my being at a play; and there she shows me her ring, which [is] of a Turky-stone[2] set with little sparks of Dyamonds, which I am to give her as my valentine, and I am not much troubled at it, it will cost me near 5*l* – she costing me but little compared with other wifes, and I have not many occasions to spend on her. So to my office, where late, and to think up my observations tomorrow upon the report of the committee to the Parliament about the business of tickets, whereof my head is full. And so home to supper and to bed.

27. All the morning at the office, and at noon home to dinner; and thence with my wife and Deb to the King's House to see *Virgin Martyr*, the first time it hath been acted a great while, and it is mighty pleasant; not that the play is worth much, but it is finely Acted by Becke Marshall;[3] but that which did please me beyond anything in the whole world was the wind-musique when the Angell comes down,[4] which is so sweet that it ravished me; and endeed, in a word, did wrap up my soul so that it made me really sick, just as I have formerly been when in love with my wife; that neither then, nor all the evening going home and at home, I was

1. A comedy by Richard Rhodes.
2. Turquoise.
3. She played the part of St Dorothea. The play was a tragedy by Dekker and Massinger, which Pepys had last seen in 1661.
4. Probably the angel's arrival at the start of Act 5, sc. 1 when music is one of the heavenly delights used to prompt the conversion of Dorothea's erstwhile persecutor.

able to think of anything, but remained all night transported, so as I could not believe that ever any music hath that real command over the soul of a man as this did upon me; and makes me resolve to practise wind-music and to make my wife do the like.

28. Up and to the office, where all the morning doing business; and after dinner with Sir W. Penn to White-hall, where we ⟨and the rest of us⟩ presented a great letter of the state of our want of money to his Royal Highness. I did also present a demand of mine for consideration for my travelling-charges of coach and boat-hire during the war – which though his Royal Highness and the company did all like of, yet contrary to my expectation I find him so jealous[1] now of doing anything extraordinary, that he desired the gentlemen that they would consider it and report their minds in it to him. This did unsettle my mind a great while, not expecting this stop: but however, I shall do as well I know, though it causes me a little stop. But that that troubles me most is that while we were thus together with the Duke of York, comes in Mr. Wren from the House, where he tells us another storm hath been all this day almost against the Officers of the Navy upon this complaint: that though they have made good rules for payment of tickets, yet that they have not observed them themselfs; which was driven so high as to have it urged that we should presently be put out of our places – and so they have at last ordered that we be heard at the bar of the House upon this business on Thursdy next. This did mightily trouble me and us all; but me perticularly, who am least able to bear these troubles, though I have the least cause to be concerned in it. Thence therefore to visit Sir H. Chomly, who hath for some time been ill of a cold; and thence walked towards Westminster and met Collonell Birch,[2] who took me back to walk with him and did give me an account of this day's heat against the Navy officers, and an account of his speech on our behalfs, which was very good; and endeed, we are much beholden to him, as I, after I parted with him, did find by my Cosen Roger, whom I went to; and he and I to his lodgings and there he did tell me the same over again, and how much Birch did stand up in our defence – and that he doth see that there are many desirous to have us out of the office; and the House is so furious and passionate that he thinks nobody can be secure, let him deserve never so well; but how[ever] he tells me we shall have a fair hearing from the House, and he hopes justice of them. But upon

1. Wary.
2. John Birch MP.

the whole, he doth agree with me that I should hold my hand as to making any purchase of land, which I had formerly discoursed with him about, till we see a little further how matters go. He tells me that that that made them so mad today first, was several letters in the House about the Fanatickes in several places coming in great bodies and turning people out of the churches and there preaching themselfs and pulling the surplice over the parsons' heads: this was confirmed from several places, which makes them stark mad, especially the hectors and bravados of the House – who show all the zeal on this occasion. Having done with him, I home, vexed in my mind and so fit for no business; but sat talking with my wife and supped with her, and Nan Mercer came and sat all the evening with us – and much pretty discourse, which did a little ease me. And so to bed.

MARCH.

2. Up and betimes to the office, where I did much business and several came to me; and among others, I did prepare Mr. Warren, and by and by Sir D Gawden, about what presents I have had from them, that they may not publish them;[1] or if they do, that in truth I received none on the account of the Navy but Tanger. And this is true to the former, and in both, that I never asked anything of them. I must do the like with the rest. Mr. Moore was with me, and he doth tell me, and so W Hewers tells me, he hears this morning that all the town is full of the discourse that the Officers of the Navy shall be all turned out but honest Sir Jo. Minnes – who, God knows, is fitter to have been turned out himself then any of us, doing the King more hurt by his dotage and fally than all the rest can do by their knavery if they had a mind to it. At noon home to dinner, where was Mercer, and very merry as I could be with my mind so full of business; and so with my wife, her and the girl, to the King's House to see *The Virgin Martyr* again; which doth mightily please me, but above all the Musique at the coming down of the Angell – which at this hearing the second time doth so still command me as nothing ever did, and the other music is nothing to it. Thence with my wife to the Change; and so calling at the Cocke ale-house, we home, and there I settle to business and with my people preparing

1. Both men were merchants who had given Pepys "presents" in return for his assistance.

my great answer to the Parliament for the office about tickets, till past 12 at night; and then home to supper and to bed – keeping Mr. Gibson all night with me. ⟨This day I have the news that my sister was married on Thursday last to Mr. Jackson; so that work is I hope well over.⟩

4. Up betimes and with Sir W. Penn in his coach to White-hall, there to wait upon the Duke of York and the Commissioners of the Treasury, W. Coventry and Sir Jo. Duncombe – who do declare that they cannot find the money we demand; and we, that less then what we demand will not set out the fleet intended; and so broke up with no other conclusion then that they would let us have what they could get, and we would improve that as well as we could. So God bless us and prepare us against the consequences of these matters. Thence, it being a cold wet day, I home with Sir J. Mennes in his coach, and called by the way at my bookseller's and took home with me Kercher's *Musica*, very well bound.[1] But I had no comfort to look upon them, but as soon as I came home fell to my work at the office, shutting the doors that we, I and my clerks, might not be interrupted; and so, only with room for a little dinner, we very busy all the day till night, that the officers met for me to give them the heads of what I intended to say; which I did, with great discontent to see them all rely on me that have no reason at all to trouble myself about it, nor have any thanks from them for my labour; but contrarily, Brouncker looked mighty dogged, as thinking that I did not intend to do it so as to save him. This troubled me so much, as together with the shortness of the time and muchness of the business, did let me be at it till but about 10 at night; and then, quite weary and dull and vexed, I could go no further, but resolved to leave the rest to tomorrow morning; and so in full discontent and weariness did give over and went home with[out] supper, vexed and sickish, to bed and there slept about three hours; but then waked, and never in so much trouble in all my life of mind, thinking of the task I have upon me, and upon what dissatisfactory grounds, and what the issue of it may be to me. With these thoughts I lay troubling myself till 6 a-clock, restless, and at last getting my wife to talk to me to comfort me; which she at last did, and made me resolve to quit my hands of this office and endure the trouble [of] it no
⟨⟨5.⟩⟩ longer then till I can clear myself of it. So, with great trouble but yet with some ease from this discourse with my

1. Athanasius Kircher's *Musurgia universalis* (1650), an influential and finely illustrated work on musicology.

wife, I up and to my office, whither came my clerks; and so I did huddle up the best I could some more notes for my discourse today; and by 9 a-clock was ready and did go down to the Old Swan, and there by boat, with T. Hater and W. Hewer with me, to Wesminster, where I found myself come time enough and my Brethren all ready. But I full of thoughts and trouble touching the issue of this day; and to comfort myself did go to the Dogg and drink half a pint of mulled sack, and in the Hall did drink a dram of brandy at Mrs. Howletts, and with the warmth of this did find myself in better order as to courage, truly. So we all up to the Lobby; and between 11 and 12 a-clock were called in, with the Mace before us, into the House; where a mighty full House, and we stood at the Barr – *viz.*, Brouncker, Sir J. Mennes, Sir T. Harvey and myself – W. Penn being in the House as a Member.[1] I perceive the whole House was full, and full of expectation of our defence what it would be, and with great prejudice. After the Speaker had told us the dissatisfaction of the House, and read the report of the Committee, I begin our defence most acceptably and smoothly, and continued at it without any hesitation or losse but with full scope and all my reason free about me, as if it had been at my own table, from that time till past 3 in the afternoon; and so ended without any interruption from the Speaker, but we withdrew.[2] And there all my fellow-officers, and all the world that was within hearing, did congratulate me and cry up my speech as the best thing they ever heard, and my fellow-officers overjoyed in it. We were called in again by and by to answer only one question, touching our paying tickets to ticket-mongers – and so out; and we were in hopes to have had a vote this day in our favour, and so the generality of the House was; but my speech being so long, many had gone out to dinner and come in again half drunk, and then there are two or three that are professed enemies to us and everybody else; among others, Sir T. Littleton, Sir Tho. Lee, Mr. Wiles (the coxcomb whom I saw heretofore at the cock-fighting) and a few others; I saw these did rise up and speak against the coming to a vote now, the House not being full, by reason of several being at dinner but most because that the House was to attend the King this afternoon about the business of Religion (wherein they pray him to put in force all the laws against

1. These were current members of the Navy Board who had also been in post during the war.
2. The report by the Committee on Miscarriages harshly criticized the Navy Board's failures in paying seamen. Pepys responded point by point, stressing that payment by ticket was a necessary wartime measure.

nonconformists and papists); and this prevented it, so that they put it off to tomorrow come sennit. However, it is plain we have got great ground; and everybody says I have got the most honour that any could have had opportunity of getting. And so, with our hearts mightily overjoyed at this success, we all to dinner to Lord Brouncker; that is to say, myself, T. Harvey, and W. Penn, and there dined; and thence with Sir Anth. Morgan, who is an acquaintance of Brouncker's, a very wise man, we after dinner to the King's House and there saw part of *The Discontented Colonell*[1] – but could take no great pleasure in it because of our coming in in the middle of it. After the play, home with W. Penn and there to my wife, whom W. Hewer had told of my success; and she overjoyed, and I also as to my perticular. And after talking awhile, I betimes to bed, having had no quiet rest a good while.

6. Up betimes, and with Sir D. Gawden to Sir W. Coventry's chamber, where the first word he said to me was, "Good-morrow Mr. Pepys, that must be Speaker of the Parliament-house" – and did protest I had got honour for ever in Parliament. He said that his brother,[2] that sat by him, admires me; and another gentleman said that I could not get less than 1000*l* a year if I would put on a gown and plead at the Chancery-bar. But what pleases me most, he tells me that the Solicitor generall did protest that he thought I spoke the best of any man in England. After several talks with him alone touching his own businesses, he carried me to White-hall and there parted; and I to the Duke of York's lodging and find him going to the parke, it being a very fine morning; and I after him, and as soon as he saw me, he told me with great satisfaction that I had converted a great many yesterday, and did with great praise of me go on with the discourse with me. And by and by overtaking the King, the King and Duke of York came to me both, and he said, "Mr. Pepys, I am very glad of your success yesterday;" and fell to talk of my well speaking; and many of the Lords there, my Lord Berkely did cry me up for what they had heard of it; and others, Parliament[-men] there about the King, did say that they never heard such a speech in their lives delivered in that manner. Progers of the Bedchamber swore to me afterward before Brouncker in the afternoon, that he did tell the King that he thought I might teach the Solicitor generall. Everybody that saw me almost came to me, as Joseph Williamson and others, with such eulogys as cannot be

1. *Brennoralt, or The Discontented Colonel*, a tragicomedy by Suckling.
2. Henry Coventry, the diplomat. Both brothers were MPs.

expressed. From thence I went to Westminster-hall, where I met Mr. G. Mountagu; who came to me and kissed me, and told me that he had often heretofore kissed my hands, but now he would kiss my lips, protesting that I was another Cicero,[1] and said all the world said the same of me. Mr. Ashburnham, and every creature I met there of the Parliament or that knew anything of the Parliament's actings, did salute me with this honour – Mr. Godolphin, Mr. Sands, who swore he would go twenty mile at any time to hear the like again, and that he never saw so many sit four hours together to hear any man in his life as there did to hear me. Mr. Chichly, Sir Jo. Duncom, and everybody doth say that the Kingdom will ring of my ability, and that I have done myself right for my whole life; and so Captain Cocke, and other of my friends, say that no man had ever such an opportunity of making his abilities known. And, that I may cite all at once, Mr. Lieutenant of the Tower did tell me that Mr. Vaughan did protest to him, and that in his hearing it, said so to the Duke of Albemarle and afterward to W. Coventry, that he had sat 26 years in Parliament and never heard such a speech there before – for which the Lord God make me thankful, and that I may make use of it not to pride and vainglory, but that now I have this esteem, I may do nothing that may lessen it.◆

24. Up pretty betimes; and so there comes to me Mr. Shish to desire my appearing for him to succeed Mr. Chr. Pett, lately dead, in his place of Maister-Shipwright of Deptford and Woolwich; which I do resolve to promote when I can. So by and by to White-hall and there to the Duke of York's chamber, where I understand it is already resolved by the King and Duke of York that Shish shall have the place. From the Duke's chamber, Sir W. Coventry and I to walk in the Matted Gallery; and there, among other things, he tells me of the wicked design that now is at last contriving against him, to get a petition presented from people, that the money they have paid to W. Coventry for their places may be repaid them back. And that this is set on by Temple and Hollis of the Parliament and among other mean people in it, by Captain Tatnell.[2] And he prays me that I will use some effectual way to sift Tatnell what he doth, and who puts him on on this business; which I do undertake, and will do with all my skill for his service – being troubled that he is still under

1. Marcus Tullius Cicero, the greatest of Roman orators. In the seventeenth century his works were used to teach rhetoric at all levels.
2. Valentine Tatnell was a naval officer. In April, a petition was presented to the Commons accusing Coventry of selling places.

this difficulty. Thence up and down Westminster, by Mrs. Burroughes her mother's shop, thinking to have seen her, but could not; and therefore back to White-hall, where great talk of the tumult at the other end of the town about Moore-fields among the prentices, taking the liberty of these holidays to pull down bawdy-houses.[1] And Lord, to see the apprehensions which this did give to all people at Court, that presently order was given for all the soldiers, horse and foot, to be in armes; and forthwith alarmes were beat by drum and trumpet through Westminster, and all to their colours and to horse, as if the French were coming into the town. So Creed, whom I met here, and I to Lincolnes Inn fields, thinking to have gone into the fields to have seen the prentices; but here we found these fields full of soldiers all in a body, and my Lord Craven commanding of them, and riding up and down to give orders like a madman. And some young men we saw brought by soldiers to the guard at White-hall, and overheard others that stood by say that it was only for pulling down of bawdy-houses. And none of the bystanders finding fault with them, but rather of the soldiers for hindering them. And we heard a Justice of Peace this morning says to the King that he had been endeavouring to suppress this tumult, but could not; and that imprisoning some in the new prison at Clerkenwell, the rest did come and break open the prison and release them. And that they do give out that they are for pulling down of bawdy-houses, which is one of the great grievances of the nation. To which the King made a very poor, cold, insipid answer: "Why, why do they go to them, then?", and that was all, and had no mind to go on with the discourse.◆

25. Up and walked to White-hall, there to wait on the Duke of York, which I did; and in his chamber there, first by hearing the Duke of York call me by my name, my Lord Burlington did come to me and with great respect take notice of me and my relation to my Lord Sandwich,[2] and express great kindness to me; and so to talk of my Lord Sandwiches concernments. By and by the Duke of York is ready, and I did wait for an opportunity of speaking my mind to him about Sir J. Mennes his being unable to do the King any service; which I think doth become me to do in all

1. Attacks on brothels by apprentices were a Shrove Tuesday custom. This year the disorder, fuelled by religious and political grievances, escalated into the worst rioting of the 1660s. It spanned five days, having started on 23 March. The ringleaders were charged with treasonously levying war against the King, and four were executed.
2. Burlington's daughter had recently married Sandwich's son.

respects, and have Sir W. Coventry's concurrence therein; which I therefore will seek a speedy opportunity to do – come what will come of it.

The Duke of York and all with him this morning were full of the talk of the prentices, who are not yet down, though the Guards and militia of the town have been in arms all this night and the night before; and the prentices have made fools of them, sometimes by running from them and flinging stones at them. Some blood hath been spilt, but a great many houses pulled down; and among others, the Duke of York was mighty merry at that of Damaris Page's, the great bawd of the seamen. And the Duke of York complained merrily that he hath lost two tenants by their houses being pulled down, who paid him for their wine licences 15*l* a year.[1] But here it was said how these idle fellows have had the confidence to say that they did ill in contenting themselfs in pulling down the little bawdy-houses and did not go and pull down the great bawdy-house at White-hall. And some of them have the last night had a word among them, and it was "Reformation and Reducement!" This doth make the courtiers ill at ease to see this spirit among people, though they think this matter will not come to much; but it speaks people's mind. And then they do say that there are men of understanding among them, that have been of Cromwell's army; but how true that is I know not.

Thence walked a little to Westminster, but met with nobody to spend any time with; and so by coach homeward, and in Seething-lane met young Mrs. Daniel,[2] and I stopped; and she had been at my house but found nobody within, and tells me that she drew me for her valentine this year; so I took her into the coach, and was going to the other end of the town with her, thinking to have taken her abroad; but remembering that I was to go out with my wife this afternoon, I only did hazer her para tocar my prick con her hand, which did hazer me hazer;[3] and so to a milliner at the corner shop going into Bishopsgate and Leadenhall-street, and there did give her eight pair of gloves,[4] and so dismissed her; and so I home and to dinner, and then with my wife to the King's playhouse to see *The Storme*; which we did, but without much pleasure, it being but a mean play compared with *The Tempest* at the Duke of York's,

1. The Duke received all profits for the sale of licences for retailing wine.
2. Wife of a naval officer.
3. "did make her touch my prick with her hand, which did make me do" (i.e. ejaculate).
4. Notionally, a valentine gift.

though Knipp did act her part of grief very well.[1] Thence with my wife and Deb by coach to Islington to the old house, and there eat and drank till it was almost night; and then home, being in fear of meeting the prentices, who are many of them yet, they say, abroad in the fields. But we got well home, and so I to my chamber a while; and then to supper and to bed.

31. Up pretty betimes and to the office, where we sat all the morning; and at noon I home to dinner, where my Uncle Tho dined with me, as he doth every quarter, and I paid him his pension;[2] and also comes Mr. Hollier, a little fuddled and so did talk nothing but Latin and laugh, that it was very good sport to see a sober man in such a humour, though he was not drunk to scandal. At dinner comes a summons for this office and the Victualler to attend a committee of Parliament this afternoon with Sir D Gawden, which I accordingly did, with my papers relating to the sending of victuals to Sir Jo. Harman's fleet; and there, Sir R. Brookes in the chair, we did give them a full account; but Lord, to see how full they are and immovable in their jealousy that some means are used to keep Harman from coming home, for they have an implacable desire to know the bottom of the not improving the first victory, and would lay it upon Brouncker.[3] Having given them good satisfaction, I away thence up and down, wandering a little to see whether I could get Mrs. Burroughs out, but ella being in the shop ego did speak con her, but she could not then go foras.[4] And so I took coach, and away to Unthankes and there took up my wife and Deb and to the parke; where being in a Hackny and they undressed, I was ashamed to go into the Tour,[5] but went round the park; and so with pleasure home, where Mr. Pelling came and sat and talked late with us; and he being gone, I called Deb to take pen, ink, and paper and write down what things came into my head for my wife to do, in order to her going into the country; and the girl writing not so well

1. The play was *The Sea Voyage* by Fletcher and Massinger. Knepp appears to have played the shipwrecked and suffering heroine Aminta. *The Tempest* meant Dryden and Davenant's adaptation of Shakespeare's play.
2. An annuity due under the will of Thomas's brother, Robert Pepys.
3. Harman was sailing back from the West Indies. The Commons wanted him back to question him about the failure to pursue the Dutch fleet after the Battle of Lowestoft in June 1665. Henry Brouncker was accused of faking an order to Harman (captain of the English flagship) to slacken sail on that occasion. He was the brother of Pepys's colleague, Lord Brouncker.
4. "but she being in the shop I did speak with her, but she could not then go abroad."
5. The internal road in Hyde Park.

as she would do, cried, and her mistress construed it to be sullenness and so was angry, and I seemed angry with her too; but going to bed, she undressed me, and there I did give her good advice and beso la, ella weeping still; and yo did take her, the first time in my life, sobra mi genu and did poner mi mano sub her jupes and toca su thigh, which did hazer me great pleasure; and so did no more, but besando-la went to my bed.[1]

APRILL.

1. Up and to dress myself; and called, as I use, Deb to brush and dress me and there I did again as I did the last night con mi mano, but would have tocado su thing; but ella endeavoured to prevent me con much modesty by putting su hand there about, which I was well pleased with and would not do too much, and so con great kindness dismissed la;[2] and I to my office, where busy till noon, and then out to bespeak some things against my wife's going into the country tomorrow. And so home to dinner, my wife and I alone, she being mighty busy getting her things ready for her journey. I all the afternoon with her looking after things on the same account, and then in the afternoon out and all alone to the King's House; and there sat in an upper box to hide myself and saw *The Blacke prince*, a very good play, but only the fancy; most of it the same as in the rest of my Lord Orery's plays – but the dance very stately.[3] But it was pretty to see, how coming after dinner and no company with me to talk to, and at a play that I had seen and went to now not for curiosity but only idleness, I did fall asleep the former part of the play but afterward did mind it and like it very well. Thence called at my bookseller's and took Mr. Boyles book of Formes, newly imprinted, and sent my brother my old one.[4] So home, and there to my chamber, till anon comes Mr. Turner and his wife and daughter and Pelling to sup with us and talk of my

1. "and kiss her, she weeping still; and I did take her, the first time in my life, upon my knee and did put my hand under her skirts and touch her thigh, which did give me great pleasure; and so did no more, but kissing her went to my bed."
2. "with my hand, but would have touched her thing; but she endeavoured to prevent me with much modesty by putting her hand there about . . . so with great kindness dismissed her".
3. A tragedy by Roger Boyle, Earl of Orrery, first acted in 1667. Like all of his plays Pepys had so far seen, it dealt with the conflict between love and honour.
4. John Pepys got the 1666 first edition of Robert Boyle's *The Origine of Formes and Qualities*. The second enlarged edition of 1667 is still in Pepys's library.

wife's journey tomorrow, her daughter going with my wife; and after supper to talk with her husband about the office and his place, which by Sir J. Mennes's age and inability is very uncomfortable to him, as well as without profit or certainty what he shall do when Sir J. Mennes [dies]; which is a sad condition for a man that hath lived so long in the office as Mr. Turner hath done; but he aymes, and I advise him to it, to look for Mr. Ackworth's place in case he should be removed.[1] His wife afterward did take me into my closet and give me a cellar of waters of her own distilling for my father, to be carried down with my wife and her daughter tomorrow; which was very handsome. So broke up and to bed.

9. Up and to the office, where all the morning sitting. Then at noon home to dinner with my people. And so to the office again, writing of my letters, and then abroad to my bookseller's and I up and down to the Duke of York's playhouse, there to see, which I did, Sir W Davenant's corps carried out toward Westminster, there to be buried.[2] Here were many coaches and six horses and many hackneys, that made it look, methought, as if it were the burial of a poor poett. He seemed to have many children by five or six in the first mourning-coach, all boys. And there I left them coming forth, and I to the New Exchange, there to meet Mrs. Burroughs; and did tomar her in a carosse and carry ella toward the park, kissing her and tocando su breast,[3] so as to make myself do; but did not go into any house, but came back and set her down at White-hall; and did give her wrapped in paper, for my Valentine's gift for the last year before this, which I never did yet give her anything for, twelve half-crowns; and so I back home and there to my office, where came a packet from the Downes from my brother Balty, who with Harman is arrived there – of which this day came the first news.[4] And now the Parliament will be satisfied, I suppose, about the business they have so long desired between Brouncker and Harman, about not prosecuting the first victory.[5] Balty is very well, and I hope hath performed his work well – that I may get him into further imployment. I wrote to him this night; and so home, and there to the

1. Thomas Turner was clerk to the Comptroller, Mennes. Pepys was encouraging him to consider the Storekeeper's position at Woolwich.
2. Davenant, manager of the Lincoln's Inn Fields Theatre, had died on 7 April.
3. "did take her in a coach and carry her toward the park, kissing her and touching her breast".
4. Balty St Michel was Deputy-Treasurer of Harman's fleet just come from the West Indies.
5. *See* 31 March 1668.

perfecting my getting the scale of music without book; which I have done to perfection, backward and forward; and so to supper and to bed.[1]

20. Up betimes and to the getting ready my answer to the Committee of Accounts to several questions; which makes me trouble, though I know of no blame due to me from any; let them enquire what they can out. I to White-hall and there hear how Brouncker is fled, which I think will undo him; but what good it will do Harman I know not, he hath so much befouled himself. But it will be good sport to my Lord Chancellor, to hear how this great enemy is fain to take the same course that he is.[2] There met Robinson, who tells me that he fears his maister, W. Coventry, will this week have his business brought upon the stage again, about selling of places – which I shall be sorry for, though the less since I hear his standing for Pen the other day, to the prejudice though not to the wrong of my Lord Sandwich;[3] and yet I do think what he did, he did out of a principle of honesty. Thence to Committee of Accounts, and delivered my paper and had little discourse; and was unwilling to stay long with them to enter into much, but away and glad to be from them, though very civil to me – but cunning and close I see they are.◆

30. Up, and at the office all the morning. At noon Sir J. Mennes and I to the Dolphin tavern, there to meet our neighbours, all of the Parish, this being procession-day,[4] to dine – and did; and much very good discourse, they being most of them very able merchants, as any in the City – Sir Andr. Rickard, Mr. Vandeputt, Sir Jo. Fredricke, Harrington, and others. They talked with Mr. Mills about the meaning of this day and the good uses of it; and how heretofore, and yet in several places, they do whip a boy at every place they stop at in their procession.[5]

Thence I to the Duke of York's playhouse and there saw *The Tempest*, which still pleases me mightily. And thence to the New

1. At this point Pepys left eight manuscript pages blank for the entries of 10–19 April. These were not completed, and instead he bound up the rough notes for them into the volume. For examples of similar notes, *see* 9–17 June 1668.
2. Henry Brouncker, facing parliament's wrath over his part after the Battle of Lowestoft, had fled to France, just as Lord Chancellor Clarendon had fled to France when impeached in 1667.
3. The Commons had impeached Penn over his role in the prize-goods scandal of 1665. Coventry had supported Penn in the parliamentary debate, emphasizing that in taking goods Penn was following his superior (Sandwich's) order
4. Ascension Day, when parish boundaries were walked and parish dinners held.
5. The object was to imprint on boys' memories knowledge of parish boundaries.

Exchange, and then home; and in the way stopped to talk with Mr. Brisband, who gives me an account of the rough usage Sir G. Carteret and his counsel had the other day before the Commissioners of Accounts, and what I do believe we shall all of us have, in a greater degree then any we have had yet with them, before their three years are out; which are not yet begun, nor God knows when they will, this being like to be no session of Parliament when they now rise.[1] So home, and there took up Mrs. Turner and carried her to Mile-end and drank; and so back, talking, and so home and to bed, I being mighty cold, this being a mighty cold day and I had left off my waistcoat three or four days. This evening, coming home in the dusk, I saw and spoke to our Nell, Pain's daughter, and had I not been very cold, I should have taken her to Tower-hill para talk together et tocar her.[2]

Thus ends this month; my wife in the country. Myself full of pleasure and expense; and some trouble for my friends, my Lord Sandwich by the Parliament, and more for my eyes, which are daily worse and worse, that I dare not write or read almost anything. The Parliament going in a few days to rise. Myself, so long without accounting now, for seven or eight months I think or more, that I know not what condition almost I am in as to getting or spending for all that time – which troubles me, but I will soon do it. The kingdom in an ill state through poverty. A fleet going out, and no money to maintain it or set it out. Seamen yet unpaid, and mutinous when pressed to go out again. Our office able to do little, nobody trusting us nor we desiring any to trust us, and yet have not money to [?do] anything but only what perticularly belongs to this fleet going out, and that but lamely too. The Parliament several months upon an act for 300000*l*, but cannot or will not agree upon it – but do keep it back, in spite of the King's desires to hasten it, till they can obtain what they have a mind, in revenge upon some men for the late ill managements; and he is forced to submit to what they please, knowing that without it he shall have no money; and they as well, that if they give the money, the King will suffer them to do little more. And then the business of religion doth disquiet everybody, the Parliament being vehement against the

1. The Commissioners' terms ran for three years from the end of the present parliamentary session. If parliament were now to be adjourned, instead of prorogued (ending the session), their term would be so much the longer. In fact the session was adjourned soon, on 9 May.
2. "to talk together and touch her." Nell Payne was Pepys's former servant and the daughter of his waterman.

nonconformists, while the King seems to be willing to countenance them: so we are all poor and in pieces, God help us; while the peace is like to go on between Spain and France, and then the French may be apprehended able to attack us. So God help us.[1]

MAY.

7. Up, and to the office, where all the morning. At noon home to dinner, and thither I sent for Mercer to dine with me; and after dinner, she and I called Mrs. Turner and I carried them to the Duke of York's House and there saw *The Man's the Maister*, which proves, upon my seeing it again, a very good play.[2] Thence called Knepp from the King's House; where going in for her, the play being done, I did see Becke Marshall come dressed off of the stage, and looks mighty fine and pretty, and noble – and also Nell in her boy's clothes, mighty pretty; but Lord, their confidence, and how many men do hover about them as soon as they come off the stage, and how confident they [are] in their talk. Here I did kiss the pretty woman newly come, called Pegg, that was Sir Ch. Sidly's mistress – a mighty pretty woman, and seems, but is not, modest.[3] Here took up Knepp into our coach and all of us with her to her lodging, and thither comes Bannester with a song of hers that he hath set in Sir Ch. Sidly's play for her, which is I think but very meanly set; but this he did before us teach her; and it being but a slight, silly, short ayre, she learnt it presently.[4] But I did here get him to prick me down the notes of the Echo in *The Tempest*, which pleases me mightily.[5] And here was also Haynes, the incomparable dancer of the King's house, and a seeming civil man and sings pretty well.[6] And they gone, we abroad to Marrowbone and there walked in the garden,[7] the first time I ever there, and a pretty place it is; and here we eat and drank and stayed till 9 at night; and so home by moonshine, I all the way having mi mano abaxo la jupe de

1. End of the fifth manuscript volume.
2. A comedy by William Davenant, first performed in this year. Pepys had been underwhelmed on seeing it a few months earlier.
3. Probably Margaret Hughes, who had a successful stage career and became Prince Rupert's partner.
4. John Banister's music was for Sedley's *The Mulberry Garden*, first performed the following day.
5. Ferdinand's song in Act 3 of Dryden and Davenant's adaptation of Shakespeare's play.
6. Joseph Haynes, an actor and later Knepp's partner.
7. Marylebone Gardens.

Knepp con much placer and freedom; but endeavouring afterward to tocar her con mi cosa, ella did strive against that,[1] but yet I do not think that she did find much fault with it, but I was a little moved at my offering it and not having it. And so set Mrs. Knepp at her lodging, and so the rest and I home, talking with a great deal of pleasure, and so home to bed.

11. Up, and to my office, where alone all the morning. About noon comes to me my cousin Sarah and my aunt Licett, newly come out of Gloucestershire, good woman, and come to see me;[2] I took them home and made them drink, but they would not stay dinner, I being alone. But here they tell me that they hear that this day Kate Joyce was to be married to a man called Hollinshed, whom she endeed did once tell me of and desired me to enquire after him. But whatever she said of his being rich, I do fear, by her doing this without my advice, it is not as it ought to be; but as she brews, let her bake.[3] They being gone, I to dinner with Balty and his wife, who is come to town today from Deptford to see us. And after dinner, I out and took a coach and called Mercer, and she and I to the Duke of York's playhouse and there saw *The Tempest*; and between two acts, I went out to Mr. Harris and got him to repeat to me the words of the Echo,[4] while I writ them down, having tried in the play to have wrote them; but when I had done it, having done it without looking upon my paper, I find I could not read the blacklead – but now I have got the words clear; and in going in thither, had the pleasure to see the Actors in their several dresses, especially the seamen and monster,[5] which were very droll. So into the play again. But there happened one thing which vexed me; which is, that the orange-woman did come in the pit and challenge me for twelve oranges which she delivered by my order at a late play at night, to give to some ladies in a box, which was wholly untrue, but yet she swore it to be true; but however, I did deny it and did not pay her, but for quiet did buy 4*s* worth of oranges of her – at 6*d* a piece. ⟨Here I saw first my Lord Ormond since his coming from Ireland, which is now about eight days.⟩

1. "having my hand underneath Knepp's skirt with much pleasure and freedom; but endeavouring afterward to touch her with my thing, she did strive against that".
2. Sarah Giles and Lettice Howlett (relatives of Pepys's mother).
3. Kate Joyce, widowed in January, married Edward Hollinshead, a tobacconist of Cripplegate, on this day. As a young woman in the innkeeping business with three children to support, she had incentives to marry quickly.
4. Henry Harris, as Ferdinand, sang the song.
5. Probably Caliban.

After the play done, I took Mercer by water to Spring-garden and there with great pleasure walked and eat and drank and sang, making people come about us to hear us, and two little children ⟨of one of⟩ our neighbours that happened to be there did come into our Arbour and we made them dance prettily.

So by water, with great pleasure down to the Bridge, and there landed and took water again on the other side; and so to the Tower, and I saw her home, and myself home to my chamber and by and by to bed.

29. Betimes up, and up to my Tanger accounts; and then by water to the Council-chamber and there received some directions from the Duke of York and the Committee of the Navy there,[1] about casting up the charge of the present summer's fleet, that so they may come within the bounds of the sum given by the Parliament.[2] But it is pretty to see how Prince Rupert and other mad silly people are for setting out but a little fleet, there being no occasion for it; and say it will be best to save the money for better uses; but Sir W. Coventry did declare that in wisdom it was better to do so, but that in obedience to the Parliament he was setting out the 50 sail talked on, though it spend all the money and to little purpose; and that this was better then to leave it to the Parliament to make bad constructions of their thrift, if any trouble should happen. Thus wary the world is grown.

Thence back again presently home, and did business till noon; and then to Sir G Carteret's to dinner, with much good company, it being the King's birth-day and many healths drunk; and here I did receive another letter from my Lord Sandwich; which troubles me, to see how I have neglected him, in not writing, or but once, all this time of his being abroad.[3] And I see he takes notice, but yet gently, of it, that it puts me to great trouble and I know not how to get out of it, having no good excuse, and too late now to mend, he being coming home. Thence home, whither by agreement by and by comes Mercer and Gayett,[4] and two gentlemen with them, Mr. Montouth and Pelham, the former a swaggering young handsome gentleman – the latter a sober citizen merchant; both sing, but the latter with great skill; the other, no skill but a good voice and a good basse – but used to sing only tavern tunes;

1. At the start of 1668 the King had instituted a standing committee to advise the Privy Council on naval matters.
2. In March, parliament had voted to supply the King with £300,000.
3. Sandwich had been away on embassy to Spain since March 1666.
4. Mary Mercer and her friend Susan Guyat.

and so I spent all this evening till 11 at night singing with them, till I tired of them because of the swaggering fellow with the basse, though the girl Mercer did mightily commend him before to me. This night yo had agreed para andar at Deptford, there para haber lain con the moher de Bagwell,[1] but this company did hinder me.

30. Up, and put on a new summer black bombazin[2] suit, and so to the office; and being come now to an agreement with my barber to keep my perriwigs in good order at 20*s* a year, I am like to go very spruce, more then I used to do. All the morning at the office; and at noon home to dinner, and so to the King's playhouse and there saw *Philaster*;[3] where it is pretty to see how I could remember almost all along, ever since I was a boy, Arethusa's part which I was to have acted at Sir Rob. Cooke's and it was very pleasant to me, but more to think what a ridiculous thing it would have been for me to have acted a beautiful woman.[4] Thence to Mrs. Pierces, and there saw Knepp also, and were merry; and here saw my little Lady Kath. Mountagu, come to town about her eyes, which are sore, and they think the King's Evil,[5] poor pretty lady. Here I was freed from a fear that Knepp was angry or might take advantage; did parlar the esto that yo did the otra day quand yo was con her in ponendo her mano upon mi cosa[6] – but I saw no such thing; but as pleased as ever, and I believe she can bear with any such thing.

Thence to the New Exchange, and there met Harris and Rolt and one Richards, a tailor and great company-keeper; and with these over to Fox-hall and there fell into the company of Harry Killigrew, a rogue, newly come back out of France but still in

1. "I had agreed to walk at Deptford, there to have lain with Bagwell's wife". However, the intended sense is probably "to go to Deptford", given Pepys's Deptford travel habits and the ways he uses "andar" elsewhere the diary. The English "at", although clear in the shorthand, would in this interpretation stem from Pepys thinking of "a" (the Spanish/French for "to"), which in other polyglot passages follows "andar".
2. Bombasine: fabric with a twilled or corded mix of silk and wool.
3. A tragicomedy by Beaumont and Fletcher, first acted c.1609.
4. Arethusa is a virtuous princess who defies her father to marry the hero Philaster. Sir Robert Coke lived at Durdans, near Epsom in Surrey. As a child Pepys had stayed nearby with John Pepys of Ashtead.
5. Sandwich's daughter, aged 6, was thought to have scrofula.
6. Pepys's own expression here is confused and there is more than one possible reading of certain shorthand symbols. Literally, "did speak the this that I did other day when I was with her in putting her hand upon my thing". Possibly intended is "did speak of that that I did the other day…". The reference is to his actions on 7 May 1668.

disgrace at our Court,[1] and young Newport and others, as very rogues as any in the town, who were ready to take hold of every woman that came by them. And so to supper in an arbor; but Lord, their mad bawdy talk did make my heart ake. And here I first understood by their talk the meaning of the company that lately were called "Ballers", Harris telling how it was by a meeting of some young blades, where he was among them, and my Lady Bennet[2] and her ladies, and there dancing naked, and all the roguish things in the world. But Lord, what loose cursed company was this that I was in tonight; though full of wit and worth a man's being in for once, to know the nature of it and their manner of talk and lives. Thence set Rolt and some of [them] at the New Exchange, and so I home; and my business being done at the office, I to bed.

JUNE.

4. Up, and to the office, where all the morning. And at noon home to dinner, where Mr. Clerke the solicitor dined with me and my clerks. After dinner I carried and set him down at the Temple, he observing to me how St. Sepulchers church steeple is repaired already a good deal, and the Fleet-bridge is contracted for by the City to begin to be built this summer; which doth please me mightily. I to White-hall and walked through the park for a little ayre; and so back to the Council-chamber to the Committee of the Navy, about the business of fitting the present fleet suitable to the money given; which as the King orders it and by what appears, will be very little, and so as I perceive the Duke of York will have nothing to command, nor can intend to go abroad. But it is pretty to see how careful these great men are to do everything so as they may answer it to the Parliament – thinking themselfs safe in nothing but where the judges (with whom they often advise) do say the matter is doubtful; and so they take upon themselfs then to be the chief persons to interpret what is doubtful. Thence home; and all the evening to set matters in order against my going to Brampton tomorrow, being resolved upon my journey, and having the Duke of York's leave again today – though I do plainly see that I can very ill be spared now – there being much business, especially about this

1. The son of Thomas Killigrew the dramatist, he had been banished from court in 1666 for spreading sexual slanders about Lady Castlemaine.
2. A well-known bawd.

which I have attended the Council about, and I the man that am alone consulted with; and besides, my Lord Brouncker is at this time ill, and Sir W. Penn. So things being put in order at the office, I home to do the like there, and to bed.

[Pepys left blank pages on which to write the entries for 5–17 June that described his journey to Brampton and the West Country. The entries were never inserted; instead, the rough notes from which they were to be written were bound into the volume. These include notes of his expenditure meant for his account-books and not his diary. Extracts from the notes are reproduced here as exactly as possible, with italics used for those words and abbreviations that were written in longhand.

After visiting Brampton, Pepys, his wife, and their party travel to Oxford.]

Tuesdy 9th.	Paid our *Guide* ⟨when came to *Oxf.*^{d} *a very sweet place*⟩ .	01 – 2 – 6
	barber	0 – 2 – 6
	book *Stonheng*[1]	00 – 4 – 0
	~~boy that showed me the college before dinner~~	0 – 1 – 0
	To dinner and then out with wife and people and landlord and to him that showed us the schools and library	0 – 10 – 0
	To him that showed us All Souls College and *Chichly's* pictures[2]	0 – 5 – 0
	So to see Christ Church with my wife I seeing several others very fine alone with *WH*[3] before dinner and did give the boy that went with me ⟨before dinner⟩	– 0 – 1 – 0
	~~After dinner with my wife and landlord to the schools~~	
	Strawberries	0 – 1 – 2
	Dinner ⟨and servants⟩	1 – 0 – 6
	After came home from the schools I out with landlord to Brazen Nose College to the butteries and in the cellar find the hand of the child of *Hales*.[4] Butler	0 – 2 – 0
	Thence with coach and people to Physic Garden[5]	0 – 1 – 0
	So to Friar *Bacons* study[6] I up and saw it and give the man	0 – 1 – 0
	Bottle of sack for landlord	0 – 2 – 0

1. Probably Inigo Jones's *The Most Notable Antiquity of Great Britain, Vulgarly Call'd Stone-Heng* (1655), of which there is a copy in the Pepys Library. It argued the henge was a Roman temple.
2. Henry Chichele (d. 1443) was founder of the college.
3. Will Hewer.
4. The mark left by John Middleton (d. 1623) of Hale, Lancashire. He was a giant wrestler who, in about 1617, had visited Brasenose. An outline of his hand was painted on a doorpost in the cellar.
5. A garden for the study of medicinal herbs.
6. A tower on Folly Bridge, which Roger Bacon (the thirteenth-century philosopher) was supposed to have used as an observatory.

Oxford mighty fine place and well seated and cheap entertainment.

At night came to *Abington* where had been a fair of custard[1] and met many people and scholars going home and there did get some pretty good music and sang and danced till supper.. 0-5-0

[They arrive at Salisbury]

Thursday 11th. And up and *WH* and I up and down the town and find it a very brave place with river go through every street and a most capacious market place. The city great I think greater then Oxford. But the minster most admirable as ~~m~~ big I think and handsomer then *Westm*r. And a most large close about it and houses for the officers thereof and a fine palace for the *Bp.* So to my lodging back and took out my wife and people to show them the town and church but they at prayers could not be shown the *Quire.* A very good *Organ* and I looked in and saw the *Bp.* my friend *D*r *Ward.*[2] Thence to the *Inne* and there not being able to hire coachhorses and not willing to use our own we got saddle horses very dear. Boy that ~~fetched~~ went to look for them 0-0-6

So the three women behind *WH. Murf.*d[3] and our guide, and I single, to *Stonehege* over the plain and some ~~prodigious~~ ⟨great⟩ hills even to fright us. Came thither and ~~them~~ find them as prodigious as any tales I ever heard of them and worth going this journey to see. God knows what their use was. They are hard to tell but yet may be told.[4] Give the shepherd woman for leading our horses. 0-0-4◆

Thence about 6 a'clock and with a guide went over the ⟨smooth⟩ plain endeed till night and then by a happy mistake and that looked like an adventure we were carried out of our way ~~and with~~ to a town[5] where we would lie since we could ~~not~~ not go as far as we would and there with ~~miser~~ great difficulty came about 10 at night to a little inn where ~~f~~ we were fain to go into a room where a pedlar was in bed and made him rise and there wife and I lay and in a truckle bed Betty Turner[6] and Willet but good beds and the master of the house a sober understanding man and I had pl[easant?] discourse with him about ⟨this⟩ country matters as *Wool* and *Corne* and other things and he also merry and made us mighty merry at supper about manning the new ship at Bristol[7] with ~~men~~ none but men whose wifes do master them. And it seems it is become in reproach to some men of estate that are such hereabouts that this is become common talk. By and by to bed glad of this mistake because it seems had we gone on as we pretended we could not have passed with

1. An eight-day fair, at which custard was the specialist dish.
2. Seth Ward, Bishop of Salisbury was, like Pepys, a Fellow of the Royal Society.
3. Will Murford, the Navy Office messenger, was one of Pepys's party.
4. Folklore said that the stones were impossible to count, perhaps due to magic.
5. Chitterne, Wiltshire
6. Daughter of Thomas Turner, clerk in the Navy Office.
7. The *Edgar*, a warship currently being built there.

our coach and must have lain on the plain all night. ⟨This day from *Salsb.* I wrote by the post my excuse for not coming home which I hope will do for I am resolved to see the *Bath*[1] and it may be Bristol.⟩

[At Bath]

Sat— 13. Up at 4 a'clock being by appointment called up to the ⟨Cross⟩ *Bath*[2] where we were carried after one another myself and wife and Betty Turner *Willet* and *WH*. And by and by though we designed to have done before company came much company came very fine ladies and the manner pretty enough only methinks it cannot be clean to go so many bodies together in to the same water. Good conversation ~~a~~ among them that are acquainted here and stay together. Strange to see how hot the water is and in some places though this is the most temperate bath the springs so hot as the feet not to endure. But strange to see what women and men herein that live all the season in these waters that cannot but be parboiled and look like the creatures of the Bath. Carried back wrap in a sheet and in a chair[3] home and there one after another thus carried (I staying above two hours in the water) home to bed sweating for an hour and by and by comes music to play to me extraordinary good as ~~ever I I~~ ever I heard at Landon almost anywhere.................................. 0 – 5 – 0
Up to go to *Bristoll* about 11 a'clock and paying my landlord that was our guide from *Chiltren*[4]................. 0 – 10 – 0
~~Set out to Bristow~~ and the *Serjt* of the Bath .... 0 – 10 – 0
and the man that carried us in chairs .... 0 – 3 – 6
Set out toward Bristow and came thither the way bad (in coach ~~e~~ hired to spare our own horses) but country good about two a'clock where set down at the Horse Shoe and there being trimmed ⟨by a very handsome fellow⟩...... 0 – 2 – 0
walked with my wife and people through the city which is in every respect another London that one can hardly know it to stand in the country no more then that. No carts it standing generally on *vaults* only dog carts.[5] So ~~to~~ to the Three Cranes tavern I was directed but when I came in the master told me that he had newly given over selling of wine it seems grown rich and so went to the *Sun* and there *Deb* going with *WH* and Betty Turner to see her uncle[6] and leaving my wife with mistress of the house I to see the key which is a most large and noble place and to see the new ship building by Bailey neither he nor *Furzer* being in town.[7] It will be a fine ship. Spoke

1. "The Bath", not "Bath", was the common seventeenth-century form of the name.
2. A bath so-called from the cross in the middle. Gentleman sat in the seats around the cross and ladies at the side under the arches.
3. A sedan chair.
4. Chitterne.
5. Sleds drawn by dogs. The vaults were mostly wine-cellars.
6. Deb Willet's uncle, William Butts, a city broker.
7. Francis Bailey was building the *Edgar* for the navy. Daniel Furzer was also a shipbuilder.

with the foreman and did give the boys that kept the cabin .... 0 – 2 – 0

Walked back to the *Sun* where I ~~will~~ find *Deb* come back and with her her uncle a sober merchant very good company and ~~is~~ so like one of our sober wealthy London merchants as pleased me mightily. Here we dined and much good talk with him................................ 0 – 7 – 6

⟨A messenger to S^r. *Jo. Knight*[1] who was not at home⟩ .. 0 – 0 – 6

Then walked with him and my wife and company ~~to~~ ⟨round⟩ the key and to the ship and he showed me the Custom House and made me understand many things of the place and led us through *Marsh* street where our girl was born but Lord the joy that was among the ⟨old⟩ poor people of the place to see Mrs. *Willets* daughter it seems her mother being a brave woman and mightily beloved. And so brought us a back way by surprize to his house where a substantial good house and well furnished and did give us good entertainment of strawberries a ⟨whole⟩ venison pasty cold and plenty of brave wine and above all *Bristoll* milk.[2] Where comes in another poor woman who hearing that *Deb* was here did come running hither and with her *eyes* so full of tears and heart so full of joy that she could not speak when she came in that it made me weep too I protest that I was not able to speak to her (which I would have done) to have diverted her tears. His wife a good woman and so sober and substantial as I was never more pleased anywhere.

Servant maid .... 0 – 2 – 0

So thence took leave and he with us through the city where in walking I find the city pay him great respect and he the like to the meanest which pleased me mightily. He showed us the place where the merchants meet here and a fine cross yet standing like Cheapside. And so to the Horse Shoe where paying the reckoning................ 0 – 2 – 6

We back and by moonshine to the *Bath* again about 10 a'clock bad way and giving the coachman................ 0 – 1 – 0

went all of us to bed.

[They travel back to London, spending a final night at Reading]

Wedn. 17th. Rose and paying the reckoning.......................... 0 – 12 – 6

Servants ⟨and poor⟩.................................. 0 – 2 – 6

Music the worst we have had came to our chamber door but calling us by wrong names we gave him nothing

June. So set out with one coach in company and through *Mydenhead* which I never saw before to *Colebrooke*[3] by noon the way mighty good. And there dined and fitted ourselfs a little to go through London anon. Somewhat out of humour all day reflecting on my wife's neglect of things and impertinent humour got by this liberty of being from me which she is never to be trusted with for she is a fool.

Thence pleasant way to London before night ⟨and find

1. Navy agent at Bristol.
2. A sweet sherry.
3. Colnbrook, a coach stage between Maidenhead and London.

> all very well to great content⟩ and there to walk with my wife. And saw ~~Mr.~~ *Sr. W P* who is well again. ~~I hear~~ Hear of the ill news by the great fire at *Berbedos.*[1]
> By and by home and there with my people to supper all in pretty good humour though I find my wife hath something in her gizzard that which waits an opportunity of being provoked to bring up. But I will not for my content sake give it. So I to bed glad to find ⟨all⟩ so well here. And slept well.

18.[2] Up betimes and to the office, there to set my papers in order and books, my office having been new-whited and windows made clean. And so to sit, where all the morning; and did receive a hint or two from my Lord Anglesy,[3] as if he thought much of my taking the ayre as I have done – but I care not a turd. But whatever the matter is, I think he hath some ill-will to me, or at least ⟨an⟩ opinion that I am more the servant of the Board then I am. At noon home to dinner, where my wife still in a melancholy fusty humour, and crying; and doth not tell me plainly what it is, but I by little words find that she hath heard of my going to plays and carrying people abroad every day in her absence; and that I cannot help, but the storm will break out, I know, in a little time. After dinner, carried her by coach to St. James's, where she sat in the coach till I to my Lady Peterborough;[4] who tells me, among other things, her Lord's good words to the Duke of York lately about my Lord Sandwich, and that the Duke of York is kind to my Lord Sandwich – which I am glad to hear. My business here was about her Lord's pension from Tanger.◆ So, my wife not speaking a word going nor coming, nor willing to go to a play, though a new one, I to the office and did much business. At night home, where supped Mr. Turner and his wife, and Betty and Mercer and Pelling, as merry as the ill melancholy humour that my wife was in would let us; which vexed me, but I took no notice of it, thinking that will be the best way, and let it wear away itself.

After supper, parted and to bed; and my wife troubled all night, and about one a-clock goes out of the bed to the girl's bed; which did trouble me, she crying and sobbing, without telling the cause. By and by comes back to me, and still crying; I then rose and would

1. At St Michael's (now Bridgetown) on 18 April; most of the town was destroyed.
2. Roughly from this point onwards to the end of the diary, the effects of Pepys's eyestrain are visible in the manuscript. The symbols and lines are more widely spaced and the handwriting is larger: this becomes more marked after early February 1669.
3. Treasurer of the Navy.
4. Wife of the former governor of Tangier.

have sat up all night, but she would have me come to bed again. And being pretty well pacified, we to sleep; when between 2 and 3 in the morning, we were waked with my crying out, "Fire!
⟨⟨19⟩⟩ Fire! in Marke lane!" so I rose and looked out, and it was dreadful; and strange apprehensions in me, and us all, of being presently burnt: so we all rose, and my care presently was to secure my gold and plate and papers, and could quickly have done it, but I went forth to see where it was, and the whole town was presently in the streets; and I found it in a new-built house that stood alone in Minchin-lane, over against the Clothworkers-hall – which burned furiously, the house not yet quite finished. And the benefit of brick was well seen, for it burnt all inward and fell down within itself – so no fear of doing more hurt; so homeward and stopped at Mr. Mills, where he and she at the door, and Mrs. Turner and Betty and Mrs. Hollworthy; and there I stayed and talked, and up to the church leads and saw the fire, which spent and spent itself, till all fear over; I home, and there we to bed again and slept pretty well. And about 9 rose; and then my wife fell into her blubbering again and at length had ⟨a⟩ request to make to me, which was that she might go into France and live there out of trouble: and then all came out, that I loved pleasure and denied her any, and a deal of do; and I find that there have been great fallings-out between my father and her, whom for ever hereafter I must keep asunder, for they cannot possibly agree. And I said nothing; but with very mild words and few suffered her humour to spend, till we begin to be very quiet and I think all will be over, and friends; and so I to the office, where all the morning doing business. Yesterday I heard how my Lord Ashly is like to die, having some imposthume in his breast, that he hath been fain to be cut into the body.[1]◆

30. Up and at the office all the morning. Then home to dinner, where a stinking leg of mutton – the weather being very wet and hot to keep meat in. Then to the office again all the afternoon; we met about the Victualler's new contract. And so up, and to walk all the evening with my wife and Mrs. Turner in the garden till supper, about 11 at night; and so after supper parted and to bed – my eyes bad but not worse; only, weary with working. But however, I very melancholy under the fear of my eyes being spoilt and not to be recovered; for I am come that I am not able to read out a small letter,

1. Ashley, the Chancellor of the Exchequer, had been operated on for a ruptured liver cyst. For the rest of his life he wore a pipe to drain the wound.

and yet my sight good, for the little while I can read, as ever they were I think.

JULY.

1. Up, and all the morning we met at the office about the Victualler's contract. At noon home to dinner; Cosen Roger, come newly to town, dined with us, and mighty importunate for our coming down to Impington – which I think to do this Sturbridge-Fair.[1] Thence I set him down at the Temple; and Commissioner Middleton dining the first time with me, he and I on to White-hall and so to St. James's, where we met and much business with the Duke of York; and I find the Duke of York very hot for regulations in the Navy, and I believe is put on it by W. Coventry and I am glad of it; and perticularly, he falls heavy on Chatham-yard and is vexed that Lord Anglesy did the other day complain at the Council-table of disorders in the Navy, and not to him.[2] So I to White-hall to Committee of Tanger; and there vexed with the importunity and clamours of Alderman Backewell for my acquittance for money by him supplied the garrison, before I have any order for paying it. So home, calling at several places; among others, the Change, and on Cooper to know when my wife shall come and sit for her picture – which will be next week;[3] and so home and to walk with my wife; and then to supper and to bed.

3.◆ I to Eagle Court in the Strand and there to a ale-house; met Mr. Pierce the surgeon and Dr. Clerke, Waldron, Turberville my physician for the eyes, and Lowre,[4] to dissect several Eyes of sheep and oxen, with great pleasure – and to my great information; but strange that this Turberville should be so great a man, and yet to this day had seen no eyes dissected, or but once, but desired this Dr. Lowre to give him the opportunity to see him dissect some. Thence to Unthankes to my wife and carried her home, and there walked in the garden; and so to supper and to bed.

1. The Cambridge fair held annually from 24 August to 29 September.
2. The Master-Attendants at Chatham dockyard were accused of malpractices. Over the coming months, Pepys would be busy fuelling the Duke's zeal for reform of the Navy Office.
3. Elizabeth sat for a miniature by Samuel Cooper over the next few weeks. This is now lost.
4. All were physicians. Richard Lower was particularly distinguished, being an expert in dissection and a pioneer of blood transfusion.

18. At the office all the morning. At noon dined at home, and Creed with me, who I do really begin to hate, and do use him with some reservedness. Here was also my old acquaintance Will Swan to see me, who continues a factious fanatic still; and I do use him civilly, in expectation that those fellows may grow great again. Thence to the office, and then with my wife to the Change and Unthankes, after having been at Coopers and sat there for her picture; which will be a noble picture, but yet I think not so like as Hales's is.[1] So home and to my office, and then to walk in the garden, and home to supper and to bed. They say the King of France is making a war again in Flanders with the King of Spain, the King of Spain refusing to give him all that he says was promised him in the treaty.[2] Creed told me this day how when the King was at my Lord Cornwallis, when he went last to Newmarket, that being there on a Sunday, the Duke of Buckingham did in the afternoon, to please the King, make a bawdy sermon to him out of the Canticles. And that my Lord Cornwallis did endeavour to get the King a whore, and that must be a pretty girl, the daughter of the parson of the place; but that she did get away, and leaped off of some place and killed herself – which if true, is very sad.

23. Up, and all day long but at dinner at the office, at work till I was almost blind, which makes my heart sad.

24. Up, and by water to St. James (having by the way shown Symson[3] Sir W. Coventry's chimny-pieces, in order to the making me one); and there, after the Duke of York was ready, he called me to his closet, and there I did long and largely show him the weakness of our office, and did give him advice to call us to account for our duties; which he did take mighty well, and desired me to draw up what I would have him write to the office. I did lay open the whole failings of the office, and how it was his duty to find them and to find fault with them, as Admiral, especially at this time – which he agreed to – and seemed much to rely on what I said.[4] Thence to White-hall and there waited to attend the Council, but was not called in; and so home, and after dinner back with Sir J. Mennes by coach, and there attended, all of us, the Duke of York, and had the hearing of Mr. Pelt's business, the maister-shipwright at

1. John Hayls had painted Elizabeth in February 1666.
2. This rumour was false.
3. A master-joiner for the navy who had made Pepys's bookcases.
4. This prompted Pepys to begin the "great letter" on failures of the Navy Office, drawn up over the next month.

Chatham; and I believe he will be put out. But here Commissioner Middleton did, among others, show his good-nature and easiness to the Maisters-Attendants by mitigating their faults, so as I believe they will come in again. So home and to supper and to bed, the Duke of York staying with us till almost night.

29. Busy all the morning at the office. So home to dinner, where Mercer; and there comes Mr. Swan, my old acquaintance, and dines with me, and tells me for a certainty that Creed is to marry Betty Pickering and that the thing is concluded; which I wonder at – and am vexed for.[1] So he gone, I with my wife and two girls to the King's House and saw *The Mad Couple*,[2] a mean play altogether; and thence to Hyde-park, where but few coaches; and so to the New Exchange and thence by water home with much pleasure; and then to sing in the garden, and so home to bed, my eyes for these four days being my trouble, and my heart thereby mighty sad.

AUGUST.

11. Up, and by water to Sir W. Coventry to visit him, whom I find yet troubled at the Commissioners of Accounts about this business of Sir W. Warren; which is a ridiculous thing – and can come to nothing but contempt.[3] And thence to Westminster-hall, where the Parliament met enough to adjourne, which they did, to the 10th of November next; and so I by water home to the office, and so to dinner; and thence at the office all the afternoon till night, being mightily pleased with a little trial I have made of the use of a Tube=spectacall of paper, tried with my right eye.[4] This day, I hear that to the great joy of the nonconformists, the time is out of the Act against them, so that they may meet;[5] and they have declared that they will have a morning lecture up again, which is pretty

1. Elizabeth Pickering was Sandwich's niece. Pepys was jealous of Creed's success, since Creed had (like him) been Sandwich's secretary.
2. *All Mistaken, or The Mad Couple*, a comedy by James Howard, probably first performed in 1665.
3. The Commissioners criticized a large navy contract made with Warren for masts in 1664. Pepys had been largely responsible for composing it.
4. He was experimenting with using a tube of black paper to help read. This followed advice in a letter that had appeared in the Royal Society's *Philosophical Transactions* of 13 July 1668.
5. The Conventicle Act of 1664 was due to expire at the end of this parliamentary session. The King did not in fact end the session until 1 March 1669, but no further meetings of parliament were held. Nonconformists now met fairly freely until the summer of 1669.

strange; and they are connived at by the King everywhere I hear, in city and country. So to visit W Penn, who is yet ill; and then home, where W Batelier and Mrs. Turner came and sat and supped with us; and so they gone, we to bed.

This afternoon, my wife and Mercer and Deb went with Pelling to see the Gipsys at Lambeth and have their fortunes told; but what they did, I did not enquire.

16. *Lords day.* All the morning at my office with W. Hewer, there drawing up my report to the Duke of York, as I have promised, about the faults of this office, hoping therein to have opportunity of doing myself [some good]. At noon to dinner; and again with him, to work all the afternoon till night, till I was weary and had despatched a good deal of business. And so to bed, after hearing my wife read a little.

18. Up, and to my office about my great business betimes. And so to the office, where all the morning. At noon dined; and then to the office all the afternoon also; and in the evening to Sir W. Coventry's; but he not within, I took coach alone to the park to try to meet him there, but did not; but there was few coaches, but among the few, there was in two coaches our two great beauties, my Lady Castlemaine and Richmond; the first time I saw the latter since she had the smallpox. I had much pleasure to see them, but I thought they were strange one to another. Thence going out, I met a coach going which I thought had Knipp in it; so I went back, but it was not she. So back to White-hall and there took water, and so home and busy late about my great letter to the Duke of York. And so to supper and to bed. This night yo did hazer Deb tocar mi thing with her hand after yo was in lecto[1] – with great pleasure.

19. Up betimes; and all day and afternoon, without going out, busy upon my great letter to the Duke of York, which goes on to my content. W Hewer and Gibson I imploy with me in it. This week my people wash over the water, and so I little company at home. In the evening, being busy above, a great cry I hear, and go down; and what should it be but Jane, in a fit of direct raveing which lasted half-an-hour; beyond four or five of our strength to keep her down. And when all came to all, a fit of jealousy about Tom, with whom she is in love. So at night, I and my wife and W Hewer called them to us, and there I did examine all the thing, and them in league. She in love, and he hath got her to promise him to marry, and he

1. "I did make Deb touch my thing with her hand after I was in bed".

is now cold in it – so that I must rid my hands of them. Which troubles me, and the more because my head is now busy upon other greater things. I am vexed also to be told by W Hewer that he is summoned to Commissioners of Accounts about receiving a present of 30*l* from Mr. Mason the timber merchant – though there be no harm in it that will appear on his part – he having done them several lawful kindnesses and never demanded anything, as they themselfs have this day declared to the Commissioners, they being forced up by the discovery of somebody that they in confidence had once told it to. So to supper, vexed and my head full of care; and so to bed.

22. Up betimes, at it again with great content, and so to office I, where all the morning; and did fall out with W. Penn about his slight performance of his office; and so home to dinner, fully satisfied that this office must sink or the whole service be undone. To the office all the afternoon again; and then home to supper and to bed, my mind being pretty well at ease, my great letter being now finished to my full content; and I thank God I have opportunity of doing it, though I know it will set the office and me by the ears for ever.

This morning Captain Cocke comes and tells me that he is now assured that it is true what he told me the other day, that our whole office will be turned out, only me; which, whether he says true or no, I know not nor am much concerned, though I should be better contented to have it thus then otherwise.

This afternoon, after I was weary in my business of the office, I went forth to the Change, thinking to have spoke with Captain Cocke, but he was not within. So I home, and took London-bridge in my way, walking down Fish-street and Gracious-street to see how very fine a descent they have now made down the hill, that it is become very easy and pleasant.[1] And going through Leaden-hall, it being market-day, I did see a woman ketched that had stolen a shoulder of mutton off of a butcher's stall, and carrying it wrapped up in a cloth in a basket. The jade was surprized, and did not deny it; and the woman so silly that took it as to let her go, only taking the meat.

23. *Lords day.* Up betimes, my head busy on my great letter, and I did first hang up my new map of Paris in my green room – and changed others in other places. Then to Captain Cocke's, thinking

1. Changes after the Great Fire had reduced the gradient.

to have talked more of what he told me yesterday, but he was not within; so back to church and heard a good sermon of Mr. Gifford's at our church, upon "Seek ye first the Kingdom of Heaven and its righteousness, and all these things shall be added to you."[1] A very excellent and persuasive, good and moral sermon; showed like a wise man that righteousness is a surer moral way of being rich then sin and villainy. Then home to dinner, where Mr. Pelling, who brought us a hare, which we had at dinner, and W How. After dinner to the office, Mr. Gibson and I, to examine my letter to the Duke of York; which to my great joy, I did very well by my paper tube, without pain to my eyes. And I do mightily like what I have therein done; [and] did, according to the Duke of York's order, make haste to St. James'; and about 4 a-clock got thither, and there the Duke of York was ready to expect me, and did hear it all over with extraordinary content and did give me many and hearty thanks, and in words the most expressive tell me his sense of my good endeavours, and that he would have a care of me on all occasions, and did with much inwardness tell me what was doing, suitable almost to what Captain Cocke tells me, of design to make alterations in the Navy; and is most open to me in them, and with utmost confidence desires my further advice on all occasions. And he resolves to have my letter transcribed and sent forthwith to the office.[2] So, with as much satisfaction as I could possibly or did hope for, and obligation on the Duke of York's side professed to me, I away into the park, and there met Mr. Pierce and his wife and sister and brother and little boy, and with them to Mullbery-garden and spent 18*s* on them; and there left them, she being again with child, and by it, the least pretty that ever I saw her; and so I away and got a coach and home; and there with wife and W Hewers talking all the evening, my mind running on the business of the office, to see what more I can do to the rendering myself acceptable and useful to all and to the King: we to supper and to bed.

29. Up, and all the morning at the office ⟨⟨where the Duke of York's long letter was read, to their great trouble and their suspecting me

1. A close recollection of Matthew 6.33. George Gifford was Professor of Divinity at Gresham College.
2. Pepys's letter to the Duke on reform of the Navy Office was to be sent as a letter from the Duke to the Navy Board (with Pepys's involvement concealed). The letter criticized the Treasurer, Comptroller, and Surveyor for failing to implement the Duke's formal instructions to the Board of 1662. "The Duke" levelled no criticisms at Pepys as Clerk of the Acts – which must have made it easier to discern the letter's origins.

to have been the writer of it⟩⟩; and at noon comes, by appointment, Harris to dine with me; and after dinner, he and I to Chyrurgeon's-hall, where they are building it new, very fine, and there to see their Theatre, which stood all the fire, and (which was our business) their great picture of Holben's,[1] thinking to have bought it, by the help of Mr. Pierce, for a little money; I did think to give 200*l* for it, it being said to be worth 1000*l* – but it is so spoiled that I have no mind to it, and is not a pleasant, though a good picture. Thence carried Harris to his playhouse, where though 4 a-clock, so few people there at *The Impertinents*[2] as I went out; and do believe they did not act, though there was my Lord Arlington and his company there. So I out, and met my wife in a coach and stopped her going thither to meet me; and took her and Mercer and Deb to Bartholomew-fair, and there did see a ridiculous, obscene little stage-play called *Mary Andrey*,[3] a foolish thing but seen by every-body; and so to Jacob Hall's dancing of the ropes, a thing worth seeing and mightily fallowed;[4] and so home and to the office, and then to bed – writing to my father tonight not to unfurnish our house in the country for my sister, who is going to her own house, because I think I may have occasion myself to come thither; and so I do, by our being put out of the office; which doth not at all trouble me to think of.

SEPTEMBER.

8. Up and by water to White-hall and to St. James's, there to talk a little with Mr. Wren about the private business we are upon in the office, where he tells me he finds that they all suspect me to be the author of the great letter; which I value not – being satisfied that it is the best thing I could ever do for myself. And so after some discourse of this kind more, I back to the office, where all the morning; and after dinner, to it again all the afternoon and very late; and then home to supper, where met W Batelier and B. Turner; and after some talk with them, and supper, we to bed. This day, I received so earnest an invitation again from Roger Pepys to

1. Holbein's *Henry VIII and the Barber-Surgeons* (c.1542). Pepys had seen the picture before it was damaged in the Great Fire. *See* 27 Feb. 1663.
2. Thomas Shadwell's comedy *The Sullen Lovers, or The Impertinents*, first performed in this year. It was showing at the Lincoln Inn Fields Theatre, where Harris acted.
3. "Merry Andrew", probably a puppet play.
4. Hall was a famous tightrope performer at fairs in the 1660s and 1670s.

come to Sturbridge-Fair, that I resolve to let my wife go, which she shall do the next week; and so to bed. This day I received two letters from the Duke of Richmond about his Yacht, which is newly taken into the King's service, and I am glad of it, hoping hereby to oblige him and to have occasions of seeing his noble Duchess, which I adore.

11. Up, and at my office all the morning. And after dinner, all the afternoon in my house with Batelier shut up, drawing up my defence to the Duke of York upon his great letter, which I have industriously take[n] this opportunity of doing for my future use.[1] At it late, and my mind and head mighty full on it all night.

12. At it again in the morning; and then to the office, where till noon; and I do see great whispering among my Brethren about their replies to the Duke of York; which vexed me, though I know no reason for it – for I have no manner of ground to fear them. At noon home to dinner; and after dinner, to work all the afternoon again; at home late and so to bed.

13. *Lords day.* The like all this morning and afternoon, and finished it to my mind. So about 4 a-clock walked to the Temple, and there by coach to St. James's and met, to my wish, the Duke of York and Mr. Wren; and understand the Duke of York hath received answers from Brouncker, W. Penn and J. Mennes; and as soon as he saw me, he bid Mr. Wren read them over with me. So having no opportunity of talk with the Duke of York, and Mr. Wren some business to do, he puts them into my hand like an idle companion, to take home with me before himself had read them; which doth give me great opportunity of altering my answer, if there was cause. So took a hackney and home; and after supper made my wife to read them all over, wherein she is mighty useful to me. And I find them all evasions, and in many things false, and in few to the full purpose. Little said reflective on me, though W. Penn and J. Mennes do mean me in one or two places, and J. Mennes a little more plainly would lead the Duke of York to question the exactness of my keeping my records – but all to no purpose. My mind is mightily pleased by this, if I can but get them to have a copy taken of them for my future use; but I must return them tomorrow.[2] So to bed.

1. The Navy Board's Principal Officers each responded individually to the Duke's letter. Pepys was therefore mounting a defence against the letter he had composed, partly to keep up the charade that he was not responsible for it.
2. He retained copies of his colleagues' responses and delivered his own reply to the Duke a few days later.

28. Up betimes, and Knepp's maid comes to me to tell me that the women's day at the playhouse[1] is today, and that therefore I must be there to encrease their profit. I did give the pretty maid Betty that comes to me half-a-crown for coming, and had a besar or dos, ella being mighty jolie;[2] and so I about my business by water to St. James's, and there had good opportunity of speaking with the Duke of York, who desires me again, talking on that matter, to prepare something for him to do for the better managing of our office, telling me that my Lord Keeper and he talking about it yesterday, my Lord Keeper did advise him to do so, it being better to come from him then otherwise – which I have promised to do. Thence to my Lord Burlington's house,[3] the first time I ever was there, it being the house built by Sir Jo. Denham, next to Clarendon-house. And here I visited my Lord Hinchingbrooke and his Lady, Mr. Sidny Mountagu[4] being come last night, come to town unexpectedly from Mounts bay,[5] where he left my Lord well eight days since; so as we may now hourly expect to hear of his arrivall at Portsmouth. Sidny is mightily grown; and I am glad I am here to see him at his first coming, though it cost me dear, for here I come to be necessitated to supply them with 500*l* for my Lord: he sent him up with a declaration to his friends of the necessity of his being presently suppli[ed] with two thousand pounds, but I do not think he will get one; however, I think it becomes my duty to my Lord to do something extraordinary in this, and the rather because I have been remiss in writing to him during this voyage – more then ever I did in my life, and more indeed then was fit for me. By and by comes Sir W. Godolphin[6] to see Mr. Sidny, who I perceive is much dissatisfied that he should come to town last night and not yet be with my Lord Arlington, who, and all the town, hear of his being come to town; and he did it seems take notice of it to Godolphin this morning. So that I perceive this remissness in affairs doth continue in my Lord's managements still – which I am sorry for – but above all, to see in what a condition my Lord is for money, that I dare swear he doth not know where to take up 500*l* of any man in England at this time upon his word, but of myself, as I believe by the

1. A benefit day for the actresses.
2. "a kiss or two, she being mighty pretty".
3. Burlington House, Piccadilly. The Earl of Burlington was Hinchingbrooke's father-in-law.
4. Sandwich's second son, aged 18.
5. In Cornwall.
6. Godolphin worked for Secretary of State Arlington and had been a secretary on Sandwich's Spanish embassy.

sequel hereof it will appear. Here I first saw and saluted my Lady Burlington, a very fine-speaking lady – and a good woman, but old and not handsome – but a brave woman in her parts. Here my Lady Hinchingbrooke tells me that she hath bought most of the wedding-clothes for Mrs. Pickering, so that the thing is gone through and will be soon ended – which I wonder at; but let them do as they will.[1] Here I also, standing by a candle that was brought for sealing of a letter, do set my periwigg a-fire; which made such an odd noise, nobody could tell what it was till they saw the flame, my back being to the candle. Thence to Westminster-hall and there walked a little, and to the Exchequer and so home by water; and after eating a bit, I to my vintner's and there did only look upon su[2] wife, which is mighty handsome. And so to my glove and ribbon shop in Fanchurch-street and did the like there; and there stopping against the door of the shop Mrs. Horsfall, now a late Widdow, in a coach, I to her and shook her by the hand; and so she away and I by coach towards the King's playhouse; and meeting W How, took him with me and there saw *The Citty Match*,[3] a play not acted these 30 years, and but a silly play. The King and Court there. The house, for the women's sake, mighty full. So I to White-hall, and there all the evening on the Queen's side; and it being a most summerlike day and a fine warm evening, the Italians came in a barge under the leads before the Queen's drawing-room, and so the Queen and ladies went out and heard it for almost an hour; and it was endeed very good together but yet there was but one voice that alone did appear considerable, and that was Seignor Joanni.[4] This done, by and by they went in; and here I saw Mr. Sidny Mountagu kiss the Queen's hand; who was mighty kind to him – and the ladies looked mightily on him, and the King came by and by and did talk to him. So I away by coach with Alderman Backewell home, who is mighty kind to me, more then ordinary, in his expressions. But I do hear this day what troubles me: that Sir W. Coventry is quite out of play, the King seldom speaking to him; and that there is a design of making a Lord Treasurer and that my Lord Arlington shall be the man; but I cannot believe it – but yet the Duke of Buckingham hath it in his mind, and those with him, to make a

1. This was Betty Pickering's match with John Creed.
2. "his".
3. A farcical comedy by Jasper Mayne, first acted c.1637.
4. Possibly Giovanni Battista Draghi, who became a celebrated musician and composer.

thorough alteration in things; and among the rest, Coventry to be out.◆ So home to read and sup; and to bed.

29. ⟨*Tuesday*⟩ *Michaelmas day.* Up and to the office, where all morning.[1]

OCTOBER.

11. *Lords day.* Up and to church, where I find Parson Mills come to town and preached, and the church full, most people being now come home to town, though the season of year is as good as summer in all respects. At noon dined at home with my wife all alone, and busy all the afternoon in my closet, making up some papers with W. Hewer; and at night comes Mr. Turner and his wife, and there they tell me that Mr. Harper is dead at Deptford, and so now all his and my care is how to secure his being Storekeeper in his stead. And here, they and their daughter, and a kinswoman that came along with them, did sup with me, and pretty merry; and then they gone, and my wife to read to me, and to bed.

13. Up and to the office; and before the office, did speak with my Lord Brouncker and there did get his ready assent to T. Hater's having of Mr. Turner's place, and so Sir J. Mennes also. But when we came to set down at the Board, comes to us Mr. Wren this day to town, and tells me that James Southern doth petition the Duke of York for the Store-keeper's place of Deptford; which did trouble me much, and also the Board, though upon discourse after he was gone, we did resolve to move hard for our Clerks, and that places of preferment may go according to Seniority and merit.[2] So, the Board up, I home with my people to dinner; and so to the office again and there, after doing some business, I with Mr. Turner to the Duke of Albemarle's at night, and there did speak to him about his appearing to Mr. Wren a friend to Mr. Turner, which he did

1. The entry for 29 September ends here, and twelve blank pages follow in the manuscript. No rough notes were inserted, as he had done on two similar occasions in April and June 1668. In the missing days, Pepys travelled to Southwick, Hampshire, to welcome Sandwich back from Spain. He visited the King who was on a progress in Suffolk. He seems also to have gone to meet Elizabeth, who was staying at Roger Pepys's house near Cambridge. They returned to London on 10 October.
2. James Southerne was one of the clerks in the Admiral's office. The next day, as Pepys desired, Thomas Turner (whose jobs included Purveyor of Petty Provisions in the Navy Office) was appointed to the storekeeper's place and Thomas Hayter (chief clerk in the Navy Office) replaced Turner in the purveyor's role.

take kindly from me; and so away thence, well pleased with what we had now done; and so I with him home, stopping at my Lord Brouncker's and getting his hand to a letter I wrote to the Duke of York for T. Hater, and also at my Lord Middleton's[1] to give him an account of what I had done this day with his man at Alderman Backwell's, about the getting of his 1000*l* paid. And here he did take occasion to discourse about the business of the Dutch war, which he says he was alway an enemy to; and did discourse very well of it, I saying little, but pleased to hear him talk and to see how some men may by age come to know much, and yet by their drinking and other pleasures render themselfs not very considerable. I did this day find by discourse with somebody, that this gentleman was the great Major-Generall Middleton, that was of the Scots army in the beginning of the late war against the King. Thence home and to the office to finish my letters; and so home and did get my wife to read to me, and then ⟨Deb⟩ to comb my head; and here I had the pleasure para touch the cosa[2] of her and all about, with a little opposition; and so to bed.

23. Up, and the plasterers at work and painter[s] about my house. Collonell Middleton and I to St. James's, where with the rest of our company we attended on our usual business the Duke of York. Thence I to White-hall to my Lord Sandwiches, where I find my Lord within but busy, private; and so I stayed a little, talking with the young gentlemen; and so away with Mr. Pierce the surgeon toward Tyburne to see the people executed, but came too late, it being done, two men and a woman hanged; and so I back again and to my coachmaker's, and there did come a little nearer agreement for the coach; and so to Duck-lane and there my bookseller's and saw his moher, but ella is so big-bellied that ella is not worth seeing.[3] So home and there all alone to dinner, my wife and W. Hewer being gone to Deptford to see her mother; and so I to the office all the afternoon. In the afternoon comes my cousin Sidny Pickering to bring my wife and me his sister's favour for her wedding;[4] which is kindly done. And he gone, I to business again; and in the evening home, there made my wife read till supper time, and so to bed. This day Pierce doth tell me, among other news, the late frolic and

1. The new governor of Tangier; appointed in 1667, he did not sail for there until September 1669.
2. "to touch the thing".
3. "his wife, but she is so big-bellied that she is not worth seeing." Mary Shrewsbury, wife of William, gave birth in late November.
4. Betty Pickering's marriage to John Creed had taken place on 6 October.

Debauchery of Sir Ch. Sidly and Buckhurst, running up and down all the night with their arses bare through the streets, and at last fighting and being beat by the watch and clapped up all night;[1] and how the King takes their parts and my Lord Chief Justice Keeling hath laid the constable by the heels to answer it next sessions – which is a horrid shame. How the King and these gentlemen did make the fiddlers of Thetford, this last progress, to sing them all the bawdy songs they could think of. How Sir W. Coventry was brought the other day to the Duchesse of York by the Duke of York to kiss her hand; who did acknowledge his unhappiness to occasion her so much sorrow,[2] declaring his intentions in it and praying her pardon; which she did give him upon his promise to make good his pretences of innocence to her family by his faithfulness to his master, the Duke of York. That the Duke of Buckingham is now all in all, and will ruin Coventry if he can; and that W. Coventry doth now rest wholly upon the Duke of York for his standing; which is a great turn. He tells me that my Lady Castlemayne, however, is a mortal enemy to the Duke of Buckingham; which I understand not, but it seems she doth disgust his greatness and his ill usage of her. That the King was drunk at Saxam with Sidly, Buckhurst, &c. the night that my Lord Arlington came thither, and would not give him audience, or could not – which is true, for it was that night I was there and saw the King go up to his chamber, and was told the King had been drinking.[3] He tells me too that the Duke of York did the next day chide Bab. May for his occasioning the King's giving himself up to these gentlemen, to the neglecting of my Lord Arlington; to which he answered merrily, that by God, there was no man in England that had heads to lose, durst do what they do every day with the King; and asked the Duke of York's pardon – which is a sign of a mad world. God bless us out of it.

25. *Lords day.* Up, and discoursing with my wife about our house and many new things we are doing of; and so to church I, and there find Jack Fen come, and his wife, a pretty black woman; I never saw her before, nor took notice of her now. So home and to dinner; and after dinner, all the afternoon got my wife and boy to read to me. And at night W Batelier comes and sups with us; and after supper,

1. Sedley and Lord Buckhurst enjoyed combining nakedness and public disorder, *see* 1 July 1663.
2. By his part in the fall of Clarendon, her father, in autumn 1667.
3. This episode was at Little Saxham, Suffolk on 7 October, part of the period missing from the diary.

to have my head combed by Deb, which occasioned the greatest sorrow to me that ever I knew in this world; for my wife, coming up suddenly, did find me imbracing the girl con my hand sub su coats; and endeed, I was with my main in her cunny.[1] I was at a wonderful loss upon it, and the girl also; and I endeavoured to put it off, but my wife was struck mute and grew angry, and as her voice came to her, grew quite out of order; and I do say little, but to bed; and my wife said little also, but could not sleep all night; but about 2 in the morning waked me and cried, and fell to tell me as a great secret that she was a Roman Catholique and had received the Holy Sacrament;[2] which troubled me but I took no notice of it, but she went on from one thing to another, till at last it appeared plainly her trouble was at what she saw; but yet I did not know how much she saw and therefore said nothing to her. But after her much crying and reproaching me with inconstancy and preferring a sorry girl before her, I did give her no provocations but did promise all fair usage to her, and love, and foreswore any hurt that I did with her – till at last she seemed to be at ease again; and so toward morning,
⟨⟨26⟩⟩ a little sleep; and so I, with some little repose and rest, rose, and up and by water to White-hall, but with my mind mightily troubled for the poor girl, whom I fear I have undone by this, my [wife] telling me that she would turn her out of door. However, I was obliged to attend the Duke of York, thinking to have had a meeting of Tanger today, but had not; but he did take me and Mr. Wren into his closet, and there did press me to prepare what I had to say upon the answers of my fellow-officers to his great letter; which I promised to do against his coming to town again the next week;[3] and so to other discourse, finding plainly that he is in trouble and apprehensions of the reformers, and would be found to do what he can towards reforming himself. And so thence to my Lord Sandwich; where after long stay, he being in talk with others privately, I to him; and there he taking physic and keeping his chamber, I had an hour's talk with him about the ill posture of things at this time, while the King gives countenance to Sir Ch. Sidly and Lord Buckhurst, telling him their late story of running up and down the streets a little while since all night, and their being beaten

1. "with my hand under her coats [i.e. skirts]; and endeed, I was with my hand in her cunny."
2. Elizabeth had spoken of this before (*see* 20 March 1664), but she never publicly converted. She received the sacrament in the Church of England on her deathbed in 1669.
3. Pepys was now to prepare the Duke's response to the Principal Officers' defences (including his own) to the Duke's letter that he had himself composed.

and clapped up all night by the constable, who is since chid and imprisoned for his pains.

He tells me that he thinks his matters do stand well with the King – and hopes to have despatch to his mind; but I doubt it, and do see that he doth fear it too. He told me my Lady Carteret's trouble about my writing of that letter of the Duke of York's lately to the office; which I did not own, but declared to be of no injury to G. Carteret,[1] and that I would write a letter to him to satisfy him therein. But this I am in pain how to do without doing myself wrong, and the end I had, of preparing a justification to myself hereafter, when the faults of the Navy come to be found out. However, I will do it in the best manner I can.

Thence by coach home and to dinner, finding my wife mightily discontented and the girl sad, and no words from my wife to her. So after dinner, they out with me about two or three things; and so home again, I all the evening busy and my wife full of trouble in her looks; and anon to bed – where about midnight, she wakes me and there falls foul on me again, affirming that she saw me hug and kiss the girl; the latter I denied, and truly; the other I confessed and no more. And upon her pressing me, did offer to give her under my hand that I would never see Mrs. Pierce more, nor Knepp, but did promise her perticular demonstrations of my true love to her, owning some indiscretion in what I did, but that there was no harm in it. She at last on these promises was quiet, and very kind we were,
⟨⟨27⟩⟩ and so to sleep; and in the morning up, but with my mind troubled for the poor girl, with whom I could not get opportunity to speak; but to the office, my mind mighty full of sorrow for her, where all the morning, and to dinner with my people and to the office all the afternoon; and so at night home and there busy to get some things ready against tomorrow's meeting of Tanger; and that being done and my clerks gone, my wife did towards bedtime begin to be in a mighty rage from some new matter that she had got in her head, and did most part of the night in bed rant at me in most high terms, of threats of publishing my shame; and when I offered to rise, would have rose too, and caused a candle to be lit, to burn by her all night in the chimney while she ranted; while [I], that knew myself to have given some grounds for it, did make it my business to appease her all I could possibly, and by good words and fair promises did make her very quiet; and so rested all night and rose with perfect good peace, being heartily

1. As former Navy Treasurer.

afflicted for this folly of mine that did occasion it; but was forced to be silent about the girl, which I have no mind to part with, but much less that the poor girl should be undone by my folly. So up,
⟨⟨28⟩⟩ with mighty kindness from my wife and a thorough peace; and being up, did by a note advise the girl what I had done and owned, which note I was in pain for till she told me that she had burned it. ⟨⟨This evening, Mr. Spong came and sat late with me, and first told me of the instrument called Parrallogram,[1] which I must have one of, showing me his practice thereon by a map of England.⟩⟩

So by coach with Mr. Gibson to Chancery-lane, and there made oath before a Maister of Chancery to my Tanger account of Fees; and so to White-hall, where by and by a Committee met; my Lord Sandwich there, but his report was not received, it being late; but only a little business done, about the supplying the place with victuals; but I did get, to my great content, my account allowed of Fees, with great applause by my Lord Ashly and Sir W. Penn. Thence home, calling at one or two places, and there about our workmen, who are at work upon my wife's closet and other parts of my house, that we are all in dirt. So after dinner, with Mr. Gibson all the afternoon in my closet; and at night to supper and to bed, my wife and I at good peace, but yet with some little grudgeings of trouble in her, and more in me, about the poor girl.

29. At the office all the morning, where Mr. Wren first tells us of the order from the King, come last night to the Duke of York, for signifying his pleasure to the Sollicitor generall for drawing up a commission for suspending of my Lord Anglesy[2] and putting in Sir Tho. Littleton and Sir Tho. Osborne (the former a creature of Arlington's, and the latter of the Duke of Buckingham's) during the suspension. The Duke of York was forced to obey, and did grant it, he being to go to Newmarket this day with the King, and so the King pressed for it. But Mr. Wren doth own that the Duke of York is the most wounded in this in the world, for it is done and concluded without his privity, after his appearing for him – and that it is plain that they do ayme to bring the Admiralty into commission too, and lessen the Duke of York.[3] This doth put strange apprehensions into all our Board; only, I think I am the least troubled at it, for I care not at all for it – but my Lord Brouncker and Pen do seem

1. Pantograph; an instrument for copying maps etc. on the same or an altered scale.
2. Navy Treasurer.
3. That is, to replace the post of Lord High Admiral (York's role) with a committee.

to think much of it. So home to dinner, full of this news; and after dinner to the office, and so home all the afternoon to do business towards my drawing up an account for the Duke of York of the answers of this office to his late great letter, and late at it; and so to bed, with great peace from my wife and quiet, I bless God.

NOVEMBER.

1. *Lords Day.* Up, and with W Hewers at my chamber all this morning, going further in my great business for the Duke of York; and so at noon to dinner, and then W. Hewer to write fair what he had writ, and my wife to read to me all the afternoon; till anon Mr. Gibson came, and he and I to perfect it to my full mind. And to supper and to bed – my mind yet at disquiet that I cannot be informed how poor Deb stands with her mistress, but I fear she will put her away; and the truth is, though it be much against my mind and to my trouble, yet I think it will be fit that she be gone, for my wife's peace and mine; for she cannot but be offended at the sight of her, my wife having conceived this jealousy of me with reason. And therefore, for that, and other reasons of expense, it will be best for me to let her go – but I shall love and pity her. This noon Mr. Povy sent his Coach for my wife and I to see; which we like mightily, and will endeavour to have him get us just such another.[1]

3. Up and all the morning at the office. At noon to dinner; and then to the office and there busy till 12 at night, without much pain to my eyes; but I did not use them to read or write, and so did hold out very well. So home, and there to supper; and I observed my wife to eye my eyes whether I did ever look upon Deb; which I could not but do now and then (and to my grief did see the poor wretch look on me and see me look on her, and then let drop a tear or two; which doth make my heart relent at this minute that I am writing this, with great trouble of mind, for she is endeed my sacrifice, poor girl); and my wife did tell me in bed, by the by, of my looking on other people, and that the only way is to put things out of sight; and this I know she means by Deb, for she tells me that her aunt[2] was here on Monday and she did tell her of her desire of parting with Deb; but in such kind terms on both sides, that my

1. Thomas Povey, a colleague from the Tangier Committee, was known for his excellent taste.
2. Deb's aunt.

wife is mightily taken with her. I see it will be, and it is but necessary; and therefore, though it cannot but grieve me, yet I must bring my mind to give way to it. We had a great deal of do this day at the office about Clutterbucke, I declaring my dissent against the whole Board's proceedings;[1] and I believe I shall go near to show W. Penn a very knave in it, whatever I find my Lord Brouncker.

4. Up, and by coach to White-hall; and there I find the King and Duke of York come the last night, and everybody's mouth full of my Lord Anglesy's suspension being sealed; which it was, it seems, yesterday; so that he is prevented in his remedy at the Council; and it seems the two new Treasurers did kiss the King's hand this morning, brought in by my Lord Arlington. They walked up and down together the Court this day, and several people joyed them. But I avoided it, that I might not be seen to look either way. This day also, I hear that my Lord Ormond is to be declared in Council no more Deputy-Governor of Ireland, his commission being expired, and the King is prevailed with to take it out of his hands;[2] which people do mightily admire,[3] saying that he is the greatest subject of any prince in Christendome, and hath more acres of land then any – and hath done more for his prince then ever any yet did. But all will not do; he must down it seems – the Duke of Buckingham carrying all before him. But that that troubles me most, is that they begin to talk that the Duke of York's regiment is ordered to be disbanded; and more, that undoubtedly his Admiralcy will fallow; which doth shake me mightily, and I fear will have ill consequences in the nation, for these counsels are very mad. The Duke of York doth, by all men's report, carry himself wonderful submissive to the King, in the most humble manner in the world; but yet it seems nothing must be spared that tends to the keeping out of the Chancellor,[4] and that is the reason of all this. The great discourse now is that the Parliament shall be dissolved, and another called which shall give the King the Deane and Chapters lands; and that will put him out of debt.[5] And it is said that Buckingham doth knownly meet daily with Wildman[6] and other Commonwealths-men; and

1. He opposed paying a victualling bill presented by Thomas Clutterbuck, consul at Livorno.
2. Ormond (who was vulnerable as an ally of Clarendon) did not lose his position until February 1669.
3. Wonder at.
4. Clarendon, the former Lord Chancellor.
5. This rumoured scheme for the sale of church lands came to nothing.
6. John Wildman, a republican who was indeed an ally of Buckingham.

that when he is with them, he makes the King believe that he is with his wenches. And something looks like the Parliament's being dissolved, by Harry Brouncker's being now come back;[1] and appears this day the first day at White-hall, but hath not been yet with the King – but is secure that he shall be well received, I hear. God bless us, when such men as he shall be restored. But that that pleases me most, is that several do tell me that Pen is to be removed; and others, that he hath resigned his place; and perticularly, Spragge tells me for certain that he hath resigned it and is become a partener with Gawden in the victualling – in which I think he hath done a very cunning thing, but I am sure I am glad of it, and it will be well for the King – to have him out of this office.[2]◆

When I came home tonight, I find Deb not come home, and do doubt whether she be not quite gone or no; but my wife is silent to me in it, and I to her, but fell to other discourse; and endeed am well satisfied that my house will never be at peace between my wife and I unless I let her go, though it grieves me to the heart.

My wife and I spent much time this evening talking of our being put out of the office and my going to live at Deptford at her brother's till I can clear my accounts and rid my hands of the town – which will take me a year or more; and I do think it will be best for me to do so, in order to our living cheap and out of sight.

5. Up, and Willet came home in the morning: and God forgive me, I could not conceal my content thereat, by smiling, and my wife observed it; but I said nothing, nor she, but away to the office.[3]◆

With Mr. Povy spent all the afternoon going up and down among the coachmakers in Cow lane, and did see several, and at last did pitch upon a little Chariott, whose body was framed but not Covered, at the widow's that made Mr. Lowther's fine coach. And we are mightily pleased with it, it being light, and will be very gent and sober – to be covered with leather, but yet will hold four. Being much satisfied with this, I carried him to White-hall; and so by coach home, where give my wife a good account of my day's work; and to the office and there late, and so to bed.

1. He had fled to France to escape impeachment.
2. Penn was the Navy Commissioner responsible for auditing the victualling accounts. He now joined Denis Gauden as a victualling contractor to the navy, resigning from the Navy Board in February 1669.
3. Pepys realized, after beginning his entry for the 6th, that the events after Deb's return that he describes under the 5th had actually happened on the 6th. He added three notes to this effect, commenting "my mind being now so troubled that it is no wonder that I fall into this mistake more then ever I did in my life before".

9. Up, and I did, by a little note which I flung to Deb, advise her that I did continue to deny that ever I kissed her, and so she might govern herself. The truth [is], that I did adventure upon God's pardoning me this lie, knowing how heavy a thing it would be for me to be the ruin of the poor girl; and next, knowing that if my wife should know all, it were impossible ever for her to be at peace with me again – and so our whole lives would be uncomfortable. The girl read, and as I bid her, returned me the note, flinging it to me in passing by.◆

10. Up, and my wife still every day as ill as she is all night; will rise to see me out doors, telling me plainly that she dares not let me see the girl; and so I out to the office, where all the morning; and so home to dinner, where I find my wife mightily troubled again, more then ever, and she tells me that it is from her examining the girl and getting a confession now from her of all, even to the very tocando su[1] thing with my hand – which doth mightily trouble me, as not being able to foresee the consequences of it as to our future peace together. So my wife would not go down to dinner, but I would dine in her chamber with her; and there, after mollifying her as much as I could, we were pretty quiet and eat; and by and by comes Mr. Hollier, and dines there by himself after we had dined. And he being gone, we to talk again, and she to be troubled, reproaching me with my unkindness and perjury, I having denied my ever kissing her – as also with all her old kindnesses to me, and my ill-using of her from the beginning, and the many temptations she hath refused out of faithfulness to me; whereof several she was perticular in, and especially from my Lord Sandwich by the sollicitation of Captain Ferrer; and then afterward, the courtship of my Lord Hinchingbrooke, even to the trouble of his Lady.[2] All which I did acknowledge and was troubled for, and wept; and at last pretty good friends again, and so I to my office and there late, and so home to supper with her; and so to bed, where after half-an-hour's slumber, she wakes me and cries out that she should never sleep more, and so kept raving till past midnight, that made me cry and weep heartily all the while for her, and troubled for what she reproached

1. "touching her".
2. It is possible Sandwich's approach was made during Elizabeth's stay at Brampton in summer 1662: *see* Pepys's comments on her return, 27 Sept. 1662. Captain Robert Ferrer was a member of Sandwich's household. Sandwich's son Lord Hinchingbrooke probably made his attempt in spring 1668 when Elizabeth was again at Brampton and he and his new wife were nearby at Hinchingbrooke House.

me with as before; and at last, with new vows, and perticularly that I would myself bid the girl be gone and show my dislike to her – which I shall endeavour to perform, but with much trouble. And so, this appeasing her, we to sleep as well as we could till morning.

13.◆ I home, and there to talk, with great pleasure, all the evening with my wife, who tells me that Deb hath been abroad today, and is come home and says she hath got a place to go to, so as she will be gone tomorrow morning. This troubled me; and the truth is, I have a great mind for to have the maidenhead of this girl, which I should not doubt to have if yo could get time para be con her[1] – but she will be gone and I know not whither. Before we went to bed, my wife told me she would not have me to see her or give her her wages; and so I did give my wife 10*l* for her year and half-a-quarter's wages, which she went into her chamber and paid her; and so to bed, and there, blessed be God, we did sleep well and with peace, which I had not done in now almost twenty nights together. This afternoon I went to my coachmaker and Crows,[2] and there saw things go on to my great content.◆

14. Up, and had a mighty mind to have seen or given a note to Deb or to have given her a little money; to which purpose I wrapped up 40*s* in a paper, thinking to give her; but my wife rose presently, and would not let me be out of her sight; and went down before me into the kitchen, and came up and told me that she was in the kitchen, and therefore would have me go round the other way; which she repeating, and I vexed at it, answered her a little angrily; upon which she instantly flew out into a rage, calling me dog and rogue, and that I had a rotten heart; all which, knowing that I deserved it, I bore with; and word being brought presently up that she was gone away by coach with her things, my wife was friends; and so all quiet, and I to the office with my heart sad, and find that I cannot forget the girl, and vexed I know not where to look for her – and more troubled to see how my wife is by this means likely for ever to have her hand over me, that I shall for ever be a slave to her; that is to say, only in matters of pleasure, but in other things she will make her business, I know, to please me and to keep me right to her – which I will labour to be endeed, for she deserves it of me, though it will be I fear a little time before I shall be able to wear

1. "if I could get time to be with her".
2. Crow, an upholsterer, was making a new bed for the couple (ordered before Elizabeth made her discovery).

Deb out of my mind. At the office all the morning, and merry at noon at dinner; and after dinner to the office, where all the afternoon and doing much business late; my mind being free of all troubles, I thank God, but only for my thoughts of this girl, which hang after her. And so at night home to supper, and there did sleep with great content with my wife. I must here remember that I have lain with my moher[1] as a husband more times since this falling-out then in I believe twelve months before – and with more pleasure to her then I think in all the time of our marriage before.

16. Up, and by water to White-hall, and there at the Robe-chamber at a Committee for Tanger; where some of us, my Lord Sandwich, Sir W. Coventry, and myself, with another or two, met to debate the business of the Molle and there draw up reasons for the King's taking of it into his own hands and managing of it upon accounts with Sir H Cholmly. This being done, I away to Holborne about Whetstones-park, where I never was in my life before, where I understand by my wife's discourse that Deb is gone; which doth trouble me mightily, that the poor girl should be in a desperate condition forced to go thereabouts;[2] and there, not hearing of any such man as Allbon, with whom my wife said she now was, I to the Strand and there, by sending of Drumbleby's boy, my flagelette-maker, to Eagle-court, where my wife also by discourse lately let fall that he did lately live, I found that this Dr. Allbon is a kind of a poor broken fellow that dare not show his head nor be known where he is gone; but to Lincoln's Inn-fields I went, to Mr. Povy's, but missed him; and so hearing only that this Allbon is gone to Fleet-street, I did only call at Martins my bookseller's, and there bought *Cassandra*[3] and some other French books for my wife's closet; and so home, having eat nothing but two pennorth of Oysters, opened for me by a woman in the Strand while the boy went to and again to inform me about this man; and therefore home and to dinner, and so all the afternoon at the office and there late, busy; and so home to supper and, pretty pleasant with my wife, to bed – and rested pretty well.

18. Lay long in bed, talking with my wife, she being unwilling to have me go abroad, being and declaring herself jealous of my going out, for fear of my going to Deb; which I do deny – for which God

1. "wife".
2. Whetstone Park was not a park at all, but a street notorious for brothels.
3. *Cassandre* was a long heroic romance by La Calprenède (first published 1642–5), available in French or in translation. Either way, it was an expensive present.

forgive me, for I was no sooner out about noon but I did go by coach directly to Somerset-house and there enquired among the porters there for Dr. Allbun; and the first I spoke with told me he knew him, and that he was newly gone into Lincoln's Inn fields, but whither he could not tell me, but that one of his fellows, not then in the way, did carry a chest of drawers thither with him, and that when he comes he would ask him. This put me in some hopes; and I to White-hall and thence to Mr. Povy's, but he at dinner; and therefore I away and walked up and down the Strand between the two turnstiles, hoping to see her out of a window; and then imployed a porter, one Osbeston, to find out this Doctors lodgings thereabouts; who by appointment comes to me to Hercules-pillars, where I dined alone, but tells me that he cannot find out any such but will enquire further. Thence back to White-hall to the Treasury a while, and thence to the Strand; and towards night did meet with the porter that carried the chest of drawers with this Doctor, but he would not tell me where he lived, being his good maister he told me; but if I would have a message to him, he would deliver it. At last, I told him my business was not with him, but a little gent[le]-woman, one Mrs. Willet, that is with him; and sent him to see how she did, from her friend in London, and no other token. He goes while I walk in Somerset-house – walk there in the Court; at last he comes back and tells me she is well, and that I may see her if I will – but no more. So I could not be commanded by my reason, but I must go this very night; and so by coach, it being now dark, I to her, close by my tailor's; and there she came into the coach to me, and yo did besar her and tocar her thing, but ella was against it[1] and laboured with much earnestness, such as I believed to be real; and yet at last yo did make her tener mi cosa in her mano, while mi mano was sobra her pectus, and so did hazer with grand delight.[2] I did nevertheless give her the best counsel I could, to have a care of her honour and to fear God and suffer no man para haver to do con her – as yo have done – which she promised. Yo did give her 20*s* and directions para laisser sealed[3] in paper at any time the name of the place of her being, at Herringman's my bookseller in

1. "I did kiss her and touch her thing, but she was against it".
2. "at last I did make her hold my thing in her hand, while my hand was upon her breast, and so did do with great delight." ("Do" here translates "hazer"; Pepys is probably using this verb, as he does elsewhere, to mean "to have sexual activity" or "to orgasm".)
3. "no man to have to do with her – as I have done – which she promised. I did give her 20*s* and directions to leave sealed".

the Change[1] – by which I might go para[2] her. And so bid her good-night, with much content to my mind and resolution to look after her no more till I heard from her. And so home, and there told my wife a fair tale, God knows, how I spent the whole day; with which the poor wretch was satisfied, or at least seemed so; and so to supper and to bed, she having been mighty busy all day in getting of her house in order against tomorrow, to hang up our new hangings and furnishing our best chamber.

19. Up, and at the office all the morning, with my heart full of joy to think in what a safe condition all my matters now stand between my wife and Deb and me; and at noon, running upstairs to see the upholsters, who are at work upon hanging my best room and setting up my new bed, I find my wife sitting sad in the dining-room; which inquiring into the reason of, she begun to call me all the false, rotten-hearted rogues in the world, letting me understand that I was with Deb yesterday; which, thinking impossible for her ever to understand, I did a while deny; but at last did, for the ease of my mind and hers, and for ever to discharge my heart of this wicked business, I did confess all; and above-stairs in our bed-chamber there, I did endure the sorrow of her threats and vows and curses all the afternoon. And which was worst, she swore by all that was good that she would slit the nose of this girl,[3] and be gone herself this very night from me; and did there demand 3 or 400*l* of me to buy my peace, that she might be gone without making any noise, or else protested that she would make all the world know of it. So, with most perfect confusion of face and heart, and sorrow and shame, in the greatest agony in the world, I did pass this afternoon, fearing that it will never have an end; but at last I did call for W Hewers, who I was forced to make privy now to all; and the poor fellow did cry like a child [and] obtained what I could not, that she would be pacified, upon condition that I would give it under my hand never to see or speak with Deb while I live, as I did before of Pierce and Knepp;[4] and which I did also, God knows, promise for Deb too, but I have the confidence to deny it, to the perjuring of myself. So before it was late, there was, beyond my hopes as well as desert, a tolerable peace; and so to supper, and pretty kind words,

1. Henry Herringman's bookshop in the New Exchange, near to Deb's current lodgings.
2. "to".
3. A punishment that marked a woman as a whore.
4. *See* the night of 26 Oct. 1668.

and to bed, and there yo did hazer con ella to her content;[1] and so with some rest spent the night in bed, being most absolutely resolved, if ever I can maister this bout, never to give her occasion while I live of more trouble of this or any other kind, there being no curse in the world so great as this of the difference between myself and her; and therefore I do by the grace of God promise never to offend her more, and did this night begin to pray to God upon my knees alone in my chamber; which God knows I cannot yet do heartily, but I hope God will give me the grace more and more every day to fear Him, and to be true to my poor wife. This night the Upholsters did finish the hanging of my best chamber, but my sorrow and trouble is so great about this business, that put me out of all joy in looking upon it or minding how it was.

20. This morning up, with mighty kind words between my poor wife and I; and so to White-hall by water, W. Hewer with me, who is to go with me everywhere until my wife be in condition to go out along with me herself; for she doth plainly declare that she dares not trust me out alone, and therefore made it a piece of our league that I should alway take somebody with me, or her herself; which I am mighty willing to, being, by the grace of God resolved never to do her wrong more.

We landed at the Temple, and there I did bid him call at my Cosen Roger Pepys's lodgings, and I stayed in the street for him; and so took water again at the Strand-stairs and so to White-hall, in my way I telling him plainly and truly my resolutions, if I can get over this evil, never to give new occasion for it. He is, I think, so honest and true a servant to us both, and one that loves us, that I was not much troubled at his being privy to all this, but rejoiced in my heart that I had him to assist in the making us friends; which he did do truly and heartily, and with good success – for I did get him to go to Deb to tell her that I had told my wife all of my being with her the other night, that so, if my wife should send, she might not make the business worse by denying it. While I was at White-hall with the Duke of York doing our ordinary business with him, here being also the first time the new Treasurers, W. Hewer did go to her and come back again; and so I took him into St. James's park, and there he did tell me he had been with her and found what I said about my manner of being with her true, and had given her advice as I desired. I did there enter into more talk about my wife

1. "I did do with her to her content".

and myself, and he did give me great assurance of several perticular cases to which my wife had from time to time made him privy of her loyalty and truth to me after many and great temptations, and I believe them truly. I did also discourse the unfitness of my leaving of my imployment now in many respects, to go into the country as my wife desires – but that I would labour to fit myself for it; which he thoroughly understands, and doth agree with me in it; and so, hoping to get over this trouble, we about our business to Westminster hall to meet Roger Pepys; which I did, and did there discourse of the business of lending him 500*l* to answer some occasions of his, which I believe to be safe enough; and so took leave of him and away by coach home, calling on my coach-maker by the way, where I like my little coach mightily. But when I came home, hoping for a further degree of peace and quiet, I find my wife upon her bed in a horrible rage afresh, calling me all the bitter names; and rising, did fall to revile me in the bitterest manner in the world, and could not refrain to strike me and pull my hair; which I resolved to bear with, and had good reason to bear it. So I by silence and weeping did prevail with her a little to be quiet, and she would not eat her dinner without me; but yet by and by into a raging fit she fell again worse then before, that she would slit the girl's nose; and at last W. Hewer came in and came up, who did allay her fury, I flinging myself in a sad desperate condition upon the bed in the blue room, and there lay while they spoke together; and at last it came to this, that if I would call Deb "whore" under my hand, and write to her that I hated her and would never see her more, she would believe me and trust in me – which I did agree to; only, as to the name of "whore" I would have excused, and therefore wrote to her sparing that word; which my wife thereupon tore it, and would not be satisfied till, W. Hewer winking upon me, I did write so, with the name of a whore, as that I did fear she might too probably have been prevailed upon to have been a whore by her carriage to me, and therefore, as such, I did resolve never to see her more. This pleased my wife, and she gives it W. Hewer to carry to her, with a sharp message from her. So from that minute my wife begun to be kind to me, and we to kiss and be friends, and so continued all the evening and fell to talk of other matters with great comfort, and after supper to bed.◆

I did this night promise to my wife never to go to bed without calling upon God upon my knees by prayer; and I begun this night, and hope I shall never forget to do the like all my life – for I do find that it is much the best for my soul and body to live pleasing to God and my poor wife – and will ease me of much care, as well as much expense.

21. Up, with great joy to my wife and me, and to the office, where W. Hewer did most honestly bring me back that part of my letter under my hand to Deb wherein I called her "whore", assuring me that he did not show it her – and that he did only give her to understand that wherein I did declare my desire never to see her, and did give her the best Christian counsel he could; which was mighty well done of him. But by the grace of God, though I love the poor girl and wish her well, as having gone too far toward the undoing her, yet I will never enquire after or think of her more – my peace being certainly to do right to my wife.◆

22. *Lords day.* My wife and I lay long, with mighty content, and so rose, and she spent the whole day making herself clean, after four or five weeks being in continued dirt. And I knocking up nails and making little settlements in my house, till noon; and then eat a bit of meat in the kitchen, I all alone, and so to the office to set down my Journall, for some days leaving it imperfect, the matter being mighty grievous to me and my mind from the nature of it. And so in to solace myself with my wife, whom I got to read to me, and so W. Hewer and the boy; and so after supper, to bed.

This day, my boy's Livery is come home, the first I ever had of Greene lined with red; and it likes me well enough.

28. Up, and all the morning at the office; where, while I was sitting, one comes and tells me that my Coach is come – so I was forced to go out; and to Sir Rd. Ford's, where I spoke to him, and he is very willing to have it brought in and stand there; and so I ordered it, to my great content, it being mighty pretty; only, the horses do not please me, and therefore resolve to have better. At noon home to dinner; and so to the office again all the afternoon and did a great deal of business; and so home to supper and to bed, with my mind at pretty good ease, having this day presented to the Board the Duke of York's letter;[1] which I perceive troubled Sir W. Penn, he declaring himself meant in the part that concerned excuse by sickness; but I do not care, but am mightily glad that it is done, and now I shall begin to be at pretty good ease in the office. ⟨This morning, to my great content, W Hewers tells me that a porter is come, who found my

1. The Duke's response to the Principal Officers' answers to the "great letter". This response was based on a draft by Pepys, with the sharp style toned down.

tally in Holborne and brings it him, for which he gives him 20*s*.⟩[1]

29. *Lords day.* Lay long in bed with pleasure [with my wife], with whom I have now a great deal of content; and my mind is in other things also mightily more at ease, and I do mind my business better then ever and am more at peace; and trust in God I shall ever be so, though I cannot yet get my mind off from thinking now and then of Deb. But I do, ever since my promise a while since to my wife, pray to God by myself in my chamber every night, and will endeavour to get my wife to do the like with me ere long; but am in much fear of what she hath lately frighted me with about her being a Catholique – and dare not therefore move her to go to church, for fear she should deny me. But this morning, of her own accord, she spoke of going to church the next Sunday; which pleases me mightily. This morning my coachman's clothes comes home, and I like my livery mightily; and so I all the morning at my chamber, and dined with my wife and got her to read to me in the afternoon, till Sir W Warren by appointment comes to me, who spent two hours or three with me about his accounts of Gottenbrough;[2] which are so confounded, that I doubt they will hardly ever pass without my doing something; which he desires of me, and which, partly from fear and partly from unwillingness to wrong the King and partly from its being of no profit to me, I am backward to give way to, though the poor man doth endeed deserve to be rid of this trouble that he hath lain so long under from the negligence of this Board. We afterward fell into other talk; and he tells me, as soon as he saw my coach yesterday, he wished that the owner might not contract envy by it; but I told him it was now manifestly for my profit to keep a coach, and that after imployment like mine for eight years, it were hard if I could not be justly thought to be able to do that.

He gone, my wife and I to supper; and so she to read and made an end of the *Life of Archbishop Laud*, which is worth reading, as informing a man plainly in the posture of the Church, and how the things of it were managed with the same self-interest and design that every other thing is, and have succeeded accordingly.[3] So to bed.

1. The tally, lost by Hewer, was worth £1,000.
2. They concerned a contract to supply masts from Gothenburg, Sweden, made in 1664.
3. Peter Heylyn's *Cyprianus Anglicus* (1668) was a celebratory biography of the royalist martyr William Laud – although this was evidently not the message Pepys took from it.

30.◆ My wife after dinner went the first time abroad, to take the maidenhead of her coach, calling on Rogr. Pepys and visiting Mrs Creed and my Cousin Turner – while I at home all the afternoon and evening, very busy and doing much work to my great content. Home at night, and there comes Mrs. Turner and Betty to see us, and supped with us; and I showed them a cold civility, for fear of troubling my wife; and after supper, they being gone, we to bed.

Thus ended this month with very good content, that hath been the most sad to my heart and the most expenseful to my purse on things of pleasure, having furnished my wife's closet and the best chamber, and a coach and horses, that ever I yet knew in the world; and doth put me into the greatest condition of outward state that ever I was in, or hoped ever to be, or desired – and this at a time when we do daily expect great changes in this office and, by all reports, we must all of us turn out. But my eyes are come to that condition that I am not able to work; and therefore, that, and my wife's desire, makes me have no manner of trouble in my thoughts about it – so God do his will in it.

DECEMBER.

2. Up and at the office all the morning upon some accounts of Sir D Gawden; and at noon abroad with W. Hewer, thinking to have found Mr. Wren at Captain Cox, to have spoke something to him about doing a favour for Will's Uncle Stevenson, but missed him; and so back home and abroad with my wife, the first time that ever I rode in my own coach; which doth make my heart rejoice and praise God, and pray him to bless it to me and continue it. So she and I to the King's playhouse, and there sat to avoid seeing of Knepp in a box above, where Mrs. Williams happened to be; and there saw *The Usurper*, a pretty good play in all but what is designed to resemble Cromwell and Hugh Peters, which is mighty silly.[1] The play done, we to White-hall; where [my] wife stayed, while I up to the Duchesses and Queenes side to speak with the Duke of York; and here saw all the ladies and heard the silly discourse of the King with his people about him, telling a story of my Lord of Rochester's having of his clothes stole while he was with a wench, and his gold all gone but his clothes found afterward, stuffed into a feather-bed

1. A tragedy by Edward Howard, first performed in 1664. In the play the usurper, Damocles, stands for Cromwell. He is abetted by the scheming flatterer "Hugo de Petra", representing Hugh Peter, a famous preacher under Cromwell.

by the wench that stole them. I spoke with the Duke of York, just as he was set down to supper with the King, about our sending of victuals to Sir Tho. Allens fleet hence to Cales[1] to meet him. And so back to my wife in my coach, and so with great content and joy home – where I made my boy to make an end of the *Reall Character*,[2] which I begun a great while ago and doth please me infinitely, and endeed is a most worthy labour – and I think mighty easy, though my eyes makes me unable to attempt anything in it. So after supper, to bed.◆

5. Up, after a little talk with my wife which troubled me, she being ever since our late difference mighty watchful of sleep and dreams, and will not be persuaded but I do dream of Deb, and doth tell me that I speak in my dream and that this night I did cry "Huzzy!" and it must be she – and now and then I start otherwise then I used to do, she says; which I know not, for I do not know that I dream of her more then usual, though I cannot deny that my thoughts waking do run now and then, against my will and judgment, upon her, for that only is wanting to undo me, being now in every other thing as to my mind most happy – and may still be so but for my own fault, if I be ketched loving anybody but my wife again. So up and to the office; and at noon to dinner and thence to office, where late, mighty busy and despatching much business, settling papers in my own office; and so home to supper and to bed. No news stirring but that my Lord of Ormond is likely to go to Ireland again, which doth show that the Duke of Buckingham doth not rule all so absolutely – and that, however, we shall speedily have more changes in the Navy. And it is certain that the non=conformists do now preach openly in houses in many places, and among others, the house that was heretofore Sir G Carteret's in Leadenhall-street, and have ready access to the King. And now the great dispute is whether this Parliament or another; and my great design, if I continue in the Navy, is to get myself to be a Parliament-man.[3]

24. A cold day. Up and to the office, where all the morning alone at the office, nobody meeting, being the Eve of Christmas. At noon home to dinner and then to the office, busy all the afternoon, and

1. Cadiz.
2. *Essay towards a Real Character, and a Philosophical Language* (1668) by John Wilkins, Pepys's Royal Society acquaintance.
3. There was no new parliament called until 1679. He stood unsuccessfully in a by-election in summer 1669, before being chosen as MP for Castle Rising, Norfolk, in 1673.

at night home to supper; and it being now very cold, and in hopes of a frost, I begin this night to put on a Wastecoate,[1] it being the first winter in my whole memory that ever I stayed till this day before I did so. So to bed, in mighty good humour with my wife, but sad in one thing, and that is for my poor eyes.

25. *Christmas day.* Up, and continued on my waistcoat, the first day this winter. And I to church, where Alderman Backewell coming in late, I beckoned to his lady to come up to us; who did, with another lady; and after sermon I led her down through the church to her husband and coach – a noble, fine woman, and a good one – and one my wife shall be acquainted with. So home and to dinner alone with my wife, who, poor wretch, sat undressed all day till 10 at night, altering and lacing of a black petticoat – while I by her, making the boy read to me the life of Julius Caesar and Des Cartes book of music[2] – the latter of which I understand not, nor think he did well that writ it, though a most learned man. Then after supper made the boy play upon his lute, which I have not done twice before sence he came to me; and so, my mind in mighty content, we to bed.

31. Up and at the office all the morning. At noon Captain Ferrer and Mr. Sheres comes to me to dinner, who did, and pretty pleased with their talk of Spain. But my wife did not come down, I suppose because she would not, Captain Ferrer being there – to oblige me by it.[3] They gone after dinner, I to the office; and then in the evening home, being the last day of the year, to endeavour to pay all bills and servants' wages &c, which I did almost to 5*l*, that I know that I owe in the world but to the public. And so with great pleasure to supper and to bed. And blessed be God, the year ends, after some late very great sorrow with my wife by my folly; yet ends, I say, with great mutual peace and content – and likely to last so by my care, who am resolved to enjoy the sweet of it which I now possess, by never giving her like cause of trouble. My greatest trouble is now from the backwardness of my accounts, which I have not seen the bottom of now near these two years, so that I know not in what condition I am in the world; but by the grace of God, as fast as my eyes will give me leave, I will do it.

1. Warm undergarment.
2. The "life" was probably the one prefixed to a translation of Caesar's *Commentaries* by Clement Edmonds (1655). Pepys owned Descartes's *Musicae compendium* in Latin and English – the latter was a 1653 translation by his colleague, Lord Brouncker.
3. It was Ferrer who had made advances to her on Sandwich's behalf. *See* 10 Nov. 1668.

1669

JANUARY.

4. Lay long talking with my wife, and did of my own accord come to an allowance of her of 30*l* a year for all expenses, clothes and everything; which she was mightily pleased with, it being more then ever she asked or expected; and so rose with much content, and up and with W. Hewer to White-hall, there to speak with Mr. Wren; which I did, about several things of the office entered in my memorandum-books; and so about noon, going homeward with W. Hewer, he and I went in and saw the great tall woman that is to be seen, which is but twenty-one years old and I do easily stand under her arms.[1] Then going further, The Turner called me out of her coach, where her mother &c was, and invited me by all means to dine with them at my Cosen Roger's mistress, the Widdow Dickenson; so I went to them afterward and dined with them, and mighty handsomely treated; and she a wonderful merry, good-humoured, fat but plain woman, but I believe a very good woman – and mighty civil to me.[2] Mrs. Turner the mother, and Mrs. Dike and The and Betty was the company, and a gentleman of their acquaintance. Betty I did long to see, and she is indifferent pretty, but not what the world did speak of her; but I am mighty glad to have one so pretty of our kindred.[3] After dinner I walked with them to show them the great woman, which they admire, as well they may; and so back with them, and left them and I to White-hall, where a Committee of Tanger met, but little to do there; but I did receive an instance of the Duke of York's kindness to me, and the whole Committee, that they would not order anything about the Treasurer for the Corporation now in establishing without my assent and considering whether it would be to my wrong or no.[4] Thence up and down the House, and to the Duke of York's side[5] and there in the Duchess's presence; and was mightily complimented by my Lady Peterborough in my Lord Sandwiches

1. She was a Dutch woman on display in Holborn, *see* 8 Feb. 1669. Pepys there gives her height at 6ft 5in., which would make him around 5ft 11in.
2. Hester Dickinson, who lived in Covent Garden, would soon marry Roger Pepys.
3. She was Jane Turner's younger daughter.
4. Pepys was Treasurer for the Tangier Committee. Regulations for civil government in Tangier were being prepared, and Pepys wanted his say in the financial arrangements.
5. Of Whitehall Palace.

presence, whom she engaged to thank ⟨me⟩ for my kindness to her and her Lord.[1] By and by I met my Lord Brouncker; and he and I to the Duke of York alone and discoursed over the carriage of the present Treasurers,[2] in opposition, or at least independency, on the Duke of York or our Board – which the Duke of York is sensible of, and all remember I believe, for they do carry themselfs very respectlessly of him – and us. We also declared our minds together to the Duke of York about Sir Jo. Minnes's incapacity to do any service in the office, and that it is but to betray the King to have any business of trust committed to his weakness – so that the Duke of York was very sensible of it and promised to speak to the King about it. That done, I with W. Hewer took up my wife at Unthankes'; and so home and there with pleasure to read and talk; and so to supper and put into writing, in merry terms, our agreement between her and me about the 30*l* a year; and so to bed. This was done under both our hands merrily, and put into W. Hewer's to keep.

12. Up and to the office, where by occasion of a message from the Treasurers that the Board found fault with Commissioner Middleton,[3] and I went up from the Board to the Lords of the Treasury to meet our Treasurers; and did, and there did dispute the business, it being about the manner of paying a little money to Chatham-yard; wherein I find the Treasurers mighty supple, and I believe we shall bring them to reason; though they begin mighty upon us, as if we had no power of directing them, but they us. Thence back presently home to dinner, where I discern my wife to have been in pain where I have been, but said nothing to me; but I believe did send W. Hewer to seek me, but I take no notice of it – but am vexed. So to dinner with my people, and then to the office, where all the afternoon, and did much business and at it late; and so home to supper and to bed.

This day, meeting Mr. Pierce at White-hall, he tells me that his boy hath a great mind to see me, and is going to school again; and Dr. Clerke, being by, doth tell me that he is a fine boy; but I durst not answer anything, because I durst not invite him to my house for fear of my wife,[4] and therefore to my great trouble was forced to neglect that discourse. But here Mr. Pierce, I asking him whither

1. Over his pension as former Governor of Tangier.
2. The Navy Treasurers, Sir Thomas Littleton and Sir Thomas Osborne.
3. Surveyor of the Navy.
4. Pepys had promised to Elizabeth never to see Mrs Pearse again. *See* 26 Oct. 1668.

he was going, he told me as a great secret that he was going to his Maister's mistress, Mrs. Churchhill,[1] [with] some physic; meaning for the pox I suppose, or else that she is got with child; but I suppose the former, by his manner of speaking it.

This evening I observed my wife mighty dull; and I myself was not mighty fond, because of some hard words she did give me at noon, out of a jealousy at my being abroad this morning; when, God knows, it was upon the business of the office unexpectedly; but I to bed, not thinking but she would come after me; but waking by and by out of a slumber, which I usually fall into presently after my coming into the bed, I found she did not prepare to come to bed, but got fresh candles and more wood for her fire, it being mighty cold too. At this being troubled, I after a while prayed her to come to bed, all my people being gone to bed; so after an hour or two, she silent, and I now and then praying her to come to bed, she fell out into a fury, that I was a rogue and false to her; but yet I could perceive that she was to seek what to say; only, she invented, I believe, a business that I was seen in a hackney-coach with the glasses up with Deb, but could not tell the time, nor was sure I was he. I did, as I might truly, deny it, and was mightily troubled; but all would not serve. At last, about one a-clock, she came to my side of the bed and drow my curtaine open, and with the tongs, red hot at the ends, made as if she did design to pinch me with them; at which in dismay I rose up, and with a few words she laid them down and did by little and little, very sillily, let all the discourse fall; and about 2, but with much seeming difficulty, came to bed and there lay well at night, and long in bed talking together with much pleasure; it being, I know, nothing but her doubt of my going out yesterday without telling her of my going which did vex her, poor wretch, last night; and I cannot blame her jealousy, though it doth vex me to the heart.

15. Up and by coach to Sir W. Coventry; where with him a good while in his chamber, talking of one thing or another; where, among others, he told me of the great factions at Court at this day, even to the sober engaging of great persons and differences, and making the King cheap and ridiculous. It is about my Lady Harvy's being offended at Doll Common's acting of Sempronia to imitate her – for which she got my Lord Chamberlain, her kinsman, to

1. Arabella Churchill, mistress of the Duke of York whom Pearse served as a surgeon.

imprison Doll;[1] which my Lady Castlemayne made the King to release her, and to order her to act it again worse then ever the other day where the King himself was. And since, it was acted again, and my Lady Harvy provided people to hiss her and fling oranges at her. But it seems the heat is come to a great heighth, and real troubles at Court about it.◆

22. Up and with W. Hewer to White-hall, and there attended the Duke of York; and thence to the Exchange, in the way calling at several places on occasions relating to my feast tomorrow, on which my mind is now set – as, how to get a new looking-glass for my dining-room, and some pewter and good wine against tomorrow. And so home, where I had the looking-glass set up; cost me *6l 7s 6d*. And here at the Change I met with Mr. Dancre, the famous lanskip painter[2] – with whom I was on Wednesdy; and he took measure of my panels in my dining-room, where in the four I intend to have the four houses of the King – White-hall, Hampton-court, Greenwich – and Windsor. He gone, I to dinner with my people, and so to my office to despatch a little business; and then home to look after things against tomorrow. And among other things, was mightily pleased with the fellow that came to lay the cloth and fold the napkins – which I like so well, as that I am resolved to give him 40*s*. to teach my wife to do it. So to supper, with much kindness between me and my wife, which nowadays is all my care; and so to bed.

23. Up, and again to look after the setting things right against dinner, which I did to very good content; and so to the office, where all the morning till noon, when word brought me to the Board that my Lord Sandwich was come; so I presently rose, leaving the Board ready to rise, and there I found my Lord Sandwich, Peterburgh, and Sir Ch. Herberd; and presently after them come my Lord Hinchingbrooke, Mr. Sidny, and Sir Wm. Godolphin;[3] and after greeting them, and some time spent in talk, dinner was brought up, one dish after another, but a dish at a time; but all so good, but

1. "Doll Common" was the actress Katherine Corey of the King's Company, so named after her role in Jonson's *The Alchemist*. She turned the role of Sempronia, an ageing courtesan and political intriguer in Jonson's *Catiline*, into an impersonation of Lady Elizabeth Hervey. Hervey was an influential figure at court and enemy of Castlemaine.
2. Hendrick Danckerts, a Dutch landscape artist whose clients included the King.
3. The illustrious guests were Lord Peterborough (former Governor of Tangier) and Lord Sandwich, two of Sandwich's sons, and his trusted associates Harbord and Godolphin.

above all things, the variety of wines, and excellent of their kind, I had for them, and all in so good order, that they were mightily pleased, and myself full of content at it; and endeed it was, of a dinner of about six or eight dishes, as noble as any man need to have I think – at least, all was done in the noblest manner that ever I had any, and I have rarely seen in my life better anywhere else – even at the Court. After dinner, my Lords to cards, and the rest of us sitting about them and talking, and looking on my books and pictures and my wife's drawings, which they commend mightily; and mighty merry all day long, with exceeding great content, and so till 7 at night; and so took their leaves, it being dark and foul weather. Thus was this entertainment over, the best of its kind, and the fullest of honour and content to me that ever I had in my life, and shall not easily have so good again. The truth is, I have some fear that I am run behind-hand in the world for these last two years, since I have not, or for some time could not, look after my accounts; which doth a little allay my pleasure, but I do trust in God I am pretty well yet, and resolve in a very little time to look into my accounts and see how they stand. So to my wife's chamber, and there supped and got her cut my hair and look[1] my shirt, for I have itched mightily these six or seven days; and when all came to all, she finds that I am louzy, having found in my head and body above 20 lice, little and great; which I wonder at, being more then I have had I believe almost these 20 years. I did think I might have got them from the little boy, but they did presently look him, and found none – so how they came, I know not; but presently did shift[2] myself, and so shall be rid of them, and cut my hayre close to my head. And so, with much content to bed.

FEBRUARY.

1. Up and by water from the Tower to White-hall, the first time that I have gone to that end of the town by water for two or three months I think, since I kept a coach – which God send propitious to me – but it is a very great convenience. I went to a Committee of Tanger, but it did not meet; and so I meeting Mr. Povy, he and I away to Dancres to speak something touching the pictures I am getting him to make for me. And thence he carried me to Mr.

1. Examine.
2. Change.

Streeters the famous history-painter over the way, whom I have often heard of but did never see him before; and there I found him and Dr. Wren and several virtuosos looking upon the paintings which he is making for the new Theatre at Oxford;[1] and endeed, they look as they would be very fine, and the rest thinks better then those of Rubens in the Banqueting-house at White-hall, but I do not so fully think so – but they will certainly be very noble, and I am mightily pleased to have the fortune to see this man and his work, which is very famous – and he a very civil little man and lame, but lives very handsomely. So thence to my Lord Bellasses and met him within; my business only to see a chimney-piece of Dancre's doing in distemper with egg to keep off the glaring of the light, which I must have done for my room; and endeed it is pretty, but I must confess I do think it is not altogether so beautiful as the oyle pictures; but I will have some of one and some of another. Thence set him down at Little Turnstile, and so I home; and there eat a little dinner, and away with my wife by coach to the King's playhouse, thinking to have seen *The Heyresse*, first acted on Saturday last; but when we came thither, we find no play there – Kinaston, that did act a part therein in abuse to Sir Charles Sidly, being last night exceedingly dry-beaten with sticks by two or three that assaulted him – so as he is mightily bruised, and forced to keep his bed.[2] So we to the Duke of York's playhouse, and there saw *Shee Would if She Could*.[3] And so home and to my office to business, and then to supper and to bed. ⟨This day, going to the play, The. Turner met us and carried us to her mother at my Lady Mordants; and I did carry both mother and daughter with us to the Duke of York's playhouse at next door.⟩

7. *Lords day*. My wife mighty peevish in the morning about my lying unquietly a-nights, and she will have it that it is a late practice, from my evil thoughts in my dreams; and I do often find that in my dreams she doth lay her hand upon my cockerel to observe what she can. And mightily she is troubled about it, but all blew over; and I up and to church, and so home to dinner, where she in a worse

1. The Sheldonian Theatre, the ceremonial hall designed by Christopher Wren, was nearing completion. Robert Streater's ceiling (which is still in position) represents Truth descending upon the Arts and Sciences.
2. The play, written at least in part by the Duke of Newcastle, is untraced. After impersonating Sedley onstage, Edward Kynaston was reportedly attacked in St James's Park by men hired by Sedley who pretended to mistake him for Sedley. "Dry-beaten" indicates no blood was drawn.
3. A comedy by Sir George Etherege, first acted in 1668.

fit, which lasted all the afternoon, and shut herself up in her closet; and I mightily grieved and vexed, and could not get her to tell me what ayled her, or to let me into her closet; but at last she did, where I found her crying on the ground, and I could not please her; but I did at last find that she did plainly expound it to me: it was that she did believe me false to her with Jane, and did rip up three or four most silly circumstances, of her not rising till I came out of my chamber and her letting me thereby see her dressing herself, and that I must needs go into her chamber and was naught[1] with her; which was so silly, and so far from truth, that I could not be troubled at it, though I could not wonder at her being troubled, if she had these thoughts. And therefore she would lie from me, and caused sheets to be put on in the blue room and would have Jane to lie with her, lest I should come to her. At last, I did give her such satisfaction, that we were mighty good friends and went to bed betimes, where yo did hazer very well con her, and did this night by chance the first time poner my digito en her thing, which did do her much pleasure; but I pray God that ella doth not think that yo did know before[2] – or get a trick of liking it. So para sleep.

8. Up and dressed myself, and by coach with W. Hewer and my wife to White-hall, where she set us two down; and in the way, our little boy,[3] at Martin my bookseller's shop going to light, did fall down; and had he not been a most nimble boy (I saw how he did it, and was mightily pleased with him for it), he had been run over by the coach. I to visit my Lord Sandwich; and there, while my Lord was dressing himself, did see a young Spaniard that he hath brought over with him, dance; which he is admired for, as the best dancer in Spain; and endeed, he doth with mighty mastery, but I do not like his dancing as the English, though my Lord commends it mightily. But I will have him to my house, and show it my wife. Here I met with Mr. Moore, who tells me the state of my Lord's accounts of his imbassy; which I find not so good as I thought – for though it be past the King and his Caball (the Committee for Foreign Affairs as they are called), yet they have cut off from 19000*l* full 8000*l*, and have now sent it to the Lords of the Treasury; who, though the Committee have allowed the rest, yet they are not obliged to abide by it. So that I do fear this account

1. Up to no good sexually.
2. "I did do very well with her, and did this night by chance the first time put my finger in her thing . . . but I pray God that she doth not think that I did know before".
3. The current footboy, Jack.

may yet be long ere it be passed; much more, ere the sum be paid. I am sorry for the family, and not a little for what it owes me. So to my wife; took her up at Unthankes, and in our way home did show her the tall woman in Holburne which I have seen before.[1] And I measured her and she is, without shoes, just 6 feet-5 inch high, and they say not above 21 years old. Thence home and there to dinner, and my wife in a wonderful ill humour, and after dinner I stayed with her alone, being not able to endure this life, and fell to some angry words together; but by and by were mighty good friends, she telling me plainly it was still about Jane – whom she cannot believe but I am base with; which I made a matter of mirth at, but at last did call up Jane and confirmed her mistress's directions for her being gone at Easter: which I find the wench willing to be, but directly prayed that Tom[2] might go with her; which I promised, and was but what I designed; and she being thus spoke with and gone, my wife and I good friends and mighty kind, I having promised, and I will perform it, never to give her for the time to come ground of new trouble; and so I to the office with a very light heart, and there close at my business all the afternoon.◆

This morning also, going to visit Rogr. Pepys at the poticary's in King's-street, he tells me that he is gone to his wife's, so that they have been married, as he tells me, ever since the middle of last week. It was his design, upon good reasons, to make no noise of it; but I am well enough contented that it is over.[3]

Despatched a great deal of business at the office, and there pretty late, till finding myself very full of wind by my eating no dinner today, being vexed, I was forced to go home; and there supped, W Batelier with us, and so with great content to bed.

18. Up, and to the office; and at noon home, expecting to have this day seen Babb and Betty Pepys here, but they came not; and so after dinner, my wife and I to the Duke of York's House to a play, and there saw *The Mad lover*, which doth not please me so well as it used to do; only, Baterton's part still pleases me.[4] But here, who should we have come to us but Bab and Betty and Talbot,[5] the first play they were yet at; and going to see us, and hearing by my boy, whom I sent to them, that we were here, they came to us hither and

1. *See* 4 Jan. 1669.
2. Tom Edwards, her fiancé and fellow servant.
3. He had married Hester Dickinson on 4 February; she was his fourth wife.
4. A tragicomedy by John Fletcher, which Pepys had first seen in 1661. Betterton played the brave general Memnon who goes mad from unrequited love.
5. Children of Roger Pepys.

happened all of us to sit by my cousin Turner and The. And we carried them home first, and then took Bab and Betty to our house, where they lay and supped, and pretty merry; and very fine with their new clothes, and good comely girls they are enough, and very glad I am of their being with us; though I could very well have been contented to have been without that charge. So they to bed and we to bed.

23. Up, and to the office, where all the morning. And then home and put a mouthful of victuals in my mouth; and by a hackney-coach followed my wife and the girls, who are gone by 11 a-clock, thinking to have seen a new play at the Duke of York's House; but I do find them staying at my tailor's, the play not being today, and therefore I now took them to Westminster Abbey and there did show them all the tombs very finely, having one with us alone (there being other company this day to see the tombs, it being Shrove Tuesday); and here we did see, by perticular favour, the body of Queen Katherine of Valois, and had her upper part of her body in my hands.[1] And I did kiss her mouth, reflecting upon it that I did kiss a Queen, and that this was my birthday, 36 year old, that I did first kiss a Queen. But here this man, who seems to understand well, tells me that the saying is not true that says she was never buried, for she was buried; only, when Henry the 7th built his chapel, it was taken up and laid in this wooden coffin; but I did there see that in it, the body was buried in a leaden one, which remains under the body to this day.

Thence to the Duke of York's playhouse, and there finding the play begun, we homeward to the glass-house[2] and there showed my cousins the making of glass, and had several things made with great content; and among others, I had one or two singing-glasses made, which make an echo to the voice, the first that ever I saw;[3] but so thin that the very breath broke one or two of them. So home, and thence to Mr. Batelier's, where we supped, and had a good supper; and here was Mr. Gumbleton, and after supper some fiddles and so to dance; but my eyes were so out of order that I had little pleasure this night at all, though I was glad to see the rest merry. And so about midnight home and to bed.

1. The tombs at Westminster Abbey were an established attraction for visitors to London, as was the body of Catherine of Valois, queen of Henry V. She had died in 1437, aged 35.
2. Glass-works.
3. The glasses vibrated in sympathy when certain notes were sung.

MARCH.

1. Up and to White-hall to the Committee of Tanger, but it did not meet. But here I do hear first that my Lady Paulina Montagu[1] did die yesterday; at which I went to my Lord's lodgings, but he is shut up with sorrow and so not to be spoken with; and therefore I returned and to Westminster hall, where I have not been I think in some months; and here the Hall was very full, the King having, by commission to some Lords, this day prorogued the Parliament till the 19th. of October next; at which I am glad, hoping to have time to go over to France this year. But I was most of all surprized this morning by my Lord Bellasses, who by appointment met me at Auditor Wood's at the Temple and tells me of a Duell designed between the Duke of Buckingham and my Lord Halifax or Sir W. Coventry – the challenge being carried by Harry Savill, but prevented by my Lord Arlington and the King told of it.[2] And this was all the discourse at Court this day. But I meeting Sir W. Coventry in the Duke of York's chamber, he would not own it to me, but told me that he was a man of too much peace to meddle with fighting; and so it rested. But the talk is full in the town of the business. Thence, having walked some turns with my Cosen Pepys, and most people by their discourse believing that this Parliament will never sit more, I away to several places to look after things against tomorrow's feast; and so home to dinner and thence, after noon, my wife and I out by hackney-coach and spent the afternoon in several places, doing several things at the Change and elsewhere against tomorrow; and among others, I did also bring home a piece of my Face cast in plaster, for to make a vizard upon for my eyes;[3] and so home, where W Batelier came and sat with us; and there, after many doubts, did resolve to go on with our feast and dancing tomorrow; and so after supper left the maids to make clean the house and to lay the cloth and other things against tomorrow, and we to bed.

1. Sandwich's 20-year-old daughter.
2. The challenger was Coventry. Henry Savile (his nephew) was acting as his second.
3. The mask was to hold paper tubes. He had read about using paper tubes to aid decayed sight in the *Philosophical Transactions* and now set about improving on those experiments. *See* 11 Aug. 1668.

2. Up and at the office till noon, when home; and there I find my company come – *viz*, Madam Turner, Dike, The and Betty Turner, and Mr. Bellwood, formerly their father's clerk but now set up for himself,[1] a conceited silly fellow but one they make mightily of – my Cosen Roger Pepys and his wife and two daughters. And I had a noble dinner for them as I almost ever had, and mighty merry; and perticularly, myself pleased with looking on Betty Turner – who is mighty pretty. After dinner we fell one to one talk, and another to another, and looking over my house and closet and things, and The Turner to write a letter to a lady in the country, in which I did now and then put in half a dozen words, and sometimes five or six lines, and then she as much, and made up a long and good letter, she being mighty witty really, though troublesome-humoured with it. And thus till night, that our music came and the office ready, and candles; and also W Batelier and his sister Susan came, and also Will How and two gentlemen more, strangers, which at my request yesterday he did bring to dance, called Mr. Ireton and Mr. Starkey; we fell to dancing and continued, only with intermission for a good supper, till 2 in the morning, the music being Greeting[2] and another most excellent violin and Theorbo, the best in town; and so, with mighty mirth and pleased with their dancing of Jiggs afterward, several of them, and among others Betty Turner, who did it mighty prettily; and lastly, W. Batelier's blackmore and blackmore-maid, and then to a country-dance again; and so broke up with extraordinary pleasure, as being one of the days and nights of my life spent with the greatest content, and that which I can but hope to repeat again a few times in my whole life. This done, we parted, the strangers home, and I did lodge my cousin Pepys and his wife in our blue chamber – my cousin Turner, her sister, and The in our best chamber – Babb, Betty, and Betty Turner in our own chamber; and myself and my wife in the maid's bed, which is very good – our maids in the coachman's bed – the coachman with the boy in his settle-bed; and Tom where he uses to lie; and so I did to my great content lodge at once in my house, with great ease, fifteen, and eight of them strangers of quality. ⟨My wife this day put on first her French gown, called a *Sac*, which becomes her very well, brought her over by W. Batelier.⟩

4. Up, and a while at the office; but thinking to have Mr. Povy's

1. Pepys's relatives Jane Turner, her sister Elizabeth Dyke, and her two daughters. Bellwood had set up as a lawyer, like Jane Turner's husband.
2. Thomas Greeting, violinist.

business today at the Committee for Tanger, I left the Board and away to White-hall; where in the first court I did meet Sir Jere. Smith, who did tell me that Sir W. Coventry was just now sent to the tower about the business of his challenging the Duke of Buckingham, and so was also Harry Savill to the Gate-house[1] – which, as a gentleman and of the Duke of York's bed-chamber, I heard afterward that the Duke of York is mightily incensed at, and doth appear very high to the King that he might not be sent thither, but to the Tower – this being done only in contempt to him. This news of Sir W Coventry did strike me to the heart; and with reason, for by this and my Lord of Ormond's business,[2] I do doubt that the Duke of Buckingham will be so fleshed, that he will not stop at anything but be forced to do anything now, as thinking it not safe to end here; and Sir W. Coventry being gone, the King will have never a good counsellor, nor the Duke of York any sure friend to stick to him – nor any good man will be left to advise what is good. This, therefore, doth heartily trouble me, as anything that ever I heard. So up into the House and met with several people, but the Committee did not meet. And the whole House I find full of this business of Sir W. Coventry's, and most men very sensible of the cause and effects of it. So meeting with my Lord Bellasses, he told me the perticulars of this matter; that it arises about a quarrel which Sir W. Coventry had with the Duke of Buckingham about a design between him and Sir Rob. Howard to bring him into a play at the King's House;[3] which W. Coventry not enduring, did by H. Savill send a letter to the Duke of Buckingham that he had a desire to speak with him – upon which, the Duke of Buckingham did bid Holmes (his champion ever since my [Lord] of Shrewsbury's business)[4] go to him to know the business; but H. Savill would not tell it to any but himself, and therefore did go presently to the Duke of Buckingham and told him that his Uncle Coventry was a person of honour, and was sensible of his Grace's liberty taken of abusing him and that he had a desire of satisfaction and would fight with him. But that here they were interrupted by my Lord Chamberlains coming in, who was commanded to go to bid the Duke of Buckingham to come to the King, Holmes having discovered[5] it.

1. The Gatehouse prison, Westminster.
2. Ormond had lost his post as Lord Lieutenant of Ireland the previous month.
3. The comedy, *The Country Gentleman* by Buckingham and Howard, satirized Coventry as "Sir Cautious Trouble-all".
4. Sir Robert Holmes had been Buckingham's second in his fatal duel against Lord Shrewsbury. *See* 17 Jan. 1668.
5. Disclosed.

He told me that the King did last night at the Council ask the Duke of Buckingham, upon his honour, whether he received any challenge from W. Coventry; which he confessed that he had. And then the King asking W. Coventry, he told him that he did not owne what the Duke of Buckingham had said, though it was not fit for him to give him a direct contradiction. But being by the King put upon declaring upon his honour the matter, he answered that he had understood that many hard questions had upon this business been moved to some lawyers,[1] and that therefore he was unwilling to declare anything that might from his own mouth render him obnoxious to his Majesty's displeasure, and therefore prayed to be excused – which the King did think fit to interpret to be a confession, and so gave warrant that night for his commitment to the Tower. Being very much troubled at this, I away by coaches homeward, and directly to the Tower, where I find him in one Mr. Bennet's house, son to Major Bayly, one of the Officers of the Ordnance, in the Bricke-tower – where I find him busy with my Lord Halifax and his brother;[2] so I would not stay to interrupt them, but only to give him comfort and offer my service to him; which he kindly and cheerfully received, only owning his being troubled for the King his master's displeasure, which I suppose is the ordinary form and will of persons in this condition; and so I parted, with great content that I had so earlily seen him there.◆

6. Up and to the office, where all the morning. Only before the office, I stepped to Sir W. Coventry at the Tower and there had a great deal of discourse with him – among others, of the King's putting him out of the Council yesterday – with which he is well contented, as with what else they can strip him of – he telling me, and so hath long, that he is weary and surfeited of business. But he joins with me in his fears that all will go to naught as matters are now managed. He told me the matter of the play that was intended for his abuse – wherein they foolishly and sillily bring in two tables like that which he hath made, with a round hole in the middle, in his closet, to turn himself in; and he is to be in one of them as maister, and Sir J. Duncomb in the other as his man or imitator – and their discourse in those tables, about the disposing of their books and

1. Coventry's challenge had been construed as conspiracy against the life of a privy councillor, and thus a felony.

2. Henry Coventry, the diplomat, was Sir William's brother; Halifax was his nephew.

papers, very foolish.[1] But that that he is offended with, is his being made so contemptible, as that any should dare to make a gentleman a subject for the mirth of the world; and that therefore he had told Tom. Killigrew[2] that he should tell his actors, whoever they were, that did offer at anything like representing him, that he would not complain to my Lord Chamberlain, which was too weak, nor get him beaten, as Sir Ch. Sidly is said to do,[3] but that he would cause his nose to be cut. He told me the passage at the Council much like what my Lord Bellasses told me. He tells me how the Duke of Buckingham did himself some time since desire to join with him, of all men in England, and did bid him propound to himself to be Chief Minister of State, saying that he would bring it about; but that he refused to have anything to do with any faction; and that the Duke of Buckingham did within these few days say that of all men in England he would have chosen W. Coventry to have joined intire with. He tells me that he fears their prevailing against the Duke of York; and that their violence will force them to it, as being already beyond his pardon. He repeated to me many examples of challengings of Privy-Councillors and others; but never any proceeded against with that severity which he is, it never amounting to others to more then a little confinement. He tells me of his being weary of the Treasury; and of the folly, ambitions, and desire of popularity of Sir Tho. Clifford,[4] and yet the rudeness of his tongue and passions when angry. This and much more discourse being over, I with great pleasure came home to the office, where all the morning; and at noon home to dinner and thence to the office again, where very hard at work all the afternoon till night; and then home to my wife to read to me, and to bed – my cold having been now almost for three days quite gone from me. This day, my wife made it appear to me that my late entertainment this week cost me above 12*l*, a expense which I am almost ashamed of, though it is but once in a great while, and is the end for which in the most part we live, to have such a merry day once or twice in a man's life.

9. Up, and to the tower and there find Sir W. Coventry alone,

1. Coventry had commissioned for his study a table with a hole in the middle, in which he could sit surrounded by papers. He had proudly shown this efficient design to colleagues, including Pepys. In Act 3 sc. 1 of *The Country Gentleman*, Sir Cautious Trouble-all shows off his similar table to Sir Gravity Empty (the privy councillor Sir John Duncombe). This ends in them whizzing round ridiculously on prototype swivel chairs.
2. Manager of the Theatre Royal.
3. Sedley's retaliation for Kynaston's impersonation of him. *See* 1 Feb. 1669.
4. Coventry's fellow Treasury Commissioner and Privy Councillor.

writing down his journall, which he tells me he now keeps of the material things; [upon] which I told him, and he is the only man that I ever told it to I think,[1] that I have kept it most strictly these eight or ten years; and I am sorry almost that I told it him – it not being necessary, nor may be convenient to have it known. Here he showed me the petition he had sent to the King by my Lord Keeper; which was not to desire any admittance to imployment, but submitting himself therein humbly to his Majesty; but prayed the removal of his displeasure and that he might be set free. He tells me that my Lord Keeper did acquaint the King with the substance of it, not showing him the petition; who answered, that he was disposing of his imployments, and when that was done, he might be led to discharge him – and this is what he expects and what he seems to desire.◆

17. Up and by water to see Mr. Wren and then Mr. Williamson, who did show me the very original Bookes of propositions made by the Commissioners for the Navy in 1618, to my great content – but no other Navy papers he could now show me.[2] Thence to Westminster by water and to the Hall, where Mrs. Michell doth surprize me with the news that Doll. Lane is suddenly brought to bed at her sister's lodgings, and gives it out that she is married; but there is no such thing certainly, she never mentioning it before; but I have cause to rejoice that I have not seen her a great while, she having several times desired my company, but I doubt to an evil end. Thence to the Exchequer, where W. Hewer came to me; and after a little business, did go by water home, and there dined and took my wife by a hackney to the King's playhouse and saw *The Coxcomb*, the first time acted; but an old play and a silly one, being acted only by the young people.[3] Here met Cosen Turner and The. So parted there from them, and home by coach and to my letters at the office, where pretty late; and so to supper and to bed.

21. *Lords day*. Up, and by water over to Southworke; and thence, not getting a boat, I forced to walk to Stangate and so over to White-hall in a scull, where up to the Duke of York's dressing-

1. He had in fact once told naval lieutenant David Lambert that he kept a diary. *See* 11 April 1660.
2. The papers provided by Joseph Williamson documented an early investigation into naval reforms, which Pepys was consulting to aid his own plans.
3. A comedy by Beaumont and Fletcher, first acted c.1608. It was performed by the less eminent members of the company who had probably obtained special permission to act on a Wednesday in Lent.

room; and there met Harry Savill and do understand that Sir W. Coventry is come to his house last night. I understand by Mr. Wren that his friends having by Secretary Trevor and my Lord Keeper applied to the King upon his first coming home, and a promise made that he should be discharged this day, my Lord Arlington did anticipate them by sending a warrant presently for his discharge, which looks a little like kindness or a desire of it; which God send, though I fear the contrary. However, my heart is glad that he is out.◆

28. *Lords day.* Lay long, talking with pleasure with my wife, and so up and to the office with Tom, who looks mighty smug upon his marriage, as Jane also doth, both of whom I did give joy.[1] And so Tom and I at work at the office all the morning till dinner, and then dined, W Battelier with us; and so after dinner to work again, and sent for Gibson and kept him also till 8 at night, doing much business; and so, that being done and my journall writ, my eyes being very bad and every day worse and worse, I home. But I find it most certain that strang drinks do make my eyes sore, as they have done heretofore always, when I was in the country, when my eyes were at the best – there strang beere would make my eyes sore.

So home to supper – and by and by to bed.

APRILL.

9. Up and by water to White-hall and there with the Board attended the Duke of York, and Sir Tho. Allen with us (who came to town yesterday); and it is resolved another fleet shall go to the Straights forthwith, and he command it. But his coming is mighty hardly talked on by the merchants, for leaving their ships there to the mercy of the Turks – but of this more in my White booke.[2]◆ I took occasion to make a step to Mrs. Martins, the first time I have been with her since her husband went last to sea, which is I think a year since; but yo did now hazer con ella what I would, though she had ellos upon her; but yo did algo.[3] But Lord, to hear how

1. Tom Edwards and Jane Birch had married on 26 March, while Pepys was away on a five-day trip to Chatham.
2. The "White booke" was his personal record of navy business and malpractices. Allin, commander in the Mediterranean, was accused of having returned home to pursue his own profits.
3. "I did now do with her what I would, though she had those upon her; but I did something."

sillily she tells the story of her sister Doll's being a widow and lately brought to bed, and her husband, one Rowland Powell, drowned, that was at sea with her husband, but by chance dead at sea, cast away – when, God knows, she hath played the whore, and is sillily forced at this time, after she was brought to bed, to forge this story.

Thence, calling at several places by the way, we home and there to the office; and then home to supper and to bed.

13. Up, and at the office a good while; and then my wife going down the River to spend the day with her mother at Deptford, I abroad, and first to the milliner's in Fanchurch-street over against Rawlinsons; and there meeting both him and her in the shop,[1] I bought a pair of gloves and fell to talk, and found so much freedom that I stayed there the best part of the morning till towards noon, with great pleasure, it being a holiday; and then against my will away and to the Change, where I left W. Hewer, and I by hackney-coach to the Spittle and heard a piece of a dull sermon to my Lord Mayor and Aldermen[2] and then saw them all take horse and ride away, which I have not seen together many a day; their wifes also went in their coaches – and endeed the sight was mighty pleasing.◆ I away home; and there sent for W. Hewer and he and I by water to White-hall to look, among other things, Mr. May,[3] to unbespeak his dining with me tomorrow. But here, being with him in the Court-yard, as God would have it I spied Deb. which made my heart and head to work; and I presently could not refrain, but sent W. Hewer away to look for Mr. Wren (W. Hewer, I perceive, did see her, but whether he did see me see her I know not, or suspect my sending him away I know not) but my heart could not hinder me. And I run after her and two women and a man, more ordinary people, and she in her old clothes; and after hunting a little, find them in the lobby of the Chapel below-stairs; and there I observed she endeavoured to avoid me, but I did speak to her and she to me, and did get her para docere me ou she demeures now. And did charge her para say nothing of me that I had vu elle[4] – which she did promise; and so, with my heart full of surprize and disorder, I away; and meeting with Sir H. Cholmley, walked into the park with him and back again, looking to see if I could spy her again in the park, but I could not. And so back to White-hall, and then back

1. The milliner and his wife.
2. A Spital (Hospital) sermon, given at Easter in Spitalfields Square.
3. Hugh May, Comptroller of the King's Works.
4. "did get her to tell me where she lives now. And did charge her to say nothing of me that I had seen her".

to the park with Mr. May, but could see her no more; and so with W. Hewer, who I doubt by my countenance might see some disorder in me, we home by water; and there I find Talb. Pepys and Mrs. Turner, and Betty too, come to invite us to dinner on Thursday; and after drinking, I saw them to the water-side, and so back home through Crutched-Friars, and there saw Mary Mercer and put off my hat to her on the other side the way; but it being a little darkish, she did not, I think, know me well. And so to my office to put my papers in order, they having been removed for my closet to be made clean; and so home to my wife, who is come home from Deptford. But, God forgive me, I hardly know how to put on confidence enough to speak as innocent, having had this passage today with Deb, though only, God knows, by accident. But my great pain is lest God Almighty shall suffer me to find out this girl, whom endeed I love, and with a bad amour; but I will pray to God to give me grace to forbear it.

So home to supper, where very sparing in my discourse, not giving occasion of any enquiry where I have been today, or what I have done; and so, without any trouble tonight more then my fear, we to bed.

15. Up and to the office; and thence, before the office sat, to the Excise Office with W. Hewer, but found some occasion to go another way to the Temple upon business; and I, by Deb's direction, did know whither in Jewen-street to direct my hackney-coachman, while I stayed in the coach in Aldgate-street, to go thither first to enquire whether Mrs. Hunt her aunt was in town, who brought me word she was not; I thought this was as much as I could do at once, and therefore went away, troubled though that I could do no more; but to the office I must go, and did, and there all the morning; but coming thither, I find Bagwell's wife, who did give me a little note into my hand, wherein I find her para[1] invite me para meet her in Moorfields this noon, where I might speak with her; and so after the office was up, my wife being gone before by invitation to my cousin Turner's to dine, I to that place; and there, after walking up and down by the windmills, I did find her and talk with her; but it being holiday and the place full of people, we parted, leaving further discourse and doing to another time: thence I away and through Jewen-street, my mind, God knows, running that way, but stopped not; but going down Holburn-hill by the Conduit, I did see Deb on foot going up the hill; I saw her, and she me, but she

1. "to".

made no stop, but seemed unwilling to speak to me; so I away on, but then stopped and light and after her, and overtook her at the end of Hosier-lane in Smithfield; and without standing in the street, desired her to fallow me, and I led her into a little blind alehouse within the walls; and there she and I alone fell to talk and besar la and tocar su mamelles; but she mighty coy, and I hope modest; but however, though with great force, did hazer ella con su hand para tocar mi thing, but ella was in great pain para be brought para it.[1] I did give her in a paper 20*s*, and we did agree para meet again in the Hall at Westminster on Monday next; and so, giving me great hopes by her carriage that she continues modest and honest, we did there part.◆

19. Up, and with Tom (whom, with his wife, I and my wife had this morning taken occasion to tell that I did intend to give him 40*l* for himself and 20*l* to his wife toward their setting out in the world, and that my wife would give her 20*l* more, that so she might have as much to begin with as he) by coach to White-hall; and there having set him work in the robe-chamber to write something for me, I to Westminster-hall and there walked from 10 a-clock to past 12, expecting to have met Deb; but whether she had been there before, and missing me went away, or is prevented in coming and hath no mind to come to me (the last whereof, as being most pleasing, as showing most modesty, I should be most glad of) I know not; but she not then appearing, I being tired with walking went home; and my wife being all day at Jane's, helping her as she said to cut out linning[2] and other things belonging to her new condition, I after dinner out again; and calling for my coach, which was at the coachmaker's and hath been for these two or three days, to be new painted and the window-frames gilt against May-day, went on with my hackney away to White-hall; and thence by water to Westminster-hall and there did beckon to Doll. Lane, now Mrs. Powell as she would have herself called, and went to her sister Martin's lodgings, the first time I have been there these eight or ten months I think; and her sister being gone to Portsmouth to her husband, I did stay and talk with and drink with Doll and hazer ella para tocar mi thing; and yo did the like para her,[3] but ⟨did⟩ not the thing itself, having not opportunity enough; and so away and

1. "and kiss her and touch her breasts; . . . did make her with her hand touch my thing, but she was in great pain to be brought to it."
2. Linen.
3. "and make her touch my thing; and I did the like to her".

to White-hall and there took my own coach, which was now come; and so away home and there to do business; and my wife being come home, we to talk and to sup, there having been nothing yet like discovery in my wife of what hath lately passed with me about Deb, and so with great content to bed.

24. Up and to the office, where all the morning; and at noon home to dinner, Mr. Sheres dining with us by agreement, and my wife, which troubled me, mighty careful to have a handsome dinner for him. But yet I see no reason to be troubled at it, he being a very civil and worthy man I think; but only, it doth seem to imply some little neglect of me.

After dinner to the King's House and there saw *The Generall*[1] revived, a good play, that pleases me well; and thence, our coach coming for us, we parted and home, and I busy late at the office and then home to supper and to bed – well pleased tonight to have Lead the vizard-maker bring me home my vizard with a Tube fastened in it, which I think will do my business, at least in a great measure, for the easing of my eyes.

25. *Lords day.* Up and to my office awhile, and thither comes Lead with my vizard, with a Tube fastened within both eyes; which, with the help which he prompts me to, of a glass in the Tube, doth content me mightily. So to church, where a stranger made a dull sermon, but I mightily pleased to look upon Mr. Buckworths little pretty daughters; and so home to dinner, where W How came and dined with us; and then I to my office, he being gone, to write down my journall for the last twelve days; and did it with the help of my vizard and Tube fixed to it, and do find it mighty manageable; but how helpful to my eyes, this trial will show me.

So abroad with my wife in the afternoon to the park – where very much company, and the weather very pleasant. I carried my wife to the Lodge,[2] the first time this year, and there in our coach eat a cheese-cake and drank a tankard of milk. I showed her this day also first the Prince of Tuscany,[3] who was in the park – and many very fine ladies. And so home, and after supper to bed.

26. Up, having lain long; and then by coach with W. Hewer to the Excise Office, and so to Lilly's the varnisher, who is lately dead and

1. An heroic drama by the Earl of Orrery; Pepys had seen it during its first London run in 1664.
2. The Keeper's Lodge in Hyde Park, where milk and cheesecakes were sold.
3. Cosimo de' Medici. He became Grand Duke of Tuscany (as Cosimo III) in 1670.

his wife and brother keep up the trade, and there I left my French prints[1] to be put on boards; and while I was there, a fire burst out in a chimney of a house just over against his house – but it was with a gun quickly put out.[2] So to White-hall and did a little business there at the Treasury-chamber; and so homeward, calling at the laceman's for some lace for my new suit, and at my tailor's. And so home, where to dinner, and Mr. Sheres dined with us, who came hither today to teach my wife the rules of perspective; but I think, upon trial, he thinks it too hard to teach her, being ignorant of the principles of lines. After dinner comes one Collonell Macknachan, one that I see often at Court, a Scotchman, but know him not; only, he brings me a letter from my Lord Middleton, who he says is in great distress for 500*l* to relieve my Lord Morton[3] with (but upon what account I know not); and he would have me advance it, without order, upon his pay for Tanger; which I was astonished at, but had the grace to deny him with an excuse. And so he went away, leaving me a little troubled that I was thus driven on a sudden to do anything herein. But Creed coming just now to see me, he approves of what I have done. And then to talk of general matters; and by and by, Sheres being gone, my wife and he and I out, and I set him down at Temple-bar, and myself and wife went down the Temple upon seeming business, only to put him off. And just at the Temple-gate, I spied Deb with another gentlewoman, and Deb winked on me and smiled, but undiscovered, and I was glad to see her.[4] So my wife and I to the Change about things for her; and here at Mrs. Barnett's shop I am told by Betty, who was all undressed, of a great fire happened in Durham-yard last night, burning the house of one Lady Hungerford, who was to come to town to it this night; and so the house is burned, new furnished, by carelessness of the girl sent to take off a candle from a bunch of candles, which she did by burning it off, and left the rest, as is supposed, on fire. The King and Court was here, it seems, and stopped the fire by blowing up of the next house.

The King and Court went out of town to Newmarket this morning betimes, for a week. So home and there to my chamber and got my wife to read to me a little; and so to supper and to bed.

Coming home this night, I did call at the coachmaker's, and do

1. These were prints of Louis XIV and other French grandees by the celebrated artist Robert Nanteuil.
2. A gun was shot up the chimney to clear it and bring down burning soot.
3. Son-in-law of Middleton, the Governor of Tangier.
4. This is Pepys's final encounter with Deb Willet in the diary.

resolve upon having the standards of my coach gilt with this new sort of varnish; which will come but to 40*s*; and contrary to my expectation, the doing of the biggest coach all over comes not to above 6*l* – which is [not] very much.

28. Up, and was called upon by Sir H. Cholmly to discourse about some accounts of his of Tanger; and then to other talk, and I find by him that it is brought almost to effect, the late endeavours of the Duke of York and Duchess, the Queen-Mother, and my Lord St. Albans, together [with] some of the contrary faction, my Lord Arlington, that for a sum of money we shall enter into a league with the King of France; wherein he says my Lord Chancellor is also concerned, and he believes that in the doing hereof, it is meant that he shall come in again, and that this sum of money will so help the King as that he will not need the Parliament; and that in that regard, it will be forwarded by the Duke of Buckingham and his faction, who dread the Parliament;[1] but hereby, we must leave the Dutch,[2] and that I doubt will undo us, and Sir H. Cholmly says he finds W. Coventry to think the like. My Lady Castlemayne is instrumental in this matter and, he says, never more great with the King then she is now. But this is a thing that will make the Parliament and Kingdom mad, and will turn to our ruine – for with this money the King shall wanton away his time in pleasures, and think nothing of the main till it be too late. He gone, I to the office, where busy till noon; and then home to dinner, where M. Batelier dined with us, and pretty merry; and so I to the office again.

This morning, Mr. Sheres sent me, in two volumes, Mariana his history of Spaine in Spanish,[3] an excellent book and I am much obliged for it to him.

1. These rumours concerned the negotiations that produced the secret Treaty of Dover in May 1670. In it, Charles agreed with Louis XIV to attack the Dutch in return for an annual subsidy and, after an additional payment, to declare himself a Catholic. The full dealings were known to very few, the prime movers being Charles, his sister Henrietta, and Louis. Buckingham knew only of a second version of the treaty, which excluded provisions concerning Charles's religion. The former Lord Chancellor Clarendon, exiled in France, was not involved at all.
2. An Anglo-Dutch alliance had been made in January 1668.
3. Juan de Mariana's *Historia general de España*, first translated from Latin into Spanish in 1601.

MAY.

1. Up betimes, called up by my tailor, and there first put on a summer suit this year – but it was not my fine one of flowered tabby vest and coloured camelott tunic, because it was too fine with the gold lace at the hands, that I was afeared to be seen in it – but put on the stuff-suit I made the last year, which is now repaired;[1] and so did go to the office in it and sat all the morning, the day looking as if it would be fowle. At noon home to dinner, and there find my wife extraordinary fine with her flowered tabby gown that she made two years ago, now laced exceeding pretty, and endeed was fine all over – and mighty earnest to go, though the day was very lowering, and she would have me put on my fine suit, which I did; and so anon we went alone through the town with our new Liverys of serge, and the horses' manes and tails tied with red ribbon and the standards thus gilt with varnish and all clean, and green raynes, that people did mightily look upon us; and the truth is, I did not see any coach more pretty, or more gay, then ours all the day. But we set ⟨out⟩ out of humour; I because Betty, whom I expected, was not come to go with us; and my wife, that I would sit on the same seat with her, which she liked not, being so fine; and then expected to meet Sheres, which we did in the Pell Mell, and against my will I was forced to take him into the coach, but was sullen all day almost, and little complaisant; the day also being unpleasing, though the park full of coaches; but dusty and windy and cold, and now and then a little dribbling rain; and what made it worst, there were so many hackney-coaches as spoiled the sight of the gentlemen's, and so we had little pleasure. But here was W Batelier and his sister in a borrowed coach by themselfs, and I took them and we to the Lodge, and at the door did give them a sullabub[2] and other things, cost me 12*s*, and pretty merry; and so back to the coaches and there till the evening; and then home, leaving Mr. Sheres at St. James's gate, where he took leave of us for altogether, he being this night to set out for Portsmouth post, in his way to Tanger – which troubled my wife mightily, who is mighty, though not I think too fond of him. But she was out of humour all the evening, and I vexed

1. The "tabby" vest was made of silk and the "camelot" (camlet) tunic probably of imported woollen fabric; the plainer "stuff-suit" was worsted cloth.
2. Sillabub: sweetened milk mixed with wine.

at her for it; and she did not rest almost all the night, so as in the night I was forced to take her and hug her to put her to rest. So home, and after a little supper, to bed.

2. *Lords day.* Up, and by water to White-hall and there visit my Lord Sandwiches, who, after about two months absence at Hinchingbrooke, came to town last night. I saw him, and very kind; and I am glad he is so, I having not wrote to him all the time, my eyes endeed not letting me. Here, with Sir Ch. Herbert and my Lord Hinchingbrooke and Sidny, we looked upon the picture of Tanger designed by Ch. Herberd and drawn by Dancre, which my Lord Sandwich admires, as being the truest picture that ever he saw in his life – and it is endeed very pretty, and I will be at the cost of having one of them.

Thence with them to White-hall, and there walked out the sermon with one or other; and then saw the Duke of York after sermon and he talked to me a little; and so away back by water home, and after dinner got my wife to read; and then by coach, she and I, to the park and there spent the evening with much pleasure, it proving clear after a little shower, and we mighty fine, as yesterday, and people mightily pleased with our coach as I perceived. But I had not on my fine suit, being really afeared to wear it, it being so fine with the gold lace, though not gay.

So home and to supper; and my wife to read, and Tom, my *Nipotisme*,[1] and then to bed.

10.♦ To St. James and there met the Duke of York, who told me with great content that he did now think he should master our adversaries, for that the King did tell him that he was satisfied in the constitution of the Navy, but that it was well to give these people[2] leave to object against it; which they having not done, he did give warrant to the Duke of York to direct Sir Jeremy Smith to be a Commissioner of the Navy in the room of Penn; which, though he be an impertinent fellow, yet I am glad of it, it showing that the other side is not so strong as it was; and so, in plain terms, the Duke of York did tell me that they were every day losing ground – and perticularly, that he would take care to keep out Childe.[3] At all

1. *Il nipotismo di Roma: or, The History of the Popes Nephews* (1669), attributed to Gregorio Leti. It argued that God frustrated the popes' desire to advance their kin, punishing their greed and sacrilege.
2. Buckingham's faction.
3. Smith, who had held multiple navy commands, was subsequently appointed in preference to the Duke of Buckingham's preferred candidate, the merchant Josiah Child.

which I am glad, though yet I dare not think myself secure, but the King may yet be wrought upon by these people to bring changes in our office, and remove us ere it be long. Thence I to White-hall, and there took boat to Westminster and to Mrs. Martins, who is not come to town from her husband at Portsmouth; so drank only at Cragg's with her and Doll, and so to the Swan and there besard[1] a new maid that is there; and so to White-hall again to a Committee of Tanger, where I see all things going to wrack in the business of the Corporation, and consequently in the place, by Middleton's going.[2]

Thence walked a little with Creed, who tells me he hears how fine my horses and coach are, and advises me to avoid being noted for it; which I was vexed to hear taken notice of, it being what I feared; and Povy told me of my gold-lace sleeves in the park yesterday,[3] which vexed me also, so as to resolve never to appear in Court with it, but presently to have it taken off, as it is fit I should. And so to my wife at Unthankes, and coach, and called at my tailor's to that purpose; and so home, and after a walk in the garden, home to supper and to bed.

12.◆ After dinner, my wife and I to the Duke of York's playhouse, and there in the side balcone over against the music, did hear, but not see, a new play, the first day acted, *The Roman Virgin*, an old play[4] and but ordinary I thought; but the trouble of my eyes with the light of the candles did almost kill me.

Thence to my Lord Sandwiches, and there have a promise from Sidny to come and dine with me tomorrow; and so my wife and I home in our coach, and there find my Brother John, as I looked for, come to town from Ellington; where, among other things, he tells me the first news that my sister is with child and far gone; which I know not whether it did more trouble or please me, having no great care for my friends[5] to have children, though I love other people's.[6] So, glad to see him, we to supper and so to bed.

1. "kissed".
2. The Earl of Middleton, Governor of Tangier, set out for the colony in September 1669.
3. Pepys and his wife had been touring in their finery in Hyde Park again.
4. This "old" and "new" play was John Webster and Thomas Heywood's early seventeenth-century tragedy *Appius and Virginia*, now adapted by Thomas Betterton.
5. Relatives.
6. Paulina Jackson's first child was named Samuel, after her brother. After Samuel Jackson defied Pepys by marrying against his instructions in 1701, Pepys made Paulina's younger son, John, his heir.

16. *Lords day.* My wife and I at church, our pew filled (which vexed me at her confidence) with Mrs. Backwell[1] and six more that she brought with her. Dined at home, and W Batelier with us, and I all the afternoon drawing up a foul draft of my petition to the Duke of York about my eyes, for leave to spend three or four months out of the office, drawing it so as to give occasion to a voyage abroad; which I did to my pretty good liking. And then with my wife to Hyde-park, where a good deal of company, and good weather; and so home to supper and to bed.

19. With my coach to St. James, and there, finding the Duke of York gone to muster his men in Hyde-park, I alone with my boy thither; and there saw more, walking out of my coach as other gentlemen did, of a soldier's trade then ever I did in my life – the men being mighty fine, and their commanders, perticularly the Duke of Monmouth; but methought their trade but very easy, as to the mustering of their men, and the men but indifferently ready to perform what was commanded in the handling their arms.

Here the news was first talked of Harry Killigrews'[2] being wounded in nine places last night by footmen in the highway, going from the park in a hackney-coach toward Hammersmith to his house at Turnam-green – they being supposed to be my Lady Shrewsbury's men – she being by in her coach with six horses. Upon an old grudge, of his saying openly that he had lain with her.

Thence by and by to White-hall, and there I waited upon the King and Queen all dinner-time in the Queen's lodgings, she being in her white pinner and apern, like a woman with child;[3] and she seemed handsomer, plain so, then dressed. And by and by, dinner done, I out and to walk in the Gallery for the Duke of York's coming out; and there meeting Mr. May, he took me down about 4 a-clock to Mr. Chevins's lodgings, and all alone did get me a dish of cold chickens and good wine, and I dined like a prince, being before very hungry and empty. By and by the Duke of York comes, and readily took me to his closet and received my petition, and discoursed it about my eyes and pitied me, and with much kindness did give me his consent to be absent, and approved of my proposition to go into Holland to observe things there of the Navy, but would first ask the King's leave; which he anon did, and did tell me

1. Wife of the goldsmith-banker Edward Backwell.
2. Disreputable courtier; son of Thomas Killigrew the dramatist.
3. Catherine wore a neckcloth and apron. She was indeed pregnant, but miscarried in June.

that the King would be "a good maister to me" (these were his words about my eyes) and doth like of my going into Holland, but doth advise that nobody should know of my going thither – but pretend that I did go into the country somewhither – which I liked well.[1] Glad of this, I home; and thence took out my wife and to Mr. Holliards about a swelling in her cheek, but he not at home; and so round by Islington and eat and drink; and so home and after supper, to bed.

In discourse this afternoon, the Duke of York did tell me that he was the most amazed at one thing just now that ever he was in his life; which was that the Duke of Buckingham did just now come into the Queen's bed-chamber, where the King and much mixed company, and among others Tom Killigrew, the father of Harry who was last night wounded so as to be in danger of death, and his man is quite dead – and there in discourse did say that he had spoke with some that was by (which all the world must know that it must be his whore, my Lady Shrewsbury) who says that they did not mean to hurt, but beat him, and that he did run first at them with his sword – so that he doth hereby clearly discover[2] that he knows who did it, and is of conspiracy with them, being of known conspiracy with her; which the Duke of York did seem to be pleased with, and said it might perhaps cost him his life in the House of Lords[3] – and I find was mightily pleased with it – saying it was the most impudent thing, as well as foolish, that ever he knew man do in all his life.

24. To White-hall, and there all the morning, and thence home; and giving order for some business, and setting my brother to making a catalogue of my books, I back again to W. Hewer to White-hall, where I attended the Duke of York and was by him led to the King, who expressed great sense of my misfortune in my eyes, and concernment for their recovery; and accordingly signified not only his assent to my desire therein, but commanded me to give them rest this summer, according to my late petition to the Duke of York. W. Hewer and I dined alone at the Swan, and thence, having thus waited on the King, spent till 4 a-clock in St. James's-park, when I met my wife at Unthankes and so home.

1. Pepys, Elizabeth, and her brother travelled on the continent for two months from late August, during which time Pepys collected naval intelligence. They visited Holland, Flanders, and France.
2. Disclose.
3. Buckingham was not prosecuted.

30. *Whitsunday.* By water to White-hall, and thence to Sir W. Coventry, where all the morning by his bedside, he being indisposed; our discourse was upon the notes I had lately prepared for commanders' instructions; but concluded that nothing will render them effectual without an amendment in the choice of them,[1] that they be seamen, and not gentlemen above the command of the Admiral by the greatness of their relations at Court. Thence to White-hall and dined alone with Mr. Chevins his sister; whither by and by came in Mr. Progers and Sir Tho. Allen, and by and by fine Mrs. Wells, who is a great beauty and there I had my full gaze upon her, to my great content, she being a woman of pretty conversation.

Thence to the Duke of York, who, with the officers of the Navy, made a good entrance on my draft of my new instructions to commanders, as well expressing his general [views] of a reformation among them, as liking of my humble offers towards it. Thence, being called by my wife, Mr. Gibson and we to the park, whence the rain sent us suddenly home.

31. [Up] very betimes, and so continued all the morning, with W. Hewer, upon examining and stating my accounts, in order to the fitting myself to go abroad beyond sea, which the ill condition of my eyes, and my neglect for a year or two, hath kept me behindhand in, and so as to render it very difficult now, and troublesome to my mind to do it; but I this day made a satisfactory entrance therein. Dined at home, and in the afternoon by water to White-hall, calling by the way at Michell's,[2] where I have not been many a day till just the other day; and now I met her mother there and knew her husband to be out of town. And here yo did besar ella, but have not opportunity para hazer mas with her as I would have offered if yo had had it.[3] And thence had another meeting with the Duke of York at White-hall with the Duke of York on yesterday's work, and made a good advance; and so being called by my wife, we to the park, Mary Batelier, a Duch gentleman, a friend of hers, being with us. Thence to the World's-end, a drinking-house by the park, and there merry; and so home late.

And thus ends all that I doubt I shall ever be able to do with my own eyes in the keeping of my journall, I being not able to do it any

1. The naval commanders.
2. Michael and Betty Mitchell's alcohol shop.
3. "I did kiss her, but have not opportunity to do more with her as I would have offered if I had had it."

longer, having done now so long as to undo my eyes almost every time that I take a pen in my hand; and therefore, whatever comes of it, I must forbear; and therefore resolve from this time forward to have it kept by my people in longhand, and must therefore be contented to set down no more then is fit for them and all the world to know; or if there be anything (which cannot be much, now my amours to Deb are past, and my eyes hindering me in almost all other pleasures), I must endeavour to keep a margin in my book open, to add here and there a note in short-hand with my own hand.[1] And so I betake myself to that course which [is] almost as much as to see myself go into my grave – for which, and all the discomforts that will accompany my being blind, the good God prepare me.

31. May. 1669. S.P.

1. He never kept the kind of diary described here. He did keep several later journals for specific purposes, such as recording his journey to Tangier in 1683.

SELECT LIST OF PERSONS[1]

ALBEMARLE, 1st Duke of (Lord Monke): Captain-General of the Kingdom
ANDREWS, Thomas: merchant and neighbour
ARLINGTON, *see* Bennet
ASHLEY, 1st Baron (Sir Anthony Ashley Cooper, later 1st Earl of Shaftesbury): Chancellor of the Exchequer
BACKWELL, Edward: goldsmith-banker
BAGWELL, Mrs [?Elizabeth]: Pepys's mistress; wife of a ship's carpenter
BALTY: Balthasar St Michel, brother-in-law and minor naval official
BATELIER, William: merchant and neighbour
BATTEN, Sir William: Surveyor of the Navy
BENNET, Sir Henry, cr. Baron Arlington, 1665: Keeper of the Privy Purse, 1661–2; Secretary of State from 1662
BETTERTON (Baterton), Thomas: actor in the Duke's Company
BIRCH, Jane: maidservant
BLACKBORNE, Robert: the senior navy official under the Commonwealth; uncle to Will Hewer
BLAND, John: merchant in the Mediterranean trade
BOOKSELLER, my: Joshua Kirton (until the Great Fire)
BOWYER, my father: Robert Bowyer, senior Exchequer colleague
BRISTOL, 2nd Earl of: politician
BROUNCKER (Bruncker, Brunkard, Brunkerd), William, 2nd Viscount: Commissioner of the Navy
BUCKINGHAM, 2nd Duke of: politician
CARKESSE (Carcasse), James: clerk in the navy's Ticket Office
CARTERET, Sir George: Treasurer of the Navy and Vice-Chamberlain of the King's Household
CASTLEMAINE, Barbara, Countess of: the King's mistress
CHANCELLOR, the: *see* 'Lord Chancellor'
CHOLMLEY, Sir Hugh: courtier, engineer
CLARKE (Clerke), Dr Timothy: royal physician
COCKE, Capt. George: Baltic merchant and navy contractor
COMPTROLLER (Controller), the: the Comptroller of the Navy (Sir Robert Slingsby, 1660–1; Sir John Mennes, 1661–71)
COVENTRY, Sir William: Secretary to the Lord High Admiral, 1660–7; Commissioner of the Navy, 1662–7 (occasionally called 'Mr' after being knighted in 1665)
CREED, John: household and naval servant of Sandwich
CREW, John, cr. 1st Baron Crew, 1661 ('Mr Crew' until 1661, 'Lord Crew' thereafter): Sandwich's father-in-law; Presbyterian politician
CREW, Thomas: Sandwich's brother-in-law; knighted 1660
CUTTANCE, Sir Roger: naval captain
DEANE, Anthony: shipwright
DEB: *see* 'Willet, Deborah'
DOWNING, Sir George: Exchequer official, Envoy-Extraordinary to the Dutch Republic, and secretary to the Treasury Commission
DUKE, the: usually James, Duke of York, the King's brother; occasionally George (Monck), Duke of Albemarle
DUKE OF YORK: *see* 'James, Duke of York'
EDWARDS, Tom: servant

1. Adapted from *The Diary of Samuel Pepys*, ed. Latham and Matthews, IX, 571–4.

EVELYN, (Eveling) John: friend, savant; Commissioner of Sick and Wounded
FENNER, Thomas (m. Katherine Kite, sister of Pepys's mother): uncle; ironmonger
FERRER(S), Capt. Robert: army captain; member of Sandwich's household
FORD, Sir Richard: merchant, navy contractor, and neighbour
FOX, Sir Stephen: Paymaster of the Army; official in the royal household
GAUDEN, Denis: navy victualler
GENERAL(S), the: Albemarle, Captain-General of the Kingdom, 1660–70; Prince Rupert and Albemarle, Generals-at-Sea in command of the Fleet, 1666
GIBSON, Richard: clerk to Pepys in the Navy Office
GOSNELL, [?Winifred]: paid companion to Elizabeth Pepys; actress
GWYN, Nell: actress (in the King's Company) and later the King's mistress
HARRIS, Henry: actor in the Duke's Company
HAYTER (Hater), Tom: clerk to Pepys in the Navy Office
HEWER, Will: servant; clerk to Pepys in the Navy Office
HILL, Thomas: friend, musician, and merchant
HINCHINGBROOKE, Viscount (also 'Mr Edward', 'the child'): eldest son of Sandwich
HOLLIER (Holliard), Thomas: surgeon
HOLMES, Sir Robert (Capt. and Major): naval commander
HOWE, Will: household and naval servant of Sandwich
HUNT, Elizabeth: neighbour in Axe Yard, Westminster
JAMES, DUKE OF YORK: the King's brother and heir presumptive (later James II); Lord High Admiral
JANE: usually Jane Birch, maidservant
JOYCE, Anthony (m. Kate Fenner, Pepys's 1st cousin): tallow-chandler and innkeeper
JOYCE, William (m. Mary Fenner, Pepys's 1st cousin): tallow-chandler
KNIPP (Knepp), Mrs: actress in the King's Company
LANE, Betty: *see* 'Martin, Betty'
LANE, Doll: Pepys's mistress; linen draper in Westminster Hall
LAWSON, Sir John: naval commander
LIEUTENANT OF THE TOWER: Sir John Robinson
LLEWELLYN (Luellin), Peter: underclerk to the Council of State, 1660; later clerk to Edward Dering, timber merchant
LORD CHANCELLOR: Edward Hyde, 1st Earl of Clarendon (often called Chancellor after his dismissal in 1667)
LORD KEEPER: Sir Orlando Bridgeman
LORD PRIVY SEAL: John Robartes, 2nd Baron Robartes
LORD TREASURER: Thomas Wriothesley, 4th Earl of Southampton
LOWTHER (Louther), Anthony: husband of Peg Penn (daughter of Sir William Penn)
MARTIN, Betty (née Lane): Pepys's mistress; linen-draper in Westminster Hall
MENNES (Minnes), Sir John: Comptroller of the Navy
MERCER, Mary: neighbour and paid companion to Elizabeth Pepys
MILL(E)S, Rev. Daniel: Rector of St Olave, Hart St; Pepys's parish priest
MITCHELL, Ann ('Mrs Michell'): bookseller in Westminster Hall
MITCHELL (Michell), Betty: wife of Michael, owner of a shop selling spirits; daughter-in-law of Ann Mitchell
MONCK (Monke), George (Lord): army officer. *See* 'Albemarle, 1st Duke of'
MONMOUTH, Duke of: illegitimate son of Charles II
MOORE, Henry: lawyer; Sandwich's man of business
MY LADY: usually Jemima, wife of Sandwich
MY LORD: usually Sandwich
NELL, NELLY: usually Nell Gwyn
PALL: Paulina Pepys; sister (sometimes spelt 'pall')

PALMER, Madam: *see* 'Castlemaine, Barbara'
PEARSE (Pierce), James: courtier, surgeon to Duke of York, and naval surgeon
PELLING, John: apothecary, musician, and friend
PENN, Sir William: Commissioner of the Navy and naval commander (father of the Quaker leader)
PEPYS, Elizabeth (née St Michel): wife
PEPYS, John and Margaret: parents
PEPYS, John: brother; student, then unbeneficed clergyman
PEPYS, Paulina (m. John Jackson): sister
PEPYS, Robert (Capt.): uncle, of Brampton, Huntingdonshire
PEPYS, Roger: 1st cousin once removed; barrister and MP
PEPYS, Thomas: uncle, of St Alphege's parish, London
PEPYS, Thomas ('the turner'): cousin; son of Thomas of St Alphege's
PEPYS, Tom: brother; tailor
PETT, Peter: Commissioner of the Navy and shipwright
PICKERING, Edward (Ned): courtier, 1662–3; Sandwich's relative and servant
POVEY, Thomas: Treasurer of the Tangier Committee, 1663–5
PRINCE, the: usually Prince Rupert
QUEEN, the: (until May 1662) the Queen Mother, Henrietta Maria, widow of Charles I; then Catherine of Braganza, wife of Charles II (m. 21 May 1662)
RICHMOND, Duchess of: *see* 'Stuart, Frances'
RIDER, Sir William: merchant
ROBERT, Prince: Prince Rupert
RUPERT, Prince: 1st cousin of Charles II; naval commander
ST MICHEL, Balthasar ('Balty'; m. Ester Watts): brother-in-law; minor naval official
SANDWICH, 1st Earl of: 1st cousin once removed, and patron; politician, naval commander, and diplomat
SHEERES (Sheres), Henry: military engineer and surveyor
SHIPLEY (Sheply), Edward: steward of Sandwich's household
SIDNY, Mr: Sidney Mountagu, second son of Sandwich
'SIR WMS. BOTH': Sir William Batten and Sir William Penn, colleagues on the Navy Board
SPONG, John: chancery clerk and, after 1662, optical-instrument maker
STUART, Frances ('Mrs Stewart'): reputedly the King's mistress; married Duke of Richmond, 1667
THE: Theophila Turner, relative
TRICE, Tom: step-son of Pepys's Uncle Robert Pepys; civil lawyer
TURNER, Betty and The[ophila]: relatives, daughters of John and Jane Turner
TURNER, Elizabeth ('Mrs Turner'): neighbour; wife of Thomas Turner of the Navy Office
TURNER, Jane ('Mrs Turner' or 'Madam Turner', née Pepys): distant cousin; married to John Turner, barrister
TURNER, Thomas: senior clerk in the Navy Office
VYNER, Sir Robert: goldsmith-banker, knighted 1665
WARREN, Sir William: timber merchant and navy contractor
WARWICK, Sir Philip: Secretary to the Lord Treasurer
WIGHT, William: uncle (half-brother of Pepys's father); fishmonger
WILL: usually Will Hewer
WILLET, Deborah: paid companion to Elizabeth Pepys
WREN, Matthew: Secretary to the Lord High Admiral, 1667–72
WRIGHT, Lady Anne (m. Sir Henry Wright): sister of Lady Sandwich

INDEX

ABOUT THE EDITORS

ROBERT LATHAM (1912–95) was Reader in History at Royal Holloway College and afterwards Fellow and Pepys Librarian, Magdalene College, Cambridge.

WILLIAM MATTHEWS (1905–75) was Professor of English at UCLA and Director of the UCLA Center for Medieval and Renaissance Studies.

KATE LOVEMAN is Associate Professor in English at the University of Leicester and author of *Samuel Pepys and his Books: Reading, Newsgathering, and Sociability, 1660–1703*.

This book is set in CASLON, designed and engraved by William Caslon of WILLIAM CASLON & SON, Letter-Founders in London, around 1740. In England at the beginning of the eighteenth century, Dutch type was probably more widely used than English. The rise of William Caslon put a stop to the importation of Dutch types and so changed the history of English typecutting.